# Labour Relations
## A southern African Perspective

Eighth edition

Founding author: Sonia Bendix
Editor: Anita de Bruyn

juta

*Labour Relations: A southern African Perspective*

Previously published as *Industrial Relations in South Africa*
First published 1989
Third edition 1996
Fourth edition 2001
Fifth edition 2010
Sixth edition 2015
Seventh edition 2019
Eighth edition 2022

Juta and Company (Pty) Ltd
First floor, Sunclare building, 21 Dreyer street, Claremont 7708
PO Box 14373, Lansdowne 7779, Cape Town, South Africa
www.juta.co.za

© 2022 Juta and Company (Pty) Ltd

ISBN 978 1 48513 157 1 (Print)
ISBN 978 1 48513 158 8 (WebPDF)

Production specialist: Seshni Kazadi
Editor: Simone Chiara van der Merwe
Proofreader: Lilané Putter Joubert
Cover designer: Simplicitas Design
Typesetter: Wouter Reinders
Indexer: Lexinfo

Typeset in ITC Veljovic Sts

# Contents

# Preface

Welcome to the eight edition of *Labour Relations: A southern African Perspective*.

This book is a tribute to Ms Sonia Bendix, the founding author of this book series.

Those familiar with the seventh edition will note that that there has been a substantial change in the structure of the book. The book has been divided into different parts to create a logical flow and to orientate the reader. This was accomplished by breaking away from larger chapters, revisiting the objectives of each chapter and sifting through the literature to ensure that the content is relevant for today's labour relations practitioners.

Furthermore, senior academics from various South African tertiary institutions and ethical backgrounds were selected to present a more comprehensive and diverse social view on South African labour relations.

Relationships are not static, and changes signal growth and development. Join us in the journey to create conducive and healthy working relationships in South Africa's workplaces.

The contributing authors

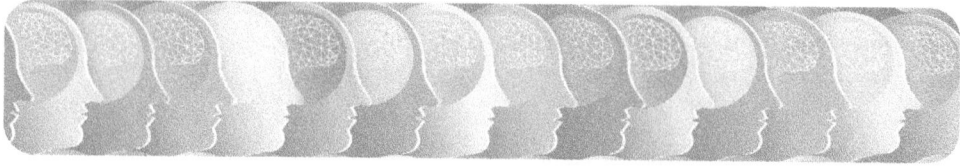

# Acknowledgements

This book could not have been completed without the assistance of numerous people. We especially wish to mention the following:

- Many of our colleagues in the labour relations field, whose research efforts have made the growth in the field possible.
- The work of Sonia Bendix, who authored the previous editions.
- The excellent editorial assistance offered by Juta & Co, particularly Leighzyl Hill, Seshni Kazadi and Simone van der Merwe.
- The staff at Juta, especially our current publisher, Jayde Butler.
- Our families, who continue to support us by providing us with time, inspiration and opportunities for continued learning to sustain this project.

# About the authors

**Professor Sonia Bendix** spent 22 years as an academic, first as a senior lecturer and later as Head of Department of Human Resource Management. During this period, she was a member of the National Standards Body for Human and Social Sciences, the Standards Generating Body for Human Resource Management and the qualifications task team for the Board of Personnel Practice. She has trained and consulted widely in industry and the public service, gaining intimate knowledge of IR/HR practices. Her other publications include *Industrial Relations in South Africa*, *The Basics of Labour Relations*, *Labour Relations in Practice and Industrial Relations and Organisational Dynamics* (co-authored with Fred Jacobs and published by Juta).

**Dr Anita de Bruyn** is a senior lecturer in human resource management, in the College of Economics and Management at the University of South Africa (Unisa). She has 30 years' industry experience in human resource management, specialising in labour relations. She joined academia in 2006. She facilitates learning on both undergraduate and postgraduate levels and is a community project leader. Her current research focus area is high-performance work practices in the new world of work, specifically labour relations. Anita is registered as a Master HR Professional (MHRP) with the South African Board for People Practices (SABPP) and a member of the Higher Education Committee.

**Professor Elsabe Keyser**, in her work in the School of Industrial Psychology and Human Resource Management at the Vaal Triangle Campus of North-West University, focuses on the labour relations field, the psychological contract and work-related outcomes. She has been involved in various research projects related to employment relations and organisational behaviour over three decades. She has published widely and is registered as an MHRP with the SABPP.

**Dr Karel Lessing** is a senior lecturer in labour relations in the Department of People Management and Development at the Pretoria-West campus of Tshwane University of Technology. He has more than 20 years' experience as a senior lecturer and his areas of research interest include employment relations, collective bargaining and negotiations. Karel is registered as an MHRP with the SABPP and a member of the Higher Education Committee.

**Dr Calvin Mabaso** is a senior lecturer at the Department of Industrial Psychology and People Management, College of Business and Economics, at the University of Johannesburg (UJ). He holds a doctorate in human resources management. His research areas include remuneration, total rewards, talent retention and employment relations. He teaches on both undergraduate and postgraduate levels. His academic work has been published in leading journals such as the *South African Journal of Human Resource Management*, *Research Journal of Business Management* and *Springer*. Calvin is registered as an MHRP with the SABPP and a member of the Higher Education Committee.

**Dr Mpho Magau** has over 25 years of human resource management experience. Most of this period was spent in the mining industry as a labour relations specialist. Since joining academia in 2011 as a lecturer in human resource management, Mpho has led curriculum development in labour relations studies and facilitated interventions aimed at maintaining trust-based relationships in the workplace. He also supervises postgraduate research in the field of labour relations. Mpho is the former deputy head of department and was responsible for co-ordinating the human resource management programme in the Department of Industrial Psychology and People Management at UJ. Mpho is a Chartered HR Professional (CHRP) with the SABPP and a member of the Higher Education Committee.

# List of abbreviations

| | |
|---|---|
| AI | artificial intelligence |
| ANC | African National Congress |
| ASGISA | Accelerated and Shared Growth Initiative for South Africa |
| AU | African Union |
| BEE | black economic empowerment |
| CCMA | Commission for Conciliation, Mediation and Arbitration |
| COSATU | Congress of South African Trade Unions |
| CUSA | Council of Unions of South Africa |
| EU | European Union |
| FEDUSA | Federation of Unions of South Africa |
| FOSATU | Federation of South African Trade Unions |
| GEAR | Growth Employment and Redistribution Strategy |
| HPCSA | Health Professions Council of South Africa |
| HR | human resources |
| ILO | International Labour Organization |
| LIFO | last in, first out |
| NACTU | National Council of Trade Unions |
| NDP | National Development Plan |
| NEDLAC | National Economic Development and Labour Council |
| NUM | National Union of Mineworkers |
| NUMSA | National Union of Metalworkers of South Africa |
| RDP | Reconstruction and Development Programme |
| SACLA | South African Confederation of Labour Associations |
| SACP | South African Communist Party |
| SACTU | South African Congress of Trade Unions |
| SAFTU | South African Federation of Trade Unions |
| SAPS | South African Police Service |
| SETA | Sector Education and Training Authority |
| TUCSA | Trade Union Council of South Africa |

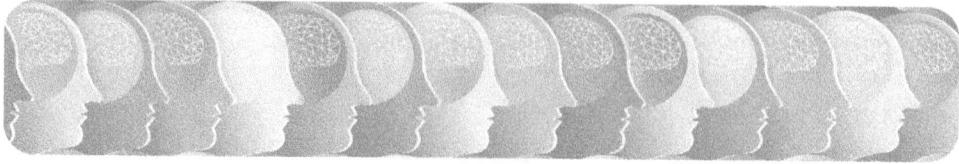

# List of useful websites

www.anc.org.za
www.busa.org.za
www.cosatu.org.za
www.ituc-csi.org
www.justice.gov.za
www.jutalaw.co.za
www.labour.gov.za
www.macrotrends.net
www.miningweekly.com
www.nationalplanningcommission.org.za
www.neasa.co.za
www.saffli.org.za
www.statssa.gov.za
www.tradeunions.co.za
www.weforum.org
www.worldbank.org/en/country/southafrica

# Table of cases

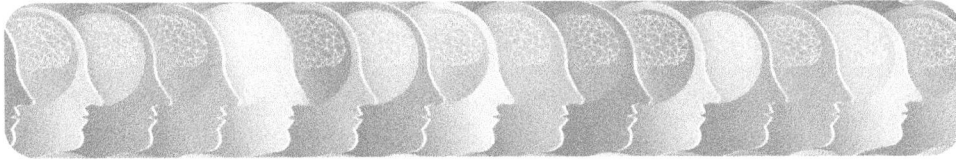

# Table of legislation

## CONVENTIONS

## RECOMMENDATIONS

# PART 1:
# Labour Relations Fundamentals

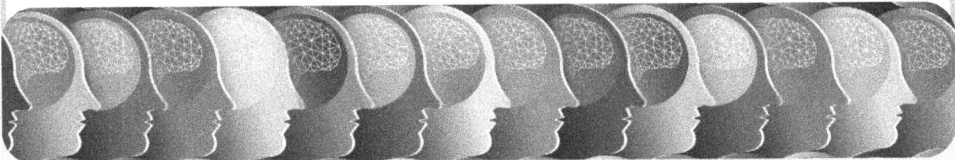

# 1

# The Employment Relationship: A Brief Introduction

➤

## INTRINSIC FACTORS REGULATING THE RELATIONSHIP

Custom and Tradition • Legislation • Mutual Agreement • Ethical Considerations: Trust, Integrity and Fairness | *The Need for an Ethical Framework* | *The Concept of Fairness*

## EXTERNAL INFLUENCES ON THE LABOUR RELATIONSHIP

The Sociopolitical System • Societal Influences • The Economic Dispensation • The Influence of Trade Unions • Additional Influences

## APPROACHES TO THE EMPLOYMENT RELATIONSHIP

Traditional Approaches | *The Unitary Approach* | *The Radical Approach* | *Pluralism* • Contemporary Approaches | *Societal Corporatism* | *State Corporatism*

## CONCLUSION

## SUGGESTED QUESTIONS/TASKS

## SOURCES

# Overview

Employment relations can only be studied once some background to the subject has been obtained and a basis for analysis and interpretation established. It is necessary, firstly, to analyse the concept and to identify the main elements. After that, the next logical step is to analyse the relationship itself and to see what sets it apart from other relationships.

The employment relationship is one in which one or more persons are employed by a private owner or work provider, by a large corporation or in the public service. Historically, the employment relationship was marked by certain negative attitudes, a great degree of depersonalisation and feelings of powerlessness among employees. These feelings arose mainly from the types of work people did as well as from traditional attitudes to work and the work situation, which evolved from the Industrial Revolution.

Attitudes to work and the work relationship did not change much with the advent of the Second Industrial Revolution, which saw the introduction of the assembly line and continued mass production. This situation began to change in the second half of the twentieth century, with the escalating use of digital technology. Since then the rate of change has been exponential, with many scientific discoveries leading to predictions of radical changes in the way business is done.

After analysing the basic characteristics of the traditional employment relationship, it is necessary to identify the parties and the roles adopted by each party, to discover how they interact and why they interact in that manner. Commonality and conflict are the two poles in the employment relationship. The parties can either co-operate and engage in participative processes, or rely on the use of power and collective bargaining. However, these processes are not mutually exclusive. Parties may move continually between the two poles established by commonality and conflict. Attention may also shift between the individual and the collective.

The way in which the parties interact will depend largely on the interaction between custom and tradition, between legal determination and mutual agreement. Integrity, trust and concepts of fairness play an important role.

In addition, there are numerous external factors which influence the manner in which the parties behave towards each other. These include sociopolitical and economic factors and the role of trade unions, as well as demographic and technological developments. The nature of the work being performed will also influence the interaction. Increasing digitalisation means that the relationship as we know it will continue to change. The Covid-19 pandemic has also affected employment relations more broadly.

Finally, we briefly discuss the three classical approaches to the relationship: unitarism, radicalism and pluralism. It must be noted that these are not necessarily practised in their purest form, and approaches may change according to circumstances. We also introduce two other approaches, namely societal corporatism and state corporatism. Additional to these approaches, various African philosophies concerning labour relations in Africa have emerged. Es'kia Mphahlele (the father of African humanism), John Langalibalele Dube (self-reliance), Mogobe Bernard Ramose (ubuntu) and Mabogo P More (black existentialism) are some of the leading philosophers in this southern branch of African philosophy.

# Understanding the Concept of Employment Relations

### From Industrial Relations to Employment Relations: Emphasising Relationship

The relationship which is the focus of this text has been variously referred to as industrial relations, labour relations and employment relations.

Labour or work relationships have existed since the first time an individual approached another to perform a task, based on the promise of payment. However, the employment relationship as a specific area of study is comparatively new. It has its origins in the Industrial Revolution and in subsequent attempts to regulate the interactions between the new types of employers and employees which evolved in industrialised society. This new work relationship was based on mass employment and mass production, and was marked by a growing division between those who owned and those who laboured. The result was a greater potential for conflict. Because workers were poorly treated overall, trade unions were formed to represent their interests and to counter the power of employers. In order to contain the conflict, bargaining processes were instituted and, eventually, governments began to pass laws to regulate the relationship. Thus, the field then known as industrial relations, was born.

Industrial relations as a concept placed emphasis on the institutionalisation of conflict by way of collective representation, collective bargaining, joint regulation and laws intended to regulate the relationship. This emphasis can be seen in most traditional definitions of the term 'industrial relations'. Clegg (1972) saw it as encompassing the rules that govern employment, the way the rules are made, changed, interpreted and administered. Flanders (1970), too, emphasised the institutionalised aspects of the relationship when he described an industrial relations system as a system of rules dealing with institutionalised and regulated relationships in industry.

These definitions, while they point to the need for the regulation of the relationship and to the fact that interactions are predominantly collective, are too narrow for our present purposes. We live in what is known as a post-industrial society, based on sophisticated economic activity, usually counterbalanced by an accountable public service and welfare systems and programmes. Our interest, therefore, lies in all relationships arising from work which contribute to, support or promote the economy, or which provide a service for or within society. Consequently, the term 'labour/work relations' – or, better still, 'employment relations' – is preferred. In the South African context too, the term 'labour/employment relations' can be used interchangeably with 'industrial relations' and is accepted by scholars. The concept of 'labour relations' is more in keeping with a post-industrialised society where the realities of white-collar service-related industries need to be accounted for.

The shift towards using employment relations as a concept does away with certain negative aspects associated with the concept of industrial relations and also broadens the scope of this field. Balnave et al (2007) note that employment relations has undergone development in recent years in response to, first, changes in the world of work and, second, the inability of industrial relations and human resource management to conceptualise these changes and the current state of play within the confines of their traditional disciplines. 'Employment relations' is a bridging term that both integrates industrial relations and human resources management and broadens the boundaries of both disciplines to encompass a wider range of stakeholder and environmental factors. Therefore, employment relations is intended to add a focus on the dimension of one-on-one individual relationships at work and to accentuate the importance of the informal dimension of the employment relationship. In this textbook, the term 'employment relations' will be used.

Employment relations is about the behaviour, interactions and psychological processes involved when people (employees) and organisations are at work. Slabbert, Parker and Farrel (2015) describe employment relations as a discipline that deals with formal rules, procedures, regulations, laws and policy decisions which shape the formal employment relationship. Furthermore, employment relations is also about the work experience, involvement and behaviour of each individual employee, and not only about a process of engagement between trade unions and employer organisations. At the organisational level, the employment relationship is more concerned with the conflict built into any employment relationship than it is with the coexistence and interdependence of the parties to this relationship. Employment relations encompasses both the individual and collective dimensions, while industrial relations and labour relations focus more on the collective dimension.

## Ambit of the Relationship

From the preceding discussion we see that, in our study of labour/employment relations, we are dealing with relationships between people within a work situation. These relationships may be of an individual or collective nature; they may differ from one society to another; and they give rise to actions, reactions, processes, rules, institutions and regulations which, in turn, will affect the relationships themselves. On the basis of this analysis, labour/employment relations as a discipline may be described as encompassing a study of:

- relationships
- the work situation and working person
- the problems and issues of modern industrial and post-industrial society
- certain processes, structures, institutions and regulations unique to this relationship.

All of these are placed or occur within a specific social, political, economic and historical context, and none can or should be studied in isolation.

## The Employment Relationship from a Historical Perspective

History plays an important role in shaping individual attitudes, societal norms and institutions. Therefore, the employment relationship should be placed in the context of one of the most important occurrences in economic history, the Industrial Revolution, and the further industrial revolutions which followed on from it.

### The First Industrial Revolution
*The Industrial Revolution as a Change Agent*
The Industrial Revolution was a social and economic convulsion which commenced in the fourteenth century, or even earlier. The most important changes at this stage were the introduction of the printing press, the invention of the steam engine and the establishment of factories, most notably in the textile industry. Because the Industrial Revolution changed the economic order, it had an immense effect on existing social structures, on the perceptions of individuals and society at large, and on working life. Together with the French Revolution, it played a major role in shaping the type of society we know today.

*Pre-industrial Society*
In pre-industrial society, work was traditionally determined. A marked division existed between wealthy landowners and peasants. Working people – with the exception of merchants and those in service – were engaged either in agriculture or in established crafts. Small communities were formed, in which labour was seen not as employment, but rather as fulfilling a particular function in society. The idea of earning a living was secondary to the fulfilment of this traditional or functional role.

Until the eighteenth century the striving for gain or excess profit, as we know it, was generally regarded as highly immoral. Heilbroner (1980) quotes the example of a sermon delivered in a Boston church in the year 1644. The minister, referring to a certain Keayne, charged with the crime of making more than sixpence profit in a shilling, goes on to expand on the following 'false' principles of trade:
- A person buys low and sells high.
- A person raises prices to make up for losses suffered.
- A person sells expensively because they bought expensively.

The above does not mean that wealth did not exist. It did, in the form of private wealth, but there was little or no attempt to put it to aggressive use – that is, to risk it in order to accumulate more capital.

## The Factory System and the Emergence of the Working Class

By the middle of the eighteenth century the old feudal order was already in decline, and the industrial era was born. This was partly due to the use of new energy sources, such as steam, and the invention of new machines which could, at a much more efficient rate, do the work previously done by hand or using handheld tools.

Moreover, society now began to accept that people by nature wanted to pursue gain, that gain was at the centre of commercial activity and that no law should exist against gain. The owners of capital established factories in which masses of workers performed relatively humdrum tasks. With the exception of a few who had special skills, workers were selling not their own products or know-how but their labour. It stands to reason that work lost much of its meaning and that working people had to search for a new identity. This was later found in the working class and through membership of trade unions.

## Effects on the Employment Relationship

New relationship patterns had to be established. Particularly during the early years of industrialisation, workers suffered great hardships. Many saw capitalist activities as based on the principle of keeping the poor poor. The idea took root that the capitalists, through their control of economic activity, had forced ordinary people into a situation where they had to abandon their traditional roles in society and sell their labour for a wage which was often below subsistence level, all to the benefit of the employer. This is a perception which, sometimes unjustifiably so, is still held by many employees today. It contributes greatly to the negative attitude many workers hold towards their employment and to the basic conflict between employer and employee.

Much has been said about the negative effects of the Industrial Revolution and little about the positive results, such as greater progress and development in all spheres and, later, a general improvement in the standard of living of all people. Our concern is mainly with the fact that the Industrial Revolution gave rise to a new type of society, centred on economic activity, and thus to 'economic man'. Employment relations, as a human science, concentrates on the latter. The most important consequences of the Industrial Revolution were, therefore:

- the removal of economic activity from the individual's personal and social life

- the depersonalisation of work and, consequently, of the employment relationship
- the polarisation between the mass of the employed, on the one hand, and the owners or managers, on the other
- the rise of working-class consciousness
- the growth of trade unionism
- negative attitudes engendered by the new dispensation
- the centrality of the role played by economic activity, causing it to become the main aspect of people's lives and one which impacts greatly on their personal, social and political lives
- the predominance of capitalism – the ownership by one or more persons of the 'tools' of production
- the consequential concept of 'selling labour'
- the disempowerment of the producers of such labour.

## The Second Industrial Revolution

By the middle of the nineteenth century the Second Industrial Revolution had already begun. This phase was marked by more and more scientific discoveries, more sophisticated technology, increased automation, the use of petroleum and electricity and the introduction of the assembly line, most notably in the production of motor cars in the late nineteenth to early twentieth century.

Even though trade unions had gained in strength and influence and there was greater socialisation of the economy, the major problems caused by industrialisation were still prevalent in the work situation. No significant reconciliation occurred between people's working lives and their personal or social lives. Work and the employment relationship were still, by and large, of a depersonalised nature. Polarisation, although perhaps not as great as before, continued to exist and the role of trade unions remained antagonistic.

## The Third Industrial Revolution

The latter part of the twentieth century saw an exponential increase in scientific discovery, resulting in the advent of digitalisation worldwide and introducing what has been dubbed the Third Industrial Revolution. Positive changes took place: improved education and training, as well as the growing tendency to flatten and decentralise organisational structures, began to blur the distinctions between different groups of employees, and between employers or managers on the one hand and 'workers' on the other. Gigantic projects emphasised the need for a team approach. It was thought that new meaning could be achieved by greater personal ownership of work and by the recognition of individual and collective value, while equalisation and team activity would improve identification and social interaction, resulting in a completely new attitude to work.

Yet, as Thompson (1986) has stated, it must be acknowledged that behind the glossy advertisements showing futuristic electronic equipment lies the reality of more routine tasks and fewer skilled jobs. Escalating automation made individuals and their labour increasingly dispensable. Global mergers and downsizing became the order of the day.

### The Fourth Industrial Revolution

The new millennium saw the onset of the so-called Fourth Industrial Revolution (4IR), an age of advanced technology based on information and communication technology (ICT). This revolution has led to changes in the labour market, with machines replacing human labour in many fields. In essence, 4IR is a continuation of digitalisation, but it is characterised by almost overwhelming scientific advances such as robotics, self-driven cars, cloning, nanotechnology and the prospect of advanced exploration of the universe.

In many ways, Thompson's (1986) prediction has come true. This is substantiated by Rifkin (2011), who predicted in 2011 that manufacturing would no longer be at the centre of economic activity and that labour costs would become less and less important. Technology has facilitated the creation of new products and services that have generated significant transformation in people's personal and professional lives, emphasising interaction between machines and people. Services, automation, robotics, artificial intelligence (AI), the Internet of Things (IoT) and additive manufacturing are elements that have shaped and are shaping business and the world of work.

Unemployment has been increasing worldwide since the turn of the century, while productivity has decreased significantly. Work is increasingly outsourced to independent experts/contractors. Experts like Rifkin, and Klaus Schwab of the World Economic Forum, have warned that organisations and governments need to change the way in which business is done. It seems that the world needs to move away from capitalism and large organisations to what is called a 'shared economy'.

The Fourth Industrial Revolution has also brought several benefits, which include increased economic efficiency; increased labour productivity; and increased productivity, flexibility and intelligence, reducing manufacturing costs while increasing returns on investments.

Ultimately, the question to be asked is whether work, in the form of salaried labour, will not eventually disappear. This would point to an entirely new social and economic order, one most of us cannot as yet conceive of. A reduction in creativity could occur due to increased automation and the disappearance of human capital from production technology. The Fourth

Industrial Revolution will affect employment relations both negatively and positively, since organisations are expected to reskill employees. While we have to be aware of possible future developments, we still need to concentrate on the work situation as it exists today and to direct our efforts at improving and possibly changing the nature of the relationship and the nature of work today.

## The Effect of the Covid-19 Pandemic on the Employment Relationship

The Covid-19 pandemic has, of course, affected employment relationships. Scholars (Blustein et al, 2020; Casale & Posel, 2020; Jain et al, 2020) have shown that the pandemic brought about an increased potential for conflict in organisations, which presents significant challenges in employment relations. The pandemic has led to huge increases in unemployment in several nations, as is widely documented (Blustein et al, 2020). South Africa is no exception: studies estimate that between 2.2 and 2.8 million individuals in the country lost their jobs between February and April 2020 due to the lockdown and widespread economic inactivity (Casale & Posel, 2020; Jain et al, 2020), exacerbating South Africa's unemployment crisis. This loss of employment has had significant implications for people's access to financial resources.

The majority of organisations have been affected by the pandemic, which has put them under extreme pressure given operational demands. South Africa is not immune to these challenges, since the majority of organisations have not been able to escape the economic impact of Covid-19, which resulted in job losses and some businesses closing down. Loss of employment or salary reductions are therefore grave issues faced by employees due to Covid-19.

Employees who did not lose their jobs during the pandemic had to deal with a change in work demands and resultant pressures, since there is a shortage of staff in the workplace due to retrenchments brought on by Covid-19. In order to curb the spread of the virus, many changes to work processes had to be introduced, such as remote working, social distancing and many others. The nature of work has thus changed substantially for most industries, leading to an increase in work demands and stress in many instances.

These new normal working routines require that employers consult with trade unions, the representatives of the workforce, on a regular basis. If trade unions are not consulted properly, conflict could escalate. Employers need to recognise the potential for conflict among employees in the current climate and ensure that they are sensitive and supportive of employees.

# Analysis of the Employment Relationship

While it shares similarities with other relationships, the employment relationship differs from other relationships in that it has an economic base (employees are selling their expertise and placing it at the disposal of the employer), is often impersonal, and is marked by negative attitudes on both sides. The relationship is also dynamic, meaning that it is ever-changing. As a result, it may be more complex than other relationships.

It is important to maintain healthy employment relationships, since they are a prerequisite for the success of an organisation. Positive employment relations are required if high performance and job satisfaction are to be achieved. Since the employment relationship is more complex, it is essential to avoid issues which might hamper the productivity of employees, or to resolve these if they do occur.

### The Employment Relationship as a Human Relationship

Labour/employment relations is concerned with people who, because of their mutual involvement in the work situation, have been placed in a specific relationship with one another. The relationship formed is a human one and, as such, will contain elements common to all other relationships – friendships, marriages, business partnerships, religious associations and political ties. The elements that make those relationships work should also promote a sound employment relationship. Consequently, like all other relationships, the labour/employment relationship will be improved by:

- mutual interests
- mutual support
- understanding
- trust
- meaningful communication
- shared goals and shared values.

Also, as in the case of all other relationships, the employment relationship is multilayered and dynamic. It changes as the status, needs, attitudes and perceptions of the parties change and as society itself evolves.

### The Uniqueness of the Relationship

The employment relationship is essentially a relationship of exchange that comes into existence when a person is employed by another party to perform work under the control and direction of the employer in exchange for some form of remuneration. The major distinguishing feature of this relationship is the fact that it arises from the need for economic activity in society and from people's need to work and to earn a living. Its uniqueness is to be found in:

- the societal and individual importance of the relationship
- the often-negative attitudes of the parties involved
- the depersonalised and mostly collective nature of the relationship itself.

## The Economic Basis of the Relationship

The basic level of the employment relationship is economic. Employees offer their expertise to the employer for a certain price. Therefore, the employer is expected to take into account economic considerations such as wages, salaries, benefits and other rewards before entering into the employment relationship. However, economic factors and markets may also have an influence on the employment relationship.

Modern society is economically oriented. The majority of our activities and institutions are centred on the economy. As a result, a person's identity is most often derived from the type of economic activity in which they are engaged. Who you are depends on what you do. Considering that at least one half of our waking hours is devoted to work, the relationships established in the work situation are among the most important aspects of modern human life.

The economic situation of employees will also differ, as some employees may come from high-income groups while others come from middle- or lower-income groups. Income differentials can affect the employment relationship; the organisation therefore needs to manage these differentials.

## Negative Attitudes in the Relationship

Despite the importance attached to work, attitudes to the employment relationship are not always positive. This phenomenon has its origins in traditional attitudes to work and to workers, and in the problems which came with industrialisation and mass production.

The performance of individuals largely depends on the relations among workers. In most cases, employees work in teams, and negative attitudes can affect feelings of collegiality and, thus, productivity. This, in turn, affects organisational performance. Conflicts and disputes can turn into major rifts among employees. It is impossible to completely control or curb such negative attitudes in the workplace. Even today these negative attitudes may persist, due mainly to the features of the employment relationship discussed next.

## The Impersonal and Collective Nature of the Relationship

The parties to the employment relationship do not usually display that sense of partnership, closeness and mutual commitment found in most other relationships. This stems from the almost involuntary and impersonal nature of the relationship.

Employees do not seek work with a particular employer because they like that employer or because they are in any way committed to the undertaking (although this may occur later). Essentially, an employee takes a job and enters the relationship merely to fulfil other, more personal, needs. Equally, the employer or the manager who represents the employer has no personal interest in the relationship or, for that matter, in the employee. The employer is not interested in the individuality of the worker or in their unique characteristics as a human being different from all other human beings; what is of interest to the employer is merely the employee's ability to perform the work required. At worst, the employer sees the worker as just another factor of production and, at best, as another replaceable member of the labour force.

Furthermore, the employment relationship is usually described in collective terms – not as a relationship between an employer and employee but as one between employers and employees. Both parties, and particularly the employee, are placed in a group context, leading to further depersonalisation. This perception of collectivism is made worse by societal divisions between those who work for others and those who own or manage. It is these divisions which led to the concept of a working class, where the word 'work' connoted not an action in itself, but the act of working for others.

The negativity often found in the employment relationship is aggravated by the fact that employees may feel forced, because of circumstances, lack of education or personal limitations, to work or to do a certain type of work, while they might prefer to be engaged in other, more attractive, pastimes or occupations. Negativity would also increase:

- if there is a markedly uneven distribution of wealth
- if employees cannot see themselves as being advantaged by the increased profitability of the undertaking
- if too much power rests with some of the participants
- if, in the extreme, employees regard the situation as an 'unfair' deal brought about by an 'unfair' system.

## The Complexity of the Labour Relationship

From the above, it becomes apparent that the employment relationship is both complex and paradoxical by nature. The relationship becomes more complex and dynamic because it exists in the broad context of various roles, rights, expectations and obligations in the workplace, either individual or collective. The relationship itself and the manner in which it is conducted are of immense importance to the individual and to society, yet both parties approach the relationship and each other with a certain amount of negativity and indifference. It is also a relationship in which perceptions of collectivity, from both sides, play an important role. The result is that personal identities are lost in the anonymity of the collective. Nevertheless, only the assertion of, and respect for, individuality can lead to personal satisfaction and meaningful relationships. It is these paradoxes which the labour/employment relations student and practitioner will be required to resolve.

## The Parties to the Employment Relationship

The labour/employment relationship is traditionally described as a tripartite relationship between employers, employees and the state. The employment relationship comes into existence as soon as one party employs another person. In this regard, the employer employs an employee and the two parties enter into an agreement.

In its basic form, the employment relationship is an economic relationship, meaning that one party is prepared to do work in exchange for some kind of reward for that work. And, as the term indicates, the employment relationship is, at its core, a relationship between the employer and employee(s). This is known as the primary relationship, while the relationship with the state forms the secondary relationship, as shown in Figure 1.1.

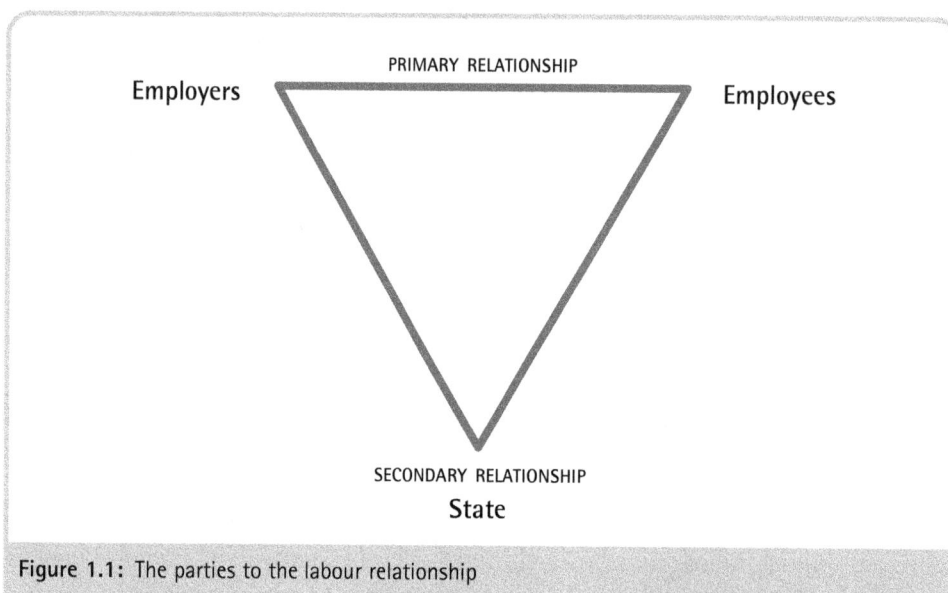

PRIMARY RELATIONSHIP

Employers                                                    Employees

SECONDARY RELATIONSHIP
**State**

Figure 1.1: The parties to the labour relationship

Also, the traditional description does not take into account the role of trade unions and employer organisations as representatives of the parties. In certain circumstances these bodies may exert as much influence over the relationship and the system built around it as does the state; thus, the labour/ employment relationship is best described as a relationship between an employer and employee/employees as the main partners, with the state, to a greater or lesser extent, playing a regulatory and protectionist role, and with unions and employers' organisations wielding, at times, substantial influence as the collective representatives of the core parties.

## Employer and Employee Roles

As in many other relationships, the roles and status of the parties to the employment relationship are, to a large extent, assigned by custom and tradition. Traditionally, the employer, owner or entrepreneur plans, decides, directs and controls, while the employee executes the orders of the owner, takes no part in decision making or planning, and is not concerned with the results of their actions. Employers are legal entities such as incorporated companies, close corporations, trusts, partnerships or entities resembling partnerships that employ people (Grogan, 2020).

The above-mentioned roles are still accepted and upheld by most participants in the employment relationship, resulting in a more or less willing acceptance of what may loosely be termed 'employer prerogative'. It can be said that the challenge to employer prerogative has lately gained impetus, but the mere fact that it needs to be challenged proves its existence. Despite changes in societal values and systems, individual beliefs and goals, and organisational and ownership structures, the roles adopted by the employer and employee remain, in essence, the same as those held at the beginning of the twentieth century.

It is important to define who the employee is in the employment relationship. According to Section 213 of the Labour Relations Act 66 of 1995, employee refers to:

> (a) *any person, excluding an independent contractor, who works for another person or for the state and who receives, or is entitled to receive, any remuneration; and*
> (b) *any other person who in any manner assists in carrying on or conducting the business of an employer ...*

This definition is in line with Section 1 of the Basic Conditions of Employment Act 75 of 1997 and Section 1 of the Employment Equity Act 55 of 1998.

Managers of large corporations, who are themselves employees, but who view themselves as representatives of the employer, have unquestioningly accepted both the traditional role of the employer and the employer prerogative. In the employment relationship, the manager, in their designated role as a representative of the organisation, and the employees interact on a daily basis. It is therefore also important to define the role of management. The management of an organisation refers to individuals or groups of individuals who are arranged in a hierarchical order according to levels of accountability and who are charged with achievement of the organisational goals through planning, organising, leading and controlling (Bartol & Martin, 1998).

Without a doubt, technological advances, the growing numbers of people working from home and increased outsourcing will lead to changes in the roles of the participants, and the erosion (or redefinition) of employer (or management) prerogative. The right of employers or managers unilaterally to plan, decide, direct and control will be increasingly challenged or will become redundant. This does not signify that no co-ordination will be required, but rather that the word 'management' will take on an entirely different meaning.

## The State as Party to the Relationship

In most societies, the state will, at the very least, provide minimum legal protection to the parties in the relationship and, if necessary, establish a framework for the peaceful conduct of the relationship. The state fulfils multiple roles in the employment relationship, which includes setting relevant policy direction in terms of political, economic and social aspects. The role of the state is to regulate the employment relationship by means of law making and to actively participate as an employer or, in some cases, as an observer.

The state is also widely involved in a dominant role in the employment relationship. The state is the major actor in the employment relationship, since it plays the role of creating and enforcing the legislation that regulates this relationship. The state further establishes social norms. It plays a structural role in that it establishes economic policies that influence the economic environment and a constitutive role in that it determines the fundamental nature of the employment relationship. The degree to which the state interferes (or is allowed to interfere) in the relationship varies from one country to the next, and will depend not only on the nature of the relationship itself but also on the predominant ideological and political beliefs of the society in which the relationship is conducted.

There is one instance in which the state becomes a full partner in the employment relationship. Because it administers a vast public sector, the state is also an employer, a role which may conflict with its other roles, namely that of legislator, conciliator and regulator. Traditionally, the state is regarded as a different type of employer from the private sector employer. The argument goes that the state is a non-profit organisation and that it gains its income from society, including its own employees. In the past this has led to the adoption of different employment relations legislation in the public sector and, often, to limitations being placed on collective bargaining and the freedom to strike in this sector; however, this is also changing.

## The Union as Party to the Relationship

The employment relationship between employers and employees is very complex and dynamic, since there are conflicting and shared interests. To safeguard the interests of these parties, both employers and employees traditionally join organisations like employers' organisations and trade unions so that they can collectively bargain on matters of mutual interest and to contain conflict. The employment relationship is therefore also, at times, described as a management–union relationship or, less frequently, as a relationship between an employers' organisation and a union or unions. This, however, does not take into account a relationship where no union or employer body exists.

The term 'union' is an abstraction for a collective of employees. Strictly speaking, a union does not have an existence independent of the totality of its members. As a social structure, it does gain a seemingly separate existence and can wield significant power, both in the relationship and in society. However, if its grassroots support were to fall away, the union would no longer exist. Thus, although unions have played, and continue to play, an important role in traditional labour/employment relations, they may not always be essential to the employment relationship.

As it is, unions continue to play a significant role in the South African system, as representatives of employee interests and rights, both at the bargaining table and in social and political structures.

## A Layered Perspective

In the preceding discussion, the employer and employee were shown to be at the centre of the relationship, with the degree of state interference varying from system to system. Unions, too, could play a dominant or merely a peripheral role in the relationship. The situation is further complicated by the fact that the state acts as an employer and thus has to regulate itself.

The role adopted by the state depends on a number of interrelated factors, two of which are the sociopolitical and economic principles of the dominant political party and the strength or acceptance of trade unions in the system. Trade unions may, in turn, wield extensive influence in the sociopolitical system. All of the above can be factored into a more multifaceted view of the relationship, as illustrated in Figure 1.2.

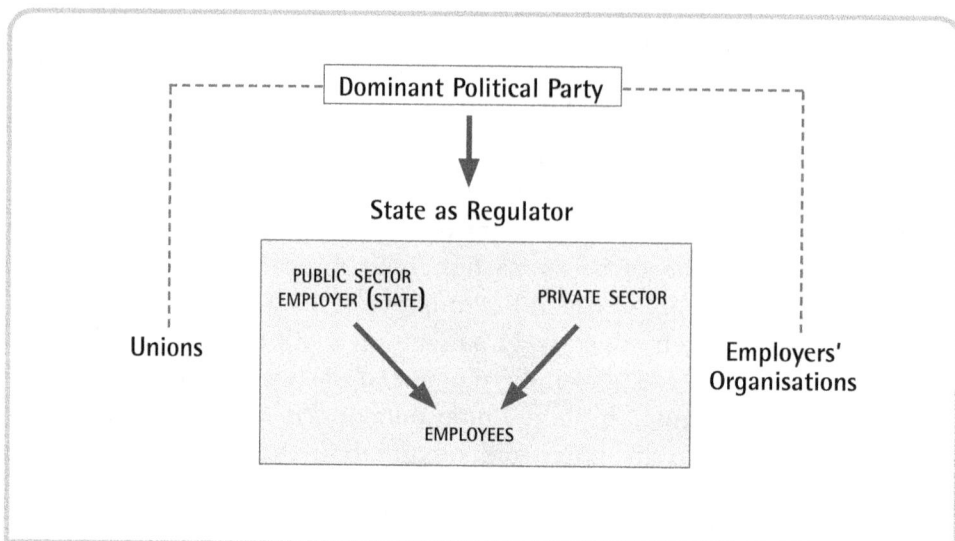

**Figure 1.2:** A multifaceted perspective of the employment relationship

## Factors Impacting on Interactions between the Parties

Numerous factors will affect the labour relationship. The most important of these are:

- the extent to which the parties acknowledge that they have common interests and agree to co-operate with one another
- the level of conflict in the relationship and the emphasis placed on collective bargaining
- the distribution of power between the parties and the type of power applied
- the degree to which participants, and union members in particular, are free to make their own decisions versus their allegiance to the collective.

From the above, an interaction model can be developed. See Figure 1.3 later in this chapter.

### Common Interests and Interdependence

In any relationship there is a certain commonality of interest. In the labour/employment relationship, commonality is found in the fact that both the employer and the employee – and the state, for that matter – have a vested interest in the continued profitable existence of the undertaking. The employer, in order to produce certain goods or services and to reap the intended profits, creates work for the employee who, in turn, accepts the work in order to gain remuneration, status and/or personal satisfaction. Consequently, both are interdependent, and both should be interested in advancing the work process to the highest possible level of efficiency as both will (or should) reap the benefits of continued profitability.

Where common interests exist, a certain measure of co-operation becomes essential. In the employment relationship, each party needs the other to achieve their own ends. Therefore, whether the parties want to or not, they co-operate in order to achieve their own goals. Although many people do not think so, co-operation still forms the basis of the relationship. If this were not the case, very little economic activity would occur. Rationally, therefore, we could assume that the relationship should be conducted in a spirit of harmony and mutual support. Unfortunately, this is not always the case, mainly for the following reasons:

- Employees in particular do not see themselves as having anything in common with the employer or manager. This view is the result of traditionally assigned roles and the behaviour associated with these roles, the negativity in the relationship, the polarisation between the parties and the perception of unequal reward.
- Commonality of interest is often overshadowed by conflict related to personal and group goals, values, interests and ideologies. The situation is made worse by social and political conflicts which intrude on the work situation.
- The employer does not see themself as dependent on a particular employee, but on the employee's labour, which, from the employer's perspective, is bought and relinquished by the employer at will.
- Most importantly, not enough emphasis is placed on processes and structures which promote co-operation in the workplace. Instead, the emphasis has fallen on the institutionalisation of conflict. This is true of both traditional theory and its implementation in practice.

Fortunately, new insights into the relationship have made practitioners realise that merely containing conflict does not develop the relationship. If development is what they want, they will have to focus on the commonality in the relationship and, therefore, on co-operative or participative processes. In South Africa, there have been attempts to balance conflict and the process of collective bargaining with co-operation and greater worker participation.

## Conflict and Collective Bargaining
### The Potential for Conflict
The potential for conflict in the employment relationship is infinite. At its most basic level, conflict can be seen in disagreements about the division of profits and benefits. Employees will want as much as possible in the form of wages, benefits and leisure, while the employer wants to maximise

profits for pay-outs to shareholders, expansion and reinvestment. On a more sophisticated level, conflict centres on matters such as:

- role and status definition
- decision-making powers
- accountability structures
- flexibility and control
- a conflict of personal values and goals, beliefs and ideologies.

### Functional and Dysfunctional Conflict

Studies in conflict prove that conflict in itself is not always bad; in effect, a certain level of conflict is functional. It prevents stagnation. Conflict in a relationship is not at issue. Such conflict will become dysfunctional only if it reaches destructive proportions, is not balanced by co-operation and is not handled in the proper manner.

In the employment relationship, it has long been accepted that conflict is endemic; consequently, processes have been devised to handle and contain conflict. This has led to the acceptance of collective bargaining as a predominant process in the relationship. Collective bargaining prevents one party to the relationship from pursuing their own interest at all costs, and thus prevents conflict from reaching unmanageable proportions. However, it can be argued that too much emphasis is placed on collective bargaining as the most preferred method of resolving conflict.

Collective bargaining, particularly distributive bargaining, results in compromise solutions and very often in a win-lose or lose-lose result. By contrast, it is generally accepted that integrative problem solving, relying on a large measure of co-operation, is a far superior method of resolving conflict, since it usually results in a win-win solution, which is more universally acceptable.

### The Power Dynamic

#### The Shifting Nature of Power

Because it is most often based on win-lose outcomes, the process of collective bargaining, as practised in contemporary labour/employment relations, relies greatly on the use of power. In fact, collective bargaining commences only when one side sees the other as holding power and the process involves continual attempts to balance or equalise power. The amount of power wielded by either party at any particular time is dependent on certain power variables. Of these, the most important are:

- dependence
- importance
- scarcity
- non-substitutability.

The more dependent an employer is on an employee, the more power that employee will wield over the employer. The more important an employee or group of employees is to an organisation, the more power will be wielded by those employees. When jobs are scarce, employers wield more power. An employee who cannot be replaced is in a position of power.

Power is never constant or held by only one party; it is continuously shifting from one party to another. In the past it was believed that the more balanced the power, the better would be the outcome. Magenau and Pruitt (1979), for example, maintained that when power is balanced, there is usually an easy agreement of high value. Unfortunately, a balance of power is often unachievable. As soon as one party sees that the other has equal power, the former will try to gain greater power. This results in continuing power competition. It is important to note this phenomenon. Most traditional employment relations and collective bargaining theories rest on the assumption of a power balance between the parties. This may, in many instances, not be possible.

The state also holds power over the work relationship. Depending on its ideological orientation, the state may decide to interfere in the relationship and may thereby equalise power between the parties or tip the scales in favour of either the employer or employees. Thus it can be said that, despite the lesser role assigned to it, the state, if it chooses to interfere to a high degree, may have overarching power in the employment relationship.

### The Predominance of Coercive Power

Much depends on the one party's perception of the other's power. Power, if it exists, must be seen to exist. Therefore, it is sometimes necessary for one of the parties to engage in an open display of power in order to persuade the other party to engage in meaningful bargaining.

In the employment relationship, the power displayed on both sides is, unfortunately, usually coercive. Employers start from a basis of power over the employee. Organisational structures, systems and processes are designed so that the employer can continue to exercise coercive power or, at best, to use negative rewards. Managers gain legitimacy based on their ability to punish or reward employees, and most work processes are established within these parameters. The most extreme form of coercive power used by management comes from the ability to withhold the opportunity to work – and, therefore, to earn a living – from the employee. This is seen in dismissals, retrenchments and lockouts.

The individual employee's power rests mainly on their value to the employer. If the employee is easily replaceable, they will, in situations where they have no legal or agreed right, not have sufficient power to counter the power held by the employer or manager. It is for this reason that laws are introduced to protect employees and that employees, particularly semi-skilled and unskilled workers, rely on the power of the collective. This is usually gained by union membership. Only if they jointly withhold their labour can they hope to match the power of the employer. Some observers believe that this is merely an illusion of power – that the very nature of organisational design ensures that managers/employers retain their power. Nevertheless, the threat by either side that it may use extreme coercive power, in the form of lockouts or strikes, forms the basis for the collective bargaining process.

*The Five Forms of Power: Referent and Expert Power as Preferred Modes of Power*
French and Raven (1959) identified five forms of power:
1. **Coercive power:** for example, the threat of punishment or harm, like in industrial action
2. **Reward power:** the ability to bestow favours on the other person
3. **Legitimate power:** obtained by being in a position of authority over another
4. **Expert power:** resting on knowledge and experience
5. **Referent power:** obtained when others identify with a person or his or her value system and look up to that person.

Of the five, coercive power is said to be the least desirable and the most primitive. Reward power is closely related to coercive power, as the threat of not bestowing a reward becomes coercive. Legitimate power relies heavily on the use of punishment and reward. This leaves expert power and referent power. To gain truly legitimate power, managers should rely not only on the authority of their positions, but also on power gained from their expertise. At the same time, each employee should gain power through their expertise. Furthermore, both parties should strive to substitute the overuse of one-sided coercive power with 'interactive' referent power, resting on shared goals, values and beliefs. In short, they should be substituting 'power over' with 'power to', because only if each individual is empowered will the organisation itself become powerful. This again points to the establishment of joint structures and processes, not necessarily to the exclusion of those designed for collective bargaining, but alongside them.

## The Freedom of the Individual versus Allegiance to the Collective
Nowadays, most work is performed on a collective basis. Consequently, enterprises are structured as collectives. In organisations there are departments, sections, management boards, production workers and administrative staff. People are viewed not as individuals but as members of a particular group.

On the employee side, this collectivity is further emphasised by the need to identify with fellow employees in order to match the power of the employer. In these circumstances it is extremely difficult for employees to assert their individuality. Tension is created between employees' need for personal recognition, advancement and satisfaction, and their need to form part of the collective. Equally, tension exists between employers and unions. In spite of their own collective emphasis, employers at times want to treat employees on a differentiated basis as individuals, while unions, being the representatives of the collective, do not want individuals to be singled out.

This tension between the individual and the collective raises a number of questions:

- Can an employer award differentiated increases on the basis of merit, or in any way treat one employee differently from another?
- Does the employer have the right to demand that an employee takes an individual decision contrary to that of the union?
- Can the employer establish direct representation by employees even where collective representation by a union is the norm?
- Does the union have the right to demand that all employees abide by a majority decision and that no differentiation be made by employers?
- Can the union insist that all employees become union members and that the employer communicate only through a representative body?

The solution is probably to achieve a balance between the interests of the collective and those of the individual, with due respect for the allegiance owed by the individual to a particular collective. If the matter is handled with sensitivity and acknowledgement of both individual and collective rights, due recognition can be given to both the collective and individual interests of employees. However, the employee may owe allegiance to two collectives, namely the company and the union. One should therefore take care that demands from the one do not clash with the interests of the other or erode allegiance to a third party.

The Interaction Continuum

From the preceding discussions it becomes evident that, in the employment relationship, we move (or can move) on a continuum between conflict and co-operation, each dynamic being underscored by its own power relations and processes (see Figure 1.3). Also, there is continued tension between the needs and demands of the organisation, the individual and the collective.

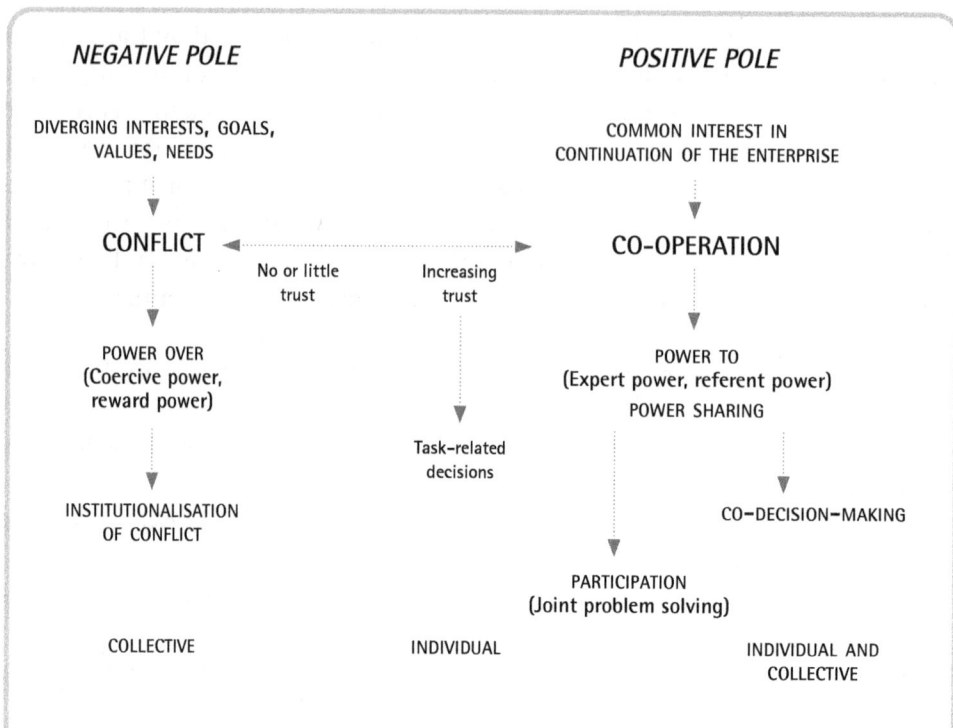

**NEGATIVE POLE**

DIVERGING INTERESTS, GOALS,
VALUES, NEEDS

↓

**CONFLICT** ◄- - - - - - - - - - - - -►

No or little    Increasing
trust            trust

↓

POWER OVER
(Coercive power,
reward power)

Task-related
decisions

↓

INSTITUTIONALISATION
OF CONFLICT

COLLECTIVE                INDIVIDUAL

**POSITIVE POLE**

COMMON INTEREST IN
CONTINUATION OF THE ENTERPRISE

↓

**CO-OPERATION**

↓

POWER TO
(Expert power, referent power)
POWER SHARING

↓

CO-DECISION-MAKING

↓

PARTICIPATION
(Joint problem solving)

INDIVIDUAL AND
COLLECTIVE

Figure 1.3: The interaction continuum

## Intrinsic Factors Regulating the Relationship

### Custom and Tradition

The manner in which the parties to a relationship behave towards each other, as well as their status and roles in the relationship, is often determined by custom and tradition. This is the case with the employment relationship, where custom has not only determined the roles of the parties but has also accorded certain rights and duties to each party. Thus, as stated earlier, managers assumed a traditional prerogative and employees traditionally obeyed without question.

The influence of custom and tradition in societal structures is strong, and any attempt to change traditional perspectives or hierarchies is vehemently resisted. Yet custom and tradition are not always correct or rational, particularly in the light of ever-changing realities. Too much reliance on custom results in stagnation and in a relationship that is out of touch with the world in which it exists. The need to question the customary way of handling work relationships, organisational design and the manner in which work is done will in the next decades become more and more important as the millennium progresses (see the discussion on the Third and Fourth Industrial Revolutions earlier in this chapter).

## Legislation

Because we cannot rely solely on custom and tradition to regulate the employment relationship – as the relationship itself is often unequal and the parties might engage in destructive practices to the detriment of society – it is usually regarded as necessary to establish a legal framework within which the labour relationship can be conducted. Consequently, the law may establish machinery for the peaceful resolution of conflict between the parties, delimit the rights of both parties and even attempt to correct perceived power imbalances. Yet in a free society the state, as legislator, can never presume to control all aspects of the employment relationship. Experience has shown that, the law notwithstanding, the parties will eventually regulate the relationship in the way they deem fit.

Having said this, if unemployment worldwide continues to escalate and technology makes more and more jobs redundant, it may well happen that the state will have to play a greater role in the way technological advancement and economic activity are handled. In the final analysis the state may even be obliged to interfere in the division of the profits emanating from such activity.

## Mutual Agreement

Since custom and tradition and the imposition of legislation may be deficient, the parties to the employment relationship also resort to mutually agreed rules and regulations as a basis for their interactions. Agreement is achieved either by the process of collective bargaining or, in more sophisticated systems, by joint structures established for this purpose. The more the parties to a relationship can agree on rules, processes and substantive issues, the less they will have to rely on the assistance or jurisdiction of external instances.

## Ethical Considerations: Trust, Integrity and Fairness
### The Need for an Ethical Framework

Usually, too little attention is paid to a system of ethics as a regulator of the employment relationship. There has been a gradual realisation of the need to conduct business along more ethical lines, but little is usually said regarding an ethical framework for the conduct of the employment relationship.

A lack of trust, which often permeates the labour relationship, is evidence of the absence of an ethical code to which both parties can subscribe. Like any other relationship, a labour relationship not founded on trust will inevitably experience difficulties. Despite the conflict and the battles of will between the parties which often exist, some measure of trust has to be established. This can be achieved if there is:

- respect for the other party
- faith in the integrity of the other party
- due recognition of the value, power, ability and legitimacy of the other party
- the assurance that neither party will abuse their position
- agreement that both parties will view situations from a balanced perspective, will not attempt any form of subversion, will keep their word and will act consistently in the light of their own beliefs and values.

This may seem like a tall order, but it is achievable if both parties operate within a mutual ethical framework and share a common work ethic.

### The Concept of Fairness

The fact that the parties often do not ensure that they are behaving fairly is further proof that ethical considerations do not predominate in the employment relationship. As a result the state may find it necessary to legislate fair labour practices. Admittedly, concepts of fairness do differ from person to person, and perceptions of fairness need to be placed in the context of particular circumstances. Yet certain neutral and universally accepted standards of fairness can be postulated. The most commonly used is the test of the 'reasonable person', although this may require a common definition of the word 'reasonable'. The question to be asked is whether others in the relationship, or an impartial judge, would regard the interaction as reasonable, and whether the party committing the action would deem it reasonable if it was committed against them.

Further criteria for fairness, as suggested by Salamon (1987), are the following:

- There should be reciprocity and balance between the parties concerned.
- One party should not obtain all the benefits to the detriment of the other.
- There should be equitable exchange of both substance and behaviours.
- Both parties should receive equal treatment and equal consideration.
- The same criteria and judgements should apply to both parties.
- The treatment of persons should, as a whole, be consistent.

South Africa's own Labour Court has repeatedly indicated that the parties should be 'perceived to be acting fairly'; in other words, that 'fair' is not 'fair' unless others see this fairness in action. This means that parties should explain their behaviours and decisions or, ideally, actually involve those concerned when decisions are being made.

The complex question of ethics, and particularly of fairness, is the subject of much debate, but it is extremely important in the conduct of the employment relationship.

## External Influences on the Labour Relationship

### The Sociopolitical System

No relationship functions in a vacuum. It is a product of time and place, and will be subject to influences from the wider society in which it exists. Conversely, the type of employment relationship established in a particular society will impact on that society. This interaction is demonstrated by the fact that the political system, based on a particular ideology, will largely determine the type of labour/employment relations system and influence the power balance between the parties. On the other hand, individual employers and employees, as voters in the political system, are able to influence the policies of government and will have a say in the type of employment relations system established.

Specific public policy, not necessarily connected to the employment relationship, will impact on the relationship. For example, in South Africa, the policy of apartheid greatly influenced employment relations. It led to unequal bargaining power and the immobility of labour, as well as divisions in, and the politicisation of, the trade union movement. The advent of the new political dispensation in South Africa in the last decade of the twentieth century has seen increased legislation by government, some of which was intended to remedy past injustices and to grant more protection to vulnerable employees.

### Societal Influences

In the social sphere, there is continual interaction between social relationships and employment relations. Employees bring to the workplace perceptions established in their subsocieties. If, for example, there are large divides of class and race in society, these will be reflected in the workplace. Similarly, tensions arising in the workplace will be carried out to the wider society, either by individuals or by organised groups such as trade unions and employers' organisations. If goodwill and co-operation predominate in the workplace, this may spread to society at large. At the micro level, problems experienced by employees in their communities – such as a lack of housing, inadequate facilities, a lack of transport and substandard education – will impact on the employment relationship or become issues in collective bargaining.

## The Economic Dispensation

Most obviously, the economic dispensation, on both a macro and a micro level, will directly influence the conduct of employment relations. The predominant economic philosophy of a particular society – that is, whether it favours free enterprise or a planned economy – will largely determine the type of employment relationship and the role of collective bargaining in the system. Other factors, such as fiscal policy, economic growth and unemployment, also exercise a strong influence, particularly in collective bargaining.

## The Influence of Trade Unions

Trade unions are the direct result of worker dissatisfaction with capitalist enterprise. Although they arise from this system, they are essentially antagonistic to it. Initially, owner- managers and the governments of the time tried to subvert these organisations, but labour unions grew in strength during the nineteenth and early twentieth centuries. Many established their own political parties or affiliations, extending their power into society at large. As such, they served to curb the previously unfettered prerogative of the entrepreneur or owner, and influenced governmental regulation of the employment relationship.

Attitudes to and behaviour within the employment relationship have been and continue to be greatly affected by trade unions. A particular employer may, in theory, favour a certain style and approach to the relationship, but the style the employer adopts will to a large extent be circumscribed by the amount of influence a trade union has on the enterprise. Equally, a government may tend to favour the employer party and the capitalist economic system, but, in a democratic system, it cannot enact legislation without due reference to a strong trade union movement. This, eventually, will also impact on the relationship at enterprise level.

Figure 1.4 illustrates the various external influences on the employment relationship.

## Additional Influences

A number of other interactive factors, such as technological development, business structure, industry concentration and labour demography, influence developments in employment relations, and particularly the collective bargaining process, but the subject matter of this chapter does not justify a more detailed discussion of these factors. It is important merely to note that the relationship and the processes emanating from it cannot be studied in isolation, once again illustrating the necessity of adopting an interdisciplinary approach.

SOCIAL STRUCTURES

POLITICAL PARTIES
PUBLIC POLICIES

INDUSTRIAL RELATIONS SYSTEM

GOVERNMENT REGULATION

LABOUR RELATIONSHIP

MORALS

TRADITION

IDEOLOGY

ATTITUDES  GOALS

ROLES

EMPLOYERS,
EMPLOYERS'
ASSOCIATIONS

VALUES  INTERESTS

SOCIOPOLITICAL
BELIEFS

PARTICIPATION

CO-OPERATION

COMMON
GOAL

CONFLICT

COLLECTIVE
BARGAINING

IDEOLOGY

ATTITUDES  GOALS

ROLES

EMPLOYEES,
UNIONS

VALUES  INTERESTS

SOCIOPOLITICAL
BELIEFS

ETHICS

CUSTOM

COMPROMISE/AGREEMENT

ECONOMIC
DEVELOPMENTS

TECHNOLOGY,
DEMOGRAPHIC CHANGES

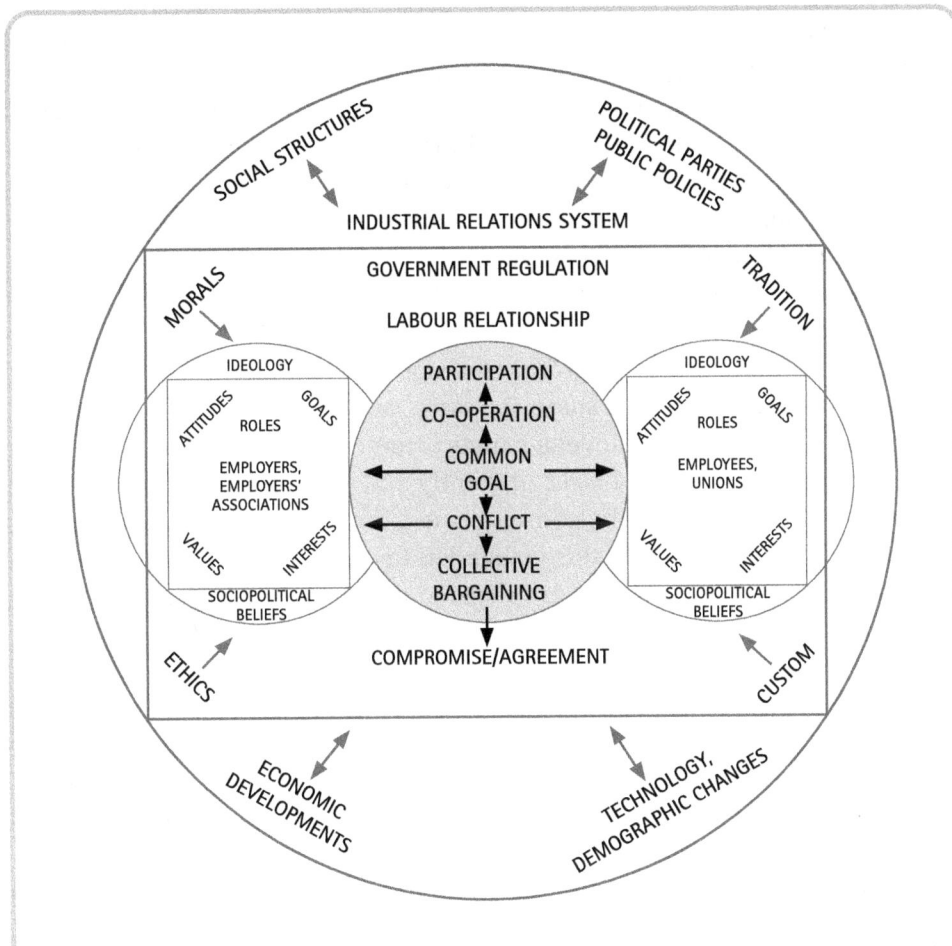

**Figure 1.4:** Schematic representation of the labour relationship

## Approaches to the Employment Relationship

Traditional theory identifies three approaches to the employment relationship. Two of these can be traced to particular ideologies, while the third constitutes an attempt to achieve a compromise between different ideological positions.

### Traditional Approaches

*The Unitary Approach*

This approach has its origins in classical liberalism, laissez-faire capitalism and the Smithian tenet of the 'common good'. It is individualist in that it does not recognise the necessity for collectives. Employees are regarded as individuals who have contracted their labour to the employer in order to gain an assured income. This approach sees the employment relationship as a long-term partnership between employees and employers with a common interest. Profitability and other organisational goals cannot be separated from fulfilling work, fair treatment and providing employees with feelings of satisfaction and addressing their other intrinsic desires. This approach is the foundation for contemporary human resource management and its focus is on creating policies that simultaneously benefit employees and employers.

This approach holds the following:

- The income of employees is assured only if the enterprise remains profitable.
- All parties should strive towards a common objective.
- Employers and employees share the same values.
- Both employers and employees support free enterprise, respect authority and perform their allotted tasks diligently and with loyalty.
- Since the system aims at the common good, there should be no questioning of the individual's place in this constellation.
- Employers or their managers are there to manage; employees are there to work.
- Employers care for their employees.
- Those who do well will be rewarded, just as those who do wrong will be punished.
- There is no real conflict of interest between employers and employees.
- Conflicts which do occur are the result of interpersonal friction or are caused by troublemakers.
- Unions are unnecessary and cause friction, as they compete with the employer for the loyalty of employees.
- Collective bargaining should not be encouraged.

It is important to note that the unitarist employment relationship does not recognise issues of structural power and conflict. Since employers and employees are assumed to share unified interests, power is unimportant and conflict is seen as a suboptimal state of affairs.

With the rise of trade unionism at the beginning of the twentieth century, the unitary approach was gradually eroded. However, the last decade of the twentieth century saw a resurgence of the liberal ideology in the form of neo-liberalism. This was accompanied by globalisation, an increased emphasis on the individual, and a worldwide decrease in trade union numbers and influence, with the result that the neo-unitarist approach gained popularity. This approach recognises collectives, but focuses on the individual. It engages in consultation and once again stresses the need to co-operate rather than to adopt positions as adversaries.

*The Radical Approach*

The radical approach is based on Karl Marx's theories regarding the ills of private ownership of the means of production and the position of the worker in the capitalist system. This approach holds the following:

- The capitalist economic system establishes political and legal structures which favour the employer.
- In this system, the power of the employer is always greater than that of the employee.
- The employee is continually exploited.
- Conflict is inherent in the socio-economic system as a whole, and not only in the employment relationship.
- Consequently, the structures established in the system will not resolve or ameliorate the conflict, but merely perpetuate it.
- Trade unionism may be necessary to conscientise the working class, but it cannot achieve equality while it is operating within the system.
- At best, trade unions, through collective bargaining, can provide continual challenges to employers while working on the political front towards the overthrow of the capitalist system.
- Victory over capitalism is the only means to achieve an equitable dispensation.

The radical approach, though perhaps not in its extreme form, is often promoted by unionists. Radical Marxism may be out of fashion, but a socialist dispensation remains the stated objective of most major employee bodies.

*Pluralism*

With the rise of trade unionism and the liberal democratic ideology, the pluralist approach was proposed as the best means of accommodating the interests of the working class in a capitalist system. Pluralism has its philosophical roots in the Hobbesian view of the human being as a selfish being who will utilise any opportunity to dominate their fellows. It rests on the conflict model of society, which proposes that, in order to prevent dominant groups from gaining absolute control and to contain conflict within manageable limits, power should be more widely distributed. It proposes multiple centres of power and the give and take of bargaining between competing centres of power. Unlike the radical approach, pluralism does not seek to abolish capitalism, but rather to reform or manage it.

Pluralism, when applied to the labour relationship, accepts the following:

- There will always be conflict between employers and employees.
- The power of the employer inherent in the relationship can be balanced by the countervailing power of the collective.

- Conflict can be contained by 'orderly' collective bargaining.
- Because a common interest underlies the relationship, some form of compromise will always be reached.
- In the process, each party may apply power tactics to persuade the other of their point of view.

It is evident that, at the extremes of the pluralist mode, the parties are essentially positional and view each other as adversaries. Power underlies the relationship, continual conflict is accepted as the norm and power lies with the collective.

The pluralist approach, albeit in varying forms, has been adopted in most industrialised countries. It has also been the dominant approach in the South African system. However, both locally and internationally, there is a marked tendency towards social market economies and a more mixed approach to employment.

## Contemporary Approaches
### Societal Corporatism
Societal corporatism is an extension of pluralism, and it is also referred to as tripartite co-operation. It refers to a system of interest representation in which the constituent units are organised into a limited number of singular, compulsory, non-competitive, hierarchically ordered and functionally differentiated categories. These are recognised or licenced by the state and granted representational monopoly within their respective categories in exchange for observing specific controls on the selection of their leaders and the articulation of their demands and support (Schmitter, 1974).

Societal corporatism incorporates aspects of pluralism through social dialogue between two main parties in employment relations. It is based on the principle that the two main parties in the employment relationship (employer representatives and employee representatives) are no longer viewed as interacting on a mainly competitive basis. In corporatism, management, employees and the state collaborate to share power through social dialogues. This power-sharing arrangement seeks to contain conflict and better manage it. An important feature of societal corporatism is institutional arrangement, allowing organised labour and employers to formulate economic policy with the state. In societal corporatism, the relationship between the state, employers and labour is institutionalised in tripartite structures, and a strong interdependence among all parties is acknowledged.

## State Corporatism

State corporatism refers to instances where the state imposes its will on the labour movement. In this case, the emphasis shifts from tripartite co-ordination and co-operation to a situation where the state adopts a paternalistic or authoritarian stance to demobilise and co-opt organised labour into the government structure. This system is found more often in underdeveloped countries.

Finnemore, Koekemoer and Joubert (2018: 13) cite Zimbabwe as an example of a country where authoritarian state corporatism has driven trade union oppression, and Namibia as a country that has witnessed paternalistic state corporatism. State corporatism is characterised by conflict between the employer and employee, and is thus considered undesirable. In most cases, trade union movements have become weak and relatively small owing to industrial development. In these countries, a large proportion of the labour force either works in the agricultural and public sector or is unemployed (Finnemore et al, 2018). While trade unions may either be small or large in terms of employee representation, it is notable that their influence may be weakened by the paternalistic and authoritarian state rule in these nations, where democratic labour practices are restricted. The state controls the trade union movement; for example, the formation of new trade unions and trade union structure is dictated by the state and involvement in political activities is forbidden.

## Conclusion

To explain the intricacies of any relationship in a single chapter is a daunting undertaking –even more so for the employment relationship, with its unique and often paradoxical characteristics and its highly dynamic nature. Therefore, the intention of this chapter has been to merely introduce the reader to the vast panorama of actions, interactions and processes which constitute the employment relationship. Specific aspects will be discussed in greater detail in later chapters.

## Suggested Questions/Tasks

1. Which aspects would you emphasise if you wanted to change the employment relationship in an organisation towards a more co-operative one, and how would you go about doing this?
2. Do some research on the Third and Fourth Industrial Revolutions. Outline a future work scenario and argue for considerable changes in the way we handle the work situation.

3. Cite the new and revised legislation the government has introduced since 1995 and analyse the reasons for such legislation.

## Sources

Balnave, N, Brown, J, Maconachie, G & Stone, R. 2007. *Employment Relations in Australia*. Milton: John Wiley & Sons.

Bartol, KM & Martin, DC. 1998. *Management*, 3rd edition. New York: McGraw Hill.

Blustein, DL, Duffy, R, Ferreira, JA, Cohen-Scali, V, Cinamon, RG & Allan, BA. 2020. 'Unemployment in the time of COVID-19: A research agenda'. *Journal of Vocational Behavior 119:* Article 103436.

Casale, D & Posel, D. 2020. 'Gender inequality and the COVID-19 crisis: Evidence from a large national survey during South Africa's lockdown'. *Research in Social Stratification and Mobility* 71: Article 100569.

Clegg, H. 1972. *The System of Industrial Relations in Great Britain*. Totowa: Rowman and Littlefield.

Finnemore, M, Koekemoer, GM & Joubert, Y. 2018. *Introduction to Labour Relations in South Africa*, 12th edition. Durban: LexisNexis.

Flanders, A. 1970. *Management and Unions*. London: Faber & Faber.

French, WL & Raven, S. 1959. 'The basis of social power', in *Studies in Social Power*, edited by D Cartwright. Ann Arbor: University of Michigan Press.

Grogan, J. 2020. *Workplace Law*, 13th edition. Cape Town: Juta.

Heilbroner, R. 1980. *The Worldly Philosophers*. New York: Simon & Schuster.

Jain, R, Budlender, J, Zizzamia, R & Bassier, I. 2020. 'The labor market and poverty impacts of Covid-19 in South Africa'. CSAE Working paper WPS 2020-14. https://scholar.harvard.edu/ronakjain/publications/labor-market-and-poverty-impacts-covid-19-south-africa (Accessed 4 November 2021).

Labour Relations Act (66 of 1995). *Government Gazette* vol 366 no 16861. Pretoria: Government Printer, December 1995.

Magenau, JM & Pruitt, DG. 1979. 'The social psychology of bargaining', in *Industrial Relations: A Social Psychological Approach*, edited by GM Stephenson & CJ Brotherton. New York: John Wiley & Sons.

Rifkin, J. 2011. *The Third Industrial Revolution: How Lateral Power Is Transforming Energy, The Economy, and the World*. New York: Palgrave MacMillan.

Salamon, M. 1987. *Industrial Relations Theory and Practice*. Hoboken: Prentice Hall.

Schmitter, PC. 1974. 'Still the century of corporatism?', in FB Pike and T Stritch (eds), *The New Corporatism*. Notre Dame: University of Notre Dame Press: 85–131.

Slabbert, JA, Parker, AJ & Farrel, DV. 2015. *Employment Relations Management. Back to Basics: A South African Perspective*. Durban: LexisNexis.

Thompson, P. 1986. *The Nature of Work*. London: Macmillan Education.

# 2

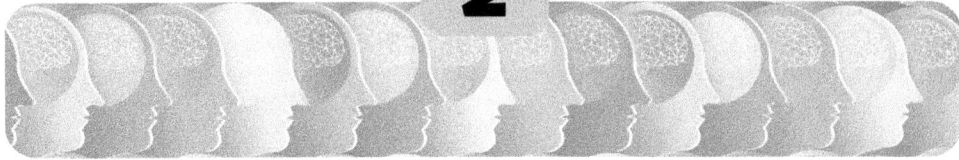

# The Labour Relations System

## Chapter Outline

➤

BACKGROUND TO DEVELOPMENTS IN THE SOUTH AFRICAN LABOUR RELATIONS LANDSCAPE

Racial, Economic and Ideological Divides • A 'Dichotomous' Ideological Approach • The 'New' Dispensation

INDUSTRIALISATION IN SOUTH AFRICA (1880–1924)

Discovery of Gold and Diamonds • Immigration and Unionisation • Industrial Action and Government Reaction • The Rand Rebellion • The 'Black/Disenfranchised' Trade Union Movement • The Industrial Conciliation Act 11 of 1924 • The Civilised Labour Policy • Analysis of Developments

THE GROWTH OF THE MANUFACTURING AND SERVICE INDUSTRIES (1925–1948)

The White and Multiracial Trade Union Movements • The Influence of Afrikaner Nationalism • The Independent Black Trade Unions • Analysis of Developments

ASCENT TO POWER OF THE NATIONALIST GOVERNMENT (1948–1970)

The Botha Commission • The Native Labour (Settlement of Disputes) Act 48 of 1953 • The Industrial Conciliation Act 28 of 1956 • The Multiracial Trade Union Movement • The All-White Labour Movement • The Independent Black Movement • Analysis of Developments

CHANGES IN LABOUR RELATIONS (1970–1990)

The Start of a New Era • The Revival of Black Employee Interests • The 1972–1973 Strike Wave • New Unions Emerge

THE BLACK LABOUR RELATIONS REGULATION AMENDMENT ACT 70 OF 1973

Consolidation of 'New' Union Power • The Wiehahn Commission • The Industrial Conciliation Amendment Act 94 of 1979 • The Reaction of the Newer Trade Unions • New Federations Established • White Opposition • TUCSA Disintegrates • Government Reaction • Analysis of Developments | *Collective Power as an Instrument for Change* | *Initial Acquiescence with Capitalism* | *Acceptance of Pluralism*

DEVELOPMENTS POST 1990

The New Dispensation • Initiatives to Kickstart the Economy • Labour Relations Policy and Legislation | *The Labour Relations Act 66 of 1995* • Labour Action • The Trade Union Movement | *Tensions in the Tripartite Alliance* | *Expectations and Actions Post Polokwane* • Collective Industrial Relations Processes | *Collective Bargaining* | *Workplace Forums* • New Legislation • Analysis of Developments | *Socio-economic Policies* | *Labour Legislation* | *The Union Movement*

ECONOMIC AND SOCIAL REALITIES IN THE NEW MILLENNIUM

The Economy • Unemployment • Inequality • Civil Unrest • Government Initiatives | *The New Growth Path Framework and the National Infrastructure Development Plan* | *The National Development Plan* | *Radical Economic Transformation* • Union Developments | *State of the Unions* | *New Unions Emerge* • Analysis of Developments | *Socio-economic Problems and Proposed Solutions* | *Union Developments* | *Labour Unrest and Collective Bargaining Arrangements* | *Approach to the Relationship*

CONCLUSION

SUGGESTED QUESTIONS/TASKS

SOURCES

# Overview

In order to understand the South African labour relations system, it is necessary first to understand how different systems come about. Labour relations systems are societal structures. This means that they are shaped by the societies in which they occur. A system consists of the various participants, the processes adopted in the relationship and the legislative framework.

The most important variable shaping a society – and, therefore, its labour/employment relations system – is the dominant ideology. In this respect, we differentiate between two ideological poles: individualism and communitarianism. These are also the foundation for different economic ideologies, resting originally on the ideas expounded by Adam Smith, at the one extreme, and Karl Marx, at the other. However, in modern society there is a tendency to convergence between these extremes. Nowadays very few societies, or their labour/employment relations systems, reflect extreme ideological stances.

In formulating policy, the government of the day will be guided largely (but not exclusively) by the dominant ideology. Other factors influencing the type and extent of government interference include the economic situation, trade union strength and the government's labour–capital bias. In any society all the variables interact in a complex manner to produce a system unique to that society.

In South Africa, industrialisation commenced with the discovery of diamonds and gold in 1867 and 1886 respectively. At the time the dominant ideology was individualistic, but because of the belief in white supremacy, other race groups were denied freedom of choice and controls were introduced to protect the position of white employees in the labour relations system. As the economy developed, the government was obliged to legislate a framework for the conduct of the relationship, but from the beginning the emphasis was on the exclusion of black African workers. This was reflected in the Industrial Conciliation Act 11 of 1924, which excluded 'pass-bearing natives' from the definition of employee, and, later, by the Industrial Conciliation Act 28 of 1956, which prevented black trade unions from achieving registered status and therefore from engaging in legal actions.

Societal forces were, however, at work and during the first half of the twentieth century there were numerous actions by workers from different race groups. Growing dissatisfaction among black workers eventually resulted in the Natal strikes of 1973, which proved that these workers could make their voices heard and which forced the government to take heed of this section of the workforce. In the years which followed, new trade unions were established, leading to the formation of the Federation of South African Trade Unions (FOSATU) in 1979 and the Council of Unions of South Africa (CUSA) in 1980. The new unions did not join the centralised bargaining bodies which had been established by the white and 'multiracial' unions. Instead, they concentrated on strong shop-floor representation, eventually gaining ground over the 'multiracial' Trade Union Council of South Africa (TUCSA).

During the 1970s, economic and political pressure from inside and outside the country increased. In response to this, and in the face of growing union militancy, the government passed the Industrial Conciliation Amendment Act 94 of 1979 (subsequently renamed as the Labour Relations Act of 1979) which gave all employees and their unions equal rights in the labour/employment relations system. This equalisation in the labour relations system served as a precursor to political democracy.

➤

In 1985 different union streams joined forces to form the Congress of South African Trade Unions (COSATU) and, shortly thereafter, the National Council of Trade Unions (NACTU). Their new-found legitimacy in the system and their participation in central bargaining bodies greatly increased the power of unions in these federations.

The government of the time legislated the framework for interactions between the parties for fair labour practices and for minimum conditions of service. The idea was to allow the parties, as far as possible, to regulate the relationship among themselves. After the African National Congress (ANC) came to power in 1994 it was, however, obliged by historic inequities to interfere to a greater degree in the conduct of the relationship. This more mandatory approach was best exemplified by the Employment Equity Act 55 of 1998 and the Skills Development Act 97 of 1998 as well as later amendments to the Labour Relations Act 66 of 1995 and the Basic Conditions of Employment Act 75 of 1997. At the same time, the new government established the National Economic Development and Labour Council (NEDLAC). This proved that it was inclined to adopt a more corporatist approach.

Despite its alliance with COSATU and the South African Communist Party (SACP), the ANC government did not adopt a socialist approach and did not engage in pro-labour mandatorism. On the economic front, it chose instead to broadly support a free-market economy, while ameliorating this with welfare initiatives. At the time of writing (2021) the government's emphasis on 'radical economic transformation' may be signalling a tendency towards far greater government intervention in the economy and also the relationship, although this may merely be a result of current political turmoil. As regards labour/employment relations, the state has hovered between institutionalised voluntarism and some strong mandatory elements – both under the umbrella of limited corporatism.

In recent years, stress lines have increasingly appeared, first in the economic and employment spheres, and now also in the political sphere. General dissatisfaction with service delivery regularly results in demonstrations. On the labour relations front, strike action has not abated. Particularly significant is the dissatisfaction of employees with the unions representing them at centralised level, as evidenced in the mining industry, and the deployment of the police to quell demonstrations. In relation to the mining industry, the government has been harshly criticised for deploying the police during upheavals; however, the government went on to play a role in bringing about an accord, one which, unfortunately, did not last long. In general, more and more voices are calling for a more co-operative system and an emphasis on workplace democracy.

# Part One: The Labour Relations System as a Societal Structure

The labour relations system operating in a particular society is a product of, and is structured by, that society. It follows that a country's labour relations system will be shaped by all the different forces in that society. Because all societies are unique, labour relations systems are not all alike. Furthermore, as a society changes, so will its labour relations system.

In this section we find out:

- how systems vary because of different roles adopted by the parties, different processes and procedures and differences in the legal framework

- the effect of ideology on a system
- the theories of Karl Marx and Adam Smith
- the roles which the state could adopt and different forms of state interference in the employment relationship.

## The Composition of a Labour/Employment Relations System

### Major Components
The main components of a labour relations system are:
- the parties to the relationship
- the processes, such as collective bargaining and workers' participation, favoured by the parties
- the legal system governing the relationship.

These components are found in all systems, but, depending on the interaction of a number of societal variables, they are present to different degrees in different systems.

### Variations in the Composition of Different Systems
*The Parties to the Relationship*
Employers, employees and the state are, in all labour relations systems, the major participants in the relationship. However, one system will differ from another in terms of the importance and the role of each participant. In certain systems the state dominates the relationship, while in others it adopts the role of junior partner. Similarly, some societies will emphasise the interests of the employer, while in others the employee may be the most important participant. The power relationship between employer and employee – and the amount of influence each has – will greatly depend on the society in which they function.

Usually, the two parties in the primary relationship, and particularly the employee party, will act through representative bodies. These organisations will differ from country to country. In one society the functioning of trade unions may be facilitated, while in another, efforts at organising may be hampered by legislation and social circumstances. Trade union members may be an integral part of one society, while in another they may be relegated to second-class citizenship. Consequently, trade union actions and goals will vary from one system to another.

*Processes and Procedures*
The predominant processes in labour relations systems are collective bargaining and the practice of workers' participation. Varying emphasis will be placed on

these processes. In some systems, the use or implementation of one or both of these is compulsory, whereas in others it is completely voluntary. Equally, collective bargaining may be conducted at a highly centralised or a highly decentralised level and may take place in an orderly or a random fashion.

There are other processes which flow from the two main processes. These include:

- dispute settlement procedures
- communication structures
- systems for the conclusion of agreements
- in-plant disciplinary and grievance procedures.

The kinds of procedure followed and the relative emphasis placed on them will also differ in line with societal constraints.

### The Legal Framework

Most obviously, the legislation governing the establishment and conduct of the employment relationship will vary from country to country. Yet there are definite similarities in labour legislation, particularly in societies which have the same ideological base. Differences in the legal framework are to be found in:

- varying degrees of compulsion
- different forms of protection granted to employers and employees
- differences in the application of the freedom of association and the right to bargain collectively
- differing concepts of fairness and differences in legislation pertaining to this concept.

Finally, certain societies may establish other laws which do not apply directly to the employment relationship but nevertheless have an effect on the system.

## Ideological Basis

### Definition

All societies rest on an ideological base. The dominant ideology of a society will largely determine the type of labour relations system in that society. Equally, a system will change in line with changes in ideology.

Hunt and Sherman (1978) define ideology as beliefs that are typically used to morally justify the economic and social relationships in a society. It may also be described as a set of common feelings or values about how relationships in society should be conducted.

Individualism versus Communitarianism: Two Ideological Poles

The greatest difference in ideology is to be found between the belief in individual freedom, on the one hand, and communitarianism on the other.

Individualism, in its absolute sense, maintains:

- Individual persons or groups in society are free to make their own choices and pursue their own goals.
- Individuals have little or no responsibility towards society.
- Society has little or no obligation towards them.
- Society is secondary to the individual.
- Society is shaped by, and composed of, individual beings.
- Government by the majority may be necessary for a democracy, but minority interests should be accommodated.
- Conflict is unavoidable, and government should establish systems to accommodate it.

By contrast, communitarianists maintain:

- Individuals are shaped by society.
- The choice and self-interest of the individual should not predominate.
- The individual's first duty is towards the society from which they emanate.
- Individual interests should always be secondary to those of society.
- It is the duty of government to shape and control society.
- Bigger government is essential.
- Minority interests are subservient to the majority.
- Conflict should be avoided in favour of co-operative effort.

## Conflicting Economic Ideologies

As mentioned in the previous chapter, the roots of modern industrial society, centring on economic activity, are to be found in the Industrial Revolution. Because a new pattern of relationships was established, it also became necessary to develop new philosophies, to explain or direct the new relationships in society. These philosophies were expounded by a new breed of economic thinkers. Their pronouncements were related to the ownership of working capital by individuals and to the consequences, whether beneficial or otherwise, of such private ownership of capital and the labour process. The most influential thinkers were Adam Smith and Karl Marx and, later, the Fabian socialists, who preceded the institutional economists.

## Adam Smith and the Free Market

### The Rise of Classical Liberalism

Classical liberalists, among whom were such eminent thinkers as Thomas Hobbes, John Locke and Bernard Mandeville, regarded human nature as essentially selfish in its striving for pleasure and avoidance of pain. The individual was seen as the fundamental component of society. Consequently, the individual needed to be free to pursue their own interests – which, in terms of the liberal ideology, would eventually benefit society as a whole.

This life view was adopted and applied to economic activity by Adam Smith, who in 1776 published his famous work, *The Wealth of Nations* ([1776] 2000). This text came to be regarded as the basis of and justification for a capitalist system.

### Support for the Market Mechanism

In Smith's view, the developments which he saw around him – where an entrepreneur brought workers together and divided their labour in order to produce more efficiently and more competitively – would eventually benefit society as a whole. As long as the market operated freely, the desire of individual entrepreneurs to accumulate profits would result in healthy competition. This, together with the rationalism of the consumer, would lead to a regulation of profits and prices. Too much profit-taking, resulting in increased prices, would result in undercutting by competitors, or to consumer resistance. This would either push the profit-taker out of the market or oblige them to lower prices. Based on what he termed the Law of Accumulation, Smith supported the amassing of profits within limits dictated by the market. He saw it as leading to investment in new ventures, new job opportunities and the development of society as a whole.

### Wages as a Product of Demand and Supply

Smith believed that wages could also be regulated by the law of supply and demand. Thus, he advised the removal of all restraints and all forms of interference in order to give free rein to price, wage and labour-market competition. Smith believed that, in a perfectly competitive labour and consumer market, all wage rates would tend towards an average rate. However, Smith did admit that factors such as skill (or a scarcity of skills), the amount of training needed for a certain job, the degree of responsibility involved and the seasonal or unpleasant nature of certain jobs might result in higher wages for some employees, and that wages could be affected by government interference in the labour market.

*The Ideal Market*

Smith promoted economic individualism in its most extreme form. He was opposed to any form of government interference in the free play of market forces. Nevertheless, he did warn against the establishment of monopolies and the effects of mass production on the creativity and morale of employees. Moreover, he maintained that no society could flourish if the majority of its citizens were poor and miserable: the total wealth of nations was equal to the sum of individual wealth. His was essentially a utopian system that presupposed a perfect market, operating in an allowed legal and moral code. In this system, the economy would respond to market demands and there would be universal and fully effective competition and a complete absence of any form of political interference.

## The Rise of Socialism and the Writings of Karl Marx
*Reaction to Capitalist Enterprise*

The capitalist system evoked reaction and criticism not only from workers, but also from eminent thinkers. Among the first of these was Robert Owen, a capitalist owner who nevertheless criticised the class divisions and oppression resulting from private ownership of capital. Owen suggested that private ownership should be abolished in favour of a system of co-operation and joint ownership. Most early socialists, such as Gracchus Babeuf, Henri de Saint-Simon, Charles Fourier and Pierre-Joseph Proudhon, rejected private ownership of the means of production and espoused a philosophy of universal equality.

*Scientific Socialism and Dialectical Materialism*

Most of the early socialist theorists were labelled 'utopian socialists' by Karl Marx since, according to him, they relied too much on rationality and morality as the basis for change. Marx commenced by analysing the ills of the capitalist system. He maintained that this system was essentially self-destructive. Its superstructure, which entrenched private property and private control of the means of production, was, according to Marx, incompatible with its economic base, namely industrial production. The latter, he explained, is an interrelated and interdependent process which demands social planning, not generally favoured by the supporters of private ownership. The result, he said, was planless production, leading to a constant disorganisation of economic activity. Because of this disruption capitalism would unwittingly breed its own successor, namely a rationally planned economy. This, in Marx's view, could be achieved only in a system in which the individual did not operate freely, but was subject to planning for the entire society.

## Marx's Theory of Surplus Value

Marx's main criticism of the capitalist system was that it reduced workers to the level of automatons who could not develop their full potential and who were measured only in terms of the exchange value of their labour. He saw labour as the most important instrument in the welfare of society, since it was the only factor creating value. In the capitalist society, people were alienated from their labour and were obliged to produce surplus value in the form of profits for the employer. Marx argued that employees provided value in excess of the amount needed to maintain themselves but were paid only the bare minimum needed to support themselves, while the surplus value created was pocketed by the employer. Also, the capitalist system ensured that the supply of labour was always in excess of market demand, thus guaranteeing continued low wage levels.

## Towards a New Order

For Marx, the solution lay in a system of common ownership, which would lead to a more equitable distribution of surplus value or profits or, at the least, would allow employees to work only long enough to supply their basic needs.

Marx emphasised the dichotomy between employer and employee in the employment relationship. He did not believe that the conflict arising from the dichotomy could be confined purely to the work situation or that a compromise could be found in the development of trade unionism and collective bargaining. He supported unionism only as necessary to conscientise the working class and lead the way to a new order. In short, Marx emphasised the necessity to change society and the system of government to a communitarian base rather than to attempt to contain employer–employee conflict in the capitalist or private property system.

## The Fabian Socialists

During the latter half of the nineteenth century, workers made political gains through parties formed to represent their interests. They also experienced an increase in real wages. This resulted in less revolutionary thinking. It was hoped that peaceful change could be achieved by using the government as an instrument of social reform. The leading thinkers were not so concerned with the fact that capitalists owned the means of production; rather, they emphasised the unequal distribution of wealth because of the unequal division of the fruits of production.

Among the most prominent of these so-called Fabian socialists were the British researchers Beatrice and Sidney Webb. As socialists, the Webbs agreed with Marx that there was a basic conflict of interest centring on control of the mode of production and, therefore, an ongoing conflict between the 'haves' and the 'have-nots'. However, in their view, this conflict could be solved through a process of gradual accommodation rather than a complete and immediate change of the existing order. Society needed legal safeguards to protect the freedom and rights of all parties and special strategies to increase the negotiating or bargaining power of the 'have nots'.

For the Webbs, the solution was initially to be found in a combination: the development of trade unions as an economic and political force, and a system of collective bargaining – a term which was, in fact, coined by them. The Webbs also rejected the idea that, in a socialist society, workers might democratically manage their own industries. Instead they proposed the appointment of professional managers, accountable to the general population.

## The Institutional/Reformist Economists

The Fabian socialists preceded the institutional/reformist economists. The concerns of these economists relate mainly to decreasing productivity and increasing global unemployment in a rapidly changing world. The reformists advocate gradual change through institutions and changing relationships between the government, business and financial institutions. Governments need to help markets work by increasing their efficiency, enforcing contracts and assisting firms to access the grid and technology. Legislation governing work should, in their opinion, become simpler and more flexible. For example, among other things, they proposed that firms should be allowed to keep 20 per cent of employees on fixed-term contracts. In short, governments should assist firms to become commercially viable.

## The 'Forward Thinkers'

As mentioned in Chapter 1, the new millennium has seen ever-increasing technological advancement, particularly in the area of automation. This has raised concerns about the nature of work in the future and theories about the changing arena of work and business. Two of the foremost thinkers in this area are Jeremy Rifkin and Klaus Schwab.

Rifkin, who is particularly concerned about the continued decline of employment and profitability worldwide, predicted the establishment of 'post-market economies'. Rifkin (1995) points out that, as the century progresses, there will be less work available and those who have work may have to share their jobs with those who are not employed. This could be achieved by, for example, legislating for a 30-hour week. Persons who then have more free time could help the government by doing voluntary work in non-profit organisations. A great deal of the more advanced work required by organisations would be outsourced to independent contractors, whom governments would have to support by ensuring access to and advancement of technological resources. Although private ownership of businesses might continue, this would be on a reduced scale and with lower profits, since inputs and outcomes would be shared with experts who provide the know-how and their services. It is envisaged that governments will play a more active role by promoting and facilitating business while at the same time promoting the interests of all sections of society. This is a view shared by Schwab (2016), who is actively engaged in assisting governments to change their approach to business and the economy.

### Towards Convergence

The tempering of extreme ideological stances on both sides of the spectrum and the pronouncements of the 'forward thinkers' support the belief that the direction for the future lies in a convergence of individualism and communitarianism and the establishment of a new ideological framework in developed societies. However, the early years of the twenty-first century have not seen much momentum in the convergence of ideologies and the establishment of more economically 'balanced' societies. Instead, globalisation has brought with it a renewed emphasis on the operation of market forces and greater concentration of resources and capital. This has been supported by what some have termed neo-liberalism, which is actually best described as 'libertarianism'. Unlike classical liberalism, it places all the emphasis on freedom and none, or very little, on responsibility. Whether this aggressive, acquisitive capital accumulation in the economic sphere can be reconciled with a more communitarian orientation in the sociopolitical arena, is debatable. This applies equally in the South African context.

## The Role of the State

### Government and the State

The state may be described as the abstraction of all the individuals in a society. It represents society at large. However, it is very difficult to picture or conceptualise the state in such abstract terms. Thus, the state is commonly seen as being embodied in systems of government. This causes the words 'state' and 'government' to be used interchangeably. In democratic systems, governments are elected by the people, but, because democracy is based on the principle of majority rule, governments so elected are not necessarily representative of all those who constitute the state. The prospect of democracy also diminishes if, as in South Africa, representatives in Parliament are not elected directly by their constituents but by the relevant political party. All of the aforementioned dimensions of the state's functions and responsibilities are enshrined in the Constitution, which, together with all other laws, covers the whole spectrum of government.

A particular government, as representative of the majority in society, will adhere to a greater or lesser degree to either a communitarian or an individualist ideology. In practice, the state (in the form of its main instrument, the government) will have a political bias, which, in a modern, economically based society, is revealed in a pro-capital or pro-labour orientation. This bias is of importance in labour/employment relations since it will, with other factors, determine the degree of state interference in the employment relationship.

## Voluntarism and Mandatorism

The extent and manner of state interference in the work relationship will, in the broadest terms, depend on whether it supports voluntarism or mandatorism. This, in turn, depends on its ideological base. If a government believes in voluntarism there will be minimal or no interference in the conduct of the relationship. Conversely, the principle of mandatorism rests on absolute or maximal government control of all aspects of the employment relationship. This would occur only in a society where government also exercises or attempts to exercise control over all economic and social forces.

At present, most societies operating to a greater or lesser degree on the free-market principle support voluntarism as the basis of their labour relations systems. Yet, in practice, absolute or pure voluntarism does not exist anywhere in the world. In all so-called voluntary systems there are mandatory elements. This is so for the following reasons:

- The government, in establishing a legal framework for society, necessarily impinges on labour/employment relations.
- Employment relationships, if left solely to the main participants (that is, employers and employees or unions), may be inequitable, making it necessary to restore the power balance.
- The conduct of labour/employment relations will impact on society and particularly on the economy.
- Labour relations also involves politics – the government, being a political instrument, necessarily interests itself in developments in this sphere.

Consequently, governments will, at the very least:
- provide the legal framework for the conduct of the labour relationship
- give minimum protection to employees and employers
- attempt to preserve labour peace
- attempt to safeguard society against extreme behaviour by either party.

## Forms of State Interference

The degree and type of interference in the labour relationship practised by a particular government will depend, interactively, on:

- its ideological base
- its political objectives
- sociopolitical and economic circumstances
- the strength of the union movement.

This results in different forms of interaction between the state and the other role players in the labour relations sphere.

### Market Individualism

In a society where the government supports an individualist ideology, is biased towards capital and adopts a laissez-faire approach to the economy; where the union movement is weak; and where the economy is relatively healthy, the tendency will be to adopt a completely hands-off approach to the conduct of the work relationship. The government will take the view that:

- employers and their employees are responsible for the way in which the relationship is conducted
- the contract of employment is the final regulator of the relationship
- market forces will sufficiently regulate employment practices.

However, the institutions and laws in such a society may favour capital and entrench property rights. Also, nothing would be done to correct the inherent imbalance in the employer – employee relationship and the unions themselves might not be strong enough to redress the situation. Therefore, in most modern societies the increased power of trade unions and general sociopolitical developments have led to the demise of market individualism.

### Institutionalised Voluntarism

In a society where the government is individualist-oriented, biased towards capital and supports the free-market system, but where trade unions are strong, it becomes necessary for the government also to accommodate the interests of employees and their unions. In essence, the government may still adopt a laissez-faire approach to the relationship, but it will accept trade unions' right to existence and it may entrench this right in legislation. Collective bargaining becomes an accepted, if not obligatory, practice and the government may go so far as to establish or endorse processes for this purpose. Disputes are accepted, as are the freedom to strike and to lock out.

To safeguard employees, the government may legislate minimum conditions of service regulations, health and safety prescriptions and regulations pertaining to workmen's compensation and unemployment. A government which has adopted this approach may set the framework for the conduct of collective bargaining, but will not oblige participants to engage in these practices. A governmental policy of this kind constitutes what is generally regarded as a voluntary approach, but it is better described as a policy of 'institutionalised voluntarism'.

## Pro-capital Interventionism

It could happen that a trade union movement becomes so strong that it poses a political or economic threat or causes a power imbalance between unions and employers. If this occurs, the government may engage in greater interference, aimed at curtailing the power of unions. This it may do by limiting their freedom to strike or restricting their activities in other spheres. The policy of pro-capital interventionism may also be adopted where a previous, labour-oriented government has, in the opinion of a new government, intervened too much on behalf of labour – for example, by nationalising industries and allowing employees too much power in the workplace. The new government will denationalise industries, encourage capital accumulation and place stronger restrictions on trade union action. This happened in the UK under the Conservative government of Margaret Thatcher.

## Corporatism

Economic or political developments may oblige a government to intervene in labour relations. In times of reconstruction or economic recession, a government wishing to kick-start the economy may request employers and employees to co-operate in its efforts to bring about economic improvement. This is what is generally known as corporatism. If the parties agree to a corporatist approach, it is implied that they will not engage in aggressive collective bargaining, that unions will limit their wage demands and that employers will limit price increases. Such a policy may be adopted with the voluntary co-operation of unions and employers. If not, an incomes policy or other restrictions and conditions may be imposed by the government.

Where all parties voluntarily co-operate to formulate labour relations and economic policies, they enter into a social contract aimed at achieving maximum benefit for all. This approach usually hovers between individualism and communitarianism, as it is meant to curtail the individual power of both capital and labour in the interests of society as a whole.

## Pro-labour Interventionism

If labour gains dominance in the government or the changed objectives of government bring about a bias towards labour, a government may intervene on behalf of labour. This happens particularly where economic ideology shifts to a more communitarian approach, seeking to incorporate social welfare principles or a social market policy. The government, through its economic policy, engages in the redistribution of wealth. This usually makes it unnecessary for the parties to engage in aggressive collective bargaining and strike action or lockout action. A policy of pro-labour interventionism will lead to greater protection and promotion of employee interests and to an extension of their rights in the workplace. Typical outflows of such a policy are compulsory employee profit-sharing schemes, workers' participation schemes and regulations regarding employee or union co-determination on boards of directors.

### Pro-labour Mandatorism

In a strictly communitarian society, pro-labour mandatorism will prevail. The government adopts an absolute bias towards labour, does not accept the free-market principle and does not encourage capital accumulation. The labour/employment relationship in its totality is under the control of the state and there is no perceived need for union action in the form of collective bargaining or protection of employee rights. Whether the government in this case does not itself become the employer is a question that could be debated.

### Pro-capital Mandatorism

Absolute mandatorism could prevail where a totally individualist government favours capital to the exclusion of labour. Since labour, which usually constitutes the majority of the national population, will have a vote in government, this is unlikely to happen in a democratic society. Nor will it be possible where there is a strong trade union movement.

A policy of pro-capital mandatorism would be marked by government intervention to curtail employee rights. This would manifest in the non-recognition of unions, in curtailment of the right to strike and in laws promoting the employer. With this policy, the circle of government intervention is closed, as the next step would be the adoption of a policy of market individualism.

### Variables Moderating Government Intervention

The compartmentalisation of levels of government intervention into seven basic types is an oversimplification of the real situation. It has been done merely to provide a framework for understanding different governmental policies and actions. In practice, there are not only exceptions to the rule, but also many fine differences of degree and numerous interacting variables. So, for example, economic circumstances or a change in objectives might lead a government to abandon one policy for another, despite its basic ideology, its capital or labour orientation, and the strength or weakness of the trade union movement. Furthermore, labour itself may become disenchanted with a labour-oriented government and may vote a capital-oriented government into power. This would lead to the adoption of a completely new policy.

Figure 2.1 attempts a schematic representation of some of the factors influencing the degree of government intervention, and tries to take into account their dynamic interaction. In Figure 2.1, the circles without arrows represent changing government bias and economic policy; the outer circle indicates the interventions which result. The circles with arrows are dynamic forces which represent, first, the growth of the union movement and, secondly, fluctuations in the economy. It can be perceived that, as trade unions grow in strength, government is gradually obliged to adapt its policy. Likewise, as governments increase their intervention, unions become weaker. Finally, the weaker the economy becomes, the more government will be obliged to intervene.

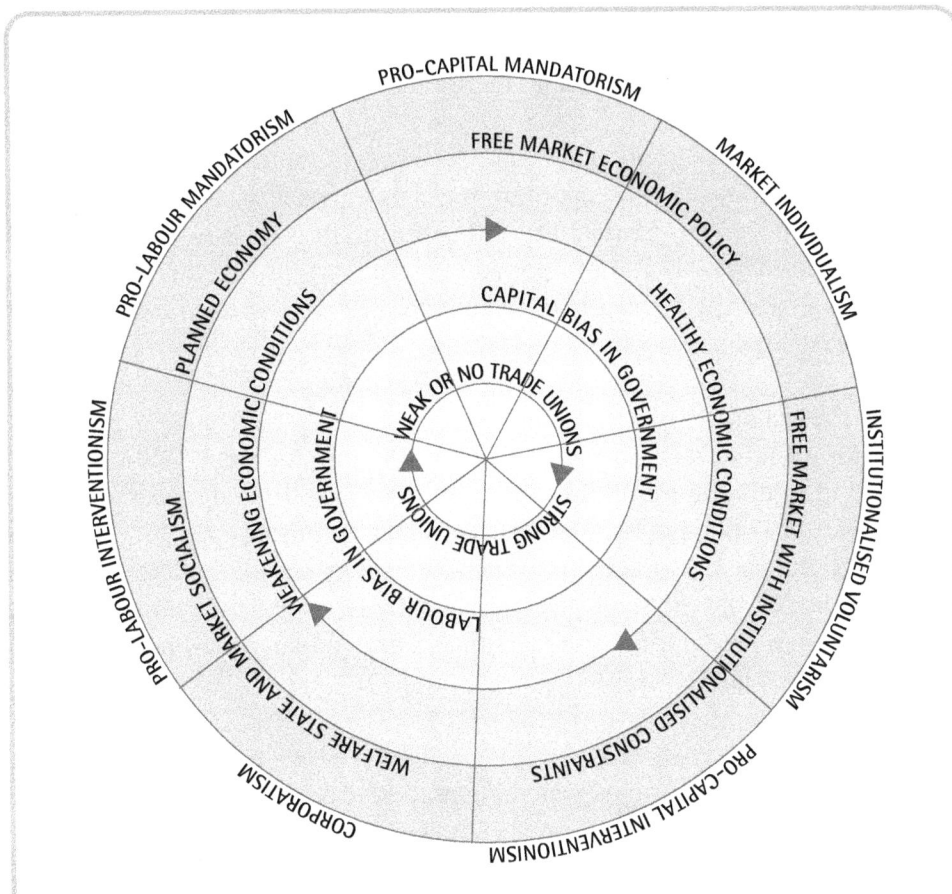

**Figure 2.1:** The cycle of state interference

## Roles Adopted by the State

Salamon (1987) divides the roles adopted by the state into four categories: employer, legislator, conciliator and regulator. Whether the state as employer intervenes in the labour relations system per se is debatable; this aspect is therefore omitted from the discussion that follows. Two more methods of intervention may be added to those of Salamon: the role of the state as adviser to the other two parties and its role as distributor of state income. In addition, the roles of state agencies such as the judiciary and the police deserve consideration.

### The State as Legislator

When it comes to the work relationship, the legislative role of the state is the most important. The state may legislate on individual rights and on collective rights; it may establish collective bargaining machinery and may prescribe statutory procedures to be followed by parties to the relationship. Generally, the type and amount of legislation will depend on a government's overall policy regarding intervention in the labour relationship. This is, in turn, dependent on the numerous interacting factors mentioned in the previous section.

### The State as Conciliator

In pursuing its objective of maintaining labour peace, a government may establish conciliation, mediation and arbitration services. The use of such facilities may or may not be made compulsory by the government. In certain instances, the government itself may interfere in disputes or act as conciliator/mediator.

### The State as Regulator

If the state wants to regulate the conduct of the employment relationship, it will have to intervene more directly in the relationship and, particularly, in the conduct of collective bargaining. The most common form of regulation is found in the establishment of an incomes policy or a complete freeze on wages and prices, but the state also regulates the relationship when it provides for compulsory recognition and bargaining and when it compels workers' participation at plant level.

### The State as Adviser

The state may set itself up as watchdog and adviser in the sphere of labour relations. In this instance the state will establish various bodies to monitor developments in labour/employment relations, to produce guidelines on the conduct of the relationship and to suggest innovations to the participants.

*The State as Controller of Income Distribution*

The state collects vast sums of money in the form of taxes and (if properly run) public enterprises. This would allow it to affect the relative positions of capital and labour. Most governments already make concessions in the form of lower taxes and other allowances for low-income earners. The state may also boost certain industries through loans or concessions and may use its financial power to bring about changes in the system. Rifkin (1995), for example, suggests that if, in the future, workers are obliged to accept shorter hours and engage in voluntary welfare work in their spare time, the state could compensate them by a reduction of or exemptions from taxes.

## The Role of the Judiciary

Despite its theoretical independence from government, the judiciary remains an instrument of the state. The function of the judiciary is to determine common law pertaining to the employment relationship and also to interpret and apply the statutes passed by government to regulate the relationship.

Problems with the normal judicial process are experienced where the judiciary is not acquainted with the intricacies of the employment relationship or with the law pertaining to it. Such problems increase when the judiciary is required to interpret concepts of fairness pertaining to the relationship. For this reason, certain governments see fit to introduce labour courts dealing specifically with labour matters.

## The Role of the Police

Essentially, the police have no role to play in labour/employment relations, as they are not supposed to side with either party. However, they do have a duty to protect the public and to prevent public disturbances. Therefore, where either of the major parties poses a threat to the public or causes a public disturbance, the police, as the law enforcement arm of the state, may intervene. Unfortunately, it is usually employees and their unions who are seen as causing a disturbance or infringing upon the rights of other individuals. Consequently, the police are often viewed as siding with the employers. For this reason and various others, police intervention should be allowed or requested only in extreme circumstances – and then only for the purpose of public protection or to prevent individuals from harming one another. Ultimately, the police force is an instrument of the state, and the latter should not allow it to be used to the benefit of either party or to promote the interests of the government in power.

### The Future Role of the State in Labour Relations

The state, with its instruments of government, represents a permanent institution which may change in nature and policy but not in essence. As explained throughout this section, the role of the state will be determined largely by circumstances. Nevertheless, where there is a shift from free-market principles to support for mixed economies or a social market system, the state may play an increasingly interventionist role in the labour/employment relationship.

### Effect of the Labour/Employment Relations System on Society

The interaction between society and the labour relations system is not a one-way process. Developments and events in the system will affect the wider society, particularly in societies where progress has been retarded.

At its most basic level, this interaction is seen in the effect that strike action has on the community and the economy. Such actions not only impede economic activity, but also cause general upheaval in society, which may have further repercussions. On the micro level, there is the case of the employee who is poorly treated and robbed of human dignity. This leads to the situation where this person is unable to fulfil their rightful role in society. Equally, polarisation in the workplace will be reflected in similar societal divisions, while collective organisation in the employment sphere leads to greater influence in the outside world. Both trade unions and employers' organisations play significant roles in the societies in which they function.

Participation and co-operation in the workplace may lead to similar co-operation between different groups in society. Training provided by the employer and the practice of social responsibility uplifts society as a whole. In many respects, the labour/employment relations system can take the lead and show those in power the route to follow.

## Part Two: The South African System

## The Industrial Revolutions

Before exploring the South African context, it is essential to remind the reader about the driving forces of prior industrial revolutions in world history, in order to facilitate a contextual understanding of how our current industrial revolution aligns with its historical predecessors. These industrial revolutions have a major bearing on labour relations.

### The First Industrial Revolution (1760–1850)

The First Industrial Revolution began in England in 1760. It involved radical innovations in production associated with the textile and clothing industry. Wool and textile frames were invented, which led to many jobs previously done by hand becoming redundant. The revolution converted the home craft of wool and textile weaving into an organised process of mass production. The supply chain and logistics were improved, since the new system linked the textile-producing towns in England. The First Industrial Revolution extended until 1850. Additionally, coal and steam energy was utilised to power steam locomotives.

### The Second Industrial Revolution (1850–1930)

The Second Industrial Revolution was ushered in by Henry Ford, who introduced the factory assembly line and the process of mass production. Production was carried out through the use of steam, gas, oil and hydroelectric power, which was used to create electrical power, resulting in the establishment of the factory system of assembly-line mass production. This system was at its peak in the 1920s. The developments during this era resulted in the invention of the electric bulb by Thomas Edison.

### The Third Industrial Revolution (1985–2007)

Rifkin (1995) coined the concept of the Third Industrial Revolution. His notion was that the internet and various renewable energy sources were intersecting to create an environmentally sustainable mass movement that could change the nature of energy creation, storage and supply.

### The Fourth Industrial Revolution (2008–2018)

The Fourth Industrial Revolution (4IR) has brought innovations such as digitalisation applications, the utilisation of robots in industry and production, three-dimensional printers, artificial intelligence (AI) and big data. Smart factories automatically adapt production conditions to current conditions and organise production plans to order demands.

4IR has brought about changes in many areas, from production relations to social relations, from cultural structures to political movements. The employment relationship and employment models have been transformed – some occupational categories have become redundant, and some are set to decrease considerably. In this context, 4IR is forcing transformation in labour markets and production methods, which has triggered changes in socio-economic and cultural structures. The efficiency of the production system has been ensured, triggering sustainable savings in terms of resources. At the same time, productivity has been increased, thereby decreasing the costs of production. The transition to automation has further decreased active human capital, which threatens labour relations.

The inevitable changes being brought about by 4IR will require a serious reassessment of both economic policy and work relations in the longer term. The automatisation of work may make a significant number of jobs obsolete, but it may also bring greater opportunities for the creation of a seamless global workforce and a different work–life balance.

### The Fifth Industrial Revolution (2019 to the present)

The onset of the Fifth Industrial Revolution (5IR) was marked by a major pandemic (Covid-19), resulting in major social change in innovation and creativity towards a more inclusive, humane society, a greater regard for environmental influence integrated to business profits and digital processes.

Society 5.0 is a concept that has grown out of Industry 4.0. The latter, dating from about 2011, is characterised by digitalisation and the further automation of processes through connected devices. For example, smart factories use a combination of cyber physical systems and human labour, with support from intelligence and automation. Society 5.0 is about personalisation. It is characterised by interdependence between machines and human beings, through the combination of human intelligence and cognitive computing.

## Background to Developments in the South African Labour Relations Landscape

### Racial, Economic and Ideological Divides

For long, South Africa was marked by historically, politically and legally entrenched racial divisions. This led, in the pre-1994 era, to the establishment of two distinct societal groups. The most obvious distinctions were to be found between the group which believed in white exclusivity and dominance and the one that subscribed to a policy of black nationalism. Positioned between these two poles there were those who supported a policy of 'separate but equal' multiracialism and others who were strongly non-racist. Distinctions also existed in economic ideology. While many South Africans were, in general, supportive of a capitalist free-enterprise system, there were also a substantial number who saw their future as secured in a more socialist, though not necessarily Marxist, dispensation.

### A 'Dichotomous' Ideological Approach

The distinctions made above are necessarily an oversimplification of the real situation. As South African society developed, extreme ideologies on both sides became diluted, but there was continued support for capitalism and the free-market system. However, the protectionism required to maintain the supremacy of the white population necessarily led to the imposition of greater restrictions on other groups, greater planning by government, and certain totalitarian practices. Thus apartheid South Africa had an unusual mixture of raw capitalism and free-market enterprise on the one hand, and selective social legislation promoting whites – and especially Afrikaners – on the other.

### The 'New' Dispensation

Following the first democratic elections in 1994, the ANC took over the reins of government. Its partners in the Tripartite Alliance – the SACP and COSATU – and many members of government held communitarian views. While broadly supporting the free-market system, the government promised to undertake a programme of reconstruction and upliftment, initially encapsulated in the Reconstruction and Development Programme (RDP). Its support of the free market – combined with efforts to change society, assist the poor and promote the previously disadvantaged – reflected a leaning towards a mixed economic or social market system.

## Industrialisation in South Africa (1880–1924)

### Discovery of Gold and Diamonds

Industrialisation in South Africa commenced with the discovery of diamonds in 1867 and of gold in 1886. Prior to these events, South Africa was mainly an agrarian society. There were, of course, merchants and craftsmen to supply the services needed by various communities, but there was no actual industrial activity. The only employment-related law was the Master and Servants Act 15 of 1856, which governed work rules, meaning crafts or services. There were no collective labour relations and no concerted attempts at organisation by workers, although there were occasional strikes before 1870.

### Immigration and Unionisation

With the discovery of diamonds and gold, there was an influx of labour, to the Witwatersrand in particular. Industrialisation was slowly commencing in the rest of the country, but the focus was on the diamond and gold mines and the industries – such as the railways, the engineering and the building industries – and the service sector established around them.

Because South Africa did not have a sufficiently skilled labour force, European (primarily British) immigrants were employed to do much of the work in this category. They brought with them the European – and mainly British – brand of trade unionism, based at that time on the ideal of a universal worker movement but balanced by the British sense of individualism. The first real unions were unions for skilled workers. The services of these workers were in high demand, and they occupied a privileged position in the labour force.

Unskilled and semi-skilled work was initially performed primarily by black people who had been obliged by the 'poverty push' to migrate to towns. After the Anglo-Boer War, they were joined by white Afrikaners who had been left without a livelihood due to the 'scorched earth' actions of the British army, which had destroyed most farms. These employees – and particularly unskilled black workers – were paid far less than their skilled counterparts.

Increased mechanisation meant that many skilled jobs could be broken down and done by cheaper unskilled or semi-skilled labour. The deskilling of work posed a threat to the skilled workforce. Their unions, which previously might have held universal socialist beliefs, began to insist on guarantees of job security for skilled workers. As a result, the first regulation instituting an industrial colour bar was introduced in 1897. It effectively prevented black African employees from becoming engine drivers. This was followed by the Mines and Works Act 12 of 1911, which reserved 32 types of jobs for white mineworkers.

### Industrial Action and Government Reaction

From the early 1900s onwards, strike action by white employees – and also by black employees –increased. The situation came to a head with a large-scale strike by white mineworkers in 1913. In the same year, black mineworkers went on strike.

These actions were followed by strikes at the railways and power stations and by a general strike of white workers in 1914. Up to that point, the government had mainly adopted a laissez-faire approach to labour relations and had interfered by the use of martial law and other measures only when security was threatened. It now realised that specific controls had to be introduced. As a result, the government passed the Indemnity Act 61 of 1961 and the Riotous Assemblies Act 17 of 1956, curtailing specific industrial actions.

In 1915, the Transvaal Chamber of Mines agreed to recognise white unions. Partly as a result of the First World War, a period of relative stability followed. In 1919, the government called a national conference of employers and employees, at which it was resolved that industrial unrest could be alleviated if employers of labour would recognise employees. Various agreements had, in the meantime, been reached between the white unions and the Chamber of Mines. The most significant one was the Standstill Agreement, whereby employers agreed that the ratio of white to black employees would never be less than 2 whites for every 17 blacks in employment.

### The Rand Rebellion

This co-operative spirit between employers and white employees was not to last. In 1920, the price of gold began to fall. General prosperity declined and a number of strikes occurred, also in the industrial and service sectors. Soon afterwards, mine employers announced that a new type of machine would be introduced. This posed a threat to skilled employees. The danger of skilled employees losing their jobs to less skilled workers increased when the Standstill Agreement was dropped. At the same time, white employees were informed that wages might have to be cut, resulting in the retrenchment of about 10 per cent of the white workforce.

In January 1922, 25 000 white miners went on strike. Because the miners later took up arms, this strike became known as the Rand Rebellion. Jan Smuts's government sent in the army and the strike was effectively crushed. By the end of the strike, 153 miners had been killed and 500 were wounded. Five thousand strikers had been arrested, four of whom were later hanged for treason. Hundreds of white miners were subsequently laid off. Those who did return to work had to be satisfied with lower wages and the deskilling of certain jobs.

### The 'Black/Disenfranchised' Trade Union Movement

As indicated, action also occurred among black African workers on the mines. This later spread to allied industries and services. The first recorded strike by black mineworkers took place in 1896, in reaction to a decision by mine managers to reduce wages. This was followed by more strikes after the Anglo-Boer War and by protest actions, such as boycotts, desertion and non-co-operation.

Following the black mineworkers' strike of 1913, a number of improvements were introduced in the mine compounds where black African employees lived, but protest action continued. As prices rose in comparison to wages, dissatisfaction among black employees spread to other industries, and this led to the formation, in 1918, of the Industrial Workers of Africa (IWA), generally believed to be the first union for black employees. Shortly thereafter, black workers decided to take action against the pass laws. This, and the subsequent strike by mineworkers, led to some improvements. However, in 1920, a massive strike by black mineworkers resulted in a tightening up of the pass laws, and in the curtailment of black mineworker resistance for some time to come.

In the meantime, the IWA had been overtaken by the Industrial and Commercial Workers' Union of South Africa (ICWU), born from the organisation of dockworkers of all races in the Cape, under the leadership of Clements Kadalie. The ICWU as such was established at a meeting of various organisations held in Bloemfontein in 1920, and by 1924 its membership had risen to 30 000, higher than that of any other workers' federation in the country. The ICWU covered a wide range of black interests. However, perhaps because of the diversity of its membership, the various factions influencing the movement and, later, government antagonism, it began to disintegrate in the late 1920s. It is still remembered as the first real black worker body, and even more so as the first mass movement among the black working class.

## The Industrial Conciliation Act 11 of 1924

The strikes by both white and black mineworkers, and those which had occurred in allied industries and services, had one important result: the government, afraid of more unrest, concluded that it needed to establish machinery for collective bargaining and the settlement of disputes. The result was the drafting of the Industrial Conciliation Act in 1924. However, this effort at institutionalising labour relations did not save the Smuts government. In the next election, the white workers, who felt that the government had sided with the mine owners, voted Smuts's South African Party out of power. The actual legislation was passed by the Pact government which followed. This government had been established by a coalition of the Labour Party and the National Party. Both parties had been brought to power by the white worker vote. It follows that, in the years to come, there would be closer co-operation between government and those workers who had the vote.

The primary purpose of the Industrial Conciliation Act of 1924 was to prevent labour unrest by providing for collective bargaining and for conciliation in the event of dispute. The Act and its subsequent amendments:

- provided for conciliation boards and industrial councils
- placed a criminal sanction on strike action which occurred without prior negotiation in these bodies
- provided for mediation and arbitration.

Industrial councils became the recognised bargaining bodies, and agreements reached by them were, if gazetted, legally enforceable.

The Act provided a very sound basis for the more orderly conduct of the employment relationship. However, no union representing black African men could register under the Act, since the definition of 'employee' specifically excluded 'pass-bearing natives'. (Black women were at that time not obliged to carry passes and were thus included under the legislation, as were certain black men in the Cape.) The exclusion had the effect that black (African) unions, not being allowed to register, were also not allowed to join industrial councils or apply for conciliation boards, and could not institute legal strike action.

### The Civilised Labour Policy

The Pact government also introduced what is generally known as the Civilised Labour Policy. This policy arose from the concern of the government at the fact that the living and moral standards of 'poor whites' in the industrial areas had deteriorated. It led to the active promotion of white employees through the provision of more opportunities at higher wages. The Civilised Labour Policy marked the beginning of an active campaign to promote the use of white, and especially Afrikaner, employees in preference to those of other race groups.

### Analysis of Developments

Because it supported capitalist endeavour, the government of the time initially engaged in a type of market individualism, at times replaced by unashamed intervention on behalf of capital. However, the demonstration of power by labour eventually necessitated a shift towards institutionalised voluntarism. The pluralist approach, centred on collective bargaining, was accepted as the best means of containing conflict in the employment relationship.

The exclusion of black male employees from the system reflected a desire by government to shape society in terms of its own vision. This can be equated with the social engineering usually prevalent in a communitarian dispensation. It also provides evidence of the extent to which sociopolitical ideology impacted on the labour relationship.

## The Growth of the Manufacturing and Service Industries (1925–1948)

### The White and Multiracial Trade Union Movements

The prosperity brought about by the gold mining industry resulted in rapid growth in the manufacturing and service sectors. This process accelerated during subsequent decades, and especially during the Second World War (1939–1945). Unionisation of employees in these industries had already occurred during the previous decade. The unions in these sectors, lacking the protectionism of the mining unions, often organised across colour lines. Among the organisers were many members of the Communist Party of South Africa (CPSA).

Soon after the Pact government had come to power in 1924, the then Minister of Labour convened a conference in Cape Town, at which a representative body for employers and another for trade unions were established. The idea was that the government should be able to consult with these bodies on labour matters. The union body formed was the South African Trades Union Congress (TUC), later to become the South African Trades and Labour Council (TLC). The TLC, established in 1930, consisted of unions and federations across the spectrum and from the various provinces. Most of the unions were registered and could participate in the official bargaining system. They were thus more favourably placed than the exclusively black unions. Yet the TLC was greatly influenced by more liberal elements.

In the years that followed, many of the TLC unions continued, under the leadership of organisers such as Solly Sachs of the Garment Workers' Union and Ray Alexander, founder of the Food and Canning Workers' Union, to institute militant action on behalf of the entire working class. By contrast, there were other unions in the TLC which wished to promote only white interests, and some which were concerned about the influence of communists and militants in their ranks.

### The Influence of Afrikaner Nationalism

During the 1930s, further political divisions began to arise. Afrikaners had for long resented the dominance in industry of the English-speaking sector and, especially, immigrant workers. This, among other things, had led to the establishment in 1918 of the Afrikanerbond (Afrikaner association), later known as the Broederbond (Brotherhood association). One of the aims of this body was to capture a share of the country's wealth for the Afrikaner nation. In 1933, JBM Hertzog's National Party and Jan Smuts's South African Party joined to establish a new party, the United South African National Party. This caused DF Malan and JG Strijdom to leave the National Party and to establish the Purified National Party, later supported by many white Afrikaner workers. The onset of the depression in 1929 and the escalating 'poor white' problem had intensified the need for greater protection and promotion of white, and especially Afrikaner, workers. Soon after its inception, the Purified National Party began a campaign to organise white Afrikaners into trade unions, establishing, in the process, the Blankewerkersbeskermingsbond (Association for the protection of white workers).

The result of these developments was a greater division in labour ranks, yet most of the unions operating in the official system still remained under the TLC. The most prominent unions differed, particularly in their attitude to other race groups. In 1948 the South African Iron, Steel and Allied Trades Association (SAISATU) left the TLC to establish the Co-ordinating Council of South African Iron and Steel Trade Unions (CCSATU). The policy of this body was to admit only all-white unions. The withdrawal of the Iron and Steel Union (Yster- en Staal-unie) was followed by that of the Mineworkers' Union and various railway staff associations. With this development, the ideal of a unified South African labour movement was finally abandoned.

## The Independent Black Trade Unions

During this period of heightened union activity, black and other disenfranchised employees increasingly flexed their industrial muscle. Despite the provisions of the Industrial Conciliation Act of 1924, the government was initially not unsympathetic to the interests of black employees, who were supported by many white people in industry.

With the disintegration of the ICWU, it was realised that organisation on a sectorial basis was more effective than general unionism, and numerous smaller union bodies were established. In 1928, these unions amalgamated to form the Federation of Non-European Trade Unions (FNETU). Some of the FNETU unions worked together with registered unions. FNETU was initially quite active, but the depression of 1929 diluted union power and in 1933 the organisation disbanded. One of its leaders, Max Gordon, went on to organise no less than 31 black unions, later co-ordinated under the Joint Committee of African Trade Unions. In 1940, Gordon was imprisoned and, because he had trained no successor, the Joint Committee began to disintegrate.

In the meantime, a Co-ordinating Committee of African Trade Unions (CCATU) had been established, covering Gordon's unions and those organised by Gana Makabeni of the Black Clothing Workers' Union. In addition, a fast-growing African Mineworkers' Union had been established. Finally, in 1942, all these unions and federations came together to form the Council of Non-European Trade Unions (CNETU). This body was to dominate the black trade union movement for the next decade. The outbreak of the Second World War brought many more black people to the industrial areas. Because they were sorely needed by employers, black workers were now able to wield more power. Numerous strike actions were initiated, and employers made various concessions to black employees.

By the end of the war, CNETU boasted a membership of 158 000 across its 119 affiliated unions. However, after peace had been declared, black African workers again became dispensable and their power declined. Government action against members of the CPSA robbed the organisation of much of its leadership. There was also a lack of grassroots involvement. The result was that, by 1950, CNETU was no longer able to wield the same influence as before.

The militancy of the non-racial and multiracial unions, and of the unions representing black African employees, had focused government attention on the problem of continuing unrest among black workers. Realising that something had to be done to curb the frustration of black employees, in 1930 the government amended the Industrial Conciliation Act (Amendment Act 28 of 1956) to provide for the extension of industrial council agreements to blacks. The Industrial Conciliation Amendment Act 36 of 1937 added to this provision, allowing for representation of black African employee interests on industrial councils by representatives of the Department of Labour. It was believed that black employees were not sufficiently 'developed' for direct representation in official bargaining bodies. Nevertheless, during this period there were continued efforts to provide some form of representation for black employees, all of which came to nought with the subsequent ascent to power of the National Party.

### Analysis of Developments

The ousting of the South African Party in the aftermath of the 1922 mineworkers' strike was proof of the need for government to consider the interests of both capital and labour, although, in this instance, the emphasis fell only on 'non-black' labour. The approach adopted by government was one of institutionalised voluntarism, counter-posed by the protection of white worker interests. The attitude towards black employees and their representatives remained, at best, paternalistic. Despite some efforts to incorporate black employees, the period reflects the growing influence of sociopolitical tensions on the labour relations system and increasing polarisation within the trade union movement.

## Ascent to Power of the Nationalist Government (1948–1970)

### The Botha Commission

The National Party came to power during the post-war slump of the late 1940s. It was a period of general dissatisfaction among people of all races. Jobs were scarce and the influx of black Africans to the urban areas had led to unrest in the townships. This, in turn, had resulted in demands for stricter influx control. Polarisation between race groups, and between English and Afrikaans speakers, had increased, setting the scene for the policies which were to follow.

The new government immediately appointed a commission, generally known as the Botha Commission, to institute an investigation into the existing labour legislation. The Botha Commission argued that, if parity representation were granted to black employees in industry, it would lead to equality between races. This would put white supremacy at stake. Nevertheless, it recommended separate bargaining bodies for black employees, but emphasised that strike action by these employees should be outlawed. The government accepted some, but not all, of the Commission's recommendations and passed the Native Labour (Settlement of Disputes) Act 48 of 1953, later known as the Black Labour Relations Regulation Act.

### The Native Labour (Settlement of Disputes) Act 48 of 1953

The main thrust of the Native Labour Act was an attempt to avert trade unionism among black workers by allowing for the establishment of workers' committees for black employees. These committees were to be established on the initiative of the employees themselves. Complaints were to be taken to the regional workers' committees, consisting of black members appointed by the Minister of Labour, under a white chairman. The regional committees were also to act as watchdogs over conditions of work for black employees and had to report to the Black Labour Board, which had an all-white membership.

The system did not prove to be very popular. Very few employees had the initiative to form committees and, even when they did, they lacked the necessary expertise to represent themselves effectively. By 1973, only 24 committees had been formally registered under the Act, although another 110 were said to exist. Nevertheless, until 1979, the committee system, with later modifications, remained the only legitimised form of black worker representation.

### The Industrial Conciliation Act 28 of 1956

Three years after the passage of the Native Labour (Settlement of Disputes) Act, the government passed the Industrial Conciliation Act of 1956 (later known as the Labour Relations Act of 1956).

This Act became the new basis for labour legislation relating to collective bargaining. It caused further polarisation in that it:

- excluded all 'Bantu' people (including black African women)
- prohibited the further registration of mixed unions (except with ministerial permission)
- placed restrictions on the registration of already mixed-race unions
- provided that such unions could not have mixed executives
- introduced a system of job reservation, whereby a particular occupation could be legally reserved for a certain race group. This clause became one of the most notorious provisions in South African labour legislation.

### The Multiracial Trade Union Movement

From 1950 onwards, the labour movement increasingly reflected the divisions which had already begun to develop in the previous era. The establishment of parallel black unions caused small craft unions to split off to form the South African Federation of Trade Unions (SAFTU). The Suppression of Communism Act 44 of 1950 robbed many of the more militant unions in the TLC of their officials and leaders, as no person listed as a communist could hold public office.

In 1954, the TLC, SAFTU and the Amalgamated Engineering Union established a joint committee, known as the Trade Union Unity Committee. Its primary purpose was to consolidate the position of the trade union movement. The new body's efforts in this direction resulted in the establishment of the South African Trade Union Council (SATUC), which in 1962 changed its name to the Trade Union Council of South Africa (TUCSA). The TLC and the Western Province Federation of Labour Unions thereafter disbanded, but SAFTU continued to exist. SATUC decided to admit only registered unions, and to work closely with black union bodies. (In 1962, it changed this decision and readmitted black unions.) The decision not to admit black (African) unions immediately caused a number of the coloured and Indian unions to leave the federation, along with their black counterparts.

In later years TUCSA became, with the conservative white unions, the major union representative on official bargaining bodies. The organisation remained multiracial and had in its ranks a number of parallel African unions. (The Industrial Conciliation Act of 1956 prohibited mixed executives, resulting in the establishment of separate coloured and Indian unions in some cases, and the establishment of racially separate branches in others.)

Although TUCSA originated from militant union roots, its accommodation of the existent system resulted in a new type of trade unionist. The system established by the Industrial Conciliation Act had led to ever-increasing centralisation of bargaining structures. Registered trade unions bargained through the established machinery, the aim of which was to avoid industrial disputes. Because agreements were legally enforceable, unionists began to spend more and more time guarding against breaches. Benefit funds were established, and many unionists found themselves overburdened by their administrative functions. In the process a large number of unions lost touch with their grassroots organisation and took on the role of bureaucrats. Added to this was an increasing acceptance of, or at least abidance by, the sociopolitical status quo. It was this estrangement from ground level which would eventually lead to TUCSA's demise. Nevertheless, TUCSA did keep the worker movement alive at a stage when it was in danger of disappearing altogether, and it did help to maintain the tradition of collective bargaining in the South African system.

### The All-White Labour Movement

The all-white Co-ordinating Council, which had been founded in the late 1940s, continued to grow. Soon after its inception, the Iron and Steel Union was joined by the Mineworkers' Union and several railway staff associations. In 1957, the Co-ordinating Council, together with SAFTU and the Federal Consultative Council of the South African Railways and Harbours Staff Associations (FCC), established the Confederation of Labour, later known as the South African Confederation of Labour Associations (SACLA). SACLA continued to promote exclusively white unions and was at the time a firm supporter of government policies. Figure 2.2 illustrates the development of the multiracial and the white labour movements in this era.

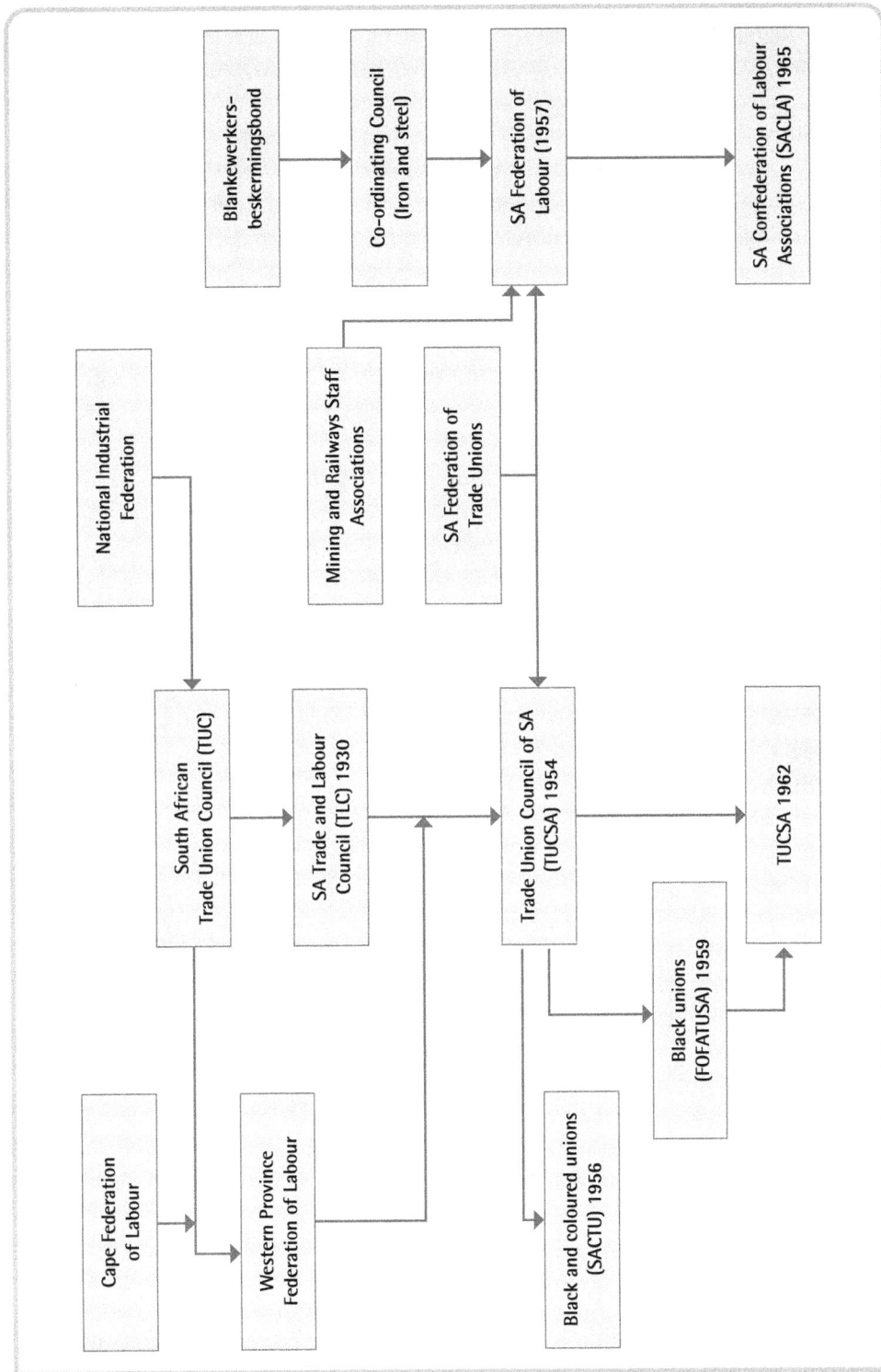

**Figure 2.2:** Development of the white and multiracial movement up to 1965

## The Independent Black Movement

The black union movement in the 1950s had its roots in CNETU, which, despite setbacks in the previous decade, had remained in existence. In 1955, the unions remaining in CNETU and the 14 unions which had split off from TUCSA combined to form the South African Congress of Trade Unions (SACTU), which has been described as the first formal alliance between unions representing Africans and unions representing other races (Friedman, 1987). Shortly after its inception, SACTU joined the Congress Alliance and from then onwards was to play a prominent role in this body.

SACTU's policy was one of grassroots organisation and shop-floor militancy. Initially it did make noteworthy gains and in 1957 staged a successful stay-away to support its 'pound a day' campaign. However, shortly after this stay-away, SACTU began to decline as a workplace organisation. Instead of progressively establishing itself as a movement able to make shop-floor gains, SACTU attempted to grow too fast in order to meet the political objectives of the Congress Alliance. Added to the lack of systematic organisation in SACTU was the fact that it suffered from government action more than other movements before it. Numerous officials were banned, and in some unions no organisers remained.

In 1960, the ANC was finally banned, and in the ensuing years more than a hundred SACTU leaders were arrested. Of those remaining, many went underground, and with this the black worker movement, at least in its overt form, disintegrated. Figure 2.3 summarises the development of the black labour movement in this era.

## Analysis of Developments

During the period under review, the paradox of a professed approach of institutionalised voluntarism counterposed by protectionism and increasing state intervention to control the black African labour force was perpetuated. The anomaly was reinforced by the provision that was made for a unitary system of workplace consultation for African employees, this in the face of a pluralist approach at a highly centralised level in the statutory labour relations system.

The repression of African representation in both the sociopolitical and industrial spheres engendered solidarity between labour representatives and political bodies representing the disenfranchised. African unions had no alternative but to become politicised and bear the consequences in the form of repression of their activities and harassment of their leaders.

While professing a liberal-democratic approach as regards non-black workers, the government resorted to totalitarian measures to control black employees and black South African citizens in general. At the same time, its professed support for free-market capitalism was countered by constraints on the majority of the population and the advancement of white, particularly Afrikaner, capital and labour.

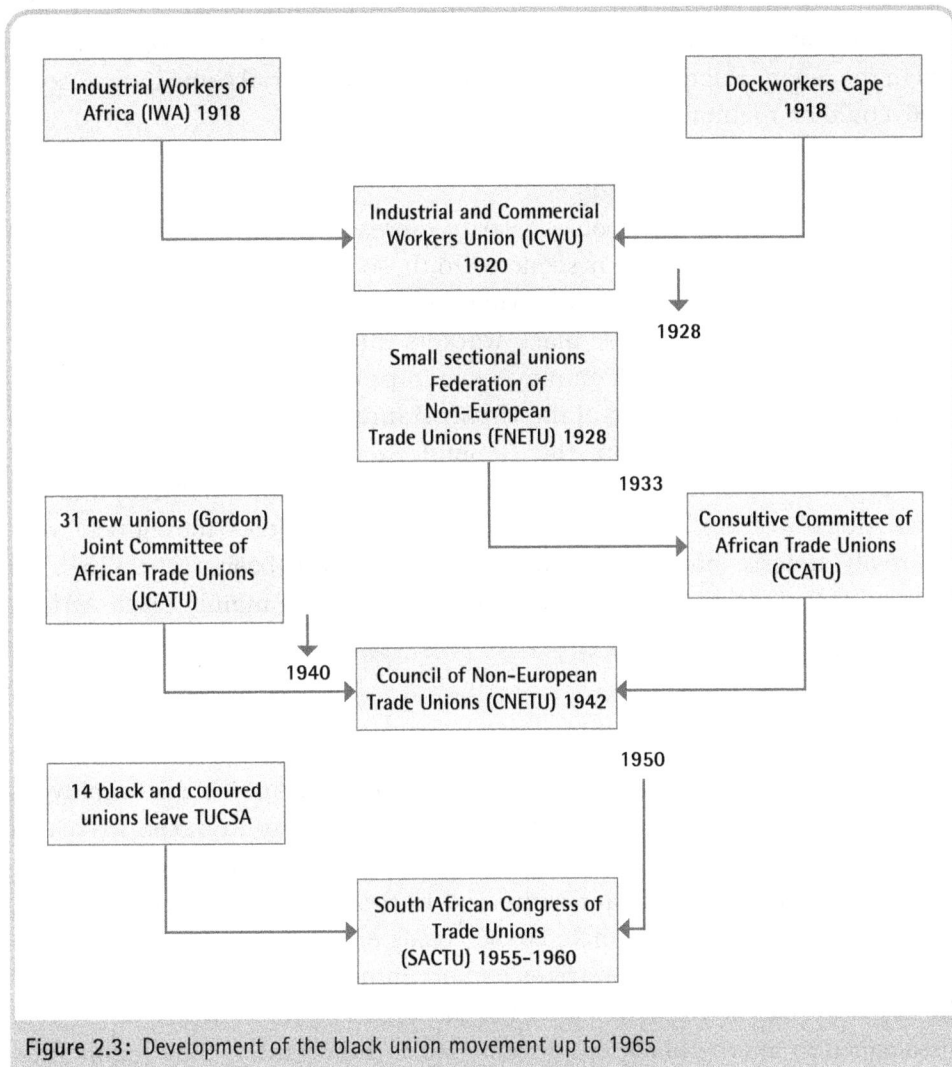

Figure 2.3: Development of the black union movement up to 1965

## Changes in Labour Relations (1970–1990)

### The Start of a New Era

The relative labour peace experienced during the late 1950s and throughout the next decade was not to last. Despite, or as a result of, the bannings and stricter pass laws imposed by the nationalist government, black Africans in general, and black workers in particular, became more conscientised regarding their rights. Furthermore, with the economy still growing, the position of the black employee became more firmly entrenched. As white workers moved up in the occupational hierarchy, black workers came in to take their place. Since this section of the population now constituted the majority of the economically active population, it was unlikely that the position of black workers in industry and in the labour relationship, as decreed by the Industrial Conciliation Act of 1956, could be maintained.

## The Revival of Black Employee Interests

During the 1960s, the only bodies overtly representing black Africans which were prominent on the labour scene were those working under the auspices of, or in conjunction with, TUCSA. However, the beginning of the 1970s saw renewed attempts to organise black workers into independent unions or, at the very least, to assist black employees to improve their working conditions. This led to the establishment of the Urban Training Project (UTP), The Wages and Economics Commission, the General Factory Workers' Benefit Fund (GFWBF), the Western Province Workers' Advice Bureau (WPWAB) and the Black Allied Workers Union (BAWU). Some of the bodies mentioned were not really unions, but together they established the basis from which an entirely new trade union movement, representative of mainly black African employees, would emerge.

## The 1972–1973 Strike Wave

By the beginning of the 1970s, black workers were no longer prepared to accept their secondary status in industry. In 1972, altogether 9 000 black employees engaged in strike actions, of which the most noteworthy were the strikes by the Putco bus drivers and those at the Durban and Cape Town docks. Yet the 1972 strikes were insignificant compared to those which occurred in 1973, when, in Natal alone, an estimated 61 000 black employees came out on strike over a very short period. The strikes had no immediate or obvious cause, and the strikers made no fixed demands, but the actions were indicative of general dissatisfaction among black employees. More importantly, they highlighted the joint power of those employees and the necessity to accommodate their interests within the labour relations system.

Although the strikes were all illegal, no arrests were made – perhaps because it was impossible to imprison all strikers and no ringleaders had emerged, or because the government was at that time being subjected to heightened criticism both from the international community and from opposition groups inside the country. Employers, for their part, reacted in various ways. Some threatened dismissal, others granted increases, while a few attempted to talk to their employees. All became aware that they did not have effective channels to communicate with their black employees.

### New Unions Emerge

The 1973 strikes added impetus to the reawakened black worker consciousness. In Natal, several new unions were established under the auspices of the GFWBF. These unions later founded the Trade Union Advisory and Co-ordinating Council (TUACC). A number of unions also emerged from the efforts of the UTP. The new unions initially concentrated on enlisting as many members as possible, but soon realised that they would have to consolidate their organisation at each plant by building up strong shop-steward representation.

A notable breakthrough occurred when the National Union of Textile Workers (NUTW) and the Textile Workers' Industrial Union (TWIU) managed, in 1974, to conclude a recognition agreement with the British-owned company Smith & Nephew. It was the first agreement of its kind since the passage of the Industrial Conciliation Act in 1924. The idea did not immediately catch on and until 1980 only four recognition agreements were concluded, yet the Smith & Nephew agreement precipitated a new development in collective bargaining.

## The Black Labour Relations Regulation Amendment Act 70 of 1973

The government reacted rapidly to the 1973 strike wave. In the same year, it passed the Black Labour Relations Regulation Amendment Act. This Act provided for the establishment of liaison committees at plant level as an alternative to the existing workers' committees. Liaison committees were to consist of representatives of employers and employees, elected on a parity basis. Their main purpose was to improve communication between employers and their black employees. Although these committees could consult on any matter of mutual interest, the liaison committees often dealt only with matters of physical hygiene or other unimportant issues. Yet the government saw these committees as a cure for all the problems which had developed.

The Act gave black employees limited freedom to strike. Disputes arising between employers and black employees had to be channelled via the black labour officer responsible for that area, to the regional Labour Committee, from there to the divisional inspector, and then to the Black Labour Board. Only once these channels had been exhausted were workers entitled to engage in legal strike action.

The provisions of the Act met with an enthusiastic response from employers. By contrast, the response from the unions was negative. Black unions saw the Act as a renewed attempt to break the power of unionism among black employees. There was, however, one loophole that the legislators did not foresee. Although organisations such as the UTP and the WPWAB did not support the committee system, they realised that they could use committees to gain entry to enterprises 'through the back door'.

The committee system for black employees was introduced in South Africa not to supplement the process of collective bargaining, but to replace it. Its introduction can be ascribed partly to the belief that black employees were not able to engage in 'responsible' collective bargaining at official level, but even more so to the fear of black union power and the fear of dominance by these bodies in the system.

## Consolidation of 'New' Union Power

Despite its initial gains, the emerging union movement soon ran into difficulties. From 1974 onwards, the government banned many of the individuals involved in the organisation and promotion of black trade unions. The bannings increased after the Soweto riots of 1976. Together with the recession which followed, they caused a decline in the momentum of trade union development. Nevertheless, the total impetus was not lost and in 1979 a number of bodies and unions involved established FOSATU. Another federation, CUSA, was founded in 1980. Together these bodies, and especially FOSATU, would dominate the South African labour scene during the next five years.

## The Wiehahn Commission

By 1976, it had become obvious that the provisions of the Black Labour Relations Regulation Amendment Act of 1973 had not solved the problem of black worker militancy. Also, South Africa's major trading partners had become more aware of the position of the black employee. The threat of sanctions and disinvestment had increased, and various codes of employment practice – notably the European Economic Community (EEC) Code, the Sullivan Code and the British Code of Employment Practice – had been issued to multinational companies in South Africa. An improved image was sorely needed, and it was in this climate that the government, in 1977, appointed the Commission of Inquiry into Labour Legislation, commonly known as the Wiehahn Commission.

The original brief of the Commission was to:
- rationalise the then existent labour legislation
- seek possible means of adapting the labour relations system to changing needs
- eliminate bottlenecks and other problems.

This was the stated brief, but, in retrospect, it appears highly probable that the Commission was specifically instructed to consider a method by which black trade unions could be controlled and incorporated into the system without creating too great a disruption.

The findings of the Commission were reported in six parts, the last report appearing some time after legislation implementing previous recommendations had been passed. By the time all the recommendations of the Commission had been implemented, the Industrial Conciliation Act, later to become the Labour Relations Act, had undergone significant amendments: the Black Labour Relations Regulation Act 48 of 1953 had been repealed, all previous legislation pertaining to training and manpower development had been consolidated into the Manpower Training Act 56 of 1981. The Shops and Offices Act 75 of 1964 and the Factories, Machinery and Building Works Act 22 of 1941 were put together and divided into what would become the Basic Conditions of Employment Act 75 of 1997 and the Machinery and Occupational Safety Act 6 of 1983 (now known as the Occupational Health and Safety Act 85 of 1993).

The Wiehahn Commission's first report was the most momentous, and the legislation which followed would bring about the most radical changes in labour relations. The report recommended, inter alia, that:

- full freedom of association be granted to all employees regardless of race, sex or creed
- trade unions be allowed to register, irrespective of their composition in terms of colour, race or sex
- stricter criteria be adopted for trade union registration
- a system of financial inspection of trade unions be introduced
- prohibitions on political activity by unions be extended
- liaison committees be renamed as works councils
- where no industrial council had jurisdiction, works councils and workers' committees be granted full collective bargaining rights
- statutory job reservation be phased out
- safeguards be introduced to protect minorities previously protected by job reservation
- the Industrial Tribunal be replaced by the Industrial Court
- fair employment practices be developed by the Industrial Court
- allowance for a closed shop be maintained
- a tripartite National Manpower Commission be established.

The first and second recommendations mentioned were, in the light of past history, the most revolutionary. The granting of registered trade union rights to black Africans, which would give them access to the collective bargaining machinery, had previously been avoided at all costs. Yet the intentions of the Commission were not as progressive as they at first appeared to be. It was believed that the new trade union movement (at that stage relatively small) would, by co-option into the system and by bargaining with other established unions on industrial councils, lose much of its impact, and that it would become more 'responsible' and perhaps even be absorbed into the established movement.

## The Industrial Conciliation Amendment Act 94 of 1979

The Industrial Conciliation Amendment Act (later known as the Labour Relations Amendment Act of 1979) introduced a new era in South African labour relations. Not all the recommended innovations were introduced forthwith, and important amendments to the Act were made in 1980, 1981 and 1982, but by 1983 the following major changes had been effected:

- The term 'employee' had been redefined to include all persons working for an employer.
- Previous provisions for racially mixed unions to have separate branches and all-white executives had been withdrawn.
- The job reservation clause (Section 77) had been repealed.
- The concept of an 'unfair labour practice' had been introduced and defined.
- Provision had been made for the establishment of the Industrial Court and the Manpower Commission.
- The name of the basic Act had been changed to the Labour Relations Act of 1956.

## The Reaction of the Newer Trade Unions

The trade unions established during the previous decade to represent black employees did not display much enthusiasm at the fact that they were now permitted to participate in the official system. Initially, most of these unions refused to register, either as a matter of principle and in protest at their previous exclusion or because they believed that registration would entail greater government control. The newer unions also stayed out of the industrial councils, in part because they resented these bodies and in part because their power base would be diluted by centralised bargaining. Instead, they organised a strong shop-floor presence and demanded recognition from individual employers.

In the early stages of the new dispensation, employers offered strong resistance to demands for plant-level bargaining. The most prevalent excuse was that they were not prepared to deal with unregistered unions – that unions should register and join the industrial councils. The result was a significant increase in strike actions, all of them illegal, culminating in the strike wave on the East Rand in early 1982. By then, some employers had relented and concluded recognition agreements with representative unions at plant level. This trend continued, so much so that plant-level bargaining soon became entrenched in the South African system.

As it became apparent that the advantages gained by registration might outweigh the disadvantages, union resistance gradually decreased. Once they had acquired registered status, and as their power base expanded to cover a substantial number of employees in particular industries, some of these unions applied for admission to industrial councils. As their power increased, they began to play a dominant role in these bodies.

### New Federations Established

As the new union movement grew, new federations came into being. The year 1985 saw the launch of COSATU, from predominantly FOSATU roots. This was followed by the formation of NACTU and the United Workers Union of South Africa (UWUSA). By 1990, total union membership, discounting the unregistered unions, had increased by one and a half million since 1980. Almost all the additional members came from the ranks of black African and coloured African employees, and most of them belonged to the newer unions.

The unions emerging in the 1980s displayed the militancy to be expected of a new movement and, particularly, of one attempting to establish itself in an entrenched system. Working in close co-operation with shop stewards, they took up every issue affecting their members. Many actions were hard fought, and strike frequency increased from 101 strikes in 1979 to 1 148 in 1987 and 1 025 in 1988. Previously, nearly all strikes which occurred had been illegal. After 1985, this trend was reversed, owing to greater sophistication on the part of the unions, a greater willingness to use the system, and more firmly established relationships. The newer unions also began to use the unfair labour practice legislation and the status quo order provision to bring Industrial Court actions against employers. All in all, the newer unions tended to dominate the labour relations arena.

From the outset the newer trade unions were intensely aware of the errors which had been committed by black trade union movements in the past. Consequently, they concentrated on worker organisation and the achievement of gains on the shop floor, rather than on mass mobilisation. However, trade union growth coincided with the mushrooming of protest movements, and trade unions, as the major representatives of the black working class, increasingly found themselves in a politically prominent position. This was to be expected since, until 1990, the trade union movement was the only legitimate public forum for disenfranchised employees. Even after the reforms by President FW de Klerk of that year and the unbanning of all political parties, the trade union movement – and particularly COSATU – remained established as a formidable political power bloc.

## White Opposition

The new dispensation in labour relations was not without its opponents. Even before the first Wiehahn report was published, white mineworkers, who had evidently been informed of its content, went on strike to protest against the inclusion of black workers in the official system. The strike was unsuccessful, but the opposition remained. Many white employees, fearful for their positions, found their political home in the Conservative Party. SACLA, now occupying a position to the right of the government, still existed. By 1983, this association, having lost more than half of its previous membership, appeared to be on the decline, but for a while it grew again as white reactionism increased.

## TUCSA Disintegrates

TUCSA was, despite its active participation in the Wiehahn Commission, the worst hit by the new dispensation. A number of TUCSA unions did open up their ranks, and most of the unions did try to service the new members by representation on industrial councils, but they lacked the grassroots organisation of the newer unions and were slower to take up issues. As the major multiracial organisation in existence before 1980, TUCSA was the first to feel the effects of the new dispensation when black and coloured members started defecting to the newer unions. TUCSA's attempts to adapt had come too late and, at the end of 1986, the organisation officially disbanded. Most of its member unions were later absorbed into a new grouping, the Federation of Unions of South Africa (FEDUSA).

## Government Reaction

The apartheid government, having set the new system in motion, appeared initially to be taken aback by it, but thereafter became increasingly inclined to let developments run their course. In 1982 the Director-General of Manpower repeatedly declared that the government believed in the principle of self-government in industry and that employers and employees should attempt to regulate their relationship in the best possible manner. Official sources began to subtly encourage employers to negotiate with recognised unions. The government was letting the system sort itself out, taking the role mainly of observer and adviser.

This policy persisted until 1988, when the government – obviously pressurised by employers and perhaps of the opinion that unions were gaining too much power – passed controversial amendments to the Labour Relations Act. These included certain codifications of unfair labour practices, some of which seemed to be directed against union actions. Also, unions could now be sued for illegal strikes undertaken by their members. The Labour Relations Amendment Act 83 of 1988 was widely opposed by the union movement. Stay-aways in protest against the Act followed, and employers came under pressure to 'contract out' of the Labour Relations Act as a totality. Following discussions between the South African Consultative Committee on Labour Affairs (SACCOLA) and representatives from COSATU and NACTU, most of the controversial clauses were withdrawn by the Labour Relations Amendment Act 9 of 1991.

## Analysis of Developments

### Collective Power as an Instrument for Change

The labour action initiated by African employees to protest against their circumstances and position within the employment relationship proves that, when faced by the collective power of employees, the government and employers are not able to exercise exclusive control over the relationship.

The institution of action on the scale of the 1973 strikes requires either extensive and effective organisation or the ability to rally workers around a cause. In this instance, the cause was presented by the negation of African rights in both the workplace and society. In an economically based society, where the majority of the adult population are either employees or aspirant employees, the workplace offers an expedient base for organisation, whether this be in pursuit of a social, political or economic cause.

Repression arouses reaction and provides unions who are able to mobilise reactionary sentiment with a strong power base. Ascent to power in the labour relations sphere proved to be a precursor to political power.

### Initial Acquiescence with Capitalism

COSATU, as the dominant union federation post 1984, did not at its inaugural congress openly challenge the capitalist free-market system. It did not, like the British Trades Union Congress (TUC) before it, state as an objective the public control and planning of industry. At that stage the federation advocated a non-racial democracy in the post-apartheid state, combined with some nationalisation of key industries. Their 'socialist' model was not orthodox Marxism; it tended towards the social democratic approach of the British Labour Party. From this it can be assumed that COSATU initially adopted a reformist rather than a radical position. Unions would be prepared to operate in the existing system provided that wealth was controlled democratically and shared fairly.

*Acceptance of Pluralism*

With the opening up of the system, all parties embraced the pluralist approach to the relationship. The unions emphasised the functionality of collective bargaining and the exercise of collective power. Because employers initially refused to recognise the newer unions (and probably because of historical realities), the approach on both sides was essentially adversarial. The SACCOLA–COSATU–NACTU Accord could be interpreted as a move towards corporatism, but it could also have been a temporary reaction to the pressures exerted by the unions.

Changes in the labour relations system pointed the way to political change. Once the government had deracialised the workplace, it was self-evident that political change would have to follow.

# Developments Post 1990

## The New Dispensation

With the unbanning of previously banned political organisations and the release of Nelson Mandela in 1990, it was evident that a new sociopolitical era had begun, and that progress towards the institution of a democratically elected government was irreversible. The De Klerk government, and thereafter the Government of National Unity, increasingly opened itself up to the major stakeholders in the labour sphere as well as to other community interests. This led, in 1993 and 1994, to the inclusion of agricultural and domestic employees under the Basic Conditions of Employment Amendment Act 137 of 1993 and, in the same year, to the Agricultural Labour Relations Act 147 of 1993, which effectively incorporated farm workers under the Labour Relations Act. A change of direction also occurred in the public sector, proved by the promulgation of the Education Labour Relations Act 146 of 1993 and the Public Service Act 103 of 1994. For the first time, the scope of labour relations was expanding to include hitherto unrepresented and often exploited workers and to acknowledge the role of the state as yet another employer.

In April 1994 the ANC, supported and bolstered by COSATU and the SACP, assumed power as the majority party in the Government of National Unity. Having come to power by the vote of the poor and previously oppressed, and having in its ranks many former trade unionists, the new government faced enormous expectations. Workers now expected the government to serve mainly their interests, forgetting that it had a far wider constituency (including also the 30 per cent or more unemployed persons). Its concerns were not confined to the workplace, but also embraced the economy in general, the need for job creation and investment, and the dire need for mammoth improvements in training, education and health services.

The fears of other sectors of society, including some in the business sector – that a government with 'socialist' partners would inevitably attempt to destroy capital and engage in an 'irresponsible' programme of nationalisation and redistribution – were not realised. The new government continued to encourage investment and express its belief in the free-market principle as the main route to economic growth. On the other hand, it attempted – by way of new economic initiatives and new education and training, housing and health policies – to uplift previously disadvantaged communities and persons. This was reflected at the micro level by the emphasis on affirmative action, black economic empowerment (BEE) and social responsibility. It was the government's stated intention to unbundle the large conglomerates and to provide opportunities for black business.

The government had to not only satisfy all sectors of society but also reconcile and reconstruct an economically and socially devastated country. At the same time it had to remain as democratic and inclusive as possible.

### Initiatives to Kickstart the Economy

Before coming to power, the ANC and its alliance partners had developed a framework, known as the RDP, for addressing South Africa's economic and social problems and redressing historical inequalities between different race groups. The RDP had as its purpose the integration of 'growth, development, reconstruction and redistribution into a unified programme' (ANC, 1994: para 1.3.6). It placed emphasis on education and training, affirmative action, job creation, programmes to address unemployment, a co-ordinated public works programme and the stimulation of both rural and urban development. The RDP was high on ideas but short on action, and it soon faded into the background, being overshadowed by the Growth Employment and Redistribution Strategy (GEAR). In 1996 the RDP offices closed their doors, although some observers believed that its principles were still being acted upon in various national departments.

The new government had also signalled its intention to create greater freedom in the South African economy, to attract local and foreign investment and to allow for the interaction of market forces. GEAR was subsequently adopted as the foundation for economic and social policy. It emphasised economic growth through investment and production. The need to redistribute wealth and to alleviate poverty was not forgotten but, in terms of GEAR, this would be achieved through economic growth, which would in turn bring about general prosperity and enable the government to engage in social upliftment programmes. GEAR was seen as necessary to boost economic growth and, in fact, the economy did grow by 4 per cent between 2000 and 2004. However, the ANC's partners in the Tripartite Alliance saw it as being in conflict with the RDP. They complained that GEAR did not place sufficient emphasis on redistribution and economic upliftment.

The improved economic situation at the beginning of the new millennium inspired President Thabo Mbeki to introduce the Accelerated Shared Growth Initiative for South Africa (ASGISA). The stated purpose of the plan was to achieve economic growth of at least 6 per cent. This, according to the International Monetary Fund (IMF), could be achieved only by trade liberalisation, improved efficiency in the labour market and improved public enterprises. The idea was to identify the six most important economic constraints and to link these with areas of intervention. However, there was no document describing in detail the initiatives to be undertaken and no means of measuring the plan's success or failure. Unfortunately, the envisaged economic growth did not happen.

## Labour Relations Policy and Legislation

After the 1994 elections, the reconstituted Department of Manpower, now renamed the Department of Labour, commenced putting its stamp on the labour relations system. A task team was established to draft a new Labour Relations Act, and in February 1995 the first 'Draft Negotiation Document' was published for comment.

In 1995 NEDLAC was established, with the aim of representing all major stakeholders and consulting on economic, labour relations and labour market policy. The government revealed its intention to continue adopting a corporatist approach by recognising NEDLAC in the proposed legislation and making the final acceptance of the draft Bill subject to consensual approval from NEDLAC.

The new government also amended the Basic Conditions of Employment Act (in the form of Act 75 of 1997) and passed the Employment Equity Act 55 of 1998 and the Skills Development Act 97 of 1998 . These Acts were intended to provide more general access to jobs and to further protect employees at the workplace, but were seen by many to be placing more responsibilities on employers and hampering employment creation.

### The Labour Relations Act 66 of 1995

The Labour Relations Act 66 of 1995 repealed the Labour Relations Act 28 of 1956 and subsequent amendments, although many of the procedures and structures contained in the Labour Relations Amendment Act 94 of 1979 were retained. The most significant changes were:
- the provision for legislated organisational rights
- the granting of the right to strike without fear of dismissal once prescribed procedures had been followed

- the limitations placed on the use of 'scab' labour
- the provision for the establishment of agency shops and closed shops
- the codification of unfair dismissals.

One of the additions to the Act was the provision for statutory workplace forums, intended to promote consultation between the parties at the workplace.

While there appeared to be a genuine desire on the part of the government to balance power, create more certainty and promote co-operation between the parties, most of the changes favoured the unions. Also, while bargaining and the choice of bargaining structure remained mostly voluntary, the Act unashamedly promoted centralised bargaining. This favoured certain larger unions rather than smaller unions and employers.

## Labour Action

Contrary to expectations, labour action did not decrease to any significant extent (from 904 strikes in 1990 to 804 in 1994). While the sectors with more established labour relations negotiated relatively peaceful settlements, major actions occurred in the health services, the police services, the municipal services and the fishing and transport industries, most of which had been granted greater freedom to strike.

The continuation of labour unrest placed both the government and the unions supporting it in a predicament. The government may have wished to curb labour unrest in the interests of promoting the economy, and some unions may have wished to co-operate. However, neither the government nor these unions could really afford to take a stand against grassroots sentiment, for fear of losing the support of their constituents to other political parties and unions.

## The Trade Union Movement
### Tensions in the Tripartite Alliance

COSATU's numerical superiority, and its political prominence before and after 1994, allowed the federation to maintain its position as the dominant union federation in South Africa. NACTU and FEDUSA did maintain substantial membership, but were not able to match or to wield the same political clout as COSATU, which relied on its alliance with the ANC and the SACP.

The government's support of free-market capitalism did not always sit well with COSATU. At the federation's policy conference in 1997, it adopted a wide-ranging declaration contrasting strongly with government policies. COSATU's criticism of the government's socio-economic policies led President Mandela to address the role of trade unions in the Tripartite Alliance. The president explained that the ANC was the leader of the Tripartite Alliance and, in so many words, cautioned COSATU not to try to usurp political power.

After 1998, relations between COSATU and the Presidency deteriorated further, owing mainly to disagreement on economic and social policy, the management style of President Mbeki and his perceived sidelining of the unions as alliance partners. It can be assumed that the trade union federation played a major role in the December 2007 'coup' at Polokwane which saw Thabo Mbeki ousted and the ascent to power of Jacob Zuma.

### Expectations and Actions Post Polokwane

COSATU, having lobbied extensively for a change in leadership, left no doubt that it did not intend to be sidelined and that it saw itself as a major player also in the sociopolitical arena. A number of former union leaders had been given parliamentary and Cabinet posts and the federation maintained that these individuals should be accountable to it as well as the government.

The federation admitted that the Alliance had become more unified under Zuma's presidency, but it did not hesitate to criticise government for failing to implement agreed policies, nor did it temper the militancy of its members. On the contrary, soon after the April 2009 elections the unions warned of massive actions if demands for pay increases were not met. Threats became actions when doctors went on strike, followed closely by municipal workers. According to COSATU, its criticisms and strike actions did not conflict with its position as Alliance partner.

## Collective Industrial Relations Processes

### Collective Bargaining

The Labour Relations Act of 1995 entrenched collective bargaining as central to the conduct of the labour relationship. This was evidenced by the granting of new organisational rights to unions, the continued provision for centralised bargaining councils, and the establishment of a compulsory bargaining council in the public service. COSATU strongly supported the move towards centralised bargaining. At its congress in 2000, the federation committed to continue its struggle for centralised bargaining and for the establishment of bargaining councils.

### Workplace Forums

Chapter 5 of the Labour Relations Act of 1995 sets out detailed provisions for the establishment of workplace forums. In terms of these provisions, forums may be established at any workplace, and should be representative of all employee levels, with the exception of senior management. Workplace forums were given the right to consultation on certain matters and co-decision-making rights on a limited number of issues.

In the *Labour Bulletin* of December 2000, Godfrey and Du Toit claimed: 'One of the most contentious issues during the NEDLAC negotiations over the new LRA was the provision for workplace forums' (2000: 13). No consensus could be reached, and eventually the Minister of Labour intervened to inform that government would not consider dropping workplace forums, as they were 'of fundamental importance to industrial relations' (Godfrey & Du Toit, 2000: 13). Workplace forums were important for 'the process of enterprise restructuring, to improve productivity and become internationally competitive' (Godfrey & Du Toit, 2000: 15).

Employers and unions were not compelled to establish workplace forums and there was little enthusiasm for their establishment. The Act provided that statutory forums could be established only at the request of a majority union or unions. The latter grouping viewed forums as a threat to collective bargaining while not granting employees any significant share in decisions.

### New Legislation

In 1997, the government passed a new version of the Basic Conditions of Employment Act. Under the new Act, maximum working hours were decreased from 48 to 45 hours per week, overtime pay increased from one-and-a-third to one-and-a-half times the normal wage, compulsory annual leave was extended from two to three weeks per annum and unpaid maternity leave from three to four months.

The Employment Equity Act 55 of 1998 was an attempt to address historical imbalances in employment and employment opportunities. It placed a prohibition on discriminatory practices and promoted the employment and advancement of designated groups.

The Employment Equity Act was followed closely by the Skills Development Act 97 of 1998 and the Skills Development Levies Act 9 of 1999. These Acts provided for a levy of 1 per cent of the payroll on all employers employing more than 50 people, and the establishment of Sectoral Education and Training Authorities (SETAs) to co-ordinate training in the different sectors.

Other Acts, such as the Protected Disclosures Act 26 of 2000, allowing for the protection of whistle blowers, and the Promotion of Equality and Prevention of Unfair Discrimination Act 4 of 2000, attempted to provide further safeguards against arbitrary action and discriminatory or corrupt practices.

### Analysis of Developments
*Socio-economic Policies*
After the first democratic elections, the South African government was faced with the following challenges:
- the globalisation of economies under the banner of neo-liberalism

- the demise of the socialist economies
- a general reaction against mandatory systems
- World Bank/IMF directives for structural adjustment programmes in African countries.

In these circumstances, the post-1994 government had little option other than to declare its support for the capitalist/free-market system. On the other hand, the history of disadvantage suffered by the majority of its constituents, and its alliance with COSATU and the SACP, obliged the government to cloak GEAR in the guise also of a distributive mechanism, to institute welfare structures and to increase spending on services, health and education.

### Labour Legislation

The dichotomy in the government's socio-economic policies was mirrored in the legislation governing the employment relationship. The Labour Relations Act, at the core of the system, was framed mainly in the voluntarist, pluralist paradigm, with the emphasis placed on free collective bargaining and self-regulation by employers and employee representatives. On the other hand, there was indirect coercion towards centralised bargaining. Also, the allowance for closed shops and agency shops ran counter to freedom of association, and reflected a preference for union hegemony over democracy.

In a situation of institutionalised voluntarism, it is generally accepted that there should be legislation granting basic substantive rights and protecting employees against injuries, accidents and unemployment. These contingencies were provided for by the Basic Conditions of Employment Act 75 of 1997, the Occupational Health and Safety Act 85 of 1993, the Compensation for Occupational Injuries and Diseases Act 130 of 1993 and the Unemployment Insurance Act 63 of 2001.

In South Africa, the need arose for additional mandatory legislation in the form of the Employment Equity Act 55 of 1998, the Skills Development Act 97 of 1998 and the Skills Development Levies Act 9 of 1999. Although these Acts were justified by the country's historical imbalances, they are not compatible with a voluntarist framework and indicate a move towards interventionism.

The South African approach to the relationship after 1994 can therefore be described as essentially voluntarist, tempered by necessary interventions undertaken in the corporatist mode.

### The Union Movement

COSATU declared its support for communitarianism, a more planned economic system, and eventual worker control or pro-labour mandatorism. However, the union movement was still ensconced in the pluralist mode. This was demonstrated by its general rejection of workplace forums and its use of collective power against both private sector employers and the government. Furthermore, the establishment of union investment companies indicated that unions were quite comfortable with the capitalist free-market system, at least for the time being.

## Economic and Social Realities in the New Millennium

### The Economy

After 2005 the South African economy failed to grow at the rate that the government might have wished.

In 2021, after having suffered the adverse effects of the Covid-19 pandemic, the South African economy recorded its fourth consecutive quarter of growth, expanding by 1.2 per cent in the second quarter of 2021 (April–June). This followed a revised 1 per cent rise in real gross domestic product (GDP) in the first quarter (January–March). Despite the gains made over the last four quarters, the economy is 1.4 per cent smaller than what it was before the Covid-19 pandemic (Stats SA, 2021).

Some experts maintain that South Africa's economic problems are only partly the result of general recessionary conditions. They explain that the state of government, economic, labour and social policies are largely to blame. The 2017–2018 Global Competitive Index (WEF GCI) ranked South Africa 61st out of 137 economies assessed – down from its ranking of 45th before 2010 (WEF, 2017). Owing to the Covid-19 pandemic, South Africa has experienced sluggish economic growth and has slipped to its lowest global competitiveness ranking yet. According to the World Competitiveness Yearbook (WCY), South Africa fell by three notches, to 59th out of 63 countries rated by the Institute of Management Development (IMD) (DEL, 2020). This 2020 ranking marks the lowest since the inception of the IMD's yearbook. South Africa fared reasonably well between 2000 and 2006 – on average 40th of 63 countries – while in 2001–2005 it was rated 37th. It is notable that South Africa's economic performance has shown a downward trend since 2007 (DEL, 2020). Particularly concerning is the fact that the country is ranked low on health provision and primary education. Even higher education is in the lower percentile. At the same time, international ratings agencies have consistently downgraded South Africa, making it a high risk for investment.

### Unemployment

According to Statistics South Africa, the country's unemployment rate hit a new record high of 34.4 per cent in the second quarter of 2021, up from 32.6 per cent in the first quarter. Moreover, the number of unemployed totalled

7.826 million people in the three months to the end of June, compared with 7.242 million people in the previous three months (Reuters, 2021). The country's persistent economic and political problems leave little hope that this situation can be remedied in the near future.

## Inequality

The Gini coefficient is an instrument used by the World Bank and other agencies to measure the degree of inequality in different countries, with a score of 1 reflecting absolute equality and one of 100 showing absolute inequality. South Africa's Gini coefficient, which has always been high, decreased only marginally from 67.4 in 2000 to 63.1 in 2011; however, in 2017 it increased again to more than 64 (Trading Economics, 2021). In fact, South Africa is now rated as the most unequal country in the world, with even Haiti and Namibia obtaining a slightly better score. At the time of writing, income distribution remained highly skewed, as 20 per cent of the population earns over 68 per cent of income, compared to a median of 47 per cent for similar emerging markets (IMF, 2020). This deterioration has happened in spite of extensive BEE and affirmative action initiatives and despite the fact that, in December 2012, black people owned 21 per cent of the top 100 listed companies on the Johannesburg Stock Exchange (JSE) (World Bank Group, 2018). This situation had not significantly improved by 2021.

As mentioned previously, there is a fairly common perception that empowerment policies benefited only a minority. This seems to be borne out by the fact that, as the Inequality Index reveals, the gap between the wealthiest black people and their poorer counterparts has increased substantially (World Bank Group, 2018).

## Civil Unrest

Democratisation created expectations of a better life for all. Unfortunately, these expectations have not been met. A large proportion of South Africans still live in dire poverty and without basic amenities. Patience with the lack of service delivery has worn thin, and the second decade of the century saw an increasing number of protest actions reminiscent of the apartheid era, with 2012 being the most protest-filled year since 1990. The situation is exacerbated by perceptions of corruption and the obvious prosperity of individuals, including political and business leaders of all race groups. The majority of municipalities in South Africa failed to obtain clear audits for the first decades of the new millennium, with poor service delivery resulting in regular civil unrest. The unprecedented looting of shopping malls in KwaZulu-Natal and Gauteng on 9–17 July 2021 claimed the lives of nearly 400 people and resulted in huge economic damage.

## Government Initiatives

### The New Growth Path Framework and the National Infrastructure Development Plan

In 2010 the government adopted the New Growth Path Framework, originating from the Department of Economic Development under former trade unionist Ebrahim Patel. Some of the stated objectives of the New Growth Path Framework were:

- to create five million jobs within ten years
- to promote a green economy
- to create more agricultural jobs
- to facilitate land transfers.

The drafters recognised the importance of a competitive economy and saw a stronger role for a competitions policy, but also for price monitoring. Nevertheless, the New Growth Path Framework is viewed as more socialist than the National Development Plan (NDP), discussed below.

The New Growth Path Framework was underpinned by the National Infrastructure Plan, which in turn resulted in the Infrastructure Development Act 23 of 2014. The central objective of the National Infrastructure Plan was to decentralise basic services and engage in strategic integrated projects, and thereby to 'transform the economic landscape'. The plan identified decentralised areas around the country and projects to be undertaken in these areas.

### The National Development Plan

The New Growth Path Framework was followed by the NDP, launched by Trevor Manuel, then chair of the National Planning Commission and Minister in the Presidency, in 2012. The NDP, for which the target date is 2030, is based on the premise of a social compact between government, business and labour, with the aim of:

- reducing poverty and inequality
- raising employment levels
- increasing investment.

The NDP, although described as high on vision but short on detail, was generally accepted by business. COSATU, while agreeing with some of the plan, described it as liberal-democratic and not advancing a radical ideological shift. The federation was not in favour of the youth wage subsidy, owing to fears that this would erode other employment. It further criticised the NDP for not putting the concept of 'decent work' at the centre, not emphasising redistribution and basing employment creation on small business promotion. For these reasons some of the COSATU unions declared themselves in favour of Patel's New Growth Path Framework rather than Manuel's NDP. The government, for its part, decided that the time for debating was past, and that there was an urgent need to proceed to actual implementation.

Despite these efforts, inequality has persisted, joblessness has remained a problem and the economy, after an initial spurt, did not grow at the desired rate. However, the government continues to set its sights on 2030 and the hoped-for outcomes.

### Radical Economic Transformation

At its Mangaung Conference in 2012, the ANC, evidently disappointed with the inability of previous plans to bring about the necessary change, declared its intention to 'radically reform' the economy. However, it was only in 2017 that a beleaguered President Zuma publicly announced that radical economic transformation of the economy had become a priority.

There is general agreement that the economy needs to transform, but little, if any, consensus on how this is to be achieved, nor is it clear what is envisaged by the government and how its objectives are to be attained.

## Union Developments
### State of the Unions

At the time of writing, South Africa has 24 registered trade union federations. Since most of these are smaller and newer federations, labour representation has been dominated by COSATU, FEDUSA and NACTU, in that order. It is obvious that old divisions, based on sociopolitical orientation, still exist. COSATU remains in the Tripartite Alliance. FEDUSA continued with the more middle-of-the-road multiracial policies of the old TUCSA unions, most of which joined this federation. NACTU is still viewed as supporter of black consciousness.

COSATU has traditionally occupied a privileged position, both as the largest federation and a member of the Tripartite Alliance. However, these very political connections opened rifts in the federation, the most obvious being that between the National Union of Mineworkers (NUM) and the National Union of Metalworkers of South Africa (NUMSA). Strong differences also arose between the then general secretary of COSATU, Zwelinzima Vavi, and the federation's president, Sidumo Dlamini. After months of speculation, in 2014, COSATU expelled its biggest affiliate, NUMSA, due to the latter's lack of support for the ANC and its criticism of NUM and of COSATU. The expulsion encouraged seven blue-collar unions, namely the South African Commercial Catering and Allied Workers Union (SACCAWU), the South African State and Allied Workers' Union (SASAWU), the Public Allied Workers Union of South Africa (PAWUSA), the Food and Allied Workers Union (FAWU), the South African Football Players Union (SAFPU) and the Democratic Nursing

Organisation of South Africa (DENOSA), to suspend their participation in COSATU activities in solidarity with NUMSA. Here, too, the conflict stemmed partly from perceptions that Vavi was not sufficiently loyal to the regime.

The conflict between COSATU and NUMSA resulted in a split, since NUMSA supported Vavi, opposing his suspension from COSATU for alleged sexual harassment in 2013. Vavi lodged an appeal against his suspension, which was reinstated by the court. However, the broken relationship between Vavi and COSATU made it impossible to work together. Loyalists trade unions affiliated to COSATU, namely the NUM, the National Education, Health and Allied Workers Union (NEHAWU), the South African Democratic Teachers' Union (SADTU) and the South African Transport and Allied Workers Union (SATAWU), put pressure on COSATU to expel Vavi. The split between NUMSA and Vavi with COSATU can be seen as the primary motive for the subsequent drive by these parties to form an entirely new federation, SAFTU. In its relatively short existence SAFTU had, by the beginning of 2018, managed to muster a membership of 800 000 from 24 unions, making it second in size only to COSATU (Nel & Kirsten, 2020). The expulsion of NUMSA from COSATU led to a significant decline in membership, from 1.9 million to 1.6 million (Kenny, 2020).

*New Unions Emerge*

Another noteworthy development in the labour sphere was the prominence gained by the Association of Mineworkers and Construction Union (AMCU). The union became a household name after the confrontation between striking mineworkers and police at Lonmin's Marikana mine in August 2012, but the history of the conflict dates much further back, to a break between certain mineworkers and the NUM.

AMCU was formed in 1999 when the executive of the NUM, under then general secretary Gwede Mantashe, disciplined and ousted from membership the local NUM chairman at the Douglas Colliery, Joseph Mathunjwa. Mathunjwa had organised a three-day sit-in by 3 000 employees, evidently without consulting the union. Soon after Mathunjwa's sacking from the union, all 3 000 employees resigned from the NUM and formed a new union under his leadership.

The union extended its membership to various platinum and gold mines. However, its efforts to gain recognition and related rights were initially thwarted by management, who maintained that workers were already represented by the NUM, which had agreed with management on thresholds of representation, effectively barring other unions from recognition. It can be safely assumed that the evident preference afforded to NUM was one of the root causes for the strike which followed at Marikana in 2012, with tragic results.

AMCU continued to grow and in 2012 claimed a membership of more than 200 000. However, members have become increasingly disgruntled at what they claim to be AMCU's lack of action to protect their interests. Additionally, the registrar of trade unions threatened to deregister the trade union in 2019, claiming non-compliance with its constitution. The registrar asked the union to submit a written submission on why they should not be deregistered; they provided sufficient evidence and were thus allowed to hold their congress.

## Analysis of Developments
### Socio-economic Problems and Proposed Solutions
The South African government continues to straddle various divides. It acknowledges the need to promote a competitive economy, but at the same time, there are growing demands for service delivery and the upliftment of the previously disadvantaged. Various experts have stressed the need to free up the economy. However, some in the ruling party's ranks and its alliance partners believe that the solution lies in greater control by government and even nationalisation – in particular of the mining sector. For some time, the government opted for a middle ground. This was borne out by the fact that both the NDP and the New Growth Path Framework indicated that their objectives could be achieved only by co-operation between the government, business and labour – in other words, by a more intensive corporatist approach.

There might be general agreement that this approach is to be preferred, but it is doubtful that the partnership would be an equal one. Consultation to achieve agreement takes time. This is proved by the fact that the plans and the legislation drafted in 2010 had, by mid-2013, not been implemented. The government, realising the urgency of the situation, has stated that it will go ahead with the NDP and plans to have achieved its objectives by 2030. This would require a more dominant and interfering role for the state, as would the rather vague objective of radical economic transformation.

### Union Developments
The period from 2012 to 2021 may well be seen as another watershed period in South African labour relations history. The rise of AMCU and ensuing events was evidence of dissatisfaction with the privileged position of the established unions and their perceived distance from grassroots interests. Events in the mining industry have long served as precursors of events in other industries, as seen in 1922 and in the rise of the NUM in the early 1970s. The NUM of today is no longer that upstart union knocking at the doors of mining companies. It has been enjoying ensconced positions at most of the major mining houses. In some cases, the salaries of its representatives are paid by

the companies and are reportedly substantial. The union is also said to enjoy a cosy relationship with government.

In general, the established unions may have become too complacent. The unions themselves have thrived financially, many now owning vast assets, and their office bearers drawing substantial salaries. Negotiations are conducted at a highly centralised level in national bargaining councils, and the main role of the union now consists of monitoring compliance with agreements. Shop-steward representation at ground level may not carry the impact it deserves. The result, as already seen, is a groundswell of resistance and demands either from a new, more active union body such as SAFTU or from the employees themselves.

### Labour Unrest and Collective Bargaining Arrangements

Government is also concerned about continuing labour unrest, particularly in the transport and mining sectors. This was confirmed by the attempt to introduce strike ballots and by the proposal for more extensive and effective dispute resolution procedures in essential services. Amendments to the labour relations legislation have introduced further changes to collective bargaining, aimed at reducing labour unrest and the number of days lost due to strikes. As it is, a significant proportion of strikes in the decade after 2011 have been spontaneous, with legal procedures not being followed. President Cyril Ramaphosa has threatened to take a stronger stance against illegal actions, but has not indicated how this will be done, short of using force, which could have dire consequences.

Additionally, the Advisory Arbitration Panel was established to resolve violent strikes and intervene in potential strikes which might cause a national crisis. The amendments to the Labour Relations Act also include new picketing rules or regulations. The Code of Good Practice: Collective Bargaining, Industrial Action and Picketing was also published; this will be discussed further in Chapter 3.

Although the government would probably wish to encourage more co-operative relations at shop-floor level by way of workplace forums, it has not done much in this direction, presumably for fear of reaction from the unions. Nevertheless, if the problems outlined above are to be addressed, a more co-operative mode would be a necessity.

### Approach to the Relationship

The labour relations system remains rooted mainly in the pluralist mode, tempered by protection mainly for employees and legal provision for trade union representation. Thus, what is essentially a system based on institutionalised voluntarism has been remoulded by pro-labour interventionism, in some instances racially based in order to advance previously disadvantaged groups.

This is similar to the approach adopted by the drafters of the 1924 Industrial Conciliation Act and their attempts to promote the interests of white workers. There are increasing signs that the government is prepared to intervene to a greater extent and put its stamp on the relationship.

After the inception of NEDLAC, the corporatist model was adopted in the drafting of policy and legislation, but it is suspected that the government and COSATU still played a dominant role. An attempt was made also to introduce a more unitarist/corporatist mode at the workplace by the introduction of workplace forums, but it did not meet with much success. Nevertheless, there is no doubt that a more co-operative mode in all spheres would greatly contribute to solving existing problems.

## Conclusion

The South African labour relations system, because of its unique societal setting, remains divided. Despite the fact that discrimination on the basis of race, sex or creed has been eliminated from labour and other legislation, the composition of the trade union movement still reflects racial and political divisions, and there is, as yet, no unified federation. The system had to adapt and develop very rapidly over the past two decades. It was and still is beset by problems in the political sphere. Although past problems are gradually disappearing, new ones have arisen, and new adaptations will be required of both employers and unions. Consequently, the labour relations system remains dynamic and subject to rapid change necessitated by developments in the labour, economic and sociopolitical arenas.

## Suggested Questions/Tasks

1. Find out in which ways the South African government acts as legislator, conciliator, regulator and adviser, and what role is predominantly played by the judiciary and the police.
2. Construct a timeline illustrating the development of unionism in South Africa. Do you see any correlation between developments in the 1970s and the most recent union developments?
3. Construct a timeline showing how the labour relations system developed. How do you see future developments and, in particular, the role of government and unions in a world where the nature of work and the role of the employer and employee will have changed significantly?

# Sources

ANC (African National Congress). 1994. *The Reconstruction and Development Programme: A Policy Framework*. Johannesburg: ANC.

DEL (Department of Employment and Labour). 2020. 'South Africa hits all time low in competitiveness ranking'. http://www.labour.gov.za/south-africa-hits-all-time-low-in-competitiveness-ranking (Accessed 5 November 2021).

Friedman, S. 1987. *Building Tomorrow Today*. New York: Ravan Press.

Godfrey, S & Du Toit, D. 2000. 'Workplace forum proposals: Opportunity or threat?'. *South African Labour Bulletin* 24(6): 13–20.

Hunt, E & Sherman, HJ. 1978. *Economics: An Introduction to Traditional and Radical Views*. New York: Harper & Row.

IMF (International Monetary Fund). 2020. 'Six charts explain South Africa's inequality'. https://www.imf.org/en/News/Articles/2020/01/29/na012820six-charts-on-south-africas-persistent-and-multi-faceted-inequality (Accessed 6 November 2021).

Kenny, B. 2020. 'The South African labour movement: A fragmented and shifting terrain'. *Tempo Social* 32(1): 119–136.

Nel, PS & Kirsten, M. 2020. *South African Employment Relations: Theory and Practice*, 9th edition. Pretoria: Van Schaik.

Reuters. 2021. 'South Africa's unemployment rate hits new record high in second quarter'. August 24, 2021. https://www.reuters.com/article/safrica-economy-unemployment-idUSJ8N2KH000 (Accessed 6 November 2021).

Rifkin, J. 1995. *The End of Work: The Decline of the Global Labour Force and the Dawn of the Post-market Economy*. New York: Putnam.

Salamon, M. 1987. *Industrial Relations Theory and Practice*. Hoboken: Prentice Hall.

Schwab, K. 2016. *The Fourth Industrial Revolution*. Cologny: World Economic Forum.

Smith, A. (1776) 2000. *The Wealth of Nations* (Modern Library E-book). London: Random House.

Stats SA (Statistics South Africa). 2021. 'The economy grows by 1.2% in Q2: 2021'. http://www.statssa.gov.za/?p=14660 (Accessed 6 November 2021).

Trading Economics. 2021. 'South Africa GINI index'. https://tradingeconomics.com/south-africa/gini-index-wb-data.html (Accessed 6 November 2021).

WEF (World Economic Forum). 2017. 'Global competitiveness report 2017–2018'. https://www.weforum.org/reports/the-global-competitiveness-report-2017-2018 (Accessed 6 November 2021).

World Bank Group. 2018. 'Overcoming poverty and inequality in South Africa: An assessment of drivers, constraints and opportunities'. Washington, DC: World Bank. https://openknowledge.worldbank.org/handle/10986/29614 (Accessed 6 November 2021).

# Labour Legislation

## Chapter Outline

➤

Injuries and Diseases Act 130 of 1993 • The Unemployment Insurance Act 63 of 2001 and the Unemployment Insurance Contributions Act 4 of 2002

## THE LABOUR RELATIONS ACT 66 OF 1995

Historical Perspective • Purpose of the Act • Government's Intentions • Ambit of the Act • Status of the Act • The Labour Relations Amendment Act 6 of 2014 • The Labour Relations Amendment Act 8 of 2018

## MAJOR PROVISIONS OF THE LABOUR RELATIONS ACT

Chapter II: Freedom of Association and General Protection | *Freedom of Association* | *Freedom from Victimisation* • Chapter III: Collective Bargaining | *Part A: Organisational Rights* | *Part B: Collective Agreements* | *Part C: Bargaining Councils* | *Part D: Public Service Bargaining Councils* | *Part E: Statutory Councils* | *Part F: General Provisions Regarding Councils* • Chapter IV: Strikes and Lockouts • Chapter V: Workplace Forums • Chapter VI: Registration of Unions and Employer Organisations • Chapter VII: Dispute Settlement | *Part A: The CCMA* | *Part B: Accreditation and Subsidisation of Councils and Private Agencies* | *Part C: Dispute Settlement under the Auspices of the CCMA* | *Part D: The Labour Court* | *Part E: The Labour Appeal Court* • Chapter VIII: Unfair Dismissals and Unfair Labour Practices | *Unfair Dismissals* | *Unfair Labour Practices* | *Retrenchments and Transfer of a Business as a Going Concern* | *Other Matters Dealt with in Chapter VIII* • Chapter IX: General Provisions | *Labour Brokers* | *Confidentiality* | *Presumption as to Who is an Employee* • *Defects and Irregularities* | *Definitions*

## THE EMPLOYMENT EQUITY ACT 55 OF 1998

Objectives of the Act • Ambit of the Act • Discrimination | *Fair and Unfair Discrimination* | *Medical and Psychological Tests* | *Applicants for Positions* | *Contraventions* • Affirmative Action | *Planning for Redress* | *Designated Employers* | *Designated Groups* | *Delegation of Responsibility* | *Consultation* | *Analysis* • The Employment Equity Plan | *Developing an Equity plan* | *Submission of Equity Plans and Reports* | *Assessment of Compliance* | *Consequences of Non-compliance* • Publication and Display of Documents • Commission for Employment Equity • Protection from Victimisation

## CONCLUSION

## SUGGESTED QUESTIONS/TASKS

## SOURCES

# Overview

Labour legislation reflects the degree of state involvement in the relationship. In a completely voluntary system, there would be no labour laws. However, no purely voluntary system can or does exist. The market is influenced by too many sociological, political and administrative factors to be able to operate freely. Moreover, its free operation might lead to unfavourable employment conditions. The parties to the labour relationship cannot be left entirely to their own devices, particularly where power is unequally distributed. Additionally, the country's history and its economic, technological and sociopolitical forces cannot be ignored, since they shape the labour relations landscape.

To be acceptable, labour laws should conform to universal standards. The best guidelines for such standards are found in the various conventions and recommendations of the International Labour Organization (ILO). Furthermore, legislation passed in South Africa cannot deviate from the principles established by the Constitution of the Republic of South Africa, 1996. As far as labour legislation is concerned, the most relevant section of the Constitution is the one outlining fundamental rights, including labour relations rights.

The employment relationship is governed, in the first instance, by the contract of employment, which is guided by common law. Parties who agree that one will work for another and be paid a certain amount have entered into a contract. From then onwards they will have certain rights and duties in terms of common law, which can be enforced in the civil courts and also in the Labour Court. A written contract will influence the decision of the courts. If there is no written contract, the courts will be guided by practice, custom and tradition. Common law does not take into account the fairness of the contract, but merely the fact that a contract has been concluded. Because of this situation, common law may be superseded by statutes, which, in South Africa, are developed in consultation with the National Economic Development and Labour Council (NEDLAC). Labour law has most recently concerned itself with employment contracts to prevent unfairness and the exploitation of vulnerable employees. Labour relations became more formalised after the great Witwatersrand strikes of 1922, after which the Industrial Conciliation Act 11 of 1924 was promulgated. The Act provided for the system of collective bargaining, the freedom to strike and a process for dispute resolution.

For our purposes, the major statute is the Labour Relations Act 66 of 1995, which also provides for delegated legislation in the form of bargaining council agreements and sectoral determinations. These may establish conditions and rules more favourable – or even less favourable – than those contained in contracts or in the labour statutes.

The Labour Relations Act sets the framework for the collective labour relationship by legislation relating to organisational rights, the registration of unions and employers' associations and the formation of bargaining and statutory councils. In order to encourage consultation and co-determination on certain issues between employers and employee representatives, the Act also provides for the establishment of workplace forums.

The legislation attempts to promote labour peace by providing a dispute settlement process and by not permitting a legal or protected strike or lockout unless the prescribed procedures have been followed. The 1995 Act introduced a new dispute settlement body in the form of the Commission for Conciliation, Mediation and Arbitration (CCMA) and replaced the Industrial Court with the Labour Court, which has higher status and more extended functions. The Act also prohibits victimisation and any interference with the freedom of association.

In all workplaces, but particularly where collective bargaining is not well established, employees are protected by the Basic Conditions of Employment Act 75 of 1997. This Act provides for maximum working hours, payment for overtime and for work on Sundays and public holidays, minimum notice periods, minimum annual leave and sick leave, the regulation of overtime and the prohibition of certain deductions.

All employees are further protected by the Occupational Health and Safety Act 85 of 1993, which provides for the appointment of safety representatives and safety committees, and which regulates safety at the workplace.

The Unemployment Insurance Act 63 of 2001 and the Compensation for Occupational Injuries and Diseases Act 130 of 1993 are, basically, insurance schemes for employees. The first-mentioned Act provides for the compulsory deduction of unemployment contributions from employers and employees. This entitles employees to certain benefits in the event of unemployment. The Workmen's Compensation Fund relies on compulsory levies paid by employers and provides for payment of compensation to employees who suffer disability as a result of an accident or who contract an illness caused by the type of work being performed.

The Employment Equity Act 55 of 1998 prohibits discrimination and compels organisations with more than 50 employees to produce an employment equity plan and show progress in instituting affirmative action measures.

## Rationale of the Legislative Framework

The purpose of labour legislation is to establish a framework for the conduct of the labour relationship and to provide, at the very least, for minimum conditions of employment. Where no labour legislation exists, the employment relationship is governed by the contract of employment. A contract can be enforced at common law, but it is generally agreed that this does not provide sufficient protection for employees. The law of contract does not deal with concepts of fairness or equity, which are crucial in the labour relationship.

Labour law must, in the first place, protect employees. The operation of the market principle, which is based only on the concepts of demand and supply, does not concern itself with the possibility of exploitation. An individual may, because of circumstances, enter into an unfavourable contract. For this reason, it is regarded as the duty of the state to legislate on minimum terms and conditions of employment and to protect the health and safety of the workforce.

In a voluntary system, labour law may also provide the framework for the conduct of the collective labour relationship. Legislation will provide for freedom of association, freedom from victimisation and the right to engage in labour action. To promote labour peace, dispute settlement procedures may also be provided. Furthermore, it may happen that each party is protected from unfair practices by the other, and that collective bargaining is promoted by the body of labour law.

Principles of social justice and the protection of society's members have led to the institution of welfare schemes in the form of legislated unemployment funds. Furthermore, in order to promote more efficient economic activity, the state involves itself in training and manpower planning programmes.

## International Labour Standards

In establishing labour legislation, governments are guided by universally accepted standards. These are best supplied by the various conventions and recommendations of the ILO, which are subsequently ratified and implemented by member countries.

Recommendations and conventions have been passed concerning almost every aspect of the employment relationship. For our present purposes, we are concerned only with those which establish the basic principles for the conduct of the relationship. These are:

- the Declaration of Philadelphia
- Convention No 87 Concerning Freedom of Association and Protection of the Right to Organise
- Convention No 98 Concerning the Application of the Principles of the Right to Organise and to Bargain Collectively.

### The Declaration of Philadelphia

The Declaration of Philadelphia reaffirms the main principles on which the ILO is based. It is generally regarded as the founding document of the ILO.

Part I of the Declaration (ILO, 1944) makes the following statements:

*(a) labour is not a commodity;*

*(b) freedom of expression and of association are essential to sustained progress;*

*(c) poverty anywhere constitutes a danger to prosperity everywhere;*

*(d) the war against want requires to be carried on with unrelenting vigour within each nation, and by continuous and concerted international effort in which the representatives of workers and employers, enjoying equal status with those of governments, join with them in free discussion and democratic decision with a view to the promotion of the common welfare.*

Part II (ILO, 1944) affirms the ideological premise of the ILO, namely that:

*all human beings, irrespective of race, creed or sex, have the right to pursue both their material wellbeing and their spiritual development in conditions of freedom and dignity, of economic security and equal opportunity.*

The third part is more specific in that it sets the ILO the task of promoting full employment and raising the standard of living of all people (ILO, 1944). This should be achieved by:

- promoting training
- facilitating the transfer of labour
- setting policies regarding wages and conditions of service
- recognising the right to collective bargaining
- promoting co-operation between management and labour to improve productive efficiency
- encouraging collaboration between workers and employers in deciding on social and economic measures
- establishing social security measures
- instituting comprehensive medical care
- protecting the life and health of workers
- making provision for child welfare and maternity protection
- making provision for adequate cultural facilities for all employees.

### Convention No 87 Concerning the Freedom of Association and Protection of the Right to Organise

Convention No 87 (ILO, 1948) enlarges on one of the founding statements of the Declaration of Philadelphia, namely that 'freedom of expression and of association are essential for sustained progress' (ILO, 1944, Part I).

The most important statements contained in Convention No 87 (ILO, 1948) are the following:

- 'Workers and employers, without distinction whatsoever, shall have the right to establish and, subject only to the rules of the organisations concerned, to join organisations of their own choosing without previous authorisation.' (Part I, Article 2)
- 'Workers' and employers' organisations shall have the right to draw up their constitutions and rules, to elect their representatives in full freedom, to organise their administration and activities and to formulate their programmes.' (Part I, Article 3.1)
- 'The public authorities shall refrain from any interference which would restrict this right or impede the lawful exercise thereof.' (Part I, Article 3.2)
- 'Workers' and employers' organisations shall not be liable to be dissolved or suspended by administrative authority.' (Part I, Article 4)

- 'In exercising the rights provided for in this Convention workers and employers and their respective organisations, like other persons or organised collectives, shall respect the law of the land.' (Part I, Article 8.1)
- 'The law shall not be such as to impair, nor shall it be so implied as to impair, the guarantees provided for in this Convention.' (Part I, Article 8.2)
- 'Each member of the International Labour Organisation for which this Convention is in force undertakes to take all necessary and appropriate measures to ensure that workers and employers may exercise freely the right to organise.' (Part II, Article 11)

The Convention speaks for itself. Essentially, it safeguards the most basic freedom in the labour relationship – the freedom to associate (or, for that matter, to disassociate) – on condition that any organisation so established does not break the law, but with the understanding that the law should not impair the freedom of association and the right to organise.

### Convention No 98 Concerning the Application of the Principles of the Right to Organise and to Bargain Collectively

Convention No 98 (ILO, 1949: Articles 1, 2.2) firstly recommends safeguards against anti-union discrimination. It recommends protection against acts which:
- make an employee or prospective employee agree not to join a union or to give up union membership
- allow an employer to dismiss an employee or otherwise prejudice them because of union membership or because of participation in union activities
- promote the establishment of workers' organisations under the domination of employers or employers' organisations
- allow employers to support workers' organisations by financial or other means.

The Convention goes on to suggest that the state should create the machinery for the establishment of employees' and employers' organisations and should provide the machinery for collective bargaining.

## The Constitutional Framework

South Africa is classified as a constitutional state, as the country is governed in terms of its Constitution (the Constitution of the Republic of South Africa, 1996), which is the supreme law of the country. South Africa is seen as autonomous or sovereign political entity based on the principles of democracy. Therefore, the interpretation and application of legislation and common law must be consistent with constitutional principles.

Chapter 2 of the Constitution sets out certain fundamental rights of all persons and makes the content of that chapter binding on 'all legislative and executive organs of State at all levels of government'. This means that no law may contain provisions which deprive individuals of these fundamental rights. The Constitution, in Section 36(1) of Chapter 2, does provide that rights may be limited by law, but on condition that the limitation is 'reasonable and justifiable in an open and democratic society based on human dignity, equality and freedom'; in addition, the limitation must not result in a negation of the essential content of the right. No rights are limitless, as the exercise of an individual's rights may impinge on the rights of others. Thus, the law may limit these rights, but cannot remove them altogether.

Section 23 of Chapter 2 in the Constitution relates specifically to labour relations and provides the following:

- 'Every person shall have the right to fair labour practices.'
- Workers have the right to form and join trade unions, and employers have the right to form and join employers' organisations.
- Workers and employers have the right to organise and bargain collectively.

Besides the section dealing with labour relations, there are other sections in the Bill of Rights which will affect labour relations and labour legislation. The following are examples:

- Section 9, dealing with equality, provides that everyone is equal before the law and has the right to equal protection and benefit of the law. It also provides protection against direct and indirect discrimination.
- Section 10 entitles every person to 'respect for and protection of his or her dignity'.
- Section 14, dealing with the right to privacy, spells out the right of persons not to be subject to searches of their person, home or property, the seizure of private possessions or the violation of private communication.
- Section 16 details the right to freedom of speech and expression.
- Section 17 grants every person the right to assemble and demonstrate with others peacefully and unarmed, and to present petitions. The right to petition or picket is not an unfettered right. This right is also entrenched in the Regulation of Gatherings Act 205 of 1993, which states that organisers of an event must give authorities (police) seven days notice, together with names, the place and the purpose of the event. The right to picket is extended to the workplace, providing registered trade unions with the authority to mobilise their members and supporters to peacefully demonstrate in support of any protected strike or in opposition of any lockouts.
- Section 18 provides for freedom of association by allowing employees to assemble and the right to form trade unions. The same right is also

entrenched in Chapter 2 of the Labour Relations Act 66 of 1995, which further allows for the limitation of the right by way of closed-shop and agency-shop agreements.

Because these rights are entrenched in the Constitution, all labour legislation and actions and processes in labour relations should be evaluated in this context. If a law or a provision in a law negates any of these rights, it may be challenged in the Constitutional Court.

## Government Policy on Labour Affairs

### Official Labour Relations Policy

The government's official labour relations policy has in the past been based broadly on the principles of voluntarism and maximum self-government by employers and employee bodies. In general, the system still functions in terms of the following principles:

- **The right to work:** All workers in South Africa have the right to provide for themselves and their families through taking part in the productive activities of the country. This right, however, places an obligation on everybody to make themselves available for work, to offer their talents and skills, and to accept such employment opportunities as are available.
- **The right to fair remuneration and conditions of service:** Every worker in South Africa has a right to fair remuneration in accordance with their skills and the effort and loyalty they devote to their employer. This right includes a limitation on the hours the worker may work in a normal day and week, and entitles the worker to overtime pay, vacation and sick leave.
- **The right of access to training and retraining:** It is the worker's right to receive training and retraining, so that they may increase their productivity and earning capacity. It is the worker's right to be fully utilised in the work for which they have been trained. The state, employers and employees are co-partners in the national training effort.
- **The right to organise and to belong to a trade union:** All employees have the right at all times to organise themselves into trade unions, to register those unions and to utilise the bargaining and conciliation machinery created by legislation. In this way a labour climate is created which promotes favourable relationships between employer and employee.
- **The right to negotiate and bargain collectively:** Collective bargaining and negotiation, in accordance with legally recognised rules, are the golden steps to the settlement of disputes between employers and employees. A spirit of mutual understanding and fairness is thereby engendered, which individual or overhasty action cannot achieve.

- **The right to protection of safety and health:** Certain occupations hold inherent dangers to safety and health, and it is the worker's right to work in the safest working environment that the employer can reasonably provide and to enjoy reasonable facilities for personal hygiene.
- **The right to security against unemployment and the payment of amounts to dependants of deceased contributors:** Workers are compelled to contribute to the Unemployment Insurance Fund and to receive compensation for loss of earnings arising from unemployment due to termination of employment, illness or maternity. Dependants of deceased contributors can also receive compensation.
- **The right to security in the event of injury on duty:** Workers are entitled to compensation against loss of earnings due to accidents or industrial diseases contracted in the course of their employment, free medical treatment and lump sums or pensions for permanent disablement. In fatal cases, pensions and an allowance for funeral expenses are paid to dependants. The onus rests on employers to submit the prescribed accident and medical reports, as well as medical accounts, to the Workmen's Compensation Commissioner.
- **The right to job security and protection against unfair labour practices:** A worker's job security lies largely in their own hands, through the dedicated performance of their duties. But the worker also has a right to job security, which is entrenched in our labour legislation. Employers may not arbitrarily change labour practices, and workers have a right to protection under the Act if their security is thus jeopardised.

## Vision and Mission of the Department of Labour

The Department of Labour has declared its vision to be the support of a labour market which promotes investment, economic growth, employment creation and decent work. To achieve this, the Department's aim has been to develop, in consultation with social partners, programmes which will:
- improve economic efficiency and productivity
- lead to employment creation
- promote sound labour relations
- eliminate inequality in the workplace
- alleviate poverty through employment.

The declared mission of the Department is to 'regulate the South African Labour market for a sustainable economy' (Department of Labour, n.d.). This it aims to do mainly by:
- putting in place the necessary legislation and regulations
- undertaking inspections to ensure that parties comply

- protecting human rights
- promoting equity.

It is noteworthy that the Department's vision emphasises economic development and job creation. There are numerous critics who argue that the very laws which the Department administers may be partly responsible for the country's poor economic growth. This was borne out in the 2017–2018 World Competitive Report, which ranked South Africa 61st out of 137 countries – 14 places lower than in the previous survey (WEF, 2017). However, the country witnessed an improvement in the rankings in 2019, when it moved up to 60th out of 141 countries (Jooste, 2019). Restrictive labour legislation is seen as one of the reasons why South Africa has become less competitive, with a concomitant inability to improve employment levels.

Creating the right balance between promotion of the economy and job creation, on the one hand, and the protection and upliftment of employees, on the other, remains a major challenge for the Department and the government in power.

## NEDLAC

NEDLAC was formed early in 1995, from an amalgamation of the National Manpower Commission and the National Economic Forum, established by the previous government. Its founding document cites its purpose to be the bringing together of labour, business, government and development actors in order to 'seek to reach consensus and conclude agreements on matters pertaining to social and economic policy' and to 'consider all proposed labour legislation' (DEL, 2019).

NEDLAC consists of four chambers: the Labour Market Chamber, the Trade and Industry Chamber, the Public Finance and Monetary Policy Chamber and the Development Chamber. The three major union federations – the Congress of South African Trade Unions (COSATU), the National Council of Trade Unions (NACTU) and the Federation of Unions of South Africa (FEDUSA) – are represented in NEDLAC on a proportionate basis, while business is represented by Business Unity South Africa. Other role players include government officials, politicians and community delegates representing, for example, women, civic organisations, rural bodies and disabled persons.

At the time of writing, rifts are increasingly appearing in NEDLAC. There is outright friction between the Black Business Council and Business Unity South Africa, under whose auspices the former was allowed into NEDLAC. These divisions rest mostly on ideological orientations. As regards the union caucus, there is growing criticism that the union federations in NEDLAC represent only a small percentage (an estimated 20 per cent) of national union membership. COSATU, previously the most influential union body in NEDLAC, has seen its position waning. A growing new body, the South African Federation of Trade Unions (SAFTU), has not yet been admitted even though it is now the second-largest union federation and is larger than both NACTU and FEDUSA combined. All in all, it would appear that NEDLAC might still be representing only a narrow band of interests in both the business and labour caucuses.

## Legal and Statutory Regulation of the Employment Relationship

### Conditions of Service

The individual contract of employment constitutes the first step in the regulation of the employment relationship. Rules of contract are established at common law, but the Basic Conditions of Employment Act 75 of 1997 does prescribe the matters that should be dealt with in the employment contract.

When the conditions set out in a contract are more favourable than those contained in a statute or agreement, the contract takes precedence. No contract can provide for conditions of service which are less favourable than those contained in:

- a statute
- a statutory agreement
- a ministerial determination
- an in-house agreement covering that employee.

The most important statute governing individual conditions of employment is the Basic Conditions of Employment Act. In addition, the Labour Relations Act 66 of 1995 provides for certain individual rights, such as:

- the right not to be dismissed without a valid reason and a fair hearing
- the right not to be victimised for trade union membership
- the right not to be arbitrarily and peremptorily retrenched.

The Occupational Health and Safety Act 85 of 1993 entitles the employee to protection from health and safety hazards, while the Unemployment Insurance Act 63 of 2001 and the Compensation for Occupational Injuries and Diseases Act 130 of 1993 entitle the employee to unemployment benefits and to compensation for injuries or diseases sustained or contracted during the course of their work.

All the above rights have to be acknowledged in the employment contract – if not explicitly, then at least implicitly. Most importantly, no contract of employment may contain conditions less favourable than those provided in the Basic Conditions of Employment Act, unless such condition has been negotiated by a bargaining council or is subject to a ministerial determination.

An agreement reached by a bargaining council will, once it has been gazetted, become subsidiary legislation, and is enforceable under the Labour Relations Act.

A bargaining council agreement assumes precedence over the Basic Conditions of Employment Act – that is, the conditions set out in a bargaining council agreement may be less favourable than all except the 'core' conditions of that Act. The core conditions are those relating to:

- maximum working hours (45)
- family responsibility leave
- health and safety
- child labour
- sick leave
- maternity leave
- annual leave.

However, a bargaining council agreement can reduce annual leave to 14 calendar days and a ministerial determination issued for industries or areas where there is no bargaining council may vary any condition of the Basic Conditions of Employment Act.

Any conditions negotiated at plant or company level must, in terms of Section 23 of the Labour Relations Act, immediately be written into the contracts of all employees covered by such agreement. Conditions contained in these agreements may never be less favourable than the Basic Conditions of Employment Act or a relevant bargaining council agreement/statutory determination.

### Other Substantive and Procedural Conditions

These relate to employee welfare and are contained in the Unemployment Insurance Act, the Occupational Health and Safety Act and the Compensation for Occupational Injuries and Diseases Act.

### Regulation of the Collective Employment Relationship

The Labour Relations Act provides the framework for the regulation of the collective relationship between employers and employees or their unions. Although it focuses on the collective relationship, the Act does provide for individual substantive and procedural rights, as contained in Chapter VI on dismissals and unfair labour practices.

## Elimination of Discrimination, Affirmative Action, Training and Development

These aspects are regulated by the provisions of the Employment Equity Act 55 of 1998 and the Skills Development Act 97 of 1998. A wider perspective on equity is also contained in the Promotion of Equality and Prevention of Unfair Discrimination Act 4 of 2000, while the Skills Development Act should be studied in conjunction with the National Qualifications Framework Act 67 of 2008.

Figure 3.1 summarises the legal and statutory regulation of the employment relationship, as has been explained in this discussion.

## The Employment Contract

### The Common-law Contract

An employment contract comes into existence when both parties agree that the employee will work for the employer. A contract may be written or verbal, or it may be understood. If no written or verbal agreement has been made, it does not mean that there is no contract. The very fact that one person is working for another means that a contract exists. Usually the parties will agree on the kind of work required and on the wage to be paid by the employer. Where this has not been spelt out, the parties can rely on accepted practice. For example, an employer who hires a labourer but does not indicate how much they will pay the labourer will be expected to remunerate the worker in terms of common practice – that is, the employer should pay the rates commonly paid for work of that kind. If no definite period of employment is stated, it is taken that the employment is indefinite. This is the difference between a permanent and a fixed-term contract.

### Rights and Duties at Common Law

Once a contract of employment has been entered into, whether in writing, verbally or tacitly, it is accepted that the parties have agreed to certain rights and duties at common law. At common law the employer should:
- pay the employee
- provide safe and healthy working conditions
- provide work for the employee
- not make the employee do work junior to the status for which they were employed
- not contract the employee's services to another employer without the employee's consent.

The reciprocal duties of the employee are to:
- perform their work faithfully and diligently
- obey reasonable orders given in the normal course of employment

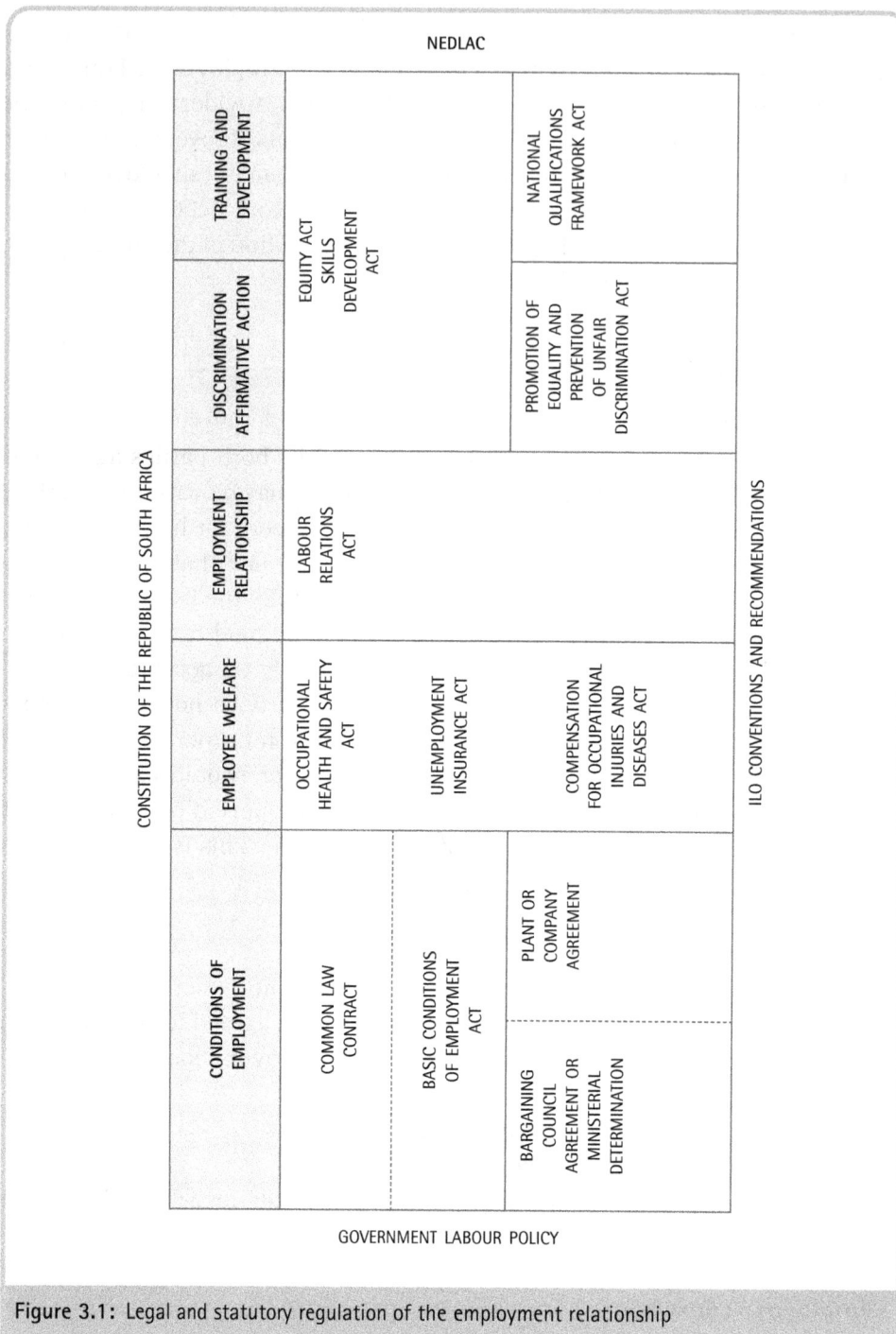

**Figure 3.1:** Legal and statutory regulation of the employment relationship

- not deal dishonestly with the property of the employer
- not compete in their private capacity with the business of the employer.

The duties of one party become the rights of the other. Thus, the employee has the right:
- to remuneration
- to work
- not to be demoted
- not to be forced to work for any other employer but their own
- to safe and healthy working conditions.

The employer has the right to expect that the employee:
- does the work to the best of their ability
- obeys reasonable orders
- is honest
- does not compete with the employer's business.

In addition, it is accepted that the employer has the right to select whomever they wish to employ. The employer can say how the work should be done and has the right to dismiss the employee if the latter's performance is not satisfactory. By accepting the job, the employee implies that they are competent to perform it and accepts that they have an obligation to work for the employer for a certain period. In most cases, this period is indefinite and will be limited only by the termination or breach of the employment contract.

### Contracts which would, at Common Law, Be Voidable

The parties may decide to enter into a verbal or written agreement. The contract they conclude may contain any provision agreed to by the parties, but they may not agree to anything which is illegal, immoral or contrary to public policy. A contract would be illegal if it contained a provision which would entail a breach of a statute or of the common law. Thus, a contract in which the employee agrees to steal for an employer would be illegal. An agreement to engage in prostitution would be both illegal and immoral. Finally, the parties may not agree on conditions of employment (including wages) which are less favourable than those prescribed by the Basic Conditions of Employment Act, a bargaining council agreement or a ministerial determination. Such contracts would be declared null and void.

Contracts are also voidable where the consent of one party has been improperly obtained by misrepresentation, coercion or undue influence. For example, the contract of a person who declares in an application that they have previous experience when in fact they have none can be cancelled by the employer. The contract can also be declared void if one of the parties does not have contractual capacity – for example, if they are under age.

If a contract does not contain any of the irregularities described, the civil courts will enforce the contract as it stands. This is the case even if the position of one party to the contract is unfavourable in relation to that of the other. It is basic to the judicial process that persons above the age of consent should be free to enter into any contract they please. As long as both parties concluded the contract of their own free will and it is not immoral, illegal or against public policy, the court will, at common law, uphold the terms of the contract, regardless of whether it is grossly unfair to one of the parties.

## Breach of Contract

Breach of contract has always been actionable in terms of the common law. The civil courts will consider precedent and statutory requirements. Where there is no specific provision by statute and no common-law precedent, the court will refer to custom or established practice to decide if breach of contract has occurred. For example, an employer who has for five years paid their employees on the 15th of each month and who unilaterally decides to pay them on the 25th may be held to be in breach of contract, even if there is no specific provision for payment on the 15th.

Section 77(3) of the Basic Conditions of Employment Act now also grants the Labour Court the right to adjudicate on matters related to the contract of employment, including alleged breach of contract.

## Termination of Contract

At common law, a contract of employment which does not contain specific conditions relating to termination may be terminated upon:
- reasonable notice by either party
- the consent of both parties
- the death or incapacity of the employee
- the insolvency of the employer.

However, notice periods are also subject to the Basic Conditions of Employment Act, which provides for:
- one week's notice if the employee has been employed for less than six months
- two weeks' notice if the employment period is longer than six months but less than one year
- one month's notice if the person has been employed for longer than a year or is a farm worker employed for longer than six months.

Common law does not oblige an employer or an employee to supply a reason for the dismissal or resignation. At common law a party merely has to give reasonable notice of the intention to dismiss or resign. By contrast, the Labour Relations Act contains detailed provisions regarding termination and reasons for dismissal, such as misconduct, incapacity, redundancy and retrenchment. It therefore safeguards employees from arbitrary and unfair termination of contract by the employer.

### The Common Law and the Employment Relationship

The common law treats the contract of employment by the same measures as any other contract. If parties to the employment relationship had recourse only to the common law, they would have to go to the civil courts, and would be able to sue only for actual financial losses. However, unlike other contracts (such as a lease or a hire purchase agreement), the employment contract leads to the establishment of a special relationship. It is usually expected that, if each party performs their duties, the employment contract will be indefinite. It follows that if termination of employment occurs, there should be a sound reason for this.

Furthermore, the employment relationship is more often than not an unequal relationship in which the employer holds more power than the employee. In these circumstances an employee might enter into a contract which will lead to their exploitation. This problem is not addressed at common law, nor is the fact that breach of an employment contract has ramifications for the employee beyond mere material damage. An employee who is dismissed may suffer loss of future prospects, loss of reputation or status and actual emotional damage.

These considerations have led to the establishment of labour statutes intended, in the main, to supplement the common law and to:
- safeguard the employee against blatant exploitation by the employer
- provide for a more equal distribution of power between employer and employee
- guard against unreasonable behaviour by either party
- allow for the establishment of collective relationships.

Thus, the employment relationship is governed not only by the common-law contract but also by the various labour statutes as well as collective agreements and ministerial determinations. Where they refer to similar matters, these supersede the common law and any conditions set out in the contract itself. See Figure 3.2 for the procedure of establishing the correct conditions of employment.

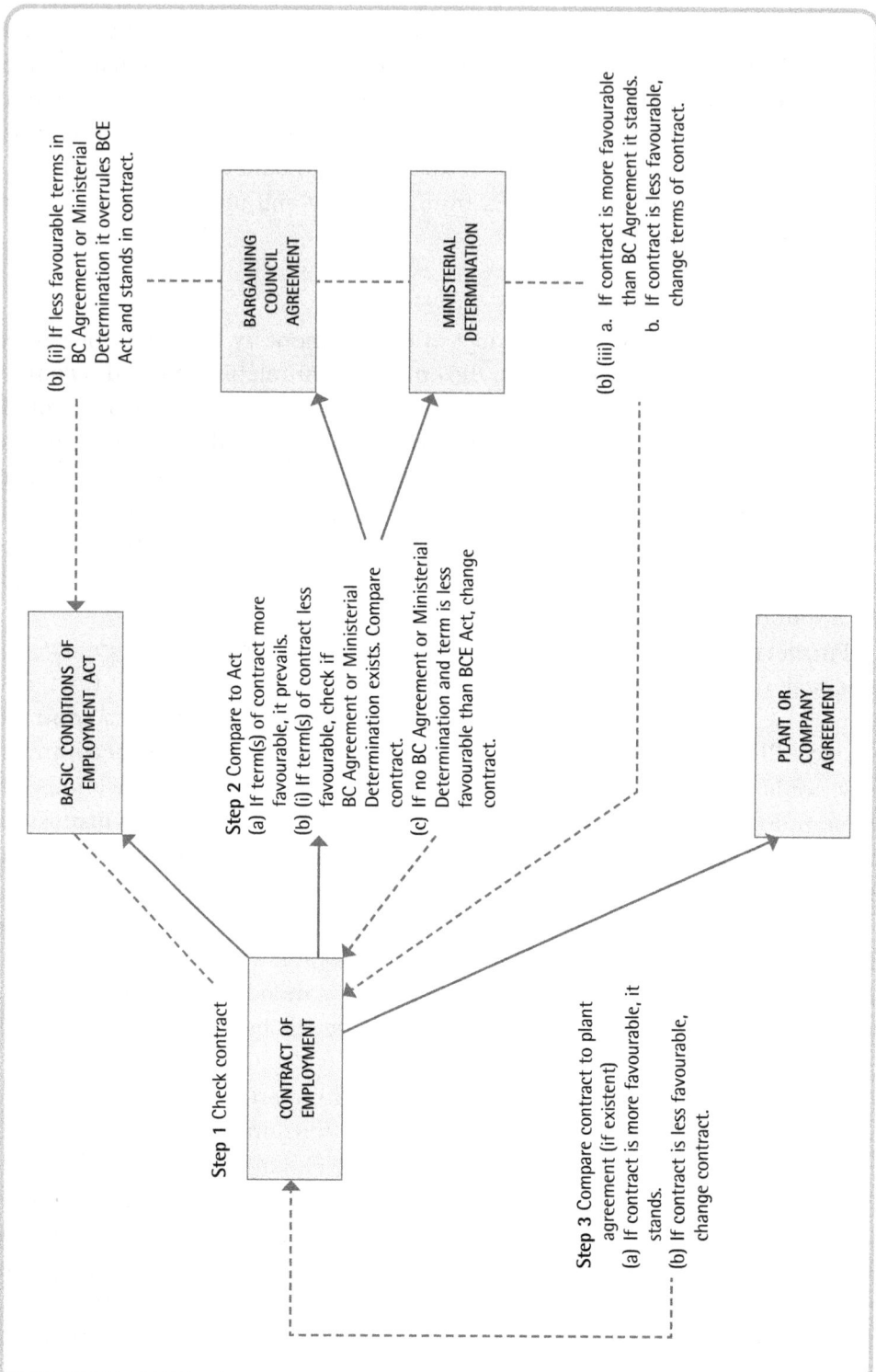

**Step 1** Check contract

**BASIC CONDITIONS OF EMPLOYMENT ACT**

(b) (ii) If less favourable terms in BC Agreement or Ministerial Determination it overrules BCE Act and stands in contract.

**BARGAINING COUNCIL AGREEMENT**

**MINISTERIAL DETERMINATION**

**Step 2** Compare to Act
(a) If term(s) of contract more favourable, it prevails.
(b) (i) If term(s) of contract less favourable, check if BC Agreement or Ministerial Determination exists. Compare contract.
(c) If no BC Agreement or Ministerial Determination and term is less favourable than BCE Act, change contract.

(b) (iii) a. If contract is more favourable than BC Agreement it stands.
b. If contract is less favourable, change terms of contract.

**CONTRACT OF EMPLOYMENT**

**PLANT OR COMPANY AGREEMENT**

**Step 3** Compare contract to plant agreement (if existent)
(a) If contract is more favourable, it stands.
(b) If contract is less favourable, change contract.

Figure 3.2: Flowchart for establishing correct conditions of employment

## The Written Contract

*Prescriptions*

Because implied and verbal contracts create uncertainty, it has become customary for new employees to receive a letter of appointment or to conclude a full contract of employment. Section 29 of the Basic Conditions of Employment Act obliges employers to issue written contracts to employees. The letter of appointment or contract must, in terms of the Act, state:

- the full name and address of the employer
- the name and occupation of the employee or a short description of their job
- the place or places where the employee is expected to work
- the date of commencement
- ordinary hours and days on which the employee is expected to work
- the wage or the wage rate and the method of calculation
- the rate of pay for overtime
- any other cash payments to which the employee may be entitled
- any payment in kind and the value of such payment
- the employee's leave entitlement (that is, annual leave, sick leave and family responsibility leave)
- notice periods in the event of proposed termination
- in case of a fixed-term contract, the date or event of termination
- any bargaining council or sectoral determination governing conditions of service
- any period of service with a previous employer that will count towards the employee's tenure.

The contract must also contain a list of other documents relating to the contract of employment, and indicate an accessible place where they may be viewed. This list would include relevant company policies and procedures, such as rules and regulations, disciplinary and grievance procedures, the retrenchment and equity policies, the relevant Acts and any agreements concluded at company or central level.

*Additional Information*

In addition to the items listed above, it is advisable to add clauses relating to the following (if applicable):

- pension/provident fund and medical aid contributions
- tax deductions in terms of directives from the South African Revenue Service (SARS)
- a confidentiality clause, if necessary.

## Requirements

The contract has to be signed and dated by both parties. This confirms that both have understood and agreed to the terms of the contract. If the employee is unable to read, the terms of the contract must be explained to them and the employee must sign to verify that this has been done.

## Omissions

If a matter is not specifically dealt with in the contract of employment, it is subject to common law or, where applicable, to the relevant statutory provisions. Thus, if a letter of appointment does not state the period of notice, it will be taken to be the period specified in the bargaining council agreement governing that industry or the period specified in the Basic Conditions of Employment Act. If no bargaining council or other agreement exists and there is no relevant legislation, the court will revert to custom and tradition.

## Persons Designated as Employees
### The Problem

Although the contract of employment forms the basis of the employment relationship, the absence of a written contract, or even the existence of a contract explicitly stating that an individual is not an employee, does not mean that the individual concerned will not be regarded as an employee and therefore not be entitled to the rights accorded to all employees.

### Definition of Employee

Section 213 of the Labour Relations Act defines an employee as:

> (a) *any person, excluding an independent contractor, who works for another person or for the State and who receives, or is entitled to receive, any remuneration; and*
> (b) *any other person who in any manner assists in carrying on or conducting the business of an employer ...*

This definition corresponds with Section 1 of the Basic Conditions of Employment Act and Section 1 of the Employment Equity Act.

### Independent Contractors versus Employees

Subparagraph (a) of Section 213 of the Labour Relations Act, as quoted above, specifies the exclusion of independent contractors from the statutory definition of employee, while subparagraph (b) seems to open up things widely. Independent contractors are excluded on the basis that they are not economically dependent on one particular client, but the problem lies in establishing whether a person who performs work for an employer is indeed an employee or would be classified as an independent contractor. By the same token, it is significant to define the employment contract (*locatio conductio operarum*) and contract of work (*locatio conductio operis*).

In addition to the persons it employs, an organisation may contract certain jobs to be performed by outside agencies. So, for example, all tasks related to security might be outsourced to a security company. The security company, as an independent contractor, provides the necessary manpower and assumes responsibility for security in the organisation. In this case, it is easy to distinguish between the employees of the independent contractor and those employed by the organisation. However, the situation becomes more complex when the entity providing the service is an individual. In such a case the person involved may appear to be acting independently, and the contract may even contain a clause to this effect, but the person may turn out to be an employee.

As indicated in the case review later on in this section (*South African Broadcasting Corporation v McKenzie*), a number of different tests have in the past been applied by the courts in order to establish whether someone is an independent contractor or is actually an employee.

In an effort to clarify the distinction between the two types of contract, in 2002 the government amended the Labour Relations Act (Section 200A) and the Basic Conditions of Employment Act (Section 83A) to specify who would be presumed to be an employee and, therefore, be covered by the relevant Acts.

A person who works for or renders services to any other person is presumed, until the contrary is proved, to be an employee. However, in order to distinguish between an employee and an independent contractor, it is essential to conduct tests. There are various types of tests:

- The **control test** is premised on the subordination of the employee to the employer in terms of the common-law contract of employment. This test assumes that an essential requirement of the employment relationship is that the employer has the right to prescribe to the employee not only what work is to be done but also the manner in which work is to be done.
- The **organisation or integration test** looks at whether a person works as part and parcel of the organisation. If the persons' work, although done for the business, is not integrated into it but only plays an accessory role, the person is an independent contractor. This test aims to determine whether the employee has been integrated into the organisation or forms an integral part of the organisation. According to this test, the employee is someone who has bound themself contractually to an organisation and who carries out work to further the organisation's objectives.
- The **dominant impression test** regards no single indicator as decisive; rather, it requires an examination of the relationship as a whole with the

aim of arriving at a dominant impression as to whether it is based on a contract of employment or a contract for the performance of independent services.

- The **reality test** emphasises three criteria: Does the employer have the right to supervise and control the employee? Does the employee form an integral part of the employer's organisation? Is the person economically dependent upon the employer? Thus, the person is an employee if one or more of the following factors is present:
  - The manner in which the person works is subject to the control or direction of another person.
  - The person's hours of work are subject to the control or direction of another person.
  - In the case of a person who works for an organisation, the person is part of that organisation.
  - The person has worked for the other person for an average of at least 40 hours per month over the last three months.
  - The person is economically dependent on the person for whom they work or render services.
  - The person is provided with tools of trade or work equipment by the other person.
  - The person only works or renders services to one person.

It needs to be stressed that the above applies only to persons earning below the earnings threshold published by the Minister of Labour. At the time of writing, the threshold was R205 433.30 per annum. It is clear that the presumption of employment was inserted to protect more vulnerable employees. Persons who qualify in terms of the threshold can approach the CCMA for an advisory award as to whether they are employees or independent contractors.

### The Code of Good Practice: Who Is an Employee?

The Code of Good Practice: Who Is an Employee? (Department of Labour, 2006) expands on the seven criteria set out above and explains what the term 'presumption' implies. If any one of the factors is present, the person may claim to be an employee. This does not mean that the claim will be automatically upheld, but rather that the onus will then fall on the employer to prove that the claimant is not an employee. Essentially, the Code urges participants to weigh up all factors and circumstances, to use the dominant impression test and to apply the guidelines set out in the *South African Broadcasting Corporation v McKenzie* case, discussed later in this chapter.

## Contract versus Reality

*State Information Technology Agency (Pty) Limited v CCMA (2008) 29 ILJ 2234 (LAC)*, heard in the Labour Appeal Court in 2008, once again illustrated that an individual may be an employee despite a contract stating the opposite. The person whose status was at issue had formerly been employed and later retrenched by the South African National Defence Force (SANDF). According to regulations and the terms of the retrenchment agreement, he could not again work for the SANDF or any of its service providers, of which SITA was one. SITA was set on employing him and, in order to circumvent the prohibitions, it was agreed that he would establish a close corporation (CC) and bill SITA for his services. The arrangement worked until SITA, having lost a major defence force contract, decided to retrench him, at which stage he laid claim to the benefits and rights of an employee.

The case was referred to the CCMA, where the commissioner held that the relationship was not one of employment. This decision was overturned by the Labour Court, which held that an employment relationship did, in fact, exist. SITA thereupon lodged an appeal against the decision of the Labour Court.

The Labour Appeal Court listed three main criteria to be applied when establishing whether an employment relationship exists, namely:

- the principal's right to supervise and control
- the extent to which the person providing a service forms an integral part of the organisation
- the extent to which the service provider is economically dependent on the organisation.

The Court found that the person was under the control of the organisation and not of the CC, that he was an integral part of the organisation and that the CC was merely a front intended to mask the real situation. SITA had, in fact, come to the court with dirty hands, and the individual in question was an employee. The considerations listed above have been absorbed into the dominant impression test.

## Persons Engaged in Illegal Activities

At common law, it is accepted that a person may not contract to perform illegal activities and that any contract to that effect is unenforceable. However, the question that arises is whether, despite the common-law tenets, an individual engaged to perform illegal work can lay claim to the benefits and rights accorded to employees in terms of labour legislation. This issue was raised at the CCMA in *Kylie v Van Zyl t/a Brigitte's (CCMA WE 7511-06)*. The applicant, a sex worker, claimed that she had been unfairly dismissed by the owner of the massage parlour at which she had been employed. Her representative argued that:

- in terms of the Constitution, every employee has the right to fair labour practices
- sex workers are not specifically excluded from the Labour Relations Act
- although prostitution is a criminal offence in terms of the Sexual Offences Act 23 of 1957, the Labour Relations Act must take preference over the Sexual Offences Act
- the Labour Relations Act can be invoked even if there is no legally enforceable contract.

The commissioner argued that the fact that sex workers were not specifically excluded from the Labour Relations Act did not mean that they were included. In his opinion, the Labour Relations Act could not be used to sanction criminal activities; neither can the Constitution be invoked for this purpose. He concluded by pointing out that the CCMA only has jurisdiction over legally enforceable contracts and therefore could not arbitrate in the applicant's dispute.

Various experts questioned the decision of the commissioner on the grounds that he should have invoked the Labour Relations Act and, especially, the definition of an employee (as quoted above). They also pointed to the Act's emphasis on the protection of vulnerable employees, arguing that sex workers are among the most vulnerable and exploited. These are valid considerations, but the counterargument would be that ignoring the common law could allow for employment contracts to commit illegal activities, for example between a Mafia boss and his henchmen.

The crux of this case is not the rejection of the common-law precept, but rather the question whether the law regarding sex workers, who are indeed among the most vulnerable and exploited, should not be revoked.

### Recent Developments Regarding the Definition of an Employee

Subsequent to *South African Broadcasting Corporation v McKenzie*, the Labour Appeal Court listed four more factors to be considered when making a decision as to whether someone is an employee:

1. The object of the contract should be that the individual renders personal services.
2. The employer chooses when and where to use these services.
3. The individual must obey the commands of the person requiring their service.
4. There is usually no date for termination of the contract, except in the case of a fixed-term contract.

## Case Review: The Independent Contract

### South African Broadcasting Corporation v McKenzie (CA8/98) [1998] ZALAC 13 (15 October 1998)

### Background

The original plaintiff, McKenzie, had been a permanent employee of the SABC from 1959 to 1968 and again from 1983 to 1986. At that stage, he resigned of his own accord. In 1988, he was approached by the corporation to take over an afternoon talk show. He agreed, and an oral contract to act as a freelancer, for which McKenzie expressed preference, was concluded. This contract was later renewed on an annual basis, as was a separate contract for another programme, which was subsequently presented by McKenzie. The contracts given to McKenzie were the standard contracts for freelancers and differed from those concluded with permanent employees.

In 1994, McKenzie was informed that, owing to a change of policy as regards the type of programmes being presented, there was 'a very real possibility' that his contract would not be renewed, and in 1995 both programmes came to an end. In the interim, McKenzie had also presented other programmes for the SABC. In each case he had been issued with a separate contract and separate fees were paid for each programme.

McKenzie disputed the termination of his contract, claiming that he was an employee and not an independent contractor. The Labour Court upheld McKenzie's claim and ordered the SABC to pay him compensation of R45 000. The case was subsequently taken on appeal by the corporation, which maintained that McKenzie was an independent contractor.

### Pronouncements

The Labour Appeal Court first explained the definition of employee as contained in the Labour Relations Act, stating that the first part of the definition, which refers to an individual working for another person and receiving remuneration, had been interpreted 'to mean a person who works for another in terms of a contract of service'. The Court noted that the second part, relating to anyone who in any manner assists in the carrying on of the business of an employer, had received 'a mixed reception', with some experts saying that it should be interpreted literally and others declaring that it should not. It was further noted that, while it had been accepted that an independent contractor was not an employee, there were still varying understandings as to when an individual would be classified as an independent contractor.

As the Court noted, a number of different tests had, in the past, been applied to establish whether a contract of service (employment) exists. The first of these was the 'supervision test', and in this regard it was explained that a contract of service cannot exist where 'there is a total absence of the right of supervising and controlling the workman under the contract, in other words, unless the master not only has the right to prescribe to the workman what work has to be done, but also the manner in which the work has to be done'.

The second test was the 'organisation test', where consideration is given to the integration of the individual in the organisation.

The third test, namely the 'dominant impression test', held that no single factor could be taken in isolation and that all conditions had to be weighed against one another. This test had been criticised as 'meaningless', but was still the one most frequently applied.

In summary, the Court identified the main differences between a contract of employment and a contract of work. These were:

- 'The object of a contract of service is the rendering of a personal service by the employee to the employer' where 'the services are the object of the contract', while a contract of work is 'the performance of certain specified work or the production of a certain specified result'.

- The independent contractor is 'not obliged to perform the work himself or produce the result himself, unless otherwise agreed upon'.

- The services of an employee are 'at the disposal of the employer', who may, at their own discretion, subject of course to questions of repudiation, decide whether or not they want them rendered, whereas the independent contractor has to produce 'a specified result' within a fixed or reasonable period.

- The employee, as a subordinate, has to obey all lawful commands of the employer, who has the right to supervise and contract, while the independent contractor is 'notionally on a footing of equality with the employer' and is 'his own master'.

- The employment contract terminates if the employee dies. In a contract of work, this is not necessarily the case.

- A contract of work terminates when the result required has been produced.

Explaining that the nature of the relationship had to be ascertained from the realities of that relationship and not by what the parties decided to call it, the Court proceeded to explore the reasons for the Labour Court's decision that McKenzie was an employee.

While the Labour Court had conceded that McKenzie was employed for fixed periods to present specific programmes at specified times, that he was paid a fixed fee per programme, that he had elected to operate as a freelancer and that he represented himself to the Receiver of Revenue as such, it had found these factors to be 'less compelling' than the following:

- McKenzie had an office with all amenities at the SABC.

- He was paid and received an annual increase.

- He was given paid leave or time off.

- For six years he devoted his productive capacity to his task.

- He kept similar office hours to other employees.

- McKenzie performed his functions under the direction and supervision of the programme manager.

- He was regarded as 'a co-employee (part of the furniture) which was not the case with ordinary freelance contributors'.

By contrast, the Labour Appeal Court pointed out that the SABC draws a clear distinction between its employees and freelancers and that the contracts are widely different. For example:

- Employees are paid a salary while freelancers receive a fee for a specific task.

- Employees contribute to group life insurance, medical aid and the pension fund. They also receive a housing allowance.

- Employees are entitled to paid annual leave and sick leave, while freelancers are not.

- Employees receive negotiated annual increases, while freelancers' fees are increased by about 10 per cent.

- Employees may be disciplined and freelancers not.

- Freelancers are entitled to take on other work, which is not the case with employees.

- Employees are subject to pay-as-you-earn (PAYE) employees' tax, while a flat 25 per cent is deducted from freelancers for tax purposes.

It was further noted that

- McKenzie had expressed a preference for freelancing, as it gave him more freedom

- except for a period of six months, he had been paid only if he presented the programme himself

- in his tax return, he had represented himself as an independent contractor and had claimed expenses against his income

- he used a letterhead in which he described his business.

It was admitted that in one instance McKenzie had been granted paid time off, but it appeared that this had been a special arrangement.

The Court concluded that 'the fact that McKenzie assisted the SABC in carrying on its business, did not in itself justify the finding that McKenzie was an employee of the SABC' and that, on the balance of probabilities, McKenzie was an independent contractor. He had known that the SABC drew a clear distinction between employees and freelancers. McKenzie did follow instructions from the programme manager and the SABC exercised control over him, but the SABC had 'the right to exercise editorial control over the programmes it broadcasts'. There had been no obligation on the SABC to provide facilities to McKenzie, and they had done so merely for convenience.

McKenzie had not been obliged to attend meetings. McKenzie could not present himself to the Receiver of Revenue as independent and then claim to be dependent. Finally, the conduct of the parties in the year before termination was 'inconsistent with an employer–employee relationship and consistent with the relationship between principal and independent contractor'.

The appeal was upheld with costs.

## Discussion

At the time, the increasing popularity of outsourcing and part-time employment rendered the issue of an independent contractor extremely important. As the Labour Appeal Court explained, the essence of the distinction between an independent contractor and an employee is to be found in the question as to whether the individual puts their services – that is, their labour or productive capacity – at the disposal of the 'employer' or whether they merely agree to provide a product or a service within a fixed or reasonable period. Added to this is the question as to whether the individual is on an equal footing with the employer or whether they have to obey the employer's lawful or reasonable commands even if these are not directly related to the job. Being on an equal footing would not stop the 'employer' from determining the type and quality of the product or service for which the individual has contracted. Finally, where an individual elects to be independent for tax purposes, they are unlikely to find sympathy with the courts.

It was further noted that an employee renders personal service, while an independent contractor delivers a result in the form of a completed product. The independent contractor may also contract with another individual or individuals to perform the work or part of it.

The differentiation between an employee and an independent contractor will become increasingly important as the nature of work changes, as more and more work is outsourced and as foreign companies employ/contract South African labour (see the case review below).

It was evidently with this situation in mind that the government added a new Section 200B to the Labour Relations Act to address what was termed 'disguised employment'. This section refers to a situation where one or more persons carry on an associated or related business by or through an employee and where the intention, directly or indirectly, is to deny the employee the protection to which they are entitled in terms of the Labour Relations Act or any other employment statute.

If more than one person is involved, the 'employers' are made jointly and severally liable for any transgression of the Acts.

## Case Review: Who Is the Employer, if Any?

*Uber South Africa Technological Services (Pty) Ltd v NUPSAW and SATAWU obo Morekure and Others (WECT12537-16, WECT10875-16, WECT14948-16, WECT875-17, WECT1503-17, WECT12614-16) [2017] ZACCMA 1 (7 July 2017)*

### Background

Uber is an international company with headquarters in the Netherlands. Their system, by which persons wishing to use taxicab services can book a taxi online, has taken the world by storm, but the way in which Uber operates has at times been controversial.

Essentially, Uber sources 'partners', or car owners, in South Africa to supply the cabs. The partners may also drive for Uber, but may in turn use other persons to drive their car or cars. The partners, as well as the individual drivers, have contracts with Uber in the Netherlands. Cars as well as drivers have to be approved by Uber.

Once a driver has been accepted, they are supplied with an app by Uber South Africa Technology Services. The app serves as the communication channel between Uber and the drivers. Uber South Africa also provides training and sets performance standards for the drivers. It has offices in Cape Town and drivers interact with the admin manager.

A driver can choose when to work and can disconnect their app whenever they want to. Although there are no minimum hours, too many cancellations may impact on the driver's performance and even lead to the app being disconnected.

Persons wishing to make use of an Uber taxi register with Uber online. They can then log in and request a cab from one point to another. Uber contacts the taxi driver nearest to the requested pickup point and relays the request to them. The driver need not accept the request, but they mostly do, because it is their way of making a living. Once the driver has accepted, Uber will invoice the customer and collect the fare. Uber pays over part of the fare to the driver, but only after it has deducted its own fee as well as that of the partner (the owner of the vehicle).

If Uber is not satisfied with a particular driver it can disconnect his app, either temporarily or permanently.

The hearing under discussion flowed from an approach to the CCMA by a number of drivers whose apps had been disconnected and who claimed that, by doing so, Uber had effectively dismissed them. In response, Uber claimed that the CCMA could not adjudicate in the matter, as the drivers were not employees but independent contractors. A decision from a senior commissioner as to whether the drivers were in fact employees then became necessary.

Uber initially maintained that the contract should be the starting point, that the contracts of both the partners and the drivers are with their head office and not with Uber South Africa Technology Services, and that the case should be heard by the International Chamber of Commerce for Conciliation and Mediation. Alternately, it was argued that the owner of the vehicle is the employer of the driver or that the driver is an independent contractor who personally negotiates with the person requesting a taxi – that Uber's role is merely to provide access to technology, for which it charges a fee. Drivers are not obliged to drive or to use the app. They can choose which passengers they will take.

On behalf of the drivers, it was argued that their contracts are not with the owners of the vehicles but with Uber. Drivers have to personally drive the cabs. Their conduct is controlled by Uber, which issues performance ratings and incentive schemes as well as policies regarding cancellations. Uber controls the conditions under which work is done as well as the pricing of fares and the deployment of drivers. Its ability to disconnect the app gives Uber ultimate control over the driver.

## Pronouncements

The commissioner commenced by noting that, because of changes to the world of work, the line between an employee and an independent contractor has become blurred. In this situation she saw it as her task to decide whom to protect, taking note of the amendments to the Labour Relations Act as well as the Code of Good Practice: Who Is an Employee?

As a start, she went back to the definition of an employee in the Labour Relations Act (see above), noting in particular that an employee was any person who receives payment from an employer and who assists in carrying out the business of an employer. It seemed obvious that the drivers did assist in carrying out Uber's business and also received payment for their fares, but only after a deduction of a fee by Uber. According to the commissioner this would not happen in the case of an independent contractor.

Pointing to the various tests used in the past to decide whether an individual was an employee, such as the control test, the organisational test and the dominant impression test, she concluded that none of these were decisive. To make a decision it was necessary not only to go by the dominant impression but also to look at 'the reality of the relationship' and to consider all factors. In this respect the commissioner noted the following:

- The contracts are with Uber and not with the owners of the vehicles.

- Drivers render personal services to Uber.

- There is no termination date in the contracts, indicating that they are indefinite.

- Although they have a certain amount of independence, drivers are under the control of Uber in that Uber sets performance standards, can deactivate a driver's app and even monitor an individual's driving by the movement of the cellphone.

- Uber controls the way business is done.

- Drivers are an essential part of Uber's service – the app is a tool, and it is the driver who provides the service.
- Uber South Africa has to approve the vehicles and provide assistance to drivers.
- Drivers are at the mercy of Uber – they are economically dependent on Uber, which is much more powerful.

The commissioner conceded that some factors pointed to the drivers being independent contractors, but added that factors such as economic realities and social justice also had to be considered.

In light of all these considerations, her decision was that the drivers are in fact employees of Uber and not independent contractors, and that Uber South Africa Technological Services, and not Uber head office, should be designated as the employer. (This was in line with her previous statement that, although they might be jointly and severally liable, the local subsidiary of the company should be regarded as the employer in order to prevent the disadvantage to employees of working for foreign organisations.)

## Discussion

This case is proof of the complexity of the situation and the fine line between an individual being regarded as an employee or an independent contractor. It also points to the use of technology as an aid in running an enterprise. According to the pronouncements of the commissioner, Uber was essentially exercising control through the use of technology and was not, as claimed, merely supplying an individual with technology which the individual could use entirely for their own purposes.

This kind of situation is bound to become even more controversial as new relationships are established and new devices are used.

For the time being, the focus will probably be on vulnerable persons, but this might change, as Section 200B is not confined to employees earning below the income threshold.

## Types of Employment Contracts
### Indefinite/Permanent Contracts
Most contracts of employment are indefinite, in that no date for termination of the contract is given. This is so because the parties expect the relationship to be a permanent one. The employee expects that, all other things being equal, they will continue in employ until they decide of their own accord to leave or until they reach pensionable age. The employer, by engaging in an indefinite or permanent contract with the employee, implicitly agrees that the employee will not be dismissed unless:
- the employee is in breach of contract
- the employee becomes too ill or incapacitated to perform their duties

- the operational requirements of the employer require a reduction of the workforce.

### Fixed-term Contracts

There are instances where the services of an employee may be required only for a specific period or for a particular project. In these instances the employer will conclude a fixed-term contract with the employee or employees in question.

Section 198B (1) of the Labour Relations Act now defines a fixed-term contract as one which will end on:
- the occurrence of a specified event
- the completion of a specific task or project
- a fixed date (but not the employee's normal retirement date).

Fixed-term contracts usually end on the date specified or with a specific event, such as the completion of a project. However, it may happen that the job takes longer than first envisaged. In that case, the contract may be extended for another specified period, but it cannot be extended indefinitely. Furthermore, in terms of Section 186 of the Act an employee on a fixed-term contract may claim that they were unfairly dismissed if:
- the employee expected the contract to be renewed on the same or similar basis and the employer did not renew the contract or renewed it on less favourable terms
- the employee reasonably expected to be retained indefinitely on the same or similar terms and they were not retained or were offered a permanent position on less favourable terms.

A fixed-term employee, like other employees, can also claim that they were unfairly dismissed if:
- the employee resigned because the employer made it impossible for them to continue
- their contract was transferred to another employer and the new conditions of service are substantially less favourable than those with the previous employer.

### Protection for Vulnerable Employees
#### The Argument for Protection

Unfortunately, there are employers who employ people mainly on a part-time basis or keep some employees on fixed-term (temporary) contracts which are renewed from period to period. This is often done to make dismissal of such employees easier and/or to impose conditions of employment different from those of permanent employees. While fixed-term contracts may be necessary in certain circumstances, the practice is open to abuse, especially of more vulnerable employees.

The Labour Relations Act now offers greater protection to employees who earn below the earnings threshold (at the time of writing, R205 433.30 per annum) in instances where such employees are given fixed-term or part-time contracts, or where their services are offered by temporary employment services (labour brokers). Section 198B(3) limits fixed-term contracts for workers in this category to three months. An employer is allowed to give employees a fixed-term contract of longer than three months only if the work is of limited or definite duration or there is another justifiable reason for fixing the contract.

A longer fixed-term contract can be justified only if the prospective employee:

- is replacing another employee who is temporarily absent from work
- is required because of a temporary increase in the workload (which should not last longer than 12 months)
- is a student or recent graduate who is employed to gain experience before entering the job market
- is working exclusively on a genuine project which will be of limited duration
- is a non-citizen who has been granted a work permit for a specified period
- is a seasonal worker
- is employed in an official public works scheme or similar job creation initiative
- is past normal or agreed retirement age
- is performing work which is funded by an external agency.

The onus will be on the employer to prove that the extension of the contract was necessary.

Any contract with vulnerable employees which exceeds three months and does not conform to the above conditions will be regarded as a permanent contract, irrespective of the wording in the contract.

Where a fixed-term contract has been extended to two years or more, the employee must be given retrenchment pay when the contract ends, unless the employer has been able to find the employee a similar position commencing immediately thereafter.

The Act further states that:

- all fixed-term contracts must be in writing
- the employer must give the reason why the contract is of extended duration.

Also, the employer must:

- not treat an employee whose contract exceeds three months less favourably than other employees doing the same or similar work
- give such employee the same access to opportunities as permanent workers
- if the employee has worked on a fixed-term contract for longer than 24 months, pay them severance pay of one week's pay per year of service or whatever higher amount is contained in a bargaining council agreement or sectoral determination.

The new provisions relating to contracts for vulnerable employees were criticised as too prescriptive and stifling job creation, which in present circumstances is a necessity. On the other hand it cannot be denied that fixed-term contracts are often abused. Moreover, there is consideration in the amendments for those instances in which fixed-term contracts may be justified. Also, the restrictions on fixed-term contracts do not apply to organisations employing fewer than 10 persons or to genuine start-ups which employ fewer than 50 persons and which have been in business for fewer than two years. Contracts which do not conform to the restrictions above may also be permitted by statute, a bargaining council agreement or another collective agreement.

In August 2018, the practice of 'rolling fixed-term contracts' again came under the spotlight when a commissioner at the CCMA ruled that Metrorail should pay R30.5 million to 260 employees who had been on multiple fixed-term contracts for a number of years. The compensation was for benefits not paid to them during their employment. Evidently, in 2005 the wage rates of the contract employees had been brought in line with those of permanent employees, but, unlike permanent employees, they were not members of the provident fund and had not received bonuses. The commissioner also ordered that they be made permanent with full benefits.

The relevant section of the Act provides that employees on contract should not be treated differently from their counterparts in permanent positions. In this case, the employees had been subjected to continued unfairness, which Metrorail attempted to justify by referring to its dire financial situation. This was an argument which the commissioner refused to accept – and rightly so, as employees should not bear the brunt of mismanagement. This having been said, it could be argued that in circumstances where there is not an urgent need for labour or where mechanisation is an option, all, or a large number, of the workers might have had no job at all. In South Africa, with its high unemployment rate, this is a distinct possibility. The tension between the need for employment and the prevention of exploitation remains.

## Part-time Employees

Section 198C of the Labour Relations Act defines a part-time employee as someone who is paid wholly or partly on the basis of time worked and who works for fewer hours than comparable employees. Comparable employees are those who are also paid, wholly or partly, according to hours worked, but are employed on a full-time basis.

The Act prohibits the employer from treating part-time employees differently from comparable employees unless there is a justifiable reason for doing so. Seniority, experience, merit, the quantity and quality of work or any other similar consideration would be regarded as justifiable reasons. The employer must also provide the part-time employee with access to training and the same opportunities as full-time employees.

The above does not apply:
- to persons who work for a particular employer for less than 24 hours a month
- during the first six months of continuous employment
- in a workplace where fewer than 10 people are employed
- where the business, as the only business of that employer, has been in operation for less than two years and employs fewer than 50 persons.

## Persons Employed by Labour Brokers

The Labour Relations Act defines a temporary employment service (labour brokerage) as one where an employee is provided to a client by a labour broker. The employee performs work for the labour broker's client but is paid by the labour broker. The Act specifies that the employee in question is regarded as the employee of the temporary employment service and not of the client. However, both the temporary employment service and the client are jointly and severally liable for any contravention of a bargaining council agreement, an arbitration award setting out conditions of service, the Basic Conditions of Employment Act or a wage determination.

Most importantly, a new Section 198A contains specific instructions regarding employees in temporary employment who earn below the threshold of R205 443.50 per annum. With regard to these employees, a temporary employment service is defined as one where the employee is provided to the client for a period of no longer than three months. If the person so provided remains with the same employer after the initial three-month period has elapsed, they will be regarded as permanent.

In August 2018 the Constitutional Court, in *Assign Services (Pty) Limited v National Union of Metalworkers of South Africa and Others (CCT194/17) [2018] ZACC 22; [2018] 9 BLLR 837 (CC); (2018) 39 ILJ 1911 (CC); 2018 (5) SA 323 (CC); 2018 (11) BCLR 1309 (CC) (26 July 2018)* ruled that employees who had been employed through a labour broker and who had continued in the employ of the client after the initial three-month period had elapsed, were permanent employees of the client (Mahlakoana, 2018).The Court's decision was hailed by the union movement as a victory over the practice of labour brokering. Various other parties were highly critical of the outcome, with some experts arguing that the judgment contradicted the section of the Act which makes the labour broker and the client jointly responsible for any violation of the employee's rights.

The majority judgment by the Constitutional Court held that 'the purpose of section 198A must be contextualised within the right to fair labour practices in section 23 of the Constitution and the purpose of the LRA as a whole'. It further held that, on an interpretation of sections 198(2) and 198A(3)(b), for the first three months the broker is the employer; subsequently, the client becomes the sole employer. The Constitutional Court judgment has made it clear that all employees earning less than the prescribed threshold will for the first three months be under the employ of the broker and after three months be under the employment of the client for an indefinite period. While the Court does not ban labour broking in its entirety, it aims to ensure that the provision of temporary services is truly temporary. Part of this protection entails that placed employees are fully integrated into the workplace as employees of the client after the three-month period. The employee automatically becomes employed on the same terms and conditions as similar employees, with the same employment benefits, the same prospects of staff development and the same job security.

## Substantive Acts

### The Basic Conditions of Employment Act 75 of 1997
The Basic Conditions of Employment Act is part of the body of statutes (Acts passed by Parliament) which regulate the labour relationship. The purpose of the Act is to ensure that all employees enjoy certain minimum conditions of employment. This is why a contract may not contain conditions which are less favourable than those contained in the Act, and why a bargaining council agreement may vary only specific provisions of the Act.

The only employees not covered by the Act are those employed by the Domestic Branch and the Foreign Branch of the South African State Security Agency, the South African National Academy of Intelligence and the directors and staff of Communications Security (COMSEC), which have their own statutes regulating these matters. Persons employed at sea will not be covered by the Act if their conditions of service are regulated by the Merchant Shipping Act 57 of 1951. People who work for less than 24 hours a month are regarded as casual employees, and are excluded from nearly all the provisions of the Act. Senior management and employees earning more than R205 433.50 per annum are excluded from certain provisions relating to hours of work.

The Act deals with the following employment conditions:

- hours of work
- leave, including sick leave, compassionate leave, maternity leave and paternity leave
- terminations and notice periods.

It also regulates administrative aspects such as the employment contract and payment and remuneration, including allowable deductions, and places a prohibition on the employment of child labour.

The Basic Conditions of Employment Amendment Act 20 of 2013 prohibits employers from taking money from employees or prospective employees for promising or offering work. Also, employers may not force employees to buy goods from the company unless this is part of a scheme from which the employee also benefits. Persons employed for shorter periods per day must be paid for at least four hours, even if they did not work for the full four hours.

The section relating to child labour has been amended to make the person who illegally employs children, as well as the person who permits or requires such labour, liable and subject to possible prosecution. The Act also allows the minister to make regulations regarding the employment of children over the age of 15, who are no longer compelled to go to school.

In November 2017 another Basic Conditions of Employment Amendment Bill passed through Parliament and went on to become the Basic Conditions of Employment Amendment Act 7 of 2018. The main thrust of the amendments was to include conditions in the National Minimum Wage Act 9 of 2018 under the definition of basic conditions of employment and to make a transgression of minimum wages prosecutable by labour inspectors. Furthermore, chapters 8 and 9 of the Act, covering sectoral determinations and the Employment Conditions Commission were repealed to make way for the National Minimum Wage Act. In February 2021, the Basic Conditions of Employment Amendment passed through Parliament.

### The National Minimum Wage Act 9 of 2018

The purpose of this new Act is to make provision for a national minimum wage and the establishment of a National Minimum Wage Commission to set minimum wage levels on an annual basis as from May 2018. The minimum wage set for that period was R20 per hour or R3 500 per month, but exceptions were made in the case of farmworkers (R18 per hour), domestic employees (R15 per hour) and persons employed on expanded public works programmes

(R11 per hour). Amendments to the minimum wages were published by the Minister of Employment and Labour in Schedule 1 and Schedule 2. The minimum wage for an ordinary hour increased to R21.69, with exceptions for farmworkers (R21.69), domestic employees (R19.09) and workers employed on expanded public works programmes (R11.93). Persons on learnerships must still be paid according to the already established schedule in terms of the Skills Development Act 97 of 1998. Additional payments or payments in kind to employees, for example in the form of transport allowances, equipment, tools, food and accommodation, cannot be counted as part of the minimum wage. Employers already paying more than the minimum may not revert to the minimum. Employers who contend that they cannot afford the minimum wage may apply for exemptions.

### The Occupational Health and Safety Act 85 of 1993

The Occupational Health and Safety Act and the regulations established in terms of the Act impose stringent health and safety conditions at the workplace. Employers who are found by inspectors to have been negligent face heavy fines or prison sentences. This conforms to the common-law principle that it is the employer's duty to provide healthy and safe working conditions. Although the Act attempts to ensure that all premises on which work is conducted are as safe as possible, it is difficult to provide by law for all eventualities. Furthermore, inspectors are not able to police every undertaking and often act only when unsafe conditions are reported to them. Health and safety campaigns have been undertaken by many unions. In the textile industry the high incidence of 'brown lung' disease among employees was publicised by unions, and serious health issues repeatedly arise in the mining industry, where safety has become a primary issue.

### The Compensation for Occupational Injuries and Diseases Act 130 of 1993

The Compensation for Occupational Injuries and Diseases Act allows for compensation to be paid to an employee who, as a result of their activities in the work situation, is partially or totally disabled or contracts an occupational disease. In the event that the employee dies as a result of the accident, injury or disease, the compensation will be paid to their dependants. The Act covers all employees, including casual and seasonal workers, and directors who have a contract of employment.

### The Unemployment Insurance Act 63 of 2001 and the Unemployment Insurance Contributions Act 4 of 2002

These Acts provide for contributions by employers and employees to the Unemployment Insurance Fund and for payment of unemployment benefits to persons who become unemployed, who are ill for lengthy periods or who give birth to or adopt a child. The Fund also provides for payments to dependants of deceased employees.

The Acts cover all employees except persons employed for fewer than 24 hours per month, certain individuals employed in national and provincial government, persons engaged in learnerships, expatriates who will be returning to their own countries and persons already receiving a pension. Although all employees contribute to the fund, compensation is capped at the earnings threshold of R205 433.30 per annum.

## The Labour Relations Act 66 of 1995

### Historical Perspective

Until 1995, the framework for the practice of labour relations in South Africa was provided by the Labour Relations Act 28 of 1956 and numerous subsequent amendments, the most significant being the Industrial Conciliation Amendment Act 94 of 1979, later known as the Labour Relations Amendment Act of 1979. The stated objectives of the 1956 Act were to prevent and settle disputes and to regulate the terms and conditions of employment.

### Purpose of the Act

The 1995 Act states that the overall purpose of the legislation is the advancement of 'economic development, social justice, labour peace and the democratisation of the workplace' (Section 1). Its intention is to achieve these aims by:

- giving effect to the fundamental rights contained in Section 27 of the Constitution
- giving effect to the duties of the Republic as a member state of the ILO
- providing a framework in which employees and their unions, and employers and employer associations can:
  - bargain collectively to determine wages, terms and conditions of employment and other matters of mutual interest
  - formulate industry/sectoral policy
- promoting orderly collective bargaining
- encouraging collective bargaining at sectoral level
- providing for workers' participation and decision making at the workplace
- providing for the effective resolution of disputes.

### Government's Intentions

It is apparent that the government was attempting to give further protection to employees and unions and yet to maintain, as far as possible, the principles of voluntarism and free collective bargaining. (The Act contains no compulsion to bargain, but does provide that disputes relating to a refusal to bargain should first be submitted to advisory arbitration.) On the whole, the Act did reveal greater government interference in the relationship. This was best exemplified by the compulsion to form workplace forums upon the request of a majority union, the onus to engage in consultation and co-decision-making with workplace forums on certain prescribed matters and the onus to disclose information required for the purpose of collective bargaining.

One of the most significant new provisions in the 1995 Act was that which protects employees engaged in a legal strike from dismissal by the employer, thus effectively granting the right to strike. Certain new provisions regarding the employment of 'scabs', or substitute workers, and the right to picket were also included. Although controversial, the insertion of these provisions was a significant victory for the unions, which had long been engaged in a battle to achieve these rights.

### Ambit of the Act

The Act covers most employees, the only exclusions being those in the SANDF, the Domestic Branch and the Foreign Branch of the South African State Security Agency.

### Status of the Act

In the event of any conflict between the provisions of the Labour Relations Act and any other law (except the Constitution), priority will be given to the provisions of this Act. The Labour Relations Act automatically supersedes the Basic Conditions of Employment Act. This exclusion explains why there are bargaining council agreements which contain conditions of employment less favourable than those provided for in the Basic Conditions of Employment Act.

### The Labour Relations Amendment Act 6 of 2014

When changes to the Act were first proposed, the explanatory memorandum grouped these under the following themes:

- the increased informalisation of labour and the need to ensure that vulnerable employees receive adequate protection and are employed under conditions of decent work
- compliance with international labour standards
- compliance with constitutional rights, including the right to fair labour practices, the right to equality (including protection from discrimination) and the right to engage in collective bargaining

- enhancing the effectiveness of bodies such as the Labour Court, the CCMA, the Essential Services Committee and the labour inspectorate
- clarifying uncertainties emanating from some of the existing provisions.

The clauses relating to vulnerable employees, conditions relating to fixed-term contracts and the clarification of issues around temporary employment services were the most important amendments in this Act. These have already been discussed above. Other important proposed amendments are dealt with in discussions on the relevant sections of the Act (see below and discussions in relevant chapters).

### The Labour Relations Amendment Act 8 of 2018

The amendments in this Act are mostly aimed at fine-tuning existing legislation with regard to matters such as bargaining council agreements, picketing rules, minimum services and the powers of labour inspectors. These are dealt with in the relevant chapters. The most significant amendment is that allowing for the appointment of an advisory arbitration panel in strike and lockout situations which have become dysfunctional and where it is believed that it is in the public interest to intervene.

## Major Provisions of the Labour Relations Act

The major provisions of the Labour Relations Act of 1995 are outlined hereunder, in the order in which they appear in the Act. Since many of the provisions are covered in chapters in this book relating specifically to their implementation in practice, not all sections are discussed in equal detail.

### Chapter II: Freedom of Association and General Protection
*Freedom of Association*
The sections contained in this chapter grant employees the right to participate in the formation of a union or federation and to join any union subject only to the constitution of that union.

Union members have the right to:
- take part in the lawful activities of that union
- participate in the election of office bearers, officials and shop stewards
- subject to the terms of a collective agreement, stand for election to any of the above positions
- if elected, hold office or carry out the functions of a shop steward (trade union representative) in terms of the Act or a collective agreement.

The same provisions apply to members of a union which forms part of a federation in respect of the election of office bearers and officials to that federation. The right to freedom of association is carried further by the provision that nobody may compel or threaten to compel an employee to become or not to become a member of a union or workplace forum or to relinquish membership of a union or workplace forum. Also, nobody may prohibit an employee or a prospective employee from exercising any rights or from participating in any activities to which they are entitled in terms of the Act.

Contracts which directly or indirectly interfere with the freedom of association are automatically void, unless the Act itself allows for the establishment of such a contract. (The latter provision is very important, as it creates a loophole for the conclusion of closed-shop agreements.)

### Freedom from Victimisation

Freedom from victimisation is ensured by the clause which states that no one may prejudice an employee because of:

- their previous, existing or prospective membership of a union or workplace forum
- their participation in the establishment of a union, federation or workplace forum
- their refusal or failure to do anything which the employer by law may not compel or allow the employee to do
- their publicising information which they may lawfully give to another person
- their assertion of any rights in terms of the Act
- their participation in any activities allowed by the Act.

Furthermore, no one may offer or promise an employee favourable treatment on condition that they waive any rights granted to them or desist from any activities in terms of the Act.

Where there is an allegation regarding victimisation or interference with the freedom of association, the complainant merely has to prove that they have been compelled, threatened, prohibited or detrimentally affected in any manner, and it is then up to the defendant (the employer) to prove that their action did not constitute victimisation.

Disputes arising from any allegations regarding victimisation or interference with the freedom of association may first be referred for mediation to the CCMA or to a bargaining council which has jurisdiction and, should the dispute not be resolved, to the Labour Court.

In the remainder of this chapter, employers are granted the same rights in respect of freedom of association and freedom from victimisation.

## Chapter III: Collective Bargaining
### Part A: Organisational Rights

This part grants unions which are 'sufficiently representative' certain rights, such as the right:

- to have access to the workplace
- to hold meetings with employees outside working hours
- to conduct an election at the workplace
- to be granted stop-order facilities.

A majority union, or two or more unions which together represent a majority of employees at the workplace, may:

- appoint shop stewards
- be given information necessary for the purpose of representation or collective bargaining
- in consultation with the employer, establish thresholds for representation (agree what percentage representation is necessary for another union also to receive recognition).

Registered unions which are party to a bargaining council will automatically have the right to access and to demand stop-order facilities at all workplaces within the registered scope of the council, regardless of the union's representation at that particular workplace. A bargaining council may also establish thresholds of representation.

The Act sets out procedures for the exercise of these rights and for the processing of disputes in this respect. Disputes involving organisational rights may be submitted for conciliation to the CCMA. If the dispute remains unresolved, the CCMA may be asked to arbitrate.

An amendment to Section 21 now allows a union (or more than one union acting jointly) which has already been granted access, and the deduction of union dues, to be granted the same rights as a majority union, subject to the following conditions:

- The trade union or unions acting jointly must have significant representation.
- There must be no other union which has been granted the same rights.
- All concerned parties must have been given the right to make inputs.

Where the rights granted arise from the union's representation at a temporary employment service, the rights may also be exercised at the workplace of the client in relation to the employees concerned.

## Part B: Collective Agreements

This section:

- deals with the enforceability of collective agreements
- provides for different types of agreement
- outlines dispute procedures in respect of agreements.

All collective agreements, whether concluded at centralised or decentralised level, are enforceable in terms of the Act. Agreements relating to substantive issues and to conduct at the workplace are applicable to:

- all members of unions
- the employers party to such agreements
- members of the bargaining unit
- persons identified in or connected with the agreement.

Collective agreements are binding on all parties for the duration of the agreement, regardless of whether or not a party remains a member of the union or employers' association. A collective agreement automatically changes the employment contract of employees covered by the agreement.

Collective agreements must contain procedures for settlement of disputes about the interpretation or application of the agreement, including a settlement agreement, and must provide for conciliation as a first resort, and thereafter for arbitration.

The Act also provides for the establishment of agency shops and closed shops. If an agency shop has been agreed to by the employer and the representative union, employees who are not members of that union but who would qualify for union membership are obliged to pay an amount equal to or less than the prescribed union dues into a fund. The fund is administered by the representative union and has to be used to advance the socio-economic interests of employees. The agency-shop agreement differs from a closed-shop agreement in that non-members do not have to join the representative union. Arrangements for closed shops and agency shops are outlined in the Act. The issue of the closed shop is extremely controversial, as it directly contradicts the freedom of association principle contained in the Act and in the Bill of Rights.

## Part C: Bargaining Councils

The Act makes extensive provision for the establishment of bargaining councils by employer and employee bodies. Both parties have to be sufficiently representative (on a national or regional basis) of a particular industry, sector, trade or occupation.

Once registered, bargaining councils have extensive powers, including the right to conclude and enforce agreements, to prevent and settle labour disputes in their area of jurisdiction and to establish pension and other funds. In addition, bargaining councils may apply to the minister to have their agreements extended to non-parties in the industry, sector or area. Before granting such permission, the minister must satisfy themself that the parties are sufficiently representative in the registered scope of the council.

If agreements are extended to non-parties, which are often smaller enterprises, the latter are obliged to pay levies and to institute the same conditions of service as those applicable to the original parties. This provision has been repeatedly criticised as partly responsible for businesses going under and for job losses. The Act does provide that non-parties may apply for exemption from the whole or part of a bargaining council agreement, but these applications are often unsuccessful. The Labour Relations Amendment Act 6 of 2014 contains changes to Section 32 of the Act which improve on the exemption process and which oblige the minister to invite representations before the agreement is extended.

## Part D: Public Service Bargaining Councils

The state may be a party to a bargaining council if it is an employer in a sector or area in respect of which a council is being established. In addition, Part D provides for a co-ordinating public service bargaining council to set the parameters for all bargaining in this sector. The Public Service Co-ordinating Bargaining Council instructs various sectors to establish their own sectoral bargaining councils. Where the operations of a particular sector are widespread, it may in turn establish subsidiary regional bargaining councils.

## Part E: Statutory Councils

According to this section, any employers' association or any union which represents at least 30 per cent of the employers or employees in a sector or area may apply for the establishment of a statutory council.

Statutory councils may apply to have their agreements regarding training and education schemes, and pension, provident, unemployment and other funds, promulgated as determinations. This means that other parties in the sector must subscribe to these schemes. Moreover, the minister may levy all employers and employees within the registered scope of a statutory council in order to cover the cost of such a council.

These provisions allow an essentially unrepresentative body to set up schemes and funds and to engage in dispute resolution for an entire sector or area.

Other provisions in this chapter include instructions for an annual review of representivity, a detailed procedure for the settlement of disputes by bargaining councils and the stipulation that bargaining councils must either become accredited as mediators and arbitrators or appoint an accredited agency to fulfil these functions. Section 56 allows a union or employers' association which has been refused membership by a council to appeal to the Labour Court, and grants the Court the power to admit such union or employers' association as a party to the council and, if necessary, to amend the council's constitution accordingly.

A final section in this part of the chapter provides that, unless other instructions are given, any dispute regarding the interpretation of organisational rights and the sections relating to bargaining and statutory councils should be referred, firstly, to the CCMA and, failing settlement, to the Labour Court.

## Chapter IV: Strikes and Lockouts

Chapter IV of the Act provides firstly that, subject to certain procedures and time limits, every employee has the right to strike and every employer the right to lock out. An employer may not dismiss employees engaged in a legal strike, but may dismiss individual employees for reasons of misconduct or operational requirements.

Statutory procedures do not have to be followed if:
- the strike or lockout is in reaction to an unprotected strike or lockout
- the employer has failed to comply with a request to reinstate terms and conditions of employment which had been unilaterally changed by the employer
- the parties have followed a disputes procedure contained in a collective agreement or a council constitution.

Strikes which conform with the provisions of the Act are regarded as protected strikes. The protection accorded to such strikers is not extended to employees who engage in an unprotected or spontaneous strike, although certain provisions are also outlined for such strikes. Secondary or 'sympathy' strikes are allowed subject to certain conditions.

The Act also sanctions picketing if the conditions and procedures set out in the Act, including the conclusion of a picketing agreement, are followed. Significantly, Section 69 of the Act has been amended to state that a commissioner is to be appointed to deal with disputes that may lead to a strike or a lockout, with the aim of determining the rules surrounding the picket. The conciliation commissioner is therefore compelled to try and secure a picketing agreement between the parties when conciliating the dispute, before the expiration of the conciliation time frame, as indicated in Section 64(1)(a). The Act states that parties to the dispute should agree on 'ground rules' prior to embarking on industrial action. This amendment is aimed at curtailing the violence and unrest which has become a norm in the labour relations landscape. The Act further indicates that if there is no picketing agreement, or if the commissioner is unable to secure an agreement between the parties, the conciliating commissioner must determine the picketing rules based on standard picketing rules as prescribed in Section 208 of the Act. The picketing rules must be issued together with any certificates of failure to settle the dispute. Trade unions may apply to the CCMA on an urgent basis for picketing rules where a dispute relates to unilateral changes to the terms and conditions of employment as indicated in Section 64(4), where the employer has failed to restore the status quo or where an unprotected lockout has been implemented. The Act also stipulates that no picket may take place in support of a protected strike or lockout without picketing rules as indicated in Section 69(6)(c). The Labour Court is empowered to suspend pickets.

Chapter IV of the Act prohibits strike action by employees engaged in essential and maintenance services. The conditions and procedures pertaining to such services and the establishment of the Essential Services Committee are outlined in the Act. (In an attempt to avert continued strike action in these services, the Labour Relations Amendment Act 6 of 2014 sets out detailed procedures for the streamlining of the Committee and its functions.)

This chapter also makes allowance for protest action to protect the socio-economic interests of employees and sets conditions for the use of substitute ('scab') labour during strike action. An employer may not employ substitute labour if the whole or part of their service has been designated as a maintenance service, nor may the employer use 'scab' labour to perform the work of any employee who has been locked out, unless the lockout was in reaction to an unprotected strike.

## Chapter V: Workplace Forums

The most innovative aspects of the Labour Relations Act are contained in this chapter, which provides for the establishment of workplace forums, upon the request of a majority union or unions, in any workplace employing more than 100 persons.

In terms of the Section 213 of the Act, a 'workplace' is 'the place or places where the employees of an employer work'.

Workplace forums are intended to:
- promote the interests of all employees at the workplace
- increase the efficiency of the workplace

- engage in consultation on certain matters stipulated in the Act
- engage in joint decision making on issues such as:
  - disciplinary codes and procedures
  - rules regarding conduct and behaviour
  - measures to protect individuals against discrimination
  - changes to the rules applicable to social benefits.

The forums must be representative of all employees, with 'employee' being defined in Section 78(a) of this chapter as 'any person who is employed in a workplace, except a senior managerial employee whose contract of employment or status confers the authority to ... represent the employer in dealings with the workplace forum'. Workplace forums are entitled to all relevant information necessary to perform their functions effectively. This would include matters such as:
- the financial and employment situation of the organisation
- overall achievements
- future plans and prospects.

## Chapter VI: Registration of Unions and Employer Organisations
In this chapter the procedures for the registration of trade unions, employers' associations and union federations are outlined in detail. All rights in terms of the Labour Relations Act are granted only to registered unions and employers' associations. A body which remains unregistered will have no status within the statutory labour relations system.

In 2015 this part of the Act was amended to fine-tune procedures in cases where a union or employers' association is not functioning properly and needs to be wound up. The Act provides that the Labour Court may, under specific conditions, order the union or federation to be wound up. The amendments allow the Court to appoint an administrator and set out the procedures involved.

Parts C and D of Chapter VI relate to the appointment of a registrar by the minister. There is an onus on the registrar to maintain up-to-date records relating to unions, employers' associations and federations, and to allow the public access to such records.

Any party aggrieved by a decision of the registrar may request a written explanation as to the reasons for such decision and/or may, within 60 days of the decision, or of the reasons being furnished, appeal to the Labour Court against such decision.

## Chapter VII: Dispute Settlement
*Part A: The CCMA*

This part makes provision for the appointment of a commission, which is to be independent of the state and of any political party, union, employers' association or federation of unions or employers' associations, and which will have jurisdiction in all the provinces to perform the functions outlined hereunder.

The CCMA should:

- attempt to settle, by conciliation, any dispute referred to it in terms of the Act
- where conciliation has not achieved the desired agreement, conduct arbitration if the Act requires this
- if any of the parties to a dispute so request, provide assistance with the establishment of workplace forums
- compile and publish information and statistics regarding its activities.

Other than the above, the CCMA may also:

- advise a party to a dispute on the procedures to be followed in terms of the Act
- assist a party to a dispute in obtaining legal advice and/or representation
- offer to settle a dispute which was not referred to it
- accredit councils or private agencies
- subsidise accredited councils and agencies
- conduct, oversee or scrutinise an election by ballot for a registered union or employers' association
- supervise or check such ballot if requested to do so by the union or employers' association
- publish guidelines as to any matter regulated by the Act
- conduct and publish research into matters relevant to its functions.

In terms of amendments to this part of the Act, the CCMA is now given the right to provide administrative assistance to employees who are lodging a dispute and who earn below the earnings threshold. It also has the right to determine whether a particular party may represent parties during proceedings at the CCMA and to set out the consequences for persons who do not attend proceedings.

*Part B: Accreditation and Subsidisation of Councils and Private Agencies*

This part empowers the CCMA to accredit and subsidise bargaining councils and private agencies as mediators and arbitrators, and sets out the conditions and procedures for such accreditation.

## Part C: Dispute Settlement under the Auspices of the CCMA

Procedures for mediation and arbitration of different types of dispute have been outlined in this part of the Act. It describes the power of commissioners in arbitration proceedings and the effect of arbitration awards, and allows for review of an arbitration award by the Labour Court.

In an attempt to improve the functioning of the CCMA and the rate at which disputes are resolved, the Labour Relations Amendment Act 6 of 2014 contained a number of amendments to this section of the Act. Amendments to sections 143, 144 and 145 of the Act are intended to streamline the execution of arbitration awards and to avoid situations where arbitrations by the Commission are unnecessarily delayed by appeals to the Labour Court.

The amended Section 147 would oblige the CCMA to arbitrate a dispute which has been referred to private arbitration but where it is established that the employee or employees concerned earn less than the earnings threshold and would have to pay all or part of the costs of the private arbitration. The same would apply if it is found that the private arbitrator is not independent of the employer.

## Part D: The Labour Court

The Act makes provision for a Labour Court to be constituted as a court of law and a court of record. As regards matters within its jurisdiction, the Labour Court has the same powers and status as a provincial division of the Supreme Court. (The 2014 amendments correct this to read 'High Court'.)

The Labour Court is presided over by a judge president, a deputy judge president and as many judges as the president, on the advice of NEDLAC and in consultation with the Minister of Justice and the judge president, may decide.

The Labour Court may make any appropriate order, including:

- the granting of urgent interim relief
- the granting of an interdict
- an order enforcing a certain action which, when executed, will correct an injustice and give effect to the primary objectives of the Act
- a declaratory order
- a compensatory award
- an order for damages relating to any circumstance covered by the Act
- an order as to costs.

## Part E: The Labour Appeal Court

The Act makes provision for appeals to the Labour Appeal Court. This Court is constituted as a court of law and equity. It, too, is a court of record and, in relation to matters within its jurisdiction, has the same status as the Supreme Court of Appeal.

### Chapter VIII: Unfair Dismissals and Unfair Labour Practices

*Unfair Dismissals*

This chapter commences by indicating that a dismissal occurs not only when an employer dismisses an employee, with or without notice. Failure to re-employ a person on a fixed-term contract on the same or similar conditions, if the employee reasonably expected this, could also be regarded as a dismissal, as could the refusal to allow an employee to return to work after maternity leave.

Dismissals are unfair if the employer fails to prove, first, that there is a fair reason for the dismissal related either to the employee's conduct, capacity or competence, or to the operational requirements of the employer, and, secondly, that the dismissal took place in terms of a fair procedure. The Act also lists certain dismissals which are regarded as automatically unfair.

Any agency charged with deciding whether a dismissal was fair will be required to take into account the Code of Good Practice appended in the Schedules. This Code contains detailed guidelines for the different types of dismissals.

*Unfair Labour Practices*

Chapter VIII of the Act also prohibits employers from engaging in unfair labour practices. Section 186(2) describes these as including:

- any unfair action relating to promotion, demotion, probation, training or the benefits afforded to an employee
- the unfair suspension of an employee or any other disciplinary action short of dismissal
- the failure or refusal on the part of the employer to re-employ a former employee where an agreement to that effect exists
- any occupational detriment, short of dismissal, suffered by an employee who has made a disclosure in terms of the Protected Disclosures Act 26 of 2000.

*Retrenchments and Transfer of a Business as a Going Concern*

The procedures to be followed in the event of retrenchments are set out in detail, as are the prescriptions for situations where the business of an employer or part of that business is transferred to another employer as a going concern. In such cases the contracts of all employers are automatically transferred to the new employer and the rights and duties of the old employer become those of the new employer.

## Other Matters Dealt with in Chapter VIII

Chapter VIII goes on to deal with procedures in unfair dismissal and unfair labour practice disputes, legal remedies and retrenchment pay.

## Chapter IX: General Provisions

The most important provisions in this chapter of the Labour Relations Act are those pertaining to the issues discussed below.

### Labour Brokers

The position regarding labour brokers has been discussed earlier in this chapter. It is necessary only to add that two or more bargaining councils can agree that a labour broker, someone in the service of a labour broker and the client of such labour broker will be covered by an agreement concluded by one of the bargaining councils or falling in the combined registered scope of such bargaining councils, provided that the agreement has been extended to non-parties.

### Confidentiality

Any person who makes public any information regarding the financial and business affairs of any other person is guilty of an offence, and subject to a maximum fine of R1 000 or a sentence to be determined by the court. This applies where such information has been obtained in any capacity by or on behalf of a council, an independent body intended to grant exemptions from collective agreements, the registrar, the CCMA or any accredited agent. This provision is not applicable where the information was made public in order to enable the person who received the information to perform their duties or act in a capacity as determined by the Act.

### Presumption as to Who is an Employee

This section has been discussed earlier in this chapter.

### Defects and Irregularities

Defects and irregularities – such as an omission in the constitution of a registered body; a vacancy in the membership of a council; or any irregularity in the appointment of a representative, a substitute or a chairperson of a council, a director or a commissioner – will not render invalid the constitution of a registered body, a collective agreement, an arbitration award, any action of the council or any action of a director or a commissioner.

*Definitions*

The following definitions are of importance:

- **Employee:** any person (except an independent contractor) working for another person or the state and who receives or is entitled to receive remuneration, or any person who in any manner assists in carrying on or conducting the business of an employer
- **Essential service:** a service which cannot be interrupted without endangering the life, personal safety or health of the entire population or part thereof (for example, Parliament and the police)
- **Issue in dispute:** in relation to a strike or lockout, the demand, grievance or dispute which forms the subject matter of the strike or lockout
- **Legal practitioner:** any person who is admitted to practise as an advocate or attorney within the Republic
- **Lockout:** the exclusion by an employer of employees from the workplace of the employer for the purpose of compelling the employees to accept a demand in respect of any matter of mutual interest between employer and employees, irrespective of whether or not in the course or purpose of such exclusion the employer breaches the contracts of employment of its employees
- **Operational requirements:** requirements based on the economic, technological, structural or similar needs of the employer
- **Protest action:** the partial or complete concerted refusal to work, or the retardation or obstruction of work, for the purpose (other than for the purpose referred to in the definition of a 'strike') of promoting or defending the socio-economic interests of workers
- **Remuneration:** any payment, in money or in kind or both, owed to a person in exchange for which that person works for another person, including the state
- **Strike:** the concerted refusal to work, whether or not the refusal is partial or complete, or the retardation or obstruction of work, by persons who are or have been employed by the same employer or by different employers, for the purpose of remedying a grievance or resolving a dispute in respect of any matter of mutual interest between employer and employee ('work', in this definition, includes overtime work, whether voluntary or compulsory).

See Table 3.1 for the major provisions of the Labour Relations Act.

**Table 3.1:** The major provisions of the Labour Relations Act

| Subject | Reference |
|---|---|
| Freedom of association<br><br>Freedom from victimisation | Chapter II and Chapter VII (Disputes) |
| Trade unions and employers' associations<br><br>Federations of trade unions or employers' associations | Chapter VI |
| Collective rights amd collective agreements<br><br>Bargaining structures | Chapter III<br><br>Schedule 1<br><br>Schedules 9 and 10 |
| Consultation<br><br>Co-decision-making and workplace forums | Chapter V<br><br>Schedule 2 |
| Strikes<br><br>Lockouts | Chapter IV<br><br>Definitions |
| Dispute settlement | Chapter VII<br><br>Schedule 4 |
| Unfair dismissals and unfair labour practices | Chapter VIII<br><br>Schedule 8<br><br>Chapter VII (Disputes) |

## The Employment Equity Act 55 of 1998
### Objectives of the Act

The Employment Equity Act has two main objectives, namely the elimination of discrimination and the promotion of affirmative action at the workplace. A number of important changes to the Act were instituted by the Employment Equity Amendment Act 47 of 2013.

The Act gives effect to Section 9(3) of the Constitution, which provides that '[n]ational legislation must be enacted to prevent and prohibit unfair discrimination', as well as to Convention 111 of the ILO. Both Section 9 (the Equality Clause) of the Constitution and Convention 111 exclude from the concept of discrimination any differentiation designed to promote, protect or advance persons previously disadvantaged by unfair discrimination. Thus, differentiation for the purpose of affirmative action would be regarded as 'fair' discrimination.

## Ambit of the Act

The Act applies to all employees and employers. However the SANDF, the Domestic Branch and the Foreign Branch of the South African State Security Agency are excluded from the term 'designated employers', as are employers who employ fewer than 50 people and whose turnover is less than the turnover threshold for that type of business. Turnover thresholds are published by the Department of Labour and modified from time to time (see Table 3.2). Local spheres of government are no longer exempted from application of the Act. Exempt employers do not have to submit equity reports (discussed below).

**Table 3.2:** Turnover thresholds (LWO, 2020)

| Sector | Total annual turnover |
|---|---|
| Agriculture | R6 million |
| Mining and quarrying | R22.5 million |
| Manufacturing | R30 million |
| Electricity, gas and water | R30 million |
| Construction | R15 million |
| Retail and motor trade and repair services | R45 million |
| Catering, accommodation | R15 million |
| Finance and business services | R30 million |
| Community, social and personal services | R75 million |
| Wholesale trade, commercial agents and allied services | R75 million |
| Catering, accommodation and other trades | R15 million |
| Transport, storage and communications | R30 million |

## Discrimination

### Fair and Unfair Discrimination

Section 5(1) of the Act enjoins all employers to promote equal opportunity by eliminating discrimination in all employment policies and practices. It further prohibits discrimination on the basis of race, gender, sex, pregnancy, marital status, family responsibility, ethnic or social origin, colour, sexual orientation, age, disability, religion, HIV status, conscience, belief, political opinion, culture, language, birth or any other arbitrary ground. Harassment can also be classified as unfair discrimination. The Employment Equity Amendment Act 47 of 2013 extends this section by stating that differentiation between persons performing the same job or work of equal value could be regarded as unfair discrimination.

In line with the Bill of Rights in the Constitution, the Act provides that measures to promote previously disadvantaged groups will not be regarded as constituting unfair discrimination; neither will differentiation based on the requirements of a particular job.

### Medical and Psychological Tests

The Act forbids medical testing of employees unless this is permitted or required by legislation or is justifiable in the light of medical facts, employment conditions, social policy, the fair distribution of employee benefits or the inherent requirements of the job. HIV testing is specifically prohibited unless declared justifiable by the Labour Court. Psychological tests and other similar forms of assessment must be scientifically proven to be both valid and reliable, must be fairly applied and should not be biased against any person or group. Furthermore, all tests will in future have to be certified by the Health Professions Council of South Africa (HPCSA) or any other body authorised by law to do so.

### Applicants for Positions

Where discrimination is concerned, applicants for a position are also regarded as employees. This happens nowhere else in labour law except in those sections of the Labour Relations Act dealing with the freedom of association and the freedom from victimisation. The significance is that any person applying for a position may question both the shortlisting of candidates and the actual selection of a candidate.

Those engaged in recruitment and selection have to prove that the shortlisting and eventual selection were conducted in terms of provable assessment criteria and that no person was unfairly advantaged or disadvantaged during the process.

### Contraventions

The existing Section 10 of the Act provides that a party who believes that they have been discriminated against by the employer can, within a period of six months, refer the alleged offence to the CCMA for conciliation. If no settlement is reached, the dispute may be referred to the Labour Court for adjudication or to arbitration if so agreed by the parties. This excludes a situation where the employee has been dismissed, in which case the dispute is submitted to a bargaining council or the CCMA for conciliation, and then to the Labour Court as stipulated in sections 187 and 191 of the Labour Relations Act.

The Employment Equity Amendment Act 47 of 2013 allows an employee who earns below the earnings threshold to submit any dispute centring on unfair discrimination straightaway to the CCMA for arbitration; any employee alleging sexual harassment is allowed to do the same. Complaints can also be brought to the CCMA instead of the Labour Court if all parties agree. Persons dissatisfied with the decision of the CCMA may appeal to the Labour Court within a period of 14 days. The amendments are evidently intended to obviate the need for these employees to go through drawn-out processes and ultimately to go to the Labour Court, which might prove expensive.

Section 11 of the Act further states that, whenever an allegation of unfair discrimination is brought by an employee, the onus is on the employer to prove that the actions were fair.

In terms of Section 60, any contravention of the Act by an employee must immediately be brought to the attention of the employer. The onus is on the employer to consult with the relevant parties and to take steps to eliminate the alleged conduct (for instance, unfair discrimination or harassment). The Act holds the employer liable should they fail to institute the necessary actions, unless it can be proved that the employer 'did all that was reasonably practicable to ensure that the employee did not act in contravention of this Act'.

Section 11 of the Act, dealing with the burden of proof, has been amended to provide that if unfair discrimination is alleged, the employer must prove, on the balance of probabilities:

- that the discrimination did not take place
- that, if it did take place, the discrimination was not unfair
- that it was otherwise justifiable.

The Act places the onus on employees who allege discrimination on 'any other arbitrary ground' to prove, on the balance of probabilities:

- that the conduct complained of was not rational
- that it amounts to discrimination
- that the discrimination is unfair.

## Affirmative Action
### Planning for Redress
In order to ensure that positive steps are taken to address demographic imbalances, Chapter III of the Act compels all 'designated employers' to:

- consult with employees regarding the equity process
- conduct an analysis of the workforce
- prepare an employment equity plan

- submit an equity report to the director-general within the periods specified in the Act
- submit a statement on income differentials to the Employment Conditions Commission.

### Designated Employers
Designated employers are defined as:
- those who employ 50 or more employees
- those who have been designated in terms of a binding bargaining council agreement
- those who employ fewer than 50 persons but whose annual turnover is above that stipulated in Schedule 4 of the Act
- organs of state, with the exception of the SANDF, and the Domestic Branch and the Foreign Branch of the South African State Security Agency.

### Designated Groups
The thrust of the employment equity analysis and plan is to identify and correct the under- representation of designated groups. Designated groups are defined to include black people, women and persons with disabilities. 'Black' is described as a generic term that includes Africans, persons of mixed race and Indians, although reporting forms issued by the Department of Labour require differentiated reporting on these groups. Furthermore, the amended Act excludes from the designated groups persons who are not South African citizens by birth or descent. This exclusion would not apply to persons who were naturalised before 27 April 1994 or those who became naturalised citizens only after that date because they were previously prevented from doing so by apartheid policies.

'People with disabilities' is defined in Section 1 of the Act as referring to 'people who have long-term or recurring physical or mental impairment which substantially limits their prospects of entry into or advancement in employment'.

### Delegation of Responsibility
The Act provides that the employer must designate a member of senior management to take responsibility for the equity process.

### Consultation
Consultation with a representative employee body is a further imperative. The Act stipulates that the employer has to consult on:
- the demographic analysis of the workforce
- the preparation and implementation of the equity plan
- the equity report.

Such consultation must be conducted with:
- a representative trade union
- the workplace forum
- jointly with a workplace forum and the trade union, if both exist
- if no trade union or workplace forum exists, with representatives elected by employees.

The body with which the employer consults must reflect the interests of all employees from all occupational levels (categories are now excluded), as well as employees from both the designated and the non-designated groups. The trade union, forum or elected body has to ensure that it complies with these requirements, or additional representatives have to be elected by those groups not represented by the union or forum.

The body established to represent employees has the right to disclosure of all information necessary to bring about effective consultation.

*Analysis*

The employer needs to collect information and conduct an analysis of all employment practices and procedures, as well as the work environment, so as to identify barriers to the employment or continued employment of designated groups. Part of the equity plan will be directed at the elimination of such barriers.

The employer must establish a demographic profile of the workforce in each occupational level in order to determine the degree of under-representation of designated groups. The employer's concern should not be with representation only, as Section 27 also obliges them to produce a statement reflecting incomes at the various levels and categories and, where 'disproportionate and discriminatory' income differentials exist, to take steps to remedy the situation.

## The Employment Equity Plan
*Developing an Equity Plan*

The employment equity plan must include affirmative action targets and, where under-representation has been identified, the numerical goals to 'achieve the equitable representation of suitably qualified persons from designated groups within each occupational level in the workforce', as specified in Section 20(2)(c).

The term 'suitably qualified' is described in Section 20(3) as dependent on:
- the person's formal qualifications
- the person's prior learning

- the person's relevant experience or their capacity to acquire, within a reasonable time, the ability to do the job
- a combination of the above.

Section 20(5) prohibits discrimination against any person solely on the grounds of their lack of the relevant experience.

In addition, the employment equity plan must contain:
- measures to identify and eliminate employment barriers, including unfair discrimination which adversely affects persons from designated groups
- measures designated to promote diversity based on equal dignity and respect for all people
- measures to accommodate persons from designated groups to ensure that they enjoy equal opportunity and are equitably represented in all occupational categories and groups (This includes preferential treatment but does not include quotas, nor does it, in terms of Section 15(4), require 'a designated employer to take any action concerning an employment policy or practice that would establish an absolute barrier to the prospective or continued employment or advancement of people who are not from the designated groups'.)
- measures to retain and develop people from designated groups and to implement appropriate training measures, including measures in terms of the Skills Development Act 97 of 1998
- the objectives for each year of the plan
- a timetable for each year, showing how objectives other than numerical goals are to be achieved
- the duration of the plan (not shorter than one year and not longer than five years)
- procedures for implementation and monitoring of the plan and the persons responsible, including senior managers
- internal disputes procedures relating to discrimination and affirmative action
- any other prescribed matter.

### Submission of Equity Plans and Reports

Once an equity plan has been formulated, it must be submitted for approval and a report on progress has to be made on an annual basis.

The prescriptions for submission have been amended. All reports now have to be submitted within 6 to 18 months after inception, and thereafter by October of each year or whatever date is prescribed by law. The director-general can ask the Labour Court to impose a fine on organisations which do not submit reports.

*Assessment of Compliance*

The employer's equity plan and efforts towards achieving equity will be judged in terms of prescribed criteria. The clause listing these criteria has been significantly modified by the Amendment Act. The criteria are now limited to:

- the extent to which the workforce reflects the demographic profile of the national and regional economically active population
- steps taken to eliminate barriers adversely affecting the employment of designated groups
- reasonable steps taken by the employer to train suitably qualified people from the designated groups
- reasonable steps taken by the employer to appoint and promote suitably qualified people from the designated groups
- steps taken by the employer to implement the equity plan.

In addition, the minister will be allowed to issue regulations setting additional criteria for particular employers. These 'regulations' may include reference to regional and national demographics which were previously listed as criteria. The latter amendment sidesteps this very controversial issue and leaves the matter up to the discretion of the minister.

It is also noteworthy that criteria relating to circumstances such as financial position, which might hamper the employer's efforts, have been removed and the emphasis has been placed on what the employer has done or is doing.

*Consequences of Non-compliance*

Besides the provision that any trade union, workplace forum or employee may report an alleged contravention by an employer, the Act also provides that labour inspectors may enter an employer's premises and question them to ascertain compliance with the Act. The inspector may first order the employer to make an undertaking to comply within a specific time frame. Where the inspector finds that the employer is not complying, the inspector may issue a compliance order which may, upon the request of the director-general, be made an order of the Labour Court.

A number of amended clauses provide labour inspectors and the director-general with extended powers where it is found that the employer has not prepared or submitted a proper equity plan or complied with other provisions. Some of the amendments are aimed at clarifying procedures, while Section 46 allows the director-general the right to apply directly to the Labour Court to impose fines on transgressors. All fines in terms of the Act have been increased threefold, with the maximum fine now standing at R2.7 million.

## Publication and Display of Documents

Once a report has been submitted, it becomes a public document. Designated employers that are public companies must include a summary in their annual financial reports, while reports from organs of state have to be tabled in Parliament.

Employers are obliged to display information on the Act in a place where it can be read by employees. In addition, they must place the most recent report, copies of a compliance order, an arbitration award or Labour Court decision relating to the Act in a prominent place accessible to all employees. Copies of the plan have to be made available to employees for consultation and discussion.

## Commission for Employment Equity

The Act provides for the establishment of the Commission for Employment Equity, consisting of a chairperson and eight other members appointed by the minister. These must include two persons nominated by organised labour in NEDLAC, two nominated by organised business in NEDLAC, two nominated by representatives of the state in NEDLAC and two nominated by community and development interests in NEDLAC.

The functions of the Commission are:
- to offer advice on codes of good practice, regulations and policy issues
- to make awards recognising achievements
- to conduct research and report to the minister on any matter related to the Act.

## Protection from Victimisation

Section 51 of the Act protects employees from victimisation resulting from the exercise of any rights conferred by the Act.

Figure 3.3 presents a schematic summary of employment equity.

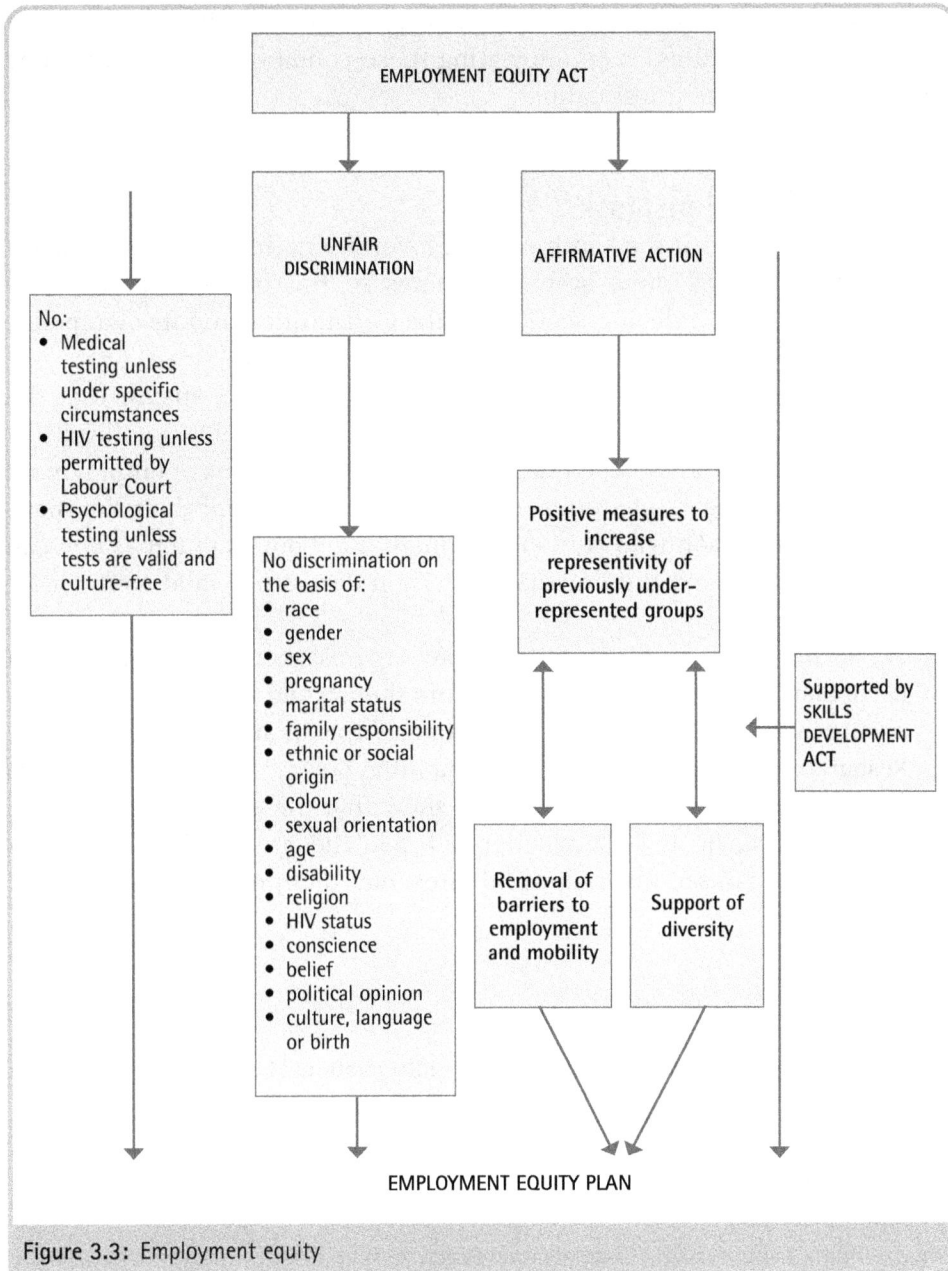

```
                    ┌─────────────────────────────┐
                    │   EMPLOYMENT EQUITY ACT      │
                    └─────────────────────────────┘
                         ↓                    ↓
          ┌──────────────────┐      ┌──────────────────┐
          │      UNFAIR       │      │ AFFIRMATIVE ACTION│
          │  DISCRIMINATION   │      │                   │
          └──────────────────┘      └──────────────────┘
```

**EMPLOYMENT EQUITY ACT**

**UNFAIR DISCRIMINATION**

**AFFIRMATIVE ACTION**

No:
• Medical testing unless under specific circumstances
• HIV testing unless permitted by Labour Court
• Psychological testing unless tests are valid and culture-free

No discrimination on the basis of:
• race
• gender
• sex
• pregnancy
• marital status
• family responsibility
• ethnic or social origin
• colour
• sexual orientation
• age
• disability
• religion
• HIV status
• conscience
• belief
• political opinion
• culture, language or birth

Positive measures to increase representivity of previously under-represented groups

Supported by SKILLS DEVELOPMENT ACT

Removal of barriers to employment and mobility

Support of diversity

**EMPLOYMENT EQUITY PLAN**

Figure 3.3: Employment equity

## Conclusion

South Africa has established a fairly comprehensive body of labour law to meet the prescriptions of the Constitution and the ILO. The proposed amendments to some of the existent statutes and the Employment Services Bill are, in the main, reactions to the continuing high unemployment rate and South

Africa's low rating on the competitive index. It remains to be seen whether the amendments will assist in alleviating these conditions or whether they will, in fact, aggravate the situation.

## Suggested Questions/Tasks

1. Do you believe that the South African government, in its role as regulator of the labour relations system, adheres to the precepts of the ILO conventions, the relevant sections of the Constitution and its own policy and mission statement? Prove your case.
2. What factors would you have to take into account to ensure that the contract you offer an employee suits your purposes and is not illegal?
3. How would you determine that the wages and conditions of employment of a certain category of employees are the correct ones for their situation?
4. Approach a person who is in employment. Find out as much as you can about their job and the organisation. Then draw up a valid contract for that employee.
5. Try to imagine a scenario where your organisation has to outsource a particular job. How would you structure the job and word the contract to ensure that the person is an independent contractor and not an employee?
6. Research the situation at the Marikana mine before the disastrous events of 2012 and present an argument to show that the situation could have been avoided, or at least ameliorated, had the proposed amendments regarding organisational rights and thresholds of representativeness been in place.

## Sources

DEL (Department of Employment and Labour). 2019. 'National Economic Development and Labour Council'. http://www.labour.gov.za/national_economic_developmnt_and_labour_council (Accessed 6 November 2021).

Department of Labour. n.d. 'About us'. http://www.labour.gov.za/about-us (Accessed 7 September 2021).

Department of Labour. 2006. 'Code of Good Practice: Who Is an Employee'. *Government Gazette* No 29445. Notice 1774 of 2006. https://www.gov.za/documents/labour-relations-act-code-good-practice-who-employee (Accessed 7 September 2021).

Employment Equity Act (55 of 1998). *Government Gazette* vol 400 no 19370. Pretoria: Government Printer.

ILO (International Labour Organization). 1944. Declaration of Philadelphia. https://www.ilo.org/dyn/normlex/en/f?p = 1000:62:0::NO:62:P62_LIST_ENTRIE_ID:2453907:NO#declaration (Accessed 6 November 2021).

ILO. 1948. 'Convention No. 87 Concerning Freedom of Association and Protection of the Right to Organise'. Legislation Online. https://www.legislationline.org/documents/id/7747 (Accessed 7 September 2021).

ILO. 1949. 'Co98 – Right to Organise and Collective Bargaining Convention'. ILO. https://www.ilo.org/dyn/normlex/en/f?p = NORMLEXPUB:12100:0::NO::P12100_ILO_CODE:C098 (Accessed 7 September 2021).

Jooste, R. 2019. 'South Africa slips in the World Bank's Ease of Doing Business Report'. Daily Maverick, 24 October 2019. https://www.dailymaverick.co.za/article/2019-10-24-south-africa-slips-to-an-all-time-low-in-the-world-banks-ease-of-doing-business-report/ (Accessed 7 September 2021).

Labour Relations Act (66 of 1995). *Government Gazette* vol 366 no 16861. Pretoria: Government Printer.

LWO. 2020. '2020 – designated employers & the Employment Equity Act'. https://lwo.co.za/2020/07/15/designated-employer-and-employment-equity-act-2020/ (Accessed 7 November 2021).

Mahlakoana, T. 2018. 'New court ruling will change the nature of labour broking in SA'. *Business Day*, 19 July 2018. https://www.businesslive.co.za/bd/national/labour/2018-07-26-new-court-ruling-will-change-the-nature-of-labour-broking-in-sa/ (Accessed 7 November 2021).

WEF (World Economic Forum). 2017. 'Global competitiveness report 2017–2018'. https://www.weforum.org/reports/the-global-competitiveness-report-2017-2018 (Accessed 6 November 2021).

# 4

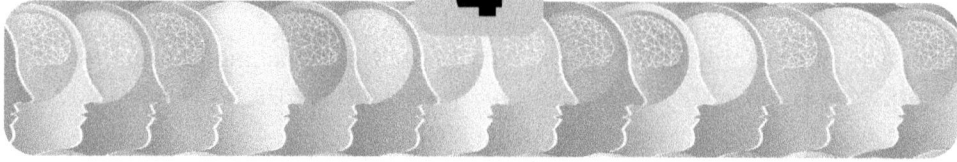

# Employment Equity

## Chapter Outline

➤

# Overview

The effective elimination of discrimination and the implementation of measures to ensure equitable representation of all races and both genders are absolutely necessary in the conduct of labour relations in South Africa. These measures have also become essential strategic considerations, as they may prove to be a means of diversifying and improving the quality of the workforce. The promulgation of the Employment Equity Act 55 of 1998 was intended to leverage employment relations to promote inclusion and diversity and eradicate unfair discrimination. This can be attained by the systematic application of human resource (HR) management processes which seek to address equity in the workplace.

The Employment Equity Act prohibits discrimination on a large number of listed grounds and any other arbitrary ground, while the Amendment Act 47 of 2013 states that different pay and conditions of employment between persons doing equal work or work of the same value may also be judged to constitute discrimination.

The Act obliges designated employers to produce and implement appropriate equity plans, designed, in the main, to promote equal employment opportunity and equitable representation for the designated groups, namely black people, women and people with disabilities. The Employment Equity Amendment Bill B14-2020 proposes various changes related to designated employers, people with disabilities, psychological testing, sectoral determinations, trade union representation and collective agreements.

As of 2020, employers who employ fewer than 50 employees will no longer fall within the definition of designated employer, regardless of their annual turnover. These employers are not required to comply with Chapter III of the Act relating to affirmative action. The definition of people with disabilities has been revised in compliance with the United Nations (UN) Convention on the Rights of Persons with Disabilities. Section 1 in Chapter 1 of the Employment Equity Act defines people with disabilities as 'includ[ing] people who have a long-term or recurring physical mental, intellectual or sensory impairment which, in the interaction with various barriers, may substantially limit their prospects of entry into, or advancement in, employment'. Additionally, the amendment has removed the requirement for certification of psychological tests and other similar assessments of an employee by the Health Professions Council of South Africa (HPCSA) or any other body authorised by law. The HPCSA is no longer obligated to provide certification, due to lack of capacity.

The Minister of Employment and Labour has been empowered to determine sectoral numerical targets. The minister can identify national economic sectors after having consulted with the National Minimum Wage Commission, with the aim of ensuring equitable representation of suitably qualified people from designated groups at all occupational levels, in all subsectors, in all regions or based on the relevant factors the minister may have determined and which apply to the employer.

The implementation of the equity plan requires consultation with representatives of all employees, an analysis of the workforce profile, and the establishment of numerical goals and concomitant strategies to achieve a more representative workforce. If the employees have a trade union representative, the employer must consult with the trade union only, and not the employees or their nominated representative, in relation to the preparation and implementation of the employment equity report. According to the 2013 amendments, the scope of the labour inspector's power has been extended; they can now request and obtain a written undertaking

➤

from the designated employer, requiring that employer to prepare an employment equity plan.

The amendment also requires the employer to work towards eliminating barriers to the employment of targeted groups, to institute measures to promote diversity and to provide reasonable accommodation for previously disadvantaged employees.

Equity plans have to be submitted to the director-general. The director-general may apply to the Labour Court to impose a fine, in accordance with Schedule 1, if a designated employer fails to prepare or implement an employment equity plan.

The process of affirmative action, like any change process, is fraught with problems and pitfalls. Perceptions as to the means of achieving equity differ, and in some instances the process is merely cosmetic. As in other change processes, the sincere commitment of all those involved is required if affirmative action is to work.

If an employer makes an offer to conclude an agreement with any organ of state to provide services or supplies, the employer must request a certificate from the minister to confirm that the employer has complied with their obligations under the Act. The minister may only issue such certificate if they are satisfied that the employer has complied with any numerical targets applicable to the employer. The minister can look at the previous three years to determine compliance or non-compliance with the Act.

The South African National Defence Force (SANDF) and the Domestic Branch and the Foreign Branch of the State Security Agency are excluded from the provisions of the Act.

## Rationale

Since the inclusion of the definition of unfair labour practice in the Labour Relations Amendment Act 94 of 1979, the concept of equity or fairness in employment practices has gained increasing importance. Despite this provision, and because of the history of discrimination in South Africa, at that time a vast number of people were still not regarded as equals in the workplace, nor were they granted equal opportunity for employment and advancement. This was demonstrated by the fact that, in the early 1990s, white males, who constituted just over 6 per cent of the total population, occupied more than 96 per cent of top positions in organisations, while the lower levels of organisational hierarchies were predominantly black (Stats SA, 2011).

In the light of South African history and the ingrained nature of prejudice and privilege in the workplace, after the advent of democracy the legislators decided to intervene actively in order not only to prevent further discrimination, but also to purposefully promote the employment and advancement of persons disadvantaged by previous policies. They believed that mere equality of opportunity (allowing free competition) would not be enough, as many contestants would commence with a handicap: in short, that true equality and equity would be achieved only by strong measures against discrimination and by the purposeful, planned placement and development of persons who had been denied equal opportunities in the past.

The Employment Equity Act 55 of 1998 complements the Labour Relations Act 66 of 1996 in two respects: as regards discrimination and affirmative action. The first legal intervention towards greater equity came in the form of the rewording of the definition of an unfair labour practice to focus specifically on discrimination. Item 2(1) of Schedule 7 of the Labour Relations Act (since deleted) had defined an unfair labour practice, inter alia, as one involving:

> *the unfair discrimination, either directly or indirectly, against an employee on any arbitrary ground, including, but not limited to race, gender, sex, ethnic or social origin, colour, sexual orientation, age, disability, religion, conscience, belief, political opinion, culture, language, marital status and family responsibility.*

Secondly, the Employment Equity Act imposes a duty on employers to adopt affirmative action with the aim of redressing the injustices of the past and promote equal representation in the workplace.

## Discrimination

### Discrimination in terms of the Employment Equity Act

Chapter II of the Act commences by placing the onus on all employers to promote equal opportunity by eliminating discrimination in all employment practices and policies. Section 6 of the Act prohibits discrimination on all the grounds listed above and adds another three grounds, namely pregnancy, HIV status and birth, while the Employment Equity Amendment Act 47 of 2013 adds the words 'or any other arbitrary grounds' to Section 6(1). According to Section 6(3), harassment is also a form of discrimination and is prohibited on any of the listed grounds. The Employment Equity Amendment Act contains a new Section 6(4), which states that different conditions of service for persons doing the same work, substantially the same work, or work of equal value may be discriminatory if based on one of the listed grounds.

The Act also protects job-seekers from unfair discrimination. Section 20(5) states that apart from being precluded from discriminating against applicants on the listed grounds, employers are not permitted to hold 'lack of relevant experience' against them. Employees who claim to have been discriminated against on an 'arbitrary' ground must prove that the ground is akin to the listed grounds.

Sections 7 and 8 of the Act provide guidelines as regards medical testing and psychological assessment.

## Disputes Centring on Alleged Discrimination

Dismissals where discrimination is alleged are automatically unfair and must be processed according to the relative provisions in the Labour Relations Act. Any other dispute related to discrimination, harassment or testing may be taken to the Commission for Conciliation, Mediation and Arbitration (CCMA) for conciliation and, if this fails, be submitted to the Labour Court for arbitration. In all these cases, except one where the employee alleges discrimination on an arbitrary ground, the employer will have to prove that the alleged actions/policies were not discriminatory. If the employee alleges discrimination on an arbitrary ground, the onus of proof lies with the employee.

A new Section 4(6)(b) in the Employment Equity Amendment Act allows an employee who alleges sexual harassment and employees who earn less than the earnings threshold prescribed by the minister (at present R205 433.30 per annum) to take their dispute straight to the Labour Court for arbitration. The Amendment Act also proposes that, if all parties agree, the CCMA may arbitrate on any disputes in this category. Persons who are not satisfied with the CCMA's decision may appeal to the Labour Court.

## Pre-employment Testing
### Medical Tests

Medical testing of candidates is permitted, but only under certain conditions. Section 7(1) of the Act permits medical testing if it is required by law, and is justifiable in the light of:

- medical facts
- employment conditions
- social policy
- the fair distribution of employee benefits
- the inherent requirements of the job.

In *IMATU v City of Cape Town (CA 13/2013) [2015] ZALAC 68 (23 April 2015)*, the respondent refused to employ a Mr Murdoch to the position of firefighter, even though he had passed the physical fitness test with flying colours. The refusal was based on the fact that he was an insulin-dependent diabetic. The City's employment policy and practice was that they do not appoint insulin-dependent diabetics as firefighters. The union argued that the City's failure to appoint Murdoch constituted, inter alia, unfair discrimination on the grounds of disability. The City's defence was that its blanket ban on employment of diabetics is fair and justified on the basis of the inherent requirements for the job of a firefighter. The Labour Court conceded that the risks inherent in hypoglycaemia were real, but ruled that this did not support the imposition of a blanket ban. The risk will vary from person to person. The Labour Court therefore held that the City had unfairly discriminated against Murdoch and had, accordingly, failed to discharge its onus of proving the fairness of the discrimination.

'The fair distribution of employee benefits' has been taken to mean that, if an employee has to belong to a medical aid or pension fund, testing might be justified, but the circumstances in which this would be so are not quite clear.

### HIV Testing

HIV testing is prohibited unless declared to be justifiable by the Labour Court. The special mention given to medical, and especially HIV, testing indicates that any discrimination based purely on an employee's medical condition has to be justified by the inherent requirements of the job.

*Joy Mining Machinery, a division of Harnischfeger (SA) v NUMSA (2002) 23 ILJ 391 (LC)* remains an important case on the issue of HIV testing. The Labour Court appeared to imply that it was necessary for an employer to obtain a Labour Court order before implementing any testing programme, even if testing was both voluntary and anonymous. The judge disagreed with the view that Section 7 prohibited employers from unfairly discriminating against employees on the basis of suffering from a medical condition. One way to reduce the likelihood of such discrimination was to limit the circumstances in which an employer may ascertain an employee's medical condition through testing.

*Hoffman v South African Airways (2000) 12 BLLR 1365 (CC)* remains the leading judgment on the issue of inherent requirements of the job and their relevance or otherwise to HIV status and HIV testing. The Constitutional Court held that the refusal of South African Airways (SAA) to employ Hoffman as a cabin attendant because of his HIV status constituted unfair discrimination. SAA was not able to discharge its onus of proving that being HIV negative is an inherent requirement for the job of a cabin attendant.

### Psychological Testing and Other Similar Assessments

These forms of assessment are allowed only if they have been scientifically shown to be valid and reliable, can be applied fairly to all employees and are not biased against any person or group.

The purpose of clauses (a) to (c) of Section 8 of the Act was to prevent the use of invalidated or culturally and linguistically biased tests, often administered by unqualified practitioners. It was not the intention to ban all forms of psychological or other similar assessments, but rather to caution test users to ensure that:

- the test is both reliable and valid (that it tests what it is presumed to test)
- as far as possible, cultural bias has been eliminated

- it does not rely for success on a privileged educational or social background
- the language used can be understood by all test subjects.

The Employment Equity Amendment Act amended Section 8 of the Act to allow for psychometric testing and other similar forms of assessment only if the tests have been certified by the HPCSA or any other body authorised to do so.

The inclusion of 'other similar assessments' could be interpreted to include polygraph examinations, as there is some controversy surrounding these.

## Harassment
### Definition
The most common form of harassment in organisations is of a sexual nature, but policies and procedures relating to this aspect should not exclude racial harassment and harassment of, for example, the disabled. Essentially, harassment is any form of behaviour, whether verbal, physical or by gesture, to which a person on reasonable grounds might object. It is particularly serious if the harasser is in a position of power.

The Draft Code of Good Practice on the Prevention and Elimination of Violence and Harassment in the World of Work (DEL, 2020) elaborates on actions which could constitute harassment and provides guidelines on handling complaints of harassment. Section 7.1.4.4(b) of the Code provides that sexual attention becomes sexual violence and harassment when:

(i) *The behaviour is persistent in, although a single incident of harassment can constitute sexual harassment; and/or*

(ii) *The recipient has made it clear that the behaviour is considered offensive; and/or*

(iii) *The perpetrator knows or ought to have known that the behaviour is regarded as unacceptable.*

Section 7.1.4.2(c) covers a wide variety of conduct, from obvious physical contact through to verbal forms such as

> *unwelcome innuendos, suggestions, hints, sexual advances, comments with sexual overtones, sex-related jokes or insults, graphic comments about a person's body made in their presence or to them, inappropriate inquiries about a person's sex life, whistling of a sexual nature and the sending by electronic means or otherwise of sexually explicit text.*

In *NUMSA on behalf of Prezens and Duferco Steel Processing (Pty) Ltd (2006) 27 ILJ 1282 BCA*, an employee was accused of writing derogatory, insulting and sexually explicit graffiti referring to a female employee on the wall of the men's toilet at work. He was dismissed for sexual harassment. The employee denied all knowledge of the graffiti. The employer relied on the evidence of a handwriting expert who identified the employee (out of 160) with a 95 per cent probability. This, with other factors, convinced the employer. At arbitration, it was held that on balance of probabilities, the employee was the author of the graffiti. The arbitrator found that the graffiti was sexually provocative, undesirable and harassing and fell within the company's code on sexual harassment. As the employer had a positive duty to create an environment free of sexual harassment and to protect vulnerable employees, dismissal was a reasonable sanction.

## Employer Liability

Section 60 of the Employment Equity Act provides that an employer who is made aware of a transgression of any provision of the Act and fails to act upon it will be deemed to have committed that transgression. This applies also to cases of harassment.

In *Mokoena & Another v Garden Art Ltd & Another [2008] 5 BLLR 428 (LC)*, it was explained that an employer becomes liable in terms of Section 60 of the Employment Equity Act only if the alleged harassment had been brought to their attention and if they failed to take proper steps to prevent further harassment of the employee concerned. In that case, the Court found that the employer had reacted to the employee's report of sexual harassment by issuing a written warning, and no further incidents had occurred. The employer was not liable for damages to the employees.

## Policy and Procedure

A harassment policy and procedure should be put in place in order to ensure that all complaints are effectively and fairly handled. Such a policy creates awareness of the issue and gives those who are subjected to harassment the reassurance that their complaints will be dealt with in a serious and sensitive manner.

Harassment is a sensitive issue. Complainants need to be assured of confidentiality and are often afraid to lodge a complaint. Therefore, harassment should preferably not be dealt with by way of a disciplinary procedure. A separate committee of respected, trusted persons should deal with this issue. Counselling of both parties is usually the first step. Nevertheless, when harassment is invidious or continuous, the matter must be handled in terms of the disciplinary process and dismissal becomes a possibility.

## Mokone v Sahara Computers (Pty) Ltd (2010 31 ILJ2827 (GNP))

### Background

In 2006 Mokone was employed in one of the company's departments. Virtually from the beginning, a male employee from another department, stating that all new persons 'had to pass through' him, made sexual overtures to her on a regular basis, at one time touching her and at another pouring water over her. She eventually confided in a male colleague whom she knew and could trust, but he advised her to drop the matter, as the person in question was 'well connected'. The advances continued and, upon the advice of another colleague, Mokone reported the harassment to the manager in her department. The latter also referred to the fact that the accused was well connected. He promised to protect her in the department, but advised her not to take the matter further, as she would probably be the one to be dismissed. However, the man continued to visit the department when the manager was not there. On one occasion, when he noticed that the manager was there, he addressed her in Tswana, threatening to have relations with her and stating that sexual harassment was for whites, and not for him. Mokone did not report the incident, as her manager had previously said nothing could be done.

At the end of 2007 Mokone did not attend the Christmas party, for fear that the person would also be there. When, a while later, the man tried to touch her buttock, she reported him to the HR department. A disciplinary hearing was held and the culprit was given a written warning. Mokone later stated that she had been dissatisfied with the outcome and had wanted to appeal, but had received no response from HR. The harassment did, however, stop.

In May 2009 Mokone resigned, citing personal reasons and that the company had failed to protect her. She subsequently visited a counselling psychologist, who later testified in court that he had found Mokone to be severely traumatised and depressed, and that the events at Sahara Computers had impacted on her social, academic, occupational and interpersonal life.

Mokone eventually took the company to court, claiming that it had failed to provide a safe working environment and that its failure to take reasonable steps to do so had been both negligent and unlawful. She claimed R150 000 for mental anguish, psychological trauma and impairment to dignity and R50 000 for counselling costs.

### Pronouncements

The North Gauteng High Court found that the second complaint (to HR) had been handled immediately, that the employee had been sanctioned and that the harassment had stopped. In that instance the company had acted appropriately. Nevertheless, the Court went on to state that if the first complaint (to the manager) had been handled properly, the harassment would have stopped much sooner. The manager should have reported the matter to HR. The fact that he did not do so proved that the company's disciplinary structures and processes were insufficient. The company had acted unreasonably by failing to ensure that proper reporting of such incidents would take place. The company was found guilty of negligence and ordered to pay Mokone R60 000 as well as her costs in bringing the case.

## The Inherent Requirements of the Job

Section 6(2) of the Employment Equity Act provides that discrimination based on the inherent requirements of a job may be regarded as fair discrimination. The International Labour Organization (ILO) also considers the inherent requirements of the job to be an acceptable reason for discrimination. Article 1(2) of the ILO's Discrimination (Employment and Occupation) Convention No 111 of 1958 affirms what is in the Employment Equity Act by providing that 'any distinction, exclusion or preference in respect of a particular job based on the inherent requirements thereof shall not be deemed to be discrimination' (ILO, 1958).

As can be seen from the case review of *Whitehead v Woolworths (Pty) Ltd (Labour Court: C122/98) Woolworths (Pty) Ltd v Whitehead (Labour Appeal Court: CA6/99)*, which follows shortly, there are different interpretations of the phrase 'inherent requirements of the job'. Where requirements such as physical fitness are essential for a particular task, the use of these as criteria for selection is not problematic. Nevertheless, it is important not to equate these requirements with stereotypes, for example that only men would have the necessary strength to become lumberjacks or that women have greater manual dexterity than men. Candidates, whatever their sex, race or age, should be assessed for the requirements and not excluded on the basis of preconceived attributes.

Requirements which are not inherent in a job are more difficult to justify. However, the courts have repeatedly stated that they will not interfere with standards set by the employer unless these are grossly unfair, and as long as the standards can be justified. Selectors need to take great care in listing competencies, requirements and criteria, and must ensure that they are justified.

Fair versus Unfair Discrimination

The Employment Equity Act itself makes provision for fair discrimination, or, to avoid the negative connotations that this word has acquired, differentiation, based on justifiable or non-arbitrary grounds.

The question is: Would discrimination be fair only if it is based on one of the grounds mentioned in the Act, namely affirmative action or the inherent requirements of the job, or will the fairness of the discrimination be judged in a wider context? The differentiation between fair and unfair discrimination is complex. Fairness of differentiation cannot be judged only in terms of the Act; it should be judged within the wider concept of fairness. This would include:

- all the circumstances
- the position of and balance between the various parties
- the interests of all parties
- the norms and interests of the organisation and society at large.

## Case Review: Arbitrary Grounds or Inherent Requirements of the Job

*Whitehead v Woolworths (Pty) Ltd (Labour Court: C122/98) Woolworths (Pty) Ltd v Whitehead (Labour Appeal Court: (CA06/99) [2000] ZALAC 4 (3 April 2000)*

### Background

In 1997, Woolworths advertised a position for a Human Resources: Information and Technology Generalist, to be based in Cape Town.

Ms Whitehead was interviewed and offered the job. She turned down the offer for reasons which are not quite clear, but which seemed to relate either to disagreement about pay or to the fact that her husband was, at that time, based in Gauteng.

Later in the same year, the job was again advertised. The new applicants included a Dr Young who, being in possession of two honours degrees, an MBA and a doctorate in which he specialised in IT, and with 17 years experience in HR and IT, was regarded as a 'star candidate'. By comparison, Ms Whitehead had a bachelor's degree in industrial psychology and far less experience. Nevertheless, Mr Inskip, for Woolworths, decided to contact Ms Whitehead to find out whether her circumstances had changed. As it happened, her husband had obtained a position in Cape Town, and it was agreed that she would be interviewed while on holiday in that city. In the meantime, a Mr Dickson had spoken to Dr Young, but he had not been interviewed by Mr Inskip.

At the interview, Ms Whitehead revealed the fact that she was pregnant. According to Ms Whitehead, Mr Inskip declared that this would not be a problem. This was denied by Mr Inskip, but what is clear is that he did not, at that stage, indicate that her pregnancy might be a problem. Ms Whitehead testified that, following the interview, she felt very confident. However, she did later admit that Mr Inskip had made it quite clear that he still had to interview other candidates and that the position could go to any one of them.

Two days later, Mr Inskip, according to Ms Whitehead, left a message for her saying he wanted to 'finalise the paperwork'. This was denied by Mr Inskip. He admitted that he did later indicate to her that his superior found her pregnancy to be an obstacle to her being placed in a permanent position and instead offered her a fixed-term contract for five months (up to the time of her confinement). When questioned about this, Mr Inskip explained that he had wanted to 'keep his options open' and had considered the possibility of later changing the fixed-term contract to a permanent one if another suitable candidate could not be found.

As it happened, Dr Young was subsequently interviewed, found suitable and appointed to the position. Ms Whitehead declared a dispute and took the matter to the Labour Court, which ruled in her favour and ordered Woolworths to pay her R200 000 in compensation. The order was subsequently overturned by the Labour Appeal Court.

## Argument

Ms Whitehead claimed that she had been unfairly dismissed and, alternatively, that she had been unfairly discriminated against on the basis of her pregnancy.

In response, counsel for Woolworths admitted that Ms Whitehead's pregnancy had played a part in the decision not to appoint her, but submitted that job continuity was a requirement for the position and that this requirement applied equally to all applicants and, secondly, that the requirement for job continuity was 'rationally and commercially justifiable'.

## Pronouncements

The case elicited four different judgments, one in the Labour Court and three in the Labour Appeal Court.

### *The Labour Court*

To counter the allegation of discrimination, Woolworths had stated that any person who could not guarantee that they would be able to work for the next 12 months would have been unacceptable. The Labour Court proceeded to explain why it did not accept Woolworths' assertion. The Court explained that Woolworths would have to show that the candidate whom they appointed could be 'guaranteed' to continue in employment for an uninterrupted period of 12 months. Since, according to the Court, no such guarantee could ever be given, the discrimination was not justifiable.

The Court then turned to the submission that the requirement for job continuity was justifiable in terms of commercial rationale. It concluded that 'the fairness or unfairness of discrimination cannot be measured against the profitability or for that matter efficiency of the business enterprise'.

In summation, the Court concluded that:

> To suggest that the requirement as in this case of uninterrupted job continuity is an inherent requirement is to distort the very concept. If the job can be performed without the requirement, as it can in this case, then it cannot be said that the requirement is inherent and therefore prohibited under item 2(2) (c) of Schedule 7 to the [Labour Relations] Act.

## The Labour Appeal Court

### Justice Zondo AJP

Justice Zondo noted, firstly, that when Ms Whitehead was interviewed for the second time, she had been informed that there were other candidates who had to be interviewed before the decision was made. When asked whether he would have offered Ms Whitehead a permanent position if he had not found another suitable candidate, Mr Inskip had replied that he probably would have. From this Justice Zondo deduced that Ms Whitehead's pregnancy did not put her 'outside the category of persons who could be offered the job'. However, if it was Ms Whitehead's case that, but for her pregnancy, she would have been appointed despite there being a better candidate, then her case was based on 'little more than a suspicion which is not supported by any evidence'. Even if Mr Inskip had thought Ms Whitehead a suitable candidate when he interviewed her, there was no reason why, after interviewing Dr Young, he should not change his mind about 'who was the most suitable for the job'.

In the light of the above, Justice Zondo found that there was 'no causal connection between her not being appointed and her pregnancy'.

### Justice Conradie JA

Justice Conradie dealt in detail with the continuity requirement and the fact that Mr Inskip had not reacted to Ms Whitehead's announcement that she was pregnant, that he had not informed her that continuity might be a problem and had, in fact, sent Ms Whitehead to consult the HR personnel on a number of matters, including maternity leave.

He then went on to question whether the job did require the uninterrupted presence of an incumbent. He decided that it was not essential and that Ms Whitehead could, as she had offered, have attended to the business during her maternity leave. There had been a failure to prove that Ms Whitehead's presence during the three months of maternity leave was 'crucial' to the effective functioning of the unit.

Justice Conradie concluded by proposing that the Labour Court's decision should be upheld, but that the amount of compensation be reduced to R140 000.

## Justice Willis JA

Justice Willis also focused on Woolworths' contention that the position required uninterrupted continuity of employment for a period of between 12 to 18 months and that, because Ms Whitehead could not fulfil this obligation, the decision not to employ her was 'a rational and commercially justifiable one'. This led to the question as to whether uninterrupted job continuity, a condition which Ms Whitehead, owing to her pregnancy, could not fulfil, was indeed a primary requirement. If it was not, then the only other plausible reason for not appointing her was that she was 'quite simply, not the best candidate'.

Justice Willis then turned to the argument, raised by counsel for Ms Whitehead, that item 2(2)(c) of Schedule 7 of the Labour Relations Act should be interpreted to read that unless discrimination was based on the inherent requirements of a particular job, it would be unfair. In Justice Willis's opinion this was not so, as it was 'not difficult to imagine situations outside of the inherent requirements of a particular job where discrimination would not be unfair'. In support of this assertion, he referred to the following factors which needed to be taken into account in establishing whether discrimination was fair or unfair:

i.   *the impact of the discrimination on the complainant*
ii.  *the position of the complainant in society*
iii. *the nature and extent of the discrimination*
iv.  *whether discrimination has a legitimate purpose and to what extent it achieves that purpose*
v.   *whether there are less disadvantageous means to achieve that purpose*
vi.  *whether and to what extent the respondent has taken reasonable steps to address the disadvantage caused by the discrimination, or to accommodate diversity.*

On the question of fairness, Justice Willis had the following to say:

*Fairness is an elastic and organic concept. It is impossible to define with exact precision. It has to take into account the norms and values of our society as well as its realities. Fairness, particularly in the context of the [Labour Relations Act], requires an evaluation that is multidimensional. One must look at it not only from the perspective of prospective employees, but also employers and the interests of society as a whole. Policy considerations play a role. There may be features in the nature of the issue which call for restraint by a court in coming to a conclusion that a particular act of discrimination is fair.*

The judge disagreed with the Labour Court pronouncement that, because no guarantee of continuity is absolute, pregnancy could not be taken into account. According to Justice Willis, 'employers must base their commercial decisions on reasonable probabilities. Risk-taking is intrinsic to enterprise. Risk is discounted, inter alia, by an evaluation of probabilities'. In his opinion, the employer 'took into account perfectly rational and commercially understandable considerations. These considerations were, in the circumstances, neither trivial nor insubstantial'.

Turning to the matter of profitability raised by the Labour Court, Justice Willis agreed that 'profitability is not to dictate whether or not discrimination is fair or unfair'. Nevertheless, it was relevant. In conclusion, Justice Willis made it quite clear that, 'as a general rule, this court views with disfavour discrimination on the grounds of pregnancy, even when it concerns applications for employment'. However, he was of the opinion that 'in respect of this issue, as with so many others, the solution does not lie with this court presenting society with unrealistic rules of law – however attractive they may otherwise seem to be. Fairness refracts when passed through the prism of reality'.

The decision of the Labour Court was overruled and costs awarded against Ms Whitehead.

## Discussion

On the most simplistic level, *Whitehead v Woolworths* points to the need for interviewing and selection to be conducted by persons knowledgeable and skilled in all aspects. These individuals should know that no indication of approval must be given to a candidate before the final decision has been made, that one does not 'hedge one's bets' by offering alternative contracts a priori and that no comments irrelevant to the selection criteria should be made or entertained. Furthermore, it points to the necessity to establish competencies and criteria beforehand and to structure both the interview and the final assessment of candidates around these. The entire issue could have been avoided had these guidelines been followed.

If it is true that Dr Young was the best candidate, then a structured interview, agreed and measurable criteria and the resultant assessment would have revealed that, and there would have been no need even to mention Ms Whitehead's pregnancy. Alternatively, if it is true that uninterrupted job continuity was an inherent requirement, this should have been spelled out beforehand and included in the criteria. Ms Whitehead would then have been informed of this aspect immediately when she announced her pregnancy. As it is, the case speaks of an ad hoc and disconnected approach to the entire recruitment and selection process.

Five main issues of principle arise from the judgments, namely:
1. the interpretation of the term 'inherent requirements'
2. the question as to when discrimination on one of the grounds prohibited by law would be regarded as fair
3. the general application of the principle of fairness
4. the acceptance or otherwise of commercial rationale as justification for a particular decision
5. the purpose of the anti-discrimination provisions.

The interpretation of fairness as closely related to societal norms raises the issue of commercial rationale as a justification for a particular decision. Numerous previous court decisions have accepted commercial rationale as a measure, yet the Labour Court was most dismissive of this argument, without, however, providing any in-depth reason for its stand, other than a passing reference to the Bill of Rights. Justice Willis, on the other hand, accepted commercial rationale as a basis for his decision and went to great lengths to explain why the courts should be careful not to impose decisions that nullified this consideration.

## Case Review: Age Discrimination

### *Evans v Japanese School of Johannesburg (Labour Court: JS387/05, 12 and 14 June; 18 September 2006)*

### Background

The applicant, a Ms Evans, was employed by the Japanese School as an English teacher in 1988. She had no written contract and nothing was said about how long she would be working for the school. At that stage there was no written retirement policy at the school. The practice appeared to be that employees retired at the age of 65, although previously some employees had worked till the age of 70.

Evidently, Evans' employers were quite satisfied with her performance and had told her on numerous occasions that they wanted her to stay. In 2002, during a meeting with one of the school committee members (at which her attorney was present), Evans indicated that she would work to the age of 65. This was evidently recorded in the minutes of the meeting. The committee members changed on a regular basis, and on another occasion, Evans told the then head of the committee that she would stay until she was 65. He smiled and nodded. Towards the end of 2003 Evans was reminded by the principal that her decision to work until 65 was on record. He added that she should not make a fuss at the CCMA, evidently referring to a medical aid issue she had taken to the Commission.

On 18 February 2004, Evans and other employees received letters stating that 60 would now be the retirement age of all employees. On receipt of the letter, Evans had a meeting with one of the main members of the school committee, during which she asked whether they still wanted her to work at the school. She received no response. Suspecting that the policy had been implemented to get rid of her, Evans addressed a letter to the committee member enquiring whether her contract would expire at the end of the school year, which was 12 March 2004. Again, she received no reply.

On 8 March, in an attempt to clarify her position, Evans wrote to the principal, stating that she was concerned that the new members of the school committee had no knowledge of previous agreements and arrangements, such as the agreement that she would retire at the age of 65, like other South African teachers. There was no response to her letter, but on 8 March the school's attorney sent her attorney a letter requesting that they meet to discuss the matter. Nothing came of this, and from March to September 2004, nothing more was said to her. Evans, who had continued to go to work every day, eventually addressed another letter, requesting a meeting. At the meeting, which took place in September 2004, Evans told the committee that she wanted to resolve the matter and felt that she was perfectly fit to go on teaching until she reached the age of 65. The head of the committee did not respond.

On 16 November, Evans received a letter telling her that she had reached the 'normal' retirement age. At the time she was 61. There had been no consultation with her. After her attorney responded, she received another letter stating that she had until close of business on 30 November to make representations. This her attorney did on her behalf. On 17 December, Evans received a letter from the principal stating that her last working day would be 21 December. As noted by the Court, after 17 years of service she was given three days' notice to vacate her post. Other employees who were also over the age of 60 continued to work at the school.

Evans subsequently filed three claims related to her dismissal. In the first claim, she requested 24 months' compensation for an automatically unfair dismissal in terms of Section 187(1)(f) of the Labour Relations Act. In the second claim, she sought damages in terms of the Employment Equity Act to the amount of R359 823.75 for loss of income between January 2005 and September 2008. Her third claim related to notice pay and allowances due to her at the time of her dismissal.

## Pronouncements

With regard to the allegation of an automatically unfair dismissal, the Court noted that the written employment contract eventually offered to Evans was silent on the question of retirement and that the school had no written retirement policy. The first intimation of any policy had been the letter addressed to employees on 18 February 2004. This letter proposed new conditions of service. The employer could not unilaterally change Evans' conditions of employment. The Court noted that, although subsection (f) of Section 187(1) declares a dismissal based on any form of discrimination, including age, to be unfair, the same section provides that a dismissal based on age will be fair if the employee has reached the normal or agreed pensionable age. In Evans' case, there was no indication that a pensionable age of 60 had been agreed upon. In the light of this, the Court found her allegation of an automatically unfair dismissal to be warranted and awarded her the maximum allowable compensation of 24 months' pay, amounting, in total, to R177 144.

The Court then turned to Evans' claim for compensation in terms of Section 6, read with Section 50, of the Employment Equity Act. The former section prohibits unfair discrimination, while the latter allows the Labour Court to award compensation to victims of unfair discrimination. It was noted that, although the Labour Relations Act and the Employment Equity Act are similar in that they both prohibit a dismissal based on unfair discrimination, the former Act places a limit on the amount of compensation to be awarded. The Employment Equity Act contains no such limitations. The Court took into account that other employees over the age of 60 were still employed by the school and the fact that Evans had been dismissed on the grounds of her age. The Court found the sum claimed by Evans to be justified. If she had not been dismissed, she would have been employed until 20 December 2008. Since Evans had already been awarded the sum mentioned above, the Court awarded her an additional R200 000 on the second claim as well as R29 524 for the three months' notice pay in terms of her contract.

## Discussion

What is interesting about this case is, first, that it dealt with age discrimination and, secondly, that claims were lodged in terms of both the Labour Relations Act and the Employment Equity Act. The relevant sections in both Acts allow employees to allege discrimination on the part of the employer, the only difference being that the Employment Equity Act does not place a limit on the compensation to be awarded by the courts.

It is strange that other employees were allowed to continue after they turned 60, indicating that there was no blanket discriminatory policy. In fact, Evans was probably being victimised for bringing a case to the CCMA, and could equally have brought her case in terms of Sections 5(1) and 87(1)(d) of the Labour Relations Act. These sections forbid the employer from engaging in practices which prevent an employee from exercising their rights.

Section 187(2)(b) of the Labour Relations Act states that it is not unfair to dismiss an employee who has reached the agreed pensionable age. This clause is the only clause in the legislation which allows a dismissal on one of the generally forbidden grounds. It merits further debate as to why persons should leave employment merely because they have reached a certain age and not because they have become less capable of performing their jobs. Countering this is the social benefit argument, namely that older employees have to leave in order to provide opportunities for new incumbents. Whether this sufficiently justifies discrimination and an incursion on the constitutional rights of individuals remains questionable. Evans had evidently not been provided with benefits and was surviving on an income from erratic part-time teaching, averaging R2 000 a month. Even if there had been an agreed policy, the question still remains whether dismissing a capable person and relegating her to a subsistence income, merely on the grounds of her age, can be regarded as fair. This question remains unanswered.

## Dalu Xolo Nicholas Sali v National Commissioner South African Police Services, Provincial Commissioner South African Police Services, Minister of Safety and Security CCT/164/13 (19 March 2014)

### Background

In 2006 Sali joined the South African Police Service (SAPS) as a police reservist. According to the information provided by Brigadier Govender (evidently the accountable manager), reservists are volunteers who perform the same functions as police officers, are given the same powers and also carry weapons. They undergo training, but are not employees and are not paid for their services.

Reservists can apply for permanent positions. However, Regulation 11(1) states that to apply for a position as member/employee of SAPS, applicants have to be between 18 and 30 years old. This regulation also covers reservists who want to apply for a permanent position. Reservists were not happy with this limitation, as many of them were already older than 30. As a result, a number of protest marches were held, obliging management to meet with the disgruntled reservists. After several meetings the reservists were informed that the limit for them to apply had been extended to age 40. However, those who applied needed to have served as reservists for at least three years.

In 2009 Sali, who by then had three years' experience as a reservist, applied for two posts, one of which stipulated that the incumbent had to be between the ages of 41 and 45. At that stage Sali's age was 41 years and 10 months. The applicants had to take tests and undergo a medical examination, all of which Sali passed. After his interview, a senior officer informed Sali that he would get the contract for the position with the 40–45-year limit and would be appointed as from January. However, in December Sali was informed that both his applications had been unsuccessful. When Sali asked for a reason, he was told that he did not qualify in terms of the age limitations.

Sali's station commissioner then wrote to the provincial commissioner, requesting that in this case the age limitation be waived. There was no response from the provincial commissioner, whereupon Sali approached the CCMA and thereafter the Labour Court.

Sali claimed that his non-appointment resulted directly from the age restrictions imposed by the SAPS. In his founding affidavit he demanded that he be appointed in the post for which he had applied and also that he be awarded R500 000 as compensation for the two years' loss in salary. He further wanted the court to rule that the SAPS should remove age discrimination from their policies.

The SAPS argued that service as a reservist did not necessarily qualify Sali to be appointed and that the age limit of 40 was, in his case, the barrier. Moreover, the SAPS claimed that the case could not be adjudicated in terms of the Employment Equity Act, as the age limits were based on legislation. Because the restriction was contained in a Regulation it was not, according to the SAPS, an 'employment policy or practice' (the term used in the Employment Equity Act).

The Labour Court agreed that the case was premised on a Regulation and that the Employment Equity Act did not apply. As a result it was, according to the Court, not necessary for it to rule on the matter. The case was dismissed and leave to appeal was denied.

Sali then bypassed the Labour Appeal Court and took his case directly to the Constitutional Court, claiming that the alleged discrimination could also constitute a contravention of the relevant clauses in the Constitution. He requested the Court to decide whether:

- leave to appeal should be granted
- Regulation 11(1) should be declared invalid in terms of the Constitution
- the decision not to appoint was based on the Regulation
- the Regulation fell outside the scope of the Employment Equity Act
- if the discrimination was not based on the Regulation, whether the SAPS had proved that the discrimination was fair.

## Argument and Pronouncements

Noting that the onus to prove that the policy was fair rested with the SAPS and not with the claimant, the Court listed the questions to be asked regarding the limitation:

- Does it differentiate between people or categories of people?
- If so, is there a rational connection related to a legitimate government purpose?
- If there is no rational connection, does it constitute a violation of the employee's rights?
- Even if rational, could it still constitute discrimination?
- Does it amount to unfair discrimination?
- Is it for a specific goal?
- If not for a specific goal, will it fit in with fundamental human rights or adversely affect these?

As regards the matter at hand, the Court expressed the opinion that it was basically a constitutional issue, but Sali had not originally raised it as such, nor was this aspect supported in the papers before the Court. Nevertheless, the Court indicated that the constitutional aspects could still be considered and that the pertinent question was whether it was in the interests of justice to grant leave to appeal.

The Court then turned to the argument brought by the SAPS that the criteria pertaining to recruits was a Regulation intended to provide for entrance and was not an employment policy or practice, as envisaged by the Employment Equity Act. It was admitted that, at first glance, the phrase 'any other employment practice' seems quite narrow; however, as the Court indicated, the definition of this term lists a wide number of practices, among them recruitment procedures, advertising and selection. Nevertheless, the Court seemed to concede that legislation, and therefore also a governmental regulation, could not be challenged in terms of the Act.

This having been said, the Court went on to point out that Section 9(3) of the Bill of Rights precludes the state from discriminating on a number of grounds, including age. Any contravention of this section would then become a constitutional matter.

From there, the Court proceeded to interrogate the new conditions pertaining to recruits and the argument made by the SAPS that these were contained in legislation. It was noted that the changes had been made following a protest march by reservists. This resulted in an agreement that the age limit of 30 would, in the case of the reservists, no longer apply.

The Court went on to explain that the national commissioner does have wide-ranging powers to waive some aspects of a particular Regulation in certain circumstances, but he does not have the power to amend the actual Regulation. This power rests only with the minister. In this case, all the national commissioner had done was to exempt recruits from the 30-year age limit. The question following on from this was whether the SAPS was correct in maintaining that Sali did not qualify in terms of the new age limit of 40. As the Court saw it, that limit could not be imposed, since there was no Regulation limiting the age requirement for recruits to 40. Although a limit of 40 had been mentioned, all that had happened was that the age limit of 30 was waived. If 40 was to be another barrier, this should have been contained in a Regulation. The waiver could not have set that limit.

From the above, the Court concluded that the SAPS and the Labour Court had been wrong in maintaining that management had acted in terms of the Regulation. In as far as it concerned applicants who were not reservists, the original Regulation still stood. The waiver of the Regulation as it applied to recruits was, in fact, policy and practice and should be judged in this light.

Having clarified this issue and accepted that the limits were an employment practice in terms of the Employment Equity Act, the Court's next question was whether the practice was fair. It noted that the age restriction had proved a barrier to many reservists, that the applicant had been treated differently from other reservists and that Sali had not been appointed because of his age. On this basis, the Court concluded that the decision must be presumed to be unfair and that it would be up to the SAPS to prove that it had been fair.

After establishing grounds for alleging discrimination, the next step was to establish whether the discrimination was fair or instituted on rational grounds. In this regard the Court described as 'rubbish' the earlier testimony by Brigadier Govender that the age limit of 30 had originally been set because during training it had been shown that older persons did not do as well as their younger counterparts. The Court pointed out that if this had been a true reason, raising the age limit to 40 went against those findings and made no sense. Moreover, in the case at hand, age apparently had no impact on academic and physical performance, yet the decision not to allow the person entry was based on the fact that he was over the age of 40 – even though the age requirement for one of the positions was that the incumbent be aged 41 to 45.

The conclusion reached by the Court was, firstly, that the SAPS had failed to prove that the refusal to appoint Sali had been fair. Moreover, a constitutional right had been violated.

The ruling by the Labour Court was set aside and the case was returned to that Court, which, the Constitutional Court said, should be asked to use its 'wide-ranging powers' to grant the appropriate relief. It was further indicated that the pleadings should include the allegation that a constitutional right had been violated.

## Discussion

The ruling was subject to a dissenting judgment, but, for our present purposes, its content is not relevant. Our concern is not so much with the legal niceties as with the attitudes and actions of the parties and the principles emerging from the judgment.

This case was included in this book because it again demonstrates that, so often, rules or regulations are instituted without any real understanding of what they mean and without their validity or purpose being questioned. In the first place, it should not have been left to the Court to explain the difference between amending a Regulation, on the one hand, and a waiver of certain conditions in a rule or Regulation, on the other. Even if management at station level did not understand the legal implications, the regional commissioner should have been able to clarify the situation. Not only did he fail to do so; he did not even respond to the request for a waiver from the station commander.

Secondly, the entire situation did not seem to strike SAPS management as questionable. Even though a new so-called limit had been set, did it not seem untoward that someone should not be appointed because he was now one year and 10 months over the 'limit' of 40, notwithstanding the fact that he was within the age range required for the post?

There is a good reason why one of the requirements for judging an action or rule is that it should be rational, meaning that it must be shown that there is an acceptable/valid reason. As it is, Brigadier Govender could not supply a rational explanation for the age restrictions and admitted that he had based his explanation on 'hearsay'. One also wonders why applicants for one of the posts had to be between the ages 41 and 45. What makes a person in that age bracket more qualified to fill post than anyone else?

As indicated in the judgment, the setting of age limits is common to many sections of the public service. This is a matter of great concern since, if this case is an example, the reasons behind these limitations may, in most cases, not be rational or acceptable. In terms of both the Constitution and the Employment Equity Act, discrimination of any kind is unlawful, unless it can be proved that it is rational. No distinction is made between different kinds of discrimination. Discrimination based on religion or family responsibility has the same status as discrimination on the basis of colour or sexual orientation. The only difference is that, in the former case, it might be justified on rational grounds, whereas differences based on innate characteristics are generally unjustifiable.

As the Court seemed to indicate, and if it is correct that Regulations cannot be questioned in terms of the Act, it may have become necessary to raise these issues in terms of the Constitution.

### The Concept of Equal Conditions for Equal Work or Work of Equal Value

As indicated earlier in this chapter, a new Section 6(4) in the Employment Equity Amendment Act 47 of 2013 now also prohibits discrimination in the conditions of service of persons doing the same work, substantially the same work, or work of equal value. However, it would have to be shown that the alleged differentiation is on one of the grounds listed in Section 6(1).

While discrimination between persons doing the same work might not be difficult to prove, this is not so easy as regards the other two criteria, and especially that relating to work of the same value. The legislators evidently foresaw the problem and the minister was tasked to establish regulations to provide guidance in assessing whether, in these cases, there are grounds for alleging discrimination.

Regulation 7 of the Employment Equity Act states that jobs are the same if they are identical or interchangeable (meaning that persons can easily move from one to the other). Even if not identical, jobs may still be the same if workers can reasonably be considered to be doing the same job. (In such cases they would probably be classified as substantially the same.) When it comes to 'jobs of equal value', the regulation states that two jobs may be of equal value if they are equal in respect of:

- responsibility for people, finances or material
- skills or qualifications
- physical, mental or emotional factors
- relevant conditions such as physical and psychological conditions and conditions relating to time and place
- any other factors relevant to particular jobs.

At the same time, the Regulation allows that differentiation may be justified on the grounds of:

- respective seniority
- length of service
- performance
- quality and quantity of work
- structural changes which may allow a demoted employee to remain at a previous salary until others catch up – see *Woolworths (Pty) Ltd v SACCAWU*

*and Others (JA56/2016) [2017] ZALAC 54; [2017] 12 BLLR 1217 (LAC); (2018) 39 ILJ 222 (LAC) (19 September 2017)*

- temporary employment for persons to gain experience
- a shortage of relevant skills
- any other relevant factors.

The Regulation reminds employers that Section 27 of the Employment Equity Act obliges them to produce an income differential statement for each level in the organisation and to indicate which measures are being taken to reduce differences.

The Code of Good Practice: Work of Equal Value also lists the grounds for differentiation and emphasises that proving that these are legitimate starts with proper job evaluation based on provable criteria.

## Case Review: Discrimination between Employees Doing the Same Work

*Pioneer Foods (Pty) Ltd v Workers against Regression (WAR), CCMA, Commissioner Johnson NO (C687/15) [2016] ZALCCT 14; [2016] 9 BLLR 942 (LC); (2016) 37 ILJ 2872 (LC) (19 April 2016)*

### Background

This case hinged on a complaint by newer employees at Pioneer that they were being paid 20 per cent less than other employees doing the same work. The employees in question regarded this as especially unfair, as some of them had already worked at Pioneer for set periods as persons supplied by a labour brokerage.

From Pioneer's side it was indicated that the employment of people in a permanent capacity had been part of an agreement with the representative union. Evidently, the union wanted Pioneer to gradually become less reliant on contract labour and to rather employ people on a permanent basis. However, the long-serving employees had been concerned that they would be earning the same as new employees. Consequently, an agreement was reached that the salaries of new appointees would be set at 80 per cent of the going rate for the first two years of employment, whereafter their wage rate would be the same as that of the older employees. These conditions would apply to all new employees and not only those who had previously been employed via a labour broker.

At the CCMA it was argued by the union, on behalf of the seven applicants in the case, that the difference amounted to discrimination between union and non-union employees, that van assistants were earning more than drivers and that the policy contravened the dictum of equal pay for equal work.

The Commissioner concluded that the differentiation was indeed discriminatory, was not rational and had been based on arbitrary grounds. Pioneer was ordered to equalise the wage rates and to pay damages to the applicants.

Pioneer then took the matter to the Labour Court.

## Argument and Pronouncements

At the outset, the Labour Court pointed out that the employees, as represented by the union, had not alleged discrimination on any of the listed grounds and that if they were to allege that the differentiation was on an arbitrary ground, they would have to prove that it was not rational and was unfair. A party alleging pay discrimination had to show that the employees were providing equal work or work of equal value. Also, they had to identify the arbitrary ground and could not just make a blanket accusation. Where differentiation was alleged, the adjudicator had to question whether the practice amounted to discrimination. If it was on a listed ground and had been proven to exist, it would be automatically unfair. If the allegation was brought on an arbitrary ground, then the arbitrator would have to decide whether it had 'the potential to impair the dignity of persons as human beings or to affect them adversely in a comparably serious manner'.

From there, the Court reviewed the reasons for the differentiation, as presented by management, concluding emphatically that nothing in the Employment Equity Act prevents an employer from adopting and implementing a rule that newer employees should be employed at a lower rate. As the Court pointed out, there is different treatment everywhere in society. Differentiation only becomes actionable if not rational and if based on one of the listed grounds.

The Court then looked at the manner in which the case had been presented, noting that there was a lack of clarity as to the grounds for the allegation of discrimination. It was not sufficient merely to state that there was discrimination. The allegation had to be linked to one of the listed grounds. That the applicants were new employees was not a listed ground, nor was the practice irrational or one which impaired the human dignity of the applicants. Furthermore, both Section 198D(2)(a) of the Labour Relations Act and the Code of Good Practice accept that length of service and seniority could be legitimate grounds for different conditions of employment.

Having dealt with the matter at hand, the Labour Court referred to the opinion expressed by the Constitutional Court that for courts to adjudicate all differences 'in every classification of rights, benefits and advantages' would be an impossible task. Persons alleging discrimination must prove that the practice has 'crossed the border of constitutional impermissibility and is unequal in the constitutional sense'. According to the Labour Court, it is accepted that a modern country cannot be regulated without differentiation, but differentiation is not necessarily discrimination.

In support of its conclusions, the Labour Court referred to the ILO's Convention No 111, which also states that if the allegation of discrimination is on an unlisted ground, the complainant will have to show that it does have the effect of 'nullifying or impairing the equality of opportunity in treatment or occupation or fundamental human dignity'.

Returning to the case at hand, the Court once again emphasised that length of service was an accepted reason for differentiation. Moreover, in the case of Pioneer, there had been an underlying reason, namely to create more permanent jobs. Also, incumbents were told at the outset that they would be paid at 80 per cent of the rate and had the choice beforehand to accept or not accept. Admittedly, the fact that the policy had been negotiated with the representative union cannot in itself be a justification. Whether it is good would, according to the Court, depend on its purpose.

The final pronouncement of the Court was that the differentiation was not irrational and that the Commissioner should have dismissed the application by the employees. As the parties would have to continue to build their relationship, no costs were awarded.

## Discussion

This was the first case to be brought in terms of the provision which includes unequal conditions of employment as a possible ground for alleging discrimination. When the Act was amended, the subclause was widely labelled as the 'Equal Pay for Equal Work' clause. The implication was that in all cases where work was equal, pay had to be equal.

This judgment, as well as the detailed Code of Good Practice, shows that the matter is not so simple. In the first place, the relevant section relates to all conditions of service and not only wages. Most importantly, and as emphasised by the Court, any allegation of inequality has to be based on one of the named reasons in Section 6(1) or on any other arbitrary reason. If the differentiation is proved to be on one of the named reasons, it will automatically be accepted as unfair. However, if the case is brought on another (arbitrary) ground, the onus will be on the applicant to prove not only that it does discriminate, but that the differentiation:

- is unequal discrimination in terms of the Constitution

- has the 'potential to impair the dignity of persons as human beings'

- can 'affect them adversely in a comparably serious manner'

- has the effect of 'nullifying or impairing equality of opportunity in treatment or occupation'.

In simple terms, the differentiation has to have a serious and noticeable effect on the employee/s.

As was so clearly stated by the Court, differentiation is common to modern society and is most often there for good reason. Differentiation does not necessarily equal discrimination. Employees need to be sure that they can prove unacceptable grounds for alleging discrimination and should not jump too readily on the bandwagon of equal pay for equal work.

## Implications of Non-discrimination Legislation for Policies, Procedures and Practices in General

The strict prohibition on discrimination places an obligation on employers to review all policies, procedures and practices in order to ensure that they do not contain or involve any form of discrimination or unjustifiable differentiation. This could be regarded as the first step of the equity process. In many instances, what used to be accepted practice may on closer examination be found to be discriminatory, pointing to the imperative to interrogate all existing practices.

Before the Labour Relations Act 66 of 1995 was promulgated, applicants for positions, and even persons applying for promotion posts in an organisation, had no or little recourse if they suspected that their failure to be appointed to a particular position was due to unfair discrimination. This left recruiters and selectors free from accountability for their decisions. In these circumstances the possibility of undesirable practices, such as nepotism, discrimination and victimisation, is self-evident.

The inclusion of applicants under discrimination provisions, and also as regards affirmative action initiatives, has greatly changed this situation. The Employment Equity Act is silent on the issue of recruitment, but the Green Paper on Employment Equity dealt in some detail with this aspect. It warned that recruitment efforts should reach all possible candidates and that word-of-mouth recruiting should be discouraged, except when it is aimed at headhunting for affirmative action candidates. In 2005, the government published the Code of Good Practice on the Integration of Employment Equity into Human Resource Policies and Practices. The Code contains, among other things, detailed guidelines relating to recruitment and selection of employees.

To guard against discrimination in selection, the shortlisting, interviewing and assessment procedures of organisations require careful review. These processes should not be left to one person. This is supported by the Code, which recommends that decisions be taken by a representative panel.

The Code further emphasises that relevant criteria should be applied in assessing candidates. The criteria can be established only if the key performance areas and the competencies required for the position have been identified. The criteria themselves should not be discriminatory. This happens when criteria such as qualifications not truly necessary to ensure competence are added as a means of excluding certain groups. Once criteria have been agreed upon, shortlisting can be completed. This is done by first ruling out applicants who do not meet the minimum requirements and, thereafter, those whose CVs do not reflect competence in the key performance areas.

The interviews and other forms of assessment should be structured in terms of the criteria which will be used to evaluate the candidates and should be the same for all persons being assessed. Questions which are irrelevant and might lead to suspicions of bias should be avoided.

Applicants have become increasingly aware of their right to question selections. It is therefore essential that records of interviews be kept, and that final selections are well motivated, so that any queries which arise may be answered in full.

## Affirmative Action

### The Legal Position
#### Definition of Affirmative Action
Section 15 of the Employment Equity Act describes affirmative action measures as 'measures designed to ensure that suitably qualified people from designated groups have equal employment opportunities and are equitably represented in all occupational levels of the workforce of a designated employer'.

#### Designated Groups
Designated groups are defined to include 'black people, women and people with disabilities', with 'black people' being defined as a generic term to include all persons not described as white. The problem with this definition is that, while it may be grammatically correct, it does not serve any purpose when it comes to affirmative action practices, since employers still have to report in terms of the different race groups (see the *Solidarity* case review later on in this chapter). The Employment Equity Amendment Act 47 of 2013 further amended the definition of 'blacks' by limiting it to persons who are South African citizens by birth or descent, who became citizens by naturalisation before 27 April 1994, or who became citizens by naturalisation after 27 April 1994 because they were previously entitled to citizenship but were prevented from claiming this right because of apartheid policies.

#### Designated Employers
The rest of Chapter III of the Act sets out the obligations of designated employers as regards affirmative action. Designated employers in the private sector are, among others, those who employ more than 50 people. According to Bill B14-2020, employers who employ fewer than 50 employees no longer fall within the definition of designated employer, regardless of their annual turnover. These employers are not required to comply with Chapter III of the Act relating to affirmative action. Schedule 4 of the Employment Equity Act indicates the following applicable turnovers (at the time this chapter was written):

- R6 million – Agriculture
- R22.5 million – Mining and Quarrying
- R30 million – Manufacturing
- R30 million – Electricity, Gas and Water
- R15 million – Construction
- R45 million – Retail, Motor trade and Repair services
- R75 million – Wholesale trade, Commercial agents and Allied trades
- R15 million – Catering, Accommodation and other Trade
- R30 million – Transport, Storage and Communications
- R30 million – Finance and Business services
- R15 million – Community, Special and Personal services

## The Nature of Affirmative Action

The term 'affirmative action' refers to the purposeful and planned placement or development of competent or potentially competent persons in or to positions from which they may have been debarred in the past. The rationale is to redress past disadvantages and to make the workforce at all levels more representative of the population, on local and national levels. Affirmative action has numerous facets. It entails:

- the search for persons with known competencies or potential to fill positions worthy of their ability
- the training and development of previously disadvantaged persons so that they may in future possess greater mobility
- continuous monitoring and adaptation of the demographic spread at all levels of the organisation.

## Duties of Designated Employers

Chapter III of the Employment Equity Act obliges every designated employer to put measures in place to promote affirmative action. These measures include:

- the elimination of barriers
- the furthering of diversity
- making reasonable accommodation for persons from designated groups
- training
- the establishment of numerical targets.

The Act, in Section 15(4), states that these measures do not include the establishment of 'an absolute barrier to the prospective or continued employment of persons who are not from designated groups'. This indicates that targets are not absolute and should be guidelines rather than quotas.

All designated employers are required to produce an equity plan, to review progress on an annual basis and to report in October of each year on progress made in implementing the plan and bringing about greater equity.

In producing the plan employers need to:

- consult with employees
- conduct an analysis of the workforce
- develop strategies and set targets to redress demographic imbalances
- report to the director-general annually on progress made towards the achievement of equity
- report on reasonable steps taken to train, appoint and promote suitably qualified persons from the designated groups
- report to the Commission for Employment Equity on income differentials in the various occupational levels and categories.

## Monitoring, Enforcement and Legal Proceeding

The Act strengthens the requirements for compliance with the provisions, as amended in 2013. There are various fines for failure to comply with the affirmative action provisions as indicated in Chapter III. Non-compliance with the provisions of the Employment Equity Act is monitored through complaints by any employee or trade union representative, the employment equity registry, labour inspections and reviews by the director general. Discretion seems to vest in the departmental inspector to decide whether to issue or not issue a compliance order or undertaking to comply. If an employer fails to comply with an order, the department will be entitled to approach the court directly. The amendments mean that there is no longer a right to review of compliance orders for employers. Additionally, an employee trade union representative may bring an allegation of non-compliance of the Act to the attention of another employee, employer, trade union, workplace forum, labour inspector or the director-general of the Commission for Employment Equity. In this regard, the labour inspector is authorised to enter the employer's premises, question staff and inspect documents, if necessary. Previously, the inspector had to first obtain an undertaking to comply from a non-complying employer; a compliance order could then be issued if there was no compliance with the undertaking to comply. Alternatively, the labour inspector could directly issue a compliance order; if there is no compliance with the order, then the labour inspector could apply to the Labour Court to make the compliance order, or any part of such, an order of the Labour Court. Schedule 1 of the Act provides for certain fines, as set out in Table 4.1, imposed for contravention of the Act.

**Table 4.1:** Schedule 1: Maximum permissible fines that may be imposed for contravening the Employment Equity Act 55 of 1998

| Previous contravention | Contravention of any provision of sections 16, 19, 22, 24, 25, 26 and 43(2) | Contravention of any provisions of sections 20, 21, 23 and 44(b) |
|---|---|---|
| No previous contravention | R1 500 000 | R1 500 000 or 2% of turnover, whichever is greater |
| A previous contravention in respect of the same provision | R1 800 000 | R1 800 000 or 4% of turnover, whichever is greater |
| A previous contravention with the previous 12 months or two previous contraventions in respect of the same provision within three years | R2 100 000 | R2 100 000 or 6% of turnover, whichever is greater |
| Three previous contraventions in respect of the same provision within three years | R2 400 000 | R2 400 000 or 8% of turnover, whichever is greater |
| Four previous contraventions in respect of the same provisions within three years | R2 700 000 | R2 700 000 or 10% of turnover, whichever is greater |

In assessing compliance, the factors that will be taken into account could include:

- national and regional demographics
- reasonable steps to appoint and promote persons from the designated groups
- reasonable steps to train persons from the designated groups
- efforts made by the employer to bring about equity and eliminate barriers.

The courts have repeatedly stated that they would hesitate to interfere where the employer has a rational equity plan established in consultation with employee representatives. This, together with the 'reasonable steps' criterion above, points to the necessity of developing a proper plan in the prescribed manner.

## Problems with Affirmative Action
### Implementation for the Wrong Reasons
Initially, most of the controversies and problems surrounding affirmative action arose not from the principle as such, but from the manner in which affirmative action was implemented. Wrong implementation occurs because organisations see affirmative action as a political imperative with which they have to comply, and not as a business objective which needs to be sustainable within the framework of the organisational objectives – one of which would be to have as effective and competent a workforce as possible.

### Targets versus Quotas
As indicated above, employers will be judged by the extent to which they have taken 'reasonable steps' to accommodate persons from the previously disadvantaged groups and are encouraged to set 'targets'. Moreover, Section 15 of the Act, which deals with affirmative action measures, specifically states, in sections 15(3) and (4), that the measures taken should include numerical goals but not quotas and that nothing in a policy or practice should be an absolute barrier to the employment or advancement of persons from the non-designated groups. As can be seen from the *Solidarity* case review discussed later on in this section, the distinction between targets and quotas is very subtle and has become quite controversial.

### Window Dressing
Persons may be appointed to positions mainly to 'window dress', usually without due consideration of their suitability for the position or the possibility of support and development. Chapter III of the Act encourages diversity in the workplace based on equal dignity and respect for all people. Arbitrary appointments leave other employees dissatisfied and are unfair to the appointees themselves, since they are either placed in meaningless positions or are unable to handle their specified tasks. This perpetuates the myth that affirmative action appointees are 'no good'. Unless affirmative action is tied to valid selection procedures that test relevant competencies or potential and are accompanied, where necessary, by a developmental programme, the myth becomes a reality.

### Shortage of Suitably Qualified Candidates
Another problem with affirmative action was that at the beginning the available pool of previously disadvantaged persons able to fulfil the requirements was too small. For example, in organisations where a need had been identified for greater representation of black people at managerial level, and where one of the requirements was a tertiary qualification, the selectors may have

encountered problems. Statistics show that the percentage of black graduates initially remained small in relation to the total population. The result was that there developed a small, highly sought-after group of people who often hopped from one opportunity to another. In recent years the situation has greatly improved.

## Too Little Emphasis on Training and Development

When the Employment Equity Act was first put into practice, one of the problems was that employers tended to look for 'ready-made products', with the possibility of emphasis being placed on quotas and paper qualifications instead of competencies, experience levels and potential. This pointed to education and training, both inside and outside the organisation, as the cornerstone of affirmative action programmes. One part of affirmative action should concentrate on career planning, training and development, or support for external education and training programmes. This is why there is a definite link between affirmative action and skills development.

## Perceptions of Reverse Discrimination

The most prevalent accusation directed at affirmative action initiatives was that they constitute reverse discrimination. Employees who had given long service and were expecting promotion were dissatisfied when an affirmative action appointee, usually from outside, was given a position which they believed they deserved.

Affirmative action becomes unfair and discriminatory only if a previously disadvantaged person is appointed 'at all costs' and without granting other persons the opportunity to compete. Discrimination occurs only when one party is intentionally disadvantaged. This would happen if an applicant or employee who is competent to do the job but does not meet the affirmative action requirements is deliberately disregarded.

Section 15(4) of the Act states that the requirement for affirmative action measures does not oblige a designated employer to institute an employment policy or practice that would be an absolute barrier to persons who are not from the designated group. All candidates should be granted the opportunity to compete and to be assessed in terms of pre-established criteria; however, an additional weighting, which should not be disproportionate to the other criteria, can be placed on affirmative action aspects. This means that the affirmative action candidate is given an edge over the other candidates. It ensures relative fairness and also satisfies the employer's need to appoint competent persons.

If the process above is to operate effectively, the use of appropriate selection techniques and suitable test or assessment material becomes imperative.

### Definition of 'Black People'

As indicated previously in this chapter, the Act states that the term 'black people' is generic and includes coloured and Indian people. However, when reporting on employment equity, these are all separate categories. The differentiation is regarded as necessary from the point of view that Africans are assumed to have been the most disadvantaged under previous policies. The Act requires that workplaces should eventually reflect the demographic profile of the population.

### Regional versus National Demographics

If the organisation is to become more representative of the population, then ideally all previously disadvantaged groups should be targeted for affirmative action. For this, planners need to be acquainted with the demographic spread of the economically active or potentially economically active population, and to compare this to their internal demographics – both in the organisation as a whole and in different job categories.

The Act refers to both national and regional demographics. It would seem most logical to base representation on the area from which the organisation draws its workforce and custom and to ensure that applying a particular demographic profile does not result in gross unfairness. In the case of *Munsamy v Minister of Safety and Security and Another (D253/03) [2013] ZALCD 5; [2013] 7 BLLR 695 (LC) (3 April 2013)*, the SAPS granted the KwaZulu-Natal division 195 promotional posts, bringing the total managerial level posts to 479. They were subsequently given a directive that the agreed ratio was 70 per cent black representation and 30 per cent white. The directive was based on the national demographics applicable at that stage. It emerged that, in order to achieve these numerical goals, Africans had to be awarded 192 posts. As there were only 195 promotion posts available, this target meant that almost 100 per cent of the proposed posts were to be given to these applicants. Munsamy, who had already been recommended for one of the posts, was informed that an African applicant would be appointed, since Indians were already, in terms of the national demographics, over-represented in KwaZulu-Natal.

In this case the Labour Court agreed that the affirmative action measure taken against Munsamy constituted unfair discrimination. The Act specifically states that there should be no absolute barrier to the appointment of any group. The use of national demographics without any further considerations, without a proper equity plan and without taking into account the demographic profile in KwaZulu-Natal was judged to be inappropriate.

The Employment Equity Amendment Act 47 of 2013 provided that the minister, in consultation with the National Economic Development and Labour Council (NEDLAC), could specify the circumstances in which national instead of regional demographics should predominate, and vice versa. Shortly after the pronouncements in the *Solidarity* case (discussed shortly), the following guidelines were published:

- Organisations with 150 or more employees should use national demographics as a guide when selecting applicants for appointment in top management and senior management, as well as for positions requiring professionally qualified persons. An average between national and regional demographics can be applied for lower levels.
- Organisations employing fewer than 150 persons can use national demographics in appointing top and senior management and regional demographics for all other levels.

It should be remembered that these are only guidelines and are not cast in stone. As the *Solidarity* case review below shows, when it comes to representation, everything is relative.

The question of relative representativeness is one of the central themes of affirmative action. Unfortunately, numerous organisations implement affirmative action policies that favour only a narrow grouping of the total spread of previously disadvantaged persons. This is bound to cause dissatisfaction. Also, demographics should provide only a guideline, since effectiveness and fairness remain important criteria for selection.

## Case Review: National and Regional Demographics and Quotas

*Solidarity and Others v Department of Correctional Services and Others (CA23/13) [2015] ZALAC 6; 2015 (4) SA 277 (LAC); [2015] 7 BLLR 649 (LAC); (2015) 36 ILJ 1848 (LAC) (10 April 2015)*

### Background

In 2010 the Department of Correctional Services finalised its third employment equity plan. According to the Constitutional Court, the plan had evidently been agreed to by most of the recognised unions. Solidarity was not a recognised union. The plan set numerical targets for the next five years, based on the national demographics for the economically active population at that time. The targets set were as follows: 9.3 per cent white males and females, 79.3 per cent African males and females, 8.8 per cent coloured males and females, and 2.5 per cent Indian males and females. The plan did allow for deviations from its prescriptions, especially where scarce skills or operational requirements were involved, but only the national commissioner has the power to allow deviations. The national commissioner also has the power to directly appoint someone to a post.

In 2011 a number of posts in the Western Cape became vacant. The litigants, who, with one exception, were coloured, had all applied for a post. Following their interviews, nine of the applicants were recommended. However, only one coloured female was eventually appointed. The rest were told that, in terms of the targets set in the plan, coloured people and white people were already over-represented at the levels in question. In fact, the strategy for the higher levels was to appoint women and black people.

The applicants were not satisfied with the decision and took the case to the CCMA. From there they approached the Labour Court, where they alleged the following:

- The failure to consider them for appointment amounted to unfair discrimination and constituted an unfair labour practice.

- The Department's 2010 employment equity plan was invalid, as it did not comply with the Employment Equity Act.

- The plan was discriminatory as applied to the litigants.

## At the Labour Court

The Labour Court agreed that the plan did not conform to the provisions of the Act. The Act referred to all black persons, but in this case no consideration had been given to the demographics of the Western Cape. This amounted to discrimination not protected by the Act. The Act also allows for proportionality, balance and fairness, requiring that both national and regional demographics be taken into account.

The Labour Court made no ruling as regards the applicants, but did order the Department to immediately take steps in order to ensure that both national and regional demographics be taken into account.

The Department then took the case to the Labour Appeal Court.

## At the Labour Appeal Court

The Labour Appeal Court indicated that, in conducting an inquiry into the equity plan, the following questions had to be answered:

- Does it target persons disadvantaged by discrimination?

- Is it designed to protect and advance persons from the designated groups?

- Does it promote the achievement of equality?

The Court then turned to the allegation by the litigants that the plan entailed quotas, which, they said, was proved by the fact that at certain levels white people were preferred while at other levels no white people were appointed.

In response to this, the Court indicated that the allowance for deviation from the plan made the numerical targets flexible, proved by the fact that from 2010 to 2012 there were 13 appointments in the Western Cape which did not conform to the targets. Furthermore, the 'suitably qualified' criterion was applied for selection. There was also consideration for the retention of special skills and for regional as well as national demographics.

The Court concluded that, although there was a weight given to certain aspects, this did not amount to quotas and there was no blanket obstacle to non-designated groups. According to this Court, the plan passed the test and the appeal was therefore dismissed.

Solidarity then took the case to the Constitutional Court.

## At the Constitutional Court

The Constitutional Court commenced by noting that both the Labour Court and the Labour Appeal Court had declared the equity plan to be invalid.

From there the Court turned to the allegation that the plan in question was based on quotas, admitting that if it rested on quotas, the plan would not have complied with the Act, and the decision not to appoint the plaintiffs would be wrong. As explained by the Court, quotas are rigid, while numerical targets are flexible. The complainants had argued that although the plan made provision for deviation, this was limited, since only the national commissioner could grant exemptions, non-compliant managers were sanctioned and there was no provision for grievances.

To this the Court responded that the plan had to be looked at holistically. The fact that deviations were allowed would indicate that the requirements were not quotas. It went on to point out that the national commissioner had wide-ranging powers and that numerous deviations had been allowed, also in the Western Cape, where deviations had been more than the 13 mentioned previously. The Court disagreed with the opinion expressed in a second judgment that the plan provided for quotas (see below). According to the Court, the fact that the plan provided for deviations proved that it was flexible and that the goals were targets and not quotas. It was also pointed out that even the litigants' 'expert' witness had agreed that the targets were flexible.

The Court then addressed the allegation that the failure to appoint the litigants amounted to unfair discrimination and an unfair labour practice, as well as their demand that the plan be declared invalid. Having summarised the duties of the employer in ensuring equitable representation, the Court singled out the duty to set numerical goals. These, however, needed to take into account both the national and regional demographics. In this case the Department had used only the national profile. In failing to also use the demographics of the region, the Department had breached a rule and had acted unlawfully. The rule requiring that regional demographics also be considered could not be disregarded. According to the Court, by not appointing the qualifying coloured applicants, the Department had engaged in 'acts of discrimination'.

The Department was ordered to reinstate all applicants, except one, who had not qualified, one who had been appointed in the meantime, and the white applicant. The orders were retrospective to the date when they should have been appointed. Where the positions for which the applicants had applied had not yet been filled, they were to be appointed to those posts and compensated for the period which had elapsed in-between. Where the posts had already been filled, the applicants would remain in their present posts but be remunerated at the level of the post for which they had applied and also be compensated as if they had been in the post from the original date.

## Minority Judgment

The minority judgment agreed with the sanction imposed, but was of the opinion that the final decision was based on very narrow grounds. This aside, the main point of disagreement was the conclusion by the Court that the Department's equity plan had set flexible targets and not quotas.

According to this judgment, one of the fundamental questions was whether the imperative to ensure full and equal enjoyment of all rights and freedoms for previously disadvantaged groups also meant that a person in this group had a right to a particular job. In this respect it was pointed out that the purpose of affirmative action is to 'promote' equality – that, in terms of the Act, this could happen by giving preference to previously disadvantaged persons, while at the same time taking into consideration the promotion of economic development and efficiency. The manner in which numerical targets had been established and implemented was not compliant with the precepts of the Act and had not taken note of all the duties of the employer as set out in the Act.

The judgment went on to explain that, although the Courts had accepted that, in pursuing equality, some persons may experience more harm than others, it should not unduly invade the human dignity of individuals. The pursuit of equity was intended to eventually produce a non-racial, non-sexist and socially inclusive society.

Referring to the numerous instances where the Constitutional Court had cautioned that implementing equity should be undertaken in a nuanced, balanced manner, the judgment indicated that one would have expected a 'thoughtful, empathetic and textured' plan, qualities which the Department's plan did not exhibit. Instead, there were only numbers, based on two ratios only, namely racial groups and a male/female category.

It was also established that the figures on which the numerical goals had been based were incorrect. In the first place it was claimed that they were based on the 2005 statistics and as such were in line with the 2006 census, but there had been no census in 2006. Furthermore, they were based on the entire South African population and not only the economically active population, as required by the Act. This was followed by 'arithmetic tables' allocating numbers to match the ratios, accompanied by instructions to the responsible officials to 'fill the gaps'.

The judgment reflects the instructions given at all levels, of which the following are a few examples:

- Level 3: Only white and Indian people
- Level 4: 9 African males and 1 African female and 1 coloured male
- Level 5: Only African females and white people
- Level 7: 684 African males, 331 African females and 10 Indian females
- Levels 11 and 12: 109 African females
- Levels 13–16: Too many African males (none to be appointed), 24 African females and 1 Indian female
- Level 14: 3 African females and 1 white female
- Level 15: 2 African females and 1 white female.

These are described as hallmarks which must apply throughout. As the judgment recorded, any form of non-compliance would be classified as a transgression and be punishable as per the guidelines of the Department of Labour, which was termed the 'watchdog' over these 'transgressions'.

These, according to the judgment, were not numerical targets, but quotas. They had 'the look, characteristics and flavour of quotas'. It was noted that, according to the dictionary definition of a quota, it is 'an allocation which is in some sense due'. If one looked at the plan, there was an allocation of persons in terms of numbers, which had to be implemented, meaning the allocations were due. Therefore, they were quotas.

As for the argument that there was allowance in the plan for deviations, the judgment pointed out that these related only to persons with special skills, such as nurses, doctors and social workers, and to operational requirements. These were special cases. The concern should be for the general application of the plan, not these special cases. As maintained in this judgment, when the national commissioner allowed deviation from the plan, they were not acting in terms of the plan but treating the deviations as exceptions to the plan. One had to ask not about the special cases but whether there was flexibility in general, and this was not the case. In fact, the plan could not be more rigid. One could not tell people without special skills that the plan was flexible.

The so-called numerical goals were, according to this judgment, not guidelines at all. Once the 'target' had been achieved there were 'rigid barriers'. All that would be taken into account were the numbers, this even though the Act leaves room for discretion, as suggested by the employment equity guidelines. There were absolute barriers to the employment of certain groups at various levels. This, according to the judgment, was the same as the apartheid policy of job reservation.

The judgment conceded that the targets could not just be discarded – that mostly they would act as guidelines – but it nevertheless indicated that they should never constitute an absolute barrier to other groups.

In conclusion, the judgment touched on the subject of national and regional demographics. It agreed that the demographic profile of organisations should reflect all the characteristics of the population. However, the policies should be rational and should not be based on only one characteristic.

The purpose of employment equity is to bring about representation and equitable access to employment opportunities. People are mainly able to access such opportunities in the place where they live. There are numerous anomalies in the national demographics related to the spread of different groups across the various provinces. These need to be taken into account. For example, the Western Cape has a population of 48.8 per cent coloured people, yet the Department's plan restricted this population group to 8.8 per cent representation. The Department had no explanation for this anomaly, which, according to the judgment, is not rational and not normal.

## Discussion

These two judgments reflect the complexity of the affirmative action legislation and emphasise the fact that no single factor can be applied without consideration of all the others.

There is a very fine line between affirmative action and social engineering. This is hinted at in the second judgment when it emphasises that the purpose of the equity legislation is to eventually bring about a non-racial, non-sexist and all-inclusive society. This implies that society, and the workplace, should not be dominated by a certain race group, as happened during the apartheid era. Concentrating on numbers only could well result in a return to the latter.

As for the issues involved in the case, it seems that some progress was made as regards regional versus national demographics, although the Regulations later issued by the minister in this regard could still be contentious. As regards targets versus quotas, disagreement remains.

## Initial Steps to Drawing up an Affirmative Action Programme
*Nomination of a Responsible Manager*

The Act stipulates that each designated employer shall appoint a senior manager to take responsibility for affirmative action. This task is not delegated to the HR department, since it is not a staff function imposed on line management, but the responsibility of all line managers. The HR or labour relations practitioner provides advice where necessary.

The designated manager takes responsibility for:
- getting the process started
- reporting to the Department of Labour
- monitoring the programme
- ensuring its success.

*The Consultative Body*

The Labour Relations Act determines that affirmative action is subject to joint decision making by management and the workplace forum. The affirmative action strategy is a change strategy and, as such, is developed like any other change policy in collaboration with all stakeholders in the organisation.

In terms of the Employment Equity Act, a representative consultative committee, which includes the union and representatives of every employee category and level and all employee groups, including the non-designated groups, is tasked with establishing affirmative action objectives and policies and planning the necessary strategies.

*Agreement on Basic Principles and Processes*

In the representative consultative committee, agreement is reached regarding:

- principles which will form the basis of their affirmative action programme
- a common understanding of affirmative action
- the meaning of the term 'representative'
- whether or when regional or national demographics or both will be considered
- the affirmative action objectives of the organisation
- broad time frames for achieving various objectives
- the recruitment and selection of suitably qualified persons
- the interpretation of the term 'suitably qualified'
- the manner in which candidates for positions are to be canvassed and selected
- the possibility of developing persons within the organisation (education and training)
- monitoring and performance appraisal systems applicable to all employees
- support systems for persons whose performance does not meet requirements
- support to be given to training and education initiatives inside and outside the organisation
- the sensitisation of other employees to affirmative action initiatives
- programmes to change attitudes.

*Involvement of All Employees*

Once a policy and strategy have been agreed upon, these are shared with all employees in the organisation – possibly via the different stakeholders on the consultative committee. Affirmative action initiatives which are implemented without proper consultation cause distrust and fear, leading either to disregard of the initiative or, at worst, to constant sabotage.

*Review of Existing Policies, Practices and Procedures*

The consultative committee interrogates all existing policies, practices and procedures for indications of discrimination, and addresses discrimination where it does exist. A review of recruitment and selection processes is usually the first step.

*Identification of Barriers*

Barriers are those aspects of the work environment which would prevent or discourage persons from designated groups from obtaining employment or would limit their opportunity for advancement. These may include, in the case of women, the working hours and the lack of childcare facilities.

*Determining the Workforce Profile*

One of the first steps is an analysis of the workforce at all levels and in all job categories in terms of race and gender, in order to identify areas in which persons from the designated groups are under-represented. Representativeness is assessed by comparing the workforce profile to the regional or national demographics, or a combination of the two, depending on the location of the business and the policy adopted by the organisation.

Once the workforce profile has been established, the organisation is ready to develop its equity plan.

## The Equity Plan
*Numerical Goals and Time Frames*

The workplace profile will have identified areas of under- and over-representation of different groups at different levels of the organisation. The plan is aimed at establishing measures to address under- and over-representation and must set time frames and specify strategies to address these problems, taking into account the threats and opportunities involved. For example, the plan must address:

- the labour turnover and retirement rate in the organisation
- the available labour pool of qualified persons
- present and planned vacancies
- the financial position of the organisation
- future plans
- conditions in the external environment
- the regional and national demographics
- opportunities presented by the skills development initiatives.

Once a realistic picture emerges, planners return to the identified areas of under-representation and agree on numerical goals and time frames, bearing in mind obstacles to the achievement of goals. The plan indicates how the goals will be achieved, and how the obstacles and barriers will be overcome.

### Other Affirmative Action Measures

The Employment Equity Act specifies that, in addition to the numerical goals, the equity plan should also reveal measures to:

- eliminate barriers – the identified barriers are listed and strategies and time frames to eliminate these are recorded
- further diversity – this calls for creative initiatives to promote and encourage diversity in the workplace
- provide reasonable accommodation for previously disadvantaged persons.

Although some of these measures may have been instituted under the elimination of barriers, it is necessary to go further and to consider strategies such as mentorship and flexi-time.

### Retention, Training and Development

It has unfortunately been the case that so-called 'prime' affirmative action candidates engage in perennial job-hopping. Alternatively, candidates leave because of a hostile climate, because they find themselves in dead-end jobs or because they are not provided with the necessary training or career development. The issue of retention may have been addressed under other measures, but it is necessary to provide specifics of the training and development to be provided, not only for targeted affirmative action candidates, but also for the total workforce. (The format of the skills development plan demands that training by race and gender be reflected in that plan.)

### Process for Implementation

The equity plan outlines the implementation process and specifies the persons responsible. Once the plan is finalised and all parties agree, the plan is made public in the organisation.

## Monitoring and Evaluation

Regular monitoring and evaluation, which may be based on specific benchmarks, should be undertaken by the persons responsible for the various aspects, as well as the consultative committee or co-ordinating structure and the senior manager who is ultimately accountable:

- The consultative forum(s) will continue to meet on a regular basis, to review progress reports.
- Developments are recorded and communicated to employees at meetings, which should take place at reasonable intervals.

- If needs be, the plan is reviewed and revised through consultation (as per Section 9 of the Code of Good Practice).

## Communication and Reporting

By law, the plan must be communicated to all participants and be open to scrutiny at all times.

It is the function of the responsible senior manager to report to the Department of Labour on equity initiatives on an annual basis and to complete the prescribed forms. The report on income differentials needs to be submitted at the same time.

## The Need for Periodic Reviews

It can be safely assumed that most existing organisations have complied with the legislation, have equity programmes in place and are reporting on a regular basis. However, creating equity is a continuous process, not only in terms of monitoring progress, but also when it comes to bringing about changes. A stage may in fact be reached where all requirements have been met and where the crunching of numbers is no longer necessary, or even where disadvantage is suffered by persons from the non-designated group. The process of organisational development (OD) is ongoing and will take different forms at different stages.

## Grievance and Dispute Procedures

Not only applicants for positions but also persons already employed may raise complaints regarding discrimination or a particular aspect of the affirmative action process. These are dealt with through special structures established under the auspices of the affirmative action committee.

Internal procedures for resolving any dispute about the interpretation and implementation of the plan are agreed upon and specified. The use of existing dispute resolution procedures is encouraged, provided that they are appropriate and, if necessary, adapted to the needs of employment equity. Alternatively, a mechanism with appropriate representation of the employer and employees may be established in order to address and resolve such disputes (as per Section 8.8 of the Code of Good Practice).

## Case Review: Compliance with Equity Provisions

*Director-General Department of Labour v Win-Cool Industrial Enterprise (Pty) Ltd (Labour Court (D731/05): 6 February; 16 April 2007)*

### Background

Win-Cool is a cut-make-and-trim factory employing 132 people. In 2003, the factory was visited by bargaining council agents, who advised the employer as to the legislative requirements. Because the owner, a Mr Liu, is a foreigner, he approached the Federated Employers' Organisation (FEOSA) to act as consultants in respect of his legislative obligations. In November 2003, his factory was visited by an agent from the Department of Labour, who reported that Win-Cool was not complying with any of the provisions of the Employment Equity Act. She obtained an undertaking from the employer that he would conform with Sections 20 (equity plan), 21(1) (submission of equity report), 25(1) (information to employees on provisions of the Act), 25(2) (displaying of all notices related to equity) and 25(3) (copy of the plan to employees). On 31 March 2004, the agent issued Win-Cool with a compliance order directing him to execute the requirements of the Act, such as, among others, consulting with employees, conducting an analysis, preparing and implementing an employment equity plan, and submitting and publishing a report. Win-Cool did not object to the order, which it was legally entitled to do, but still failed to comply. Finally, in October 2005, an application was made to have the compliance order made an order of the Court. A similar application had been made in October 2004 but had been withdrawn.

Evidently, Win-Cool had first asked FEOSA to deal with its compliance, and, on 29 October 2004, the consultants delivered an equity report to the Department. (At the time of the hearing, this report could not be found.) In January 2005, Mr Liu had 'consulted' with the employees, advising them of the Employment Equity Act and its consequences. He later submitted a letter from the employees in which they expressed 'anger and unhappiness' at the 'case of the Employment Equity Act plan' and the fear that they would lose their jobs. Win-Cool argued that the company had always sought to comply with the order and had even used consultants to assist the company. Its workforce was made up as follows: one coloured senior official or manager; nine African and two coloured technicians, all male; and 120 African females in 'elementary' positions.

### Pronouncements

According to the Court, 'mechanical compliance with the prescribed processes is not genuine compliance with the letter and spirit of the EEA. Compliance is not an end in itself. The employer must systematically develop the workforce out of a life of disadvantage'.

The Court noted that the company had not voluntarily complied with the Employment Equity Act and that it was only after the first application was launched that any attempt was made at submitting a plan. The plan itself had not followed on from interaction with the employees and contained nothing more than a workforce profile and numerical goals. The employer should have consulted with the workforce before submitting the plan and report. He should not have relied on consultants; instead, he should have 'assigned a manager' to take responsibility for employment equity.

The Court concluded that Mr Liu had abdicated his responsibility to consultants who were not as knowledgeable as they should have been, that he only made an effort when litigation was imminent, that he appeared 'manifestly reluctant' to transform the workplace and that he had held only one consultation with employees. There was not enough information for the Court to consider all factors, but what the Court did consider seriously were the concerns of the workforce. With this in mind it imposed a relatively light fine of R300 000, of which R200 000 was suspended on condition that Win-Cool fulfilled its obligations in terms of the compliance order. No costs were ordered.

## Discussion

The application of the strict terms of the Employment Equity Act to an organisation such as Win-Cool appears equal to demanding silver service at a McDonald's. Taking into account the so-called 'letter' from the employees, it is to be questioned whether consultation with the workforce would lead to any better plan than that already presented by Win-Cool. Equally, the nature of the organisation and the work performed may not lend itself to much in the way of development or to 'quality jobs'. As it is, except for the absence of white people, the workforce appears to have been quite representative, particularly of the most previously disadvantaged, namely black women.

The taking of such formal steps in situations such as this corroborates the argument that South African labour law is too restrictive and counters employment creation. South Africa's unemployment rate is of great concern, yet some legislation, and particularly the manner in which it is implemented, does not protect employees but instead threatens their livelihoods. What, after all, prevents Mr Liu from taking his business elsewhere? This is not to say that employers should be left to do as they please. What it means is that those empowered to monitor the implementation of the law should be made aware that nothing, including a law, is absolute. There are always grey areas and there are times when they should use their discretion instead of doggedly following the letter of the law.

In Mr Liu's case, informal advice and assistance or the introduction of union representation might have accomplished more than a compliance order and a fine of R100 000, which could have gone as a bonus to employees.

Admittedly, Mr Liu may not have been treating employees as well as he should.

This having been said, employment equity should not be used to remedy other problems. If Mr Liu was running a sweatshop and not treating his employees properly, this could have been dealt with via the Basic Conditions of Employment Act or the Labour Relations Act. Changing the demographics of the workforce would not have solved the problem.

## Implementing the Affirmative Action Plan
### Selection and Appointment of New Incumbents

The starting point for implementation of the equity plan is the existing and future manpower plan of the organisation. If a position becomes vacant, the equity plan is consulted and the demographics in that job category is studied, in conjunction with the demographics of the organisation as a whole. It may then be decided to advertise that preference will be given to a person from a previously disadvantaged group, or even to headhunt for such a person with the aim of encouraging them to apply. However, this can never be an absolute imperative, since someone from that group with the necessary competencies and experience may not be available to fill the position.

The inherent requirements of the job are central to the selection procedure, and capable candidates cannot be excluded simply because they are not from the preferred group. Because certain groups were disadvantaged as regards education, and also because educational qualifications are not necessarily indicative of competence, these should not, in the case of non-academic or non-professional jobs, constitute the primary criteria. Selectors have to identify the competency requirements of the job and to establish methods whereby such competencies can be tested or assessed. Here the HR department plays an important role.

A common understanding of the term 'suitably qualified' is required. This can be based on:

- formal qualifications
- experience
- the potential to perform the job within a reasonable time.

### Using Weighted Criteria for Selection

Once criteria have been established and assessment techniques developed, a weighting is attached to each criterion. This is where affirmative action candidates can be given an edge by adding membership of a previously disadvantaged group as a criterion and applying a special, proportionate weighting to this. If the demographics have proved that particular groups are less represented in the organisation or job category, the weighting given, for example, to black females could be heavier than that assigned to white females.

*Advertising Vacancies*

Advertisements should list the competencies and experience levels required and should reach as wide an audience as possible. Selectors may actively canvass persons whom they may regard as possible incumbents, but it is not advisable to engage in 'poaching' from other organisations. This merely sustains the elitism of the already employed. It is preferable to approach persons who may not yet be occupying a position at a particular level but who display the potential to grow into the job. These persons should know that they will be competing with others for the position.

*Interviews and Assessments*

All interviews should follow the same pattern, with due regard to (but not overcompensating for) differences in personal experience, culture, language and so forth. The total 'scores' obtained by candidates in tests, assessments and interviews serve as guidelines to identify the best candidates. Once this has been done, the selection panel discusses the merits and demerits of each case, bearing in mind the affirmative action objectives. An affirmative action candidate who may score slightly less than another candidate, but who has displayed the potential to develop into the position, will then in all probability be appointed over the other candidate who may, at this stage, be slightly better, but not that much better. It should not happen that a mediocre or poor affirmative action candidate is appointed in preference to an outstanding person who was not previously disadvantaged or was previously 'less disadvantaged'. This is detrimental both to the organisation and to the appointee, who may not be able to prove themself worthy of the position.

*Targeting All Levels of the Organisation*

The focal point of affirmative action need not necessarily be the higher-level jobs in the organisation. This does not mean that concerted efforts should not be made to change the demographics at these levels, nor that a supposed lack of candidates should be used as an excuse, but organisations should not concentrate merely on such appointments. Their efforts should be directed equally at future manpower requirements and to developing persons from both inside and outside the organisation so that they may eventually fill positions which are bound to be vacated or created.

The developmental aspect of affirmative action is complex. Manpower needs have to be established, and persons with potential identified or appointed. Thereafter, a suitable programme is developed for these persons. Various problems may arise; for example, the persons identified may eventually prove unsuitable, or other employees may be unhappy at not being granted the same opportunity. To avoid dissatisfaction, developmental programmes must be instituted for as wide a group of employees as possible, and not only for new appointees. It must be made clear that eventual promotion will depend on competencies achieved.

### Integrating Employees into the Organisation

All new incumbents, and not only affirmative action appointees, should be properly integrated by way of an effective induction programme. However, in the case of affirmative action candidates, there may be circumstances which dictate that their integration be monitored. This must be done in a sensitive and careful manner, as the purpose is not to treat these candidates differently or specially, but rather to ensure that unnecessary obstacles to their integration are removed. If affirmative action candidates have been properly selected, they will more than likely accomplish their own integration.

### Monitoring and Performance Appraisal

All new employees, whether appointed in terms of an affirmative action policy or not, may be placed on probation and their performance monitored on an ongoing basis. The Labour Relations Act outlines a procedure for this. All employees need to be informed of the standards required and given regular feedback as regards their performance. If they do not meet expectations, they should be given the necessary assistance and training. Any employee who still does not perform satisfactorily may eventually be dismissed.

### Career Planning and Career Development

In all organisations, one facet of manpower planning is succession planning and career development. If this is properly done, it offers an ideal route for developing previously disadvantaged persons from both inside and outside the organisation to fill more important positions. Initiatives in terms of the Skills Development Act 97 of 1998 support this development.

Selecting one or two people and grooming them for future positions may prove unsatisfactory. The training provided should be both general and specific, so that candidates who are not eventually selected for the targeted positions may apply for other positions. This is a long-term strategy but, if the country is to develop a pool of trained manpower, it must be seen as one of the most important aspects of affirmative action.

One of the criteria by which an employer's progress is judged is the extent to which there is support for training and development of existing employees and also persons on learnerships.

*Further Strategies*

Where it has been found that few vacancies are likely to occur, it may be necessary to offer voluntary retrenchment to certain persons, while taking care that necessary skills are retained.

## Challenges when implementing Employment Equity
*Ensuring fairness*

Some employers may believe that they fulfil equity requirements if they appoint mainly black males or, on the other hand, mainly black and white females. This does not reflect the true spirit of the equity legislation. A balance should be sought between racial and gender representation and the appointment of other disadvantaged persons. Also, the non-designated group cannot be automatically excluded.

The *Henn* and *Willemse* cases are interesting examples of how our courts view this balance. In *Henn v SA Technical (Pty) Ltd (2006) 27 ILJ 2617 (LC)*, the applicant for a job, a white female, was rejected because of employment equity demographics. The respondent conceded that it had discriminated against the applicant on the basis of her race, but argued that it was obliged to apply affirmative action measures; therefore, she was not unfairly discriminated against. The Labour Court was satisfied that the respondent's conduct was not contrary to its policy, and that it was justified in giving preference to African females who were suitably qualified. According to this Court, the respondent was entitled to discriminate on the basis of race, as it was complying with affirmative action as provided for in Section 6(2)(a) of the Employment Equity Act.

However, in *Willemse v Patelia NO and Others (J1161/2004) [2006] ZALC 92; [2007] 2 BLLR 164 (LC) (19 October 2006)*, the acting director-general had rejected the recommended applicant because he did not fit into the required demographic profile. The Labour Court regarded the following factors as relevant:

■ The targets as regards gender and race had already been met.
■ The criterion was the level of the post, not the department as a whole.
■ The applicant's disability had been disregarded.

Acting Judge Deon Nel found that the applicant, Dr Willemse, a white male, had been unfairly discriminated against when the Department of Environmental Affairs and Tourism refused to promote him on grounds of gender and race. The Court held that the applicant be appointed in that post and also that he be paid the salary and benefits he would have received had he been appointed earlier.

*'Suitably Qualified'*

As indicated previously, Section 15(1) of the Employment Equity Act describes affirmative action measures as measures designed to ensure that suitably qualified persons from designated groups have equal employment opportunities and are equitably represented in all occupational categories and levels in the workforce of a designated employer. A candidate will be regarded as suitably qualified if they have one of the following attributes:

- Formal qualifications
- Relevant experience
- The potential to perform the job within a reasonable time.

The problem is, first, how to assess potential and, secondly, how to interpret the phrase 'a reasonable time'. The concept of 'reasonable time' was discussed in *Public Servants Association (PSA) obo Karriem v South African Police Service (SAPS) & Another (2007) 28 ILJ 177 (LC)*. The PSA alleged that the SAPS had failed to comply with its obligations in terms of Section 20(4) of the Employment Equity Act. In deciding on the appointment in question, it did not review all the factors for consideration as set out in Section 20(3) of the Act, namely:

- formal qualifications
- prior learning
- relevant experience
- the capacity to learn how to do the job within a reasonable time.

The PSA alleged that the SAPS had breached its obligation to implement affirmative action measures in terms of Chapter III of the Act and in terms of its own employment equity plan, in that it had failed to appoint Ms Karriem, notwithstanding the fact that she was suitably qualified and a coloured woman. The respondent had promoted a white policewoman over a coloured policewoman. Ms Karriem alleged that she had been unfairly discriminated against on the basis of race and the capacity to acquire, within a reasonable time, the ability to do the job.

The Court noted that there had been objective justification for the appointment of the white female based on consideration of all the relevant factors. The Court therefore held that the applicant had not suffered unfair discrimination. This again proves that the mere fact that an individual is competent or can become competent and belongs to a certain group does not guarantee candidacy. The qualifications and demographic profiles of other individuals also have to be considered and each weighed against the other.

The measurement of potential is made more difficult in terms of the care which has to be exercised in using psychological testing or similar forms of assessment. What is necessary is to decide beforehand on the indicators of potential, to use a proven instrument directed at assessing that potential and to be clear as to the time required to develop such potential. When immediate performance at a particular level is required, it would hardly be feasible to consider the aspect of potential. On the other hand, when the opportunity to develop exists, consideration of potential becomes important. The interpretation of 'a reasonable time' therefore depends on the position and the needs of the organisation.

*Internal Recruitment*

Internal recruitment is appropriate when adequate training and development initiatives have been undertaken over time and resulted in strong internal capacity. This may happen when the company is in a growth phase and a fair number of jobs are being created or where internal resources meet most or all requirements of the vacancies and the organisation has clear policies and procedures regarding promotions, transfers and internal movements. Internal recruitment will be acceptable if existing employees from the designated groups are able to fill promotion posts and where it results in the rectification of demographic imbalances. Where an organisation does not have enough potential candidates from the designated groups in its own ranks, an internal recruitment policy cannot be used as an excuse for perpetuating imbalances.

*Candidates-in-waiting and Contract Employees*

Persons already employed may have had their career paths mapped out for them, preventing the appointment of new candidates for future posts. Equally, employees in contract posts may have the expectation that they will receive preference should a permanent position become available. This may stand in the way of appointing affirmative action candidates.

The 2014 amendments to the Labour Relations Act impact on this situation. In terms of the amendments, an employer must provide an employee on a fixed-term contract with the same access to opportunities to apply for vacancies as it would provide to an employee employed on an indefinite employment contract. Where an expectation of renewal or of a permanent position has been created, the dismissal of these employees could be regarded as unfair. These changes also need to be borne in mind when implementing equity.

*Retrenchment and the Last-in-first-out Principle*

Because in many organisations affirmative action initiatives have been recent in nature, these appointees may be the first to be nominated when people to be retrenched are selected in terms of the last-in-first-out (LIFO) principle. This could upset the equity initiative. It is therefore necessary to ascertain whether the proposed retrenchments will create further demographic imbalances. If this is the case, a certain quota of designated employees may need to be excluded from the retrenchment exercise.

### Employing the Disabled

Often, the nature of the work required is such that it cannot be undertaken by disabled persons, nor can the work or workplace be modified to cater for such persons. In these instances, the organisation could consider outsourcing certain tasks to institutions for the disabled, where the work can be performed in more conducive surroundings.

The problems mentioned are not exhaustive. The achievement of equity is bound to involve numerous questions, some of a more general nature and others related to particular organisations.

## Case Review: Affirmative Appointments

*Public Servants Association of SA & Others v Minister of Justice and Others (Transvaal Provincial Division: 4 March 1997)*

### Background

The case arose from the existence of 30 vacant positions in the offices of the state attorney. Prior to the placement of the advertisements for the positions, a meeting had been held between the minister, an employee from the state attorney's office, and various others. The purpose of the meeting was to discuss the staffing of the vacant posts. During the meeting it was proposed that a number of posts be reserved for affirmative action candidates. The employee concerned objected to such senior posts as state attorney being reserved and suggested that existing employees should be promoted on merit. This would create vacancies at the assistant state attorney level, which could then, where possible, be filled with affirmative action candidates. His suggestion was rejected, but he was told that existing employees could also apply for the senior posts. Immediately following the meeting, the employee asked one of the management team whether it would be worthwhile for white males to apply. The reply was that they would be wasting their time.

The eagerness to appoint affirmative action candidates evidently arose from the injunction in the Interim Constitution that a broadly representative public service should be established and from the fact that, in December 1994, the Public Service Staff Code, as contained in the Public Service Act 103 of 1994, had been amended to provide for affirmative action initiatives. However, in terms of the Code, this was to be undertaken only after rationalisation of a particular department and upon presentation of an approved management plan. There was a further injunction to give effect to the affirmative action initiative in a 'balanced' manner and adopting a 'comprehensive, well-planned and structured approach'.

The Department had not yet engaged in rationalisation, nor had it developed a manpower plan. Instead, it chose to gain the approval of the Minister of Public Affairs (the second respondent in the case) to go ahead with affirmative action initiatives as a matter of urgency. In the process it did not consult with the union representing employees.

A large number of the union's members, all white males, applied for the vacant positions. One of the applicants occupied the position of deputy state attorney, while all the others who joined in the dispute were senior state attorneys or senior assistant state attorneys. Experience ranged from 15 to 26 years, and some had been recommended for extraordinary promotion.

As the Court later noted, none of these applicants were invited to an interview, and their applications were considered only for the purpose of rejection on the basis of their race and gender. Instead, three women were interviewed, one of whom had qualified five years before and had only a year's experience in the office of the state attorney, although she had spent four years in private practice.

The PSA had written to management during the process to question the implementation of a non-negotiated initiative, but had been told that it was not a matter of mutual interest. The union thereupon sought an interdict or declaratory order to prevent the Department from continuing with the process.

## Pronouncements

The Court dealt in detail with the credentials of the applicants, Section 212(2) of the Interim Constitution and the relevant sections of the Public Service Act. It also took into account the argument of the union that there had been no explanation of the selection process, that there was no evidence of targeted recruitment at entry level, that there was no provision for existing employees affected by the process, as had been agreed upon, and that affirmative action could not be used as the sole criterion.

The judgment commenced by questioning whether there had been discrimination. The Court referred to *Taylor v Hogg* (CA317/17) [2018] ZAECGHC 64 (10 August 2018) to explain that, for an act to be regarded as discriminatory, it has to be on grounds of immutable personal characteristics. General disadvantage is not required, but particular disadvantage has to be shown – 'the individual must show that he or she has suffered a disadvantage by reason of his or her possession of certain characteristics'. This led the Court to express the opinion that 'the facts fully justify the conclusion that the white male applicants for the state attorney posts have been discriminated against on those very bases. They are white and male'. The next question was whether such discrimination had been unfair.

The Court noted that the Constitution had deliberately singled out affirmative action initiatives as not necessarily being unfair. Nevertheless, the Court underlined the fact that these initiatives are subject to limitations. Having indicated that the onus was on the Department to prove that the measures had not been unfair, it went on to explain that the term 'adequate protection and advancement' meant that:

- objectives, as well as the means of achieving these, were reviewable

- measures should not go 'beyond the adequate'

- merely labelling certain measures as affirmative action measures would 'not suffice'.

Having noted that the question of affirmative action was not in dispute, but rather the Department's way of implementing it, the Court returned to the argument that the 'process of promoting a representative public service is in any event permitted and required by S212(2)(b) which demands a public administration broadly representative of the South African community'. In the opinion of the Court this was 'not an automatic licence to discriminate against others'. In order to disprove the allegation of unfair discrimination, the following were necessary:

- Measures must have been designed – this was the opposite of a 'haphazard or random action'.

- The measures had to be designed to achieve something – there had to be a causal connection between measures and objectives.

- The measures had to provide for the adequate protection and advancement of previously disadvantaged groups – with 'adequate' meaning 'equal in magnitude and extent', 'commensurate in fitness, sufficient, suitable'.

The adequate protection and advancement should be aimed at enabling groups or persons to equally enjoy rights and freedoms – with the word 'equal' connoting that 'interests of targeted persons or groups are not taken into consideration in vacuo, but also with regard to the rights of others, and the interests of the community and the possible disadvantages that the non-targeted persons or groups may suffer'.

Measures had to be evaluated 'in the light of the professions' – they needed to take into account the career-oriented nature of the public service and the necessity to function in terms of fair and equitable principles.

While a broadly representative public service was being promoted, an efficient service also had to be achieved, with the word 'promote' not meaning 'to achieve overnight'. In the Court's opinion, 'a broadly representative public administration can, in terms of S212, not be promoted at the expense of an efficient administration', to which the public and the taxpayer, including targeted persons or groups, are entitled. The Court could envisage circumstances in which both objectives could be achieved – when, for example, candidates from the targeted and non-targeted groups had 'broadly' the same qualifications and merit, and the former was then preferred.

In enquiring whether the requirements mentioned had been met, the Court came to the conclusion that the measures were not designed – they were 'haphazard, at random and overhasty'.

At this point, the Court digressed to question the basis on which it had been decided to earmark the posts. Evidently the Department had decided that representativeness must 'as soon as possible be instituted at all levels of the civil service' and this had resulted in 'the earmarking of posts, in some cases, at or near the very top of the pyramid in a professional department like the State Attorney's office'. The Court was of the opinion that this was not expressly called for by the Constitution' and that it would be unsuitable for targeted persons, other persons such as those in the position of the applicants, and of society at large if posts were earmarked for certain groups without considerations of efficiency.

The Court concluded that affirmative action had been implemented 'without any discernible rationale, which in fact amounted to the exclusion of all the other applicants on the basis of their race and gender'.

## Discussion

In the first place, this case highlights the necessity for an agreed policy and plan before any affirmative action initiatives are undertaken. Secondly, it rejects the common practice of excluding certain categories of applicants from the outset. As happened in this case, such a practice may lead to allegations, and proof, of discrimination. For this reason, positions should not be advertised as affirmative action positions. It can be stated that, in selection, cognisance will be taken of the organisation's equity targets, but that these will be weighed with other criteria.

Overall, the judgment reveals that affirmative action initiatives, like all strategic initiatives, should be placed in context and that consideration should be given to the efficient functioning of the organisation, the effect on other employees, the pool of labour available and the effect that a wrong placement may have on the affirmative action candidate.

## *Du Preez v Minister of Justice & Constitutional Development & Others (South Eastern Cape Local Division sitting in its capacity as an Equity Court (368/2004): 8 December 2005; 13 April 2006)*

### Background

During May 2002, the Magistrates Commission advertised vacant positions for court magistrates in various districts, including Port Elizabeth, where two posts were available. The Commission advises the minister on the appointment of judicial officers and is supposed to ensure that judicial officers are appointed 'without favour or prejudice'. Du Preez, a white male with 19 years' experience as a magistrate and holder of a BJuris, LLB and master's degree in public administration, was one of the applicants for a position. He did not make the shortlist. Two black female candidates with lesser qualifications and experience were nominated by the Commission.

In terms of the Magistrates Act 90 of 1993, magistrates are judicial officers who are independent of the public service and are not employees as defined by the Employment Equity Act. Consequently, Du Preez brought an action in terms of the Promotion of Equality and Prevention of Unfair Discrimination Act 4 of 2000, which is very similar to the Employment Equity Act but also applies to the wider public. Du Preez claimed that he had been discriminated against on the basis of race and because of the 'irrational, unreasonable and unconstitutional criteria' applied by the committee responsible for shortlisting the applicants for the vacant positions.

From the affidavits presented to the court, it emerged that, despite the fact that the profile of each candidate had been presented to the committee, applicants were scored on only three criteria: qualifications, race and gender. According to the commission, these criteria were being applied in all areas in view of its commitment to achieve a more representative judicial service. However, in Port Elizabeth the criteria were weighted in such a way that, as Du Preez put it, it was 'impossible for a white male to compete against a black woman'. Both scored one point under qualifications. For his 19 years' experience he was allocated three points, while the black female with two years' experience received one point. On race and gender, he scored a nil while she scored three points for race and three points for gender, giving her a total of eight points against his four. Du Preez contended that this made him a victim of unfair discrimination and sought an order setting aside the criteria used to shortlist candidates as well as an order directing the commission to re-advertise the positions and to use criteria which are 'constitutionally sound and which ... do not constitute an absolute barrier to any prospective candidate as a result of race and/or gender'.

## Pronouncements

The Court noted that two candidates, both with less than two years' district court bench experience, had been recommended for the vacancies in Port Elizabeth and that both these candidates were black females. It was also pointed out that the candidates were shortlisted solely on the results on the score sheets. The Court then went on to compare the relevant clauses relating to discrimination in the Constitution, the Employment Equity Act and the Promotion of Equality and Prevention of Unfair Discrimination Act, concluding that they were in essence the same. Of relevance was the fact that even though affirmative action measures might not necessarily disadvantage others, there would be instances where they do have that effect. The Court was of the opinion that the 'affirmative action' clauses could not be viewed as permitting discrimination in all circumstances where equality was being pursued. If this were the case, then persons disadvantaged by affirmative action measures would have 'no protection under the equality rights guaranteed by the Constitution'.

The Court then turned to Section 13 of the Promotion of Equality and Prevention of Unfair Discrimination Act, which stipulates that if the applicant has presented a prima facie case of discrimination, the onus then falls on the employer to prove that the actions undertaken were fair.

In terms of sections 14(2) and (3) of the same Act, the following criteria must be applied by persons tasked to determine whether the action was fair:

- The context in which the discrimination occurred
- Whether the discrimination reasonably and justifiably differentiates between persons according to objectively determinable criteria intrinsic to the activity concerned
- Whether the discrimination impairs, or is likely to impair, human dignity
- The impact, or the likely impact, of the discrimination on the complainant
- The position of the complainant in society: whether they suffer from patterns of disadvantage or belong to a group that suffers from such patterns of disadvantage
- The nature and extent of the discrimination
- Whether the discrimination is systemic in nature
- Whether the discrimination has a legitimate purpose
- Whether and to what extent the discrimination achieves its purpose
- Whether there are less restrictive and less disadvantageous means to achieve the purpose
- Whether and to what extent the respondent has taken reasonable steps to address the disadvantage which arises from, or is related to, one or more of the prohibited grounds, or to accommodate diversity.

In analysing the case at hand, the Court, as a first step, had to decide whether Du Preez had made a prima facie case for discrimination. The Court concluded that there had been discrimination, which would be regarded as unfair unless the respondent could prove otherwise.

As a second step, the Court turned to the question as to whether the discrimination had a legitimate purpose. It noted that, according to the evidence presented, there was indeed a real need to bring about greater equity in the bench of the Port Elizabeth regional court, where, of the 13 posts already filled, nine were held by white males, one by a white female and one by an African male. The Court also looked at the commission's policy as regards the achievement of equity and its implementation of the policy. It concluded that the commission's policy was not 'haphazard or random' and that the discrimination had a legitimate purpose.

The Court nevertheless went on to explain that it must 'ask itself whether the discrimination reasonably and justifiably differentiates between persons according to objectively determinable criteria, intrinsic to the activity concerned'. In the opinion of the Court, the main criterion in this case would have been experience; this is because sitting on the bench demands insight and maturity, and there is 'no substitute for experience'. As the Court put it: 'The regional court bench has an important position in the administration of justice. It is of cardinal importance that public confidence in the criminal justice system be fostered and maintained by appointment to the regional courts of suitably qualified and sufficiently experienced persons.' The Court pointed out that, because of the scoring system, Du Preez's lengthy experience actually 'counted for nought'. The other applicants were said to meet the minimum requirements only because experience other than that of magistrate was taken into account.

The committee's failure to have sufficient regard for experience was not the only shortcoming in the shortlisting process. The committee had failed to take the profile and CV of each candidate into account. Furthermore, they should have had regard for the other criteria by which candidates would be judged in the final selection. These include, among others, legal knowledge, leadership and management skills, language proficiency and communication. All in all, the Court concluded: 'There is a patent disproportionality in a selection policy based on race and gender to the absolute exclusion of all other qualities required for a position as responsible and important as that of regional magistrate. Such policy is irrational within its own terms and objectives.'

The final point to be deliberated was the applicant's contention that the criteria adopted constituted an absolute barrier to his being considered on merit for the position. In this respect the Court referred to Section 15(4) of the Employment Equity Act, which provides that nothing in the section relating to affirmative action requires an employer to place an absolute barrier on the prospective or continued employment or advancement of persons from the non-designated group (white males). The Court concluded: 'The inflexible modus operandi of the committee comes four-square within the situation of absolute inclusion of designated group members to the absolute exclusion of non-designated group members.' The formula effectively frustrated the applicant's ambition for advancement and denied him benefits concomitant with such promotion. Because the formula was part of departmental policy, the discrimination was judged to be endemic.

The final verdict was that the Department had failed to prove that the discrimination was fair. The Court set aside the criteria which had been utilised and ordered the commission to re-advertise the vacancies for the position of regional magistrate. Costs were awarded against the Department.

## Discussion

This case addresses one of the most important issues arising from the equity legislation, namely the question as to whether, if apparently justified by an employment equity plan, positions can be reserved outright for members of a previously disadvantaged group to the exclusion of all others. From the case review above, it is clear that while nothing in the equity legislation prohibits this, such action may be challenged in terms of the unfair discrimination clause; further, rights obtained by equity legislation are always subordinate to those contained in the Constitution, in which the right to equality and the right not to be discriminated against are primary rights. The Court once again confirmed that fairness is a complex concept, that no rights are absolute and that each action will be judged in terms of its particular circumstances and the totality of precepts applicable to the situation.

# Conclusion

Affirmative action is a dynamic, organic process. Policies, strategies and progress should be constantly reviewed and, if necessary, adapted in terms of changing circumstances and demands. Moreover, it should be remembered that, while equality should be pursued, no societal structure can be a perfect mirror of its population.

Most recently, it was reported that the Minister of Employment and Labour had informed Parliament that, according to the South African Human Rights Commission (SAHRC), the Employment Equity Act is unconstitutional. No further details have been provided, but as the SAHRC has to approve all legislation, it may be that the Act will have to be revised.

## Suggested Questions/Tasks

1.  Source another case dealing with targets as against quotas and compare its findings with the two judgments in the *Solidarity* case review in this chapter.
2.  Draw up an equity policy and procedure for your organisation under the following headings:
    a.  Policy objectives (what you aim to achieve with this policy)
    b.  Definition of terms (define all the important concepts)
    c.  Policy statements (the principles which constitute the basis of the policy)
    d.  Possible obstacles (to the achievement of equity)
    e.  Processes (those that need to be instituted in order to overcome the obstacles, achieve the objectives and put the principles into practice)
    f.  Procedures (a step-by-step outline of the exact procedure for each process, for instance checking existent policies and practices, appointing a committee, and so forth)
    g.  Allocation of responsibilities.
3.  Approach an organisation and request their equity plan (which should be open to scrutiny). Write a report on the plan, setting out the reasons why it conforms/does not conform to best practice.

# Sources

DEL (Department of Employment and Labour). 2020. 'Draft code of good practice on the prevention and elimination of violence and harassment in the world of work'. Government Notices, No 896, 20 August 2020. https://www.gov.za/sites/default/files/gcis_document/202008/43630gon896s.pdf (Accessed 6 November 2021).

Employment Equity Act (55 of 1998). *Government Gazette* vol 400 no 19370. Pretoria: Government Printer.

Employment Equity Amendment Act (47 of 2013). *Government Gazette* vol 583 no 37238. Pretoria: Government Printer.

ILO. 1958. 'Discrimination (Employment & Occupation) Convention No 111 of 1958'. https://www.ilo.org/dyn/normlex/en/f?p=NORMLEXPUB:12100:0::NO::P12100_ILO_CODE:C111 (Accessed 10 September 2021).

Labour Relations Act (66 of 1995). *Government Gazette* vol 366 no 16861. Pretoria: Government Printer.

Stats SA (Statistics South Africa). 2011. 'Census 2011'. Statistical release P0301.4. Pretoria: Stats SA.

# 5

# Labour Economics: Theories and Application

## Chapter Outline

# Overview

In a publication by the South African Board for People Practices (SABPP) entitled 'SABPP labour market scenarios 2030: People and work – How will the South African labour market change over the next 14 years?', it is stated:

> Projections concerning the South African labour market into the future are almost invariably gloomy. It seems that unemployment will not reduce significantly and the shortage of skills which hampers strategy execution for many South African organisations will not improve any time soon as the education system from early childhood to university fails to meet the needs of both young people and employers. One of the major factors influencing how the labour market develops is the economy, and at present, debate over the economy is marked by entrenched ideological differences between politicians, business leaders, union leaders and other key stakeholders, and an apparent inability to dialogue constructively to find an accepted way forward. (Meyer, 2016: 1)

To understand the current South African labour market and the future possibilities for this labour market, we need to understand the fundamental aspects of labour economics. Labour economics is an independent field and cannot be covered in-depth in this chapter. However, labour relations and human resource (HR) practitioners need to be acquainted with the most critical labour market theories, since they affect wage levels and explain unemployment dynamics.

Labour economics theories provide insights regarding individual and social behaviour that help us understand essential aspects of our lives. If we know the fundamentals of labour economics, we will better understand the vast array of social problems, policies and programmes in South Africa and on the continent. Together with social partners, such as trade unions and employers' organisations, governments have sought to develop policies and programmes that focus on labour market challenges. Macroeconomic differences between countries, and the labour market's reactions to employment policies and wages, usually follow similar trajectories, but idiosyncratic features may have additional implications for particular countries.

Before we can look at theories, policies and problems, it is essential to understand the basic concept of labour economics. According to Ehrenberg and Smith (2012: 1), labour economics 'is primarily concerned with employers and employees' behaviour in response to the general incentives of wages, prices, profits and nonpecuniary aspects of the employment relationship, such as working conditions'.

Labour economics can be conducted at different levels, namely:

- **Positive economics:** Economic theory is used to analyse 'what is' – where economists look at people's behaviour from a positive economics analysis viewpoint.
- **Normative economics:** Analysis is done to determine 'what will/would be'.

Questions determining 'what is' are related to positive economics and questions determining 'what will/would be' are related to normative economics. An example of the first type of question is: 'What is the effect of a 12 per cent increase in the minimum wage on the youth unemployment rate?' An example of the second type of question is: 'Should the government raise the minimum wage by 12 per cent?'

➤

Both positive and normative economics make use of models to focus on substantive issues of interest. Positive economics uses models to understand human behaviour, make predictions, and formulate statistical hypotheses that can be empirically tested. Normative economics uses models to examine the implications of various economic models and principles.

The positive economic theory of behaviour states that individuals respond favourably to benefits and negatively to cost. Individuals consider both benefits and cost when making decisions. The following basic assumptions are seen as part of positive economics:

■ **Scarcity:** Individuals and society do not have all the resources to meet all their needs and wants.
■ **Rationality:** People are rational; therefore a person pursues an objective through utility maximisation.

People strive toward the goal of achieving happiness to the extent possible, given the limited resources available to them.

In terms of classical labour market theory, the labour market is assumed to function in the same manner as other markets. According to this theory, wage and employment levels are determined by the law of supply and demand, as usually happens in product markets, where scarcity leads to higher prices (real wages) and oversupply to lower prices.

Neo-classical theory is a broad theory which focuses on demand and supply, which are the driving forces behind the production and consumption of goods and services and the pricing of products. The theory emerged around the beginning of the 1900s to compete with the earlier theories of classical economics (see detail discussion below). Neo-classical theorists adopted and adapted the classical theory, emphasising employers' and workers' maximising behaviour and proposing the principle of aggregate production and aggregate demand for labour as a better basis for analysing the labour market and explaining unemployment. Neo-classical theory suggests the notion of an auction market, in which employees are competing for jobs and employers bid to attract and retain labour services (McConnell, Brue & Macpherson, 2015). For example, in South Africa, bargaining councils and minimum pay scales set by the government oblige smaller firms to pay higher wages than they otherwise would, thereby preventing them from employing more employees than they currently do or than they did in the past.

Simultaneously, the institutionalists questioned the use of theoretical models to explain the realities of the labour market and instead conducted empirical studies that, they claimed, showed that internal markets in organisations/institutions operated independently of the external labour market.

The remedies suggested to solve unemployment will be influenced by the labour market theory to which the proponents subscribe. Thus, proponents of the free flexible market will suggest that government and union interference in the labour market (labour market rigidities) is mainly responsible for high unemployment levels. On the other hand, those adopting a more radical stance will blame capitalism and the free-market system. This is of relevance in Chapter 6, which deals with the problem of unemployment in South Africa.

Labour relations practitioners are also concerned with the effect of collective bargaining and wage determinations on wage levels. Other important issues include the effects of discriminatory labour practices and labour mobility, or the lack of it, on the overall composition of the labour market and the wage levels which are established for different groups.

➤

Some new research areas have developed in recent decades, including personnel economics, which uses microeconomic principles to clarify the HR practices of organisations. For example, it focuses on how workers should be paid (eg piece rates or bonuses) and not only on how much they are paid.

The field of personnel economics originated from labour economics. Lazear (1999) explains that personnel economics is a branch of labour economics aimed at understanding the use of economics within the firm's internal workings (Lazear, 1999: 200). Personnel economics is seen as a subdiscipline that uses econometrics and economic theory to examine issues of interest in the HR field. For example, within the HR field, managers need to decide to make use of costly employees in order to retain and attract new employees. Personnel economics originated from labour economics to motivate employees (Grund et al, 2017). Personnel economics examines the employment relationship and interaction between employees and firms, managers and subordinates, or colleagues (Lazear & Oyer, 2013).

As mentioned by Grund et al (2017), personnel economics is characterised by the following three core principles of economics:

1. Personnel economics focuses on employees and firms as rational maximising agents. As a result, they are continually interacting with one another within and beyond the firm. Lazear (2000: F612) has argued that 'the success of personnel economics is in large part a result of simply assuming maximisation because doing so allows the analyst to express complicated concepts in relatively simple, albeit abstract, terms'.
2. It operates within the framework of the concept of equilibrium.
3. It allows for welfare comparisons. Personnel economics focuses on employees' attempts to maximise utility and organisations' efforts to maximise profits, resulting in positive welfare outcomes (Lazear & Shaw, 2007).

Personnel economics has also included non-standard preferences, which is the subject of much of behavioural economics. For example, personnel economists consider the 'extensions of the individuals' utility function where the assumption of a purely egoistic *homo oeconomicus* is replaced by an alternative, but still maximising, view of *homo reciprocans*' (Grund et al, 2017: 102). This work extends personnel economics to consider fairness considerations and intrinsic motivation, social preferences for equality or equity, and gender differences in decisions and behaviour.

Personnel economics is related to labour/industrial relations (when considering the role of bargaining councils, unions and other labour market institutions), industrial organisation and organisational behaviour (Grund et al, 2017: 102).

Some ideas remain fundamental when explaining how labour markets function. The concept of human capital remains an integral feature of contemporary labour economics. In the new millennium, the increased prevalence of automation and digitalisation, bringing radical changes in the nature of work and thereby in demand for certain types of labour, has obliged experts to rethink traditional theory and traditional approaches to the problem of unemployment. Although the basic principles of demand and supply will remain, those in power will have to find more innovative solutions in the future.

# The Importance of Labour Economics

Labour economics has an influence on people's decision making regarding their lives, even though some of the decisions are being made even if the person is not actively involved in the labour market. This, for instance, happens when one gains an understanding of the factors influencing an individual's decision on how long to stay in full-time education and when is the best time to retire (Drinkwater, n.d.).

In the 1980s, McConnell and Brue (1986) emphasised that labour economics is an essential field, as socio-economic issues depend on current labour-related issues such as strikes, productivity levels of employees, rising unemployment, wage–price inflation and greater mechanisation. All of these are the concern of labour economists. The major part of national income is distributed in the form of wages. Since wage earners constitute the core of economic activity, it is important to understand how wage levels are established and their effect on the economy in general. This necessitates a study of the wage and labour markets, which display characteristics different from those of product and capital markets.

Drinkwater (n.d.) explains that labour economics has been influenced tremendously by microeconomic techniques. The influence is evident not only in traditional labour market issues, but also in the focus on issues than were not previously seen as explicit economic dimensions. The study of traditional labour markets included factors such as the labour demand decisions of organisations and the behaviour of trade unions. Areas that were not focused on previously included migration, discrimination and household decisions (fertility, divorce, allocation of time to activities) (Drinkwater, n.d.). Another important concern, particularly in the South African context, is the level of unemployment. Traditionally, high unemployment was attributed to flaws in or interference with the labour market, but other theorists ascribe unemployment to economic factors and misplaced economic policies.

Aspects of labour economics can be found within microeconomics and macroeconomics. Microeconomics focuses on the workings of individual markets; in this chapter, we explicitly look at the demand and supply of labour. Macroeconomics, on the other hand, deals with fundamental economics, such as unemployment. See Figure 5.1 for an overview of labour economics within microeconomics and macroeconomics.

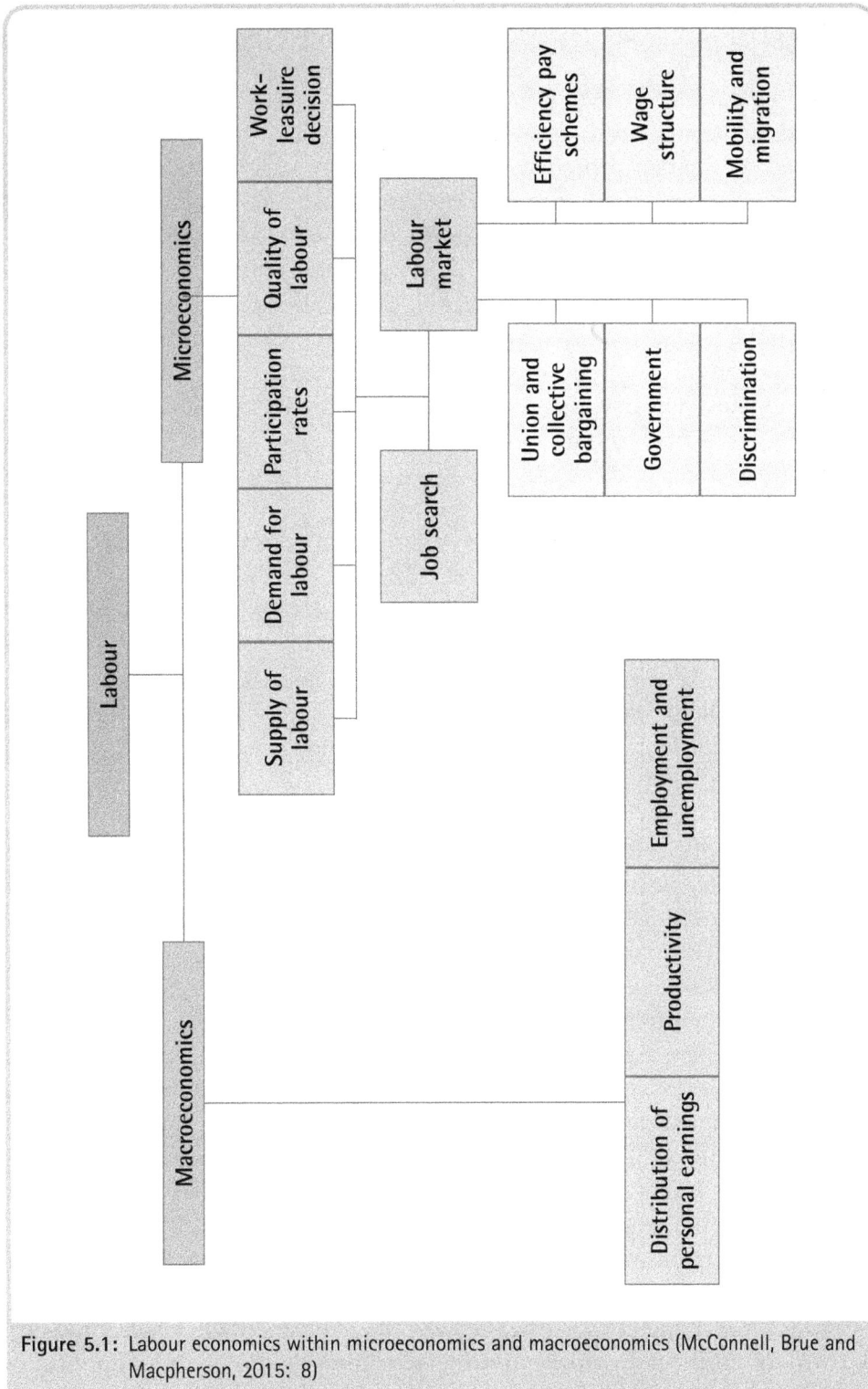

**Figure 5.1:** Labour economics within microeconomics and macroeconomics (McConnell, Brue and Macpherson, 2015: 8)

# Classical and Neo-classical Labour Market Theory

## Classical Labour Market Theory

Classical labour market theory has its origins in the writings of Adam Smith, who used the market principles of demand and supply to demonstrate that the wage rate would be determined by the interaction between the demand for and the supply of labour (see figures 5.2 to 5.4). Smith maintained that if the market functioned freely, it would continually adjust to a point where demand matched supply. Therefore, the classical economists believed that there would be no unemployment in a perfectly functioning market. If unemployment did occur, it would be temporary.

As Reynolds, Masters and Moser (1986) confirm, the following assumptions are made in classical labour market theory:

- The wage rate, and nothing else, determines the attractiveness of a particular position.
- All vacancies are filled through the market and not by internal promotion.
- All employees are the same if they can do the same job.
- There is full knowledge among potential employees of job opportunities, wage rates and job characteristics.
- Employers, likewise, have full knowledge of potential employees.
- The economic motive overrides all others.
- The market is competitive; there is no restriction or collusion.
- Everything else in the economy remains constant.

## Characteristics of the Classical Labour Market

Although the labour market is, in the classical labour market theory, equated to other markets such as capital and product markets, it has particular characteristics. Reynolds et al (1986) list the following as unique characteristics of the labour market:

- **Market multiplicity:** Reference is usually made to the labour market, but this market comprises many different markets, such as various skill levels, occupations, age groups, sexes, industries and geographical regions. The various markets are, to some extent, interchangeable, yet barriers to mobility do exist. It is these barriers that nowadays constitute a central concern in labour economics.
- **No central clearing house:** Goods may be processed through a central exchange, but there is no such clearing house for employees, who cannot be centrally collected and then apportioned on demand. Thus, when we speak of a specific market in a particular area, the concept is mainly theoretical.
- **Lack of standardisation among workers:** While various applicants might apply for the same position, they will vary in ability, intelligence,

motivation, physical characteristics, social behaviour and specific skills. Hence, they are not all equally suited for the position. A particular concern of labour economics is the development of human capital to broaden the potential labour market.

- **Temporary nature of the employment relationship:** Once a purchaser buys goods for consumption, the goods become the buyer's property. This is not so with the employment relationship. Either the employer or employee may decide to terminate the relationship. This leads to greater fluidity and unpredictability in the labour market.
- **Complexity of the employment package:** The price paid for labour and the value received may be far higher than the actual wage rate. Employees receive tangible and intangible benefits in pensions, housing, work satisfaction and personal growth. In applying the law of supply and demand to the labour market, these benefits are not considered.

## The Neo-classicists

By the end of the nineteenth century, labour market theorists had begun to realise that the perfect labour market concept was unrealistic and that the theory that existed could not account for the complexity of the concept. This was the premise adopted by the neo-classicists, who claimed to have injected realism into classical theory. Although they used the classical models of demand and supply, they believed that output and employment were determined by 'real' forces, of which the most important were aggregate demand and aggregate production. Aggregate demand in the economy was based on business expectations of future profitability.

In South Africa the neo-classical approach has historically been the dominant approach, and it persisted after the constitutional change in 1996. This approach has caused further imbalances, increasing poverty, unemployment and socio-economic inequalities as a result of industrial unrest, as has been seen, for example, in the mining sector.

The four main pillars of the neo-classical approach are the following (Őnday, 2016):

1. **Division of labour:** The classical theory assumes that if a job is broken into its simplest components, the employee will become more specialised when doing their part of the job. As a result of employee specialisation, the organisation will become more efficient.
2. **Scalar and functional processes:** The scalar process provides a scale for the grading of duties according to the degree of responsibility or authority. It generates superior–subordinate relationships within the organisation. The functional process deals with the division of the organisation into specialised departments.

3. **Structure:** The position of the employee within the organisation is important, as each position is assigned a certain level of authority (line or staff) and a specific task. Efficiency depends on the how the task is accomplished, which in turn determines the effectiveness of the organisation.

4. **Span of control:** This refers to the number of subordinates that a manager can exercise proper control over. This depends on the different levels which can be effectively supervised by a manager/superior. A wide span yields a flatter structure, whereas a short span results in a tall organisational structure.

The neo-classical economists maintain that minimum wages are harmful to employment and interfere with the efficient working of markets. Labour market policies, such as a national minimum wage, are used in different countries to decrease poverty and inequality (Patel, Khan & Englert, 2020). Stigler (1946) questioned the notion that a national minimum wage reduces poverty and argued instead that it reduces employment. Bhorat et al (2016) looked at the impact of the national minimum wage in the early 2000s on youth employed in key sectors in South Africa. They found an insignificant but negative impact on youth employment in agriculture, with some increases in the retail and taxi sectors and no adverse effects in four other sectors.

According to the neo-classicists, who were also supporters of the free market, neither monetary theory nor fiscal policy could counter unemployment. This could only be done by increasing aggregate demand in the economy and by education and on-the-job training. Thus, the emphasis was on economic growth and the allocation of a given set of resources. The neo-classical economic perspective asserts the following (Patel et al, 2020: 150):

■ Employers will respond to the increased cost of doing business by cutting jobs, reducing working hours and hiring fewer new employees.

■ Minimum wages are harmful to employment and interfere with the efficiency of the labour market.

■ Employees and employers almost have complete information on employment possibilities and wages on the market.

■ In an economic sense, both the employee and employer are rational. The employer strives for maximum profit and the employee for maximum satisfaction in the form of wages.

■ Individual decisions do not influence wages, as every employer and employee forms just a small portion of the labour demand.

■ No obstacles exist to labour force mobility and other production factors.

- Employers and employees act individually in making decisions regarding pay or employment, without agreement with other employers and employees.
- The labour market is economically movable, as labour in a specific market is changeable and uniform.

Like classical theorists, the neo-classicists supported the concept of a freely functioning market. They believed that the market would eventually return to equilibrium, but that this would take longer than the classical school proposed. They decried any interference with the market, particularly the undesirable effects of government legislation and union interference. They may therefore be described as proponents of what is nowadays termed flexible labour markets.

The neo-classical school was not without its critics, some of whose ideas were later incorporated into the neo-classical theory. Thus, while retaining its fundamental principles, the neo-classical theory's ambit was widened to include imperfect competition models and concepts such as a fair wage and an efficiency wage (a wage higher than the market rate to encourage loyalty and productivity).

Although in modern times thinking on the labour market is also approached from psychological, sociological and historical perspectives, and incorporates ideas from other labour market theories, the classical and neo-classical approaches still form the basis of labour market analysis.

## Labour Market Models

### The Law of Demand and Supply

The theory of labour demand and supply is based on the same principles as price theory. However, the latter theory's basic assumption is that there is a direct, inverse relationship between price and demand – that as the price increases, the quantity demanded will decrease.

In the context of the labour market, as the price of labour (wages) increases, the quantity of labour demanded will decrease. The demand schedule obtained from this premise is illustrated in Figure 5.2. The demand curve slopes upward to the left. According to Figure 5.2, 50 units of labour would be demanded at a wage rate (price) of R3.00 per hour, but should the wage rate rise to R6.00 per hour, the quantity demanded would decline to 20 units. The consequences of this on the level of employment are, in theory, self-evident.

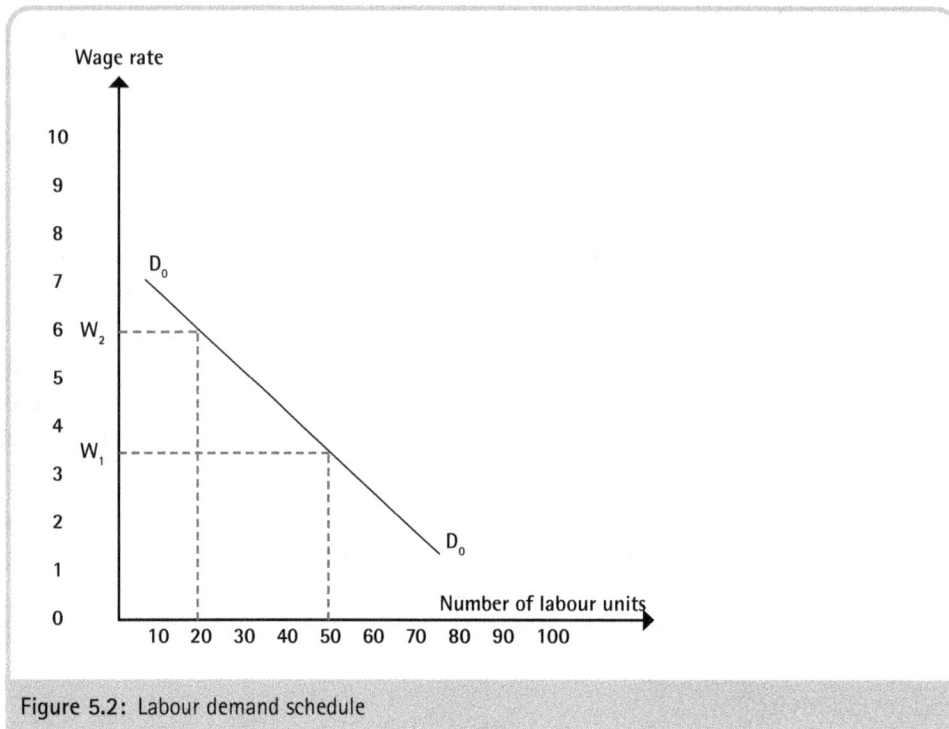

**Figure 5.2:** Labour demand schedule

The second principle of price theory is that supply stands in a direct, straightforward relationship to price. The lower the price, the smaller will be the quantity of goods or services offered to the market. In terms of labour supply, this means that the number of people prepared to do a certain job will decrease directly related to a decrease in the wage level. As a result, the supply function illustrated in Figure 5.3 is obtained. In terms of Figure 5.3, 70 workers would offer themselves at a wage of R7.00 per hour, while, at a rate of R3.00 per hour, the supply of labour would drop to 30 workers.

Market Equilibrium

In a perfectly competitive market, equilibrium is achieved at the point where the supply curve intersects with the demand curve. Equilibrium price and equilibrium quantity of labour demanded and labour supplied are determined by the interaction of market demand and supply. This is illustrated in Figure 5.4, where equilibrium would be achieved if there was a demand for 40 people at a rate of R4.00 per hour and 40 people offered themselves for employment at this wage rate. This situation arises under conditions of perfect competition, which are rarely achieved in practice. Free-market economists believe that there is, nevertheless, always a tendency towards the restoration of equilibrium.

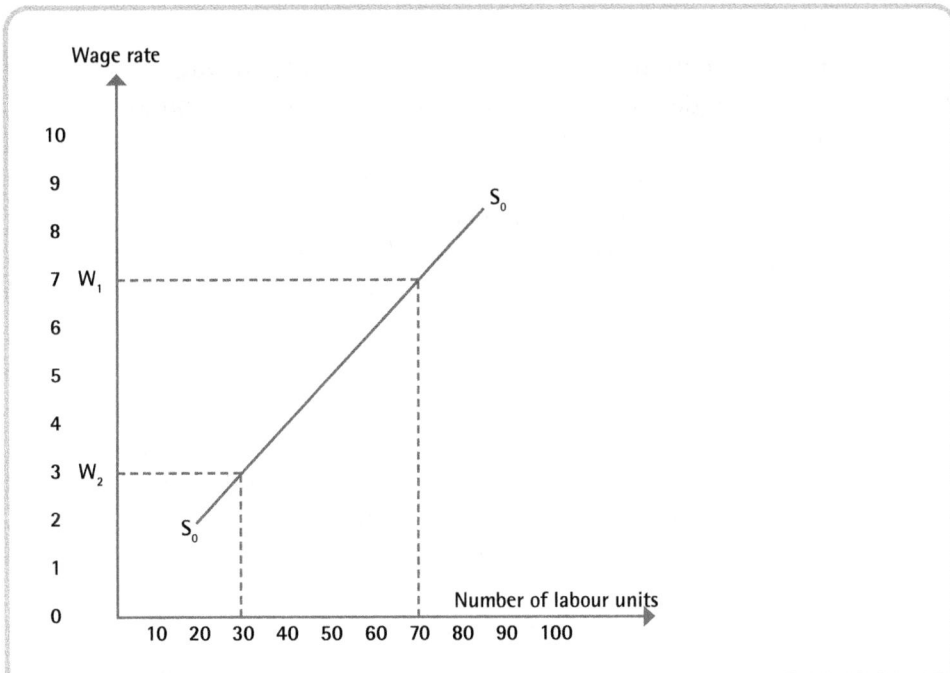

**Figure 5.3:** The supply function of labour

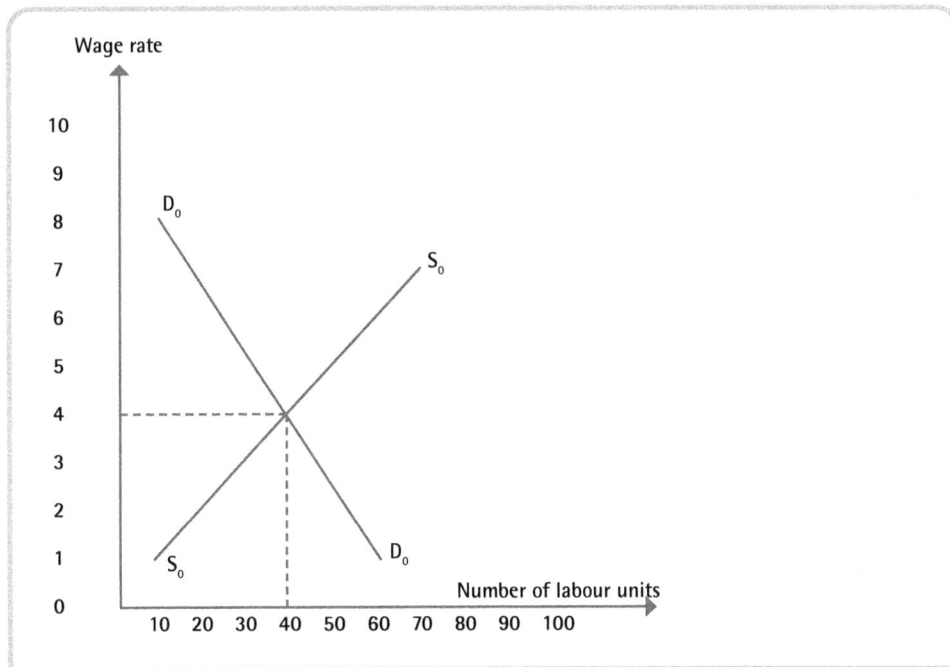

**Figure 5.4:** Equilibrium supply and demand

## Shifts in Demand

Demand for and supply of labour are not related only to wage levels. Total demand is a derived demand. It depends, inter alia, on demand for goods or services in the product market. Thus, an increase in, for example, the demand for particular goods and services will lead to an increase in the quantity of labour demanded. This will occasion a shift in the demand curve to the right of its original position (illustrated by a shift from $D_0$ to $D_1$ in Figure 5.5). If the supply curve remains constant, the consumers of labour (employers) will have to pay more to obtain further quantities of labour. This could entail overtime pay or the offer of higher wages in order to draw more suppliers (labour units) to the market. Thus, a new wage rate ($W_2$) is established.

On the other hand, if the demand for goods and services suddenly decreases, the total demand for labour will decrease. The demand curve will shift to the left of its original position (illustrated by the shift from $D_0$ to $D_2$ in Figure 5.5). If the supply of labour remains constant, the consumers of labour will be able to pay less for smaller labour quantities. A new wage rate ($W_3$) is established. This happens because there is greater rivalry among workers, some of whom will be prepared to accept lower wages. It also means that unemployment in that labour market will increase or that people will leave that market to find employment in other areas.

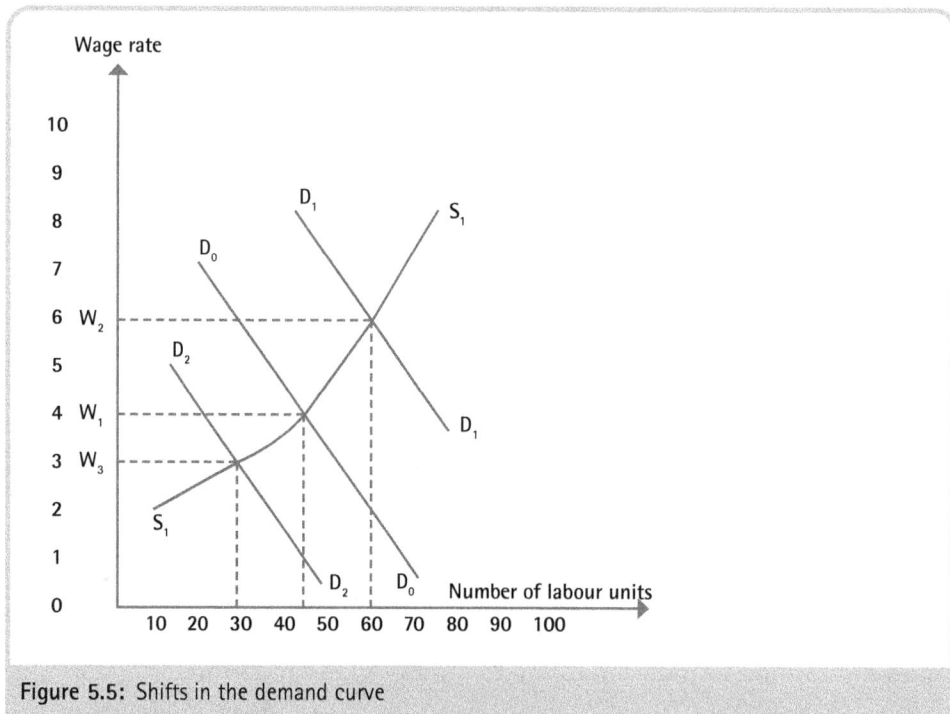

**Figure 5.5:** Shifts in the demand curve

## Shifts in Supply

Shifts may also occur in the supply curve, for example with emigration or migration. A general decrease in labour supply occasions a shift of the supply curve to the left ($S_1$ in Figure 5.6). Where demand remains constant, this results in a higher wage rate ($W_2$) being established for smaller quantities of labour (an argument similar to that of an increase in demand). An increase in the supply of labour relative to demand causes a shift in the supply curve to the right ($S_2$) and a lower wage rate ($W_3$) for higher quantities of labour.

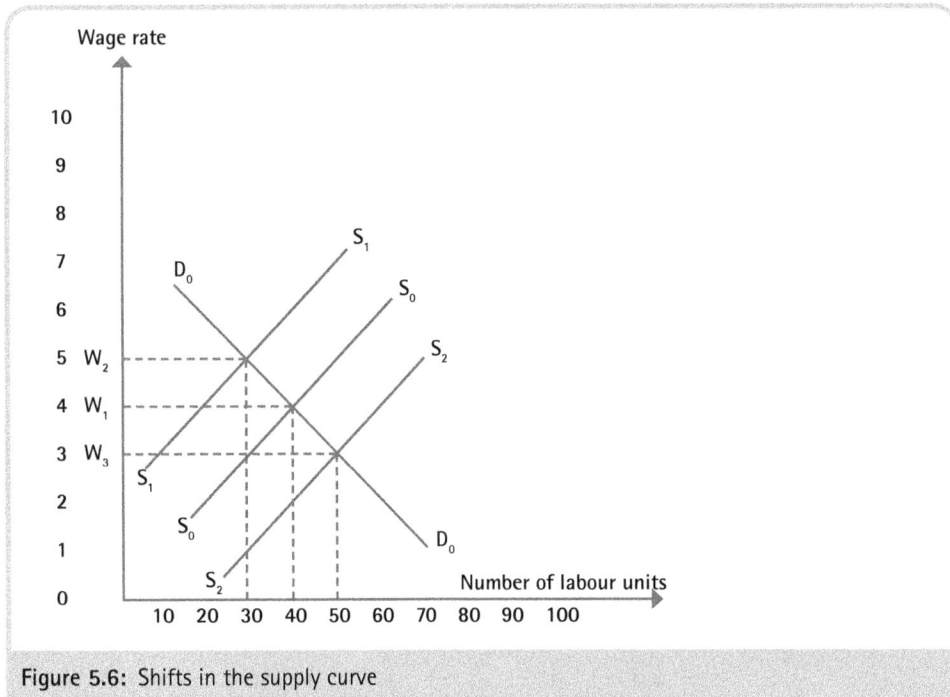

**Figure 5.6:** Shifts in the supply curve

## Movement to Equilibrium

According to free-market theorists, if all other things remain equal, the wage rate established by shifting demand and supply will be of a temporary nature since, as indicated earlier, there is always a tendency towards the restoration of equilibrium. Thus, if too many employees offer themselves for a particular job and the supply curve shifts to the right, competition or rivalry will occur among labour suppliers. As a result, certain workers will be prepared to accept lower wages, leading to a decreased average price of labour (wages). Because workers are now prepared to accept lower wages, employers are prepared to take on more labour. Therefore, there is a gradual move along the demand curve to a new equilibrium situation, where the price (wage) is lower than in the perfect equilibrium situation but higher than it would have been at the first level of supply – that is, when a situation of oversupply arose. The quantity demanded was greater than the original demand but lower than the actual supply.

Similarly, in a situation of excess demand, the employer may look for alternative means of production. If this is not possible, they may offer a higher wage to attract extra labour units. As a result, more persons will offer themselves for that occupation and, with increased competition, the price of labour will drop and a new equilibrium will be achieved, where the price is higher than in the perfect equilibrium situation but lower than it would have been at the first level of demand – that is, when the shift in the demand curve arose. This is reflected in Figure 5.7.

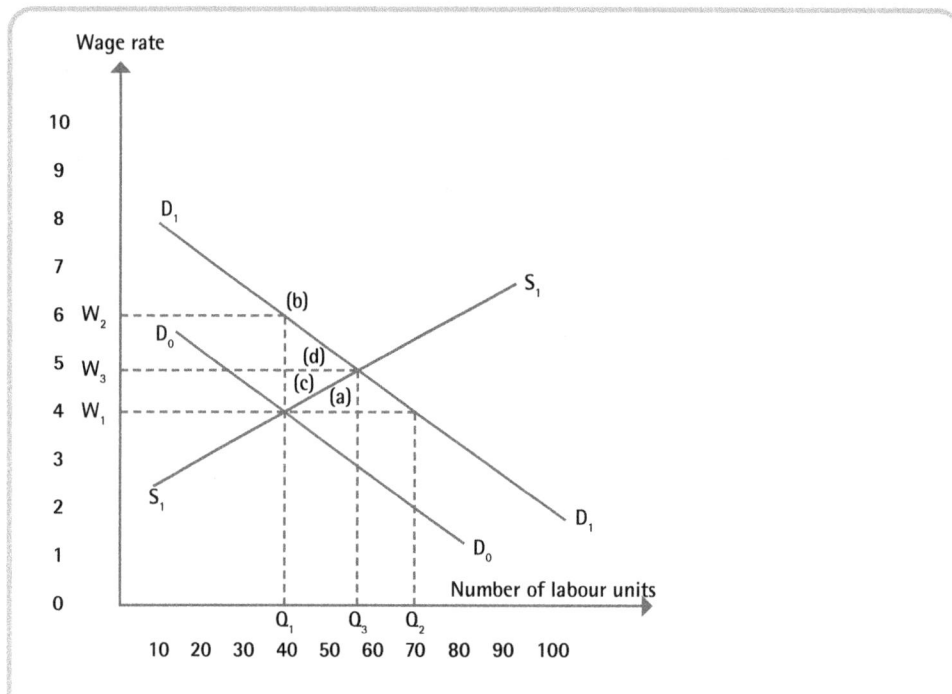

**Figure 5.7:** Establishment of equilibrium

If the general demand for labour increases, occasioning a shift in the demand curve to the right ($D_0$ to $D_1$), it means employers are demanding more labour quantities at the same wage rate (a). Since the additional quantity of labour demanded cannot be obtained at the equilibrium wage, $W_1$, the rate is increased to $W_2$, illustrated by (b) in Figure 5.7. This attracts more labour to the market, occasioning a movement, illustrated by (c), along the supply curve. Since more employees are prepared to offer their services, there is increased competition, and the wage rate will decrease from its previous high at point (b). A new equilibrium is established, resulting in a new wage, $W_3$, which is higher than the perfect equilibrium wage but lower than the wage necessitated by the original increased demand. Similarly, the quantity of labour demanded and supplied ($Q_3$) is higher than the perfect equilibrium quantity ($Q_1$), but lower than the quantity demanded when the original shortage arose ($Q_2$).

## Reasons for Shifts in Demand and Supply
### Demand
Fick and Hugh (1987) list the following as factors causing shifts in the demand curve:

- **An increase in the number of employers:** This may happen in a particular industry when a number of new employers enter the market. The demand for labour of a particular type then increases. This will cause a shift of the demand curve to the right, leading to the establishment of a higher wage rate for labour.
- **An increase in the income of employers:** This may come about if the business of employers suddenly becomes particularly lucrative, resulting in higher profits, or if the employer is subsidised when they employ more people. The cost of labour would, in relative terms, become cheaper to the employer. This might result in a shift of the demand curve to the right.
- **Preference for a certain type of employee:** There are occasions when, for various reasons, employers decide that a particular kind of employee is best suited for the job at hand. This may occur in the case where women are found to be better at executing a certain task, or it could result from an affirmative action programme or from technological developments necessitating the importation of labour. An event of this kind would occasion a shift to the right in the demand for that kind of labour and a shift to the left as regards the rest of the labour market.
- **The possibility of using alternatives to labour:** Technological development leads to the possibility of capital investment in other ways of producing goods and services which would replace labour and, in the long term, prove more cost-effective. This will decrease the demand for labour or for a particular type of labour, resulting in a shift of the demand curve to the left and a subsequent decrease in the wage rate.
- **An increase in the cost of labour:** If the price of labour increases for any reason (such as a minimum wage determination, the granting of union wage demands, or the imposition of a payroll tax), employers may, in the longer term, look for alternatives to labour. This would cause a shift in the demand curve to the left, a situation which will contribute to increased unemployment.

*Supply*

Shifts in the supply curve can occur for the following reasons:

- **Oversupply or undersupply of labour:** If, in general, the market is oversupplied (for example, if there are too many unskilled workers as a result of immigration by people with poor educational qualifications), the supply curve will be shifted to the right. Conversely, a general shortage of labour (for example, in time of war) will cause a shift of the supply curve to the left.

- **The amount of training needed to perform a certain job:** Training of any kind is an expense, also for the individual undergoing such training. The result is that, as the level and difficulty of training increases, the supply of labour of a particular type decreases. This will result in a shift to the left in the supply curve for that type of labour and a higher wage rate than the average.

- **Attractiveness of certain positions:** Work which has a high public image or offers a great deal of flexibility is usually more attractive than other occupations. Unless there are special skills involved, this will result in an influx of persons to that occupation, leading to a shift to the right in the supply curve.

- **Degree of hardship or risk involved:** Occupations which require difficult or dirty work, or which entail a certain amount of risk, are less likely to draw potential employees. This leads to an upward shift in the supply curve relating to that particular occupation. Few applicants offer themselves and wages are higher than the average. A good example is the high wage rate paid to lumberjacks in the Canadian bush, or to men prepared to work on oil rigs at sea. However, where unemployment is at a high level, these jobs might be sought after by a large number of persons with low-level skills and may therefore be poorly paid.

- **Union activities:** A union may limit the supply of labour to the market, for example by controlling the intake of apprentices, leading to a shift to the left in the supply curve.

- **Discriminatory policies:** Where certain positions are reserved for people of a particular age group, race or sex, the supply of labour is limited in those occupations, while there is an oversupply of labour in unreserved occupations. This occasions an upward shift in the supply curve in respect of the reserved occupations and a downward shift in respect of open occupations. Privileged employees will command higher wages, whereas those less fortunate and facing strong competition for jobs have to be satisfied with lower wage rates.

The factors mentioned above contribute towards the creation of an imperfect market. The reasons for these imperfections range from variables such as economic conditions, educational facilities, demographic influences, government policy, overpopulation, discriminatory practices, union activity, technological development and a lack of labour mobility, to personal preferences and the desire for leisure.

## Elasticity of Demand and Supply

The law of demand and supply postulates that as the price of labour increases, the quantity of labour demanded will decrease and, equally, that as the price decreases, the quantity supplied to the market decreases. Yet, there are instances where the quantity demanded or supplied is not responsive to price; hence the concepts of elastic and inelastic demand or supply. Where the quantity demanded can be rapidly adapted, the demand is elastic. Where the quantity demanded cannot easily change, the demand is said to be inelastic.

The degree of elasticity in demand for and supply of labour constitutes an important consideration in the bargaining situation. Naturally, employers will favour circumstances in which demand is elastic, but supply remains inelastic. The union would favour the reverse situation.

### Elastic and Inelastic Demand

The varying positions of elastic and inelastic demand are illustrated in Figure 5.8. The equilibrium wage ($W_e$) corresponds with equilibrium quantity demanded ($Q_e$). When wages increase from $W_e$ to $W_n$ there is a change in quantity demanded:

- from $Q_e$ to $Q_1$, where demand is relatively inelastic ($D_i$)
- from $Q_e$ to $Q_2$, with unitary demand ($D_u$)
- from $Q_e$ to $Q_3$, with relatively elastic demand ($D_e$).

Therefore, one sees that the employer is more sensitive to an increase in wages in situations where demand is relatively elastic ($D_e$). In these situations, higher wages result in a significant decrease in demand ($Q_3$).

In terms of the inelastic demand curve ($D_i$), demand will diminish only slightly ($Q_1$), despite a steep increase in wage price. This is particularly important when looking at employment levels. With inelastic demand, employment levels remain relatively constant, even if a significant increase in wages is negotiated by the union.

Demand will be more inelastic if:
- labour is essential and irreplaceable
- the employer has to produce a certain number of units
- labour costs do not constitute a large proportion of total costs
- the supply of capital and other non-labour factors is also constant.

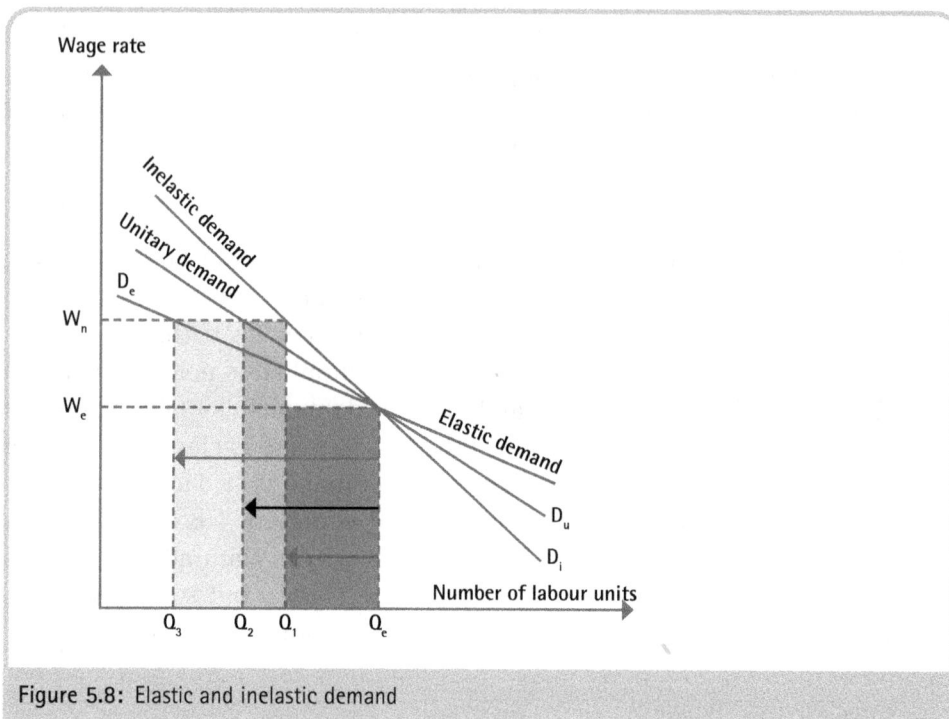

**Figure 5.8:** Elastic and inelastic demand

The effect of elastic and inelastic demand on employment levels is best illustrated by observing the effects of a wage determination on employment levels under elastic and inelastic demand conditions, as illustrated in Figure 5.9. As can be seen, where the demand for labour was elastic, the higher wage rate imposed led to a significant decrease in the number of people employed. Where the demand for labour was inelastic, the decrease in employment was insignificant. In absolutely inelastic conditions, the demand curve would be vertical. The imposed minimum wage rate would have no effect on employment levels.

*Elasticity of Supply*

Where the number of labour units supplied changes rapidly with a change in the wage rate, supply is described as elastic. If, on the other hand, the number of units supplied remains relatively constant, the supply is said to be inelastic. Elastic and inelastic supply curves are illustrated in Figure 5.10. As seen from the inelastic supply curve ($S_i$), supply decreases only marginally (from $Q_e$ to $Q_1$), despite significant changes in the wage rate from $W_e$ to $W_n$. In the elastic supply curve ($S_e$), the quantity supplied will decrease rapidly from $Q_e$ to $Q_3$, with minimal changes in the wage per hour.

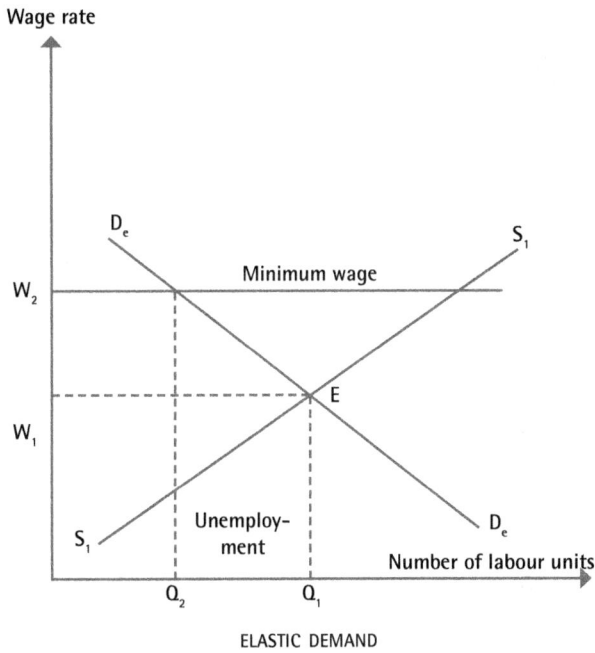

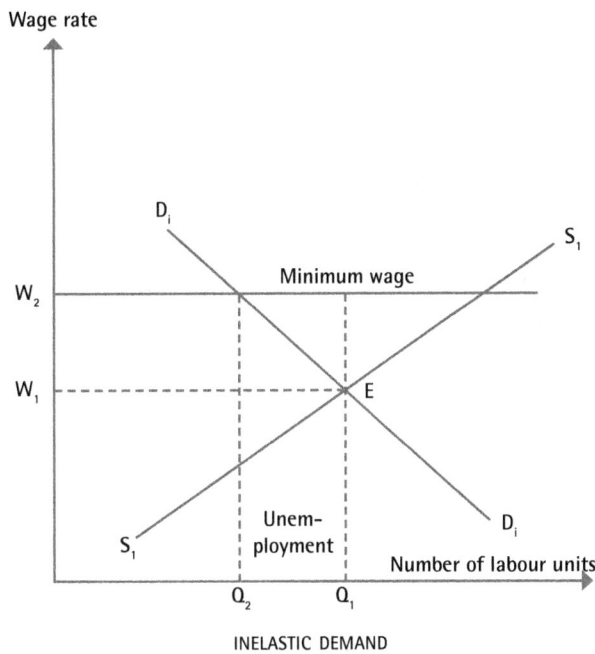

**Figure 5.9:** Employment levels as affected by wage determination in elastic and inelastic demand conditions

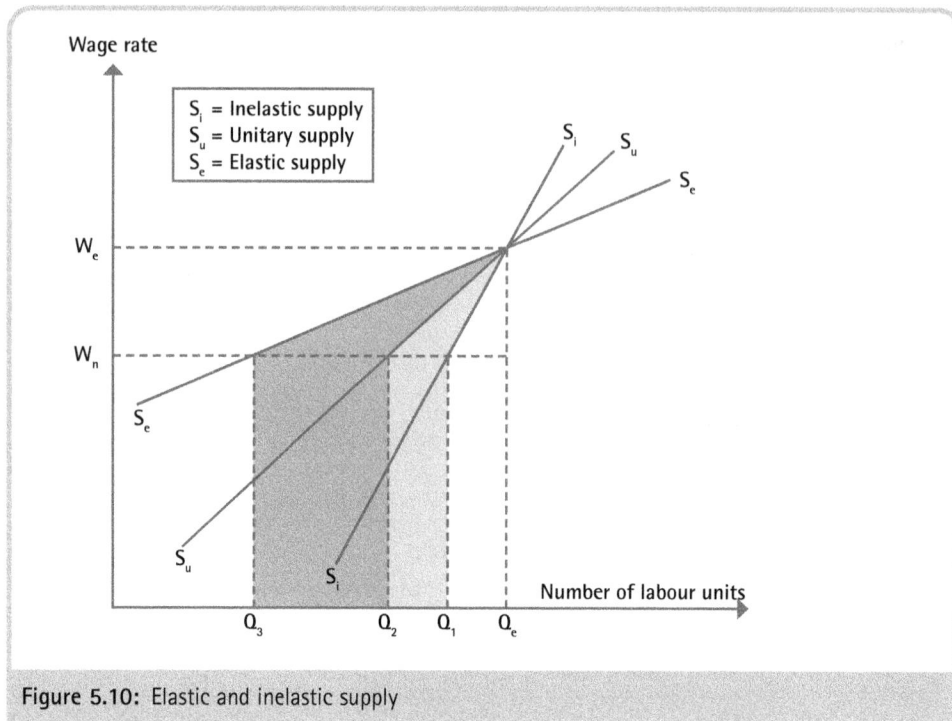

Figure 5.10: Elastic and inelastic supply

Inelasticity of supply can be caused by:

- a closed labour market – found, for example, in the apprenticeship system
- market discrimination
- the immobility of labour
- a shortage of training in certain skills.

It has an important effect on labour relations in that an inelastic supply can lead to wage fixing, either by employers or unions, whereas an elastic supply leads to more competitive wages.

### The Law of Diminishing Returns
*Premises*

The law of diminishing returns postulates that, in any process, a stage is reached at which the input of an additional unit brings a marginally declining return. It is usually applied to the use of labour in the production process, but may also be applied to individuals, in the sense that there will be a point where an employee decides that it is not worth giving up more of their leisure time in exchange for a higher income. It is also used inversely to illustrate that a union's pursuit of higher wages may ultimately be negative in that it may lead to a loss of employment and of union membership. This is the rational maximising behaviour emphasised by the neo-classicists.

*The Marginal Productivity/Utility of Labour*

It is common practice for producers of goods or services to attempt to increase their productive output by increasing labour units – that is, the number of people employed. However, marginal productivity theory proposes that, if the other major production factor, such as capital in the form of machinery or available space, remains constant, a stage will be reached where each additional unit of labour will produce marginally less than the previous unit. For example, if a machine or process was designed for operation by three persons or, at the maximum, five persons, then greater total output could be obtained by using another two operators, but each operator after the third will produce marginally less than those before him. This development is illustrated in Table 5.1.

Table 5.1: Total and marginal output per labour unit

| Number of labour units | Total output | Marginal output | Average output per labour unit |
|---|---|---|---|
| 0 | 0 | – | – |
| 1 | 12 | 12 | 12 |
| 2 | 26 | 14 | 13 |
| 3 | 42 | 16 | 14 |
| 4 | 57 | 15 | 14.25 |
| 5 | 70 | 13 | 14 |
| 6 | 80 | 10 | 13.3 |
| 7 | 86 | 6 | 12.3 |
| 8 | 86 | 0 | 10.75 |
| 9 | 84 | –2 | 9.3 |
| 10 | 81 | –5 | 8.1 |

From Table 5.1, it is evident that if only one labour unit is employed, available facilities are completely underutilised. The addition of another labour unit adds substantially to the total output and the marginal output of the second unit (what that unit contributes to the total output) is higher than that of the first unit (14 versus 12). Optimal marginal output is achieved when three units are employed, but the organisation may still benefit from employing one or two additional units, as total production still increases substantially and there is a relatively slighter decline in marginal output and, initially, a slight increase in the average output per unit. Any additional employment after the sixth unit requires careful consideration. At the eighth unit, total output remains constant, while marginal output is zero. The addition of the ninth and tenth units results in a negative return. To employ any additional units after the seventh would not be cost-effective. The progression as depicted in the table is graphically illustrated in Figure 5.11.

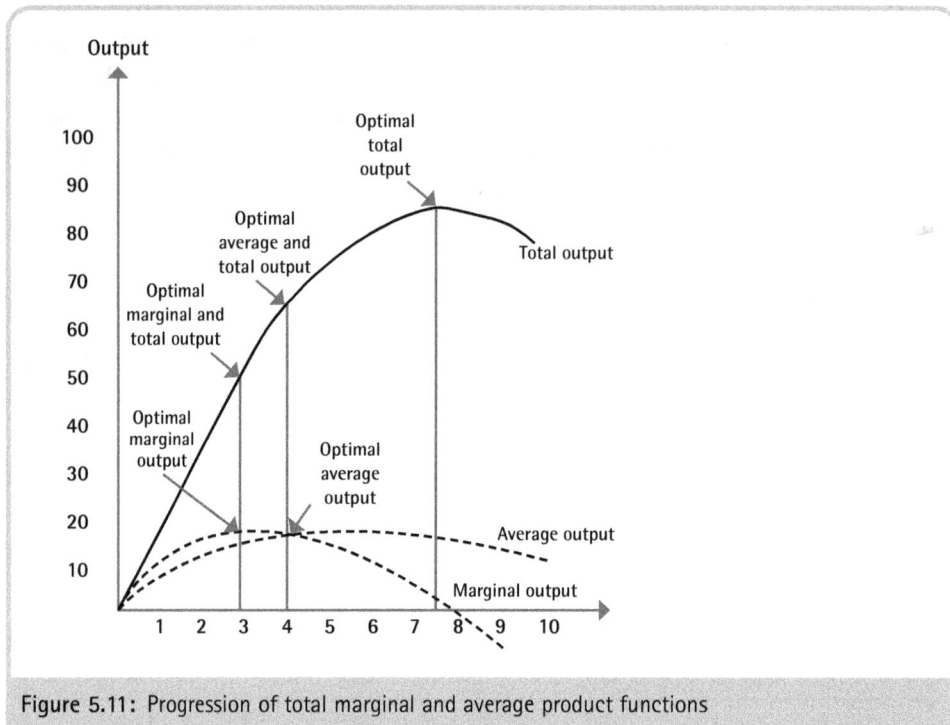

**Figure 5.11:** Progression of total marginal and average product functions

*Implications*
Marginal productivity theory underscores the fact that an increase in employment cannot be achieved without the necessary economic growth, increased capital investment or expanded production. Moreover, an employer cannot be expected to employ more than the optimal number of employees at which output per unit would be maximised. Conversely, a limitation on wages or a wage subsidy does not necessarily lead to substantially higher employment levels, since, whatever the wage rate, employers will cease to add additional units of labour once they have achieved maximum productive capacity.

## Application of Demand and Supply During the Covid–19 Pandemic
At the time of writing, a great many lives had been lost due to the Covid-19 pandemic. The demand and supply framework can be utilised to explore the effect of precipitous population decline, such as that witnessed during a

pandemic. In Figure 5.12, the pre-pandemic equilibrium is located at point E. The mortality rate shifted the labour–supply curve to the left, from S to S'.

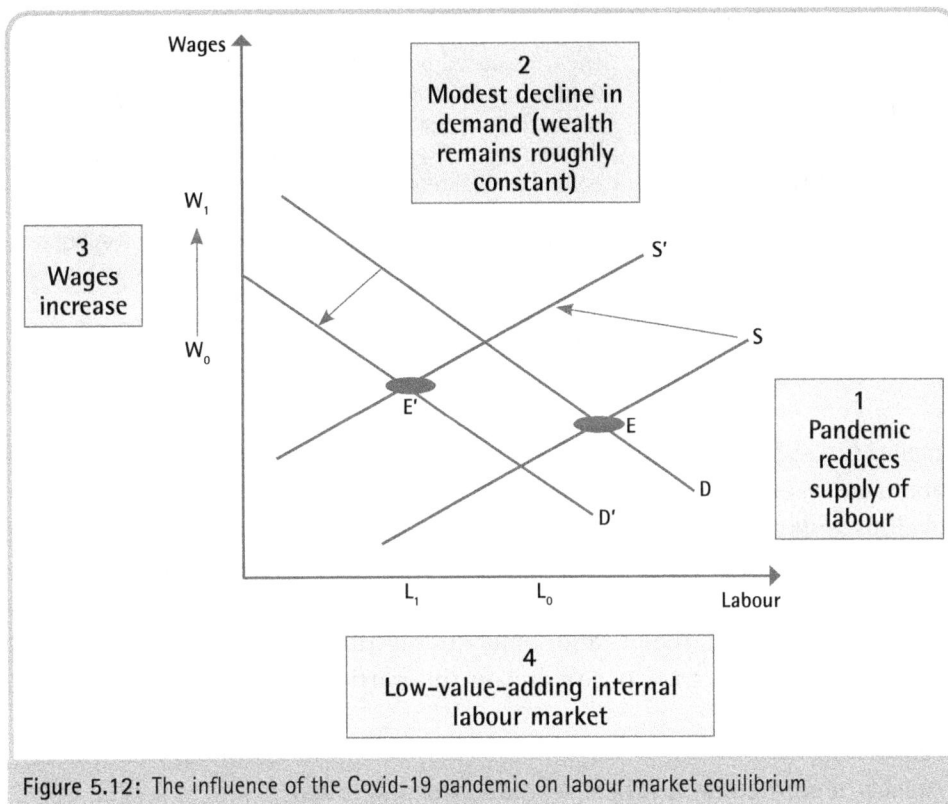

Figure 5.12: The influence of the Covid-19 pandemic on labour market equilibrium

The pandemic led to a reduction in the demand for labour in South Africa, as movement restrictions were placed on individuals. The effect was mitigated because the total demand for goods depends on the economy's real wealth and not just on the number of people per se. A significant proportion of wealth – held in the form of livestock, land and property – was unaffected by Covid-19. However, the decline in the supply of labour was greater than the reduction in the derived demand, which led to a modest shift in the labour–demand schedule.

## Contemporary Labour Market Theories

Contemporary labour market theories can be divided into labour market segmentation theories, theories based on delays in adjustment to the labour market, and theories based on wage flexibility, as shown in Figure 5.13.

| CONTEMPORARY LABOUR MARKET THEORIES | | |
|---|---|---|
| **Segmetation theories**<br>Dual labour market theory<br>Internal and external market theory<br>Traditional division of labour market sectors | **Theories based on delays in adjustment to the labour market**<br>Human capital theory<br>Natural unemployment rate theory<br>Labour market search theory | **Theories based on wage flexibility**<br>Efficient work theory<br>Insider–outsider theory<br>Non-accelerating Inflation Rate of Unemployment (NAIRU) |

**Figure 5.13:** Contemporary labour market theories (Jarmolowicz & Knapinska, 2011: 278)

## Labour Market Segmentation

Labour market segmentation is seen as one of the key labour market developments observed globally in recent years. According to the International Labour Organization (ILO, n.d.), segmentation takes place where the labour market is divided into different segments and submarkets, distinguished by different characteristics and behavioural rules. According to the ILO (n.d.), segmentation may occur due to the particularities of labour market institutions, such as:

- governing contractual arrangements (permanent or temporary contracts)
- a lack of enforcement (along formal/informal lines)
- types of employees concerned (such as migrant and non-migrant workers).

Research and advice on the topic of segmentation, according to the ILO (n.d.), aim to identify:

- important labour market segments across countries
- the degree of transitions between various segments
- the consequences of segmentation for efficiency and equity outcomes of the labour market
- the viability of policies aimed at alleviating the negative consequences of segmentation.

### The Dual Labour Market Theory

During the late 1960s and early 1970s, American economists known as the dualists directed their attention to poverty and unemployment among employees in inner-city areas known as 'ghettos' or 'slums'. The theory focuses on the existence of two separate labour markets, with limited or no mobility between the two markets. The two markets, namely the primary and secondary markets, are not defined by specific industries or occupations but by a set of general features.

The primary market is governed by an internal market and contains the privileged members of the labour force. This sector is made up of employees who received relatively high wages and enjoy good working conditions, job security, mobility along the seniority track, opportunity for promotion and administration of work rules and regulations (Doeringer & Piore, 1971: 165–169; Piore, 1969: 102; Piore, 1970: 55). The formations of trade unions to protect their members' interests is another characteristic of primary sector employment.

The secondary sector is characterised by variability and a personal relationship between employees and supervisors. This creates nepotism, which often leads to arbitrary discipline. Furthermore, it is characterised by jobs that do not require specific types of skills. The labour pool is complicatedly undifferentiated, a homogeneous mass of raw labour power. There is little or no labour training, and if training is provided, it is in the absence of trade union protection and grievance procedures. There is no seniority privileges and no codification of work rules, as seen in the primary sector. This sector has poor job security, or none at all, and few promotion prospects (Uys & Blaauw, 2006).

The South African labour market is divided between employees employed within the core sector (insiders) and those who are not (outsiders). Van der Berg, according to Uys and Blaauw (2006), has divided the dual labour market into three sectors:

1. *Core-sector employees are 'well-paid in the formal sector of the economy, namely the manufacturing sector, public sector as well as other industries and services (excluding domestic workers) that form part of this core sector.*

2. *The modern marginal sectors represent the part of the economy where low wages are being paid or where migrant labourers dominate. These sectors include domestic work, commercial agriculture and the mining sector.*

3. *The periphery consists of employees in the informal sector, subsistence agriculture and the unemployed. (Van den Berg, 1992: 5)*

The South African labour market consists of employees in the well-paid formal sector and the periphery ( Bhorat et al, 2001: 10; Braude, 2005: 402–407; Uys & Blaauw, 2006; Van der Berg, 1992: 5).

In South Africa, minimum wages policies have been introduced. According to Piek and Von Vintel (2018: 2):

*South Africa's dual imperative of employment creation and inequality reduction introduces a policy tension: minimum wages potentially exert opposite pressures on both outcomes. A 'blanket approach' – as embodied by a national minimum wage – could be beneficial for large-scale inequality reduction (including sectors that wage floors have not covered); a sector-specific approach could take into account vulnerabilities that can mitigate job losses in some segments of the economy.*

### The Internal and External Labour Market Theory

Doeringer and Piore (1971) define the internal labour market as an administrative unit, such as in a manufacturing firm where a set of administrative rules governs the pricing and allocation of labour. The internal labour market is regulated by norms and procedures and not only by the economic forces of the external labour market. The external labour market is seen as the areas which are not covered by the internal market. Figure 5.14 illustrates the segmentation of the internal and external markets in South Africa into six segments (Kraak, 2009):

- **Segment 1** is structured primarily through the state's developmental actions and policies and agencies in the fields of science, industry, technology, and education and training. Sectors within South Africa that fall in this category are mainly the public sector. An example is the Council for Scientific and Industrial Research (CSIR) and nuclear energy plants such as Koeberg in the Western Cape.
- **Segment 2** consists of top-end jobs. The focus is on individual development, including prior qualifications and diverse experience.
- **Segment 3** is the high-value-adding internal labour market. Here, the focus is on the internal procurement and development of human capability, largely through intensive training activities provided by the employer, and the maximisation of the production process through incremental improvements. Higher knowledge is obtained through the up-scaling of the production process, including work re-organisation, new technology and human capital development.
- **Segment 4** is the low-value-adding internal labour market, characterised by a low level of training. Production is carried out by a network of contractors who make finished goods for retailers, who buy in bulk.
- **Segment 5** is the flexible external labour market characterised by bottom-end jobs. Here, experience is required rather than qualifications, and skills are important.
- **Segment 6** is the state-sponsored low-skilled development strategy, representing the informal economy in South Africa. This segment is

described as the 'ghetto' of South African society. The state's labour market policy triggers sustainable economic activity that requires largely low skills input but is labour-intensive.

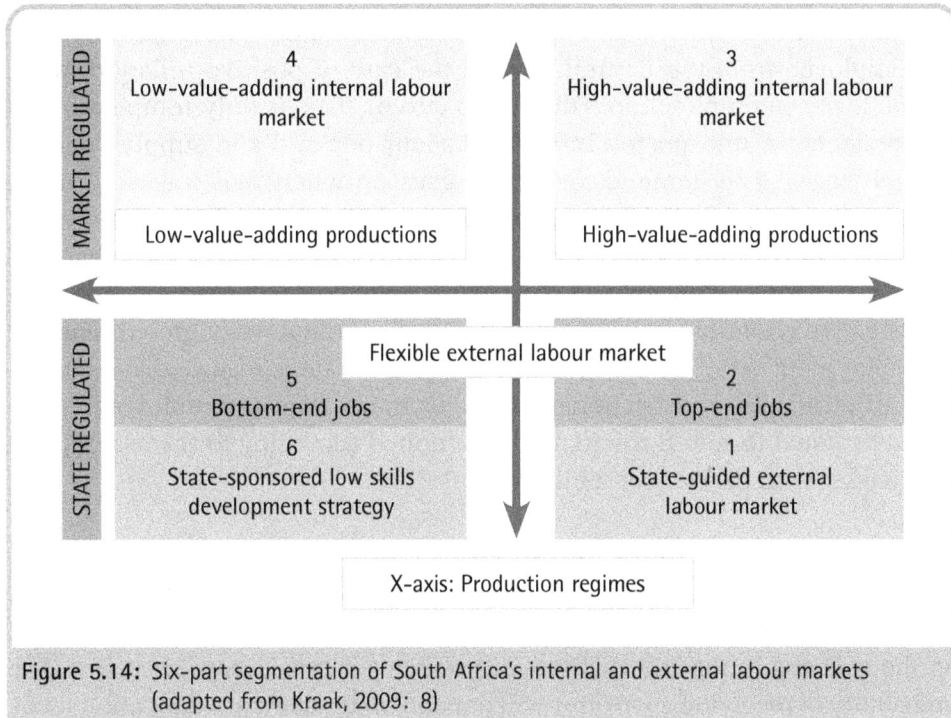

**Figure 5.14:** Six-part segmentation of South Africa's internal and external labour markets (adapted from Kraak, 2009: 8)

*Traditional Division of Labour Market Sectors*

Labour markets are divided according to various criteria, such as professional, spatial and demographics. These sectors function independently of each other due to the heterogeneous nature of labour demand and supply.

## Theories Based on Delays in Adjustment to the Labour Market

*The Human Capital Theory*

This theory was formulated in the early 1960s. Becker, Murphy and Tamura (1990) believed that wage differences resulted from differences in employees' human capital, based on their skills, professional qualifications, education levels and professional experience. An employee who possesses a desired qualification would be given a more prestigious position, with better pay and less workplace insecurity. This has an impact on labour mobility, as employees with universal qualifications may be more willing to change workplaces, and employees with specific qualifications would rather stay in their workplaces.

*The Natural Unemployment Rate Theory*

This theory was developed by Friedman and Phelps in the 1960s. The natural rate is also known as NAIRU, or the non-accelerating inflation rate of unemployment. The word 'natural' means the rate that results from equilibrium in the markets; unexpected inflation may push the employer and employee from the natural rate. In the case of positive inflation, there will be lower unemployment (the Philip curve). This is only temporary and is dependent on unexpected inflation. Labour demand and supply depends on real wages. The demand for labour goes up when real wages go down and supply goes up when real wages go up. Thus, according to Friedman, inflation can obscure price changes in such a way that it seems that real wages go up for employees and down for employers (Coleman, 2013). There is a negative relationship between the rate of nominal wage growth and the unemployment rate. The natural unemployment rate is regarded as a certain level of structural and frictional unemployment. The unemployment rate would be equal to zero if the market functioned according to the assumption of a market with perfect competition.

*The Labour Market (Job) Search Theory*

The probability of a person transitioning out of unemployment depends, first, on the probability that the individual will receive a job offer and, secondly, on the probability that the individual (job-seeker) will accept the offer. The probability of receiving a job offer will depend on the person's education level, experience and skills and on local demand conditions (Rasool & Botha, 2011). According to the job search theory, highly educated unemployed individuals can encounter problems finding an acceptable job (Groot & Oosterbeek, 1990).

## Theories Based on Wage Flexibility

*The Efficient Work Theory*

This theory is also known as the motivating job theory, the theory of work versus efficiency, and the efficiency-shaping wage theory. In this scenario, employers define fixed wages that are higher than the wage balance in the market, because they are willing to pay higher wages in order to raise efficiency. It is assumed that if an employer increases wages, labour productivity will also increase, as employees feel motivated and loyal to their work if they receive higher pay. The argument is that if employees receive higher wages than the market-clearing levels, they have more to lose if they are made redundant (Shapiro & Stiglitz, 1984).

*The Insider–Outsider Theory*

According to this theory, workers are divided into two groups (Jarmolowicz & Knapinska, 2011):

1. Insiders are employees associated with the trade union. These employees' positions are relatively strong and protected.
2. Outsiders are employees who are not associated or who are unemployed. Outsiders are influenced directly by the risk of losing their jobs and wages being lowered by insiders.

*The Non-accelerating Inflation Rate of Unemployment*

The non-accelerating inflation rate of unemployment is commonly known as NAIRU. The term entered the field of macroeconomics in the 1970s, during a period of rapid and rising inflation (Ball & Mankiw, 2002). Kabundi, Schaling and Some (2016: 1) have estimated

> *a Phillips curve for South Africa in a flexible framework which allows the relationship between inflation and real activity to change over time. Besides the slope of the Phillips curve, inflation persistence, which represents the degree to which current inflation depends on past inflation, varies too. In addition, we estimate the inflation target, the target bands, and the non-accelerating inflation rate of unemployment (NAIRU). Given that South Africa is an open economy with a flexible exchange rate, it is appropriate to control for supply shocks such as import prices or the exchange rate. We implicitly account for these factors by allowing for variation in the variance of the error term of the estimated equation.*

## The Effect of Collective Bargaining on Wage and Employment Levels

The question as to whether bargaining power has any effect on real wage levels remains controversial. Some theorists believe that the effect of bargaining on wage levels is minimal, since the wage will always tend to revert to the competitive market price. Alternatively, entrepreneurs will respond by raising prices in order to compensate for the higher wage bill, resulting in a wage–price spiral.

In certain exceptional cases, inelasticity of demand may lead to unions negotiating significantly higher wage levels, but general elasticity of demand will prevent wages from increasing disproportionately to the market value. If they do, employment levels might drop.

The conclusion that demand for labour is generally elastic arises, according to Dobbs (1996), from the assumptions that the supply of capital is elastic (that if wages increase, capital invested will shrink) and from the fact that entrepreneurs can substitute labour with machinery/technology. Except during boom conditions or where increases are matched by higher productivity, the elasticity of capital will decrease the quantity of labour demanded and can lead to an increase in unemployment.

These arguments are countered by those theorists who maintain that the market wage is not necessarily a 'natural' wage, but is determined by the percentage which the entrepreneur wishes to retain for themselves and their shareholders. Therefore, increased wages need not be offset by diminishing capital investment and employment, but rather by decreased profits. They maintain that there is no real proof that increased wages significantly affect investment.

Dobbs (1996) also suggests that wage increases, although they may lead to greater unemployment, may profit the working class in general in that, for example, an employee's spouse or working-age children may not be obliged to work. Most importantly, wage bargaining raises employees above the exploitation level, for if they remain at that level, they will continue to accept wages below the market rate.

The general conclusion is that, although wage bargaining may not have a significant impact on overall wage levels, it is necessary in order to prevent exploitation arising from imperfect competition in the labour market and monopolistic practices by employers. Where there is a strong labour movement or free competition, it is unlikely that wages will drop far below subsistence level. On the other hand, the upper limit to which wages are raised by unions may depend on sociopolitical factors rather than on purely economic ones.

## The Effect of Wage Determinations on Employment Levels

Wage determinations can have a two-way effect on wage levels in that they can either establish a minimum rate higher than the market rate or limit wage increases to an acceptable level. It is generally held that the imposition of a minimum wage which is above the market rate will lead to a decline in employment levels, as illustrated in the section on supply and demand. This need not always be the case. The manner in which demand will react will depend, first, on its degree of elasticity. Secondly, minimum wage regulations have what Reynolds et al (1986) call a 'shock effect'. Organisations subject to a minimum wage regulation may be shocked out of organisational inefficiency, resulting in higher production levels and obviating the necessity to reduce employment levels. Similarly, in some circumstances, minimum wages may offset the monopsonist power of employers, in cases where the entrepreneur is the sole employer of labour.

Wage policies aimed at limiting increases in wage levels are usually introduced to stabilise the economy and promote employment. Unless other factors are regulated, the policy may not be successful. As illustrated by marginal productivity theory, limiting wage levels may not lead to significantly higher employment levels. Economic growth or capital investment should be stimulated simultaneously if employment is to increase. The theory also presupposes that the supply of labour is adequately trained to fill new jobs which are established.

## Labour Markets in the Future

In various other chapters in this text, mention is made of the effect that digitalisation and scientific progress have had and are having on the nature of work, work organisation and, ultimately, the nature of the labour market. According to Blix (2017), digitalisation will affect all aspects of social policy, but the most significant effect will be on the labour market. With advances in automation and technology, there will, as he puts it, be increasing competition between labour and machines, with the middle level of the labour market being the most affected.

Many of the more advanced countries have started showing negative economic growth, with wages stagnating while the Gini coefficient continues to rise. This would indicate that traditional theories about labour supply and demand may no longer provide the answers and the necessary strategies. The role played by unions in ensuring fair wage rates is diminishing. More and more jobs will be outsourced and entrants to the labour market will need to improve their skills constantly. Governments will have to keep ahead of the change process and adapt their policies accordingly.

This does not mean that labour market theory will become obsolete, but the ingredients and constellations will change, as will the proposed solutions.

### Possible Scenarios for the South African Labour Market up to 2030

The SABPP has identified two important scenarios of possible changes to the South African labour market in terms of what they define as 'rules of the game' and 'key uncertainties' (Meyer, 2016: 12):

1.  The extent to which South African employers and unions will adopt or reject the new world of work.
2.  The extent to which stakeholders within the labour market can collaborate to find new ways to influence the future jointly.

The SABPP (Meyer, 2016: 12) further mentions that:

> *One of the immediate key uncertainties discussed here was the adversarial nature of relationships between employer and organised labour created by the legislative framework for collective bargaining and the need to amend labour legislation to curb the right to strike in the light of the high level of intimidation and violence taking place and the need to remedy the financial devastation occasioned by protracted strikes which are no longer in the best interest of the parties. The current status quo gives unions an unfair advantage.*

The SABPP has also named a few 'flags to watch', namely (Meyer, 2016: 16):
- NDP implementation of the 'new world of work'
- technological innovation implemented by employers, both public and private
- the extent to which secondary and tertiary education can adapt to the 'new world of work', through measures such as practical and vocational training
- the extent to which businesses in the informal sector can transition to the formal sector
- employees' freedom to move between formal and informal work.

The SABPP (Meyer, 2016: 16) suggests that reaching an inclusive and collaborative approach to the labour market can be done through:
- the resolution of centralised bargaining structures in favour of the 'new world of work'
- the adoption of co-determination practices at the level of employers
- giving consideration to corruption and anti-competitive practices
- reaching agreements on industrial action rules between the parties, which would lead to a decrease in violent strikes
- utilising the power of organised business, labour and government in order to reach and implement transformative agreements.

## The South African Labour Market During Covid-19

A World Bank economic report of 2021 made various suggestions for South Africa, the first being that young entrepreneurs should help with the job crisis that has been worsened by the Covid-19 pandemic. The second suggestion is related to self-employment, which could halve the country's unemployment rate. The report points out that South Africa's self-employment rate is at only 10 per cent, whereas countries such as Mexico, Brazil and Turkey have a rate of 30 per cent. Thirdly, the government needs to implement policies that can revitalise the job market, create a climate of inclusivity after the Covid-19 pandemic and preserve macroeconomic stability (World Bank, 2021).

The Covid-19 pandemic and the associated lockdown led to record unemployment, as many businesses closed, leading to millions unable to seek work as a result of lockdown regulations. The rate of unemployment among women was 36.8 per cent in the second quarter of 2021, compared to 32.4 per cent among men, according to the official definition of unemployment (Stats SA, 2021) (see Figure 5.15).

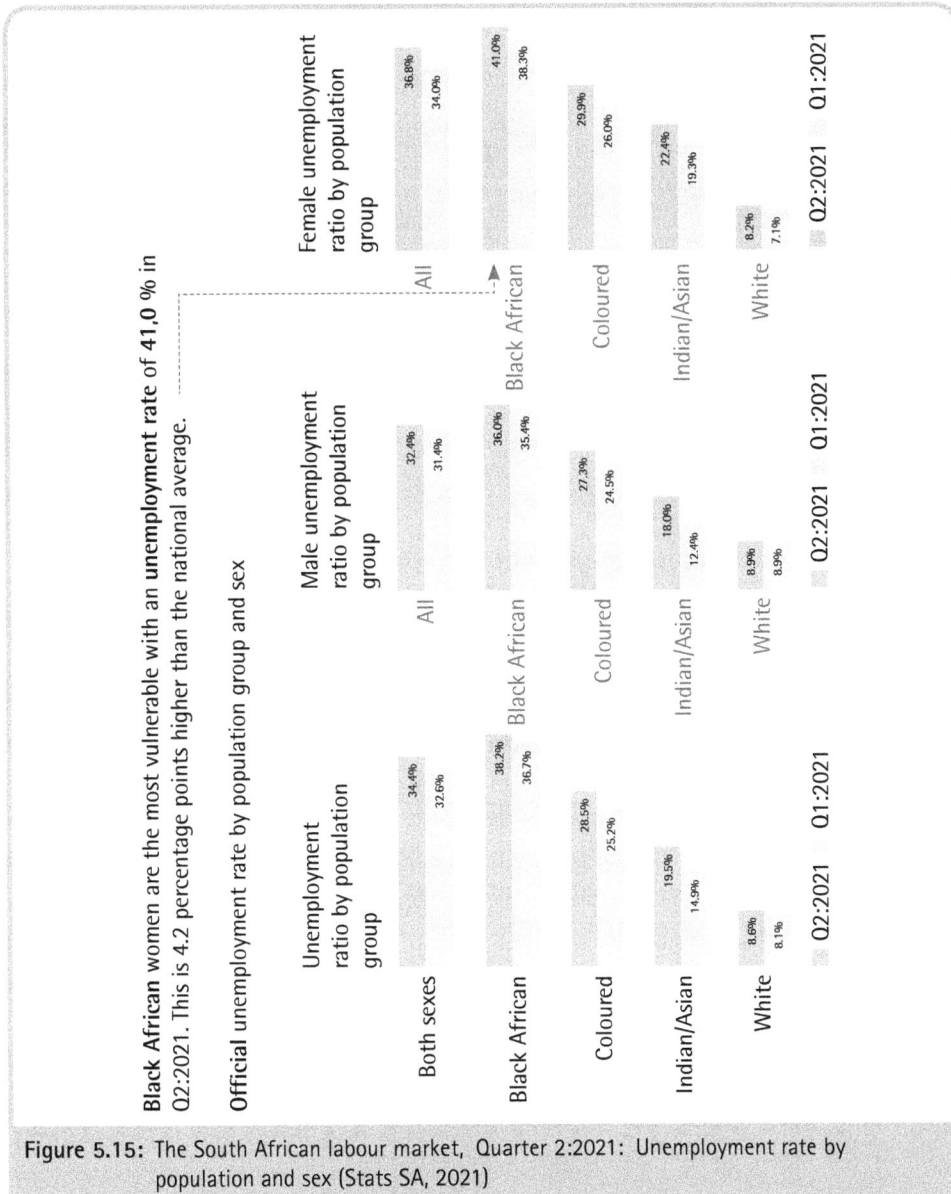

**Figure 5.15:** The South African labour market, Quarter 2:2021: Unemployment rate by population and sex (Stats SA, 2021)

There were many changes in working conditions during the Covid-19 pandemic. Many workers were temporarily absent from work, with or without pay or at reduced pay. Teleworking or remote working arrangements became the norm those able to work from home, and in other instances the location of work was changed in some way. Restrictions on movement during the pandemic led to a significant proportion of the working-age population being economically inactive, as they could not look for a job during that time. There were also changes to the hours of work, with some employees working excessive hours and others having their hours reduced.

## Conclusion

Perhaps more so than any other market, the labour market functions in terms of a set of complex variables. No single variable can be considered in isolation and the application of theory to practice would entail a detailed study of the circumstances surrounding a particular labour market.

## Suggested Questions/Tasks

1. Explain what labour economics is.
2. What is the difference between labour economics and personnel economics?
3. A union and management are deadlocked on substantial wage increases for lower-level employees (as has been happening in the mining industry). Using the theory discussed in this chapter, as well as your own further reading, present and support the following arguments:
   a. The argument from management's side as to why high wage increases would not ultimately benefit either party or the country.
   b. The argument from the union's side, countering management's argument.
4. Do you believe that the application of classical and neo-classical labour market theory is appropriate in the South African context? Write a reasoned (deductive) essay supporting your case and pointing to the way forward.
5. There is controversy surrounding the National Minimum Wage Act 9 of 2018. Conduct a debate, based on labour market theory, arguing the pros and cons of this Act.
6. Write an essay on the different economic theories and apply these theories to the South African labour market. Motivate which theory you think the parties to the labour market need to follow.

7.  Critically discuss the SABPP's view with regard to the future of the labour market up to 2030 (Meyer, 2016).
8.  Explain in detail how the Covid-19 pandemic has influenced the South African labour market.
9.  Why is it important to predict the future of labour markets?

## Sources

Ball, L & Mankiw, NG. 2002. 'The NAIRU in theory and practice'. *Journal of Economic Perspectives* 16(4): 115–136.

Becker, G, Murphy, KM & Tamura, R. 1990. 'Human capital, fertility, and economic growth'. *Journal of Political Economy* 98: S12–S70.

Bhorat, H, Caetano, T, Jourdan, B, Kanbur, R, Rooney, C, Stanwix, B & Woolard, I. 2016. 'Quantitative analysis investigating the feasibility of a national minimum wage for South Africa'. Development Policy Research Unit, University of Cape Town. http://www.dpru.uct.ac.za/sites/default/files/image_tool/images/36/Publications/Working_Papers/DPRU%20WP201601.pdf (Accessed 14 September 2021).

Bhorat, H, Leibbrandt, M, Maziya, M, Van der Berg, S & Woolard, I. 2001. *Fighting poverty: Labour markets and inequality in South Africa*. Cape Town: UCT Press.

Blix, M. 2017. 'The effects of digitalisation on labour market polarisation and tax revenue'. *CESifo Forum* 18(4): 9–14. Available: www.cesifo-group.de/DocDL/CESifo-forum-2017-4-blix-digitalisation-welfare-state-december.pdf (Accessed 14 September 2021).

Braude W. 2005. 'South Africa: Bringing informal workers into the regulated sphere, overcoming apartheid's legacy', in *Good Jobs, Bad Jobs, No Jobs: Labor Markets and Informal Work in Egypt, El Salvador, India, Russia, and South Africa*, edited by T Avirgan, L Bivens & S Gammage. Washington, DC: Economic Policy Institute: 369–490.

Coleman, TS. 2013. 'The natural rate of unemployment'. Draft, 16 December 2013. https://harris.uchicago.edu/files/naturalrate_1.pdf (Accessed 9 November 2021).

Dobbs, M. 1996. *Wages*. London: James Nisbett & Co.

Doeringer, P & Piore, M. 1971. *Internal Labour Markets and Manpower Analysis*. Lexington: Lexington Books.

Drinkwater, S. n.d. 'Labour economics'. https://whystudyeconomics.ac.uk/during-your-study/module-choices/labour-economics/ (Accessed 9 November 2021).

Ehrenberg, RG & Smith, RS. 2012. *Modern Labor Economics: Theory and Public Policy*, 11th edition. London: Routledge.

Fick, R & Hugh, SH. 1987. *The Theory and Practice of Industrial Relations in South Africa*. Johannesburg: Hodder & Stoughton Educational Southern Africa.

Groot, W & Oosterbeek, H. 1990. 'Optimal investment in human capital under uncertainty'. Research Memorandum 9014, Department of Economics, University of Amsterdam.

Grund, C, Bryson, A, Dur, R, Koch, AK & Lazear, EP. 2017. 'Personnel economics: A research field comes of age'. *German Journal of Human Resource Management* 3(2): 101–107.

ILO (International Labour Organization). n.d. 'Labour market segmentation'. https://www.ilo.org/global/topics/employment-security/labour-market-segmentation/lang--en/index.htm (Accessed 14 September 2021).

Jarmolowicz, W & and Knapinska, M. 2011. 'Labour market theories in contemporary economics'. *Transformations in Business and Economics* 10(2): 268–280. https://www.researchgate.net/publication/287512084_Labour_market_theories_in_contemporary_economics (Accessed 14 September 2021).

Kabundi, A, Schaling, E & Some, M. 2016. 'Estimating a Phillipps curve for South Africa: A bounded random walk approach'. ERSA Research Brief. May 2016. https://www.econrsa.org/system/files/publications/research_briefs/research_brief_68.pdf (Accessed 14 September 2021).

Kraak, A. 2009. 'The relevance of segmented labour market theory'. Eastern Cape Socio Economic Consultative Council (ECSECC) Working Paper Series No 7. East London: ECSECC.

Lazear, EP. 1999. 'Personnel economics: Past lessons and future directions', presidential address to the Society of Labor Economists, San Francisco, May 1, 1998 *Journal of Labor Economics* 17: 199–236.

Lazear, EP. 2000. 'The future of personnel economics'. *The Economic Journal* 110: F611–F639.

Lazear, EP & Oyer, P. 2013. 'Personnel economics', in *Handbook of Organizational Economics*, edited by R Gibbons & J Roberts. Princeton, NJ: Princeton University Press: 479–519.

Lazear, EP & Shaw, AL. 2007. 'Personnel economics: The economist's view of human resources'. *Journal of Economic Perspectives* 21(4): 91–114.

McConnell, CR & Brue, SL. 1986. *Contemporary Labour Economics*. New York: McGraw-Hill.

McConnell, C, Brue, SL & Macpherson, D. 2015. *Contemporary Labor Economics*, 11th edition. Dubuque, IA: McGraw-Hill Irwin.

Meyer, M. 2016. 'SABPP labour market scenarios 2030: People and work – How will the South African labour market change over the next 14 years?'. Johannesburg: SABPP.

Önday, O. 2016. 'Classical to modern organization theory'. *International Journal of Business and Management Review* 4(2): 15–59.

Patel, L, Khan, Z & Englert, T. 2020. 'How might a national minimum wage affect the employment of youth in South Africa?'. *Development Southern Africa* 37(1): 147–161.

Piek, M & Von Fintel, D. 2018. 'Sectoral minimum wages in South Africa: Disemployment by firm size and trade exposure'. Working Paper WP19/2018. Stellenbosch: University of Stellenbosch.

Piore, MJ. 1969. 'On-the-job training in the dual labor market: Public and private responsibilities in onthe-job training of disadvantaged workers', in *Public-Private Manpower Policies*, edited by A Weber, F Cassell & W Ginsburg. Madison: Industrial Relations Research Association: 101–132.

Piore, MJ. 1970. 'Jobs and training', in *The State and the Poor*, edited by S Beer & R Barringer, Cambridge, MA: Winthrop: 53–83.

Rasool, F & Botha, CJ. 2011. 'The nature, extent and effect of skills shortages on skills migration in South Africa'. *South African Journal of Human Resource Management* 9(1): Art 287.

Reynolds, LG, Masters, SH & Moser, CH. 1986. *Labour Economics and Labour Relations*. Hoboken: Prentice-Hall.

Shapiro, C & Stiglitz, JE. 1984. 'Equilibrium unemployment as a worker discipline device'. *American Economic Review* 74(3): 433–444.

Stats SA (Statistics South Africa). 2021. 'South Africa labour market is more favourable to men than women'. http://www.statssa.gov.za/wp-content/uploads/2021/08/Unemployment-by-population-group-final.jpg (Accessed 14 September 2021).

Stigler, GJ. 1946. 'The economics of minimum wage legislation'. *The American Economic Review* 36(3): 358–365.

Uys, MD & Blaauw, PF. 2006. 'The dual labour market theory and the informal sector'. *Acta Commercii* 6(1): a122.

Van der Berg S. 1992. 'Confronting Unemployment in South Africa'. (Occasional paper no 6.) Stellenbosch: Stellenbosch Economic Project.

World Bank. 2021. 'South Africa economic update: South Africa's labor market can benefit from young entrepreneurs, self-employment'. 13 July 2021. https://www.worldbank.org/en/country/southafrica/publication/south-africa-economic-update-south-africa-s-labor-market-can-benefit-from-young-entrepreneurs-self-employment (Accessed 14 September 2021).

**6**

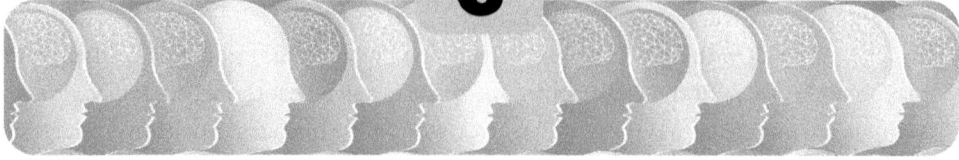

# The South African Labour Market

## Chapter Outline

➤

# Overview

A working paper of the Southern Africa Labour and Development Research Unit (SALDRU) has the following to say about the importance of the labour market in South Africa and the effects of the 2020 lockdown instituted to contain the spread of the novel coronavirus (Ranchhod & Daniels, 2021: 44):

> The labour market in South Africa has been shown by researchers to be the primary institution for determining a number of socio-economic welfare measures. Finding a formal sector job is strongly correlated with exiting from poverty, and losing one has a big impact on falling back into poverty. Thus, vulnerability to job loss is itself an important aspect of a household's general well-being. In addition, South Africa is widely considered to be one of the most unequal countries in the world, and the primary driver of economic inequality is also mediated through access to formal sector employment ... Our main findings are that the period from February to April of 2020 saw an unprecedented decrease in employment. In our sample of over 6000 adults aged 18 to 59, the fraction of the sample that was conventionally classified as employed decreased from 57 per cent in February to 48 per cent in April. If we further exclude temporarily absent workers, this fraction decreases further to 38 per cent. Thus, about 1 out of every 3 people that were employed in February in our sample either lost their job because of the lockdown, or did not work and received no wages during April. This has extremely large implications for poverty and welfare.

As seen above, the working paper of the Southern Africa Labour and Development Research Unit (SALDRU) has explained the importance of the labour market in South Africa and the effects of the 2020 lockdown instituted to contain the spread of the novel coronavirus: for a labour market to function effectively, a balance has to exist between the demand for and the supply of labour. In an ideal market, there would be a perfect balance, but no such market exists. The market system is beset by labour market imperfections, leading either to supply not meeting demand or, more generally, to an oversupply in relation to demand (unemployment).

According to neo-classical theory, the ability of an economy to grow in relation to the population and to create new jobs is a prime factor determining employment levels. However, imperfections in demand and supply may still be caused by a lack of mobility, particularly on the part of labour, abnormally high wage rates (leading to a decrease in demand), disproportional population growth, monopsonist practices, government regulations and, as some modern theorists would have it, by the existence of dual or segmented labour markets.

The South African labour market suffers from endemic structural unemployment. The economy cannot absorb all work-seekers and, often, those positions which are available cannot be filled by the unemployed, owing, in some cases, to a lack of skill, but also to structural inequities arising from historical and sociopolitical factors.

In an attempt to engender economic growth, the post-1994 government adopted the Growth, Employment and Redistribution (GEAR) strategy, aimed at both growth and redistribution. Although economic growth, even if minimal, did occur, there was no marked increase in employment and foreign investment was disappointing. More recently, investor confidence has been affected by perceived labour market rigidities in the form of labour legislation, the influence and militancy of the trade union movement, the crime rate and government inefficiencies.

➤

The government released the New Growth Path Framework on 23 November 2010 and the National Development Plan (NDP) on 15 August 2012. Both were aimed at economic development and more employment opportunities. The results of these initiatives were not immediately visible, but some aspects, such as various infrastructure programmes and the youth wage subsidy, were implemented.

In August 2017 the government announced yet another plan, namely radical economic transformation (RET). This plan deviated from the previous ones in that it emphasised the need to expand ownership of land and even to expropriate land without compensation. The means by which the objectives of the plan will be achieved needed and still needs clarification.

In 2020 the World Economic Forum develop a Covid Action platform, based on three priorities:
1. Galvanising the global community for collective action
2. Protecting people's livelihoods and facilitating business continuity
3. Mobilising co-operation and business support for the Covid-19 response.

The South African response to Covid-19 led to the National Treasury Supplementary Budget Review of 2020, containing a stimulus package for the economy aimed at mitigating the damages caused by Covid-19 and the concomitant lockdown. The country's GDP growth rate was revised from 8 per cent to a contraction of 7.5 per cent in 2020, and is forecast to grow at 2.8 per cent in 2021, slipping to 1.4 per cent in 2022 (Republic of South Africa, 2020).

As shown in Figure 6.1, the International Labour Organization (ILO) has stated that 8.8 per cent of global working hours were lost in 2020 due to the Covid-19 pandemic, compared to the fourth quarter of 2019. This is equivalent to 255 million full-time jobs – approximately four times the number lost during the 2008/2009 global financial crisis. The down-turn of lost working hours are a result of reduced working hours for those in employment or 'unprecedented' levels of employment loss, hitting 114 million people. The ILO indicated that 71 per cent of these employment losses (81 million people) came in the form of inactivity rather than unemployment, as people left the labour market because they were unable to work because of pandemic restrictions, or as they simply ceased to look for work (ILO, 2021).

In the meantime, unemployment remains a serious problem in South Africa, as does the economy, which has not grown as might be expected. Initiatives to promote economic growth and market competitiveness should become a priority, as well as informed research into future labour market requirements and planning for that market. Figure 6.2 illustrates the unemployment levels in South Africa from January 2018 to January 2021.

As explained by PwC (2021: 14) in the box on page 269, different economic growth scenarios have an impact on employment recovery.

The Covid-19 pandemic is expected to reverse the progress made globally to reduce poverty over the past two decades globally and, globally, almost 90 million people will fall below the poverty threshold during 2020 to 2021 (PwC, 2021). See Table 6.1 (page 270) for estimates of real gross domestic product (GDP) for 2020 and projections for 2021 to 2022.

➤

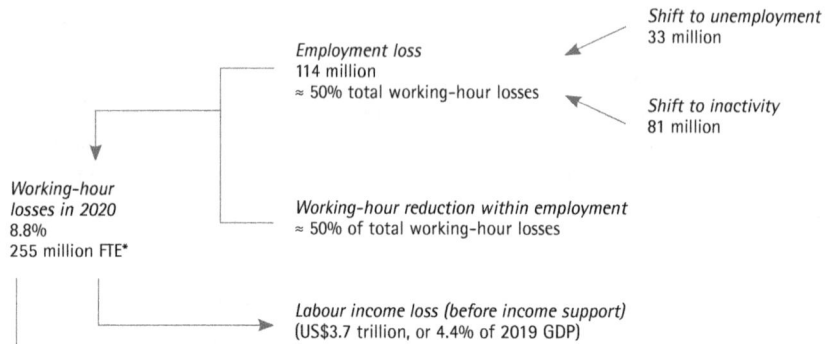

**Working-hour, employment and labour income losses 2020**

Employment loss
114 million
≈ 50% total working-hour losses

*Shift to unemployment*
33 million

*Shift to inactivity*
81 million

Working-hour
losses in 2020
8.8%
255 million FTE*

Working-hour reduction within employment
≈ 50% of total working-hour losses

Labour income loss (before income support)
(US$3.7 trillion, or 4.4% of 2019 GDP)

**Working-hour losses: quarterly trends in 2020 and projections for 2021**

|  | 2020 quarterly | | | | 2021 projection | | |
|---|---|---|---|---|---|---|---|
|  | Q1 | Q2 | Q3 | Q4 | Baseline | Optimistic | Pessimistic |
| % | 5.2 | 18.2 | 7.2 | 4.6 | 3.0 | 1.3 | 4.6 |
| FTE* (million) | 150 | 525 | 205 | 130 | 90 | 36 | 130 |

*FTE: Full-time equivalent jobs (assuming a 48-hour working week)

**Figure 6.1:** Working hours, employment and labour income losses in 2020 (ILO, 2021: 1)

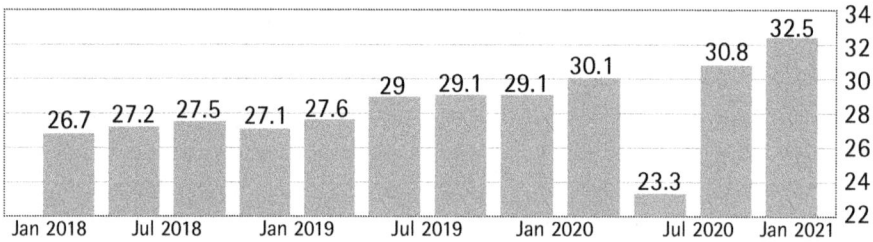

**Figure 6.2:** South Africa unemployment rates from January 2018 to January 2021 (Trading Economics, 2021)

Fewer than 500 000 jobs will be recovered this year, with a long road ahead to reduce the unemployment rate (see Figure 6.3).

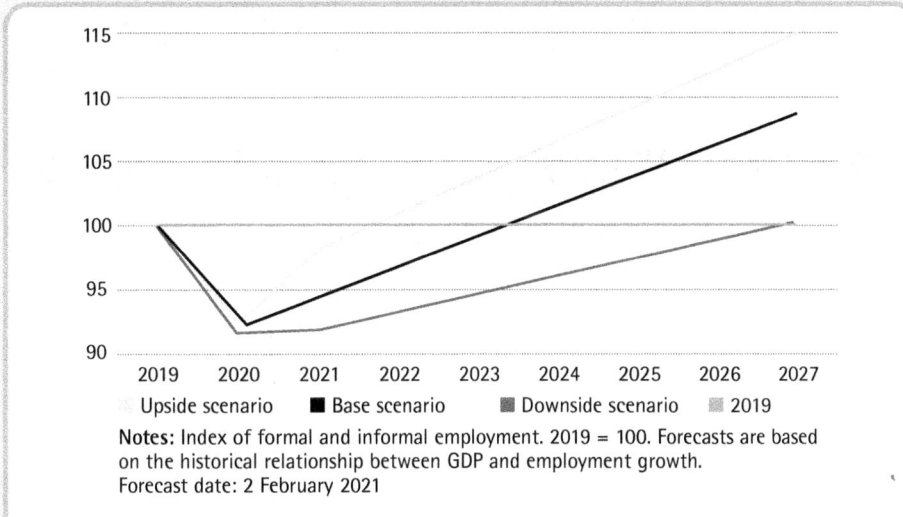

**Notes:** Index of formal and informal employment. 2019 = 100. Forecasts are based on the historical relationship between GDP and employment growth.
Forecast date: 2 February 2021

**Figure 6.3:** Index of formal and informal employment

Different economic growth scenarios have a significant impact on the trajectory of the employment recovery. For example, PwC's modelling shows that under the baseline scenario, South Africa's Economy will add only 467 000 jobs in 2021. However, achieving the upside scenario would lift this number to more than 900 000. Conversely the downside scenario sees just 109 000 jobs recovered this year.

The baseline scenario sees employment returning to 2019 levels (ie prepandemic) by 2024. However by then, a large number of new workers will have been added to the labour force. As such, PwC expects the narrowly defined, unemployment rate to decline only slowly, from an estimated 35.1 per cent in 2020 to 33.6 per cent in 2024. However, if the recovery is closer to the downside scenario, the unemployment rate will continue to rise after year's increase, approaching 40.0 per cent by the end of the decade.

South Africa already faced significant challenges with poverty, inequality and unemployment prior to the Covid-19 pandemic with an unemployment rate among the highest in the world. To avoid further exacerbation of these challenges, South Africa's economic recovery needs to be robust. Budget speech 2021 could establish a foundation to support this economic recovery.

**Table 6.1:** Real GDP estimates for 2020 and projections for 2021 to 2022 (adapted from BusinessTech, 2021)

| Real GDP | Estimate (%) | Projections (%) | |
|---|---|---|---|
| | 2020 | 2021 | 2022 |
| World output | −3.5 | 5.5 | 4.2 |
| Emerging markets and developing economies | −1.1 | 8.3 | 5.9 |
| Emerging and developing Asia | −1.1 | 8.3 | 5.9 |
| China | 2.3 | 8.1 | 5.6 |
| India | −8.0 | 11.5 | 6.8 |
| ASEAN-5 | −3.7 | 5.2 | 6.0 |
| Emerging and developing Europe | −2.8 | 4.0 | 3.9 |
| Russia | −3.6 | 3.0 | 3.9 |
| Latin America and the Caribbean | −7.4 | 4.1 | 2.9 |
| Brazil | −4.5 | 3.6 | 2.6 |
| Mexico | −8.5 | 4.3 | 2.5 |
| Middle East and Central Asia | −3.2 | 3.0 | 4.2 |
| Saudi Arabia | −2.6 | 3.2 | 3.9 |
| Sub-Saharan Africa | −2.6 | 3.2 | 3.9 |
| Nigeria | −3.2 | 1.5 | 2.5 |
| South Africa | −7.5 | 2.8 | 1.4 |

In 2020, the IMF approved USD4.3 billion in emergency financial assistance to South Africa under the Rapid Financing Instrument (RFI), in an effort to assist the authorities to address health challenges and the severe economical impact of the Covid-19 pandemic (BusinessTech, 2021).

# The Labour Force and Related Concepts

We have already discussed the classical labour market theories which underpin the free-market approach to both employment levels and wage setting. As indicated, the concept of an absolutely free market is largely theoretical, since it presupposes no government interference, perfect competition and absolute flexibility and mobility on the part of both labour and capital. There is no country where the market is allowed an absolutely free rein, and therefore no country with a perfect labour market. As later theorists indicated, wage rates or wage costs are distorted by factors other than demand and supply. Equally, employment levels are subject to numerous influences. Nevertheless, in systems which broadly support free-market principles, an interrelationship does exist between demand and supply, and wage rates are broadly determined by such interrelationships.

Indicators related to the economically active population (EAP) are used to analyse and describe the supply of labour in two ways:

1. As a basis for the formulation, implementation and monitoring of microeconomic and macroeconomic policies and programmes.
2. In human resource (HR) development planning.

The analysis of the EAP provides a basis to monitor trends in the economy and the employment situation of a country. To understand unemployment and underutilisation/underemployment, it is important to look at the EAP. The unemployment rate is used to assess the current performance of the economy and is crucial for analysing the labour market, together with labour demand statistics such as job vacancies, filled jobs, labour cost, compensation, and training needs, and contextual statistics such as economic growth, investment, population growth and skills training (AfDB, 2012).

According to Article 8 of the 13th International Conference of Labour Statisticians (ICLS) Resolution (1982), the 'labour force, or "currently active population", comprises all persons who fulfil the requirements for inclusion among the employed or the unemployed'. According to AfDB (2012), the labour force framework (see Figure 6.4), persons in the population are classified into three groups, namely the employed population, the unemployed and the population outside the labour force.

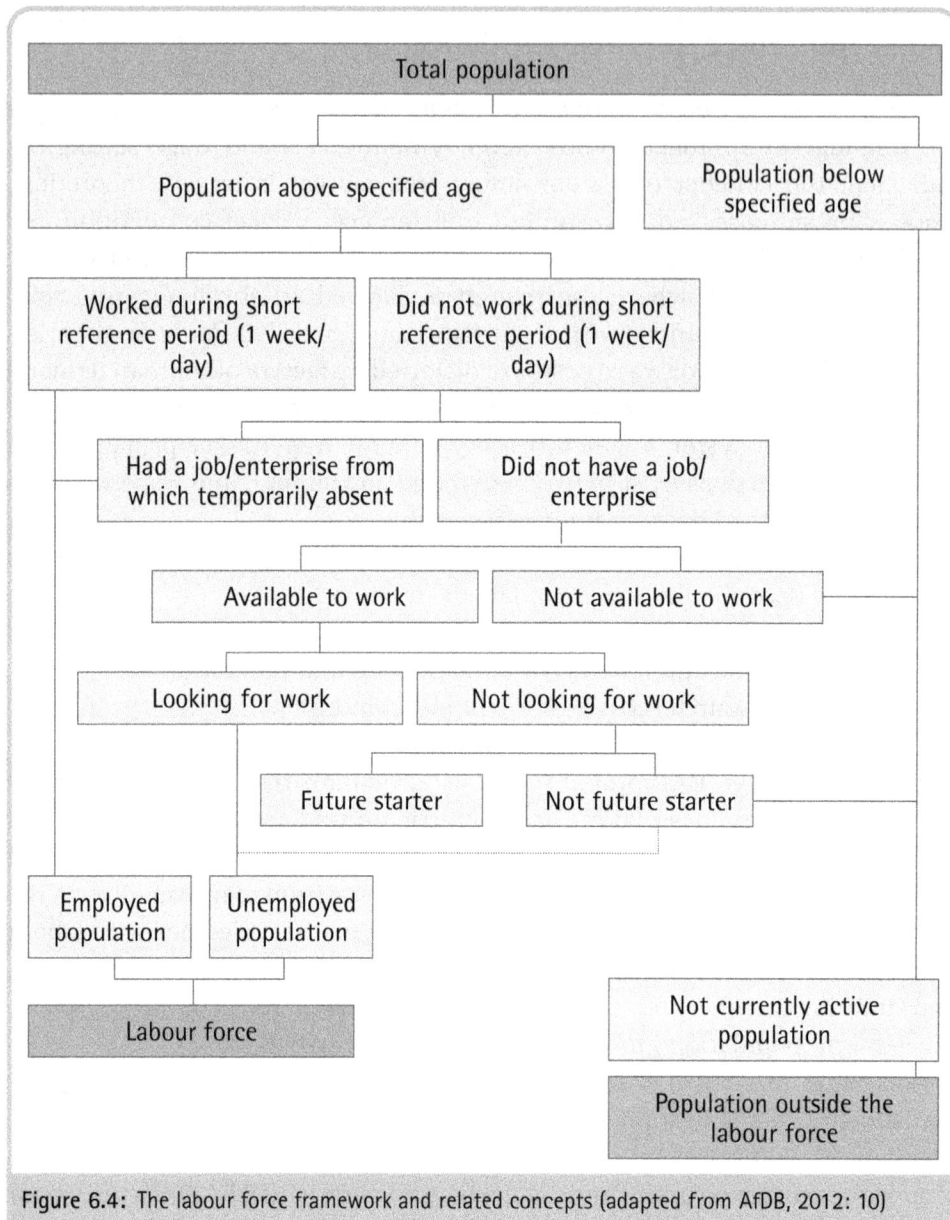

**Figure 6.4:** The labour force framework and related concepts (adapted from AfDB, 2012: 10)

## The definition of 'employed' persons

According to Article 9 of the 13th ICLS Resolution (ICLS, 1982: 1-10):

(1) *The employed comprise all persons above the age specified for measuring the economically active population who, during a specified short reference period of either one week or one day, were in the following categories:*

(a) *'paid employment'*

(a1) *'at work' persons who, during the reference period, performed some work for wage or salary, in cash or in kind;*

(a2) *'with a job but not at work': persons who, having already worked in their present job, were temporarily not at work during the reference period and had a formal attachment to their job.*

(b) *'self-employment':*

(b1) *'at work': persons who, during the reference period, performed some work for profit or family gain, in cash or in kind;'*

(b2) *'with an enterprise but not at work' persons with an enterprise (which may be a business enterprise, a farm or a service undertaking) who were temporarily not at work during the reference period for any specific reason.*

(2) *For operational purposes, the notion of 'some work' may be interpreted as work for at least one hour.*

## Unemployment and Underutilisation/Underemployment

### The Nature and Definition of Unemployment

There are many definitions of unemployment. Some researchers regard the unemployed as all potential labour without a fixed position, while others concern themselves only with active work-seekers who are unable to find jobs.

Sadie (1980) defines the unemployed as all those who are temporarily or indefinitely laid off without pay and those without a job who are available for employment and are seeking work. This definition does not take into account the large number of 'underemployed' in South Africa. These underemployed included for example people do work for a few hours a week and who form part of a large percentage of the economically active population and whom the ILO view as 'vulnerable employees'. (Underemployment is discussed in greater detail in the following subsection.) A broader definition of unemployment is that which describes the unemployed as all those who are willing and physically and mentally able to work, but who cannot find work, those who find only partial work and those who have given up.

The following is an extensive definition of unemployment, according to the ILO (2000: 86–87):

(1) The 'unemployed' comprise all persons above a specified age who during the reference period were:

(a) 'without work', ie were not in paid employment or self-employment;

(b) 'currently available for work', ie were available for paid employment or self-employment during the reference period; and

(c) 'seeking work', ie had taken specific steps in a specified recent period to seek paid employment or self-employment. The specific steps may include registration at a public or private employment exchange; application to employers; checking at worksites, farms, factory gates, market or other assembly places; placing or answering newspaper advertisements; seeking assistance of friends or relatives; looking for land, building, machinery or equipment to establish own enterprise; arranging for financial resources; applying for permits and licences, etc.

According to Statistics South Africa (Stats SA, 2021a: 12) there are two definitions of unemployment: the official definition and the expanded definition:

Unemployed persons according to the Official definition are those (aged 15–64 years) who:

a) Were not employed in the reference week; and

b) Actively looked for work or tried to start a business in the four weeks preceding the survey interview; and

c) Were available for work, ie would have been able to start work or a business in the reference week; or

d) Had not actively looked for work in the past four weeks, but had a job or business to start at a definite date in the future and were available.

Unemployed persons according to the Expanded definition are those (aged 15–64 years) who:

a) Were not employed in the reference week; and

b) Were available to work but did not look for work either because they are discouraged from looking for work or did not look for work for other reasons other than discouragement.

In Figure 6.5 we see that, according to the Quarterly Labour Force Survey (QLFS) for quarter 2 of 2021 (Stats SA, 2021b), the labour force participation rate increased by 1.1 percentage points from 56.4 per cent in Q1 of 2021 to 57.5 per cent in Q2 of 2021.

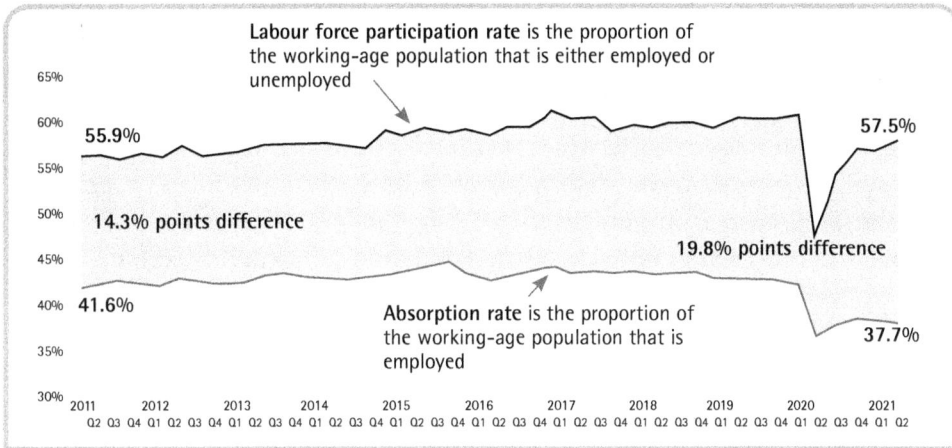

**Figure 6.5:** Labour force participation and absorption rate (adapted from Stats SA, 2021b)

In Figure 6.6 we see the narrow unemployment rate by gender. Unemployment is continuously higher among women than it was among men, reaching approximately 34.3 percent of the total labour force during Q4 of 2020 (Hill, Lilenstein & Thornton, 2020). The vertical line marks the year 2008, the year of the global financial crisis and the year when the survey instrument in South Africa changed from the LFS to the QLFS.

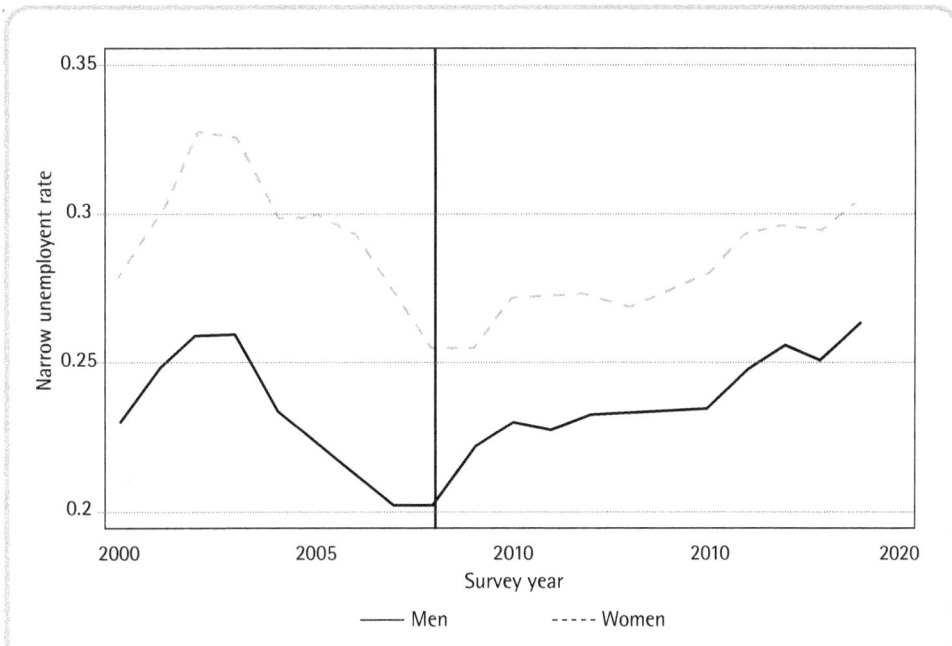

**Figure 6.6:** The narrow unemployment rate in South Africa by gender, 2000–2020 (adapted from Hill et al, 2020: 7)

For many decades the unemployment rate has been reported as the single most important indicator of how an economy is performing, but other employment statuses, such as 'disguised' unemployment, hardly received any attention. Disguised unemployment is when some jobs have economic characteristics intermediate between fair unemployment and employment. For example, part-time and casual employment can have adverse effects on individuals' income and access to benefits such as health and pension protection.

## Underutilisation and Underemployment

Unemployment does not capture other possibilities of labour resource wastage. Underutilisation is associated with individuals who are not working but who are willing to and able to work, whether they are classified as outside of or in the labour force (Mitchell & Carlson, 2000). Hauser (1974) developed a labour utilisation framework to measure visible and invisible underemployment, as shown in Table 6.2.

**Table 6.2:** The labour utilisation framework and the standard labour force (adapted from Hauser, 1974: 5; Sugiyarto, 2007: 6)

| Labour utilisation framework | Standard labour force |
|---|---|
| Total workforce | Total labour force |
| Sub-unemployed, including discouraged | Unemployed |
| Unemployed | |
| Utilised inadequately by:<br>■ Hours of work<br>■ Income level<br>■ Mismatched workers regarding occupation and education | Employed |
| Adequately employed | Employed |

As seen from Table 6.2, the labour utilisation framework recognises different categories of economically inadequate employment, based on income (poverty-level pay, hours of work – involuntary part-time work) and a mismatch between workers' education levels and their jobs (underutilised skills).

Why do we need to look at underemployment?

> *A focus on employment rather than unemployment as an indicator of labour market performance would give an advantage of being more*

*comprehensive since the employment rate covers all people, including the inactive population, in its denominator, other than the unemployment rate which disregards the inactive population altogether.* (Mncayi, 2020: 3)

The components illustrated in Figure 6.7 allow for the identification of three separate measures of labour underutilisation:

1. **Time-related underemployment:** This occurs when an employed worker is willing to work and available to work, but the hours of work are insufficient in relation to an alternative employment situation (ILO, 1998). As explained by the international standards, persons in time-related underemployment are persons who, during the reference period used to define employment, have complied with the following three criteria:
   a. They were willing to work additional hours.
   b. They were available to work additional hours.
   c. They have worked less than working time, as indicated by a threshold.
2. **Unemployment**
3. **Marginal attachment:** Persons who are neither working nor currently looking for work, but who want to work and are available to work and have looked for work sometime in the last 12 months. Discouraged workers are seen as marginally attached, as they have a job-market-related reason not for working.

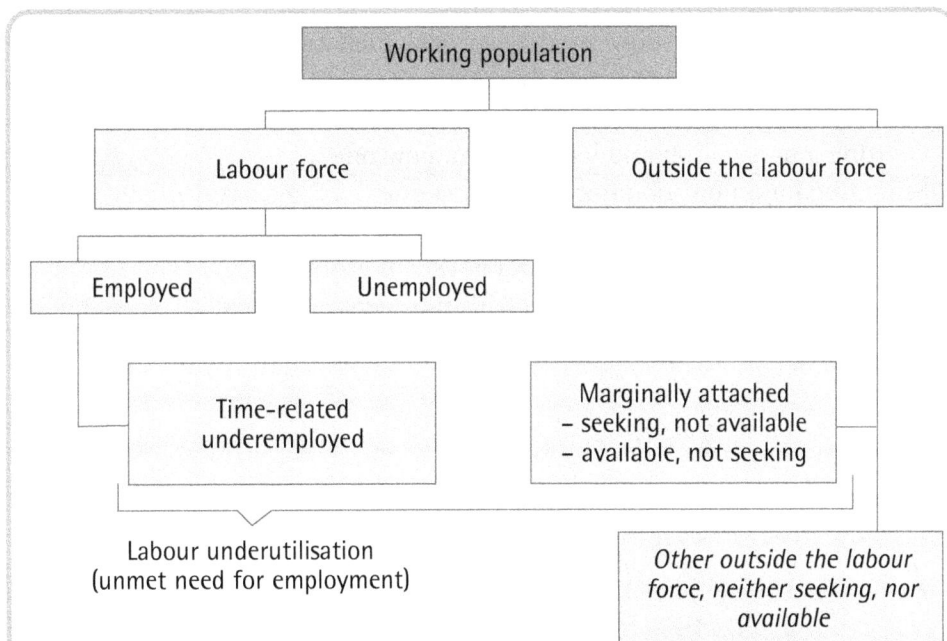

**Figure 6.7:** Components of labour underutilisation (ILO, 2013: 19)

These three measures, when used separately, allow for more detailed monitoring of labour market cycles, as each component is expected to respond differently at different stages of the business cycle and in different settings. These measurements may be combined to produce overlapping measures, such as an extended unemployment rate, and as an indicator of labour underutilisation.

## Classification of Unemployment

Unemployment can, in terms of the main reason for its occurrence, be broadly divided into frictional unemployment, cyclical unemployment, structural unemployment and seasonal unemployment.

### Frictional Unemployment

This type of unemployment occurs where existent vacancies could be filled by the unemployed, but where these persons, owing to geographical location, a lack of information or dissatisfaction with the wages offered, do not apply for the positions. Sometimes, communication regarding available positions does not reach the target market of unemployed persons or the information is not widely disseminated. Frictional unemployment can be combated mainly by:
- ensuring continual and correct exchange of information
- establishing a central 'clearing house' for vacancies and applications
- improved vocational guidance.

According to the stock-flow model, as explained by McConnell, Brue and Macpherson (2015), (see Figure 6.8), people are continuously engaging in one or more of the following:
- Quitting a present job and looking for a new one
- Searching for a new job after having lost one
- Entering the labour force to seek work for the first time
- Re-entering the labour force after a period of absence
- Leaving a job to start another job within the next 30 days.

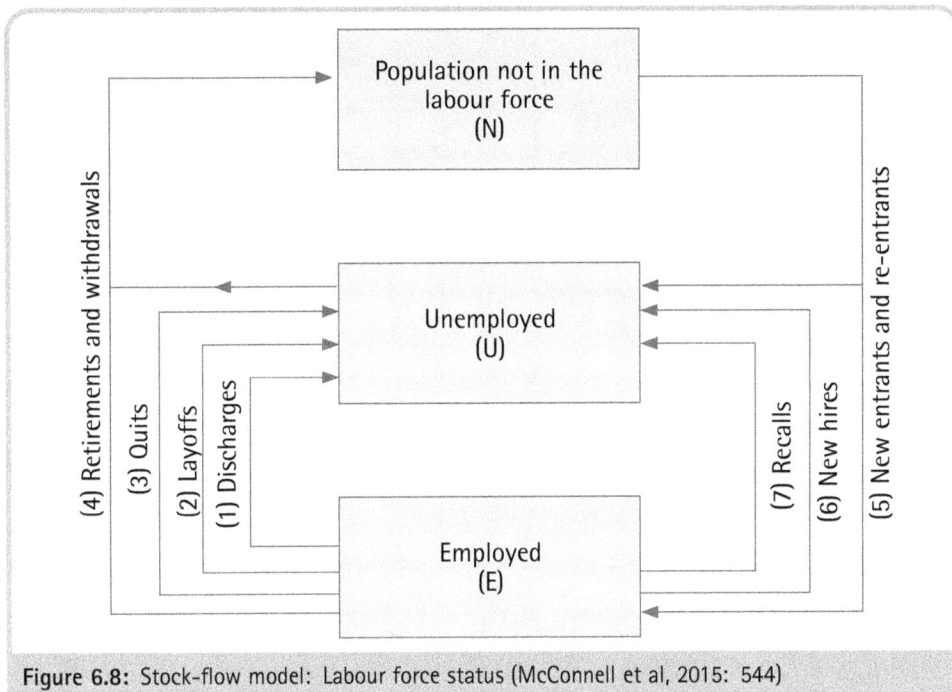

**Figure 6.8:** Stock-flow model: Labour force status (McConnell et al, 2015: 544)

From Figure 6.8 it is clear that at any given time there is a stock of people in each of the boxes representing a category of the labour force. This stock is simultaneously being replenished and depleted by numerous flows out of and into each category. The population not in the labour market (N) are those people who are discouraged workers (workers who, after having unsuccessfully looked for a job, have become discouraged to look for jobs and have abandoned their job search) and underutilised workers (workers who have accepted employment in occupations paying lower wages than those they would qualify for during a periods of full employment) (McConnell et al, 2015: 542). The labour market is not like an auction market; it never fully clears. At any moment there is a great amount of frictional unemployment, as not all active job-seekers will have found acceptable employment and not all employers will have filled all job vacancies.

As seen in Figure 6.9, South Africa's unemployment rate increased by 7.5 percentage points between Q2 (23.3 per cent) and Q3 (30.8 per cent) of 2020 (Stats SA, 2020). During the lockdown in Q3 of 2020, more than 73.6 per cent who were working for companies/organisations were expected to work from home.

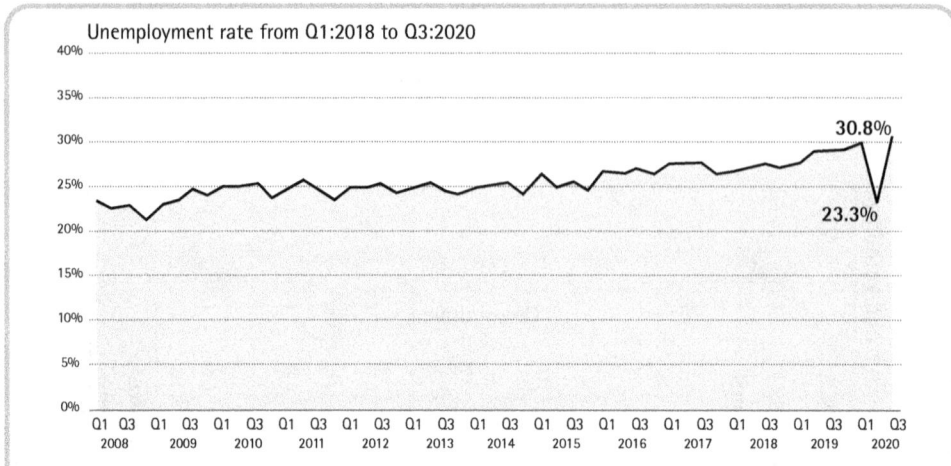

Figure 6.9: Unemployment rate, South Africa, from Q1 of 2008 to Q3 of 2020 (Stats SA, 2020)

## Demand-deficient Unemployment or Cyclical Unemployment

Cyclical unemployment is encountered when labour employed during peak economic cycles becomes redundant during periods of economic recession. As business activity declines, there is a corresponding decrease in employment levels. Employment usually increases when the economy recovers. As seen in Figure 6.10, if there is a decline in the aggregate demand for employment, then the employment level will decrease, as illustrated by D to $D_1$.

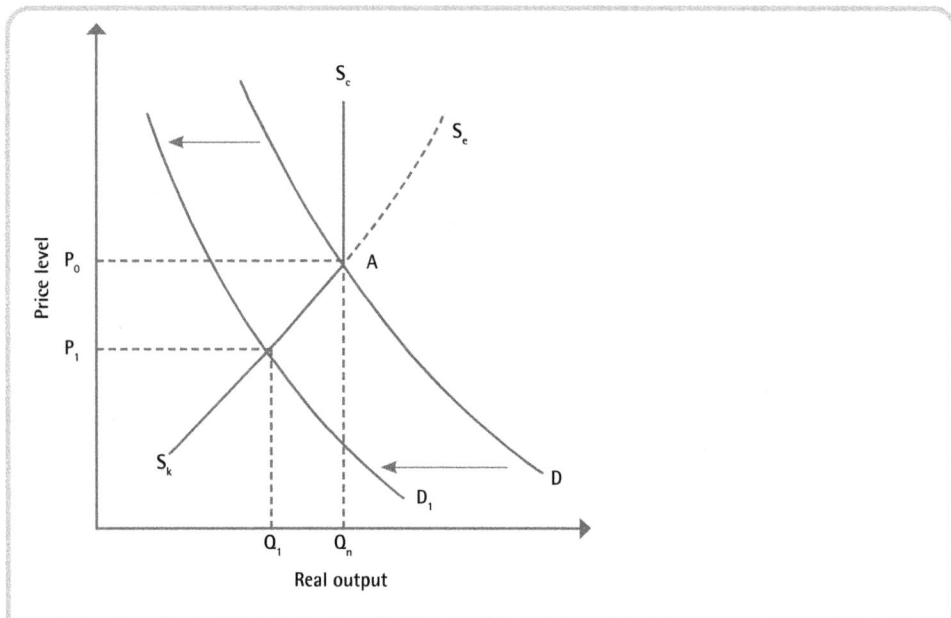

Figure 6.10: Aggregate supply and demand (McConnell et al, 2015: 555)

In Figure 6.11 there is a reduction in the demand for labour ($D_L$ to $D_{L1}$), meaning that if the supply decreases, the demand curve will shift to the left. The aggregate supply curve shows how much output is supplied by firms at different price levels. In Figure 6.11 the decline results in demand, that results in involuntary demand-deficient unemployment.

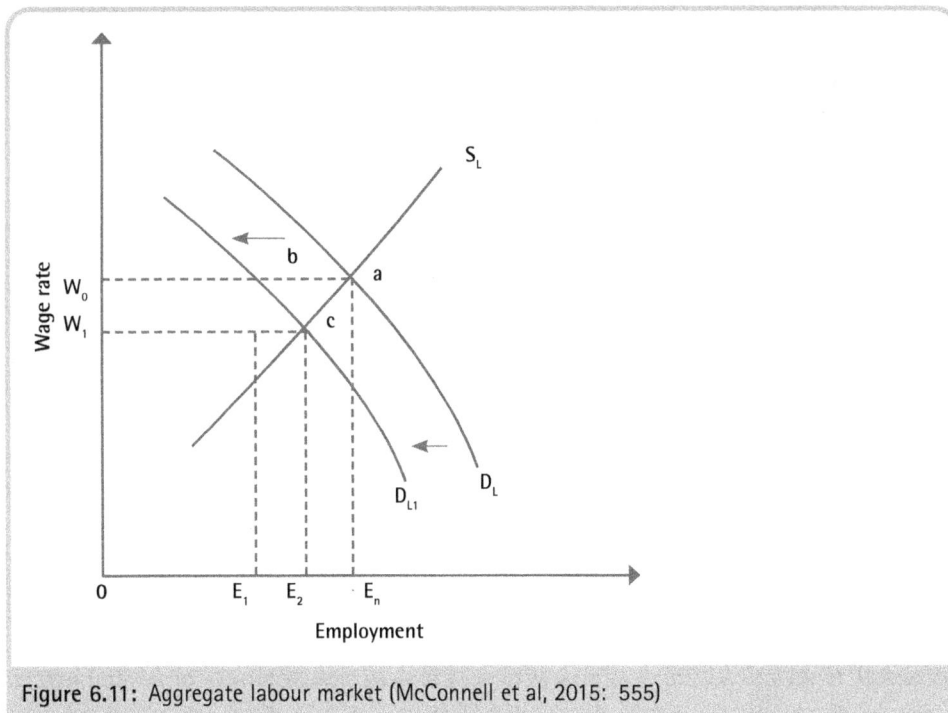

**Figure 6.11:** Aggregate labour market (McConnell et al, 2015: 555)

### Structural Unemployment

This is the most deep-rooted of all forms of unemployment. An oversupply of labour in relation to demand is the main cause of structural unemployment. Structural unemployment may be divided into two types. The first occurs when the economy cannot absorb all work-seekers. The second occurs where the available labour does not possess the qualifications or the skills necessary to take up the vacant positions that exist. This could be the result of basic inadequacies, such as lack of education and training in the labour force, or of technological advancements causing existing skills to become obsolete.

In September 2020, Boingotlo Gasealahwe made the following comment about the structural unemployment rate in South Africa (BusinessTech, 2020):

> A lot of the second-quarter job losses [due to the hard lockdown] should
> be reversed once the economy opens up, but the question is by how

*much and how soon? We think the recovery will be protracted given the weak growth outlook.*

*We also expect a slight uptick in the structural unemployment rate as some who were laid off during the crisis remain permanently unemployed.*

There are different causes for structural unemployment (Pettinger, 2019):

- **Geographical immobility** occurs when employees are unable to move from areas of high unemployment to areas where there is a labour shortage. For example, it may be difficult for people to leave an area as a result of family attachments. Geographical unemployment can be overcome, as government and employers could offer housing benefits to help the unemployed to take up jobs in other areas.
- **Occupational immobility** occurs when there are changes in the economy and a resultant shift in the demand for skilled employees. For example, after the closure of a manufacturing firm, employees with certain skills may struggle to find employment in a new industry where different skills are required. This can be overcome by education and training. Skills development programmes by Sector Education and Training Authorities (SETAs) can help with vocational training such as plumbing, bricklaying or other kind of skills required by a specific industry.

### Seasonal Unemployment

Seasonal unemployment occurs where jobs are performed only at certain times of the year, for example seasonal fruit picking. Persons employed in this type of work may be unemployed for the rest of the year but will probably be employed again in the new season. As mentioned by Izaks, Avenant and Van Schalkwyk (2018), seasonal unemployment is a phenomenon in rural areas and in industries such as leisure and tourism, construction, farming and retailing, where the demand, employment and production are seasonal. In South Africa many adults are part of the seasonal unemployment pattern. Unemployment in rural areas results in underdevelopment, poverty, ill health and psychological distress.

## Balancing Demand and Supply

### Labour Market Perfection

In a perfectly competitive or perfectly balanced labour market, the number of persons willing to work and willing to accept the rate offered would equal the number of persons required. This means that economic activity, in the form of production and services, would provide jobs at acceptable rates of pay for most members of the EAP (those who are able and willing to work). It also means that as the pool of economically active persons grows, the economy will grow accordingly.

*The question arises: How realistic is the model of a perfect labour market?* In practice, it is problematic for employees to move from one employer to another. Employees could incur significant costs when moving between jobs. Employers have a degree of monopsony power, which enables them to pay wages less than the competitive equilibrium. This monopsony power is stronger in circumstances of unemployment (Pettinger, 2019).

The state of the economy has a significant impact on the functioning of the labour market. However, the economy is not solely responsible for the health or otherwise of the labour market or for prices (wages) paid within this market. The labour market is composed of a number of different markets in different sectors, both industry- and job-wise, which require different skills.

Flexibility and mobility of labour contribute to the efficacy of the labour market. Job-seekers need to be both vocationally and geographically mobile in order to optimise the opportunities available. This is particularly important in the modern era, where the nature of work is changing continuously, a development which will make effective, flexible and relevant education and training all the more necessary.

Social factors, such as population growth, housing, health and transport, have an effect on the labour market. A lack of adequate housing not only prevents mobility to areas where labour is required, but also prevents those who have inadequate housing from working properly or bettering their skills. A healthy population contributes to a healthy labour market, while adequate public transport allows for greater labour mobility and decreases the non-wage cost of labour. Where the population growth exceeds economic growth, the labour market is unable to support all entrants. Conversely, a marked decrease in population, particularly among the economically active, will adversely affect the economy and therefore the labour market.

The most prevalent social impediment is the inability of certain sectors of a population to equip themselves through education and training to meet the labour market's existing and future demands. This occurs in markedly uneven societies or those where governmental policies and initiatives are either lacking or ineffective.

## Labour Market Imperfection: Major Causes of Unemployment

As indicated above, labour markets which fail to match supply with demand, result in unemployment. However, the utopian ideal of a perfectly balanced labour market has never been achieved. This is so both in those systems which support the free-market principle and those which prefer a government-controlled economy. In the latter instance, labour markets may be balanced by training and allocating labour where necessary, but this may happen at the cost of economic decline and unacceptable wage rates. Economic recession leads to a decline in demand and subsequent unemployment.

Where the free-market approach has been adopted, labour market imperfections are endemic to the system. One of the main reasons is the fact that free-market economic systems are prone to cyclical downturns, leading in turn to a decrease in demand and the laying off of those who are already employed. This gives rise to cyclical unemployment, which is usually temporary but could last for a number of years. There are economies which never achieve the necessary growth. These economies are or become unviable, rendering them unable to absorb the number of work-seekers and resulting in structural unemployment. Structural unemployment also occurs where work-seekers do not possess the required skills. It follows that structural unemployment occurs more frequently in countries where the economy is weak, where population growth exceeds economic growth and where there is insufficient education and training. This is usually accompanied by a lack of adequate housing and proper health care facilities. South Africa unfortunately suffers from chronic structural unemployment, exacerbated by cyclical unemployment.

In 2013, the root causes of unemployment in South Africa were reported as being (Government Communications, 2013):

- the legacy of apartheid and poor education and training
- a labour demand–supply mismatch
- the 2008/2009 global recession
- the role of trade union federations in government and their demands for higher wages, which may lead to a decline in new employment
- a general lack of interest in entrepreneurship – young people engaging in entrepreneurial account for less than 6 per cent of the total youth population (18–34 years)
- slow economic growth, which means that the rate of new job creation is also slow.

## Capital Mobility and the Labour Market

The free-market principle presupposes that both labour and capital are allowed maximal mobility or flexibility. This means that employers are free to substitute labour with machines or technology, thereby decreasing labour demand in relation to supply. The competitiveness inherent in the free-market system often obliges employers to introduce new technology in order to achieve improved efficiencies. Equally often, rising labour costs result in machines being employed as substitutes for labour. Capital may also attempt to achieve maximum flexibility through flexible employment practices such as the use of casual and temporary labour, flexible wage rates and outsourcing. Attempts by governments to regulate these actions are viewed as interference and as leading to labour market rigidity. This problem is bound to grow as employers are forced by competition and economic necessity to replace traditional production with more up-to-date processes and techniques.

The mobility principle also presupposes that capital is free to go where the other factors of production – land and capital – are both cheap and abundant, and where labour does not make excessive demands on the employer or engage in labour action. Thus, investors will look to those countries with the least possible labour regulation. Unfortunately, this very often leads to exploitation of workers in those countries.

## Wages and Employment Levels

The market-based wage-price theory assumes that there is a direct, inverse relationship between the price of labour and the demand for labour – that as the wage price of labour increases, the demand for labour will fall, leading to increased unemployment. Conversely, as the supply of labour increases in relation to demand, the price of labour will fall.

Basing their argument broadly on these assumptions, employers warn that 'unrealistic' wage demands by employees or their unions will result in growing unemployment. By the same token, they expect labour to cap wage demands in times of rising unemployment.

Wage demands alone do not account for labour costs. Regulated conditions of employment in the form, for example, of leave, sick leave, maximum working hours and payment for overtime add to these costs, as do levies on employer wage bills. It is argued that these, too, may contribute to unemployment.

There is no doubt that unrealistic wage demands and other rigidities in the labour market do influence employment levels. On the other hand, the absolutely free play of market forces can result in gross human rights abuses and in the intolerable exploitation of labour. A delicate balance has to be maintained between the protection of employees from exploitation and the institution of basic worker rights on the one hand, and employment creation on the other.

On the opposite side of the spectrum are those theorists who propose that the starting point should be the demand for consumer goods. As wage and salary earners normally constitute the majority of consumers, the argument is that higher wage rates would raise consumer demand, resulting in increased economic activity and, therefore, increased employment. It may also increase national savings, leading to increased local investment. Theories of this nature are not popular in existing market-driven economies, but do have some merit and should be balanced against the absolute reliance on employment demand principles.

## Productivity and the Labour Market

The productivity levels of those employed in the labour market will eventually affect total employment. The reason for this is the relationship between productivity and economic prosperity. The more productive the workforce, the greater will be the economic benefits enjoyed by the country as a whole. Furthermore, a reputation for productivity encourages investment, both locally and from external sources. Productivity is engendered by a positive work ethic, sound organisational relationships and relevant education and training.

In November 2021, the CEIC reported that South Africa's labour productivity increased by 12.93 per cent year-on-year (YoY) in June 2021, compared to the previous quarter where growth was only 6.42 per cent. South Africa's labour productivity growth data are updated quarterly. These data have been published since March 2009, averaging at 0.02 per cent. The data reached an all-time record low of –4.04 per cent in June 2020 and a high of 12.93 per cent in June 2021. These data are calculated by the CEIC by utilising labour productivity growth from quarterly employment and real GDP (CEIC, 2021).

## Demographic Changes and the Labour Market

If the population of a country grows at an excessive rate, the economy will eventually have to grow accordingly to absorb the increasing number of persons entering the labour market. If this does not happen, unemployment levels will rise and a large number of persons entering the labour market will not be able to find work.

The major cause of population growth is an increase in the birth rate. In the first quarter of 2021, the birth rate for South Africa was 19.662 births per 1 000 people, a 1.67 per cent decline from 2020, while the mortality rate was 9.441 (United Nations, 2021). If the mortality rate of a country remains constant, this would mean that an economy which has full employment would not have to grow at all to accommodate new work-seekers. On the other hand, an economy with high unemployment rates would need to curb the birth rate still more in order to first absorb the existing and potential work-seekers. (The idea of curbing population growth is, however, highly controversial.)

Population increases or decreases are also brought about by immigration and emigration. When national unemployment levels are high, immigration is usually discouraged, as it places an additional burden on the labour market. On the other hand, if capital can move wherever it wants, it could be argued that the same should apply to labour.

Emigration from one national labour market to another is a cause for concern, as the result may be a structural imbalance in the markets left behind by emigrants. This is particularly so where highly skilled persons emigrate from a market which cannot easily replace those skills or where the existing stock of skilled labour is insufficient.

Just as population growth may give rise to market imbalances, so too may a sudden or gradual reduction in the population. The loss of a large number of skilled and economically active persons has a detrimental effect on the economy, which cannot produce as optimally as before. The labour market becomes imbalanced, since the number of prime providers of labour and skills is drastically reduced.

A further consideration is the fact that people are generally living much longer today than in the past. This places a strain on those wage earners who have to support ailing relatives and who therefore have to seek more income. It also leads to a situation where older people are staying in employment longer than before and thereby lessening the opportunities for new entrants to the labour market.

A balanced labour market further presupposes that all persons, irrespective of race or gender, should be able to work if they desire to do so. Discrimination and cultural norms often militate against this principle in practice.

## Monopsonist Practices

Monopsonist practices exist where one employer or a number of employers in collusion are able to set wage levels, thus preventing the free play of demand and supply. This may occur where a number of large employers dominate the market, where employers form cartels or even where powerful employers matched by weak unions regulate wages through bargaining councils.

# The Government and the Labour Market

## Government Policies

The political, economic and social policies adopted by a particular government largely determine the economic well-being of the society, and therefore influence the labour market in terms of employment levels. Depending on its orientation, a government can allow for maximum market flexibility of producer, consumer and labour markets or impose regulations which introduce protectionist measures, such as import and export controls or minimum wages. These may lead to rigidities in the market.

Equally, a government can attract investment by, for example, deregulation, incentives for business start-ups and lowering company tax. Social policies such as housing, health, crime prevention, transport, and education and training all eventually have an impact on the labour market.

In formulating policy and legislation, a democratic government needs to carefully balance the interests of capital and labour. Undue protectionism of, say, employees or society at large may result in inflexible labour markets, with consequent unemployment. On the other hand, complete non-regulation inevitably leads to exploitation and destruction of both the social fabric and the environment.

### The Government as Employer

Governments are themselves employers and providers of services. In certain quarters, it is argued that governments need to absorb the excess supply of labour by employing persons for diverse social services and by increasing government spending not only on arms and other instruments of war, for instance, but also on social services. However, government activities are non-economic activities. They do not contribute to the GDP. Government revenue is obtained from the taxation of economic activity. Therefore, undue increases in government spending will inevitably lead to increased taxation, which will, in turn, adversely affect investment and the labour market. Also, one criterion for measuring the health or otherwise of an economy is the proportion of government spending in relation to gross national income and expenditure. When this ratio is too high, the economy loses credibility.

This having been said, labour market changes and problems are also the business of government. Where society as a whole is being or might be adversely affected, it is the government's duty to be continually aware of possible problems and to step in when the situation so requires.

Role-players consulted on National Minimum Wage adjustment

Monday, February 22, 2021
Employment and Labour Minister Thulas Nxesi has reiterated that the adjustment of the National Minimum Wage rate was the outcome of an extensive consultation process.

The Minister on Monday made the comment in response to the outcry on the newly adjusted National Minimum Wage (NMW) rates.

The department last week announced that the NMW increased to R21.69 per hour from R20.76 from March.

The minimum wage is a tool to ensure that vulnerable workers do not fall below the poverty line and it is designed to reduce inequality and huge disparities in income in the national labour market.

"As we have pointed out before, the minimum wage is really what it says it is. But it is not based on thumb-suck but a well thought out process that allows all the interested parties to have a voice.

I have noted with concern the objections from some stakeholders on the adjustment of the NMW and recognize the reality that the COVID-19 pandemic has had a harsh impact on most employers," said the Minister.

Nxesi said the NMW Act however accordingly permits employers that are genuinely unable to pay the proposed adjustment to utilise the exemptions procedures in order to be exempted from the NMW.

In amending the minimum wage this year, the department said the Minister had considered all legal requirements, the report of the commission as well as different inputs from stakeholders. This, reads the statement, was based on these and the results of the initial research undertaken on the impact of the introduction of the national minimum wage.

With regards to the inputs received in response to the notice published by the NMW Commission on its recommendations, stakeholders were divided in their recommendations.

Some supported the recommended adjustments, arguing for an above inflation increase as well as immediate equalisation of the domestic and worker sectors.

"Indeed some stakeholders were against the recommended adjustment based on impact that it will have on employment/ unemployment, low economic growth, the impact that COVID-19 has had on the operations of businesses as well as the high production costs for farmers who will have to bear the brunt of the increase," said Nxesi.

Research conducted by the Development Policy Research Unit (DPRU) at the University of Cape Town and the University of Johannesburg's Centre for Social Development in Africa (CSDA), found that there has been no negative impact on employment as a result of the introduction of the national minimum wage.

However, they said the reason for that could be due to employers already adjusting almost two years prior to implementation.

Also, research found that the introduction of the national minimum wage led to a statistically significant increase but smaller than expected improvement in wages for the workers it covers and generally there was broad compliance in agriculture, with slightly lower levels in domestic work. Unfortunately, employees considered that the minimum wage for farm and domestic workers was too low.

"The domestic worker sector on the other hand, judging by the findings of the Quarterly Labour Force Survey was severely impacted by the initial levels of lockdown and therefore the recommendation was to increase the minimum wage to 88% of the national minimum wage which translates to R19.09 per hour as of 1 March 2021," said the Minister – **SAnews.gov.za**

(Source: SA News, 2021)

# South African Labour Market Initiatives 1994–2008

As previously indicated, the South African labour market suffers from endemic structural unemployment. For the post-1994 government, addressing labour market needs was among its most important priorities.

## The Tripartite Alliance

There was initially a measure of disagreement among the parties to the Tripartite Alliance – the ANC, the Congress of South African Trade Unions (COSATU) and the South African Communist Party (SACP) – regarding the best strategies to solve the country's economic and labour market problems. This is illustrated in Table 6.3.

Chapter 6: The South African Labour Market    287

**Table 6.3:** Differing approaches among the Tripartite Alliance partners, July 1998

| Policy | ANC | COSATU | SACP |
|---|---|---|---|
| Fiscal policy | Discipline and reducing budget deficit to 3 per cent of GDP. Growth rate of 6.1 per cent. | Flexible bands for deficit and revenue targets.<br><br>Expand demand for locally produced goods and services. Reduce national debt. | More generous attitude to budget deficit.<br><br>Macroeconomic policy subordinate to developmental growth strategy. |
| Monetary policy | Control inflation. Encourage domestic savings and investment with high interest on saving. Phase out exchange controls. Facilitate loans from banks for foreign investors. | Stimulate demand by lower interest, redistribution through taxation and export promotion. Establish capital controls.<br><br>Discourage speculative investment by exchange control and taxes on short-term capital gains. | Slice interest rates drastically. Review removal of exchange controls. Instead take into account the vagaries of speculative pressure on the currency. |
| Industrial policy | Promote export-oriented growth. Remove tariffs and lure foreign investors with tax breaks. Promote small enterprises. | Selective tariff barriers to save jobs. De-emphasise small business as engine of job creation. Punish retrenchments with tax disincentives. Oppose demutualisation. | Regulate financial sector. 'Intercept' demutualisation. |
| Social and sectoral policy | Redistributive budgets in favour of poor (through GEAR). Partnerships with voluntary service organisations. Affordable alternatives for social grants. | Security system and social wage for poor and unemployed. Free public health, housing, transport for destitute – obtained from taxes on wealth. Solidarity tax on companies for development. | Promoting co-operative and elective ventures. Everyone's basic needs provided for. |

➤

| Policy | ANC | COSATU | SACP |
|---|---|---|---|
| Land reform | Agricultural development as key to distribution of income. | State-sponsored land redistribution. Collective bargaining extended to farms. Stop all retrenchments and evictions from farms. | State plays big role in agricultural and related industries. Land made available for co-operatives. |
| Labour market | Regulated labour market flexibility. Flexible bargaining structures – differing standards. Wages not to rise faster than productivity and inflation. | Abandon labour market flexibility, deregulation and capping of wage increases. Extend unemployment insurance or institute basic income grant for the poor. | Democratise labour market. Absence of social strife, inequality and provision of adequate human resources will bring investment. |
| Job creation | Job creation from three sources: economic growth, government programmes and labour market reforms. Private sector as biggest job creator. | Dramatically expand mass public work programmes, including housing. Moratorium on retrenchments. | Moratorium on retrenchments. Heavy investment in training and development. |
| Public sector | Aim to create more than 300 000 jobs by 2000. Private sector involvement in matters such as housing. | Extend and improve public service to disadvantaged. Avoid cutting jobs in public service. | Restructure for efficiency and development. Avoid cutting jobs. |

**Table 6.4:** Reconstruction and recovery plans of the Tripartite Alliance partners as of 2020 (SA News, 2020)

| ANC | COSATU | SACP |
|---|---|---|
| Job creation is key to economic recovery.<br><br>While some of the interventions build on the strengths of existing programmes, the stimulus also includes new and innovative approaches.<br><br>This includes a focus on what government terms 'social employment'.<br><br>Government is working from the premise that there is no shortage of work to be done to address the many social problems in the society. | The aim is to support the considerable creativity, initiative and institutional capabilities that exist in the wider society to engage people in work that serves the common good. This work cuts across a range of themes, including food security, ending gender-based violence, informal settlement upgrading and much more. | Supplement the efforts of the public sector, allowing for greater scale and social impact as well as new forms of partnership with diverse social actors.<br><br>The stimulus includes a new national programme to employ teaching and school assistants in schools. Schools are making these appointments right now, delivering new opportunities in every community across the length and breadth of the country.<br><br>Public employment is not just for unskilled work, as it has a cross-cutting focus on graduates, with opportunities for nurses, science graduates, artisans and others.<br><br>The stimulus will also protect jobs in vulnerable sectors that have been hit hard by the pandemic.<br><br>Support will be provided to early childhood development practitioners, mainly self-employed women.<br><br>Over 74 000 small farmers will also receive production input grants. |

## Growth, Employment and Redistribution and the Reconstruction and Development Programme

When the ANC-led government came to power, it was faced with a neo-liberal revival worldwide and the need to compete in the global economy. In light of this, in June 1996 the government adopted GEAR as a framework for economic development. This, it was believed, would bring about the necessary job creation. By including the aspect of redistribution, the government signalled that it was not discarding the principles of the Reconstruction and Development Programme (RDP) and was adopting a two-pronged approach.

The RDP placed emphasis on redistribution, the opening up of previously suppressed economic and human potential in urban and rural areas, education and training, affirmative action, and public works and programmes which would address unemployment. GEAR, on the other hand, emphasised economic growth. This would be achieved by adopting the free-market approach and by encouraging local and foreign investment. It was believed that, in a democratic dispensation, redistribution would flow from such growth.

Comins (2021) reports that, according to a global PwC report of 2020, 'Forty-one percent of South African CEOs are "very confident" about their own organisation's prospects for growth in 2021'. This survey comes after the global recession in 2020, which led to a 3.5 per cent decline in the world GDP and a GDP contraction of 7 per cent in South Africa. In the South African context, Comins (2021) further explains:

> South African companies continue to see China (27%) and the UK (27%) as key to growth, but are also looking to other African countries for opportunities such as Ghana (11%), Nigeria (11%) and Kenya (8%).
>
> In view of South Africa's rising inequality and employment challenges, it was concerning that 51% of SA CEOs (compared to 37% globally) reported that they had reduced staff in the past 12 months and that 41% (compared to 21% globally) plan to do so in the year ahead.
>
> The proportion of South African CEOs expecting to reduce staff has exceeded those expecting to increase it for the first time, and by a margin of 25 percentage points. This is unprecedented in the history of the survey. The survey findings are based on the economic outlook at the time, namely, a level 3 lockdown period, issues arising from the rollout of vaccinations, as well as load shedding.

South African government and business need to amend and improve labour legislation to promote employment opportunities, job creation and job sustainability, as this will help to ameliorate chronic poverty by limiting or reducing inequality and reducing unemployment in South Africa. In recent years, the South African government has introduced transformative entrepreneurial interventions among black youth, such as broad-based entrepreneurship activities and ventures to address unemployment, poverty and inequality (Odeku & Rudolf, 2019). Other programmes that the government has implemented to combat youth unemployment include the wage subsidy system in 2014 known as the employment tax incentive, according to which a tax credit was given to employers if they employed young persons below the age of 30 years and low-wage workers who receive a wage below R6 000 a month. Despite government intervention to increase youth demand and youth education and skills levels, these policies have not resulted in a systematic improvement in employment of the targeted youth (Ebrahim & Pirttilä, 2019).

Keynesian economics sees job creation programmes as the cornerstone of reducing unemployment and inequalities. Economic growth is important, but it is insufficient on its own to reduce unemployment, inequality and poverty.

### The Accelerated Shared Growth Initiative for South Africa

In February 2006, President Thabo Mbeki (2006) announced the launch of the Accelerated Shared Growth Initiative for South Africa (ASGISA), which was intended, in Mbeki's words, to provide 'a limited set of interventions intended to serve as catalysts to accelerate shared growth and development' (Mbeki, 2006). ASGISA was given a budget of R370 million. Among its proposals for growth were:

- an increase in public sector capital investment from 6 to 8 per cent of GDP
- massive capital spending by Transnet and Eskom
- government capital expenditure to increase by 15 to 20 per cent every year
- public investment to increase threefold (which would have necessitated an increase in private sector investment from R219 billion to R316 billion, while realistically it was only possible for private sector investment to increase to R264 billion).

There were high hopes of delivery, but barely a year later the panel of international experts appointed to advise on the initiative declared that it would be virtually impossible to achieve ASGISA's target of 6 per cent growth per annum by 2014 unless the most binding constraints were eliminated. These included:

- currency volatility
- inefficiencies in the national logistics system
- skills shortages
- limited market competition
- a burdensome regulatory environment
- deficiencies in state organisation.

(It is interesting to note that the two entities on which government placed its hope for improving economic performance, namely Eskom and Transnet, have, in fact, drained the state coffers and over the past years have come close to complete collapse.)

The Economic Recession of 2008

The year 2008 saw the worst worldwide economic crisis in history up to that point, and South Africa followed the rest of the world into a recession. Between October 2008 and March 2009, GDP fell by 1.5 per cent, with mining being the hardest hit. By the end of 2009, Stats SA indicated that almost a million jobs had been lost during the course of that year.

Like the rest of the world, in 2009 South Africa looked forward to some improvement in 2010. In this it was encouraged by a report from UK Trade and Investment, which placed South Africa fourth on its list of key emerging markets as regards investment potential. Unfortunately, the expected growth did not materialise.

Currently, the grim effects of the Covid-19 pandemic in South Africa led to GDP figures that are a crushing blow for the country's economy, and South Africa has fallen into its third recession since 1994.

## Variables Impacting on Employment Levels

### Labour Market Regulation

It is obvious that, to achieve its objectives, the post-apartheid South African government had to interfere more directly in the labour market. However, this could bring its own problems. Overregulation of the labour market by government or by centralised union–management agreements may result in inflexibility. This means that the wage price of labour will remain relatively constant or increase despite market fluctuations in demand and supply. When demand is, by comparison, elastic, it will decrease if the wage price remains high. Employers then either mechanise or invest elsewhere, thus reducing demand and contributing to unemployment.

The cost of labour includes not only the actual wage price, but also other costs in the form of benefits, insurance funds, levies on employment or total salary bill, leave and sick leave provisions.

### Small, Medium and Micro-enterprises

Some observers view the development of the small, medium and micro-enterprise (SMME) sector as the 'engine' of employment creation. Initially, the South African government also regarded this as one of the prime avenues for job creation. However, very often this sector operates at the subsistence level. Thus, while the establishment of SMMEs, and particularly micro-enterprises, may give some of those who were previously unemployed enough to live on, it hardly serves to engender massive employment or substantial economic growth. Moreover, trends in world production markets may not favour the establishment of very small enterprises unless these form clusters or co-operatives or are contracted to larger enterprises for specialised tasks. The dearth of personal savings and relatively high interest rates in South Africa also make it difficult for small entrepreneurs to acquire capital. Similarly, the low standard of education in the country fails to equip would-be entrepreneurs with the necessary life and business skills.

It is further held by various critics that legislation affects the development of small business, in that red tape and agreements impact on all businesses – regardless of size – often deterring would-be entrepreneurs.

## Education and Training

Griffiths and Jones (1980) define education as a process which creates human capital, and they emphasise the close relationship between human capital and economic progress. In this respect the fact that a large percentage of the South African population is functionally illiterate is extremely disturbing.

The establishment of the South African Qualifications Authority (SAQA) and the National Qualifications Framework (NQF), the implementation of the Skills Development Levies Act 9 of 1999, and the restructuring of higher education were all intended to address the existing imbalances and to partially alleviate the problem of structural unemployment. Unfortunately, training in terms of the Skills Development Act did not deliver as expected and, although the education system expanded, primary and secondary education are still reported to be unsatisfactory.

## Productivity

South Africa ranks very low on the global competitiveness register. This is attributable to ineffective use and development of human resources and to a lack of productivity on the part of those in employment.

The productivity problem has many probable causes. Among these are insufficient education and training and a high labour turnover. Productivity problems not only render South African products uncompetitive as against those of other countries, but generally discourage investment. This happens particularly if labour costs are, by comparison, relatively high. Productivity did increase, in relative terms, between 2000 and 2008, but much remains to be done.

## Migration, Emigration and Immigration

After 1994 the lifting of influx controls resulted in a steady flow of work-seekers from rural to urban areas. This placed a strain on the provision of housing and other facilities and raised unemployment levels in urban areas. Services and industries in urban areas were unable to provide employment to all new job-seekers. As unemployment and crime are closely related, crime figures in urban areas escalated. This, in turn, had an adverse effect on the economy.

In addition to internal migration there are also immigrants who have entered South Africa in the hope of finding a better future, many of them doing so illegally. Many of these have added to the ranks of the unemployed.

In contrast to immigration, there has also been an outflow of mostly skilled or qualified persons. A large number of qualified South Africans – nurses, doctors, teachers, engineers, artisans and technicians – all possessing skills which South Africa desperately needs, have emigrated and now reside in other countries.

### Labour Action

Union actions, in the form of wage demands and concomitant actions when negotiations deadlock, have had an effect on the economy and on investor confidence. Since the early 1980s, South African unions have adopted a militant style, sometimes in reaction to the recalcitrance of employers. Strike figures from the 1980s compared unfavourably with those of the country's major trading partners and those countries with whom it competes for investment. This led to the World Bank calling on the government to 'rein in the unions'. Events since 2000 – and particularly during 2012 and 2013 – hold out little hope of a decrease in union militancy and concomitant labour action.

### Crime

A circular relationship exists between crime and unemployment. As the crime rate increases, investor confidence wanes. Decreased economic growth leads to higher levels of unemployment; the unemployed, unable to sustain themselves, may eventually turn to crime.

It can therefore be postulated that, as unemployment decreases, the crime rate will drop, but the problem lies with fuelling the necessary economic growth while crime prevails. Crime affects every aspect of society, and also business. While the 'poverty push' to crime is understood, it can be argued that poverty will not be alleviated before crime is taken in hand.

## Employment Initiatives Post 2008

### The Joint Initiative for Priority Skills Acquisition and the Human Resource Development Strategy

In 2006, realising that all other efforts were not producing the skills required, the deputy president, Phumzile Mlambo-Ngcuka, announced the formation of the Joint Initiative for Priority Skills Acquisition (JIPSA), meant to place emphasis on the skills required by the economy and to foster, with business and labour, opportunities for individuals to acquire these skills.

JIPSA was a short-term measure, and in April 2009 it was announced that it would be replaced by the Human Resource Development Strategy for South Africa (HRDS), which was approved by government in 2010. The top priorities of the HRDS were to:

- eradicate adult illiteracy
- ensure that children and youths remain in education and training until they reached 18
- enable all entrants to the labour market to access education and training
- ensure that immigration reflected an inflow of persons with priority skills
- ensure that education was equitable in terms of race, gender, disability and geographic location.

Most of the initiatives mentioned were too broad to be termed strategies and although each had some impact, the problems remained.

## The New Growth Path Framework

In 2010 the government adopted the New Growth Path Framework, originating from the Department for Economic Development under former trade unionist Ebrahim Patel. The stated objectives of the Framework were to:

- create 5 million jobs within 10 years
- promote a green economy
- create more agricultural jobs
- facilitate land transfers
- promote mining and beneficiation of products
- establish state mining companies in competition with the private sector
- bring about reindustrialisation in manufacturing
- promote tourism and other income-generating sectors
- bring about improvements in government
- promote stronger partnerships between government, the private sector and organised labour.

The drafters recognised the importance of a competitive economy and saw a stronger role for a competitions policy, but also for monitoring prices. Nevertheless, the New Growth Path Framework was viewed as more socialist than the NDP, which followed it.

The New Growth Path Framework was underpinned by the National Infrastructure Plan. The central objective of the plan was to decentralise basic services and engage in strategic integrated projects and thereby 'transform the economic landscape'. The plan identified decentralised areas around the country and projects to be undertaken in these areas. It was believed that it would create a significant number of jobs, unlock opportunities, integrate human settlements and lead to a more balanced economy.

## The National Development Plan

The New Growth Path Framework appears to have been absorbed into the NDP, launched by the planning minister, Trevor Manuel, in 2012. The NDP, for which the target date is 2030, is based on the premise of a social compact between government, business and labour, with the aim of (NPC, 2012):

- reducing poverty and inequality
- raising employment levels
- increasing investment.

More specifically, the plan aims to (NPC, 2012):

- increase employment from 13 million in 2010 to 24 million in 2030
- significantly reduce the Gini coefficient
- reduce the share of households (39 per cent) living on R419 per month
- increase the share of national income owned by the poorest, from 10 to 40 per cent
- raise per capita incomes, from R50 000 to R120 000 per annum
- achieve economic growth of 5.4 per cent
- increase fixed investment from 17 to 30 per cent.

These objectives are to be achieved by (NPC, 2012: 34):

- broadening access to employment
- ensuring a stronger social wage
- improving transport systems
- creating a more professional public service
- promoting private investment in labour intensive industries
- increasing public infrastructure development by 10 per cent
- promoting competitiveness in exports
- promoting accountable education
- instituting a national health system
- encouraging youth employment through a tax incentive or subsidy for learnerships.

The drafters of the plan saw its primary challenges as being (NPC, 2012: 34):

- the poor quality of school education
- inadequate infrastructure
- the lack of inclusive development
- too great a reliance on resources

- an inadequate public health system
- uneven and poor-quality public service
- high levels of corruption
- societal divides.

The NDP has been described as high on vision but short on detail. It was generally accepted by business, but COSATU, while agreeing with some of its contents, described it as liberal-democratic and not advancing a radical ideological shift. The federation was also not in favour of the youth wage subsidy, owing to fears that this would erode other employment. It further criticised the NDP for not putting the concept of 'decent work' at the centre, not emphasising redistribution, and basing employment creation on small business promotion. For these reasons some of the COSATU unions declared themselves in favour of Patel's New Growth Path Framework rather than Manuel's NDP.

The government, for its part, decided that the time for debating was past and that there was an urgent need to proceed to actual implementation. The first steps towards implementation of the plan were contained in the Infrastructure Development Act 23 of 2014, which made provision for an Infrastructure Co-ordinating Commission headed by the president. The function of the Commission is to oversee the implementation of strategic integrated projects and ministers must take responsibility for specific projects. Infrastructure is defined in the Infrastructure Development Act 23 of 2014, Schedule 1, Section 7(1)(a), as 'installations, structures, facilities, systems, services and processes' and its development should lead to economic and social upliftment. Strict criteria as to the type of projects to be undertaken are contained in the Act. Some progress has been made in infrastructure development, but lack of adequate resources may have prevented the programmes from becoming as successful as anticipated.

Radical Economic Transformation
At its National Policy Conference in July 2017, the ANC, under a beleaguered President Jacob Zuma, announced its plan for what it termed 'radical economic transformation' (RET). This, it was claimed, constituted the second phase of the transition from apartheid. It was envisaged that the proposed shift in focus would bring about economic transformation; promote growth and development; increase state-led infrastructure development, with the emphasis on local content and local companies; and ensure macroeconomic stability. According to a statement issued at the time, the plan is aimed at bringing about change in the way ownership is structured and in how the economy is managed and controlled, with a focus on women and girls and the poor.

More specifically, the objectives of the plan are to:
- reduce unemployment, particularly among the youth
- return land to the people
- increase black ownership and control of the economy
- activate small businesses and co-operatives
- raise levels of investment
- strengthen social justice
- improve the employment impact of infrastructure projects
- reduce inequality in employment
- dismantle monopolies
- assert South Africa's interests in the global economy
- improve integration into the African economy
- stimulate inclusive growth.

Some aspects of the plan, in particular that relating to land restoration, raised concern, resulting in a negative effect on the economy and on sentiment among investors. On the whole it constitutes yet another instance of high ideals without sufficient analysis of the obstacles and clear guidelines as to their achievement. It also fails to consider future changes in the nature of work and therefore future labour market requirements.

## The Reality on the Ground

It is emphasised by Brothwell (2020) that South Africa lost one million jobs in the recession of 2008. This financial crisis took a substantial toll on employment, not just locally but also internationally, where over a period of 18 months roughly over 34 million job losses were experienced worldwide. The current recession is potentially more threatening than the one in 2008, as we have experienced the Fourth Industrial Revolution. At the time of writing, the South African economy had slipped into a technical recession and was experiencing low levels of economic growth. Furthermore, the technology-driven Fourth Industrial Revolution continues to increase the potential of redundancy in a variety of jobs. Increased automation has resulted in various unskilled jobs being made redundant.

Financially, the outlook is bleak, with the economy showing a negative growth rate of 0.8 per cent for the period 2017 to 2018 and a drop of 2.2 per cent in the first quarter of 2018. South Africa's GDP growth rate for 2020 was –6.96 per cent, a decline of 7.11 per cent from 2019 (World Bank, 2020). In terms of competitiveness, in 2017 the country was ranked 61st out of 137 countries, down 14 places from its previous ranking. From 2019 to 2020, South Africa fell by four notches to 62th out of 64 countries as rated by the Institute for

Management Development (IMD, 2021). South Africa's government coffers have come dangerously close to depletion, owing partly to misspending and corruption, and many state enterprises will need substantial assistance if they are to survive. In these circumstances it is doubtful whether the labour market problems can be adequately addressed unless emphasis is firstly placed on economic growth and security.

Both the ILO and the World Bank have expressed concern at the state of the South African economy and the high level of unemployment. It is obvious from the statements by these bodies that they do not regard the steps taken or planned to be sufficient to rectify South Africa's situation. The World Bank believes that, while the economy may grow around 2 per cent in the period up to 2030, it will not meet the 5.4 per cent growth envisaged by the NDP, nor will the projected employment levels be achieved (World Bank, 2021). The present and projected money supply does not allow much space for further expansion.

Added to the problems outlined above is the fact that union wage demands are for increases above the rate of inflation. Moreover, militant action, particularly by unions in competition with others, has not abated. It is understandable that wage demands should be aimed not merely at matching inflation but also at improving the situation of, in particular, the working poor. However, union actions often have a boomerang effect in that protracted strikes eventually affect the economic viability of organisations and result in retrenchments, as happened at the Lonmin mines.

## Planning for the Future

Ensuring that South Africa does not sink further in terms of economic depression and unemployment will require extensive and ongoing research and analysis. The battle should be on two fronts, the first being the existing problems of poverty and unemployment and the second the predicted changes in the labour market. The purpose should be to establish strategic priorities, to question previously held assumptions and to identify areas where employment will decrease as against those where it will grow. For example, South Africa continues to rely heavily on the mining and manufacturing industries as being among its main sources of economic and employment growth. In reality, predictions regarding the future nature of industry and work point to these becoming less important in the face of increasing scientific inventions.

According to Blix (2017), the changes brought about by digitalisation will have an effect across the board on social policy, with the labour market being the most affected. He quotes Frey and Osborne (2013), who estimated that half the existent jobs in the USA would be automated within the two decades up to 2033. This does not mean that human work will disappear, but the content and context of work will change. Technological improvement will favour high-level skills and 'cognitive social abilities'.

It is evident that resolving the existing problems and ensuring preparedness for the changes to come will require not only economic means, but also appropriate and diverse skills development and education. Relying on previous standardised university and other qualifications may not bring the necessary results. Employees themselves should also take responsibility for continually upgrading their skills to meet new job requirements. As Blix (2017) has warned, those who are slow to upgrade their skills will experience faster wage stagnation.

The anticipated changes in the nature of work will lead to greater casualisation and to an increasing number of persons acting as independent contractors. This will oblige the government to rethink existing laws and arrangements in order to ensure proper protection for all concerned. In fact, the role of government may become bigger rather than smaller.

## Conclusion

South Africa is not the only country faced with the problem of rising unemployment, although the situation in this country may be worse than in many others. Unemployment is on the increase worldwide. It is a situation which should arouse concern in every quarter, since it could eventually lead to a breakdown of the social fabric. Unemployment breeds poverty and poverty breeds crime. It also breeds resentment on the part of those who suffer deprivation against those who enjoy a more affluent life. This, throughout history, has been the cause of major wars. As mentioned by Bendix (2019), Adam Smith stated that no nation can prosper if the majority of its citizens are poor and miserable. Equally, the world cannot prosper or continue as is if the ranks of the unemployed continue to grow.

## Suggested Questions/Tasks

1. In March 2021 Bhekizizwe started work in an expanded public works programme (EPWP) in the iLembe district in Kwazulu-Natal. Last night he was talking with his friends, who also work with him in the same EPWP, around a fire. They all received their pay slips at the end of April 2021, but they are unhappy about the payment, as they expected more (at least the same as other workers in the country that receive a minimum wage). They also thought that, as they were working for the government, they would receive a transport allowance. Consult *Government Gazette* No 44136, published on 8 February 2021 (available at https://www.gov.za/

documents/national-minimum-wage-act-annual-review-and-adjustment-national-minimum-wage-2021-8-feb), to help you to answer the following questions:

    a.    Explain what you understand about the minimum wages set by government, as indicated by the *Government Gazette* No 44136.

    b.    Indicate whether their wages were correctly determined.

    c.    Are Bhekizizwe and his friends entitled to a transport allowance?

2.    Define unemployment, focusing on the South African definition(s) of unemployment.

3.    Summarise the major strategies of the New Growth Path Framework and the NDP.

4.    Compare the New Growth Path Framework and the NDP to ASGISA, GEAR, and the RDP.

5.    In which ways, if any, do the New Growth Path Framework and the NDP differ from and improve on previous initiatives?

6.    List the five major factors contributing to unemployment in South Africa and suggest strategies for addressing these.

7.    Explain how the productivity levels of those employed in the labour market will eventually affect total employment.

8.    Study the initial approaches by the ANC, COSATU and the SACP, as detailed in Table 6.3. Which of the suggestions have already been implemented and which should be implemented?

## Sources

AfDB (African Development Bank). 2012. 'African Development Report 2012: Towards Green Growth in Africa'. Accra: AfDB.

Bendix, S. 2019. *Labour Relations in Practice*, 3rd edition. Cape Town: Juta.

Blix, M. 2017. 'The effects of digitalisation on labour market polarisation and tax revenue'. *CESifo Forum* 18(4): 9–14. Available: www.cesifo-group.de/DocDL/CESifo-forum-2017-4-blix-digitalisation-welfare-state-december.pdf (Accessed 14 September 2021).

Brothwell, R. 2020. 'South Africa lost 1 million jobs because of the 2008 recession – here's why this one could be even worse'. BusinessTech, 4 March 2020. https://businesstech.co.za/news/technology/379079/south-africa-lost-1-million-jobs-because-of-the-2008-recession-heres-why-this-one-could-be-even-worse/ (Accessed 14 September 2021).

BusinessTech. 2020. 'South Africa's scary unemployment figures are coming'. 28 September 2020. https://businesstech.co.za/news/business/436153/south-africas-scary-unemployment-figures-are-coming/ (Accessed 16 September 2021).

BusinessTech. 2021. 'IMF forecasts South Africa's GDP will grow 3.1% in 2021'. 6 April 2021. https://businesstech.co.za/news/business/481071/imf-forecasts-south-africas-gdp-will-grow-3-1-in-2021/ (Accessed 18 November 2021).

CEIC. 2021. 'South Africa labour productivity growth'. https://www.ceicdata.com/en/indicator/south-africa/labour-productivity-growth (Accessed 16 September 2021).

Comins, L. 2021. 'SA CEOs predict a return to economic growth in 2021 – PwC survey'. The South African, 18 March 2021. https://www.thesouthafrican.com/news/sa-ceos-predict-a-return-to-economic-growth-in-2021-pwc-survey/ (Accessed 18 November 2021).

Ebrahim, A & Pirttilä, J. 2019. 'Can a wage subsidy system help reduce 50 per cent youth unemployment? Evidence from South Africa'. WIDER Working Paper No 2019/28, United Nations University World Institute for Development Economics Research (UNU-WIDER), Helsinki. https://www.wider.unu.edu/publication/can-wage-subsidy-system-help-reduce-50-cent-youth-unemployment (Accessed 18 November 2021).

Frey, CB & Osborne, MA. 2013. 'Future employment: How susceptible are jobs to computerisation?'. Oxford Martin School, University of Oxford. Working Paper. https://www.oxfordmartin.ox.ac.uk/publications/the-future-of-employment/ (Accessed 16 September 2021).

Government Communications. 2013. Insight Newsletter issue 13. Pretoria: GCIS. https://www.gcis.gov.za/content/resourcecentre/newsletters/insight/issue13 (Accessed 18 November 2021).

Griffiths, HR & Jones, RA. 1980. *South African Labour Economics*. New York: McGraw-Hill.

Hauser, P. 1974. 'The measurement of labour utilisation'. *Malayan Economic Review* 19: 1–17.

Hill, R, Lilenstein, K & Thornton, A. 2020. 'Job spells in an emerging market: Evidence from apartheid and post-apartheid South Africa'. WIDER Working Paper No 2020/27. The United Nations University World Institute for Development Economics Research (UNU-WIDER), Helsinki. https://www.econstor.eu/bitstream/10419/229251/1/wp2020-027.pdf (Accessed 18 November 2021).

ICLS (International Conference of Labour Statisticians). 1982. 'Resolution concerning statistics of the economically active population, employment, unemployment and underemployment'. Adopted by the 13th International Conference of Labour Statisticians (October 1982). https://ec.europa.eu/eurostat/ramon/coded_files/ecacpop_en.pdf (Accessed 16 September 2021).

ILO (International Labour Organization). 1998. 'Resolution concerning the measurement of underemployment and inadequate employment situations'. Adopted by the 16th International Conference of Labour Statisticians. Geneva: ILO. https://www.ilo.org/global/statistics-and-databases/standards-and-guidelines/

resolutions-adopted-by-international-conferences-of-labour-statisticians/ WCMS_087487/lang--en/index.htm (Accessed 16 September 2021).

ILO. 2000. 'Current International Recommendations on Labour Statistics'. https:// www.ilo.org/global/publications/ilo-bookstore/order-online/books/WCMS_ PUBL_9221108465_EN/lang--en/index.htm (Accessed 16 September 2021).

ILO. 2013. 'Resolution concerning statistics of work, employment and labour underutilization'. https://www.ilo.org/global/statistics-and-databases/standards-and-guidelines/resolutions-adopted-by-international-conferences-of-labour-statisticians/WCMS_230304/lang--en/index.htm (Accessed 18 November 2021).

ILO. 2021. 'ILO Monitor: COVID-19 and the world of work. 7th edition. Updated estimates and analysis'. https://www.ilo.org/wcmsp5/groups/public/---dgreports/---dcomm/documents/briefingnote/wcms_767028.pdf (Accessed 30 October 2021).

IMD. 2021. 'IMD world digital competitiveness ranking 2021'. https://worldcompetitive ness.imd.org/ (Accessed 30 November 2021).

Izaks, F, Avenant, J & Van Schalkwyk, I. 2018. 'Exploring the lived experiences of seasonally unemployed parents in the Gouda area'. *Social work* 54(2): 210 – 224.

Mbeki, T. 2006. 'State of the Nation Address'. February 3, 2006. Cape Town: Parliament of South Africa. https://www.sahistory.org.za/archive/2006-president-mbeki-state-nation-address-3-february-2006 (Accessed 1 December 2021).

McConnell, CR, Brue, SL & Macpherson, DA. 2015. *Contemporary Labor Economics*, 11th edition. New York: McGraw-Hill Education.

Mitchell, MF & Carlson, E. 2000. 'Beyond the unemployment rate – labour underutilisation and underemployment in Australia and the USA'. Working paper no 00-06. Centre of Full Employment and Equity, University of Newcastle Callaghan.

Mncayi, NP. 2020. 'An analysis of underemployment amongst young people in South Africa: The case of university graduates'. DPhil dissertation., North-West University.

NPC (National Planning Commission). 2012. 'National Development Plan 2030: Our future, make it work'. Pretoria: The Presidency.

Odeku, KO & Rudolf, SS. 2019. 'An analysis of the transformative intervention promoting youth entrepreneurship in South Africa'. *Academy of Entrepreneurship Journal* 25(4): 1–10.

Pettinger, T. 2019. 'Wage determination in perfectly competitive labour market'. Economics help, 28 November 2019. https://www.economicshelp.org/labour-markets/wage-determination/ (Accessed 16 September 2021).

PwC (PriceWaterhouseCoopers). 2021. 'South Africa's economic outlook: What can Budget 2021 do to help?'. https://www.pwc.co.za/en/assets/pdf/sa-economic-outlook-february-2021.pdf (Accessed 18 November 2021).

Ranchhod, V & Daniels, RC. 2021. 'Labour market dynamics in South Africa at the onset of the Covid-19 pandemic'. *South African Journal of Economics* 89(1): 44–62.

Republic of South Africa. 2020. 'Supplementary Budget Review 2020'. Pretoria: National Treasury. Treasury.

Sadie, JL. 1980. *Labour Demand and Supply*. Stellenbosch: Kosmo Publishers.

SA News. 2020. 'Job creation is key to SA's economic recovery'. 19 October 2020. https://www.sanews.gov.za/south-africa/job-creation-key-sa%E2%80%99s-economic-recovery (Accessed 16 September 2021).

SA News. 2021. 'Role-players consulted on National Minimum Wage adjustment'. 22 February 2021. https://www.sanews.gov.za/south-africa/role-players-consulted-national-minimum-wage-adjustment (Accessed 16 September 2021).

Stats SA. 2020. 'South Africa's unemployment rate increased by 7,5 percentage points to 30,8% in Q3:2020 compared to Q2:2020'. http://www.statssa.gov.za/wp-content/uploads/2020/11/Unemployment-rate-for-Q3-data-story.jpg (Accessed 16 September 2021).

Stats SA. 2021a. 'Quarterly labour force survey. Quarter 1: 2021'. Statistical release P0211. Pretoria: Stats SA. https://www.statssa.gov.za/publications/P0211/P02111stQuarter2021.pdf (Accessed 18 November 2021).

Stats SA. 2021b. 'Quarterly labour force survey. Quarter 2: 2021'. Statistical release P0211. Pretoria: Stats SA. http://www.statssa.gov.za/publications/P0211/Presentation%20QLFS%20Q2_2021.pdf (Accessed 18 November 2021).

Sugiyarto, G. 2007. 'Measuring underemployment: Establishing the cut-off point'. ERD working paper no 92. Asian Development Bank.

Trading Economics. 2021. 'South Africa unemployment rate'. https://tradingeconomics.com/south-africa/unemployment-rate (Accessed 16 September 2021).

United Nations. 2021. 'South Africa death rate 1950–2021'. https://www.macrotrends.net/countries/ZAF/south-africa/death-rate (Accessed 18 November 2021).

World Bank. 2020. 'South Africa GDP growth rate 1961–2021'. https://www.macrotrends.net/countries/ZAF/south-africa/gdp-growth-rate (Accessed 18 November 2021).

World Bank. 2021. 'Building back better from COVID-19, with a special focus on jobs'. 13 July 2021. https://www.worldbank.org/en/country/southafrica/publication/south-africa-economic-update-south-africa-s-labor-market-can-benefit-from-young-entrepreneurs-self-employment (Accessed 18 November 2021).

# PART 2:
# Labour Relations Contexts

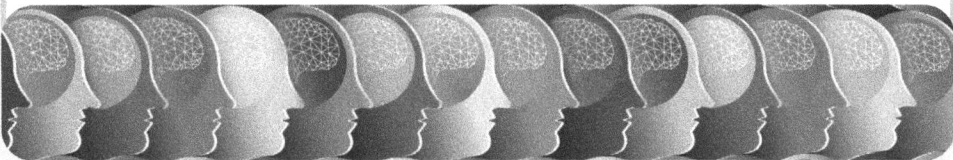

# 7

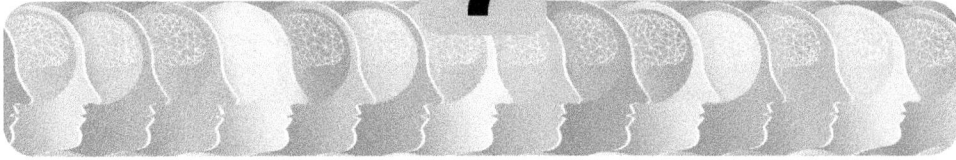

# Mobilising and Organising Representation in the Workplace

## Chapter Outline

➤

# Overview

Holgate, Simms and Tapia (2018) asked whether there is a difference between mobilising and organising parties in the workplace. Considering the international workplace landscape, the old debates around issues such as declining trade union presence, standard employment contracts, specified organisational rights, legal workplace definitions and predetermined employer networks are being challenged by this question – and this is set to continue during the Covid-19 pandemic. While it takes time for social change to result in the building of a new future, labour practitioners are challenged to consider the opportunities and new possibilities created by adapting to various workplaces, workplace cultures and different engagement processes. Trade unions, employers' and state organisations, processes, bodies of knowledge, roles, purposes and formats were all nurtured and developed over the last four industrial revolutions. The cognitive, creative process of adjusting to the realities of the different industrial revolutions, and now the protracted Covid-19 pandemic, challenges the long-held theory that we have become accustomed to. For the purpose of providing a base from which new strategies for these parties can develop, this chapter serves as a reminder of the theory regarding the development of players in the workplace.

In the South African labour relations system, we deal mostly with collectives. Consequently, the two main participants in the relationship – employees and employers – should be described in their collective forms.

The collective with the highest profile is the union. Unions are both the reactive and the proactive participants in the relationship. They often initiate action, to which employers or employers' associations, and sometimes also the state, react. Any attempt to understand labour processes requires an understanding of unions – of what they are, what they try to achieve, what methods and strategies they use and how they are organised.

Unions initially arose because employees needed to counter the power of employers, particularly on the economic front, but nowadays unions have far wider objectives and use diverse strategies. Also, although unions may be democratically founded and structured, there is a very real danger that they may eventually be dominated by a few individuals. Equally, shop stewards, as representative of the union at the place of work, may at times assert their independence from the union.

Unions do not act alone. The other party, namely the employers, does not necessarily need to form collectives to deal with the union. However, they may, for various reasons, prefer to do so. Employers' associations may not hold as high a profile as unions, but they do play an important role in labour relations, both in the sphere of collective bargaining and as a mouthpiece for employers in an industry or sector.

The legal position of unions is based on the principle of voluntarism. There is no legal obligation on unions to register, but unions who are not registered do not enjoy the privileges and rights granted by the Labour Relations Act 66 of 1995.

Unions also negotiate with employers for additional rights. One of these is the appointment of full-time shop stewards, who have a particular role to play in organisations.

People (members) organise themselves into trade unions. Local trade unions may be affiliated with local trade union federations. These federations may in turn also be affiliated with international federations. International federations in turn may belong to global union federations and trade union advisory committees.

➤

Like unions, employers may register employers' organisations. The main purpose of these organisations is to engage in centralised collective bargaining with unions.

Lastly, the state, as the third party in the employment relationship, plays a range of roles and executes various functions. The traditional roles of the state have been particularly challenged in the current era, characterised by increasing globalisation, economic instability and neo-liberalism. The South African state has so far attempted, through the National Economic Development and Labour Council (NEDLAC), to involve all parties in the formulation of labour and economic policy and legislation; however, it may now be reconsidering the effectiveness of this approach.

In line with international political, social, legalistic and economical changes since the First Industrial Revolution, the concepts known today as the state, the employer/employers' organisation and the employee/trade union have developed over time and may not carry the same meaning in all countries. When critising and analysing the conduct and development of these parties in a particular historic era from a labour relations perspective, it is prudent to judge and appreciate the development of these parties against the realities of that time, and to build on such an understanding taking into account the realities of the current era.

## Part One: The State as the Third Party in the Relationship

## The Corporatist Approach

With the advent of a new political dispensation in 1994, the trade union movement demanded the broadest possible consultation. As early as 1991, it was noted in the Laboria Minute – recording an agreement between the Congress of South African Trade Unions (COSATU), the National Council of Trade Unions (NACTU) and the government – that extensive consultation must be carried out on the legislative framework for regulating labour relations (Webster & Forrest, 2020).

Shortly afterwards the National Economic Forum was established, with a view to gaining the input of business and labour regarding proposed economic reforms. At the beginning of 1995 this body was replaced by NEDLAC. In establishing NEDLAC, the government signalled its intention to adopt a more corporatist approach.

Von Holdt (2002) describes corporatism as an institutional framework in which the economic and social decision making of society incorporates the labour movement and which generally leads to greater co-operation between the state, labour and capital and greater capacity to negotiate on common objectives. He also notes that corporatist policies are likely to be introduced in a situation where labour supports the government, but where government believes that economic activity must be promoted by free enterprise in order to also safeguard the interests of business.

In 2020, the focus of the South African government was on:

- strengthening the African agenda and regional integration
- consolidating global economic, political and social relations
- developing and managing state-owned properties in the form of foreign missions
- providing foreign policy
- reinforcing and promoting the country as a responsible producer, possessor and trader of defence-related products and advanced technologies
- promoting the New Partnership for Africa's Development (NEPAD) as a socio-economic flagship programme of the African Union. NEPAD's four primary objectives are to eradicate poverty, promote sustainable growth and development, integrate Africa in the world economy and accelerate the empowerment of women
- engaging with NEPAD, as well as BRICS, IBSA, the UN General Assembly and the African Union (AU)
- applying labour legislation, processes and procedures with state employees.

Following the corporate approach of the state, several processes, laws and institutions were put in place to assist the state in fulfilling its mandate. These include the Department of Employment and Labour, whose role it is to reduce unemployment, poverty and inequality through a set of policies and programmes developed in consultation with social partners. These policies and programmes are aimed at:

- achieving improved economic efficiency and productivity
- creating employment
- ensuring sound labour relations
- eliminating inequality and discrimination in the workplace
- alleviating poverty in employment.

## The Need to Reassess

The existing economic and social problems in South Africa continue to be a cause for concern. The reasons for this situation are many and do not apply only to South Africa. However, other countries in a similar position have managed to weather the economic storms far more successfully than South Africa has. Internally, the reasons are varied; they range from ineffective or indecisive government policies to rampant corruption, defective planning in the areas of education and health provision, and continuing inequality.

Yet it cannot be denied that labour relations and the role of unions and employers in a society have a significant impact on the economy and on perceptions among potential investors. This is therefore the topic discussed in the rest of this chapter.

## Part Two: Trade Unions and Employers' Organisations

## Trade Unions as Collective Organisations

### Definitions

The concept of 'trade union' has different meanings in different countries, and may sometimes even be confused with other concepts such as 'labour unions' and 'trade federations'. For the most current definition of a trade union, it is advisable to consult the most current labour legislation.

For instance, in Zimbabwe the Labour Act defines a trade union is defined as a body that represents or advances the interests of employees as regards their employment. In Namibia, according to the Labour Act 11 of 2007, a trade union refers to an association of employees whose principal purpose is to regulate relations between employees and their employers. In South Africa a trade union is defined, in Section 213 of the Labour Relations Act, as 'an association of employees whose primary purpose is to regulate relations between employees and employers including any employers' organisation'. Notice the subtle difference in the orientation of different neighbouring countries on the concept of trade unions.

### Origins

In medieval times, skilled workers organised themselves in guilds. However, with the dawn of the Industrial Revolution in Britain in the late eighteenth century, the trajectory was set for varying trade disputes, which were handled intermittently by different stakeholders. The so-called Friendly Societies were established in Britain around this time by craftsmen, who contributed a small amount each week and were then entitled to receive benefits in case of sickness, retirement, unemployment or death. These societies were very localised. To deal with trade disputes in an orderly fashion, the Combination Acts of 1799 and 1800 were passed. These Acts prohibited employees from forming collective bodies, and as a result the Friendly Societies had to operate in secret. In essence, they did not have enough power to make an impression on employers.

In 1824, the British government repealed the Combination Acts. A new Act, passed shortly thereafter, allowed workers to combine to protect their interests and even, within limits, to strike. At this stage, the state took its first steps towards instituting some form of protection for workers. It placed certain prohibitions on the use of child labour, later extending these to the employment of women on the mines. Subsequently, a number of unions were established, mostly by skilled workers. Many of the unions formed did not last long, first because of poor organisation and, secondly, because unionism was still generally resisted by the state and by employers. It was only after 1850 that the first real trade unions were established, and these were organised mainly among craftsmen.

This was the picture at the beginning of the twentieth century. By that point, trade unions of various kinds had established themselves as a permanent feature.

Today, accelerated industrialisation has led to trade unions proliferating in most economically advanced societies throughout the world, with trade union density being the highest in the Nordic countries.

As far as South Africa is concerned, there have been two notable armed labour revolutions, namely the Rand Rebellion of 1922 (the Rand Revolt or Red Revolt) in Fordsburg, Johannesburg, and, more recently, the Marikana Massacre of 16 August 2012 in the North West province. Both these historic events were dealt with in relatively similar ways by the state, and both resulted in significant political, social and legislative labour relations transformations.

Two significant trade union formations developed from the Rand Rebellion. The first is known today as Solidarity. It was founded on a religious base and focused on independence from the state (at that stage, Britain) – that is, an attitude of not waiting for the state to provide. The second is Industrial Workers of Africa (IWA), which was founded on a political and socialistic basis.

## Trade Union Classification

Traditionally, three categories of trade unions have been identified:
1. Occupational unions, described as 'niche' trade unions by Smale (2020)
2. Industrial/sectoral unions
3. General unions.

However, it is to be noted that the classification of unions is not absolute. As circumstances change, new constellations may evolve.

### Occupational unions

Occupational unions are so called because their membership derives from employees in a certain occupation. They can be broadly classified into craft unions, promotion unions, unskilled and semi-skilled unions and white-collar/professional unions.

## Craft Unions

The first occupational unions established were the craft unions. The main characteristic of these unions is their concern for and protection of the skilled status of their membership. Craft unions found their power in the skills of their members and in their ability to restrict entrance to the craft which they represented. Their strength lay not in numbers, but in the fact that their members occupied strategic positions in an undertaking and were not easily replaceable.

The dilution of skills by the introduction of technology has had the result that very few craft unions still exist, but some have managed to survive. An example of a surviving craft union is the South African Typographical Union (SATU), which serves the printing, newspaper and packaging industry. It also happens to be the oldest craft union in this country.

## Promotion Unions

A variation of the craft union is the promotion union. This type of union also recruits among workers with a particular skill, but the skill is one that is achieved by on-the-job training and promotion rather than by an apprenticeship. An example of a promotion union was the United National Transport Union (UNTU), established for the railways. The power base of promotion unions is the same as that of craft unions, namely the strategic importance and skill of the workers they represent. In recent years many promotion unions, like craft unions, have been absorbed into industrial or sectoral unions.

## Unskilled and Semi-skilled Unions

To fill the void left by craft and promotion unions, unions were established to represent unskilled and semi-skilled workers in certain industries. These unions restricted their membership to so-called lower-level employees, who then represented a specific occupational interest. This happened particularly in South Africa, where there was a historical correlation between skill and race and where the interests of African workers were not represented by craft and promotion unions, or even industrial unions.

Unions representing semi-skilled and unskilled workers do not have the strategic power of craft and promotion unions. Their power lies in mass organisation and in preventing the use of replacement labour. As union organisation and the fragmentation of skills increased, many of these unions amalgamated with craft and promotion unions to form larger industrial unions.

*White-collar or Professional Unions*

The last type of occupational union is one which is established to represent the interests of professional, white-collar workers. Traditionally, there has always been a difference in interests between these and so-called blue-collar workers. Non-manual workers have also been slower to organise. This may be ascribed to the fact that white-collar workers often perceive themselves as being closer to management.

With the shift to service industries in the economies of many developed countries, there has been a marked increase in white-collar unionism. Most of these unions will only organise workers in a particular industry or sector, but some, especially those representing certain professions, may organise across industries or sectors. Of all the occupational unions, these are the ones which have managed to maintain a significant presence. An example is the Banking, Insurance, Finance and Assurance Workers Union (BIFAWU).

## Industrial or Sectoral Unions
*Rationale*

The purpose of an industrial/sectoral union is to represent all the workers in a certain industry or sector, or at least as many workers as possible in that industry. These unions arose mainly out of the need of unskilled and semi-skilled workers to also have representation, but they later came to encompass all workers in a particular industry, with the rallying call 'one shop, one union'.

Industrial unions arose as a direct result of the dilution and fragmentation of crafts and skills, but they may also have a sociopolitical purpose. According to Salamon (2018), industrial unionism was originally intended to enable the working class to exercise greater control at the workplace and in society.

*Advantages*

Industrial/sectoral unionism has definite advantages, in that it:

- leads to stronger unions
- helps to eliminate inter-union competition
- reduces the number of unions with which employers have to bargain
- facilitates correspondence between union organisations and employers' organisations
- facilitates centralised bargaining
- leads to improved industrial/sectoral planning.

For the union, it has added advantages: officials can gain expertise in the workings of a particular industry/sector, and the union's power base, through its ability to institute strikes across an entire industry or sector, is greatly enhanced.

In South Africa, COSATU adopted the concept of one union per industry as a definite objective, for both organisational and sociopolitical reasons.

Examples of trade unions keeping to a particular industry are the South African Municipal Workers' Union (SAMWU) and the Independent Municipal and Allied Trade Union (IMATU) in local government.

### General Unions

Klikauer and Campbell (2021) state that general trade unions allow virtually any type of worker to join as a member, irrespective of sector, skill or occupation. These unions originated both from the politically inspired ideal of organising the entire working class into one body and from the need to represent non-skilled workers without reference to industries/sectors, or to form amalgamations of unions operating in different industries/sectors. In theory, their membership is open to any employee. However, many general unions have tended to adopt a particular industrial or sectoral pattern, as proved by a name such as Transport and General Workers' Union (TGWU).

## Trade Union Objectives

### Major Goals

The basic goals of trade unions all over the world generally fall into the following categories, which fall broadly under the banner of 'decent work' for their members:

- Wages: Protection of wages, minimum wages, protection of worker claims (at employer's insolvency)
- Employment security
- Social policies, such as reasonable accommodation for housing and traveling
- HIV/AIDS and pandemic-related work policies
- Job regulation: reasonable working hours, rest, paid leave, night work – contributing towards a work – life balance
- Equality of opportunity and treatment, including protection from arbitrary and discriminatory action
- Social security: Access to sustainable pension/provident funds
- Social justice: Giving workers access to a fair share of the wealth that they have helped to generate
- Training and development of members/employees and prospective members, such as vocational guidance and training
- Advancement of indigenous people and tribes in the workplace
- A safe and healthy work environment and access to health care
- Equality in the workplace with regard to gender, parental and other rights.

### Economic Concerns

Maintaining and improving the economic status of their members remains one of the major functions of trade unions. A union which does not obtain economic gains may soon lose its members.

However, unions – and particularly large industrial or sectoral unions – which attempt to improve the economic position of their members at all costs could, in the long term, bring about a decline in general economic conditions, which would adversely affect their members. For this reason, unions may sometimes temper their demands or even co-operate with government and other agencies by temporarily freezing wage demands for the purpose of improving the general economy. Also, if a union keeps demanding ever-increasing wages, this may lead to staff reductions. In essence, a union cannot pursue its economic objectives without reference to the total situation.

### Sociopolitical Involvement

Finally, it is important to remember that trade union members have a stake in the social and political systems in which they function. Trade unions necessarily have to represent the interests of their members in these spheres. Thus, to say that trade unions should not be 'political' would be unrealistic. Trade unions constitute a very potent political force, and most trade unions do engage in political action of some kind or another. The evolutionary role of trade unions within existing sociopolitical structures has been best demonstrated in those countries where grassroots opposition to governments in power became so strong that trade union leaders were obliged to become political campaigners. However, once these leaders entered the political arena, they could no longer be classified as trade unionists, even though they still relied on trade union support.

## Methods by which Unions Attempt to Achieve Their Objectives

### Different Strategies

The means by which unions seek to achieve their objectives are as diverse as the objectives themselves. The method used will often depend on the objective which is being pursued. Methods of achieving objectives include:

- collective bargaining with employers
- collective action
- representation and involvement in the undertaking
- affiliations with other bodies by, for example, forming federations or alliances
- collective bargaining with government (by the threat of a general strike, union federations can force government to listen to them)

- representation on local, national and international bodies
- representation on legislative and policy-making bodies
- political involvement (governments listen to unions which can bring in votes)
- representation on benefit funds such as pension and medical aid funds.

### The 'Power' Objective

For the union, achieving power is both an objective and a means by which it can achieve other objectives. The union's power will depend on:

- the solidarity of its membership (their willingness to engage in collective action)
- the depth and extent of its organisation (the larger and the better organised a union is, the more power will it wield)
- the skill and expertise of the negotiators
- the sympathy it gets from other bodies in both the labour relations and sociopolitical spheres
- its ability to influence government, business or even international agencies.

## The Organisation and Management of Trade Unions

### Trade Union Structure

There is, in most unions, a hierarchical structure similar to that found in business undertakings.

Looking from the bottom upward, the following structure pertains:

- **The general membership:** Members of different organisations form the broad base of the union.
- **Shop stewards:** Officials are elected by members in each undertaking (their constituency) to represent their interests with management.
- **Shop steward committees:** These are elected in individual undertakings or by members from different undertakings in the same area.
- **Local branches**: These are at the centre of trade union organisation. Their functions are to:
  - co-ordinate union activity in the area
  - recruit new members
  - act as intermediaries between members and the upper levels of the hierarchy.
- **The regional committee:** This committee, which does not necessarily exist in all unions, consists of representatives from the branches. It co-ordinates the activities of branches and acts as an intermediary between branches and the national committee.

- **The national committee:** Headed by the national executive and national chairperson/president, this committee establishes policy and strategy and generally directs the union's activities. Members are either elected by the national congress or come from regional or branch committees.
- **The national congress:** This body consists of representatives elected by grassroots membership via branches. It is supposed to be the ultimate policy and decision-making body in the union. The national congress usually meets on an annual or bi-annual basis, but special meetings may be called if circumstances warrant.
- **Federation:** A trade union may be affiliated with other trade unions under an umbrella body, where they share similar interests.
- **International bodies:** Federations of different countries may be affiliated with each other under an umbrella body to create a global force to promote specific worker interests.

## Trade Union Management

Union management is a complex and difficult task, and the manner in which it is tackled will vary from union to union.

### Management by the People

The management of a trade union rests with the various executives at branch, regional and national level. Since the persons serving on these committees are normally elected by trade union members, it can be said that the members manage the union.

A typical union constitution will state that changes in union policy and fundamental decisions may be made only by a general congress of trade union members or (in the case of larger unions) by a general congress of representatives from each region. The purpose is to ensure that the highest decision-making authority remains vested in the members themselves.

### Officials and Organisers

In keeping with the above policy, unions may not grant officials, such as general secretaries, or organisers appointed from outside a vote in committee or executive decisions. These officials are, in effect, employees of the union. They may advise elected office bearers and union members but may make no determinations.

### Problems with Trade Union Democracy

The principle of member management and control is an ideal which may not always be achieved in practice. This is so for various reasons:

- Unions may be dominated by certain factions or office bearers who pursue their own interests and not those of the general membership.
- Officials and organisers will influence – and even control – union members. They have greater expertise and knowledge and spend all their time on union business.
- There are many day-to-day decisions which have to be taken by individuals, committees or executives, and in these cases they do not have the opportunity of first obtaining the approval of the general membership.
- Most importantly, trade union members are sometimes apathetic. They do not always actively participate or take an interest in union affairs, except when a crisis arises.
- Finally, individuals appointed to important positions in the union hierarchy will hold substantial power. They are able to influence a vast number of people and, because of their positions, may become public figures. This may result in a 'power complex', where the individual perceives themself as more important than the union or its members – at the cost, very often, of democracy and the welfare of the general membership.

Numerous theorists have stated that unions move in a continual cycle, from democracy to oligarchy and back to democracy. A union or union federation which was originally established on a democratic basis may eventually be dominated by a few skilled or powerful individuals. This phase will continue until members become dissatisfied with the situation, whereupon there will again be an initiative towards democratisation. Unfortunately, and almost inevitably, certain individuals will again achieve dominance, and so the cycle continues.

Despite the problems mentioned, trade unions do attempt to conduct their affairs along democratic lines. The most effective safeguard against undemocratic action is to be found in the greatest possible involvement of members at all levels of the organisation. For this reason, unions which take democracy seriously will:
- attempt to involve shop stewards in negotiations
- report back as often as possible
- ensure that office bearers on the national executive are drawn from as wide a base as possible.

## Other Organisational Issues
### 'Responsible' Leadership
The principle of union democracy may prove a problem to employers who insist on rapid decision making and on union leaders keeping their members 'under control'. A union which insists on continual report-back may not be able

to give an immediate decision, and a leader who represents the interests of the members and abides by the majority decision cannot 'control' the members.

Thus, the management call for union leaders to act 'responsibly' may contradict the democratic principle on which unions are based.

### Trade Union Discipline

A union is a collective which the individual joins of their own accord. Having joined, the member is subject to the rules and decisions of that collective. Should the individual disagree, they are free to withdraw their membership, but they may not act in an individual capacity or distance themself from union decisions at will. This applies particularly to office bearers of the union.

## The Shop Steward

### The Role of the Shop Steward

Most unions insist that members at every workplace elect shop stewards from among their own ranks and that management recognises such shop stewards as the legitimate representatives of the union members in their employ.

The shop steward plays a pivotal role in union organisation. The shop steward performs union duties in the course of their employment and is the one office bearer who can directly represent workers' interests to both management and the union. Figure 7.1 illustrates the pivotal role played by the shop steward in the communications network.

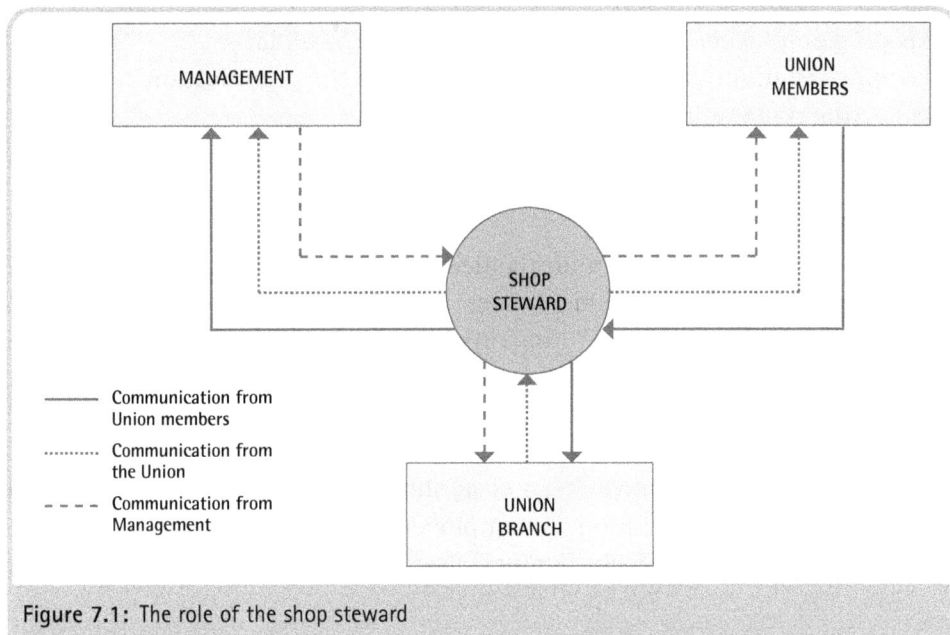

**Figure 7.1:** The role of the shop steward

## Qualities of a Good Shop Steward

It is clear that a shop steward plays a very important role in the employment relationship, especially in the workplace where they are functioning. For this very reason a shop steward must have certain qualities that will enable them to operate effectively. The shop steward should:

- have the respect and trust of the union, fellow employees and management
- be an effective communicator
- be able to make independent, objective judgements and to reach rapid decisions
- be committed, diligent and fair-minded
- be knowledgeable in union, employee and even management affairs.

## Shop Steward Duties

The duties of a shop steward will include:

- recruiting new members
- assisting and representing members in grievance and disciplinary procedures
- consulting and negotiating with management on plant-level matters
- obtaining mandates from members before and during these negotiations
- assisting with the organisation of ballots, such as strike ballots
- ensuring that management adheres to wage and other agreements
- organising and attending union meetings at plant level and branch level
- participating in workplace forums or committees
- participating in health and safety committees
- advising fellow employees
- keeping employees informed of union policies and plans
- keeping the union informed of the situation in the organisation
- collecting trade union dues
- working at branch level.

## Shop Steward Rights

Shop stewards perform their union duties in their free time but will be called on to perform certain functions during normal working hours. Their job at the workplace may have to be interrupted to bring an urgent matter to the attention of management, to negotiate with management or to represent fellow members during the conduct of grievance and disciplinary procedures. Thus, shop stewards are allowed greater flexibility than other employees and will be permitted to leave their posts at short notice if a workplace-related matter requires their attention. As employees, they need to ask permission to leave their place of work, but permission should not be unreasonably withheld. Also, a law or agreement may provide for shop stewards to be given time off for training or to attend to union business.

### Full-time Shop Stewards

In some countries the law or agreements may provide for the appointment of full-time shop stewards. The number of full-time shop stewards will usually depend on the size of the organisation. Suitable persons are nominated by the union, which makes recommendations to management. The shop stewards are appointed for a specific period, and they usually continue to be paid the wages that they were receiving in their previous positions. Once the agreed period has expired, the incumbent may be reappointed. If not, they will return to their previous job.

The appointment of full-time shop stewards can contribute significantly to stabilising relationships at the workplace. The only problem for management is that the shop steward's normal job will have to be filled on a temporary basis, but this obstacle is not insurmountable.

## Trade Unionism in the Twenty-first Century

Trade unions arose out of the necessity to protect employees from exploitation in societies where employers held absolute power and where governments were not overly concerned with the general welfare of the population. Their role was essentially antagonistic in that they had to battle, often against great odds, for every concession. The second half of the twentieth century saw a gradual breaking down of class structures, a more general spread of ownership (also to employees), the introduction of laws protecting workers from exploitation and even, in some countries, the passing of laws mandating a degree of joint decision making by employers and employees.

Consequently, trade unions were faced with the dilemma of balancing antagonism with co-operation. In certain instances, trade unions managed to achieve some balance by separating their bargaining function from their co-operative and co-decision-making function.

In the last years of the twentieth century, the issue of globalisation started to gain prominence. Globalisation gives capital, and thereby business, greater mobility. Investments can be withdrawn easily and businesses can be moved elsewhere. Technology poses a threat to traditional jobs and trade unions may see their traditional membership base reduced, divided, individualised and dispersed.

By 2010 the worldwide economic crisis of 2008 had obliged a rethinking of globalisation and global capital. It highlighted the problem of escalating unemployment, the growing divide between rich and poor and the dangers of allowing international finance free rein. Added to this were the effects of digitalisation and the outsourcing of jobs, all of which may lead governments to consider greater interference in the economy and, indirectly, in the labour relationship.

More recently, the Covid-19 pandemic highlighted the need for social protection, the problems posed by social inequalities and the need to improve general health and safety awareness.

Concern on the part of governments may give unions greater prominence as lobbyists and increase their leverage both in the workplace and in society at large. Conversely, governments may regulate to such an extent that unions lose much of their relevance. What is clear is that governments will expect greater co-operation from unions in regulating the work situation. Union demands for decent wages could be directly linked to rising job losses, but it is unlikely that unions will trim their demands as the poor continue to get poorer. It is equally unlikely that businesses will continue to absorb high labour costs and not compensate by way of outsourcing and greater use of technology. The problem is far from straightforward and will require a more sophisticated approach than the existent labour market and labour relations theory can provide.

## Employers and Employers' Organisations

There are also organisations which represent business in a wider framework, such as Business Unity South Africa (BUSA) the National Employers' Association of South Africa (NEASA) and the National Organisation for Employers South Africa (NOESA).

### Management as Representative of Employers

Labour relations theory uses the term 'employer' or 'employer representative' as against 'employee' and 'employee representative'. However, the use of the word 'employer' is misleading. Nowadays, very few business undertakings are owned and managed by a single employer/owner. Generally, they are either private or public companies owned by shareholders, headed by a board of directors and run by a management team. The shareholders are the actual employers, but they take no active part in the day-to-day running of the company's affairs. Therefore, they are rarely seen as the employers. Instead, the word 'management' is now used synonymously with 'employer'.

### Employer Goals

Employers and members of management are bound by the common goals of maximising the profit potential of the undertaking, ensuring the future of the enterprise, expanding the market, satisfying customers, utilising resources efficiently and looking after employees. The primary goal remains that of maximising profit potential. However, organisations are also stakeholders in states, which creates a duty on employers to consider the manner in which economic wealth is created. The United Nations' Sustainable Development Goals (SDGs) suggest that employers need to reconsider the manner in which wealth is created. Economic profit needs to be balanced by aspects such as reducing inequalities, ensuring responsible consumption, and so forth (United Nations, n.d.). These issues usually bring management into conflict with employees and unions.

Employers or management will also insist on their right to manage. Yet nowadays most employers are aware that the profit motive cannot be pursued to the detriment of employees and that managerial prerogative is not absolute. The issue is now one of degree rather than principle.

## Attitude towards Unions

There is little doubt that the majority of employers would, if they could, have no unions in their organisation. They would prefer to run their businesses as they see fit, to gain the commitment (if possible) of their employees and even to engage in some form of joint decision making with the employees themselves, provided that this is at the employer's initiative (the unilateral management perspective). However, since unions are endemic to the pluralist system, employers have had to accept them as such and have learnt to live with them – if not in absolute harmony, then at least as peacefully as possible.

## Collective Employer Bodies

Because employers have interests other than the regulation of the employer–employee relationship, employers may belong to various organisations, some of which play no role in labour relations.

One form of employer organisation is the chamber of commerce or industry, which will have as members the majority of employers from a geographic area. The purpose of a chamber of commerce or industry is to serve as a forum and to represent the interests and opinions of business in engaging with government and other sections of the community. A chamber will attempt to cover all facets of business and will, consequently, also deal with manpower matters and labour relations issues. The chambers serve as useful representational, liaison and advisory bodies and may succeed in promoting healthier relations, but they do not actively intervene in the employer–employee relationship and do not engage in collective bargaining. The only employer bodies dealing with the relationship are those specifically designed to do so.

## Employers' Organisations

In contrast to the employee, an employer may not need to combine with other employers in order to hold power in the labour relationship. The employer's power is derived from their ability to hire and fire, from the fact that they determine wages and increases and from the authority vested in them.

Employers will focus on 'collective' labour relations only in reaction to unionism. However, dealing with a union or unions individually is time-consuming and may also place the employer at a disadvantage, particularly if they are not skilled in negotiation. Consequently, employers have established bodies to deal with labour relations issues and to engage in collective bargaining with unions. These are known as employers' organisations.

### Reasons for Forming/Joining Employers' Organisations

The most common reasons for forming or joining employer's organisations are to:

- balance the collective power of the unions
- standardise conditions of service in an industry
- put wages out of competition (prevent unions from using agreements with one employer as a basis for better agreements with another)
- protect the interests of employers who may not be able to afford high remuneration packages
- have negotiations conducted by persons with expertise
- have the employer's interests represented at a macro-level.

### Functions of Employers' Organisations

The most common functions of employers' organisations are to:

- provide a forum for the development of a co-ordinated strategy in dealing with organised labour
- negotiate with unions for the purpose of standardising minimum wages and conditions of service and procedures in an industry or sector
- assist members by providing them with information on issues such as procedures, legislative changes, handling of labour action and the administration of collective agreements
- provide a co-ordinated system of employee benefits such as pension funds and medical aid schemes
- co-ordinate training and development in the industry
- lobby government to pass legislation which serves the interests of employers
- liaise with trade union federations at a centralised level over issues of national interest

- engage the media as a means of promoting support for the policies and position of the employers' organisation on various issues and also counteract any unfavourable publicity.

### Organisation and Management of Employers' Organisations

The organisational structure and management of employers' organisations resembles that of a union, although they do not have to engage in the same efforts to recruit new members as unions do. Their aims and their methods of achieving their aims may also be more limited than those of a union.

Employers' organisations are made up of the various employers in an industry or sector, who may come together on an area, regional or national basis. Membership of an employers' organisation is voluntary.

A national or regional organisation may have sub-organisations at various levels. The ultimate authority and decision-making power of an employers' organisation is vested in the general meeting. Here, general policy is established, general directions are given and mandates are granted. A problem encountered in employers' organisations is that large companies tend to dominate these bodies. This happens particularly where votes in the general meeting are granted in proportion to the size of an employer's business.

### The Future Role of Employers' Organisations

In countries where there is a preference for plant-level bargaining instead of centralised negotiations, employers' associations as bargaining bodies are becoming less relevant. Yet they are likely to remain in one shape or another, if only to represent the joint voice of employers vis-à-vis the unions and government, to advise members, and to provide continued benefits.

## Part Three: Employee and Employer Representation in South Africa

## The Legal Position

### Voluntarism with regard to Registration

In keeping with the principle of voluntarism, trade unions and employers' organisations in South Africa have not been subject to control in that they were not, and still are not, obliged to register in terms of the Labour Relations Act 66 of 1995. However, all rights accorded to parties in terms of the Act (such as the rights to access, to hold meetings on the employer's premises and to elect shop stewards) are accorded only to registered bodies. This most certainly encourages all active unions, as well as employers' associations, to register. By implication, an unregistered union, although it may enter into an agreement with an employer, has no statutory rights.

## The Registration Process

The prescriptions for the registration of trade unions and employer organisations (which are essentially the same) are contained in sections 95 to 106 of the Labour Relations Act.

A trade union may apply for registration on the prescribed form provided that it:

- selects a name which cannot be confused with the name or shortened name of another registered union
- has adopted a constitution with the required provisions
- has a physical address in the Republic
- is independent. (A trade union will be regarded as independent if it is not under the direct or indirect control of any employer or employers' organisation and if it is free from any type of influence or interference from an employer or employers' organisation.)

An application for registration must be made on the prescribed form and be accompanied by a copy of the union's constitution and any other information which may be of use to the registrar. In terms of Section 96(5) of the Labour Relations Act, the constitution of a union must contain provisions relating to:

- a statement that the union is an association not for gain
- qualifications for membership
- conditions under which membership will be denied
- membership fees, and the method by which these fees will be determined
- termination of membership
- cancellation of membership
- appeals against withdrawals of membership rights, procedures for such appeals and the naming of a body to hear appeals
- the calling of meetings, including the quorum required and the taking of minutes
- the method by which decisions will be taken
- the position of secretary and the duties involved in that position
- other office bearers, officials and shop stewards and their respective duties
- the procedure by which office bearers and shop stewards will be nominated
- the procedure for the nomination, election and appointment of officials
- the removal of office bearers, officials and shop stewards, procedures for appeals against such removal and the designation of a body by which appeals can be heard
- the circumstances in which a vote by ballot should be held

- the holding of a vote by ballot before a strike is called
- a prohibition on the disciplining of a member or the cancellation of membership where the member refuses to take part in a strike which has not been subjected to a ballot, or where a majority of persons involved did not vote in favour of a strike
- the deposit and investment of funds
- the application of funds
- the date on which the financial year will end
- procedures for amendments to the constitution
- procedures whereby the union can, by resolution, be liquidated.

All the above provisions, except those relating to shop stewards, apply also to the constitutions of employers' organisations.

Once convinced that the applicant conforms to the requirements, the industrial registrar will register the union (or employers' organisation, as the case may be).

Registration gives the union/employers' organisation the status of a juristic person and protects members from obligations and liabilities incurred by the union/employers' organisation. This means that a member, office bearer, official or shop steward cannot be held personally responsible for losses suffered by anybody as a result of the actions undertaken by a member, office bearer, official or shop steward on behalf of the union. Registered unions can apply for entry to a bargaining council and are more easily granted recognition by employers.

## Obligations

Every registered trade union or employers' organisation is obliged to:
- keep a register of members, listing names and membership fees paid
- keep proper financial records and records in respect of its income and expenditure, assets and liabilities
- within six months of the financial year end, prepare annual statements of income and expenditure and an end-of-year balance sheet
- submit its financial records and financial statements to an annual audit
- obtain a written report from the auditor, in which the auditor indicates whether the union has adhered to its constitution as regards financial matters
- table the financial statements and the auditor's report for inspection by members, and present these documents to a meeting of members or their representatives
- keep all financial records, substantiating documents, records of membership fees or levies paid by members, income and expenditure statements,

balance sheets and auditor's reports, in original or reproduced form, for a period of at least three years
- keep a register of members
- keep minutes of meetings for a period of three years
- retain ballot forms for at least three years from the date on which the ballot was conducted and, by 31 March each year, supply the registrar with a certified membership list
- supply the registrar, within 30 days of its receipt, with a certified copy of the auditor's report and the financial statements
- within 30 days of the election of national office bearers, supply the registrar with the names and work addresses of these office bearers
- inform the registrar within 30 days of any change of address.

## Union and Shop Steward Rights
The sections of the Labour Relations Act which deal with organisational rights provide for the election of shop stewards (union representatives) by a majority union or unions and also spell out the rights of shop stewards and union office bearers at the place of work. In terms of subsections 14(4) and (5), shop stewards of majority unions are entitled to:
- assist employees during disciplinary and grievance procedures
- monitor the employer's adherence to the Act
- check on the implementation of binding collective agreements
- report any transgression of the Act or an agreement to the employer, the union and/or a responsible authority
- perform any other function agreed upon between the union and the employer
- take reasonable time off to fulfil their functions or to receive training.

Sections 11 to 22 of the Labour Relations Act provide majority unions with wide-ranging rights, including access to the workplace, the right to hold meetings on the premises, the right to stop-order facilities and the right to time off for office bearers. Some, but not all, of these rights also apply to unions which have sufficient representation.

## Exercising Organisational Rights
If a registered trade union wants to exercise any of the organisational rights granted by the Act, the union should:
- notify the employer in writing that it wants to exercise one or more of the organisational rights at the workplace
- specify which rights it wishes to exercise

- identify the workplace in which it wants to exercise these rights
- provide proof of its representativeness.

The employer and the union should meet within 30 days to try and conclude a collective agreement which will stipulate the manner in which the union will exercise its organisational rights.

Normally the employer will firstly ask the trade union for proof of registration and the union will have to submit a certified copy of its registration certificate. The next step will be a membership verification exercise to determine how many employees the trade union actually represents in the workplace. Should it be established that the union is either sufficiently representative or a majority trade union, the parties will then draw up the agreement and spell out the specifics with regard to organisational rights and the manner in which the union will be able to exercise these rights.

Any dispute regarding organisational rights should be referred to the Commission for Conciliation, Mediation and Arbitration (CCMA), which will try to settle the dispute first through conciliation and, should conciliation fail, through arbitration.

## Part Four: The South African Trade Union Movement – A Historical Perspective

## The Position: 1950–1994

The development of the various streams of the South African trade union movement since the beginning of the twentieth century is outlined in Chapter 2. As described in that chapter, the all-white and multiracial movement, as embodied by the South African Confederation of Labour Associations (SACLA) and the Trade Union Council of South Africa (TUCSA) respectively, had been established in the 1950s. The non-racial movement, representing mainly black employees, which had been established in the same period under the banner of the South African Congress of Trade Unions (SACTU), had by 1960 disintegrated (or gone underground), and it was only at the beginning of the 1970s that the black and non-racial trade union movement re-emerged under the auspices of the various worker aid societies established in what were then the provinces of Natal, Transvaal and the Cape. By 1980 these unions had already made their mark on the South African labour relations scene. They had introduced a new dimension into South African labour relations by concentrating on strong shop-floor representation and recognition at plant level.

## CUSA, FOSATU and Other Significant Unions

In April 1979, the majority of the newer unions had joined forces to establish the Federation of South African Trade Unions (FOSATU), the first non-racial trade union federation representing mainly black workers since the demise of SACTU. Soon afterwards, in 1980, some of the remaining unions established the Council of Unions of South Africa (CUSA).

At the beginning of the 1980s there were, in addition to these two bodies, also individual unions which played an important part in bringing about change. Among these the most prominent were the non-racial Cape Town Municipal Workers' Association (CTMWA), the Western Province General Workers' Union (which shortly afterwards became the General Workers' Union [GWU]) and the Food and Canning Workers' Union/African Food and Canning Workers' Union. Furthermore, the Black Allied Workers' Union (BAWU), founded by black consciousness activist Drake Koka, had split into BAWU, still maintaining the black consciousness ideology, and the South African Allied Workers' Union (SAAWU), espousing non-racialism and finding its base mainly in the highly politicised East London area. With the emergence of the 'new' unions, South Africa had once again a union movement reflective of the entire spectrum of South African society and of the various political orientations within that society.

## The Community-based Unions

Among the unions established in the 1980s were those which found their power not only in shop-floor organisation, but also through gaining the support of the community. SAAWU was the forerunner of this movement. Very soon, efforts to organise the same workers led to rivalry between the community-based unions and the older emergent unions, which were concentrating on shop-floor issues.

The community-based unions did not emphasise worker leadership to the same extent as the 'older' unions such as the GWU and the FOSATU affiliates. The community-based unions were to some extent dominated by certain full-time officials. These differences in organisational methods and attitude hampered efforts towards unity among the newer unions in the early years of the new decade.

The position became even more difficult after the establishment of the United Democratic Front (UDF) in August 1983. This body immediately concentrated on gaining worker support. In the union movement, divisions arose over the question of affiliation to bodies such as the UDF. While SAAWU, the Motor Assembly and Component Workers' Union of South Africa (MACWUSA) and even CUSA immediately became affiliated to the UDF, FOSATU and the GWU remained resolutely independent of any sectoral political affiliation, even if they vigorously supported the objectives of a national resistance movement.

## The Black Consciousness Unions

The black consciousness wing of the trade union movement had already been established in the 1970s by BAWU, but this body remained weak. This led the Azanian People's Organisation (AZAPO), established in 1977, to seek the support of the Consultative Committee of Black Trade Unions (CCOBATU). In May 1984, these bodies launched the Azanian Confederation of Trade Unions (AZACTU). AZACTU disclaimed formal links with AZAPO, but it was clearly the trade union branch of this movement.

## Unionisation on the Mines

The unionisation of black workers was not as immediate and rapid in the mining industry as in the manufacturing sector. By 1982, mine employers, overtaken by events in other sectors, had started granting limited access to unions representing black and coloured mineworkers. In late 1982, CUSA, which had been approached by individuals organising black mineworkers, decided to launch a union in the mining industry. The result was the formation of the National Union of Mineworkers (NUM), with Cyril Ramaphosa as general secretary. Under his leadership the NUM grew rapidly to become, by 1985, the largest union representing black workers.

## Unity Moves and the Formation of COSATU

In August 1981 and April 1982, representatives of the then emergent unions came together in Cape Town to discuss trade union unity. Not much was achieved, because of differences on the question of registration. While many of the FOSATU unions were willing to register, unions such as the GWU regarded registration as a route to co-option by employers and the government. In July 1982, another round of unity talks were held, which ended in deadlock.

Nevertheless, in April 1983 a steering committee was formed to establish the principles for a new federation, but new differences arose on the issue of industrial versus general unionism. The community-based unions and CUSA, which favoured general unionism, did not provide the information necessary for demarcation plans, in line with the other unions' idea of establishing strong national industrial unions.

In the meantime, certain CUSA unionists had become concerned at the fact that those involved in the unity initiative had not emphasised black leadership. Also, the unions affiliated to the UDF formed an interest group separate to the core unity unions, such as the FOSATU unions and the GWU. The AZACTU unions had, for the first time, been invited to join in the unity movement, but differences regarding the question of non-racialism came to the fore, and AZACTU did not attend subsequent meetings. Shortly afterwards CUSA also withdrew from the unity initiative, stating that it had reservations about participating in discussions where black leadership was not enforced as a principle (Webster, 1987). CUSA's withdrawal resulted in the NUM's disaffiliation from this body, as it wished to be part of the new federation.

The remaining bodies found common ground in the principle of non-racialism. Furthermore, agreement was finally reached on the principle of industrial unions, with various unions declaring themselves willing to amalgamate in order to establish single-industry unions. Other principles accepted were worker control, representation on the basis of paid-up membership and co-operation on a national level. The new federation, COSATU, was eventually launched on 30 November 1985. It originally consisted of 449 279 paid-up members in 33 unions, including 9 former UDF affiliates.

### Trade Unionism under Inkatha

The Inkatha movement, established in what was then Natal, had always been eager to garner trade union support. Upon the formation of Inkatha, Chief Mangosuthu Buthelezi had invited newly formed unions to join the movement, but the trade unions had by then gained in strength and they evidently saw no reason to forge closer ties with this movement, although many of their members also belonged to Inkatha. In June 1984, Chief Minister Buthelezi noted that Inkatha's membership was dominated by peasants and workers and that the movement wanted to share its power with workers (Southall, 1986). By then, discernible rifts had emerged between Inkatha and the unions operating in Natal, one of the reasons being Buthelezi's opposition to FOSATU's disinvestment stand. In spite of this lack of support, Buthelezi persevered and 1 May 1986 saw the inauguration of the United Workers' Union of South Africa (UWUSA). This body had its origins with a group of dissatisfied FOSATU members in the Richards Bay–Empangeni area. It was established with a view to increasing Inkatha's involvement in the worker movement and in opposition to the COSATU unions.

At its inauguration, UWUSA claimed to have a membership of 85 000, but it had not at that stage organised at any specific plants. The federation gained limited recognition in Natal, but UWUSA never made a real impact on South African labour relations.

### NACTU

After the withdrawal of AZACTU and CUSA from the unity initiative, it was evident that a new black consciousness alliance was in the making. In October 1986, CUSA and AZACTU merged to form CUSA/AZACTU, later to be known as NACTU. The alliance was in many senses an unlikely one, as CUSA was not as extreme in its black exclusivity stand as the AZACTU unions.

## The Demise of TUCSA

The gradual demise of TUCSA has already been described in Chapter 2. Despite efforts by individual TUCSA unions to accommodate the black African workforce, the organisation eventually proved itself unable to adapt completely to changing circumstances. As time passed, numerous unions which had opened up their ranks to black employees found their membership of TUCSA to be a hindrance rather than an asset. The unions which remained formed two groupings: those representing white-collar and supervisory workers, and those representing mainly skilled workers in the textile, leather and garment industries. In 1986, some textile and leather unions left TUCSA, and at the end of that year TUCSA was dissolved.

## FEDUSA

In 1985 the Federation of South African Labour (FEDSAL) was revived. It represented mainly non-manual white workers but also had a substantial black membership. FEDSAL formed the basis for the establishment, in April 1997, of the Federation of Unions of South Africa (FEDUSA). Formed from an amalgamation of FEDSAL and the Federation of Organisations Representing Government Employees (FORGE), FEDUSA also absorbed the unions belonging to the Federation of Independent Unions (FITU), a loose federation of ex-TUCSA unions.

## Sociopolitical Orientations

It is impossible to speak of the South African trade union movement without reference to parallels in the sociopolitical sphere. In South Africa, with its history of incisive political and social divisions, it would be totally unrealistic to expect unions to operate regardless of political considerations. Up until the 1990s, the union movement had been the only legitimate voice of the disenfranchised section of the population. It was to be expected that this section would use its industrial muscle also to raise political demands and grievances, and that emerging political organisations would woo the worker movement because of the powerful base from which it operated. Thus, by 1990, the South African trade union movement, despite all protestations to the contrary, still reflected the divisions within the sociopolitical spectrum.

# The New Dispensation: Important Developments and their Antecedents

## Dominant Constellations

According to statistics supplied by the South African Department of Employment and Labour there were, by mid-2016, 138 registered unions and 22 federations in South Africa. However, most of the larger unions were affiliated to one of the dominant federations, namely COSATU, FEDUSA or NACTU. Together, these three federations represented more than 3 million employees, with COSATU membership standing at approximately two-thirds of the total. These are also the three union bodies which still represent organised labour at NEDLAC.

Another body which should be mentioned is the Confederation of South African Workers' Unions (CONSAWU), established in 2003. It is one of four national trade union centres in South Africa, and it is affiliated with the International Trade Union Confederation (ITUC). CONSAWU, which recruits workers from all race groups, has set as its main goals the eradication of poverty, exploitation and discrimination and urges all workers to join trade unions. However, some see it as the successor of the all-white SACLA, especially since Solidarity, which originally represented mainly white worker interests, became one of its affiliates. It is inevitable that certain union bodies may still be tainted by their previous affiliations, but a great deal of levelling has taken place in the last 20 plus years and workers of all colours are in the same position. As it is, by 2016 CONSAWU's membership reached a not inconsiderable figure of around 200 000. Most recently it has challenged NEDLAC on its refusal to allow CONSAWU representation on that body.

Probably the most significant recent development in this context has been the formation of the South African Federation of Trade Unions (SAFTU) (see later in this chapter).

## COSATU

### Aims and Objectives

The aims and objectives of Cosatu include to fight for worker rights through securing social and economic justice for all workers. They also aim to influence clear economic policies in order for the creation of wealth to be democratically controlled. They emphasise the restructuring of the economy, the achievement of just standards of living, social security and fair conditions of work for all (COSATU, n.d.).

## Organisational Structure

COSATU emphasised the principle of trade union democracy, resting on maximum participation by union members, equality of membership and decision making from the bottom upwards. It is COSATU's stated policy that workers should be represented on all committees. COSATU is comprised of the following structures:

- The National Congress
- The Central Committee
- The Central Executive Committee
- The Provincial Congress
- The provincial executive committees
- The provincial shop steward councils
- The local shop steward councils
- The Lower Executive Committee.

Full-time paid officials should have no vote, and negotiations are supposed to be conducted by shop stewards with the assistance of union officials – although very often this does not happen in practice.

## COSATU and the Union Dilemma

Many of the trade unions established during the 1970s had deliberately avoided overt involvement with political bodies – first, because it might elicit reaction from some members; secondly, because it would detract from their shop-floor organisation; and, thirdly, for fear that, like the SACTU unions, over-involvement would eventually lead to their disintegration as a union movement.

These unions saw their battle as centring on the economic upliftment of workers, which, they believed, could later lead to sociopolitical upliftment. They also placed emphasis on democratic structures. According to Friedman (2000), the union leaders were of the opinion that they would not win economic equality if a black elite simply replaced the white elite, and if the black elite were the leaders of political movements. However, with the formation of COSATU, it was accepted that this body would have to play both an economic and a political role. As Maree (1993) stated, COSATU was not a political party, but it realised that it had a political responsibility.

As was later proved, COSATU did play a major role in bringing about a new political dispensation. The issue which followed and which is still relevant was whether COSATU, as a supporter of the majority party in government, should put the interests of the government and society at large above the interests of its members or whether, regardless of the effects, it should promote only the well-being of its members – who, after all, constitute a relatively small portion of South African society.

*Positions and Stances within the Changed Political Dispensation*

With the unbanning of various political parties in February 1990, it was surmised that the new legitimacy granted to the South African Communist Party (SACP) and the ANC would take the pressure off COSATU in the political sphere. However, COSATU was by that time a very potent political force, unlikely to surrender its position on the political stage. Secondly, COSATU had throughout committed itself to improving the position of its members, not only at the workplace but also in society at large. Consequently, and despite its previous commitment to non-affiliation, COSATU formed a broad alliance with the ANC and the SACP, with a view to influencing the negotiation process around a new political dispensation. Cyril Ramaphosa, one of the most prominent COSATU officials, was appointed as chief negotiator for the ANC and soon assumed a leadership position in the party.

COSATU's role in the Tripartite Alliance initially strengthened its position. However, much debate at that time centred on the political implications. Some union leaders objected to what they perceived as COSATU's 'junior status' in the Alliance and the ANC's failure to consult COSATU before making certain policy decisions. Others feared that a close alliance with the ANC and SACP would endanger COSATU's independence and, in a future dispensation, make it beholden to a political party. The question was whether COSATU should:

- become entrenched as the labour wing of the ANC or SACP, requiring any future government to obtain a mandate from the trade union movement before instituting legislation affecting workers
- form its own political party
- remain independent and concentrate on restructuring industries and the economy by extended centralised and national bargaining.

The argument for independence was based on the belief among some trade union leaders that any form of political allegiance would endanger the independence of the trade union movement.

*Problems within the New Dispensation*

Having made a pact with the ANC, COSATU put all its energies into ensuring an ANC victory in the 1994 elections. More than 20 leading figures in COSATU were released to stand for Parliament, while numerous others later left of their own accord in order to take up new positions which were being offered by the government and in business. This 'brain drain' continued as reforms took place in the civil service and society at large.

Some of the remaining union leaders were dissatisfied with the fact that top union officials had been released without ensuring their accountability to the union movement. It was subject to speculation whether these ex-unionists would continue to promote a labour agenda.

In the immediate post-election period, unions were faced with heightened expectations and militancy at grassroots level and, on the other hand, with a government which expected them to curb this militancy in the interests of the country as a whole.

### National Congress, 1994

At its national congress in 1994, COSATU delegates again dwelt on the accusation that they constituted a labour elite. The congress devoted considerable time to the question of independence as well as to the Reconstruction and Development Programme (RDP). Unions said they would be prepared to sacrifice, as long as the RDP also promoted worker interests. It was eventually decided that COSATU would remain in the Tripartite Alliance and even try to strengthen it, but that parties and government should be totally independent when it came to policy and action (Maree, 1998). There was general agreement that it was not in the interest of workers to withdraw from the Alliance at that stage, although the federation's affiliation would be reviewed from time to time.

### Continued Pressure on the Tripartite Alliance

After the first democratic elections the new government's continued attempts to create an investor-friendly economic climate led to a discernible policy rift between it and the union movement, which was still intent on giving priority to the RDP.

Reporting on the COSATU policy conference in May 1997, Buhlungu (2005) commented on the fine balancing act that organised labour had to perform in choosing between loyal opposition to the ANC and action that would pose a threat to the Tripartite Alliance.

In his report to the 50th National ANC Conference in 1997, President Mandela addressed the role of trade unionism within the Alliance. He acknowledged the part played by trade unions in the liberation struggle, but stressed the eventual role of the ANC as the leader of this movement. According to Mandela, some trade union leaders had 'never been able to find a home within political organisations of national democratic movements. Effectively, they have therefore treated the trade union movement as an alternative political formation through which they would pursue both their trade union and political aspirations'. Trade unions were representatives of the material interest of workers who, he indicated, were in a relatively privileged position, while the SACP represented the working class in general. By contrast, the government represented 'the people as a whole'. President Mandela concluded that a need existed to 'deal with the complex question of the interconnection between the role of the progressive unions as representative of the interests of their members and the role of these unions as an important part of the progressive movement for the fundamental and sound transformation of our society' (Mandela, 1997).

The major points of contention between the government and the union movement at the time were the former's adoption of the Growth, Employment and Redistribution Strategy (GEAR), its perceived neglect of the RDP and the privatisation of public enterprises.

### The Alliance Summit of April 2002

COSATU's anti-government position on economic policy, HIV/AIDS and privatisation resulted in widespread speculation on the possible disintegration of the Tripartite Alliance. A measure of reconciliation between the parties was evident during the Alliance summit held in April 2002. The summit affirmed that the working class was the 'major motivating force' and emphasised the need to adopt a more inward-looking economic policy. Despite the pronouncements at the summit, it became increasingly clear that COSATU was not happy with President Thabo Mbeki's government and that, if no change occurred, the Tripartite Alliance might fail.

### Impetus for Change

As already mentioned, the first years of the twenty-first century saw a marked deterioration of the relationship between COSATU and the government, as led by President Mbeki. The main points of contention between the parties were the perceived neo-liberal leanings of the government, Mbeki's stance on HIV/AIDS and the treatment meted out to Jacob Zuma. As a consequence, COSATU started moving closer to the SACP and openly supported Zuma, who was facing prosecution for alleged corruption.

In July 2007, Mbeki, addressing the ANC policy conference, warned the SACP, and indirectly COSATU, not to attempt to tell government what it should and should not do. Noting that the ANC was not a socialist party and had never sought to prescribe to the SACP as regards the latter's policies, Mbeki in so many words told the SACP to toe the line or to carve out its own path (Pillay, 2008). The possibility of the SACP fielding its own candidates for the 2009 elections had been discussed, both within the SACP and COSATU. In 2005, the president of COSATU, Willie Madisha, highlighted the reason for continued partnership with the Alliance. He pointed out that the affiliation allowed COSATU to exercise influence on legislation and it prevented them from operating in isolation as a trade union (COSATU, 2005).

In the end, both COSATU and the SACP decided to continue what some termed their 'parasitic' relationship with the ANC and to work for change from the inside.

An opportunity for change was presented by the ANC's 52nd National Conference, held at Polokwane in December 2007. Before the conference, both COSATU and the SACP lobbied vigorously to oust Thabo Mbeki and to elect Jacob Zuma as president of the ANC. Not all in the federation were in agreement with the support lent to Zuma. Divisions arose between pro-Mbeki and pro-Zuma factions. The National Union of Metalworkers of South Africa (NUMSA) had already criticised COSATU's attacks on President Mbeki in 2006. The union suggested that the federation should instead concentrate on dismantling white monopoly capital.

### Lobbying for New Policy Directions

In the run-up to the Polokwane conference, COSATU General Secretary Zwelinzima Vavi spoke critically of the ANC's draft policy documents. According to Vavi, the documents implied 'that there was nothing inherently wrong with market-driven capitalism as long as capitalists were encouraged to behave ethically and not seek selfish advantages' (Tabane & Robinson, 2007). Vavi was concerned that the documents:

- minimised the class struggle
- did not place sufficient emphasis on the contribution made by workers to economic well-being
- gave the ANC itself no 'proactive role' in strategy and policy development
- elevated the government's role in the labour relationship to that of referee between capital and labour.

These criticisms indicated that COSATU would prefer a more interventionist form of government.

After the victory of the Zuma faction at Polokwane, COSATU set about formulating its economic vision for the future. The federation proposed, among other things, that decent work, greater equity and the eradication of poverty be set as primary objectives, that the economy be diversified and that it moves away from reliance on resource exports (COSATU, n.d.). In what was described by Draper, Disenyana and Gilberto as 'a backward leap to command economics' (2010: 249), COSATU went on to suggest that:

- trade protection measures be put in place
- the state support certain sectors of the economy
- the rand be devalued in order to achieve trade balance
- more state-owned firms be established

- the Reserve Bank lower interest rates and move away from inflation targeting
- a radically expanded public works programme be undertaken.

### Post-Polokwane Realities

COSATU's aggressive stance surprised both observers and the government. The latter indicated that it expected its alliance partner to engage in talks rather than take to the streets, while analysts wondered how COSATU could claim to be close to government and yet take such drastic action. COSATU's response was that its position in the Alliance did not mean that it should not take action and be critical of government actions, and that its primary duty was to its members and the poor.

### Developments Post 2010

The formation and history of COSATU have been dealt with in some detail because, as the major federation and one that is on close terms with government, its policies and actions have important implications in both the political and economic spheres.

During the presidency of Jacob Zuma, COSATU's attitude towards the government softened, although some officials still openly criticised government actions and policies. The most outspoken of these critics was the general secretary, Zwelenzima Vavi. It was also reported that Vavi did not see eye to eye with Sidumo Dlamini, the president of the federation and evidently a staunch supporter of President Zuma. In September 2013, Vavi was placed on special leave and later suspended following an alleged incident involving a female employee of the federation. The move was viewed by many in the federation as a vendetta against persons not absolutely 'loyal' to the presidency. NUMSA, supported by eight other COSATU unions, subsequently lodged an appeal against Vavi's suspension. In the interim the general secretary of NUMSA, by then the largest union in COSATU, publicly stated that there were two camps in COSATU, namely a capitalist camp and a socialist camp, and that the divisions were hampering economic development. The union threatened to withdraw from COSATU. Shortly before the 2014 elections, the courts ordered that Vavi be reinstated. There were fears that this would lead to further disruptions, but an intervention by Cyril Ramaphosa, then occupying the position of deputy president of the Republic, managed to achieve an uneasy accord. However, NUMSA still signalled that it might consider forming its own political party. As it is, both Vavi and NUMSA were later expelled from COSATU.

*The Mining Industry*

To add to COSATU's problems, the position of what had previously been its biggest union, the NUM, was increasingly threatened by the Association of Mining and Construction Union (AMCU). AMCU's gaining of majority representation at Lonmin, where the Marikana strikes erupted, resulted in the company cancelling its recognition agreement with the NUM. The perception of some observers was that the NUM held a favoured position with government, which attempted to negotiate an accord in the industry.

Despite attempts to neutralise it, AMCU extended its efforts to capture the mining industry and has since become an important player in that arena. AMCU has not confined itself to negotiating with the mine owners. Of late it has increasingly brought the plight of all the people in that area to the forefront. While originally remaining independent, it has joined NACTU, in which it is bound to play an important role.

### FEDUSA

FEDUSA was established in 1997 by the amalgamation of two federations, namely FEDSAL and the Federation of Organisations Representing Civil Employees (FORCE). FEDUSA focuses on the rights of workers and on improving working conditions and wages.

### NACTU

NACTU was formed through a merger between AZACTU and CUSA that took place in 1986. Its main aim is action against capitalism. Its orientation is non-racialism, worker control, working-class leadership and financial accountability. Office bearers cannot be office bearers of political parties.

### SAFTU

SAFTU represents 30 unions working to create an independent, campaigning and democratic trade union federation. Their focus is on a living minimum wage, jobs for all, good housing, land ownership and free education. They are a revolutionary and socialist-oriented federation.

## Employers' Organisations

### Collective Bargaining Organisations

The Labour Relations Act 66 of 1995 provides for the formation and registration of employers' organisations for the purpose of centralised collective bargaining with a union or unions in bargaining councils. The process for the registration of employers' organisations is essentially the same as that relating to trade unions (described previously).

An updated list of employer's organisation status can be obtained from the Department of Employment and Labour at http://www.labour.gov.za/DocumentCenter/Pages/Employer-organisations--September-2020.aspx.

In line with the unions' strategy of promoting strong national industrial or sectoral unions, and the fact that bargaining councils are structured in the same way, employers' organisations are usually also registered as representative of particular industries, sectors or trades.

As the employer party in bargaining councils where agreements which may be applicable to an entire industry are negotiated, these bodies occupy an important place in the labour relations and national arena. In addition to their bargaining function they also serve to:

- co-ordinate employer initiatives in the industry
- represent the interests of employers in the industry in engaging with government and other bodies
- provide advice to members.

In the larger industries, there may be separate employers' organisations in the various regions or sub-groups and these will, in turn, be affiliated to federations which co-ordinate initiatives in the industry and have an even stronger voice with government. An example of such a body is the Steel and Engineering Industries Federation of South Africa (SEIFSA).

## Non-registered Bodies

Another body that is important in the collective bargaining sphere is the South African Chamber of Mines. The Chamber is not registered as an employers' organisation, and it has functions other than that of collective bargaining, but it has traditionally bargained with mining unions on behalf of employers in the mining industry. There are large mines which have recognised unions in their operations and who may negotiate on certain issues directly with these unions, but bargaining on wages and conditions of service has generally been co-ordinated by the Chamber.

## Other Employer Bodies
### Business Chambers

Other employer bodies which involve themselves in labour relations (although they do not engage in bargaining per se) include chambers of business, commerce and industry.

The South African business community is not large in comparison to that of European countries, but it too displays the divisions prevalent in South African society. Despite some efforts at unification, the following bodies still exist:

- Regional chambers of business, which were established from the amalgamation of the historically dominant chambers of commerce and chambers of industry in various parts of the country; these now resort under the South African Chamber of Commerce and Industry (SACCI)
- Regional *sakekamers* (business chambers) under the Afrikaanse Handelsinstituut (AHI)
- Regional associations for black businesspeople, co-ordinated by the National African Federation of Chambers of Commerce (NAFCOC)
- The Foundation for African Business and Consumer Services (FABCOS)
- The National Small Business Chamber
- The Minara Chamber of Commerce, which represents Muslim business-people and entrepreneurs.

Business chambers traditionally have a voice with government as regards labour affairs and, through their national bodies, submit comments or make representations relating to developments in this sphere.

### Business Unity and the Black Business Council

The need for an organisation to represent business in general on bodies such as NEDLAC resulted in the formation of two new bodies, namely:

- Business South Africa (BSA), with SACCI and the AHI as major members
- the Black Business Council (BBC), which had as members both NAFCOC and FABCOS.

Subsequently in 2003, these two bodies amalgamated to form BUSA. Both BUSA and the BBC profess to be non-racial and BUSA has as one of its objectives the promotion of broad-based black economic empowerment (BBBEE). However, while BUSA stresses the promotion of business interests in general, the BBC places major emphasis on the unification and promotion of black business. This body also aims to establish links with the labour movement and NGOs.

In spite of their differences, the formation of these bodies has given business a strong voice when dealing with government and labour.

# Conclusion

The participants in the employment relationship are at a point where important decisions have to be made. The outcome of those decisions will determine whether the path thereafter is upward or downward. As the world of work continues to evolve, the role players, their roles and their associations also need to evolve to be fit for purpose in the new world of work.

## Suggested Questions/Tasks

1. Consider any trade federation in South Africa. Design a three-level hierarchy to illustrate its current trade union membership (below) and its international membership (above). Also include other trade federations belonging to the same international body (confederation). Explain what the differences between the various levels are.
2. Consider the African Union (AU) and the European Union (EU). How do these bodies differ from a South African trade union?
3. Consider the AU's Agenda 2063 (see https://au.int/agenda2063/goals) and the UN's Sustainable Development Goals for 2030 (see https://www.un.org/sustainabledevelopment/). Select three aspects which could have an influence on the employment relationship and provide your reasoning for selecting these aspects.
4. Consider the role of stakeholder theory in employment relations and its application to corporate social responsibility.
5. The nature of employment relations actors in global supply chains influences the governance structures that need to be adopted and the implications of these global supply chains for employment relations systems. Discuss the influence on global supply chains of the elements of employment relations, corporate social responsibility and the labour relations approach to multinational corporations.
6. You and others working in the same industry have decided to form a union to protect your interests. Describe the steps you would follow and draw up the documents required for the eventual registration of your union.
7. Form different groups to debate the following propositions:
   a. COSATU has/has not lived up to its founding principles.
   b. The 'marriage of convenience' in the form of the Tripartite Alliance is/is not to the benefit of any of the parties and a divorce would/would not be the best solution.
   c. Corporatism will/will not work in the South African context.

d.  The best solution for South Africa's problems is to free up the labour relations system completely/for the government to exert greater control over employees and trade unions.

e.  The next 10 years will/will not see the demise of COSATU.

f.  Research the composition of unions in SAFTU. Then compare these unions and their strategies to those of the COSATU unions. Which of these two will be more relevant in the future? Give reasons for your answer.

g.  Progressive Automatum decides that it will no longer manufacture certain small parts and will enter into a contract with Small Automatum (Pty) Ltd to manufacture and supply these parts. However, since Small Automatum does not have the necessary employees, Progressive Automatum will 'lend' it some of its better people. Although they will be paid by Small Automatum, these persons will be guided by the factory manager at Progressive Automatum, who reserves the right to inspect their work from time to time. At Small Automatum employees are also expected to work on Saturdays, which is not the case at Progressive Automatum. All seems to go well until Small Automatum decides that it can save money by reducing the number of workers. What do you think will happen next and what will be the outcome?

h.  Progressive Automatum decides that it can no longer sustain its advertising department and offers the two persons in the department the option to freelance for the company. Progressive Automatum agrees to give them all their advertising business, but because it is such a competitive field, it wants the ex-employees to agree that they will work only for Progressive Automatum. The sales manager at Progressive will pop in from time to time to check on progress. Comment.

## Sources

Buhlungu, S. 2005. 'Union–party alliances in the era of market regulation: The case of South Africa'. *Journal of Southern African Studies* 31(4): 701–717.

COSATU (Congress of South African Trade Unions). n.d. 'Aims and objectives'. http://mediadon.co.za/aims-objectives/ (Accessed 4 October 2021).

COSATU. 2005. 'COSATU 3rd Central Committee'. https://sarpn.org/documents/d0001517/index.php (Accessed 4 October 2021).

Draper, P, Disenyana, T & Gilberto, B. 2010. 'South Africa', in *Governments, Non-State Actors and Trade Policy-Making: Negotiating Preferentially Or Multilaterally?*, edited by A Capling & P Low. Cambridge: Cambridge University Press: 249–283.

Friedman, G. 2000. 'The political economy of early Southern unionism: Race, politics, and labor in the South, 1880–1953'. *The Journal of Economic History* 60(2): 384–413.

Holgate, J, Simms, M & Tapia, M. 2018. 'The limitations of the theory and practice of mobilization in trade union organizing'. *Economic and Industrial Democracy* 39(4): 599–616.

Klikauer, T & Campbell, N. 2021. 'Global minimum wage'. Znet. https://zcomm.org/znetarticle/global-minimum-wage/ (Accessed 22 September 2021).

Mandela, N. 1997. 'Report by Nelson Mandela to the 50th National Conference of the African National Congress (ANC)'. 16 December 1997. http://www.mandela.gov.za/mandela_speeches/1997/971216_ancd.htm (Accessed 20 September 2021).

Maree, J. 1993. 'Trade unions and corporatism in South Africa'. *Transformation* 21: 24–54.

Maree, J. 1998. 'The COSATU participatory democratic tradition and South Africa's new parliament: Are they reconcilable?'. *African Affairs* 97(386): 29–51.

Pillay, D. 2008. 'COSATU, the SACP and the ANC post-Polokwane: Looking Left but does it feel Right?'. *Labour, Capital and Society/Travail, capital et société*: 4–37.

Salamon, E. 2018. 'Temporary labor convergence: Newsworkers mobilize massive community support to organize the newspaper chain, 1963–1966'. *Journalism Studies* 19(12): 1730–1749. https://doi.org.10.1080/1461670X.2017.1301780.

Smale, B. 2020. *Exploring Trade Union Identities: Union Identity, Niche Identity and the Problem of Organising the Unorganised*. Bristol: Bristol University Press.

Southall, R. 1986. 'A note on Inkatha membership'. *African Affairs* 85(341): 573–588.

Tabane, R & Robinson, V. 2007. 'ANC: to the left, to the left?' *Mail & Guardian*, 22 June 2007. https://mg.co.za/article/2007-06-22-anc-to-the-left/ (Accessed 22 September 2021).

United Nations. n.d. 'Sustainable development goals'. https://www.un.org/sustainabledevelopment/ (Accessed 17 September 2021).

Von Holdt, K. 2002. 'Social movement unionism: The case of South Africa'. *Work, Employment and Society* 16(2): 283–304.

Webster, E. 1987. 'The two faces of the black trade union movement in South Africa'. *Review of African Political Economy* 14(39): 33–41.

Webster, E & Forrest, K. 2020. 'The role of the ILO during and after apartheid'. *Labor Studies Journal* 46(4): 325--344. https://doi.org/10.1177/0160449X20967098.

# 8

# Workplace Democracy and Worker Participation

## Chapter Outline

# Overview

The term 'workplace democracy' describes systems for enabling the exercise of power by workers or their representatives and for granting self-management to workers through a range of institutional solutions. The objectives pursued by means of workplace democracy are broad and range from the self-organisation of work in the production unit to strategic decisions concerning hiring policies, product development, or social and environmental values (Frega, Herzog & Neuhäuser, 2019: 1).

In recent years, the International Labour Organization (ILO) and the International Organization for Standardization (ISO) have significantly increased their influence on the concept of 'democracy' in the 'world of work' around the world. In South Africa, organisations of relevance are the Institute of Directors of South Africa (IoDSA) and the King Committee, the National Economic Development and Labour Council (NEDLAC), the South African Board of People Practices (SABPP) and the South African Institute of Chartered Accountants (SAICA).

## The ILO and Workplace Democracy

The ILO has slightly changed its orientation towards workplace democracy since its centenary in 2019, by focusing on the promotion of social dialogue and governance among stakeholders at the workplace.

Social dialogue is defined by the ILO as the promotion of democratic involvement of the main stakeholders – governments, employers' associations and workers' organisations – in the governance of the world of work. The ILO indicates that social dialogue promotes social justice, inclusive economic growth, improved wages and working conditions and sustainable enterprises. Tripartism is defined as the interaction of government, employers and workers (through their representatives) as equal and independent partners to seek solutions to issues of common concern (ILO, 2021b).

The main approaches utilised to ensure social dialogue include (ILO, 2021b):
- dispute prevention and resolution
- collective bargaining
- negotiations and consultations
- framework agreements.

Certain prerequisites need to exist in order for social dialogue to be effective. These include (ILO, 2021b):
- commitment, will and a workable level of trust for the stakeholders to engage with each other
- a functional and enabling legal and institutional framework
- respect for collective bargaining enablers, such as the right to freedom of association.

## The ISO and Workplace Democracy

The ISO has developed international standards to provide innovative solutions to global challenges, which include leadership in workplace democracy (ISO, 2021). Specific management systems standards that have a bearing on workplace democracy include:
- ISO standard range 26000 (social responsibility)
- ISO standard range 31000 (risk management)

➤

- ISO standard 30431: 2021: human resource management – leadership metrics cluster
- ISO standard 30414: 2018: human resource management – guidelines for internal and external human capital reporting
- ISO standard: human resource management.

These standards are specifically designed to achieve the development goals of both the African Union (AU) and the European Union (EU) and are supported by all member states, including South Africa.

### The King Committee and Workplace Democracy

In South Africa, corporate governance is directed by the King IV Report (IoDSA, 2016). This report suggests a range of principled and outcomes-based guidelines to ensure that tripartite stakeholders (government, employers' associations and workers' organisations) display an attitude, mindset and behaviour of ethical leadership in dealing with each other, their community and the environment around them in a focused and transparent manner. Also see the King IV practice notes, IP policy and report endorsement on the IODSA website (https://www.iodsa.co.za).

### Other South African Professional Bodies and Workplace Democracy

Professional bodies ensure that their members comply with the statutory regulations of the audit committees (SAICA) and ensure human resource (HR) compliance with the principles of the King IV Report (SABPP).

### NEDLAC and Social Partnership

Until the 1950s, free collective bargaining was, with a few exceptions, the focal point of most developed labour relations systems. During the last 30 to 40 years of the twentieth century, a gradual shift of focus occurred. The reason for this was, first, the fact that free collective bargaining, entailing also the freedom to strike, involves high social and economic costs and leads to a polarisation between capital and labour. Secondly, very few undertakings still belonged to single entrepreneurs. This change towards more diffused ownership made it more difficult to distinguish the employer/owner as a separate entity. Thirdly, and more importantly, sociopolitical values and ideologies had changed. Capitalism and the absolute rule of the market principle had been mellowed by considerations of social justice and egalitarianism, and by a greater level of interference by governments as protectors of social interests. Also, employees themselves became more aware and more knowledgeable, and aspirations increased. This was accompanied by a greater concern for people in society and in the world of business. The result was a demand for the widening of workplace democracy, in the form of increased employee participation both in the decision-making process and in the profits of the undertaking.

Since the establishment of NEDLAC, the tripartite stakeholders and community organisations have established a formal and legal structure to deal with economic, labour and development issues, as well as other related challenges facing South Africa (NEDLAC, 2020: 5).

# What Is Worker Participation?

There is a lack of agreement on the definition and scope of worker participation. The concept of worker participation differs based on the scientific field from which it is viewed and based on the particular stakeholder interest, as illustrated in Figure 8.1.

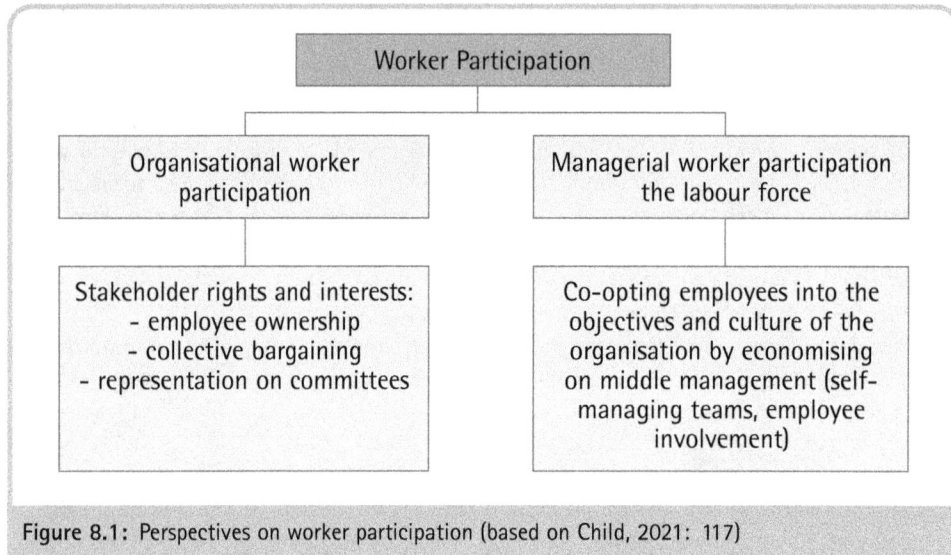

```
                    ┌─────────────────────────┐
                    │   Worker Participation   │
                    └─────────────────────────┘
            ┌───────────────────┴───────────────────┐
┌───────────────────────────┐         ┌───────────────────────────┐
│   Organisational worker    │         │ Managerial worker participation │
│       participation        │         │      the labour force      │
└───────────────────────────┘         └───────────────────────────┘
┌───────────────────────────┐         ┌───────────────────────────┐
│ Stakeholder rights and     │         │ Co-opting employees into the │
│ interests:                 │         │ objectives and culture of the │
│  - employee ownership      │         │ organisation by economising │
│  - collective bargaining   │         │ on middle management (self- │
│  - representation on       │         │ managing teams, employee    │
│    committees              │         │ involvement)                │
└───────────────────────────┘         └───────────────────────────┘
```

**Figure 8.1:** Perspectives on worker participation (based on Child, 2021: 117)

Child (2021: 117) proposes that:

> *the focus of organisational worker participation is on stakeholder rights and reflecting their interests (through governance provisions such as representation on boards, co-determination); ensuring a fairer distribution of rewards (eg collective bargaining, employee ownership, representation on remuneration committees); and counteracting abuses of hierarchical power.*

He notes that managerial worker participation includes (Child, 2021: 117):

> *co-opting employees into the objectives and culture of the organisation (through consultation); improving productivity and economizing on middle management (eg, self-managing teams, employee involvement); and promoting innovation.*

## Principles of Worker Participation

Alongside the principles for the implementation of democracy in the world of work published by national and international bodies, López-Arceiz and

Bellostas (2020: 311) propose that governance practices (for individual workers and also the organisation), sound management systems, transparency and accountability for behaviour should ideally be infused in strategies, processes, policies and decision making at the workplace.

Therefore, only those forms of participation where employees share in decisions, or are able to influence the actions of the employer/management, will be regarded as relevant in the present context.

## Trade Union Representation versus Worker Participation

It could be argued that workplace democracy is best practised by the institutionalisation of free collective bargaining. Bargaining does limit the authority and prerogative of management, but it also allows for the representation of employee interests as against those of the employer. Through the process of collective bargaining, trade unions and employees can engage in joint regulation of workplace-related affairs and may jointly solve problems. Nevertheless, it is preferable to distinguish between the two concepts, since the following differences do exist:

- Trade union representation usually places emphasis on employer–employee conflict, whereas worker participation tends to promote co-operation (although elements of conflict and co-operation exist in both practices).
- Trade union representation rests on the bargaining relationship, while worker participation is based on consensus and the perception of a social and economic partnership.
- A system of worker participation presupposes that the right of employees to share in the decision-making process is accepted. By contrast, collective bargaining recognises the right of the employer to manage and to take important decisions; unions merely challenge these decisions.

In many developed systems, participation and collective bargaining are complementary processes. While free collective bargaining continues, participation is instituted to extend employee influence and to deal with aspects which were omitted from the collective bargaining process or are not suited to collective bargaining.

The differentiation between the collective bargaining function and the participation function does not mean that trade unions and their office bearers cannot be involved in worker participation schemes. In the majority of systems where participation has been introduced, trade unions play an important, and sometimes dominant, role. Also, the shop steward, being involved in workplace affairs, may act in both a collective bargaining and a participative capacity. However, participation may also place unions in a dilemma in terms of their traditional role as antagonists and challengers of managerial decisions.

## Dimensions of Worker Participation

South Africa has a unique history in terms of demands for the implementation of worker participation. As one of the younger democracies in the world, developments in the economic and social areas of society need to be in place before the more advanced forms of worker participation can be implemented in South African organisations. Bischoff, Masondo and Webster (2021: 376) note that since the advent of democracy in South Africa, steady progress has been made to move away from the adversarial class struggle approach towards a more participatory and co-operative labour relations system.

The degree of control that workers have depends on the extent to which an employee or stakeholder is allowed to influence decisions in the organisation. On the one end of the spectrum are decisions about which employees are merely informed. On the other hand are those decisions for which employees take ownership and responsibility, as they are in control. As illustrated in Figure 8.2, the issues over which that control is exercised can range from ordinary tasks to more strategic organisational decisions, which could include company direction and conditions of employment.

### Organisational Level of Control

Some decisions only affect a particular job, while other decisions have an impact on a number of sections, departments or even the whole organisation or industry. For some decisions, an employee merely needs to inform another employee, while other decisions require the opinions of other stakeholders. In South Africa, the implementation of these decisions is governed by the relevant collective bargaining agreement. This may range from information sharing to consultation, stakeholder information sessions and even, eventually, to co-determination on certain matters.

### Information Sharing

Some authorities list information sharing as a form of participation. By information sharing is meant the dissemination of information, or communication from management to employees and from employees to various levels of management. It is generally believed that a continual two-way flow of information alleviates the fear of the unknown on the part of employees and leads to greater acceptance, involvement and commitment. Although any form of participation most definitely rests on full and continuous sharing of information, mere information sharing is not a participation method in the true sense.

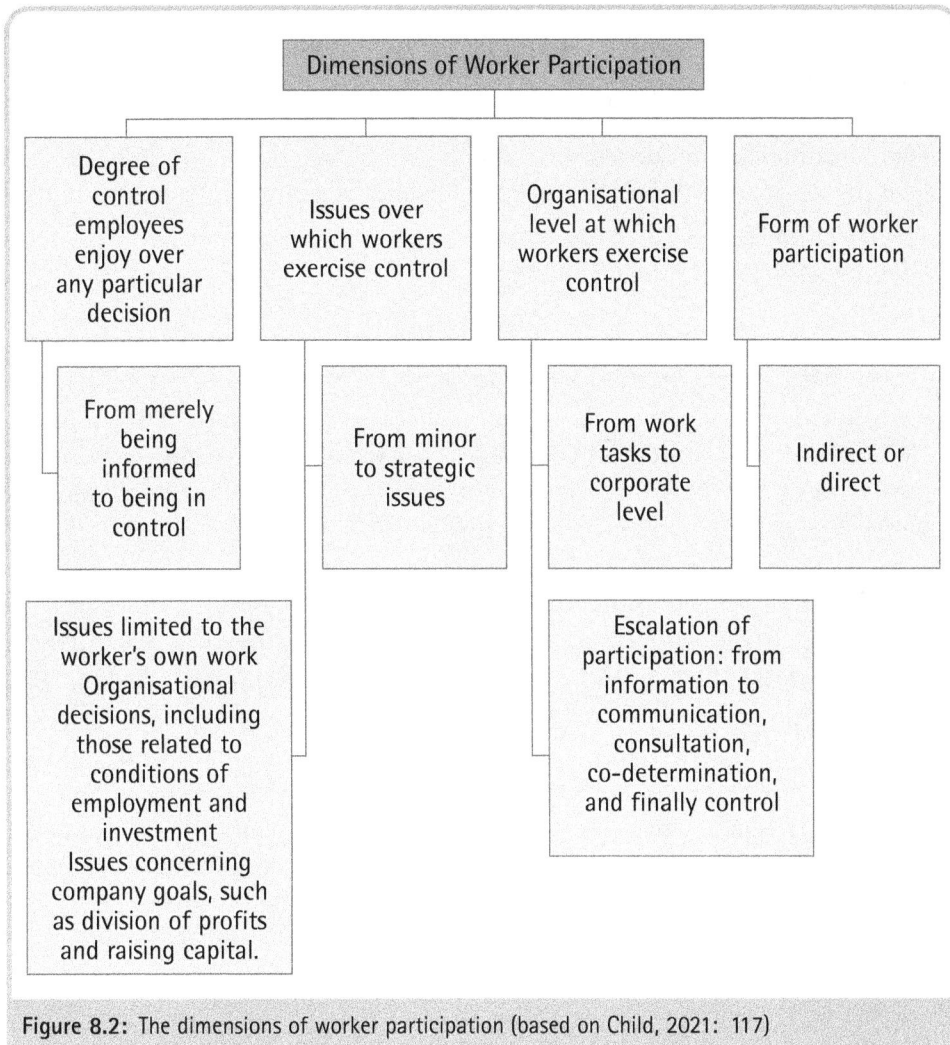

**Figure 8.2:** The dimensions of worker participation (based on Child, 2021: 117)

## Forms of Participation: Indirect and Direct Participation

*Direct Worker Participation*

The ILO (2021a) states that employees may participate in decision making either directly, or indirectly through their representatives (trade unions or elected employee representatives). Direct participation may be on an individual basis, for example through job enrichment, job enlargement or job rotation. It may also be on a group basis. Quality circles, briefing groups and suggestion and communication schemes are typical forms of employee involvement where employees become more engaged in their direct work environment (Charles, Francis & Zirra, 2021). Teamwork constitutes a form of group-based direct participation.

Direct worker participation, if properly implemented, could:

- increase employee satisfaction
- encourage individual responsibility and discretion/judgement
- lead to immediate feedback
- give the employee the feeling of having made a significant contribution to the total process
- create a climate for social interaction.

Managers and supervisors may fear a loss of control and authority, but this need not be the case, particularly if leadership by management is effective and regular meetings are conducted.

The independent work group does allow the employee a certain measure of control over the working environment, but if participation is restricted to this activity, it remains at a relatively low level.

### Indirect Worker Participation

Indirect participation refers to collective participation by way of employee representation on formal structures of consultation and negotiation. The ILO (2021a) notes that indirect worker participation is a system of worker participation in management decision making that is conducted through workers' representatives. Examples include collective bargaining; employee representation on joint consultative committees, bargaining councils, statutory councils and workplace forums; and employee members of boards of directors. Collective bargaining, bargaining councils, statutory councils and workplace forums are regulated by the Labour Relations Act 66 of 1995.

#### Plant-level Committees

The use of plant-level committees is one of the most popular forms of employee participation, but many such committees are not truly participative. Plant-level committees may take many forms, such as shop-floor, shop-unit, plant-level or even enterprise-level committees.

Management and employees may decide to form any kind of committee to deal with specific issues. The most prevalent type of committee so formed is that which deals with matters of health and safety. In many societies, including South Africa, the law regulates the establishment of safety committees and prescribes the powers of workers' representatives.

*Joint Decision Making on Supervisory Boards*

The principle of joint decision making by employees on supervisory boards or boards of directors is a common practice in a number of Western European countries. It is supported by a draft directive to this effect issued by the European Economic Community in 1992 but is not yet a general practice in South African organisations. The policy allows for employee-directors, elected by employees or trade unions, to be appointed to supervisory boards or boards of directors. These boards decide on general policy for the organisation and its management team, but do not usually function in an executive capacity – that is, they are not involved in the day-to-day running of the organisation.

In countries where one board fulfils both the policy-making and executive functions, there is a general resistance to the appointment of worker-directors. It is feared that if worker-directors are involved in the management function as well, there will be continual confrontation between employee and managerial representatives, and urgent decisions may be delayed. The general perception is that, while it may be acceptable to involve employees in long-term decisions and policy formulation, they lack the expertise to function at management level.

Representation on supervisory boards is very rarely based on equity. Most commonly, employee representatives constitute one-third of the board, with the other two-thirds being made up of directors elected by the shareholders. Alternatively, the remaining directorial seats could be divided between shareholder-directors and independent experts.

The appointment of worker-directors to supervisory boards does bring about employee participation at the highest decision-making level of the enterprise. A more balanced perspective is achieved and more equitable decisions may be taken. Worker-directors are able to represent the interests of employees at this level and to put forward alternatives to managerial proposals. In essence, such worker-directors have a share in controlling and supervising the functions and policies of management. However, the fact that parity representation is not granted begs the question as to what degree of influence worker-directors can exert. It reflects the belief that the final decision should rest with the shareholders or, at least, with shareholders and appointed experts. It is also possible that some trade unions would want this kind of co-responsibility.

*Financial Schemes*

Note that the different financial schemes from which profit is realised are taxable according to the South African Revenue Services (SARS). Equally, the risk of loss from such a scheme is also shared among the participants in such schemes. Two examples of financial schemes are the following:

- **Profit-sharing schemes (equity shares):** The introduction of profit-sharing schemes shifts the emphasis from workers having a share in decision making and work processes to them having a share in the financial rewards generated by employers and employees in the organisation. Profit-sharing schemes provide for a fixed proportion of company profits to be paid to all employees, either individually or to a fund established for the benefit of the employees. Schemes of this nature are intended to bring about a fairer distribution of wealth. They may also act as an incentive to employees to cut costs and increase productivity and could result in greater co-operation. However, unless profit sharing is accompanied by other participative practices, the employee will not gain greater control over their working life, and participation – in the decision-making sense – will not be achieved.
- **Employee share schemes:** Employee stock ownership plans (ESOPs) are employee benefit plans that give employees an ownership interest in an organisation (Nicol, 2021: 21). To ensure broad-based transformation in the South African economy, the Department of Trade, Industry and Competition (DTIC), through NEDLAC and the Industrial Development Corporation (IDC), promotes broad-based ownership schemes, including discussions of workers' representation at board level and proposals to amend the legislation, particularly the Companies Act 71 of 2008. By April 2021, more than 150 000 South African employees were part owners of the companies they worked for through shareholding in those firms, with more than R100 billion having been transferred to those employees. Examples of companies who have recently instituted ESOPs are Pepsico South Africa, AB InBev South Africa, Astron Energy, Vodacom, Sasol and Kumba Iron Ore.

*Co-operative Enterprises*

The Co-operatives Act 14 of 2005 defines a co-operative as 'an autonomous association of persons united voluntarily to meet their common economic and social needs and aspirations through a jointly owned and democratically controlled enterprise organised and operated on co-operative principles'.

For a co-operative to be a legally recognised entity, it has to be registered at the Companies and Intellectual Property Commission (CIPC). Profits, known as surplus in a co-operative, are divided among members. Each member receives a portion of the surplus, depending on the amount of business the member did with the co-operative.

While thousands of co-operatives are registered annually, very few are successful. The majority fail due to a lack of skills and of proper management.

# Benefits of Worker Participation

Child (2021) suggests that employee participation can benefit the organisation on various levels:

- **Economic benefits:** Participation can enhance competence and so increase productivity, innovation and organisational effectiveness.
- **Social contribution:** The centralisation of political and hierarchical power in states and organisations has contributed to rising economic inequality and insecurity which, in turn, provokes high levels of stress and serious social tensions. With the emergence of the Fourth and Fifth Industrial Revolutions, the ability of employees to partake in decision making through the use of technology has been driven to the forefront.

# Disadvantages of Worker Participation

## The Managerial Perspective

In any type of participative scheme, it is the employer who will give up some of their traditional prerogative. The most frequent objection voiced by employers to participation is that shared decision making leads to lack of control, that it is a time-consuming process and that, as a result, managerial efficiency may be detrimentally affected.

Employers fear that employees may not have the same objectives as the employer and that, particularly where employees share in higher-level decisions, they will place their preference for economic benefits and for leisure above the long-term interests of the organisation. Employees may not see that if they do this, they themselves will be disadvantaged in the long term. Employers may also object to the fact that it is usually the responsibility of the employer to equip the employees with the skills which will allow them to participate effectively in organisational decisions.

## Union Concerns

Unions are generally concerned that joint responsibility and accountability for decisions will dilute the union's traditional role as challenger of managerial decisions. This conflict between co-operation and antagonism is the greatest dilemma faced by unions, especially where participation is introduced at higher decision-making levels. A union which was party to one decision by management might find it very difficult to oppose management in other areas. Co-operation thus generally detracts from the union's role as the antagonist.

Unions which adopt the radical perspective will resist participation on the grounds that it does not change the capitalist system but leads to the co-option of employees within the existing framework. Trade unions are particularly suspicious of direct employee participation which is not balanced by a form of indirect or representational participation. In direct participation, employees are treated as individuals, and commonality of interests, as well as the combined power of employees, is diluted. Furthermore, while the direct forms of participation might encourage commitment and higher productivity, they do not greatly increase the amount of influence employees are able to wield in the undertaking.

On a more practical level, unions may fear that the introduction of participation schemes will eradicate the traditional boundaries between unions, and that the inclusion of non-unionised employees in such schemes will dilute union power. There is also the problem of the role conflict which might be experienced by shop stewards who participate at the higher decision-making levels.

## Implementing a Participation Scheme

### General Guidelines

Salamon (1987) offers the following useful guidelines regarding the implementation of participation within an undertaking:

- The employer/management should approach participation without any preconceptions.
- There should be consultation with employees or their unions before the scheme is developed so that a joint strategy may be formulated.
- Both sides (employees and employers/managers) should commit themselves to consultation and shared decision making.
- Participation should not be merely a boardroom policy but an overall managerial strategy.
- Participation should be instituted from the bottom upwards as well as from the top downwards.
- Supervisors and junior managers should be actively involved in the scheme and also in higher-level managerial decisions.

### The Need for Training

Participation schemes cannot be introduced without the necessary training. Both managerial and employee representatives need to be trained in the utilisation of participative structures and methods. Employees in particular will have to be given extensive information on the operation of the enterprise. They will need to gain the necessary knowledge and confidence to participate, to conduct meetings and to question and evaluate managerial plans and decisions. Both parties will have to learn to approach each other in completely new ways.

### Participation as an Ongoing Process

Participation is a developing process. Participation in one area will lead to demands for its extension to other areas. Salamon (1987) suggests that no limits should be set. Management should accept that once a participation scheme has been introduced, there is no area which might not, in future, be open to co-operative decision making.

## Conclusion

The concept of workplace democracy is one of the most relevant contemporary labour relations issues. The shift towards corporate ownership, the convergence of socialist and capitalist principles in society, and the questioning of traditional institutions and values have made it necessary to reassess the roles of the employer and employees in the enterprise. Differences in perceptions as to the depth and breadth of democracy will continue to exist and will be a point of contention between employees, unions and management, and among individual unions. Nevertheless, some form of compromise will have to be achieved between collective bargaining and co-operation, between management's desire to manage effectively and employees' desire to be party to decisions affecting them, and, finally, between the capitalist–individualist orientation of most employers and the socialist–collectivist ideologies of numerous employees and unions.

The need for greater co-operation on all fronts becomes particularly relevant in view of South Africa's labour market and economic challenges and the as yet unknown changes that will surface in the coming decades.

## Suggested Questions/Tasks

1.  Critique the following statement by Ellerman and Gonza (2021: 63):

    *Workplace democracy is the old idea that each private organisation should be a democratic organisation, a small republic whose citizens are the people working in it. This idea has surfaced again and again over the last century and half but is still little known. Workplace democracy, in its essence, is based on the abolition of the employment relations, the hiring, employing, renting or leasing of people. If the renting of people is abolished, then there can only be labor hiring capital in workplace democracies instead of capital hiring labor in the early twenty-first century's human rental organisations.*

2. Consider the various ISO standards that could have a bearing on workplace democracy. Briefly indicate their applicability to workplace democracy in South Africa.
3. Consider the King IV Report (IoDSA, 2016). Briefly indicate its applicability to workplace democracy in South Africa.
4. Differentiate between the various forms of direct and indirect worker participation and recent examples thereof.

## Sources

Bischoff, C, Masondo, T & Webster, E. 2021. 'Workers' participation at plant level: A South African case study'. *Economic and Industrial Democracy* 42(2): 376–394.

Charles, J, Francis, F & Zirra, CTOP. 2021. 'Effect of employee involvement in decision making and organization productivity'. *Archives of Business Research* 9(3): 28–34.

Child, J. 2021. 'Organizational participation in post-covid society: Its contributions and enabling conditions'. *International Review of Applied Economics* 35(2): 117–146.

Co-operatives Act (14 of 2005). *Government Gazette* vol 482, no 27912. Pretoria: Government Printer.

Ellerman, D & Gonza, T. 2021. 'Less-known supporters of workplace democracy'. *Journal of Participation and Employee Ownership* 4(1): 63–85.

Frega, R, Herzog, L & Neuhäuser, C. 2019. 'Workplace democracy: The recent debate'. *Philosophy Compass* 14(4).

ILO (International Labour Organization). 2021a. 'Forms of worker's participation'. https://www.iloencyclopaedia.org/part-iii-48230/labor-relations-and-human-resource-management/item/202-forms-of-workers-participation (Accessed 20 October 2021).

ILO. 2021b. 'Social Dialogue and Tripartism Unit (DIALOGUE)'. https://www.ilo.org/global/about-the-ilo/how-the-ilo-works/departments-and-offices/governance/dialogue/lang--en/index.htm (Accessed 20 October 2021).

IoDSA (Institute of Directors of South Africa). 2016. 'How to access the King IV Report'. https://www.iodsa.co.za/page/king_iv_report (Accessed 20 October 2021).

ISO (International Organization for Standardization). 2021. 'About us'. https://www.iso.org/about-us.html (Accessed 20 October 2021).

López-Arceiz, FJ & Bellostas, AJ. 2020. 'Nonprofit governance and outside corruption: The role of accountability, stakeholder participation, and management systems'. *Nonprofit Management and Leadership* 31(2): 311–333.

NEDLAC (National Economic Development and Labour Council). 2020. 'Nedlac Founding Declaration'. https://nedlac.org.za/wp-content/uploads/2020/11/Nedlac-Founding-Declaration.pdf (Accessed 20 October 2021).

Nicol, M. 2021. 'Bothersome BEE'. *New Agenda: South African Journal of Social and Economic Policy* 79: 21–28.

Salamon, M. 1987. *Industrial Relations Theory and Practice*. Hoboken: Prentice Hall.

# 9

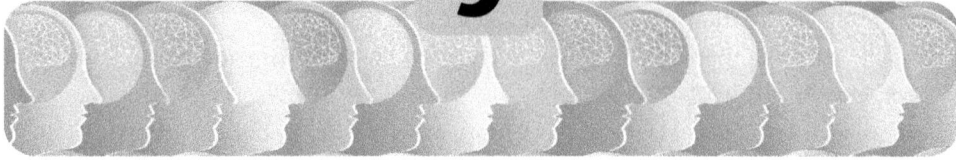

# Negotiation and Social Influence

## Chapter Outline

➤

INITIATING COLLABORATIVE NEGOTIATIONS

Challenges in Implementing Collaborative Negotiations

APPROACHES TO THE NEGOTIATION PROCESS

PREPARING FOR NEGOTIATION

The Initiator of the Negotiation Process • The Negotiation Planning Sheet • Negotiation Conventions • Setting Goals and Objectives • Delimiting the Area of Negotiation • Selecting the Negotiator(s) | *Single Person or a Negotiation Team* | *The Chief Negotiator* | *Roles Assigned to Team Members* • Identifying the Main Issues • Defining the Interests • Establishing the Bargaining Range | *The Importance of Establishing Bargaining Ranges* | *The Area of Interdependence* | *Employee/Union Considerations when Setting Limits* | *Employer Considerations when Setting Limits* | *Other Factors Determining Limits Set* • Information Gathering | *Current Conditions* | *Statistical Indicators* | *Organisational Position* | *Knowledge of the Other Side* • Establishing Resistance and Target Points • The Settlement Range • Risk Assessment | *Cost–Benefit Analysis for Management* | *Cost–Benefit Analysis for Employees/the Union* | *Weighing Costs against Benefits* • The Contract Zone | Costing of Contracts • Developing Strategies • Obtaining a Mandate • Testing the Water

CONDUCTING NEGOTIATIONS

Overview of the Negotiation Process • The Opening Phase | *Establishing Climate* | *Establishing Positions* | *Feeling out the Other Party* • The Body of the Negotiation Process | *Bringing Argument* | *Countering the Other Party's Argument* | *Displaying Commitment* | *Granting Concessions* | *Caucusing* | *Impasses* | *Deadlock* | *'Final' Offers/Demands* | *Threats and Bluffs* | *Sanctions* • Closure

NEGOTIATION MANOEUVRES

AGREEMENTS: THE OUTCOMES OF SUCCESSFUL NEGOTIATION

Types of Agreements | *The Agreement to Bargain* | *Wages, Conditions of Service and Procedures* | *Subject-related Agreements* • Monitoring Agreements • Enforceability of Agreements

DISPUTES AND COERCIVE ACTION

CONCLUSION

SUGGESTED QUESTIONS/TASKS

SOURCES

## Overview

According to the World Economic Forum's 'Future of Jobs' report, around half of the current employees in the world would need to be reskilled by 2025 for the future world of work. The soft skills required include analytical thinking and innovation, the ability to learn on the run, complex problem solving, critical thinking and problem solving, creativity, leadership and social influence, technology use and development, resilience, stress tolerance and flexibility (Whiting, 2020). From this list it is evident that the traditional skill of 'negotiation' is no longer on the list. It has been replaced by a greater umbrella of social influence and leadership.

Social influence encompasses the ability to persuade others and reach agreement. Social influence is based on the social institutions in which we function – like workplaces, religious organisations, trade unions and political parties – and how we interact and modify our behaviour to fit in. The relationship between negotiation, social influence and persuasion still needs to be researched in greater depth.

## Part One: Negotiation Fundamentals

## Definition and Scope of Labour Negotiations

Khan and Baldini (2019: 19) regard negotiation as one of the fastest and cheapest alternatives to dispute resolution, not only in the context of international business but also for resolving interpersonal disagreements. Ebner et al (2017) suggest a process of seeking agreement or decision, involving co-ordination between parties to reach an agreement in the presence or absence of certain factors. They add that in order to arrive at a meaningful definition of negotiation, the parties need to prepare for negotiations. There also needs to be some sort of relationship structure between the parties, some form of action between the parties (like communication) and some form of result achieved (like an agreement or demand accepted).

Scope, according to Lexico (2021), suggests the 'opportunity or possibility to do or deal with something'. The scope of negotiations changes with the subject field under discussion. If one intends to negotiate the buying or selling of a house or vehicle, the legal scope of that transaction should be understood and adhered to by the parties. That scope looks different from the negotiations that would take place if one intends to enter into a traditional wedding, as in that instance one would need to understand the intricacies and legal arrangements around such a wedding. Similarly, the legal scope to approaching negotiations in labour relations is regulated by labour legislation, which includes the Constitution of the Republic of South Africa, 1996. This implies that one should ideally not attempt workplace negotiations without a thorough understanding of these applicable legislations.

The debate about the difference between negotiations and bargaining has been ongoing for centuries. Semantically, 'negotiation' stems from the fifteenth-century Latin words *neg* (not) + *otium* (leisure), meaning 'to communicate with another or others in search of mutual agreement'. Only from the early sixteenth century a slight nuance was added: 'to successfully arrange for or procure by negotiation' (Online Etymology Dictionary, 2021b). This definition suggests a present act. The concept 'bargain', on the other hand, stems from the French and German words *bargaignier* and *borgēn*, meaning 'to pledge goods in business'. Only later a slight nuance was added in the form of 'to pledge/arrange for beforehand' (Online Etymology Dictionary, 2021a). Ideally, in labour relations we strive to reach agreements before dispute situations become unmanageable.

## Negotiation Theory

Lande (2017) investigated the body of knowledge regarding negotiation theory and found that it is derived from various theoretical perspectives and various disciplines. The main theories include identity theory, social interaction theory, field theory, human needs theory, rational choice theory, transformation theory and mutual gains theory.

## Issues which Trigger Negotiation

Negotiation topics are as varied as the issues and problems arising from the collective bargaining relationship. Negotiations may be conducted to resolve differences regarding the dismissal of a single employee or the intended retrenchment of a group of employees, or to settle a grievance brought by an individual. Periodically, major negotiations are conducted to determine wage levels and conditions of service and to resolve other important issues. Besides these major negotiation sessions, negotiations will be undertaken with every dispute which arises, and will have to be instituted or continued should a strike or lockout occur.

## Motivations for Negotiation

The structure of negotiations flows from the motivation for negotiation. Carnevale and De Dreu (2006) developed a taxonomy of five types of motivations to negotiate:
1.  The **aspiration motivation** is concerned with the desired outcome of the negotiations.

2. The **identity motivation** is concerned with the image resulting from the negotiations.
3. The **initiation motivation** is related to the motivation of the other party at the beginning of the negotiations.
4. The **social motivation** is concerned with the distribution of outcomes.
5. The **epistemic motivation** is related to understanding the issues and negotiators' interests.

## Environmental Factors Influencing Labour Negotiations

Negotiations are influenced by environmental factors, in the form of:
- the economy
- public policy
- political influences
- societal influences
- demographics
- the role of the media
- technological advances.

Developments in these spheres contribute to determining:
- the content and progress of negotiations
- the power balance between the parties
- the role of government in the process
- the attitude adopted by one party towards the other.

## Economic Influences on Labour Negotiations

### Macroeconomic Influences
Kochan (1980b: 23) stated: 'All theories of collective bargaining start with a set of economic variables. The economic constraints, pressures and incentives influence all of the other components of the collective bargaining system.'

### Government Policy
The government's overall economic policy will set the stage for collective bargaining and will determine the importance attached to this process in a particular labour relations system. Most importantly, the monetary policy of a government will affect the conduct and content of negotiations. It is this monetary policy which largely determines the rate of economic growth and, with it, inflation and unemployment rates. These, in turn, affect the expectations of employees and the bargaining power of unions.

## Economic Prosperity

In times of economic prosperity, the expectations of employees will rise. More importantly, labour will be in high demand and unions will have greater bargaining power. This may lead to increased demands by unions and to aggressive negotiation, even though employers are better able to meet union demands in these circumstances than in times of economic recession.

The bargaining range will be quite narrow, but because unions hold more power, wage rates will probably show a marked increase. This holds the danger of a rise in unemployment, since the increase in labour costs may lead employers to attempt to achieve the same production levels with a smaller workforce or to decide to mechanise. If this occurs, unions may again have to limit demands.

## Economic Adversity

In times of economic adversity and rising unemployment, union bargaining power diminishes, because labour becomes more dispensable. As a result, the demands and expectations of employees may, on the face of it, have to be more realistic, and there may have to be a more co-operative relationship at the bargaining table. Yet negotiations are still likely to be lengthy and, at times, hard fought. The problem is not straightforward, as economic downturns will not necessarily result in less militancy and lower demands by unions. Whether unions moderate their demands will also depend on societal factors such as growing poverty and inequality, and on the unions' position in that society.

## The Inflation Rate

A high inflation rate or a consistent increase in the consumer price index (CPI) will inevitably lead to demands for higher wages and for agreements to contain escalation clauses, whereby wage levels automatically increase by a certain percentage for every year of the agreement. If, at the same time, there is no increase in productivity, and if the government engages in expansionary policies, a still higher inflation rate may result. Prices will increase with the increase in wages, giving rise to a wage–price spiral which may be difficult to break. Employers will expect unions to take the initiative by limiting their demands, but unions will first want to see prices decreasing.

## Microeconomic Factors

Kochan (1980a) cites various micro-economic factors as important in the bargaining process. These factors are discussed below.

*Elasticity of Demand*

Marshall (2013) originally postulated the theory that the power of trade unions will increase as the demand for labour becomes more inelastic. If the demand is inelastic, increases in wages will not result in a reduction of the workforce, and the bargaining power of the union thus remains constant. Inelasticity of demand may occur when:

- labour cannot be easily replaced
- the demand for the final product will not change
- the supply of other factors of production is static
- labour costs constitute only a small proportion of total costs.

If an employer is unable to continue the work process without certain employees (or a certain number of employees), or if the union has organised workers throughout the market, unions representing those employees hold additional power. If, for whatever reasons, the product (eg bread) remains in demand, the union need not be concerned that an increase in wages will affect employment levels. Similarly, if an employer is not able to substitute other factors for labour – in the form, for example, of capital investment in technology – unions are stronger. If the cost of labour is relatively low in comparison to the overall costs of production, the employer will more readily agree to increased remuneration for employees.

*Labour Market and Product Competition*

Where an industry is concentrated and where a number of employers compete for labour in a tight market, unions can exercise greater leverage. Conversely, if the product is highly competitive, and particularly if there is no centralised bargaining system, the employer may engage in aggressive wage bargaining for fear that increased labour costs will price the product out of the market.

*Profit Margins*

The last factor mentioned by Kochan (1980a) – namely, the level of profit in an undertaking – may be controversial, but it can happen that an employer who has higher overall profit margins or increased productivity is more ready to meet wage demands than an employer who is not in the same position. The economic factors mentioned are all interactive, not only with one another, but also with other influences on the negotiation process. Together they will determine the content and success of the negotiations.

## Public Policy

The government, through its legislative framework, sets the parameters for collective bargaining. It does so by, in the first place, establishing minimum conditions of employment and by the regulation of such matters as health and safety at the workplace. These minimum standards are used as guidelines for further bargaining by those involved in negotiations.

Secondly, a government may guide the collective bargaining process by:

- making provision for statutory bargaining bodies
- providing for the statutory enforcement of collective bargaining agreements
- establishing statutory dispute settlement machinery and mediation or arbitration services
- limiting the freedom to strike or lock out
- enforcing bargaining with a representative union
- delimiting bargaining units.

If the statutory machinery provides for centralised bargaining bodies, the employers and unions may be obliged or may prefer to adopt this bargaining structure. Equally, they might be obliged to use the statutory dispute settlement machinery or may prefer to do so instead of establishing their own.

Thirdly, a government may limit the rights of either party by, for example, legislation regarding the organisation and management of unions and employers' organisations; by limiting sympathy actions, picketing and boycotts; and by 'fair labour practice' legislation. For example, a government could oblige unions to institute strike ballots. It could legislate for payment of damages in cases of unjustified labour action and could declare the failure to bargain 'in good faith' an unfair labour practice.

A government can, by its overall policies and legislation, greatly affect the bargaining relationship. Should it treat one sector of society more favourably or as inferior, this would spill over into the labour relationship and affect the bargaining power of that group.

## Political Influences

Strong political divisions in society, or a high degree of politicisation in certain sectors, will eventually also be reflected in the issues raised at the bargaining table and in the attitude of the bargaining partners towards each other. Where the bargaining partners are diametrically opposed in their political viewpoints, or where one partner sees the other as political opposition, bargaining becomes more aggressive and less co-operative. Where politicisation is intense, political issues are added to the bargaining agenda. These may range from demands for the celebration of political holidays to insistence that employers take a political stand on certain issues.

## Societal Influences

The societal influences on the bargaining relationship are many and varied. Social and cultural divisions between employer and employee could, if these are very distinct, lead to tensions between the bargaining partners and create sensitive areas in the negotiation process. Group divisions in a community, whether of a social or religious nature, may lead to divisions among employees. This could cause tension at the workplace and further complicate the bargaining process.

Problems experienced in particular communities – such as insufficient housing, inadequate childcare or other facilities, poor education and lack of or insufficient transport – will make their way to the bargaining table in the form of demands for benefit and other schemes, or for social responsibility programmes. An employer could be expected not only to care for their own employees, but also to show some responsibility towards the community from which the labour force is drawn.

## Demographic Influences

Demographic changes in the composition, average age, predominant gender or average educational level of a workforce, and other developments, such as greater urbanisation or decentralisation of industry, will have a direct influence on worker expectations and on employee attitudes towards jobs and unions. This will, in turn, be reflected by changes in union composition and union objectives and, therefore, in bargaining relationships and negotiation issues.

As the workforce on average becomes younger, less emphasis may be placed on job security and more on personal development, and unions may have more militant supporters. Women, too, have become more vociferous in their demands and are particularly sensitive to discriminatory practices. A workforce which is, on average, more highly educated may stress job enrichment and opportunities for leisure rather than increased wages.

All these developments will affect the strength and bargaining power of unions. In some instances, union membership may increase, whereas in others it will show a decline. The more rapid the change and the more heterogeneous the membership of a union becomes, the more difficult it becomes for the bargaining process to accommodate the various interests.

Urbanisation results in greater population density and, consequently, in easier organisation for trade unions. Greater urbanisation is also accompanied by intensified social problems, especially as regards housing. These problems are certain to be brought to the bargaining table.

## The Role of the Media

The press, as an opinion-forming medium, has an active influence on negotiations, in both the long and the short term. On the negative side, press involvement can detrimentally affect actual negotiations and complicate the bargaining relationship. The press helps to shape the initial opinions and standpoints of the parties and their attitudes towards other parties. The public is influenced by the press and the body public may, by collectivised opinion or the application of pressure, play a role in the negotiation process. The press may disproportionately emphasise issues and disputes between the parties or misreport events, thus heightening conflict situations and hampering the progress of negotiations.

## Technological Advances

The effects which technology has on negotiations can be divided into two types, namely:

1. the influence of technology on the work process and on the employee who performs that work
2. the effect on employment levels.

It is commonly believed that mass-production technology alienates the employee from their work, minimises social interaction and, in general, has a dehumanising influence. This results in demands by unions for the humanisation of the work process by, for example, increased job content, whole process tasks, work groups and access to psychological counselling for employees. Demands of this nature become problems or issues at the bargaining table and could be subjected to distributive or integrative bargaining.

The ever-present threat posed by technological development to the job security of employees is a constant point of debate between employers and unions. Technology may be purposely introduced by an employer in order to diminish trade union power. At the very least, unions will demand to be consulted on the introduction of new technology and to be assured of compensation should employees be retrenched. In more sophisticated systems, this would be followed by the demand for employee retraining or re-education, so that employees themselves are able to man any new machinery which might be introduced.

As indicated in earlier chapters, the new millennium has seen escalating technological and scientific developments which threaten to change the very nature of work and traditional employment. Many traditional jobs may disappear, and employers will increasingly outsource special aspects of the business. Employees with the necessary expertise may well become business partners. Unions may not necessarily disappear, as some have predicted, but will have to reassess their priorities and strategies. Negotiations, where they do occur, will probably be at more centralised levels, perhaps even involving the government.

## Effects of Collective Negotiations on the Environment

Just as environmental influences affect the negotiation process and its outcome, so also the process itself influences developments in the environment. This is particularly the case in the economic sphere, where agreement on higher wages or other benefits and consequent price increases may contribute to inflationary trends in the economy. Repeated, disruptive strike action may negatively affect the economy and societal relationships and may necessitate measures limiting the rights of parties.

Socially, the results of collective bargaining are most obvious, especially if parties negotiate social improvement schemes or employers become involved in education and housing problems. On the negative side, conflicts and problems arising in the negotiation process will be carried out to the wider society and may result in community actions against employers in the form of product boycotts, blacklisting by communities and tensions between various sectors of the community.

## Part Two: Factors Contributing to the Effectiveness of the Process

## Individual Skills, Interactions and Perceptions

The degree of success achieved during a particular negotiation process will depend to some extent on:

- the skill of the negotiators
- the willingness or perceived willingness of either party to engage in coercive action
- the degree of commitment to reaching a final agreement
- the expectations and needs of both parties
- the parties' past relationship
- the knowledge that each party has of the other and of prevailing circumstances
- the amount of trust existing between the negotiators.

# Power and Influence

## Using Different Forms of Power

The conduct and outcome of distributive negotiation is ultimately dependent on the power balance between the parties. Coercive power is at the basis of the bargaining relationship and is the form of power most frequently applied by the parties. Nevertheless, according to French and Raven (1959), various types of power may be applied during the negotiation process:

- **Legitimate power** is applied by ensuring that the chief negotiator is a person who holds a senior position in either employer/management ranks, the union hierarchy or the employee collective. Alternatively, the negotiator could refer to a principal who is an individual with legitimate power, or to an outsider who holds legitimate power in society. In a negotiating team, important issues could be addressed by an individual who holds legitimate power in that sphere.
- **Reward power** can be used on an individual or a collective basis. A negotiator may point to the collective rewards which can be achieved from agreement.
- **Coercive power** is used when negotiators employ threats and bluffs; when they demonstrate displeasure by, for example, walking out of the negotiation session; or when they play on the fears of the other party.
- **Expert power** is one of the best forms of power to utilise in negotiations. This type of power depends on the knowledge and skill of the negotiator. Expertise is demonstrated by creating awareness of a negotiator's experience and background, by citing facts and figures and by the manner in which information is presented and arguments are countered. Expert power can also be enhanced by calling on persons with expertise in particular areas to make presentations during negotiations.
- **Referent power** is regarded as the most beneficial form of power. To utilise this kind of power, the negotiator would have to be someone with whom the other side can identify, despite their differences. This is why employers may choose to appoint an outside consultant as chief negotiator, in the belief that the union team will more easily identify with that person than with a member of management. Referent power may also be gained by referring, in argument, to persons with whom the other side can identify, or by operating within the context of shared values and beliefs. This, of course, is the ideal negotiating situation.

## Strategies for Gaining Power

During the negotiating process itself, parties may gain power if they:
- set relatively high aspirations and commit themselves to these

- have the support of their constituents or principals
- gain support from the community
- can make the other party look bad
- ensure that time is on their side
- are willing to take risks
- have knowledge of, and can resort to, the law
- have sufficient information and skill
- can create dominance (particularly by displaying knowledge and skill)
- persuade the other party of their commitment
- maintain contact with constituents and principals
- demonstrate strength by letting the other side know what measures can be taken
- point to the benefits of co-operation and the importance of maintaining a favourable image
- show that they have contacts outside who are willing to support them
- act courageously at all times.

## Profile of a Successful Negotiator

For a number of years, Rackham and Carlisle (1978a; 1978b) conducted various studies with the purpose of identifying the attributes of successful negotiators. Their observations proved the following:

- When planning for negotiations, skilled negotiators considered a wider range of options and outcomes than those who were less skilled.
- While all negotiators tended to concentrate on conflict areas, skilled negotiators gave far more attention to areas of possible co-operation than did the average negotiator.
- Both skilled and less skilled negotiators tended to concentrate on short-term objectives, but successful negotiators paid more attention (twice as much) to long-term objectives.
- Skilled negotiators established upper and lower limits during their planning sessions, whereas those less skilled tended to plan around a fixed point.
- Less skilled negotiators established rigid sequences beforehand, whereas the skilled negotiators were more flexible in this respect.
- More successful negotiators seemed to avoid irritating expressions such as 'unfair', 'unreasonable', 'uncaring', etc.
- Skilled negotiators did not make immediate counterproposals as frequently as those who were less skilled.
- Average negotiators engaged in defence–attack spirals on a much more frequent basis than did skilled negotiators.

- Skilled negotiators usually warned the other party of the kind of statement they were going to make – for example, by saying that they intended to make an offer. Less skilled negotiators tended to say 'I disagree' more often than their skilled colleagues, who, instead, would commence with reasons and explanations.
- More successful negotiators frequently tested understanding and summarised their own and the other party's arguments.
- Skilled negotiators questioned the other party far more frequently than did their less skilled colleagues.
- While average negotiators tended to concentrate on facts and figures, more successful negotiators explained how they felt about the other side and its arguments.
- Skilled negotiators backed up their arguments with an average of 1.8 reasons, whereas those who were less skilled used an average of three reasons per argument.
- Finally, it was found that more than two-thirds of the successful negotiators spent time after the negotiations reviewing what had happened and thus learning from experience, while less than half of the average negotiators had acquired this habit. Perhaps this, more than anything else, accounts for the high rate of success experienced by the first group in comparison to the second.

## Important Qualities of Successful Negotiators

The best negotiator is not the most forceful or aggressive character in the union or management team. The most important qualities required by a negotiator are:

- sensitivity to the needs, feelings and perceptions of all concerned
- tact – not needlessly antagonising the other side
- a readiness to listen, particularly to the other side
- the ability to interpret non-verbal cues such as facial expressions
- discretionary judgement – for example, knowing when to stand firm, when to concede and when to use particular arguments
- flexibility – being willing to adopt different strategies and approaches
- the ability to handle information
- the ability to present a persuasive, reasoned argument
- superior thinking and planning skills
- in-depth knowledge of the issues at hand
- good communication skills
- the ability to withstand pressure and stress
- the ability to earn the respect of the other party.

A negotiator intent on winning at all costs is not the most effective. A total triumph by one party involves the complete defeat of the other. This is bound either to elicit a counterreaction or to lead to more conflict at a later stage. The effective negotiator will also consider the other party. The negotiator may, and is entitled to, pursue the interests of their own party as single-mindedly as possible and, in the process, to use aggression and threats. However, they should do so without totally antagonising the other party and without causing the opposing side to lose face completely.

## Part Three: The Negotiation Process

## Negotiation Models or Subprocesses

The seminal work of Walton and McKersie (1965) identified four main negotiation models or subprocesses for negotiations, namely distributive negotiation, integrative negotiation, attitudinal restructuring/structuring and intra-organisational bargaining.

### Distributive Negotiation

This model is also referred to as value-taking, competitive, positional, adversarial, zero-sum or hard negotiations. Negotiators following this model strive to gain the best possible outcome for themselves (Lande, 2017: 91). The orientation of this form of negotiation is separate bargaining outcomes and gaining wins on each outcome. A distributive negotiation orientation can normally be identified by the demand for a fixed type of outcome or a fixed amount.

Because the relationship focus is short term, there is little information sharing, but there may be threats and ultimatums – a typical win-lose orientation. Each party's mandate is typically their resistance point and bargaining base. A classical South African example was the origins of the Marikana Massacre, where the inflexible demand for a R12 000 salary signalled a typical distributive negotiation.

### Integrative Negotiation

Unlike distributive bargaining, this joint-problem-solving orientation is characterised by congruent interests. This win-win, interest-based, co-operative, problem-solving model has a more long-term intent related to a relationship between the parties. Variable amounts and agenda items signal this negotiation model (Lande, 2017: 92). The relationship between the parties is collaborative, which is the main mandate for negotiations.

### Attitudinal Restructuring/Structuring

This approach uses various forms of influence to shape intergroup attitudes. This form of negotiation refers to the interpersonal relations between the parties and their level of trust (Hennebert & Pérez-Lauzon, 2019).

### Intra-organisational Bargaining

Intra-organisational bargaining refers to internal conflicts that need to be resolved throughout the bargaining process (Hennebert & Pérez-Lauzon, 2019). Collective bargaining or negotiation with the other side will always be preceded by negotiations with other people in the organisation and, in the union's case, with union members. Such intra-organisational negotiation will continue as long as the negotiations themselves last.

The task of formulating a joint strategy or position will fall mainly on the shoulders of the chief negotiator. In order to achieve the necessary co-ordination, the chief negotiator will have to:

- identify the issues
- establish the needs of all concerned (particularly those of their own and the opposing organisation)
- gather as much information as possible
- negotiate with their own team, their principals and other concerned persons in the organisation.

Only once consensus has been achieved can the actual planning of negotiations commence. Entering negotiations with an unco-ordinated team, or without the support of principals/members, is looking for trouble.

## Preconditions for Collaborative Negotiations

As mentioned earlier in this chapter, the traditional approach to negotiation is adversarial in nature. Each party adopts a particular position, which it guards at all costs. The objective of negotiators using this traditional approach is to urge the other party to move as far as possible towards their own position, and to concede as little as possible. This results in an extremely narrow approach to negotiation – along a straight line between the position of one party and that of the other, with much game-playing and posturing in between. There is little or no consideration of alternative solutions, and each strives to gain as much as possible at the expense of the other. Personalities and egos become involved and, very often, the outcome relies on a contest of wills rather than on the realities of the situation. This description may be extreme, as most negotiations will also involve some attempt at collaboration, but it serves to typify the dominant aspects of positional or adversarial negotiation. A more fully collaborative or integrative approach to negotiation would, of course, be preferable and would lead to outcomes which are of greater value for both parties. However, for such collaboration to exist, certain preconditions are required.

### Recognising the Legitimacy of the Other Party

If parties are to engage in collaborative negotiations, each should, in the first place, recognise the legitimacy of the other party. Each party should:

- display respect for the other party's needs and interests
- approach the negotiations openly and honestly
- be willing to share information and to work towards a solution
- believe that together they can and will find the best possible solution.

### Emphasis on Common Interests

Collaborative negotiations further require that, although there may be different goals and perspectives, and although these must be respected, common interests predominate. For this to happen, both parties should be accorded equal value and status. One party should not be pleading with or demanding from the other. This means that, in an organisational setting, both management and employees should view themselves as joint stakeholders and the organisation as their point of common interest.

### Trust as an Important Component

Parties will have to share their needs, interests and fears, which in turn necessitates a trust relationship. Such trust is built by:

- engendering psychological closeness
- displaying openness and honesty
- emphasising similarities and interdependence
- displaying positive attitudes, including a desire to co-operate
- minimising power differentials and avoiding the use of power
- focusing on problems instead of arguing positions.

Collaborative negotiation does not rely on positioning or, therefore, on absolute mandates. Negotiators have to be trusted by their constituents and be given far greater flexibility and decision-making powers than would be granted in an adversarial situation. Therefore, not only the negotiators but also the different constituents have to trust each other. Clearly such a relationship cannot be built up overnight, and will be supported by a history of collaboration and goodwill in other areas. Also, it is easier to build a relationship of this kind in a decentralised situation where parties continually work closely together.

## Communication

As always, the successful establishment of a collaborative relationship will depend on continual clear and accurate communication and the furnishing of all relevant information by the parties concerned.

## Initiating Collaborative Negotiations

Collaborative negotiations may commence with a statement of positions; however, instead of concentrating on positions, concessions and demands, the parties explore the needs, interests and concerns behind these positions. In other words, the problems have to be separated from the positions, and also from the negotiators themselves.

In most cases, it is preferable not to state positions at all, but rather for both parties to put their concerns and objectives on the table. These are then placed in the organisational context and explored within the framework of prevailing circumstances. However, before this can be done it might be necessary to sideline hardliners in each group and to establish the correct climate through levelling conferences, pre-meetings and training in problem-solving skills. This is important since, once concerns have been placed on the table and depersonalised, the parties basically adopt a problem-solving mode.

### Challenges in Implementing Collaborative Negotiations

The collaborative mode is a complex process to which the very sketchy outline above does not do justice. It requires far more detailed study and continued building of the relationship by both parties. In some instances, the parties may not be capable of this on their own, and a facilitator may be required during the initial stages. Also, both parties may be reluctant to relinquish power positions. Taking power, especially coercive power, out of the picture in negotiations requires a definite paradigm shift, which may not be easy to achieve.

## Approaches to the Negotiation Process

Historically, there are five types of analytical approaches to the phases of negotiation (Zartman, 1988: 31–38):

1. **Structural analysis** is based either on how parties position themselves in relation to an issue (resource possessions) or on their ability (power) to ensure that their chosen option prevails.
2. In **strategic analysis**, the parties focus on what (the value) they want to achieve (preferred choice), rather than on how they will achieve their outcome. The assumption is that parties are equal or symmetrical. Typical examples are found in game theoretic matrices and standard

strategic models. For example, the Prisoner's Dilemma game and Chicken Dilemma game are symmetrical.

3. In **process analysis**, the outcome is reached by the parties, by means of a range of careful comparative calculations of costs regarding concessions on a party's position and the positions of the other parties.

4. **Behavioural analysis** involves the determination of a negotiated outcome through the parties analysing the different personal characteristics of the individual negotiators, like personalities.

5. In **integrative analysis**, the perception and performance of each party at the end of each negotiation session is evaluated, and the conceptualisation of an issue is used to reach mutually accepted outcomes.

However, recently De Oliveira Dias (2020) proposed matrix evaluation based on the dimensions of negotiation processes, mainly focusing on the number of issues and value creation via a mutual gains approach. This matrix suggests that the evaluation of the process depends on the individual, the complexity of the negotiations, and social-psychological and communication processes within the phases of the negotiation process:

- **Individual processes:** These include individual differences between parties, what motivates and differentiates parties, as well as the mental models with which the parties approach the negotiations.

- **Complexity of the negotiation:** The more complex the negotiation is, the higher the type of negotiation – in other words, two-party and single-issue negotiations versus multi-issue and multi-party negotiations. Similarly, the context of negotiations will have an influence on the approach taken to the negotiation process. Some examples of different contexts include management–trade union negotiations, peace negotiations and hostage negotiations.

- **Social-psychological processes:** These include the influence of power, trust, culture, gender, ethics and the number of parties in the negotiation process.

- **Communication processes:** The dynamics of technologically enabled communication between parties will be different to that of face-to-face communication. The frequency of interaction will also influence the negotiation process.

## Preparing for Negotiation

### The Initiator of the Negotiation Process

Traditionally, the initiative for starting the negotiation process has come from the union or employees, either by way of a set of demands or in the form of grievances raised by employees. However, the reverse could and does occur.

The employer may act as initiator in order to gain certain concessions from, or institute arrangements with, the employees or the union. Whoever the initiator may be, the proposals made by one side are certain to be met with counterproposals from the other or by an agreement to meet for the purpose of negotiation.

Depending on the nature and extent of the issues, the ensuing negotiation could be conducted at various levels and may be very limited or extensive, as would be, for example, negotiations around wages and conditions of employment. For the present purposes it is assumed that the negotiations are of the latter kind.

### The Negotiation Planning Sheet

In order to put their plans into concrete form, negotiators may choose to draw up a negotiation planning sheet. This will list the issues, the bargaining parameters, the projected costs, the areas of concession and matters which are non-negotiable. A planning sheet of this kind provides all members of the negotiating team with the necessary information for reference purposes during the actual negotiations.

### Negotiation Conventions

Before engaging in negotiation, both parties should understand the protocol applicable to this process. The practice of negotiation requires, in the first place, recognition of the right of each party to state its case, to make proposals and counterproposals and to raise arguments and counterarguments. The chief negotiator speaks and makes decisions on behalf of their team, but other team members may also speak, either when called upon or at their own request.

In properly conducted negotiations, both sides acknowledge the need for compromise. At the same time, each recognises the right of the other to pursue their own targets as aggressively as possible, even to the point of threatening coercive action.

The art of negotiation relies on professional behaviour. There is consideration for the other side, and correct manners are maintained at all times. It is accepted that no petty harangues will take place and that no personal attacks will be made, and that negotiators on either side will not lose their tempers. For this reason, negotiations normally follow a formal procedural pattern. The chief negotiator on either side is the one to be addressed. An agenda is drawn up, minutes are taken, time periods are set and there is an opening and closing address. In all negotiations each side has a right to request a caucus or the opportunity to report back to its principals or members.

When conducting negotiations, all participants should have equal status. It is accepted that existing agreements will be upheld, and that movement will come from both sides. Negotiations should be conducted fairly and in good faith. This means that:

- an offer, once made, should ideally not be withdrawn, as withdrawal results in the party being seen as not trustworthy
- verbal offers and agreements are taken as given
- there should be no denial of something which has been accepted
- both sides should display willingness to negotiate
- there can be no outside or informal settlement of a negotiable issue
- confidential or privileged information may not be abused by either party during negotiations or at a later stage
- the other party should be left with some credit
- no trickery should be employed in the final agreement
- agreements will be implemented as they stand.

## Setting Goals and Objectives

It is important to know what the negotiation team wants to achieve (its goal), as this will have a direct and indirect effect on the choice of strategy the party will follow.

Planning and strategising is usually preceded by the establishment of certain broad objectives and, if possible, calculated guesses as to the objectives of the other party. The objectives are described as 'broad' in the sense that they refer not to targets to be reached during negotiation, but rather to:

- the overall objectives of the negotiation process
- the general objectives of management and the union
- the specific objectives of negotiators.

The overall objective of negotiation is usually to achieve the fairest and most acceptable settlement. This notwithstanding, there are particular circumstances in which the overall objective may be to take a principled stand or to display strength. This usually happens when the other party has in the past displayed an exaggerated sense of its own power or when too many concessions are perceived to have been made.

Whatever the overall objective, it is important that it is clearly defined and is kept in mind by the entire negotiating team. It is this objective which will set the tone for the negotiations and which will keep negotiators on course.

During negotiations, management's main concern will be with turnover, profits before and after tax, tax concessions, profit margins, reinvestment, growth, expansion, dividends declared, competitiveness, productivity, market retention, control and cost savings. An appreciation of these concerns by the union can facilitate negotiation and result in better arguments. Equally, management should understand and appreciate the union objectives and should plan arguments and counterarguments in light of these objectives.

Generally speaking, unions want to improve the situation of their members, in terms of continued employment and security, job satisfaction, a happy workforce and acknowledgment of employee rights. Management, on the other hand, wants production to continue and improve and the operation to run with as few problems and difficulties as possible. Understanding these general and specific objectives leads to better strategising and to more reasonable behaviour during negotiations.

### Delimiting the Area of Negotiation

Before negotiations commence, each party should establish:

- what it wants to achieve
- what it is likely to achieve
- to what extent it is prepared to concede
- what the other side will want to achieve
- what the other side is likely to achieve
- what the other side is likely to concede.

This allows negotiators to make optimistic and pessimistic projections for each issue, particularly the substantive ones, and gives some idea of what a realistic outcome would be.

One overall objective of negotiation remains, and that is the desire of both parties to maintain and, if possible, improve their relationship. Whatever their individual aspirations, the parties undertake negotiations principally as a means of ensuring the continuity of the relationship.

### Selecting the Negotiator(s)

*Single Person or a Negotiation Team*

Any negotiation requires the appointment or selection of the person or persons most suited to conduct the negotiations. The type of issue and the nature of both employer/management and union organisation will determine the type and number of persons appointed. These will be selected on the basis of their expertise or their involvement in the issue at hand. Thus, a management negotiating team could consist of the production manager, the financial manager, the company secretary and one or two foremen, while the union team may consist of an organiser, one or two officials and some shop stewards. The preferred practice is to keep the team as small as possible. Too large a negotiating team might encumber negotiations and make it more difficult to reach consensus.

*The Chief Negotiator*

Where negotiations are to be conducted by a negotiation team, it is customary to appoint a chief negotiator. The chief negotiator is usually chosen on the basis of their experience, expertise and knowledge of both their own organisation and the other party. The chief negotiator's task is to:

- co-ordinate and lead the negotiating team
- get to know the other party
- advise their principals in preparing an objective strategy
- arrange and lead meetings
- continually report back and refer to their principals
- within limits, reach decisions during negotiations on behalf of their principals.

If the chief negotiator is to carry out their task successfully, they will have to establish a sound relationship with their principals, their teammates and the other side. They should have the trust and confidence of all involved, and particularly of their principals.

*Roles Assigned to Team Members*

Some teams may decide to cast each team member in a specific role. One may act as the aggressor and another as the pacifier, while yet another maintains the position of expert and adviser throughout the negotiations. This is not always necessary, as long as the team co-ordinates effectively, and one team member is designated as listener. It is necessary that one person, trained in listening and observation skills, refrains from talking and instead sits back to observe innuendoes, subtle gestures and reactions. This person is the one who, from time to time, may call for a caucus in order to inform their teammates of their observations. This person may also act as recorder, but in larger teams it is preferable to appoint another team member to record all the important arguments and decisions.

## Identifying the Main Issues

Once demands have been posted or proposals and counterproposals have been made, the negotiating team will, as one of its first tasks, attempt to identify the issues to be subjected to negotiation. This is necessary, as not all the issues may be immediately recognisable. In certain cases, demands or proposals are in misleading language, or one demand raises another issue.

Note that single-issue negotiations tend to lean towards a distributive negotiation strategy, whereas multiple-issue negotiations lend themselves towards more integrative negotiations.

Issues should be listed in order of priority and it should be specified whether they can be linked together or separated from each other to obtain more leverage for settlement. The list of issues established at this early stage may later be amended and priorities may change, both after intra-organisational bargaining has occurred and after the initial encounter with the other side. Negotiators need to establish the bargaining range of the prioritised issues prior to establishing possible bargaining mixes.

## Defining the Interests

Understanding the underlying interests and needs of one's own team, and those of the other party, could have a determining influence in preparing for a mandate or refining a settlement. These aspects are normally reflected in the agenda or notice to negotiate from a party. One needs to look out for language use indicating a focus on relationship, process or the substantive description of interest, as this provides an indication of the other party's focus. Also, in preparation one should consider what alternatives are available if one's party's interests are not met, or the item is not included on the agenda for discussion. These alternatives are known as a party's BATNA (best alternative to a negotiated agreement).

## Establish the Bargaining Range

The upper and lower limits of one party may be entirely unrealistic and there may be no commonality at all with the limits set by the other party. This will result in both sides having to go back to the planning stage before actual negotiations can commence. It is therefore necessary to establish a more specific bargaining range. The bargaining range will be widely delimited by what is generally known as the area of interdependence.

### The Importance of Establishing Bargaining Ranges

It may be asked if the preliminary establishment of bargaining and settlement ranges is necessary, and whether it would not rather be advisable for each side to make as realistic an assessment as possible and to establish a contract zone forthwith. This is usually not possible, first because perceptions of reality are established gradually and may change during negotiations. Secondly, the contract zone established depends to some extent on the negotiation process.

### The Area of Interdependence

The area of interdependence is that range – say, in wages – within which it is worth each party's while to try to maintain the relationship; in essence, it is the range in which it is worth continuing with the negotiations.

The outer limits of this area are set by the points at which either party would terminate a potentially advantageous relationship. For example, employees might be unwilling to continue working for the undertaking or engage in protracted actions if the wage rate is set at lower than R30 per hour. On the other hand, if the employer is forced to pay more than R60 per hour, they might look for alternatives such as giving up the operation, mechanising or moving to another area where labour is cheaper. Thus, principally, the area of interdependence establishes or limits the bargaining range, as illustrated in Figure 9.1.

*Employee/Union Considerations when Setting Limits*
In practice, the outer limits of the area of interdependence may be pushed even lower in the case of employees and higher in the case of employers. The decision by employees on whether it is worthwhile to continue in employment might be affected by:
■ their mobility or lack thereof
■ their knowledge of the labour market
■ the extent to which the market is decentralised
■ the employees' experience in a particular type of work
■ the fact that they may lose benefits or seniority rights
■ their skill levels
■ the rate of unemployment.

*Employer Considerations when Setting Limits*
The employer, on the other hand, may go beyond their upper limit after considering such factors as the costs of replacement, of severance and of moving. The employer's upper limit, or whether they will go beyond their upper limit, will also depend on the union's control of the labour market. Should the union control the entire market, the employer may have no option but to agree to union demands; however, this may eventually lead the employer to mechanise, in which case the union will have gained in the short term and lost in the long term.

*Other Factors Determining Limits Set*
It is generally believed that high or higher upper limits will be established if:
■ demand is inelastic
■ there is a national rather than a local product market
■ the operations of the employer are of a large scale
■ multi-unit companies are involved
■ it is not easy for the organisation to relocate
■ the products are diverse.

The area of interdependence will further be affected by what is known as mutually created gain. Negotiation is not merely a divisive process. It creates additional value and mutual benefit. In the long term it will lead to trust and confidence between the parties. They may form a unique combination, which will provide social satisfaction for both.

In addition to mutually created gain, there are subjective utilities and disutilities to consider. Although a union may have higher wages as its main objective, it will also consider the subjective disutility of enforcing its demands at all costs, as this may lead to problems in later negotiations and even to a drop in employment. In the same way, the employer who does not want to pay higher wages might consider the subjective utility of having a happier and more satisfied workforce and a favourable image in the industry.

The area of interdependence cannot be rigidly established. There are many factors which would influence employees to accept less than their limit and employers to offer more than their limit. In practice, a skilled negotiator will not attempt to push the other party to these limits, as it greatly endangers the relationship.

A negotiator will always set their own limits slightly lower or higher than the limits of the party they represent. This is done because they would lose credibility with their party and might even lose their job if they negotiate around the party's outer limits. The position is thus as illustrated in Figure 9.1.

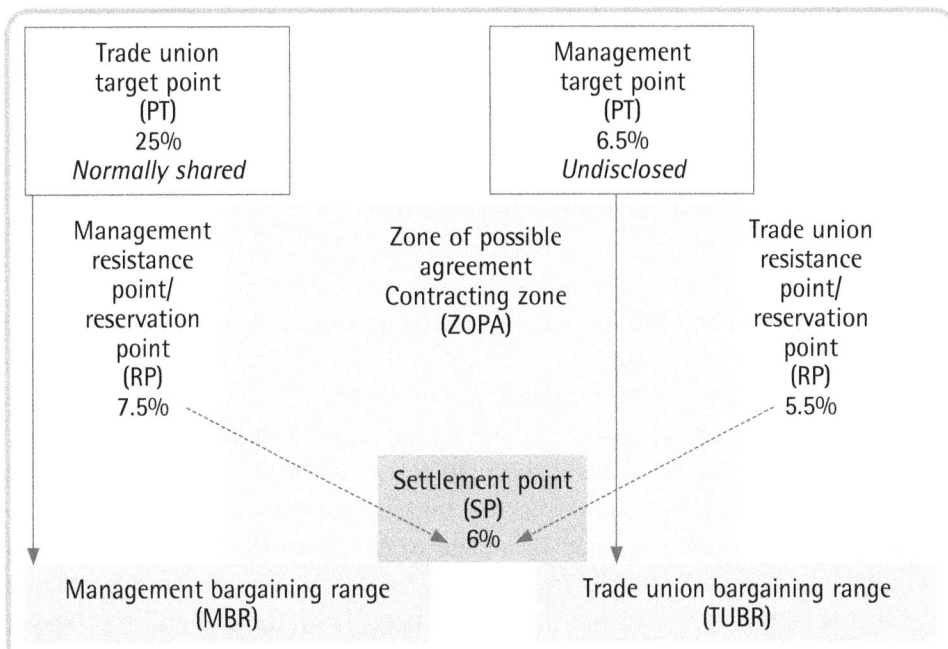

Figure 9.1: Setting limits during negotiations

## Information Gathering

In both the preparation for and the actual conduct of negotiations, information may prove the key to success. The negotiating team should have all the necessary information at its disposal before negotiations commence. This includes information relating to current conditions, its own organisation and the other side. Comprehensive information leads to realistic goal setting, good strategic planning and persuasive argument and counterargument. The types of information needed are discussed below.

### Current Conditions

Economic, social and political conditions will influence the conduct of negotiations and the bargaining power of each party. Negotiators should know whether prevalent economic developments will favour the other party and whether social or political conditions could play a role in the negotiation process.

In wage negotiations, economic conditions are particularly important. Negotiators need to take into account:
- inflation levels
- cost-of-living indices
- levels of economic activity
- business cycles
- industry trends
- economic forecasts
- unemployment levels
- the labour market
- current trends in wages and prices
- wages negotiated in related undertakings
- household and minimum subsistence levels
- wage determinations and arbitration awards.

### Statistical Indicators

The following statistical indicators are most frequently used during substantive negotiations:
- **CPI:** This reflects the increased price of goods and services used by an average family, and is calculated by taking approximately 600 consumer goods and services, weighting them in terms of importance, establishing a base year and then calculating the percentage increase from month to month and from year to year. It is used to calculate the inflation rate and to adjust prices and wages. However, there are certain inherent problems with this statistic, in that the household used is imaginary and the basket of goods is therefore not always typical. Also, it does not take into account direct taxation. In dealing with lower-level income groups, it is often

advisable to supplement this statistic with the food price index, which may be more relevant.

- **Inflation rate:** The inflation rate is wider and more general than the CPI, and can therefore be lower. In essence, it shows by how much money has devalued over a certain period, and is calculated by taking all prices into account and expressing increases on a percentage basis. It is usually calculated on a month-by-month and year-by-year basis, expressed as a 12-month moving average.

- **Producer price index (PPI):** Previously called the wholesale price index, this shows the increased price of a representative basket of goods required by producers, including capital and intermediate goods. It reveals the increase in the price of imported goods more effectively, and is often used by management to prove an escalation in capital and production expenses.

- **Gross domestic product (GDP):** This statistic reflects the total price of goods and services produced in a country, but does not include unrecorded and non-market activity. It is used to measure the degree of economic activity in a country from one year to another and to compare this with that of other countries.

- **Per capita income:** This refers to the average income per person in a particular country, and is calculated by dividing the total income by the number of people. It is used to compare earnings with those in other countries and to measure economic progress, but the problem is that it does not indicate how income is distributed.

- **Real wages:** The real wage lag is the loss suffered when prices rise without a concomitant rise in wages. Thus, if the inflation rate is 15 per cent per annum, a wage of R100 in January will amount to a real wage of R85 by December.

- **Minimum subsistence level (MSL) and household subsistence level (HSL):** MSL determines how much a family of a certain size (usually five or six) needs just to survive, and HSL determines how much they need to subsist reasonably. It is calculated by taking the price of an average basket of goods – but, again, the problem is that the basket is arbitrary and does not allow for any other expenditure except necessities. Nowadays, MSLs and HSLs are mostly discredited, with unions preferring to use a 'decent wage' as the basic criterion.

*Organisational Position*

No negotiator can enter into a negotiation situation without full knowledge of the organisation they represent. The management negotiator should have sound knowledge of:

- the organisational needs for profit, control, stability and expansion
- the organisation's present position as regards profitability
- plans for the future
- the ratio of labour costs to total costs
- the operation of each department
- the production process
- the management styles adopted in every department.

The negotiator needs this knowledge so that they do not make commitments which, in practice, prove to be unrealistic or out of line with general policy.

From the union side, the union negotiator has to be fully informed about the organisation they represent. In union circles it is not necessary to stress this point as emphatically. A union is established for the sole purpose of representing the interests of its members, mainly by the process of collective bargaining; consequently, negotiation is one of its main tasks.

*Knowledge of the Other Side*

From the management side, it is essential to study the union, to know, for example:

- its policy, strategy and past history
- its successes and failures
- its proneness to strike action
- its affiliations
- the support it may receive
- its present position and intentions.

The union, in its turn, will study the company as regards:

- its managerial style
- the industry within which it operates
- its past history
- its internal and external organisation
- the work process
- profitability levels, wage structures and labour costs.

More sophisticated unions will obtain information from the annual reports of a company and its competitors, or they may request that the company's books be opened for inspection by union officials.

## Establishing Resistance and Target Points

The considerations outlined above are not separate steps but form part of an integrated process, the purpose of which is to establish target and resistance points. From these, the settlement range will eventually be obtained.

A target point is the point at which a negotiator would like to conclude negotiations. It is based on:

- the highest estimate of what is needed or possible
- the most optimistic assumptions regarding the probability of success
- the most favourable assessment of the negotiator's bargaining skill.

Resistance points are based on:

- the lowest estimate of what is needed or possible
- the most pessimistic assumptions regarding the possibility of success
- the least favourable assessment of the negotiator's bargaining skill.

Resistance points are also those at which a party is likely to stop negotiations. In labour relations that is the point where a union is likely to consider strike action and management could consider a lockout.

The target and resistance points of both parties will be established within the perceived bargaining range.

## The Settlement Range

The settlement range is the perceived area between the resistance points of both parties. A positive settlement range (one in which there is a likelihood of agreement) is achieved if the union's resistance point is lower than management's resistance point.

In order to estimate the settlement range, it will be necessary to make a calculated guess as to the target and resistance points of the other party. This is done by:

- studying the demands of that party
- drawing from past experience and other agreements reached
- estimating the benefits and costs of agreement as against the benefits and costs of disagreement to both parties.

It is obvious that, as actual negotiation progresses and more information is obtained, perceptions of the settlement range may have to be adapted. Nevertheless, it is useful to project the settlement range before entering into negotiations, as it assists in the establishment and modification of the party's own targets and points the way to the type of strategy to be adopted.

If the projected settlement range is negative, preliminary efforts will have to include establishing a more positive zone for negotiation. This may be done if the party modifies its own resistance and target points or it may be achieved by placing subtle pressure for modification on the other party.

## Risk Assessment

When attempting to establish realistic upper and lower levels, it is useful to hypothetically calculate the costs and benefits of non-settlement for both sides. Representatives should estimate what they will gain and what they will lose if settlement is not reached at a certain point. Equally, they need to project the potential benefits and costs to the other side. This may lead to a party rethinking its limits. Alternatively, benefits and costs relating to one negotiation issue may be offset against those derived from another issue.

### Cost–Benefit Analysis for Management

The costs which management could incur by not settling include:

- losses suffered as a result of a strike, a go-slow or a work-to-rule
- a decline in productivity
- lack of involvement by employees
- loss of time
- loss of market segment
- a poor public image
- lack of credibility in the community
- high labour turnover
- legal action
- a breakdown in the relationship
- tougher bargaining in the future
- eventual loss of face when forced to settle.

Benefits of not settling could include:

- savings incurred by not conceding
- the establishment of precedents
- less administration
- time gained for reassessment
- opportunity to use stockpiles
- face-saving
- a greater willingness by the other side to make concessions in the future.

### Cost–Benefit Analysis for Employees/the Union

By not conceding, employees, as represented by unions, may:

- lose wages should there be a lockout or a strike
- in the long term, lose more than they gain by going on strike
- face tougher bargaining the next time around

- suffer a breakdown in the relationship
- eventually lose face.

However, by not conceding they may:
- eventually obtain a better deal
- establish a precedent and a power base for the future
- start off from a more advantageous position during the next round of negotiations
- enjoy increased solidarity and greater commitment from members.

### Weighing Costs against Benefits

Bargaining power can be calculated by weighing one's own and the other party's costs of disagreeing as against benefits derived. Bargaining power could also be calculated by assessing the cost of settlement to the other party. If the cost of a certain settlement is disproportionately high in relation to the benefits, it is unlikely that the party involved would readily agree. The bargaining power of the other party consequently decreases.

### The Contract Zone

The contract zone is that area within the settlement range which will be delimited as the final area of negotiation. The area in which the contract zone is established will depend on the skill of the negotiators on each side and the power of the parties. In the example of a positive settlement range illustrated in Figure 9.1 earlier in this chapter, the contract zone will probably be between 5.5 and 6.5 per cent if management has more skill and power. Conversely, it will be between 6 and 7.5 per cent if union negotiators are more skilful and can exert more pressure.

### Costing of Contracts

Especially where substantive issues are concerned, it is necessary for management to calculate the cost of the projected contracts, both at the most pessimistic level and from a realistic perspective. Costing would have to be undertaken where negotiations hinge on extended leave benefits, fringe benefits, pensions, training and other matters of this kind. However, ideally, consultations around dismissal for operational reasons and substantive negotiations should always be dealt with separately as a good faith labour relations practice.

It is advisable to draw up various alternative packages and to cost these accordingly. The costing of individual factors and of the total contract makes it easier to reach decisions regarding affordability, the possibility of trading off one benefit against another and the possibility of staggered increases.

Moreover, total contract costs constitute a powerful argument in persuading the other party to lower its demands or to raise its offer.

## Developing Strategies

Once target and resistance points have been established, strategic planning for negotiations can proceed. In developing strategies, negotiators will decide:

- which issues to address first
- which arguments should be raised
- when and where concessions can be made
- which issues or targets will be non-negotiable.

In making these decisions, it is useful to appoint one of the negotiating team as 'devil's advocate', or to test arguments on an outsider.

At this stage negotiators will also plan:

- the initial approach to the other side
- the tone to be adopted
- the role of the various negotiators
- the probable order of negotiations.

Possible coercive action is another aspect which requires close attention. All major negotiations should be preceded by contingency planning for a strike by employees or a lockout by employers.

Timing, too, is important. From management's perspective it might be strategically expedient to negotiate when there is a downturn in production, when employees want a rapid settlement and when management has time to spare. This, of course, would not be beneficial to the union. Equally, unions would not wish to negotiate when management is not busy and can therefore prolong negotiations, nor do they favour negotiations at the beginning of the financial year or when an annual increase date is imminent.

## Obtaining a Mandate

Before any preparations for negotiation can commence, the chief negotiator or their negotiating team should obtain an initial mandate from the principals or, in the case of a union, its constituents. This will probably not be the final mandate for negotiations, but it will establish a framework within which planning can take place. For the union negotiators, it would entail bringing a management demand to their membership or, most often, establishing the needs and demands of their members. Management negotiators will obtain direction from their principals and broadly establish the size of the package which the principals are prepared to offer. A mandate is never absolute, and it may change as preparations and negotiations progress.

### Testing the Water

Before entering into more detailed preparation for negotiation, it is advisable to test the water. This entails finding out more about the other side's intentions and objectives, establishing how committed they are to their demands, how much support they have and how they would react to certain proposals. Initial probing can take the form of casual questions, informal talks and parallel remarks (saying something 'by the way'). It can also be used to give the other side an idea as to whether their demands will be acceptable or not.

## Conducting Negotiations

### Overview of the Negotiation Process

Negotiations commence with an *opening encounter*, which sets the climate for negotiations and is usually of a formal nature. After the rules have been established and the agenda has been formulated, each party attempts by various tactics to establish the position of the other side, without itself revealing too much. It may become necessary even at this stage for the parties to reassess their positions and strategies in light of what they have learnt from the other party.

The opening encounter is followed by the actual *body of the negotiation process*, a period of argument and counterargument during which both parties will engage in hard bargaining in an attempt to modify the perceptions of the other and to initiate movement towards their own targets. Concessions will be made and demanded, pressure will be applied, joint problem solving may occur and the commitment of both parties to their respective positions will be revealed. From time to time, one or the other party may request a caucus to reassess its position or to engage in further planning. Negotiators will keep their principals or members informed, and may periodically request the adjournment of negotiations to allow for feedback or consultation.

From here, negotiations will gradually move to a *stage of crisis*, where pressure is increased in an attempt to extract more concessions. Sanctions are more seriously considered, impasses are frequent and deadlock may eventually be reached. Before this occurs, the parties may seriously search for alternatives and the bargaining range will have narrowed down considerably.

In the final stage, or *closing encounter*, agreement may have been reached on some issues but not on others. The decisions taken should be carefully summarised and recorded, since they will form the basis of the written agreement. Any incorrect wording or misconceptions may give rise to disputes in the future. Once a written agreement has been drawn up, it should be studied and signed by both parties – but only after each has ensured that their understanding of the provisions is correct. On issues where agreement has not yet been reached, both sides will start pushing for closure.

Negotiations do not always proceed smoothly. Most often they are marked by withdrawal or the threat of withdrawal, or they may be interrupted by labour/industrial action. These may bring an end to the negotiation process; however, most commonly, negotiations are resumed after reassessment by each side.

## The Opening Phase
### Establishing Climate
The opening phase of negotiations has a great impact on the rest of the proceedings, as it is during this stage that the climate for the entire negotiation process is established. Usually, both parties will attempt to establish a positive framework for the negotiations and emphasise common ground or point to mutual gain to be achieved from the negotiations. At the same time, each will be assessing the other's attitude and position, and a great deal of careful listening takes place.

### Establishing Positions
During the initial stages of negotiation, much time is devoted to establishing one's own position and attempting to discover the real position of the other party. Skilled negotiators will, from the outset, attempt to establish a position of dominance. This they do by making a very firm offer or demand and displaying great commitment. It is not necessary at this stage to engage in any lengthy arguments.

The opening offer or demand could be disproportionately low or high, or it could be more realistic. Some practitioners argue that an exaggerated opening bid allows more room for manoeuvring, but it is also dangerous, as it could be summarily rejected and have the effect of hardening attitudes and detracting from the credibility of the negotiator. Another suggested policy is to follow up an extreme opening bid with a more realistic one which, although still low or high, will then be more acceptable to the other side. This could prove useful, but could still detract from the credibility of the negotiator, particularly if they have already displayed firm commitment to their initial offer/demand. The negotiator would then have to find a very good reason for changing their stance so rapidly. The best approach is probably to set high but realistic targets and to negotiate around these for some time.

### Feeling out the Other Party
While confirming their own position, the negotiator tries to establish the degree of commitment on the other side. For this reason, it is advisable not to

talk too much during the initial stages of a negotiation session. Karas (1970) suggests that a good negotiator will attempt to discover more about the other side by:

- asking leading or loaded questions
- eliciting responses from persons other than the chief negotiator in the opposing team
- suggesting that the negotiators' party would like to receive more information
- trying to find out which are the other party's hard and soft lines
- noting reactions to statements and questions
- above all, listening to what the other party is saying.

The other party will, at the same time, be attempting to establish the negotiator's position. Consequently, the negotiator should be careful not to give too much away. They do so by deferring questions from the other party – for example, by asking for clarification, deflecting the question, providing ambiguous or selective answers or breaking down the question. The purpose is to gain time to think and to avoid intuitive answers or too many explanations.

## The Body of the Negotiation Process
### Bringing Argument

Arguments constitute the core of the negotiation process and should be carefully prepared. It is better to bring one strong argument rather than a range of weaker ones. Not all arguments supporting a particular point of view should be made from the beginning.

The beginning and the end of a message are the most important. The negotiator should first state their point of view, then supply the reason and follow this up with a summary or reiteration of their position. They will also be more persuasive if, from the outset, they take into account different points of view and provide counterarguments.

Arguments should be brief and to the point. Conclusions should be clearly stated, and the message can be repeated as often as possible, even by different members of the negotiating team.

Sound argument requires sound knowledge, and if the chief negotiator themself does not know enough about a particular issue, they should defer to another member of the team or, if allowed, use the services of an expert. Points of view may be backed up by illustrations, statistics or written communications.

The negotiator should aim at persuading the other party that they will benefit from agreement. This can be done by pointing to the disadvantages that would ensue if no agreement is reached and even by subtle threats and bluffs. They should try to find common ground, emphasise this, and attempt to make their stance sound as reasonable as possible.

When negotiations revolve around a multitude of issues, it is preferable to commence with an issue which is easier to settle and, if possible, to link easier issues with more difficult ones.

### Countering the Other Party's Argument

The attention devoted to the presentation of the negotiator's own argument should be equalled by that devoted to the countering of the other party's argument. The negotiator adopts a critical stance, by:

- questioning the assumptions, statements of fact and conclusions of the other side
- challenging inconsistencies
- taking note of omissions
- pointing to emotionally biased arguments.

It is usually not advisable to reject the argument of the other party immediately, but the negotiator could:

- question the speaker's credibility
- point to the consequences of the proposal
- enlarge on the other party's weaknesses
- suggest that the other party revise its case.

During the entire process of argument and counterargument, the skilled negotiator will:

- seek clarification from the other side
- from time to time, summarise their own and the other party's point of view
- ensure that there is mutual understanding of matters dealt with
- at the same time measure progress.

### Displaying Commitment

In order to gain the necessary dominance, a negotiator should display commitment to their position. However, this commitment should not be rigid, particularly during the initial stage of negotiations. Instead, the negotiator should persuade the other party that they sincerely believe their offer/ demand to be fair and that only very sound argument from the other side will convince them to change their stance. As the negotiator moves nearer to their resistance point, their commitment should become firmer, but they should not be absolutely inflexible unless they have decided that they are prepared to take the consequences.

*Granting Concessions*

It is expected that, during the negotiation process, both sides will make concessions; however, a trade-off of concessions on a one-for-one basis is not always necessary or advisable. The skilled negotiator will not commence granting concessions until they have the full picture and have felt out the other party – unless they have purposely opened with an exaggerated offer or demand and intend to make a large initial concession in order to bring movement.

Usually, concessions are granted slowly, commencing with concessions on smaller issues and moving gradually to larger ones. An initial unwillingness to grant concessions signals commitment and firmness, but care should be exercised that positions do not become hardened. Concessions on particular items may be larger at the beginning and become smaller as negotiators move closer to each other, although a larger concession may be made towards the end to signify a final offer. A good strategy is to link concessions to previous ones, and to indicate that a concession is now expected in return.

In some instances, a concession from the other side may not be accepted immediately. The negotiator will indicate that it is insufficient and suggest that it be revised.

The number, type and rate of concessions will eventually depend on bargaining power, and the good negotiator will make concessions only if forced to do so or if they wish to bring about movement. However, they should remain flexible, always bearing in mind the golden rule of concessions, according to Karas (1970): do not give too much too soon, too much too late, or too little too late.

*Caucusing*

Periodic caucuses are necessary in order to reassess, replan or consider a concession made by the other side, but they are also a sound bargaining strategy.

The temporary withdrawal of one party allows the other time for consideration, particularly during moments of heightened tension. The other party may become uncertain and decide to move from previously held positions. Parties should agree on the approximate duration of caucuses and, where extensions are required, it is good form to ask permission.

*Impasses*

Impasses may be reached at any point during hard bargaining. These are not deadlocks; rather, in this case both sides are still prepared to move, but neither wants to move first. It is left to the skilled negotiator to bring about new movement, preferably by the other side. This the negotiator may do by:

- changing from a competitive to a co-operative mode
- changing the shape of their own package

- letting the other side know that they (the other party) cannot afford to remain where they are
- suggesting a change in the other party's package
- encouraging the other party to move by indicating that, if they do, the negotiator might also move
- limiting issues, summarising developments and pointing to areas requiring movement
- suggesting that both parties move together by making a concession linked to one from the other side
- suggesting that both parties refer back to their principals or constituents
- providing the other party with the necessary face savers.

Where tension is high, it might be advisable to move to another agenda item for the time being, to call for a caucus, to introduce a red herring or to use humour. Usually impasses arise because one or both sides become overcommitted. If this is the case, the negotiator should search for a means by which the other party can graciously move from their overcommitted position.

### Deadlock
Deadlock is reached when neither party is prepared to move any further. Both are prepared to declare a dispute and to risk sanctions from the other side. Deadlocks merely test the strength and commitment of the parties. They serve to soften positions and to initiate new movement. This is proved by the fact that most dispute procedures provide for renewed negotiation.

### 'Final' Offers/Demands
Once the parties approach the expected contract zone, 'final' offers or demands are put on the table, with the purpose of achieving a settlement which is as near to the negotiator's target as possible. Final offers should be presented in such a manner that the other party is convinced of their seriousness. The offer/demand should be clear, firm and precisely phrased, but it can be linked to alternatives and time spans.

The other party must be allowed time to think. This is generally achieved by timing final offers and demands to coincide with the end of a particular negotiation session. When a final offer or demand is made by the other side, the negotiator should never accept immediately and should not overreact. By listening carefully, the negotiator will convince the other party that they are taking the matter seriously. In essence, final offers are not always final.

*Threats and Bluffs*

A threat serves as a reminder that one party can initiate sanctions against the other. A bluff, on the other hand, is a threat which that party has no intention of carrying out or is unable to carry out. Bluffs should not be engaged in without proper consideration, as the other side may call the bluff, leading to loss of face for the initiator. Threats, too, should be carefully planned and should not be of a spontaneous or idle nature. The other party should be convinced that the threat will, in fact, be executed. Karas (1970) suggests that negotiators should gradually raise the level of threats and should set an example by putting minor threats into action. Threats should be implied rather than spoken, mild rather than enormous, rational rather than emotional.

One of the best methods of countering a threat is to oblige the other party to articulate it. Very often the party will hesitate to do so, as they are then committed to carrying out the threat. The negotiator could also pretend that the threat is harmless, or that they have not heard it at all. Alternatively, the negotiator could face the threat head on and prove to the other party that its execution will in fact harm both parties.

*Sanctions*

In union–management negotiations, the ultimate sanction is a strike or a lockout, but less severe sanctions may be instituted when impasses or deadlocks are reached. These include a display of antagonism, temporary walkouts from negotiations, demonstrations, bad publicity, work-to-rules, go-slows and overtime bans. Sanctions are applied in escalating order, according to the severity of the situation.

Closure

Most negotiations will reach a stage where one or both parties realise that they are close to an agreement. One method of nudging the other party towards a final settlement is to agree in principle but to ask for something in addition, or to set certain conditions. The negotiator could also attempt to lure the other party into settlement by offering a deal, granting minor concessions or engaging in flattery. Alternatively, the negotiator could assume that agreement has been reached and start noting down the details or summarising the main points. Where the other party continues to hold back, the negotiator could express surprise at the fact that a settlement cannot be reached under the circumstances, point to the dangers or costs of not settling, or threaten to withdraw all other concessions if a final agreement is not reached (only if the negotiator has made the concessions conditional on a final settlement).

The negotiator should be assertive, even a little aggressive. They should not talk too much and should display a positive attitude. Once agreement has been reached, a document reflecting the terms and conditions is drawn up and signed by both parties.

## Negotiation Manoeuvres

In the previous section, discussion was about the art of negotiation. It is necessary also to mention the tactics which some negotiators, intent on gaining the upper hand, may apply. Many of these are negative by nature and, while they may prove useful in the short term, do not necessarily guarantee high-value outcomes. The following are among the best-known manoeuvres:

- **Deadlines:** Certain broad time limits for negotiations should be established. However, the skilled negotiator will not be coerced into meeting narrow deadlines, since these create unnecessary pressure. In the urgency of the moment, negotiators sometimes concede too readily, only to regret their actions once the agreement has been signed.
- **Limited authority:** A negotiator may, when faced with a difficult decision, hide behind the excuse that they do not have the necessary authority to make the decision. While all negotiators will from time to time refer back to their principals or constituents, they should have decision-making power within the parameters of their mandate. The best way to deal with a party who continues to plead limited authority is to request that they obtain a wider mandate or that they be replaced by someone capable of making the necessary decisions.
- **Statistics and averages:** Statistics do serve a purpose in that they may support an argument or point of view, but there are negotiators who will attempt to overwhelm the other party with statistical information which may have no meaning at all. Those subjected to this overuse should remember the adage, 'There are lies, lies, lies and statistics'. Statistics may be interpreted in many ways, and for every statistic there is often another which proves the opposite.
- **'Funny money':** Closely associated with the abusers of statistics are those who play around with figures to prove their arguments. By juggling figures, they attempt to show losses and gains which actually do not exist in practice – much like a trade union that tells management that they have saved the organisation a certain amount per employee per hour by not working overtime and still making the product.
- **Body language:** During negotiations the skilled negotiator will closely observe also the subtle, non-verbal communication from the other side. Much is revealed by looks, body movements, posture and gestures. The negotiator should, however, be aware that if the other party is skilled, they may be purposely misleading them. The negotiator may pretend boredom

by drumming their fingers or a pencil on the desk, try to appear confident and dominant by standing with their hands on their hips, or assume an indifferent attitude by placing their feet on the desk and staring out of the window. It is best not to pay too much attention to such actions.

- **Shock tactics and irritants:** A negotiator may attempt to put the other party off their stride by doing or saying something which the negotiator knows will shock the other party, or through irritating behaviour. In the process of recovering from the shock or distraction, the other party may readily concede on an issue, because the other party is not concentrating fully on the matter at hand.

- **Fatigue:** One tactic often used is to continue negotiating until the other party virtually drops from fatigue and, in their desire to end the negotiations, readily comes to an agreement.

- **Change of pace:** Negotiations usually proceed at a relatively even pace, but a negotiator may, at a certain point, speed up the process in an attempt to rush the other party into settlement.

- **Deliberate errors:** Particularly when summarising the other party's argument or the points of agreement, a negotiator may deliberately make an error. If the other party does not listen carefully, that party may agree that the summary is correct, thus weakening their own position.

- **Changing negotiators:** A change of negotiators may be resorted to with the purpose of gaining time, since the new negotiator is not up to date with developments during negotiations and a great deal of backtracking has to occur. It is disturbing for the other party to suddenly have to deal with a new person. There should be an agreement that no changes will be made without the consent of both parties.

- **The 'bad cop, good cop' trick:** Here one member of the team purposely acts in an aggressive manner and harangues the other side. When a crisis is reached, another member of the team steps in with a much kinder approach. The other party is usually more willing to deal with the second negotiator, who then starts from an advantageous position.

- **Addressing the weakest member:** Where a negotiator is unable to elicit sufficient information from the other side or where they are of the opinion that there is some disagreement in the other team, they may attempt to elicit comments or answers – or even agreement – from the weakest member of the other team. Alternatively, the negotiator may harangue this person in the hope of breaking them down.

- **The defence–attack spiral:** Certain negotiators deliberately initiate attacks on the other party, hoping that they will react defensively. This leads to a defence–attack spiral which detracts from the real issues. A skilled negotiator will absorb such emotional attacks and wait for the right moment to make their own, more rational, counterattacks.

- **Acted emotions:** Negotiators may be very good actors who can act out emotions such as frustration, anger, disappointment and sadness at will. It is best to allow emotional outbursts, whether acted or not, to subside and not to react intuitively to these.
- **Killing with kindness:** There are negotiators who treat the other party with such kindness that it is difficult for these persons to oppose or argue with them. The purpose is to change enemies to allies, thereby weakening the stand of the other side.
- **Interruptions:** Interruptions can prove very useful, particularly when negotiations are progressing unfavourably for one's own side or when a party needs time to reconsider but does not wish to request a caucus. Experienced negotiators will determine beforehand that no interruptions should occur.
- **'Red herrings' or straw issues:** Here the negotiator deliberately introduces one or more issues which are of no real importance to them but on which they spend an inordinate amount of time. This may distract the other party from the more important aspects of the negotiations.

As mentioned, many of the manoeuvres described here have negative effects and they should therefore be used with care.

## Agreements: The Outcomes of Successful Negotiation

The purpose of collective bargaining is to reach agreement. Minutes are kept during negotiation meetings. Once agreement has been reached, a formal agreement is drawn up and signed by both parties.

### Types of Agreements
#### The Agreement to Bargain
The first type of agreement to be reached between the parties to the bargaining relationship is the agreement to bargain. Thus, the recognition agreement or the constitution of a bargaining association, both of which contain basic procedures for the conduct of the bargaining relationship and for the settlement of possible disputes, forms the cornerstone of the relationship.

#### Wages, Conditions of Service and Procedures
Certain substantive conditions of employment may be subject to further negotiation at regular intervals. Therefore, it is preferable that these be contained in a separate agreement. Wages in particular are subject to regular

amendment. This is why, in certain bargaining relationships, a main agreement might cover basic procedures dealing with grievances, discipline, lay-offs, retrenchment and consultation on technological innovation, as well as basic substantive conditions of employment such as hours of work, benefits and holiday pay, while another agreement will cover wages and other substantive conditions which may change from time to time. Alternatively, the main agreement could merely be amended after each negotiation session, or wages could constitute a schedule attached to the main agreement.

### Subject-related Agreements

Besides the recognition agreement and substantive wage agreements negotiated from time to time, a union with a strong plant-level presence may wish to become involved in health and safety issues, or to negotiate agreements covering certain eventualities, such as retrenchment and the introduction of new technology. Also, the employer, if they wish to introduce changes in the organisation and desire the co-operation of the union and the employees, may enter into the necessary agreements with the union. One such agreement is the productivity agreement.

## Monitoring Agreements

Once an agreement has been reached and signed by both parties, it will be necessary to obtain all-round commitment to its successful implementation. Legal enforcement of an agreement or the declaration of a dispute becomes necessary only when one of the parties has acted in bad faith. Where good faith exists, the concern is more with monitoring the agreement to see that it works. Consequently, follow-up meetings may take place in order to discuss problems which have occurred, or to renegotiate decisions which have proved unimplementable in practice.

It is the task of the chief negotiator on each side to ensure that the members of their organisation are acquainted with the terms of the agreement and that they adhere to these. The employer has the duty to inform members of management of the agreement and to train managers and supervisors in its implementation. The union, on the other hand, should furnish its members with accurate information and urge acceptance of the terms agreed upon. Management, too, may play some part in disseminating information to employees.

Both sides, through their appointed agents, will monitor the implementation of the agreement by the other side and, should any breach occur, will raise this immediately with those responsible for implementation.

### Enforceability of Agreements

In South Africa, Section 23 of the Labour Relations Act 66 of 1995 provides for the enforceability of all collective agreements. Disputes about the implementation of collective agreements are submitted to the Commission for Conciliation, Mediation and Arbitration (CCMA) for conciliation. If this fails, either party may request that the dispute be submitted to arbitration. Furthermore, Section 23(4) provides that any party to an indefinite agreement may withdraw from such agreement after giving reasonable notice. In the case of fixed-term agreements, such as wage agreements, the parties are subject to the agreement for its duration, unless its implementation becomes impossible.

## Disputes and Coercive Action

Where voluntarism predominates and where the freedom to strike is recognised, disputes and coercive action by either party form an integral part of the collective bargaining process. Negotiation does not always end in agreement. While agreement may eventually be reached, the process could be marked by repeated disputes and actions along the way. The reason for this is self-explanatory. At times of complete disagreement between the parties, the coercive power of each party is again brought into play. Employers will attempt to oblige acceptance of their terms by withholding the opportunity for work, while employees will attempt to achieve the same ends by the joint withholding of their labour from the employer or by otherwise damaging the business of the employer.

Thus, actions in the form of lockouts, strikes, go-slows, work-to-rules and product boycotts may flow from the negotiation process. They are not intended to put an end to negotiation, although, in the extreme, they may. Their purpose is to serve as pressure tactics in the negotiation process. Figure 9.2 illustrates the development of the negotiation process from the inception of the relationship to the point of agreement, via the display of coercive power.

## Conclusion

The art of negotiation is not easily acquired. In general, the conduct of a negotiation session requires a great deal of knowledge, hard work, preparation and practice, and the outcome of a particular negotiation session is never certain until the final agreement has been signed. It is impossible within the context of this book to devote full and detailed attention to the actual practice of negotiation.

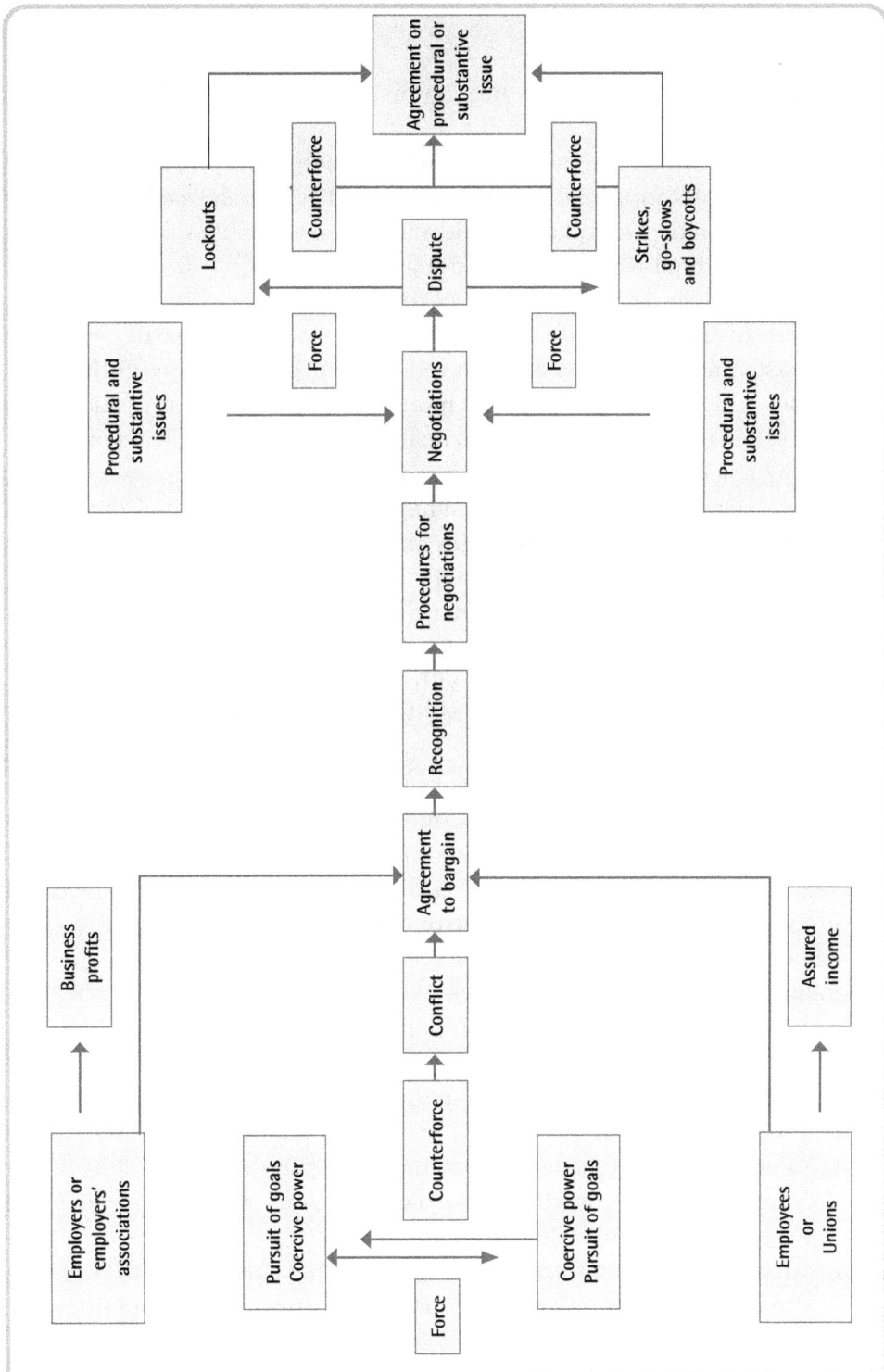

Figure 9.2: Development of the negotiation process

## Suggested Questions/Tasks

1. In your opinion, how can negotiators utilise social influence in the workplace?
2. Consider a unionised workplace where there have been substantive retrenchments in the last six months. Identify and define a number of challenges in the workplace and develop three workable solutions for one challenge. Propose how you would share your findings with management.
3. Following huge job losses at a workplace where there is evidence of a history of impasses and adversity between conflicting parties, you are requested to negotiate to arrange reduced working hours with the trade union, within the next calendar month. Explain how you would equip yourself to remain resilient and to deal with the stress of the negotiations.
4. Follow a salary negotiation between parties on a media source of your choice. Discuss the parties' original negotiation strategies, how the parties responded to each other's strategies and if the strategies changed. What is the settlement point compared to the opening positions of each party?
5. Prepare a negotiation planning sheet.
6. Follow a salary negotiation between parties on a media source of your choice. How did the parties deal with deadlock/impasse?
7. Many administrative processes are likely to be replaced by streamlined, web-based self-service processes with very little human involvement. What meaningful alternative learning paths would you suggest for unemployed administrative personnel, considering their administrative skills, to ensure continued decent employment?
8. Think of a situation in which you and your group would be involved in negotiations with another party. (This need not necessarily be a labour management negotiation.) Submit a written report, including the following:
   a. Describe your situation, the other party and the issues involved.
   b. List the persons you would involve in your negotiation team. (Explain why you have selected them and what their roles will be.)
   c. Assess how strong (powerful) you are in relation to the other party and explain why (consider also the other party's strengths).
   d. Explain where you think your contract zone will be and how you reached that conclusion.
   e. Establish whether there would/would not be a possibility of reverting to a more collaborative mode and give reasons for your opinion.

# Sources

Carnevale, PJ & De Dreu, CK. W. 2006. 'Motive: The negotiator's raison d'êetre', in *Negotiation Theory and Research*, edited by LL Thompson. Evanston: Psychosocial Press: 55–76.

De Oliveira Dias, M. 2020. 'The four-type negotiation matrix: A model for assessing negotiation processes'. *British Journal of Education* 8(5): 40–57.

Ebner, N, Lande, J, Matz, D & Schneider, AK. 2017. 'The definition of negotiation: A play in three acts'. *Journal of Dispute Resolution* 1: Article 4.

French, J & Raven, B. 1959. *The Bases of Social Power*. Ann Arbor: University of Michigan Press.

Hennebert, MA & Pérez-Lauzon, S. 2019. 'The practice of collective bargaining in the private sector in Quebec (Canada): The changing "rules of the game"'. *Industrial Relations Journal* 50(3): 240–255.

Karas, CL. 1970. *The Negotiating Game*. New York: Thomas Y Cromwell.

Khan, MA & Baldini, GM. 2019. 'Understanding the scope and importance of negotiation', in *The Palgrave Handbook of Cross-Cultural Business Negotiation*, edited by MA Khan & N Ebner. Cham: Palgrave Macmillan: 19–51.

Kochan, TA. 1980a. *Collective Bargaining and Industrial Relations*. Homewood: Richard D Irwin.

Kochan, TA. 1980b. 'Industrial relations research: An agenda for the 1980s'. *Monthly Labor Review* 103(9): 20–25.

Lande, J. 2017. 'Taming the jungle of negotiation theories', in *The Negotiator's Desk Reference*, edited by C Honeyman & A Kupfer Schneider. St Paul, MN: DRI Press: 87–105.

Lexico. 2021. 'Scope'. https://www.lexico.com/definition/scope (Accessed 6 September 2021).

Marshall, A. 2013. *Principles of Economics*, 8th edition. London: Palgrave Macmillan.

Online Etymology Dictionary. 2021a. 'Bargain'. https://www.etymonline.com/word/bargain (Accessed 6 September 2021).

Online Etymology Dictionary. 2021b. 'Negotiate'. https://www.etymonline.com/search?q=negotiate (Accessed 6 September 2021).

Rackham, N & Carlisle, J. 1978a. 'The effective negotiator – Part 1: The behaviour of successful negotiators'. *Journal of European Industrial Training* 2(6): 6–11.

Rackham, N & Carlisle, J. 1978b. 'The effective negotiator – Part 2: Planning for negotiations'. *Journal of European Industrial Training* 2(7): 2–5.

Walton, RE & McKersie, RB. 1965. *A Behavioural Theory of Labour Negotiations*. New York: McGraw-Hill.

Whiting, K. 2020. 'These are the top 10 work skills of tomorrow – and how long it takes to learn them'. World Economic Forum, 21 October 2020. https://www.weforum.org/agenda/2020/10/top-10-work-skills-of-tomorrow-how-long-it-takes-to-learn-them/ (Accessed 6 September 2021).

Zartman, IW. 1988. 'Common elements in the analysis of the negotiation process'. *Negotiation Journal* 4(1): 31–43.

# PART 3:
## Labour Relations Subprocesses

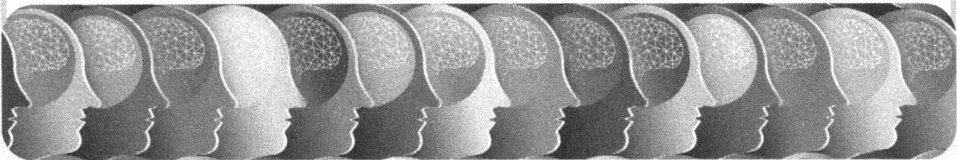

# 10

# Conflict Management

## Chapter Outline

# Overview

As all individuals have different personalities, conflict in their daily interactions is unavoidable. During interactions, if one person imposes their opinions and views on the other, this may cause unhappiness, resentment and rejection, subsequently leading to conflict. This is also seen when individuals join groups with the intention of strengthening the sense of their own identity or in some cases to exercise control over their own destiny.

Groups are interdependent, with members forming relationships with one another and most often sharing scarce resources. Progressively, and as a group storms, some members may apply tactics to prevent others from achieving their goals, to threaten their identity or to control the resources, most likely culminating in conflict. Inevitably, this results in a power play between the group members. Competence, capability and the level of commitment of members also affect how different groups interact and relate to each other. Where each group perceives the other as holding power, they may decide to institute procedures to regulate their relationship. This happens in collective bargaining, for instance, where parties representing different groups apply different types of power – such as legitimate, coercive and information power – to impose themselves.

Where resources or control are unevenly distributed, a structural imbalance occurs. The party which is relatively disadvantaged may seemingly submit to the other, but conflict will remain covert and manifest itself in different forms, such as through sabotage or a go-slow in the case of a labour relations context. Where there is strong power competition, a trigger incident may well lead to overt, serious conflict, which can be expressed through the withdrawal of labour by employees or by the employer suspending the provision of benefits perceived to be privileges and not rights.

The virtual work environment has also brought its own challenges affecting group dynamics. The geographically dispersed nature of interaction through electronical means and cultural heterogeneity can negatively affect communication patterns and stifle decision-making processes. Conflict is then expressed through non-responsiveness and lack of participation.

Whether conflict will be resolved or escalate depends on the existence of moderators or aggravators, and on the history of the relationship, the degree of trust between the parties and the manner in which the parties communicate with each other. If there are numerous 'aggravators', and if this is compounded by a poor relationship and inadequate communication, the conflict is bound to escalate until a stage is reached where the parties are not able to come to a settlement without outside assistance. The factors which prove that conflict is escalating may themselves cause further escalation.

Where conflict has reached unmanageable proportions, a third party will have to intervene through facilitation or mediation. The mediator may have the authority to impose a settlement, as in the case of arbitration, but this does not always resolve the conflict. A settlement essentially requires both parties to comply with the order of the intervening third party, but this outcome will not necessarily make both parties happy. The third party's purpose would be to move the conflicting parties to a position where they agree on a mutually acceptable solution. This is a very complex and time-consuming process, but one which in the end may yield the best results.

# The Conflict Phenomenon

## Conflict and Commonality as Endemic to Relationships

The term 'conflict' denotes the meeting of opposing forces or persons. In essence, every person stands in opposition to others in the attempt to guard their own or personal interests. As unique human beings, individuals will strive to uphold their individual identities, which are different from those of other persons in a group. Therefore, conflict is endemic to all relationships. However, people do share many common traits, interests, values and goals, and they seek to form relationships with those with whom they can find common ground. It is this commonality that strengthens the relationship, and which enables the parties to handle conflict in a constructive manner.

Conflict can occur in most group development stages, such as forming, storming, norming, performing and adjourning. In particular, conflict is likely to manifest in the early stages of group development, when groups are forming and storming. During the normalisation, performance and adjourning stages, it is expected that commonality will prevail, and individuals will put their differences aside and pursue common interests.

## Group Formation

As social beings, individuals' sense of identity is further strengthened by their membership of a group or groups. People join a particular group because it is reflective of their own ideology, values, interests and goals. The shared identity of the group enhances their identity.

Alternatively, an individual may join a particular group not so much for the commonality among the group members, but because membership of the group allows the person to gain some form of control over their destiny. With this comes the fulfilment of more basic physical, social and economic needs.

Membership of a group grants the individual a particular place in society, different and opposing to that of other individuals. Even in the group itself, individuals and sub-groups will stand in opposition to each other, giving rise to intragroup conflict; however, again, commonality will usually ensure the constructive handling of such conflicts. Groups also develop their own cultures, norms and rules, which will be different from those of other groups and are often not understood or recognised by other groups.

The following is evident from the foregoing:

- Humans have a natural tendency towards group formation.
- Groups so formed will have goals, values, interests, cultures, norms and even ideologies which are different from those of other groups.

- The achievement of both an individual and social identity and of some sense of control over a person's own destiny is as important as the fulfilment of people's basic needs for food, shelter and security.

## Group Storming

Storming can be characterised by the dominance of one group over another, an unwillingness to co-operate and share information, and in some cases even elements of complete withdrawal. A low level of consensus will emerge, with both groups maintaining their independence and identities. While it may appear as if there is something wrong in the relationship during this stage, tension and potential conflict should in fact be expected during storming; however, great awareness of the negative effects is required. To reiterate, conflict is inevitable, and the relationship will normalise over time. At that point the parties' level of performance will improve as group members or groups mature enough to realise the impact of divergence and the importance of maximising commonality.

## Intergroup Relationships

Groups form part of a wider societal order and may themselves seek alignment with other groups with whom they share common interests, goals, values or ideology. On the other hand, they may have to coexist with other groups despite not having much in common with them. They may have to establish relationships with these groups, either because they depend on one another or because they rely on the same, often scarce, resources.

Another important factor in these relationships is communication, which should in fact help overcome differences between group members. In these instances, based on perceptions, preconceived notions and stereotypes, group members may prefer communication mechanisms that intimidate or seek to destabilise the other in order to pursue their own interests. The relationships formed are not those to which the group members would be naturally inclined, and they may even enter them with great reluctance. Yet, even here, some commonality of interests exists, although it may not be openly acknowledged. It is between such groups that conflict, if not correctly handled, may reach unmanageable proportions.

## Heterogeneous Groups

A growing phenomenon in recent years is the need to embrace diversity in group composition. This refers not only to race or gender, but also to heterogeneity related to competence, capability, experience and networks, all of which can translate into group effectiveness. Heterogeneity in groups is beneficial in that it promotes group interdependence and information sharing. There tends to be less competition in heterogenous groups.

## Virtual Groups

The digital world has revolutionised intergroup relationships. Instead of physical or face-to-face interactions, groups located in different geographical areas have to meet virtually, which can affect members' thought processes, disrupt the exchange of information, reduce the quality of decision making and, consequently, create incompatible wishes or even irreconcilable priorities. These conflicting expectations may result in group members preserving their independence, becoming less confident in the decision-making process and generally becoming suspicious of what the other group members are doing or saying on the other side of the electronic communication line.

To re-emphasise, just as in normal face-to-face intergroup interactions, it is essential for virtual groups to focus on common goals instead of differences, as a focus on the latter may lead to their relationship becoming disrupted by a distributive (win-lose) approach instead of being characterised by integrative deliberations (concern for the other group members).

## Intergroup Conflict

The possible sources of conflict between non-aligned groups include differences as regards values, interests, goals, ideologies, cultures and norms. If a particular group was able to pursue its own interests and goals in the framework of its own ideology, culture and norms, it would never come into open conflict with another group. Unfortunately, this would be possible only if each group inhabited its own island. Societal (and now global) existence obliges people to interact and share resources. Groups cannot exist in isolation and are usually interdependent. Thus, inevitably, the goals and interests of one group will come into conflict with those of another.

The manner in which such conflict is handled will largely depend on:
- the nature of the relationship which was formed
- the availability or otherwise of resources for each group
- the fulfilment of basic and other needs
- the acknowledgment by each group of the other's identity and legitimacy
- the effectiveness of the communication between them
- their acknowledgement of interdependence or common interests
- their perceptions of the other party
- the contextual framework in which decisions are expected to be taken by the groups collectively.

## Power Realities in Intergroup Conflict

Where one group forms an obstacle to the achievement of another group's goals, or where both compete for the same resources, power becomes an important factor. Each party will try to muster as much power as it can in order to achieve its goals or maintain its interests in opposition to those of the other party. This results in a power battle between the parties, which, if allowed to, may culminate in unmanageable conflict.

If they want to prevent conflict and the concomitant power battles, the parties need to engage in rational and objective problem solving or use processes to reach some form of settlement. This can happen only if:

- the parties have established a relatively healthy relationship
- they acknowledge their interdependence and common interests
- they are subject to the same legal framework
- norms and ideology are not in absolute conflict
- each party acknowledges that the other holds power
- collective problem-solving mechanisms are in place.

Collective bargaining is an example of the type of process which can be established between opposing parties. These processes rest on the acknowledgement by one party that the other party also holds power and that they may each inflict harm on each other.

However, very often one party holds less power or is perceived as holding no power. This is usually the result of a structural imbalance between the parties. Different groups occupy different places in society, hence the concepts of class and status. The place which a group occupies may give it a position of dominance over other groups. This is usually accompanied by control over resources, with resultant inequalities.

The greater the structural imbalances, the greater the potential for conflict, but where one group is dominant, the other group(s) may not yet hold enough power to counter the power of that group. Consequently, the latter group(s) may seem to surrender. Yet conflict will remain hidden and, since no individual or group is completely powerless, the weaker group(s) will continue to build a power base until such time as it (they) can openly confront the dominant group.

## The Trigger Incident

In a situation of power abuse, divergent interests, covert conflict or continued power competition, it may happen that an insignificant trigger incident leads to major conflict. The mistake often made is to concentrate on the events related to the trigger incident instead of dealing with the conflict inherent in the relationship. It is necessary to analyse the relationship as a whole in order to establish the underlying causes of the conflict situation. Only once this has been done can the conflict be effectively managed or resolved.

### Psychological Contract Breach

Defined as the perception that a promise has been broken, psychological contract breach occurs when either employees or employers feel that expectations regarding certain obligations are not being fulfilled. These tacit expectations are normally formed right at the beginning of an employment relationship, at times during the interviewing process. After officially joining the organisation, and once they realise that their expectations are not being fulfilled, employees with common interests can form a group or affiliate with a trade union to act against the employer in respect of the perceived broken promises. Unmet expectations break down trust and prevent co-operation. This could potentially escalate into conflict that might get out of hand if concerted efforts are not undertaken to clarify misunderstandings.

## Variables Determining Conflict Levels

Anstey (1999) lists a number of variables which will collectively determine whether conflict, once triggered, will remain at a relatively low and manageable level or will escalate to unmanageable and even violent proportions. These 'moderators' and 'aggravators' are interactive, and no variable should be seen in isolation.

### Causes or Antecedents of Conflict

Where the cause of the conflict is found in the inability of one party to achieve satisfaction of an interest not involving a basic necessity, conflict levels may remain relatively low, as will the potential for escalation. On the other hand, the possibility of the conflict escalating is high if:
- a party's identity is threatened
- one party feels that they have lost control over their own destiny
- values (often emanating from ideological beliefs) are at issue
- one party cannot fulfil their basic needs
- power struggles develop between the parties.

### The Number of Issues

Conflict is usually moderate if one or a few matters are at issue. However, the type of issue is also important. Matters such as an attack on identity or denial of basic needs can in themselves lead to heightened conflict. Too many interest-based issues may also raise the level of conflict.

### Recognition of Legitimacy

One of the greatest causes of conflict escalation is the failure of one party to recognise the legitimacy of the other party, or the legitimacy of the issues raised by the latter. Conflict increases if one party refuses to acknowledge that the other party occupies a legitimate place in society (or the organisation), that they have the right to raise issues and that the issues themselves may be legitimate. This should be understood in relation to the fact that non-recognition of legitimacy denies the identity of the other party and their right to exercise control over their destiny.

### Intra- and Intergroup Dynamics

Where there is high group cohesion and pressure on group leaders to deliver desired results, conflict levels tend to rise. The more closely knit the group, the greater will be the support for the leader in instances where the leader threatens to use, or actually does use, coercive power. In fact, a highly cohesive group may urge a leader to take actions which the leader themself might otherwise not consider wise.

The degree of cohesion in a group often stands in direct relation to its isolation from other groups. Groups which have little or no contact with other groups turn in upon themselves. In these cases there is no cross-cutting group membership (where some members from two different groups are also joint members of a third group).

### Leadership

The type of leadership in a group influences the level of conflict. Where a leader is power-hungry, aggressive and inflexible, conflict will escalate. On the other hand, flexibility on the part of the leader promotes more peaceful and rational settlements. It may happen that a leader needs to entrench their position. They may be losing their following and may 'create' issues in order to draw the group together under their leadership. If this is the case, the person attempting to facilitate a resolution could either allow another, more generally acceptable, leader to emerge or allow the existing leader the necessary credibility to make them feel secure in their position.

### Aspirations

Where aspirations or expectations are high, the potential for conflict escalation increases. This can also happen if the group has been promised certain benefits, either by those in control or by their leadership. If these do not materialise, there will be general discontent and the potential for conflict.

## Size of the Threat

If the threat from the other party is relatively insignificant, conflict can normally be confined to manageable proportions. The greater the threat, the greater the possibility of escalation.

## Uncertainty

Human beings have a desire for certainty – to know where they are placed and to have some idea as to what the future holds. The individual's desire for certainty is rooted in the need to exercise some measure of control over their own destiny.

In times of change or when the group is kept ignorant of future plans, the potential for conflict increases. Uncertainty is often caused by ineffective communication, rumour-mongering and an overactive organisational grapevine. Moreover, trust-based and transparent relationships tend to lead to less uncertainty.

## Common Norms/Standards

Where norms or standards of behaviour are established by mutual agreement, or where both groups subscribe to the same norms, these can be applied to prevent extreme or unacceptable behaviours. If, for example, all people in a society support the rule of law and respect the lawmakers and law enforcers, crime is more easily controlled. The opposite is, of course, also sometimes true, especially in South Africa.

Acceptance of mutually agreed standards and the establishment of processes to enforce the law rely on the consensual application of power. If one party imposes the standards, the other party may regard this as an abuse of power and reject the standards so established, even if they essentially agree with these standards.

## Reciprocity

Reciprocity refers to an interchange of behaviour, and it is one of the standards of fairness. It means that both sides must be prepared to give. If the relationship is not reciprocal, the party which does most of the giving will look for ways to re-establish a balance. This they will do by developing their power base, withdrawing co-operation and even by inflicting harm on the other party.

Reciprocity stands in an inverse relationship to structural imbalance. The less reciprocity there is, the greater will be the structural imbalance and potential for conflict escalation.

Interaction between Aggravators and Moderators

It has become evident that the 'aggravators' and 'moderators' do not function in isolation. The existence of a number of aggravators will exponentially increase the potential for or level of conflict. However, this may be partly nullified by strong moderators. Furthermore, the history of the relationship, the communication between the parties and their perceptions of each other will provide the framework for any situation which arises and will partly determine the course to be adopted.

## Broken Promises: Psychological Contract Violation

Following countless attempts to secure a job, Zandile Kamogelo eventually landed herself a new position as a sales executive at InkaMatt (Pty) Ltd. She considered this an opportunity that she would use to contribute to the growth of the company and advance her career in the retail environment. As part of the selection process, Zandile was subjected to various assessment processes for determining whether the much-needed chemistry between herself, the job and the organisation was present. In fact, according to her, one thing that attracted her to this company was its compelling employee value proposition, which included InkaMatt's commitment to learning and development, its flexible work arrangements and its competitive remuneration packages for attracting and retaining talent.

Three weeks after taking up her new position, Zandile enquired from her manager, Mr Matt, about the flexible work arrangement. She said that during her interview, the human resource (HR) manager, Ms Inga Mogale, had indicated that employees in the sales division qualify for one day out of office per week in exchange for achieving a sales target of 100 per cent. In response, the sales manager indicated that this option is not viable given the nature of the business, as customers come on site to view and purchase vehicles. This was not well received by Zandile, who felt that the company had violated a tacit expectation which had influenced her final decision to join the organisation. Zandile became disgruntled and gradually lost confidence in her manager, as she felt he was unreliable and untrustworthy.

## Dimensions and Components of Conflict

The dimensions of conflict are those aspects that provide a framework for diagnosing the root causes and types of conflict, as well as analysing how conflict escalates. These aspects relate to the situation and individual behaviour, including sociocultural (culture, perceived status and class) potentialities, that affect our interpretation of the meaning of reality and the social norms we use to judge reality. A conflict space is therefore intangible and delineated by how conflict develops and evolves over time, and is subject to the components discussed below.

### Structure
The structure of conflict relates to the allocation of resources, unequal power distribution, geographical constraints, and the organisational hierarchy, all of which create sociocultural distance between parties and lead to tendencies of opposition. The greater the distance, the more likely it is that parties will oppose each other. For instance, a potential for conflict between management and employees exists where the latter feel less empowered in the relationship. Likewise, management may develop a tendency to oppose the demands of employees if the cultural norms of the latter are perceived to be counterproductive.

### Deep-rooted Conflict
Deep-rooted conflict originates from potent identity factors such as race, religion, culture, language and so on, which people use to mobilise against unequal distribution of resources or power. Conflict arising from these deep-rooted factors is characterised by win-lose adversarial interactions. Often, a party in this situation will be willing to relinquish their power only if they perceive that greater benefit lies in co-operation.

### Values and Norms
The impact of standards of behaviour (norms) on conflict has already been dealt with in the previous sections. Coupled with these are the beliefs each party hold about the other and their opinions regarding matters of mutual interest. The greater the distance between the beliefs of the two parties, the greater are the chances that conflict may endure indefinitely, causing damage to the relationship.

### Balancing of Interests
Inherently, parties in the employment relationship are continuously involved in a struggle to balance their interests. These interests vary over time and evolve as new expectations emerge, which ultimately changes the structure of the conflict. A collaborative act will be triggered by the willingness of the parties to find commonality.

### Communication
Information plays a crucial role in reducing or even eliminating conflict. Lack of access to information or an excess thereof, together with differing interpretations, has the potential to escalate conflict. Moreover, parties should

be encouraged to select and use relevant information with clearly defined goals in joint problem solving and decision making.

## Signs of Conflict Escalation

Where there are few inhibiting factors, or where conflict is badly handled, the conflict tends to escalate. Anstey (1999) identifies a number of signs which serve as indicators that conflict is escalating. It is interesting to note that these indicators of escalation at the same time serve to further raise conflict levels.

As conflict escalates, the following will occur:

- The number of issues increases and may reach a point where the original issue is overshadowed by a myriad other complaints.
- As issues increase, demands become bigger.
- Parties hear only what they want to hear. They give and receive selective information.
- Communication can break down completely.
- Coalitions are formed among different groups and with parties not involved in the original conflict situation.
- The relationship between the parties becomes more adversarial, as they view each other as enemies.
- The group itself becomes more closely knit, as its members see themselves as threatened by the common enemy. In the extreme, they develop a mob identity.
- The other party is stereotyped, even demonised. This de-individualisation of the persons in the other group accounts for the fact that persons who engage in acts of violence often see these as justifiable. The perpetrators themselves relinquish their individuality by their membership of the mob. Equally, they do not see the members of the other group as individuals, but as part of a malicious force.
- As conflict escalates, group members may turn against those leaders who want to resolve the conflict, the result being a change in the leadership structure, where the 'hawks' replace the 'doves'.
- Coercive action by one party elicits a reaction from the other, leading to increasingly violent behaviours.

Conflict which has escalated to unmanageable proportions feeds on itself. It escalates in ever-widening circles. Also, some persons or groups actually thrive on conflict. It becomes the focus of their being. Consequently, they may resist any attempt at de-escalation or resolution of the conflict situation.

# Standard Approaches to Conflict Resolution

## Resolution versus Settlement

In the employment relationship, the parties usually see an agreement of some kind as ending the conflict between the parties. This could be a misconception. The kind of settlement reached by, for example, the adversarial collective bargaining process may take the form of a compromise, often achieved because one party holds more power than the other. In these situations, one or both parties may remain dissatisfied, which heightens the potential for further conflict. Therefore, it cannot always be said that the conflict has been resolved. To achieve resolution of conflict there should be:

- no coercion of one party by the other or by a third party in the form of an arbitrator or enforcer
- mutual satisfaction with the outcome
- a reduced possibility of further conflict
- an improvement in the relationship, which should thereafter be placed on a sounder footing.

If possible, disputes should be resolved by the parties themselves. Where this does not happen it becomes necessary for a third person or body to intervene. Such intervention can take numerous forms.

## Authoritarian Intervention

Where conflict is deep-rooted or has escalated to unmanageable proportions, it will be impossible to resolve without the intervention of a third party. In situations where the parties are inflicting harm upon each other and where behaviour is of a violent or disruptive nature, it may be necessary first to use authority structures in order to restore a sense of order. This will not resolve the conflict, but it will allow for conflict resolution processes to be set in motion. The authorities used should be those respected by both parties. (See the section entitled 'Recognising Differing Paradigms'.) Once the violence has subsided, attempts at resolution can begin.

## Conciliation, Mediation and Arbitration

In labour relations, third-party intervention usually takes the form of conciliation, mediation or arbitration. It is, on the whole, best suited to the resolution of conflict about the rights of either party. While third-party intervention may result in settlement, it may not necessarily resolve the conflict, or it may leave both parties dissatisfied, upon which they have the option to refer the dispute to the Labour Court. Third-party facilitation is regarded as a more effective intervention in addressing endemic or deep-rooted conflict between different groups.

## Third-party Facilitation

### The Nature of Facilitation

A facilitator may commence with conciliation, the purpose still being that the parties should eventually resolve the conflict themselves. However, the facilitator does not merely bring the parties together – they re-educate the parties and support them through the process of achieving a solution. The facilitator is not merely an intermediary, but more a participant and a guide, although they never dominate the process. This requires vast experience and great skill on the part of the third party and is usually a time-consuming process.

### Basic Principles of Facilitation

Conflict resolution is an interactive process and, as such, requires interactive interventions and resolution. The parties should, from the beginning, be encouraged to take ownership of the process and to interact with each other in a manner different from that adopted previously.

Secondly, although conflict and the causes of conflict appear overt, conflict has subjective roots. It is necessary to deal with, and perhaps change, the subjective orientations of both parties. This refers particularly to their perceptions of the conflict, each other and themselves. They should also be made aware of how their own prejudices, preferences and paradigms influence their view of the conflict and of the other party.

### Engaging in Facilitation
#### *Understanding the Conflict*

Before a third party can engage in facilitation, they should gain an understanding of the conflict, and particularly of the issues and problems which caused the conflict to escalate to existing levels. The third party needs to analyse all facets of the situation and understand the history of the conflict and of the relationship.

#### *Recognising Different Paradigms*

Khorasani and Almasifard (2017) explored differing paradigms in management sciences, as depicted in Figure 10.1. Paradigms emanate from ideological beliefs, norms and value systems, with implications for conflict in labour relations.

## CLASSICAL MANAGEMENT THEORIES

**Scientific Management Theory**
Improvement of production depends on standardising methods of working, usage of machinery and workers bringing different sets of skills
Frederick W Taylor (1856–1915), Henry L Grant (1861–1919), Frank B Gilbreth (1868–1924), Lillian EM Gilbreth (1878–1972), Morris L Cooke (1872–1960)

**Bureaucratic Management**
Effective and efficient management of the organisation depends on clear lines of authority, with formalised processes and procedures regulating the manner in which taks are carried out
Max Weber (1864–1920): charismatic, traditional, rational-legal organisations

**Administrative/Process Management Theory**
The successful functioning of the entire organisation relies on how tasks are structured and how work groups are organised. Functional departments facilitate the productivity of employees at the operational level.
Henri Fayol (1841–1925): management role theory

## BEHAVIOURAL MANAGEMENT THEORY

Concerns the company's efforts to understand the employee in terms of their motivation, expectations, needs and interests, which contributes towards productivity improvement

Hugo Münsterberg (1863–1916): applied psychology; Kurt Lewin (1890–1947): group dynamics; Chester Barnard (1886–1961): executive functions; Mary P Follet (1868–1933): sociology; George E Mayo (1880–1949): employee motivational theory; Douglas McGregor (1906–1964): theory X&Y; Abraham Maslow (1908–1970): hierarchy of human needs.

## GREAT DEPRESSION

The state of economic collapse or catastrophe causing unemployment; deflation leading to poverty and inequality
John Maynard Keynes.

## ORGANISATION ENVIRONMENT/SYSTEMS APPROACH THEORY

The organisation operating as a total whole, with interdependencies between different components

Ludwig von Bertalanffy (the whole is better than individual parts); Peter Senge (learning organisations)

## CONTINGENCY MANAGEMENT THEORY

Considers situational factors in organisations (both internal and external) in the process of organising a business

Tom Burns and George Stalker; Paul Lawrence, Jay Lorsch, Joan Woodward; Alfred Chandeler

## INFORMATION REVOLUTION THEORY

Information is an economic activity that provides organisations with a competitive advantage

**Figure 10.1:** Paradigm shifts in management sciences (summarised and adapted from Khorasani & Almasifard, 2017)

When the paradigms in which one party operates are directly opposed to those of the other party, any attempts which the parties themselves make to solve the conflict are bound to fail. In these situations the parties will make progress only if they acknowledge that they are coming from different perspectives and if each agrees to move away from their own paradigm and meet on neutral ground. Given the strong influence of ideology, values and norms, this is an almost impossible task for the parties themselves. It usually requires a third, neutral party to create awareness of the different approaches to the problem and to present an alternative approach.

In the employment relationship, the most distinct conflict of paradigms occurs where one party supports individualism, private property and the free-market system and the other leans towards a more communitarian approach. This difference in paradigms is reflected in the formation of 'radical' and 'conservative' camps, with the radical party not accepting the status quo in a capitalist/free-market system and the conservative party attempting to preserve the existing order.

It is obvious that parties at these extremes will differ on ways of handling particular conflict situations. Such attempts are resisted by the communitarian/radical grouping, which views its position as legitimate and the enforcers of norms, rules or the law as illegitimate. From their perspective, their own community organisations, or others holding the same beliefs, are more legitimate. In situations like this it is unwise to rely on entrenched societal or organisational institutions and processes to quell or settle the conflict. Unless each party understands the other's frame of reference, the conflict cannot be resolved.

*Identifying Different Needs and Goals*
Since most deep-rooted or unmanageable conflicts arise from clashing needs and goals, broken promises or structural imbalances, these should be identified at the commencement of the conflict intervention. Physical needs such as those for food, water, shelter and clothing are not difficult to identify; neither is the need for security in both the physical and the social sense. Besides these, individuals and groups also need:
- a sense of dignity and own identity
- to participate in groups and in society
- to feel that they are in control of their own destiny
- to feel that they are respected (the legitimacy issue)
- to know that they do have some power
- to have psychological security
- to be able to predict the effects of their actions
- to enlarge the range and quality of satisfactions available to them

- the freedom of choice
- a sense of their own worth and integrity
- the confidence that society or the organisation holds a fair measure of hope
- the prospect that their aspirations may be fulfilled.

Unless the intermediary understands the needs of the parties and creates an understanding of the other's needs, the process of resolution cannot begin. Some conflicts may arise from one party's need for excessive power or from a 'subordinate' party's need to create a power balance. Even where power is not overtly sought, the power play between conflicting parties cannot be ignored. Power cannot be taken out of the equation, but parties should understand that all sides hold power of some kind or other. What they should be seeking should not be power over the other party, but the power to achieve their goals and satisfy their needs. If both parties are empowered to achieve all or some of their goals, there is no need for a power play between the parties.

### Differentiating between Rights and Obligations

In most conflict situations, parties tend to equate interests with rights, to insist on supposed rights or to dwell on rights that they already have but which the other party does not acknowledge. (Imagine, for example, a union's reaction to management's insistence on its right to make decisions.) To achieve successful resolution, the issue of rights has to be excluded. One party cannot insist on rights which the other party does not accept or acknowledge. It is preferable to focus on the obligations which parties might have, both towards each other and towards other societal or organisational players.

### Emphasising Commonality

It is natural that, in a conflict situation, the differences between the parties will be emphasised and the commonalities or common interests overlooked. It is the task of the facilitator to search for, and create renewed awareness of, common interests or goals and to shift the emphasis away from points of difference. Also, neither party may be willing to acknowledge their dependence on the other. Unless this happens, the power play between the parties will continue.

### The Continuation of the Relationship

The most important of the initial questions is whether both parties wish to continue and even develop the relationship. If one or both have no desire to do so, attempts at a resolution may prove futile. However, the mere fact that the parties have agreed to come together points to a wish for continuance. This should then be emphasised.

## Initiating Facilitation

*Identifying the Issues and the Parties and Gaining Trust*

Before commencing with facilitation, all parties involved in or influencing the conflict should be identified. The persons most overtly engaged in the conflict may not be the only ones involved, and if they alone are present, the conflict may continue to be fuelled from outside. It is customary for the facilitator to meet with each party beforehand in order to gain a thorough understanding of the issues.

From the outset, the facilitator should focus on gaining the trust of the various parties. They need to be assured that the facilitator is neutral yet knowledgeable, and able to guide them towards the resolution of the conflict. However, at the same time they should be made aware that the solution lies with them and not with the facilitator. The facilitator will merely help them to achieve resolution. At this stage the facilitator will be listening to the parties and gaining an impression of the past relationship, the issues and the stances or perceptions of each party.

*Bringing the Parties Together*

The parties are brought together at a venue removed from the actual conflict situation. Experience shows that behaviours change when persons are placed in a different setting. It also removes them from the comfort zone of their own support systems and from an environment which may reinforce their particular perceptions.

*The Behavioural Contract*

The conflict is not addressed before the parties have agreed on a behavioural contract. The parties commit themselves to the process and agree that they will not engage in aggressive behaviours, will demonstrate respect for each other and will engage in honest and open communication. Parties need to know that:
- no individual will be vested with authority
- nobody will be granted special privileges
- judgement will not be passed on any communication, irrespective of its source.

*Other Requirements*

It may be necessary first to train the parties in problem-solving techniques by using a fictitious case and also to instil the rules of controlled communication – that is, communication where ideas, thoughts and even feelings are expressed without excessive emotion and without engaging in defensive or aggressive behaviour.

It is in this initial stage that the tone for the entire process is set. Meetings should not be too formal, nor so informal that there is no order. The tone can be quite light, and it is useful to introduce humour, but there should always be an underlying seriousness and a sense of purpose.

## Engaging in Joint Problem Solving
### *Listing the Issues*
The parties need to explore, define and delimit the conflict. The interests and viewpoints of both parties should be explored, and the key issues identified. The facilitator should not prevent any person from expressing feelings as long as this is done in a controlled manner and is mediated so that it does not threaten other parties. In fact, if properly handled, expressing emotions may serve to de-escalate the level of conflict. It should be made clear that, although these emotions are what the party is feeling, the purpose is to change those perceptions and feelings by an enhanced understanding of the other party. Here it could be useful to let the parties change positions and to explore what they would feel if they were in the other party's position. Where perceptions, ideological stances and value systems influence the conflict, the facilitator attempts to change those subjective orientations or, at the very least, create an understanding of the role played by these in the conflict situation.

In all probability, a diversity of issues will be raised, some of them old grievances and others entirely new. The facilitator needs to keep the parties on track by constantly guiding them back to the main issues. If there is agreement as to what these are, the parties should progress to joint information-gathering on these issues. The facilitator assists by contributing facts and information of their own.

### *Defining the Problem*
Once the issues have been explored and defined, the parties should jointly define the central problem. This requires expert guidance, as the tendency is to define the problem in terms of the issues, while the two may not be synonymous. For example, two persons who are in conflict because the one wants to go to the cinema and the other to a rugby match will be inclined to say that the problem is that they want to do different things, while the actual problem may be that they have only one car or that the two events are taking place at the same time. This is what differentiates a problem from an issue. Attempts to resolve the issue would result in a compromise by one of the parties, while the solution to the problem may be to explore other forms of transport or to establish whether the film will be showing at another venue at another time. This example is simplistic, but it illustrates the necessity of making a clear distinction between issues and positions on the one hand and

the problem on the other. It also demonstrates that focusing on the problem depersonalises the issues and allows the parties to move away from their respective positions.

Where there are a number of diverse issues, a problem statement may have to be developed for each issue. However, most commonly, the issues can be compacted into one or two all-encompassing problem statements.

Great care should be exercised that the parties or one of the parties does not already, at this stage, put forward solutions. The facilitator needs to explain that the process has just begun and that no partisan solution is acceptable.

### Agreeing on Criteria

If a proposed solution is to be acceptable to all parties, it will have to be evaluated in terms of agreed criteria. These criteria will indicate whether the solution is feasible and acceptable to both groups. Criteria could include, for example, such matters as cost-effectiveness, the statement that the solution must impose minimal harm on all parties or an undertaking that there should be no threat to the environment.

The establishment of criteria depersonalises proposed solutions and allows for rational argument regarding the merits and demerits of such solutions.

### Generating Options

The next step is to encourage the parties to generate as many options or alternative solutions as possible. This can be done by brainstorming or the nominal group technique. All suggestions are recorded, and no evaluation or criticism of a suggested solution is allowed. The facilitator could add solutions or rephrase the solutions offered.

The processes used allow for depersonalisation of the proposed solutions. It is unlikely that when the solutions are put up for scrutiny and evaluation they will be attributed to particular persons. Participants must be encouraged to be as creative as possible and given the assurance that no suggestion, however improbable, will be discarded without evaluating its merits.

### Evaluating Solutions

The proposed solutions are posted up or printed and opened to general discussion. Participants are encouraged to raise concerns with particular solutions, but the concerns should not be partisan by nature. Thereafter, the solutions are evaluated in terms of the criteria, and those which prove the least feasible are immediately discarded. Further discussion around the remaining solutions, which may entail redefining the solutions or obtaining more information, should result in a consensual decision as to the most feasible option. Consensus entails the agreement of all parties. If there is no consensus, clarification and information-sharing must continue until such agreement is reached. If this is not achieved, the conflict will not have been resolved.

## Planning Implementation

A solution may seem feasible in theory but prove unfeasible in practice. Consequently, the process cannot end before implementation plans have been established jointly. Obstacles to implementation need to be identified by, for example, a SWOT (strengths, weaknesses, opportunities and threats) analysis, whereafter strategies to overcome the obstacles are developed.

If the solution proves to be completely impractical, it is replaced with one of the other options generated and the process is repeated.

The fact that the parties work together in formulating strategy and planning for implementation strengthens the change in the relationship, which should have started developing already during the generation of the problem definition and its solution.

## Problems Bedevilling the Process

The joint problem-solving process may seem relatively straightforward, but in practice it is often difficult to implement, owing to particular stances by individuals or groups. One of the main problems is that there is a tendency to maintain role identity and to look for authoritative leadership. In management–employee sessions, managers and employees alike tend to act and speak within the framework of their traditional roles. Employees defer to the 'boss' or are afraid to speak honestly in the employer's presence. It requires great skill on the part of the facilitator to move participants from these stances and to equalise relationships, but if this is not done, there can be no honesty, innovation or creativity and the process will fail. The facilitator should, in a non-threatening manner, 'neutralise' any individual or group displaying a tendency to dominate the process.

Just as there are some who would dominate, there are others who are intractable and remain over-committed to their own positions or solutions. Persons who are not willing to consider alternatives should be sidelined as far as possible, or members of the same group who are more flexible could be requested to intervene.

The greatest problem in implementing a co-operative approach to conflict resolution is the prevalence of the power factor. Either parties are afraid that, by engaging in the process, they will be relinquishing their power base, or they would rather risk engaging in a coercive process where they might lose but also have the prospect of winning. When parties are intent on power competition, a joint problem-solving process is not feasible.

## The Role of the Facilitator

It has become evident from the above that the facilitator takes responsibility for the process, but not for the solution. The facilitator's role is to:

- defuse the conflict
- set the stage for the exploration of each party's interests and subjective orientations
- set and control the agenda
- harvest ideas
- provide detached overviews
- review concepts
- show connections between different ideas and solutions
- provide knowledge and information when necessary
- keep the discussions at a logical level
- get the parties to acknowledge each other's interests, values and beliefs
- almost imperceptibly control behaviour and communication
- prevent any person or party from becoming over-committed to a position or solution and thereby entrapped in a conflict situation
- by the facilitator's very presence, shift the focus from the parties to the problem.

## Facilitator Competencies

The facilitator needs to have a thorough grasp of the legal framework underpinning the nature of conflict and demonstrate the following essential competencies:

- Patience and tolerance
- An understanding of the problem
- The ability to co-ordinate the thinking process
- Well-developed communication and interaction skills
- An awareness of non-verbal communication expressed by participants
- The skill required to manage the participants' diverse thinking styles
- The ability to keep the group on track and to ensure that there is no deviation from the assigned goals
- The ability to use time and space to support group problem solving
- The ability to apply effective methods and techniques to build collaborative problem-solving
- The skill required to facilitate group-self awareness
- An attitude of encouraging trust and neutrality
- The ability to evoke creative group problem solving
- The ability to plan, organise, co-ordinate and be results-driven.

## Conclusion

The phenomenon of conflict, together with the power phenomenon, which underlies it, is extremely complex. There are so many variables affecting the prevalence and escalation, or otherwise, of conflict, and particularly intergroup conflict, that detailed study and considerable experience are required before successful resolution can be achieved.

## Suggested Questions/Tasks

1. Outline the concept of conflict and its features.
2. Differentiate between conflict management and conflict resolution.
3. Explain the conflict process and its effects on employment relations management.
4. Devise ways of managing conflict in the workplace effectively.
5. Describe a situation of heightened conflict about which you have read extensively, which you have witnessed or in which you yourself have been involved. Thereafter:
   a. Analyse the conflict.
   b. Identify the factors which led to the escalation of conflict.
   c. Identify the main participants and the stances adopted.
   d. Describe how you would go about preparing for a facilitation of the conflict.
   e. List the possible issues which the parties would raise.
   f. Provide a step-by-step description of the process you would follow after generating the problem statement.
   g. Describe how you would ensure that the eventual solution is the best possible one and acceptable to all parties.
   h. Provide details on how the facilitation would differ from the traditional confrontational (aggressive bargaining) approach.

## Sources

Anstey, M. 1999. *Managing Change: Negotiating Conflict*. Cape Town: Juta.

Khorasani, ST & Almasifard, M. 2017. 'Evolution of management theory within 20 century: A systemic overview of paradigm shifts in management'. *International Review of Management and Marketing* 7(3): 134–137.

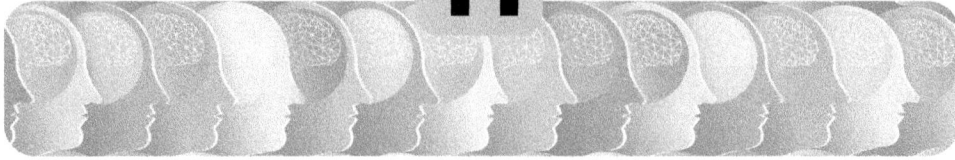

# Dispute Settlement

## Chapter Outline

OVERVIEW

PART ONE: THE NATURE AND SCOPE OF LABOUR DISPUTES

TYPES OF LABOUR DISPUTE

Disputes of Right • Disputes of Interest • Individual and Collective Disputes

THE STRUCTURE OF THE DISPUTE SETTLEMENT PROCESS

DISPUTE SETTLEMENT METHODS

Conciliation • Mediation | *Definition* | *Purpose* | *Appointment of a Mediator* | *Characteristics of a Good Mediator* | *The Role of the Mediator* | *Methods and Approaches to Mediation* | *The Mediation Process* | *The Effectiveness of Mediation* • Arbitration | *Definition* | *Types of Arbitration* | *Mediation–Arbitration and Conciliation–Arbitration* | *Advisory Arbitration* | *The Effectiveness of Arbitration*

PART TWO: DISPUTE SETTLEMENT IN TERMS OF THE LABOUR RELATIONS ACT

DISPUTE SETTLEMENT BODIES

The CCMA | *Legal Position* | *Functions* | *Management* | *Rules for the Conduct of Proceedings before the CCMA* | *Conciliation by the Commission* | *Mediation in the Public Interest* | *Arbitration by the CCMA* | *Representation at Arbitration Proceedings* | *Arbitration Awards* | *Variation and Review of Arbitration Awards* • Accredited Bargaining Councils and Private Agencies • The Labour Court | *Composition and Status* | *Jurisdiction* | *Functions* | *Proceedings and Representation of Parties* • The Labour Appeal Court • Routing of Different Types of Dispute

TYPES OF DISPUTE AND MEANS OF SETTLEMENT

Interference with the Freedom of Association • Refusal to Grant Organisational Rights • Interpretation or Implementation of Collective Agreements • Refusal to Admit a Party or Parties to a Bargaining Council • Disputes about Statutory Determinations • Interpretation and Implementation of the Act as regards Organisational Rights and Bargaining Bodies • Disputes of Interest in Essential Services • Automatically Unfair Dismissals or Dismissals Related to Retrenchments, Closed-shop Membership or Participation in an Illegal Strike • Dismissals Related to Misconduct, Incompetence and Incapacity (Including Constructive Dismissal) • Unfair Labour Practice Disputes • Workplace Forums (Including Joint Decision Making and Disclosure)

➤

# Overview

Negotiations do not always end in mutual agreement. Disagreements give rise to a situation in which the parties are said to be in dispute.

Two kinds of labour dispute exist, namely disputes of right and disputes of interest. Disputes of right do not arise from and are not usually subject to negotiation; instead, they are entrenched in law or agreements. These disputes are eventually submitted to arbitration or legal adjudication, although attempts are made, through conciliation, to get the parties to settle. Disputes of interest, on the other hand, can usually not be settled by legal determination. Consequently, other methods of dispute settlement have to be established for such collective conflicts.

Disputes of interest arise when the conflict cannot be resolved in the normal negotiation forum or when one side has refused to negotiate at all by resorting to coercive power, in the form of a strike or a lockout. This kind of action is detrimental to both parties and their relationships, and also to society at large; hence, it should be avoided by exploring dispute settlement procedures.

Dispute settlement procedures may be agreed upon between the parties themselves, or the state may put procedures and systems in place for the settlement of disputes, such as the Labour Relations Act 66 of 1995. The state's main concern is to protect the public interest and to promote economic activity by maintaining labour peace. The procedures it introduces are aimed at minimising or eradicating the need for labour action. At the very least, they oblige the parties to consider a possible resolution before any action is undertaken. Experts disagree on the extent to which the state can force the parties to use the legislated machinery and also the extent to which it can prohibit or limit strike action. The degree of compulsion and limitation varies from one system to another.

Dispute settlement procedures such as conciliation, mediation and arbitration are most frequently used in attempts to settle labour disputes. Conciliation and mediation allow for the negotiation process to continue and for the parties themselves to reach a settlement. In arbitration, on the other hand, a determination is made by a third party, such as the Commission for Conciliation, Mediation and Arbitration (CCMA), which seeks to prevent coercive action. The type of dispute settlement procedure chosen and the methods preferred will depend on the nature of the dispute, the needs of the parties and the particular labour relations system in question.

In South Africa, the Labour Relations Act provides the official dispute settlement processes, aimed at the promotion of collective bargaining, the maintenance of labour peace and the promotion of fair labour practices through the CCMA, the Labour Court, and a Labour Appeal Court. The Act sets out detailed procedures for different disputes of rights and further separates unfair dismissal from other unfair labour practices. With some exceptions, unfair dismissals are referred to the CCMA or a bargaining council for conciliation or arbitration, rather than to the Labour Court. In certain instances, modified procedures are instituted for the public sector. Disputes of interest may first be referred to conciliation or mediation; if this fails, parties may choose voluntary arbitration or engage in protected strike or lockout actions.

So far, the dispute settlement machinery has functioned relatively effectively, despite certain areas requiring improvement. As relationships between employers and unions have matured, arrangements have been made for private settlement of disputes of right, for example by resorting to private arbitration as an alternative to the use of the official processes. This alleviates the heavy burden on the CCMA and the Labour Court.

## Part One: The Nature and Scope of Labour Disputes

The definition of a labour dispute varies from country to country, but most definitions refer to a labour dispute as a dispute between an employer and their employees or the union. The subject matter of a labour dispute is usually limited to so-called matters of mutual interest – that is, matters which could be regulated jointly by the employer and their employees or those which affect employees.

For the present purpose, a labour dispute is defined as a continued disagreement between employers and employees/ex-employees or their unions in respect of any matter of common/mutual interest, any work-related factor affecting their relationship, or any processes and structures established to maintain such relationship.

Thus, disputes may arise from:
- the failure to agree to the establishment of a relationship
- disagreement about procedures
- the failure to agree on terms and conditions of employment
- the failure to abide by the terms of an agreement
- a denial of the other party's rights
- the refusal by the employer to disclose information to the trade union as determined by the Act
- poor treatment of the other party
- any other action or event which negatively affects the relationship.

In this definition the word 'continued' is important. The mere raising of a demand or a grievance does not constitute a labour dispute. A dispute will arise only if there is no final agreement on a demand or if an issue is not settled in a manner satisfactory to both parties.

## Types of Labour Dispute

### Disputes of Right
A right is something to which a party is entitled by law, by contract, by agreement or by established practice. In the labour relationship, rights are ensured by:
- common law
- labour legislation
- the terms of the employment contract
- legally enforceable agreements
- customary practices at the place of work.

Disputes of right do not arise from failed negotiations, but rather from contravention of the law, a contract or an agreement. Disputes of right will centre on issues such as:

- the failure of one party to abide by the contract of employment
- the failure to implement legally determined conditions and procedures, such as minimum working hours and prescribed notice periods
- the failure to implement the terms of a legally enforceable agreement
- the non-implementation of an arbitration award or wage determination
- a transgression of any other legal determination, such as the prohibition on victimisation or interference with the freedom of association
- a transgression of the common law
- a unilateral change in accepted or customary practices or undue withdrawal of labour or employment benefits
- unfair dismissals and unfair labour practices in terms of the Labour Relations Act.

Although attempts may be made to settle disputes of right by negotiation and other methods before, and even after, an official dispute has been declared, the final recourse in these disputes is to judicial adjudication or arbitration, under the auspices of the Labour Court or the CCMA.

### Disputes of Interest

An interest is something which a party is not yet entitled to, but to which it would like to become entitled. Whether the interest is achieved will depend on how the party can persuade the other to grant the concessions.

Interests are subject to negotiation, and once agreement has been reached, the interest becomes a right. Disputes arising from interests, which would subsequently become rights, must be settled through formal processes. For instance, an employee who has the right by law to two weeks' leave per year may not be satisfied with this minimum provision, because their interest is to be granted annual leave of four weeks. To achieve this, the employee, or their representative or union, would engage in negotiations with the employer. If the employer eventually agrees and the new terms are written into a contract of employment or a legally enforceable collective agreement, the interest becomes a right. Disputes of interest arise when no agreement on demands or grievances can be achieved. Any matter causing conflict between an employer and an employee and which is not regulated by law, agreement or custom can give rise to a dispute of interest.

### Individual and Collective Disputes

Disputes arising in the workplace can be either individual or collective-oriented. Individual disputes may occur in the event where an employee feels dissatisfied about the employer's unilateral change to terms and conditions of employment or if the employer determines that the employee has failed/ is failing to comply with the required standards of performance or code of conduct. In this case, either party can institute legal proceedings to force the other to conform.

Collective disputes may, for instance, arise in situations where the trade union acting on behalf of employees lodges an official complaint against the employer for failure to adhere to the collective agreement, or where the employer demands a collective of employees to comply with such agreement. Collective disputes can be settled through the dispute resolution mechanisms that are provided for in the agreement or dealt with in terms of the dispute resolution procedure as determined by the Labour Relations Act.

## The Structure of the Dispute Settlement Process

Negotiations at company, industry or national level may at times result in a dispute where the parties disagree and are not willing to compromise on their demands. Such an impasse requires the intervention of a third party, considering that the parties in the dispute may have exhausted all possible means to avoid the deadlock. Now, according to the dispute settlement structure depicted in Figure 11.1 below, the formal process will begin, with either party referring the dispute to the CCMA or the bargaining council for resolution.

How the dispute is resolved depends on the type of and the choice of mechanisms jointly selected by the parties. The next sections will unpack the key processes required to settle disputes.

## Dispute Settlement Methods

### Conciliation

The Oxford Reference Dictionary (1991) defines 'conciliation' as 'the act of procuring goodwill or inducing a friendly feeling. In the context of labour disputes, conciliation can be referred to a formal or informal attempt by a third party to restore a feeling of satisfaction to any party in dispute'. In the settlement of labour disputes, conciliation thus entails the procuring of renewed goodwill. This is achieved by establishing a forum for parties who are in conflict or have failed to reach agreement to come together and attempt to settle their differences.

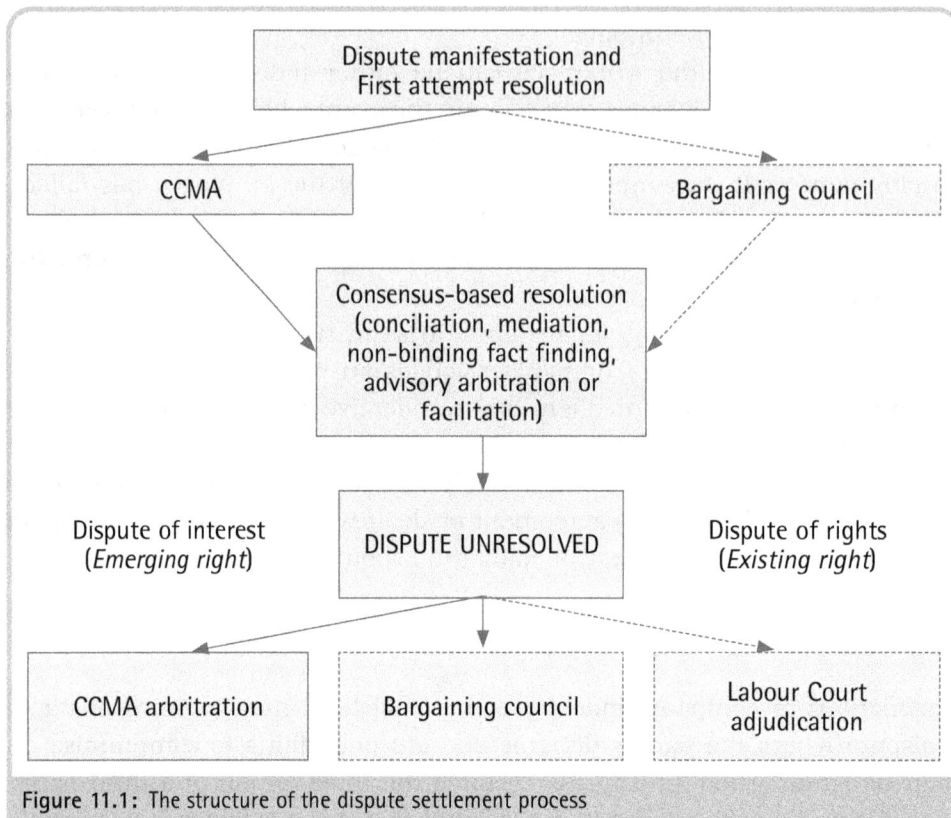

**Figure 11.1:** The structure of the dispute settlement process

Conciliation is undertaken by a third party (or conciliator), who may be a functionary of the CCMA or from a private entity. The third party may act as chairperson during the conciliation meetings and will try to appease the parties by making proposals; however, they cannot actively interfere or make any decisions regarding the matter in dispute.

Essentially, conciliation is the continuation of negotiations between the two parties, but, in this instance, the negotiations form part of the dispute settlement procedure, and are undertaken in the presence of a third party. Failure to conciliate may lead to coercive action or to further steps in the dispute settlement process.

The advantage of conciliation is that it extends the negotiation process by allowing for settlement between the parties without the interference of external agents. Where a procedure requires conciliation before any action can be undertaken, both parties have time to cool off. They can then approach each other in a friendlier manner and seriously attempt to settle before engaging in an action which might eventually destroy the relationship.

In practice, most third parties conducting conciliation do mediate to some extent – that is, they try more creative methods to bring the parties together.

The distinction between the two processes has become somewhat blurred. Often, what happens in conciliation also happens in the mediation process. In fact, the Labour Relations Act defines conciliation very broadly to include mediation, where the presiding officer or third party must determine a process to attempt to resolve the dispute through mediation, conducting a fact-finding exercise and making recommendations to the parties. Now let's elaborate on the topic of mediation to distinguish this process from conciliation.

## Mediation
### Definition
Vettori (2015: 357) defines mediation as a flexible process, conducted confidentially, in which a neutral person assists the parties to work towards a negotiated agreement of a dispute or difference, with the parties ultimately being in control of the decision to settle and the terms of resolution. Mediation can also be defined as a voluntary, third-party intervention method aimed at resolving conflict and exploring solutions (SHRM, 2021). Mediation is therefore the active intervention by a third party, or third parties, in an attempt to get a settlement.

The difference between mediation and conciliation is that in mediation, the third party always maintains neutrality and impartiality by working together with the parties as an integral partner to assist in finding the best amicable solution. The mediator plays an active part in the process by facilitating discussion between the parties and the representation of the parties' interests. In doing so, the mediator guides the parties towards a suitable solution that is fair, without imposing the mediator's own solution which they perceive as workable. The parties in the mediation play an active role by identifying commonalities and possible solutions based on each other's proposals before seeking the intervention of the mediator in finding the best possible solution. Mediation differs from arbitration in that a mediator acts only in an advisory and conciliatory capacity. The mediator has no decision-making powers and cannot impose a settlement on either party.

### Purpose
Mediation is intended to facilitate negotiation during a dispute of interest or to help parties come to an agreement in disputes of right. Sometimes, situations arise in which the parties are incapable of agreeing on rights or of continuing negotiations on their own. Introducing a neutral person, especially an experienced negotiator, could diffuse tensions and help the parties to achieve a settlement. In particular, mediation serves to narrow the gap in the settlement range.

As a mediator does not belong to either party, both parties will more easily reveal their actual positions to the mediator. Consequently, the mediator's estimation of the settlement range might differ from that established by the participants, and they could persuade one party to move closer to the other within that range. Also, a mediator might more easily elicit concessions from either party. This promotes a trade-off and, possibly, settlement. As an outsider who is not directly involved in the conflict between the two parties, and as an individual with wider knowledge, the mediator brings new perspectives to the dispute.

### Appointment of a Mediator

A mediator may be appointed by the parties themselves or by governmental or other dispute settlement agencies.

If the parties themselves appoint a single mediator, such person must meet with the approval of both sides and their neutrality should be beyond question. Where there is no neutral person available, or if the parties cannot agree on a particular mediator, each side may appoint a mediator of its choice. Each mediator will meet with their own side, whereafter the two mediators will come together and attempt to formulate a possible settlement.

### Characteristics of a Good Mediator

An effective mediator will have broadly the same qualities as a good negotiator, but they should possess these qualities to a greater degree. Ideally, they should have a proven record of success in negotiations.

A mediator, if they are to be successful, must in the first place elicit the trust, acceptance and co-operation of both parties or of the party they represent. The parties will accept the mediator only if the person has sufficient credibility and if the parties are assured that the mediator can be entrusted with confidential matters.

Intelligence, discernment and practicality are essential qualities in mediation. A mediator should be able to identify problems and offer workable solutions. To do this, the mediator needs to:

- be knowledgeable in all matters related to the negotiations
- be acquainted with the organisational structures, strategies and attitudes of both parties
- have up-to-date knowledge of labour legislation, collective agreements or determinations
- be up to date with the latest economic, sociopolitical and technological developments
- be tactful and diplomatic
- be sensitive to nuances

- have the necessary powers of persuasion
- be an effective communicator
- be a critical thinker with the ability to collate and analyse information objectively
- have a strong character, since they may need to nudge the participants towards an agreement.

In practice, an individual of such high calibre is not easily found. A mediator may not possess all the characteristics described, but they should possess some of them, as the success of the mediation process will depend partly on the qualities of the mediator.

### The Role of the Mediator

Based on the qualities and competencies described above, the mediator must in all attempts try to persuade the parties to realise what their commonalities are. Setting this context, especially at the beginning of the mediation, and in fact throughout the mediation process, will ensure that the parties converge in critical problem solving and decision making instead of focusing on their differences. Therefore, the mediator must:

- assist the parties, without deciding or imposing their position on the parties, and without being seen as arbitrating on the matters
- push for a settlement that is in the best interests of the parties, but without applying pressure
- patiently assist the parties to craft an amicable solution by not personalising the process in order to register a success for the mediator themself
- allow the parties to control the content while the mediator facilitates the process
- stimulate creative problem solving by helping the parties to identify and articulate their interests, needs and priorities in the process of seeking acceptable solutions.

### Methods and Approaches to Mediation

Mediation encourages social dialogue between the parties and forms part of the dispute resolution framework as stipulated in the Labour Relations Act. However, the Act does not provide clear guidelines, regulations, methods and approaches to mediation. This leaves the mediator with the task of applying best practice and the freedom to select and apply the best possible methods. These approaches, which are based on international best practice, can include, but are not limited to, the following:

- In **settlement mediation**, the mediator works to bring the parties away from their positions towards a compromise.

- **Facilitative mediation** promotes communication between the parties to help identify interests and needs and to highlight areas for trade-offs, without proposing or imposing a solution. Rather, compromise is encouraged in order to arrive at a mutually acceptable settlement.
- **Evaluative mediation** is based on the mediator's assessment of the parties' positions. The mediator attempts to pacify both parties by proposing the best possible solutions.
- **Therapeutic mediation** focuses on the underlying causes of the problem or dispute, with a view to improving and maintaining future stakeholder relations.
- **Relationship by objectives** (RBO) is an in-depth process of conflict or dispute resolution where the parties involved, under the guidance of a mediation expert, jointly identify action steps and measures to improve the relationship.

The choice and application of these methods will depend on the climate of mediation, and mediators may even use a combination of these approaches in line with the topics at hand. Quite significantly, the mediator must constantly assess the mediation climate; they must avoid being rigid, and rather become agile in the application of context-relevant approaches.

### The Mediation Process

Kochan (1980) divided the mediation process into three stages: introduction and establishment of credibility, steering the negotiation process and movement towards a final settlement.

During stage 1 – introduction and establishment of credibility – the mediator plays a more passive role than at any other time during the mediation process. The mediator's main task is to gain the trust and acceptance of the parties. They should believe that the mediator will be capable of assisting them and is a person on whom they can rely at all times. An experienced mediator will initially leave most of the talking to the disputing parties, but will listen attentively and ask probing questions. The mediator's main objectives at this stage will be to:
- diagnose the causes of the dispute
- identify the issues in order of priority
- pinpoint the obstacles to a possible settlement
- gain an impression of the different attitudes held by the parties
- estimate the relative power between the parties.

Once the mediator's position is entrenched and they have sufficient background knowledge, the mediator will attempt to persuade the parties to resume negotiations or to steer negotiations in a different direction. This could happen after the mediator has supplied the parties with a different perspective or removed some of the obstacles to continued negotiation.

During stage 2 – steering the negotiation process – the mediator intervenes more actively in the process, by offering advice to the parties and by attempting to establish the actual resistance point of each party and areas in which compromise could be reached. The mediator will encourage proposals and counterproposals, and if a solution seems possible, they will gently urge the parties towards accepting it. If emotions run high and tension is manifesting, the mediator should split the parties into separate rooms for private consultation, or caucus by obtaining joint consensus with the parties. During these caucuses, the mediator must encourage the parties to share new information that will help in reaching common ground, but must at the same time maintain confidentiality to avoid compromising themself.

At this stage, the mediator may become more assertive and, through their behaviour, exert pressure on the participants to accept a certain solution. However, this should be carefully timed and the mediator should be sure that the parties are ready to consider a settlement. A mediator who comes over too strongly at the wrong time may antagonise one or both of the parties and lose much of the ground already gained. At the worst, the mediator could be rejected by one or both of the parties.

During stage 3 – movement towards a final settlement – an experienced mediator will know when to exert pressure towards a final settlement. During this phase the mediator would, most probably, conduct intensive negotiations with both parties in an attempt to persuade them to face reality and adjust their positions. The mediator may also become more forceful than at any other stage. However, timing and diplomacy are extremely important. It frequently happens that only the diehards in one or both parties prove an obstacle to final settlement. Getting chief negotiators to subdue militants in their own ranks could help.

During the final stages the mediator may suggest, or draft proposals for, a settlement. The mediator should make sure that they are not identified too closely with these proposals. If either or both of the parties reject the proposals and they see these as coming from the mediator, they may also reject the mediator. Once a final settlement has been reached, the mediator remains to assist the parties in drafting an agreement and to ensure that both sides are satisfied with its terms and conditions.

The process of mediation, more so than negotiation, is dynamic and finely tuned. A mediator has to be extremely flexible and inventive. Also, the mediator must be continually on their guard against interference by their own values. They should ensure that they do not attempt to impose on the parties the settlement which they regard as correct; rather, the mediator should find the settlement which is acceptable to both parties. Preferably, under the mediator's guidance, the parties themselves should formulate a favourable settlement.

## The Effectiveness of Mediation

It is difficult to establish whether mediation is generally effective or not, since in many instances it is not possible to decide if a settlement would in any event have been reached by the parties. The test of effectiveness lies in the satisfaction of the parties involved, which is often difficult to achieve. Remember, the mediation outcome is achieved after both parties reach common ground by compromising on their demands. They may therefore not necessarily be totally and equally satisfied with the outcome. Mediation ultimately depends on the willingness of the participants to come to an agreement. The most a mediator can achieve is to advise or persuade the parties towards agreement. Nevertheless, it is generally assumed that mediation does facilitate agreement and that it is most effective in situations where:

- owing mostly to lack of experience, negotiators have overcommitted themselves to a particular stand
- the dispute centres on issues or procedures such as dismissals
- the impasse is the result of intra-organisational conflicts between the members of one or both parties
- hostility between members of the opposing parties is the major reason for the continuation of conflict
- the parties are strongly motivated to attempt settlement
- external pressures are being placed on the participants to end the dispute
- coercive action is threatened
- other commitments encourage a settlement of the existing dispute.

Mediation has proved less successful where:

- conflict has reached a high level of intensity
- matters of principle are at stake
- the dispute originated from a negative settlement range
- the dispute concerns economic issues
- the dispute becomes politicised and issues of concern are clouded by irrelevant matters
- there is an inability to pay on the one side and high expectations in the face of eroded wages on the other.

Ultimately, the effectiveness and success of mediation depends as much on the commitment of both parties to a peaceful settlement as on the skills of the mediator.

## Successful Mediation Through RBO

One of the landmark evergreen cases on mediation took place between Mercedes-Benz South Africa and the National Union of Metalworkers of South Africa (NUMSA) in 1989. The former Independent Mediation Services of SA (IMSSA) and Tokiso Dispute Settlement (the agency) facilitated the process.

In this case, the relationship between Mercedes-Benz and NUMSA had been very strained and difficult for a number of years. IMSSA became involved with the parties when it mediated a dispute over the termination of the employment of certain union members, who were found to have participated in acts of misconduct during a demonstration in the plant. The dispute was settled through mediation and, in terms of the settlement agreement, the parties committed themselves to an RBO exercise to set their relationship on a new footing. A team of five IMSSA mediators ran the process. At an initial site visit at a Mercedes-Benz plant, they found workers with wooden AK47s on their backs. At lunchtime, there were mock bayonet charges on effigies of management. White supervisors were carrying real weapons and the atmosphere on the shop floor was one of deep antagonism and hostility. This was the late 1980s, and the political climate was still highly oppressive.

The RBO took place at a neutral country hotel venue, over four days. The company was represented by its chairman, numerous board members and 40 other managers from various levels in the company. The union was represented by two senior full-time union officials and 30 shop stewards from various plants around the country. The team of mediators constructed a mini-parliament and the parties engaged each other on a range of matters of concern to them, including:

- compliance with the recognition agreement
- racial discrimination
- political issues
- the development of a sound basis for future negotiations between the parties
- selection, training and development of employees
- the quality and nature of supervision
- social responsibility of the company
- consultation and participation by employees in decision making within the company
- timekeeping
- job security
- the carrying of weapons in plant
- the management of political demonstrations in plant.

The mediators guided the debate along constructive lines. The parties were given full opportunity to voice their opinions and were encouraged to set objectives to overcome the problems in their relationship. Consensus was reached on a series of 30 objectives to do this, and action plans were developed to give effect to the objectives. Responsibility was assigned to specific individuals and groups within each party to execute the action plans. Time limits were placed on this process. In the course of the process, a change in attitude towards one another was perceptible on the part of individuals within each party and an atmosphere developed that was far more conducive to sound industrial relations.

Workers and management spoke to each other in a way that was cathartic and moving, both sides speaking of the humiliation they had suffered at the hands of the other, and showing the hurt this had caused them. One of the union representatives, who was to become president of NUMSA, said: 'It was the first time in our lives as a labour movement to sit and open our hearts to management and management to labour. IMSSA made it possible for the real issues to be looked at and we are still feeling the positive effects'. A Mercedes-Benz senior executive agreed with this positive assessment:

> The IMSSA third party intervention at Mercedes-Benz was a watershed in the company's industrial relations history. Despite a history of emotionally explosive and uncontrollable industrial relations which had paralysed the manufacturing plant for years, the parties were able to craft their own ground-breaking constitution, the boundaries of the practices institutionalising the relationship have been severely tested since then on many occasions but it has been the commitment to the structures from both sides coupled with the spirit of the RBO process that has enabled Mercedes-Benz to enter the 'new South Africa' with confidence and commitment to a long-term future in this magnificent country.

The RBO programme has become an abiding feature of our labour relations system, with literally hundreds of interventions having taken place in the 24 years since the seminal experience at Mercedes-Benz.

Source: Adapted from Euwema et al, 2019: 301–302

## Arbitration

*Definition*

Arbitration entails the appointment of a third party (the arbitrator) to act as adjudicator in a dispute and to decide on the terms of settlement by following a stringent resolution process.

Arbitration differs from conciliation and mediation in that it does not promote negotiation or dialogue between parties. Instead, a third party actively intervenes in the dispute and takes over the role of decision maker. The arbitrator listens to and investigates the demands and counterdemands on both sides, and decides on a final settlement. The parties may submit their individual proposals for a settlement to the arbitrator, but the final decision is made by the arbitrator. Whatever settlement the arbitrator imposes will become binding on the parties concerned. The parties' only recourse is the Labour Court, to which they can refer the arbitration outcome for review.

### Types of Arbitration

The first differentiation to be made is between judicial arbitration and interest arbitration:

- **Judicial arbitration** is conducted in disputes of right and is undertaken by courts of law or other judicial and semi-judicial bodies.
- **Interest arbitration** centres on the issues raised in the collective bargaining forum. It can be conducted by arbitrators appointed by government or a bargaining council. Alternatively, the parties themselves may appoint an arbitrator or they might decide to make use of an independent arbitration service.

Kochan (1980) also distinguishes between conventional and final-offer arbitration (the latter being package- or issue-related) and between arbitration conducted by a single arbitrator or by a panel of arbitrators.

Conventional arbitration leaves the arbitrator free to impose the settlement of their choice, while in final-offer arbitration (also termed 'pendulum arbitration') the arbitrator studies the final offers of each party and selects one of the proposals for final settlement.

Pendulum arbitration may be based on the total package offered by each party, or it could be based on the offers made by the parties on each issue. In issue-by-issue arbitration, the arbitrator may, for instance, select the final offer of the union on one issue and that of the employer on the other. Pendulum arbitration has the advantage that the parties know that extreme demands or minimal offers will be immediately rejected by the arbitrator and are therefore inclined to modify their proposals and to assess the situation more realistically.

The final question regarding arbitration is whether the parties will accept determination by one arbitrator or whether they would prefer the decision to be made by an arbitrator and an assessor from each side, or by a panel of arbitrators. If they choose a panel of arbitrators, such a panel might consist of a number of neutral persons. Alternatively, the panel could be chaired by a neutral person, assisted by two or more arbitrators who are selected on a parity basis by each side. It is generally preferable to limit the number of arbitrators.

## Mediation-Arbitration and Conciliation-Arbitration

Parties could also be given a choice between 'mediation-arbitration' (med-arb) and 'conciliation-arbitration' (con-arb), which are very similar. The arbitrator initially performs the function of a conciliator or mediator. Before attempting arbitration, the conciliator or mediator urges the parties towards settlement; arbitration will be conducted only if the parties themselves fail to reach an agreement. The use of a hybrid process combining mediation and arbitration offers parties the opportunity to come to an agreement; if the process is not successful, the mediator can act as an arbitrator.

There may be complications entailed in this process, as a mediator or conciliator will have gained the confidence of the parties. The mediator will have more and different information from that which would be given to an arbitrator, who judges only in terms of the facts of the case. To avoid this complication, the arbitrator could first reach a decision as arbitrator, but not disclose this to the parties, and then go over to mediation in an attempt to persuade them into a voluntary settlement of their own. This would then be known as arbitration-mediation. In terms of a con-arb, as entrenched in the new amendments of the Labour Relations Act, the third party will first conciliate on the matter and move immediately to arbitration in one sitting should the parties not reach settlement in conciliation. This process is cost-effective and helps to reduce delays in handling labour disputes. However, the Act allows for parties to object to the use of the same presiding officer who conducted the conciliation to arbitrate on the same matter in a con-arb.

## Advisory Arbitration

Advisory arbitration occurs where the parties are not bound to abide by the decision of the arbitrator. In such instances it is hoped that the decision of the arbitrator will encourage a change in positions.

## The Effectiveness of Arbitration

That arbitration is effective in ending disputes is self-evident. Once an arbitration award has been made, the parties are obliged by law to discontinue their dispute and to abide by the terms of the arbitration award, even if they are not satisfied. However, arbitration may not succeed in resolving the conflict. One or both parties might be dissatisfied with the award and, while they may adhere to the terms, the continued conflict may surface in other ways.

Where interest disputes are involved, arbitration may be a poor option, because it does not extend the negotiation process and takes the decision-making power out of the hands of the parties. In some instances, it may be seen as favouring one party over the other, resulting in further dissatisfaction or conflict.

Arbitration, particularly in interest disputes, can be subjected to overuse, or what is commonly called the 'narcotic effect'. Parties who have frequently taken disputes to arbitration tend later to use it as a first, rather than a last, resort. When a dispute arises, no negotiation is attempted and the issue is immediately subjected to arbitration. In other instances arbitration may have a 'half-life' effect in that the parties become disenchanted with the outcome of arbitration and resort to other means of settlement.

Arbitration tends to detract from the credibility of negotiators, particularly those acting on behalf of the union. Negotiators are viewed as having given over their power to the arbitrator, and may lose their standing with their members or their principals.

Despite these disadvantages, arbitration is a popular method of dispute settlement, particularly if, in the case of a dispute of interest, the parties want to avoid coercive action at all costs. In such instances, participants may more readily accept the decisions of a credible third party who has special power rather than a proposal of settlement from the other party or a mediator.

The arbitration process can be more effective if it provides for pendulum arbitration on an offer-by-offer basis, instead of independent decision making by the arbitrator. Also, a tripartite panel of arbitrators may produce a more balanced decision than a single individual. Generally, voluntary arbitration is more effective than compulsory arbitration. Parties who choose to go to arbitration show greater commitment to a settlement by working together with the arbitrator.

In some instances, arbitration may be a viable alternative to coercive action. It is particularly effective where conflict has reached unmanageable proportions, and where the parties are strong enough to resist allegations of surrendering their roles as negotiators by participating in arbitration.

## Part Two: Dispute Settlement in Terms of the Labour Relations Act

## Dispute Settlement Bodies

### The CCMA
*Legal Position*
The Labour Relations Act provides for the establishment of the CCMA, which is independent of the state and of any political party, union, employer, employers' association or federation of unions or employers' associations.

*Functions*

The functions of the CCMA are to:

- attempt, by conciliation or mediation, to resolve any dispute referred to it in terms of the Act
- arbitrate on disputes referred to it
- provide assistance in the establishment of workplace forums
- provide advice regarding procedures in terms of the Act
- assist any party to a dispute in obtaining legal advice, assistance or representation
- offer to conciliate in a dispute not referred to it
- accredit bargaining councils and private agencies to engage in dispute settlement
- conduct, supervise or scrutinise elections for a union or employers' association
- publish guidelines regarding any matter regulated by the Act
- conduct and publish research concerning any matter related to its work and regarding sexual harassment
- compile and publish information and statistics concerning its activities
- provide advice and training to any party regarding the conclusion of
  - collective agreements
  - workplace forums
  - the prevention of disputes and grievances
  - disciplinary procedures
  - procedures relating to dismissal
  - restructuring of the workplace
  - a programme for affirmative action.

*Management*

The CCMA is managed by a governing body, consisting of a chairperson and such other members as are nominated by the National Economic Development and Labour Council (NEDLAC) and appointed for three years, as well as an appointed director (who may not vote at meetings). The NEDLAC nominations comprise one independent person as chairperson, three persons proposed by labour, three by employers and three by the state.

The CCMA may charge fees for conducting or supervising an election or for giving advice or assistance to any party.

*Rules for the Conduct of Proceedings before the CCMA*

The CCMA has established rules of conduct to regulate the administration of dispute proceedings. The rules provide the requirements pertaining to the filing and serving of documents, the conciliation of disputes, the conduct of con-arb, how to request arbitrations, pre-dismissal arbitration, condonation for failure to comply with the rules as well as guidelines regarding applications for subpoenas. Although the rules are cut and dry, should some new and important issue arise during the conciliation, con-arb or arbitration, the CCMA may adjourn the proceedings in order to afford any party time to prepare their defence. This, of course, may be objected to by either party, leaving the commissioner to make a determination.

## Conciliation by the CCMA

If a dispute is submitted to conciliation, the commissioner appointed to the case should attempt to achieve a resolution within a period of 30 days from the date of referral. The Labour Relations Amendment Act 8 of 2018 provides that the commissioner or the parties could apply to the director for an extension, which should not be longer than five days and should be granted only under special circumstances.

At the commencement of conciliation, the commissioner sets out the procedures to be followed, which could include mediation, fact finding (providing detailed, concrete information on issues subject to dispute) and advisory arbitration. In essential services the parties have the option, within seven days of referral, to agree on the commissioner to be appointed and on the procedure to be followed.

At the end of the 30-day period, or whatever longer period may have been agreed upon, the commissioner must issue a certificate declaring that the dispute has been resolved or that it remains unresolved. A copy of this certificate must be served on both parties, while the original is handed to the CCMA.

Where both parties agree, a commissioner may, immediately after conciliation has failed, engage in arbitration.

## Mediation in the Public Interest

A new Section 150(1) in the Labour Relations Amendment Act 6 of 2014 gives the commission the right to appoint commissioners to conciliate in matters of public interest, irrespective of whether the issue in dispute has or has not been referred to a bargaining council or the CCMA. This the commissioner may do this with the consent of the parties or without their consent, if the commissioner decides that it is in the public interest to do so.

Before appointing a commissioner, the director must consult with the parties and the secretary of the bargaining council which has jurisdiction over the parties. The director may also appoint two persons from the governing body to assist the commissioner. One such person should be nominated by the employer party and one by the employee party.

Even if conciliation is being attempted, either of the parties may still engage in a strike or a lockout.

A follow-up to the amendment is contained in the Labour Relations Amendment Act of 2018, which provides that a high-level panel may intervene in disputes where a strike or a lockout seems imminent, if it is in the public interest to do so.

### Arbitration by the CCMA

Where conciliation has failed, the CCMA is obliged to undertake arbitration, if the law provides for it and when requested to do so by one of the parties. The parties have 90 days from the date on which the certificate of non-resolution was ordered to apply for arbitration by the CCMA.

Arbitration may be undertaken by the same commissioner who engaged in conciliation and mediation of the dispute, but, as explained in an earlier section, this might prove problematic. The Act provides that any party may object to the appointment of the same commissioner. Also, parties may, by agreement, express their preference for certain commissioners by providing a list of not more than five names within 48 hours after the issue of a certificate stating that conciliation has failed. (In the case of a dispute in essential services, the limit is seven days.)

In certain cases, the parties may apply to the director of the CCMA for the appointment of a senior commissioner to undertake arbitration. The director may decide to do so after considering:
- the questions of law arising out of the dispute
- the complexity of the dispute
- the existence of conflicting arbitration awards relevant to the dispute
- the public interest.

Parties who have an agreement to engage in pre-dismissal arbitration may have this performed by an accredited private agency, a bargaining council or the CCMA.

During arbitration proceedings, the parties are entitled to offer testimony, to call witnesses, to cross-examine the witnesses of the other party and to direct closing argument to the commissioner. Where an applicant party is not present for the proceedings, the commissioner may cancel the arbitration. Where the respondent does not attend, the commissioner may conduct the arbitration in absentia or postpone the arbitration to a later date. During the arbitration, the arbitrator also considers the law of evidence to decide on which facts relate to the case, to rule out hearsay evidence, and to determine the credibility of material evidence used. The arbitrator may order a party to refrain from using leading questions that deliberately solicit an intended or expected answer from the witness without allowing them to outline the sequence of events pertaining to the case.

An arbitrator may at any stage (but with the consent of the parties) cease arbitration and engage in conciliation).

A new Section 158(1B) in the Amendment Act of 2014 prevents the Labour Court from reviewing a decision or ruling made during arbitration or conciliation proceedings by the commissioner or an accredited bargaining council before the dispute has been finally determined, unless the Court believes that it may be just and equitable to review the decision or ruling. Moreover, if the parties agree and if it is expedient to continue with proceedings, the Court may sit as an arbitrator, but the ruling it makes must be one which an arbitrator would have been entitled to make.

### Representation at Arbitration Proceedings

As in conciliation proceedings, parties appearing before the CCMA for arbitration may represent themselves or be represented by a director; a trade union member, official or office bearer; or an official or office bearer of the employers' association. In arbitration proceedings they may also be represented by a legal practitioner. However, if the case centres on dismissal for misconduct, incompetence or incapacity, legal representation is not allowed, unless all parties and the commissioner consent or unless the commissioner concludes that legal representation should be allowed. The decision to allow legal representation should be based on the nature or complexity of the dispute, the comparative ability of the parties and the public interest.

### Arbitration Awards

Once the arbitration has been finalised, the commissioner has 14 days to make an award. (If the dispute involves an interest related to an essential service, the commissioner has 30 days from the time of referral, or whatever longer period may be agreed upon.)

The award must briefly state the reasons for the decision. Copies of the award must be served on all parties, while the original is lodged with the Labour Court. The commissioner is empowered to make any award which complies with the Act. Arbitration fees can be collected from an employer where it is found that a dismissal was procedurally unfair. An arbitration award is final and binding and, once verified by the director, can be made an order of the Labour Court.

*Variation and Review of Arbitration Awards*

Reviews of arbitration awards may be requested only where it is alleged that:

- the commissioner was guilty of misconduct regarding their duties as an arbitrator
- the commissioner committed a gross irregularity
- the commissioner exceeded their authority
- the award was improperly obtained.

A party to a dispute may, within six weeks of receiving a copy of an award that the party believes has been improperly made, request that the Labour Court review the award. Where corruption is cited as the reason for the request, the applicant has six weeks from the date on which the corruption was discovered.

The Labour Court may suspend the award pending its decision. It may eventually set the award aside and settle the dispute in a manner which it deems fit or issue an order setting out the procedure to be followed in resolving the dispute.

The Labour Relations Amendment Act of 2014 provides that the Labour Court should hand down its decision as soon as is reasonably possible.

## Accredited Bargaining Councils and Private Agencies

One of the functions of a bargaining council is to attempt to resolve any disputes within its area of jurisdiction. In support of this, Section 51(3) of the Act provides that any party to a dispute which falls within the jurisdiction of a council may refer the dispute to the council. This body must then engage in conciliation and, if necessary, arbitrate the dispute.

A bargaining council or private agency must apply to the governing body of the CCMA to be accredited as conciliators and arbitrators. If accredited, the nominated officials have the same powers as a commissioner. However, councils or private agencies will not be accredited to adjudicate on any dispute centring on:

- disclosure of information to unions
- organisational rights
- the interpretation and application of collective bargaining agreements
- agency-shop and closed-shop agreements
- statutory council agreements
- cancellation of a council's registration
- demarcation
- picketing
- co-decision-making
- information to be given to workplace forums
- interpretation of the provisions relating to workplace forums.

In broad terms, these bodies deal with disputes of interest and disputes relating to dismissals, unfair labour practices and the freedom of association.

Should the controlling body decide to accredit a council or agency, it will enter its name in a register of accredited agencies and furnish the applicant with an accreditation certificate.

### The Labour Court
#### Composition and Status
The Labour Court is a court of law and equity which, as regards matters within its jurisdiction, has the same powers as the High Court. It is also a court of record. It consists of a judge president, an assistant judge president and as many judges as the Minister of Labour, acting on the advice of NEDLAC and in consultation with the Minister of Justice and the judge president, may determine.

#### Jurisdiction
In terms of Section 157 of the Labour Relations Act, the Labour Court has, except when the Act provides otherwise, exclusive jurisdiction in all matters that, in terms of the Act or any other law, have to be determined by the Court. Furthermore, the Court has concurrent jurisdiction with the High Court as regards an alleged or threatened violation of a fundamental right as per Chapter 2 of the Constitution of the Republic of South Africa, 1996, if the violation relates to employment and labour relations or to any dispute over an executive act or conduct by the state in its capacity as employer.

#### Functions
The Labour Court may issue any appropriate order, granting any of the following:
- Urgent interim relief
- An interdict
- An order providing for an action to be carried out which will help remedy an injustice or give effect to the main objectives of the Act
- A declaratory order
- An order for compensation
- An order for damages
- An order for costs.

The Labour Court may also:
- order implementation of any provision of the Act
- declare any accord or arbitration award to be an order of the Court
- request the CCMA to conduct an investigation or to report to the Court

- settle a dispute between a member and their union or an employer and their employers' organisation regarding the implementation of the collective body's constitution
- review the performance of any function provided for in any action of the state as employer
- hear an appeal against a health and safety inspector in terms of the Occupational Health and Safety Act 85 of 1993
- perform any activities necessitated by the Labour Relations Act or any other Act.

A new Section 103A(1) in the Labour Relations Amendment Act of 2014 gives the Court the power to order that an administrator, who may be a commissioner, be appointed to administer a trade union or employers' organisation if the party concerned or the registrar requests it to do so or if it is found that the trade union or employers' organisation has failed to fulfil its functions or that there is serious mismanagement.

### Proceedings and Representation of Parties

Generally, all proceedings of the Labour Court must be conducted in open court, but the Court may exclude the public or specific persons from proceedings in any circumstances where a provincial division of the Supreme Court would be entitled to such exclusion.

A party to the proceedings may represent themself or be represented by:
- a legal practitioner
- a director or employee of the employer
- an official or office bearer of the employee's registered union or employers' association
- a designated agent or official of a bargaining council
- an official of the Department of Labour.

### The Labour Appeal Court

A party subject to a decision of the Labour Court may apply for leave to appeal against such decision. Should permission to appeal be granted, the party requesting such permission must lodge an appeal within 21 days of the date on which leave to appeal was granted.

The Labour Appeal Court is a court of law and equity. It should be the highest court of appeal against any decision made by the Labour Court.

The Court comprises the judge president and assistant judge president of the Labour Court, as well as three judges from the same court. Appeals are heard by any three judges from the panel as designated by the judge president;

however, a judge who heard a case which is subject to appeal may not act as chairperson during the appeal.

During proceedings, the Court may hear further evidence, which may be oral or given by way of affidavit, and it may decide to refer the case back to the Labour Court for the hearing of further evidence. After deliberation, the Labour Appeal Court may decide to confirm or amend the decision of the Labour Court, or to reject the decision and to give any other decision which it deems appropriate.

### Routing of Different Types of Dispute

The Labour Relations Act distinguishes between many different types of dispute, but essentially all disputes of right may be submitted first to conciliation by either the CCMA or a bargaining council, and thereafter to arbitration by one of the above or, in certain instances, to a final determination by the Labour Court. Disputes of interest, too, may be submitted first to conciliation by one of the bodies mentioned above, but after that the parties, except those in essential services, are free to resort to voluntary arbitration or to engage in a legal strike or lockout. However, the Labour Relations Amendment Act of 2018 contains a new Section 150, which allows the director of the CCMA to appoint a commissioner to arbitrate in a dispute which has not been referred to it if it is in the public interest to do so.

The Act widens the definition of 'conciliation' to include fact finding, mediation and even advisory arbitration.

The procedures to be followed in specific types of dispute are outlined in Table 11.1. Certain disputes may be referred to the CCMA only if there is no bargaining council which has jurisdiction, but there are other disputes which must be referred to the CCMA and not to a bargaining council.

## Types of Dispute and Means of Settlement

### Interference with the Freedom of Association

A dispute where interference with the freedom of association is alleged may be referred first for conciliation by the CCMA or a bargaining council having jurisdiction and thereafter, if the dispute remains unresolved, to the Labour Court for final determination (see Figure 11.1).

An applicant who alleges victimisation or interference with the freedom of association has to prove that a certain action (for example, dismissal) has been taken against them. The employer will then have to prove that they did not interfere with the freedom of association of the employee, or that they did not victimise the employee. Thus, the employer will have to show other good reasons for their actions or for their treatment of the employee.

**Table 11.1:** Dispute routes: Final resorts

| DISPUTES CONCILIATED BY A BARGAINING COUNCIL OR THE CCMA | |
|---|---|
| Freedom of association (freedom from victimisation) | To the Labour Court |
| Dispute of interest in essential services | Arbitration by a bargaining council or the CCMA |
| Dismissals relating to incapacity, incompetence or misconduct | Arbitration by a bargaining council or the CCMA |
| Automatically unfair dismissals | To the Labour Court |
| Dismissals for participating in an unforced strike for reasons related to a closed shop | To the Labour Court |
| Dismissals relating to reasons for retrenchment | To the Labour Court |
| Unfair labour practices (excluding discrimination) | Arbitration by a bargaining council or the CCMA |
| Unfair labour practices entailing discrimination | To the Labour Court |
| **DISPUTES CONCILIATED ONLY BY THE CCMA** (not referred to a bargaining council even where one has jurisdiction) | |
| Type of dispute | Route if unresolved |
| Organisational rights | Arbitration by the CCMA |
| Collective agreements (interpretation and application where there is no agreed procedure) | Arbitration by the CCMA |
| Closed-shop agreements and agency-shop agreements | Arbitration by the CCMA |
| Disputes relating to refusal to bargain | Advisory arbitration by the CCMA, then possible strike action |
| Request for picketing agreement | Determination by the CCMA |

| DISPUTES CONCILIATED ONLY BY THE CCMA (not referred to a bargaining council even where one has jurisdiction) | |
|---|---|
| Breach of picketing agreement or refusal of right to picket | To the Labour Court |
| Determination by statutory councils | To the Labour Court |
| Application and interpretation of law regarding organisational rights and bargaining councils | To the Labour Court |
| Workplace forums | Arbitration by the CCMA |

Refusal to Grant Organisational Rights

Where a union informs the employer that it wishes to exercise its organisational rights in terms of the Act, a meeting has to be held within a period of 30 days, with the purpose of establishing an agreement between the parties. Should no such agreement be reached, either party may refer the dispute to conciliation by the CCMA. If conciliation is unsuccessful, the dispute may be submitted to arbitration by the CCMA. The CCMA must make a determination within a period of 14 days.

A commissioner may, on their own initiative or at the request of the employer, cancel the organisational rights of another union already operating at the workplace if the commissioner is of the opinion that that union is no longer representative.

Interpretation or Implementation of Collective Agreements

Every collective agreement (except an agency-shop, closed-shop or settlement agreement) must provide for a procedure by which disputes regarding the interpretation or implementation of the agreement can be resolved. Such procedure should provide for conciliation as a first step, followed by arbitration. Where there is no disputes procedure in the agreement, where the procedure is not yet operative or where one party blocks the use of the procedure, either of the parties may refer the dispute to the CCMA. The CCMA will attempt conciliation and, should this fail, either party may request that the CCMA engage in arbitration.

The same procedure will apply in the case of agency-shop and closed-shop agreements, except that any person bound by an arbitration award relating to the administration and application of funds obtained under an agency-shop or closed-shop agreement may appeal to the Labour Court against such an award.

A different procedure applies where an employee has been dismissed because of their refusal to join a closed-shop union or because of the cancellation of an employee's union membership.

### Refusal to Admit a Party or Parties to a Bargaining Council

Any registered union or employers' association may apply in writing to be admitted as a party to a bargaining council. The application should set out details regarding the applicant's representativeness, the reasons why the applicant should be admitted to the council and any other relevant information in support of the application.

The council then has 90 days in which to decide whether or not to grant admission. Should it refuse admission, it must within the next 30 days supply reasons for such refusal. The applicant union or employers' association may then apply to the Labour Court for an order granting it admission to the council. The Court may admit the applicant to the council, amend the constitution of the council or make any other order which it deems fit.

### Disputes about Statutory Determinations

When a dispute arises concerning the interpretation of a determination made on behalf of a statutory council, any party may refer the dispute in writing to the CCMA. The CCMA will attempt conciliation and, failing this, either party may request that the CCMA arbitrate on the dispute.

### Interpretation and Implementation of the Act as regards Organisational Rights and Bargaining Bodies

These disputes may be referred first to the CCMA for conciliation, and thereafter to the Labour Court for legal adjudication.

### Disputes of Interest in Essential Services

When a dispute of interest occurs between parties in a designated essential service, the dispute may be referred to a bargaining council having jurisdiction or, where no council exists, to the CCMA. The council or CCMA will attempt to conciliate the dispute but, if no resolution is achieved, either party may request that it be subjected to arbitration by the CCMA or the council.

Arbitration must be conducted within a period of 30 days. If the arbitration award involves the state and has financial implications for the state, the minister may within 14 days table the award in Parliament. Parliament may then decide that the award should not be binding, in which case the dispute is referred back to the CCMA for conciliation and, should this fail, for eventual arbitration.

## Automatically Unfair Dismissals or Dismissals Related to Retrenchments, Closed-shop Membership or Participation in an Illegal Strike

A dismissal will be automatically unfair if:
- it involves victimisation
- it resulted from the employee's participation in a legal strike or protest action
- the employee has been dismissed for refusing to do the work of a co-worker who is on strike
- it has resulted from refusal by the employee to agree with an employer demand concerning a matter of mutual interest
- it resulted from the employee's exercising or declaring their intention to exercise any right in terms of the Act
- it is related to the pregnancy of an employee
- it is based on discrimination.

Disputes centring on such dismissals, as well as disputes relating to dismissals arising from retrenchments, participation in an illegal strike or non-membership of a closed-shop union, may first be referred to a bargaining council having jurisdiction or, if no bargaining council exists, to the CCMA. Referral has to take place within a period of 30 days from the date of dismissal, but an extension can be condoned by the council or CCMA. The body concerned has 30 days in which to conciliate the dispute. If no settlement is reached the employee may refer the dispute to the Labour Court for adjudication.

## Dismissals Related to Misconduct, Incompetence and Incapacity (Including Constructive Dismissal)

Disputes relating to the above-mentioned dismissals must also, within a period of 30 days from the date of dismissal (or a longer period if condoned), be referred to a bargaining council or, if there is no bargaining council or the bargaining council is not accredited, to the CCMA. The body in question will attempt to resolve the dispute by conciliation. If this fails or if a period of 30 days has elapsed since the referral of the dispute, the employee may request the bargaining council or the CCMA, whichever is applicable, to engage in arbitration. This it must do within a period of 14 days.

Alternatively, if one of the parties so requests, the director of the CCMA may refer the dispute to the Labour Court. This the commissioner will do only after considering the reasons for the dismissal, whether a question of law has arisen, the complexity of the dispute, the existence of conflicting arbitration awards and the public interest. A decision by the director to refer the dispute is final and binding.

The Labour Relations Amendment Act 12 of 2002 provides for a joint conciliation and arbitration process in cases where the dismissal is related to probation. A hearing will have to be held within 30 days and the council or CCMA must inform the parties that, if conciliation is unsuccessful, arbitration will commence immediately unless the dispute is withdrawn or there is reason for postponement.

### Unfair Labour Practice Disputes

Where an unfair labour practice is alleged, any party may refer the dispute to a bargaining council having jurisdiction or, failing this, to the CCMA. Either body will attempt to conciliate the dispute. Should the dispute remain unresolved and if it involves discrimination, making it automatically unfair, it will be referred to the Labour Court. Any other unresolved unfair labour practice dispute may be referred to the CCMA or a bargaining council for arbitration. However, if an unfair labour practice dispute centres on an occupational detriment suffered after making a protected disclosure, the employee may request that the case be heard by the Labour Court.

### Workplace Forums (Including Joint Decision Making and Disclosure)

Any dispute relating to the establishment and functioning of workplace forums, co-decision-making with forums and the disclosure of information to forum members may, in the absence of an agreed procedure relating to disputes on that particular issue, be referred to the CCMA for conciliation and, should this fail, to arbitration.

## Remedies for Unfair Dismissal

In any actions involving an alleged unfair dismissal (excluding an alleged constructive dismissal), the employee merely has to prove that the dismissal occurred. The onus will then fall on the employer to prove that the dismissal was fair. The Labour Court or an arbitrator may order the employer to do one of the following:
- Reinstate the employee with effect from the date of dismissal
- Re-employ the employee in the same or a similar position from any date following the dismissal
- Pay compensation to the dismissed employee.

The first option should be to reinstate the employee, unless:

- for good reason, the employee does not want to be reinstated
- it has become impossible to continue the relationship
- it cannot reasonably be expected of the employer to reinstate the employee.

Where a dismissal is automatically unfair or resulted from unfair retrenchment or redundancy, the Labour Court can make any other award which it deems fit.

Section 194 of the Labour Relations Act sets limits to the amount of compensation which can be ordered. The Act firstly stipulates that compensation must be 'just and equitable'. If the dismissal was automatically unfair, a maximum of 24 months' remuneration may be ordered. In other unfair dismissals and unfair labour practices the maximum is 12 months. (This is not the case with cases relating to matters heard in terms of the Employment Equity Act 55 of 1998, where no limits are set.)

## Establishing In-house Procedures

Employers and employees or their unions may decide among themselves on a procedure to be followed in the event of a dispute arising. Such procedures could specify:

- the manner in which a dispute is to be declared (this includes notice to the other party and a specification as to whether or not the declaration should be in writing)
- time limits for replying to the allegations or claims of the first party
- arrangements for negotiation meetings to attempt settlement
- time limits for negotiation (for example, a procedure may specify that if negotiation does not result in settlement within a period of two weeks, the parties may take recourse to other measures)
- other methods of dispute settlement, such as mediation or arbitration, which will be used by the parties
- whether a distinction will be made between disputes of right and disputes of interest, and whether different settlement procedures will be used in each case
- whether or not disputes of right will be submitted to private arbitration, to the dispute settlement machinery established by the government, or to legal action
- whether or not the right to a strike or lockout is admitted and, if it is admitted (or legally allowed), the limitations set and safeguards provided (for example, an employer may agree not to dismiss illegal strikers before a specified period has elapsed, or a union may undertake to remove illegally striking employees from the premises of an employer).

The dispute settlement processes established by private agreement may be described as private, plant-level or bargaining-level procedures. Such procedures are particularly popular where a system of plant-level recognition of unions exists. Where a party seeks to use procedures established by the government, the first question to be asked is whether the parties themselves tried to find a resolution and whether organisational procedures were used.

## Conclusion

The use of the dispute settlement mechanisms provided for in the Labour Relations Act remains largely voluntary. The parties or a party may, in most cases, decide to refer the dispute to the CCMA, a bargaining council or accredited agent, but may equally decide, even in a dismissal dispute, to follow other agreed procedures. Dispute settlement by the CCMA places a greater financial burden on the state, and the problem is to find sufficient persons with the necessary expertise to handle the workload of the CCMA.

The specific procedures outlined for every dispute may seem confusing, but it must be kept in mind that all disputes first have to be submitted to conciliation. This is usually undertaken by the CCMA, but, in the case of freedom of association disputes, interest disputes, dismissal disputes, illegal strikes and unfair labour practices, conciliation is undertaken by a bargaining council, if one has jurisdiction in the particular industry or sector. If conciliation fails, matters relating to freedom of association, admission to bargaining councils, the interpretation of the law regarding organisational rights, bargaining bodies, picketing, automatically unfair dismissals, retrenchments, dismissals for illegal strikes and dismissals resulting from non-membership of a closed-shop union go to the Labour Court. The CCMA, or a bargaining council where it has conciliated a dispute, arbitrates on the remaining issues.

## Suggested Questions/Tasks

1. John Smith works for a company which manufactures gates. Although the company is not a member of an employers' organisation, it has quite sophisticated labour relations procedures, including a detailed disputes process which makes provision all possible attempts to find a solution. John has been in the company's employ for the past 10 years and was promised that he would be appointed to the next promotion post which becomes available. However, when this happens, a much younger and less experienced colleague is appointed. John is very unhappy and lodges a grievance, but it is not resolved to his satisfaction.

a. What would John's next step be? How would he classify his problem? Provide details of the process and the possible dispute-settling mechanisms which could be employed. Explain how these would work.

b. After the first step the situation remains unresolved. What would John's next step be? Provide details of the process and the persons involved.

c. The second step proves unsuccessful and the matter progresses to the next step. What would this be? Who could be present and what process would be undertaken?

d. John is not satisfied with the outcome of the previous step. Does he have any further recourse? If so, subject to which conditions?

e. Give your own opinion on possible ways to resolve the problem.

2. Write your own case study involving a rights dispute. Exchange case studies with a fellow student. Provide a reasoned judgement of the other student's case study.

## Sources

Euwema, MC, Medina, FJ, García, AB & Pender, ER (eds). 2019. *Mediation in Collective Labor Disputes*. New York: Springer.

Kochan, T. 1980. *Collective Bargaining and Industrial Relations*. Homewood: Richard D Irwin.

Oxford Reference Dictionary. 1991. Oxford: Oxford University Press.

SHRM (Society for Human Resource Management). 2021. 'Managing workplace conflict: Mediation'. https://www.shrm.org/resourcesandtools/tools-and-samples/toolkits/pages/managingworkplaceconflict.aspx (Accessed 20 October 2021).

Vettori, S. 2015. 'Mandatory mediation: An obstacle to access to justice'. *African Human Rights Law Journal* 15(2): 355–377.

# 12

# No-fault Terminations: Incapacity, Retrenchments and Redundancy, and Mergers and Transfers

## Chapter Outline

OVERVIEW

THE CONCEPT OF NO–FAULT TERMINATIONS

DISMISSAL DUE TO ILL HEALTH OR INJURY

Temporary Incapacity • Permanent Incapacity • Alcohol or Substance Abuse • Abuse of Sick-leave Provisions

RETRENCHMENT AND REDUNDANCY

Rationale • Retrenchment versus Redundancy • Recommendations by the ILO • The Legal Requirements • Retrenchment Policy and Procedure • Notice of Intention to Retrench • Consultation | *The Requirement for Consultation* | *Consultation when Establishing Policies and Procedures* | *Timing of Consultation* | *Parties to be Consulted* | *Matters for Consultation* • Consideration of Alternatives | *Natural Attrition* | *Transfers and Retraining* | *Cutting Back on Time Worked* | *Voluntary Retrenchment/Retirement* | *Temporary Reductions in Salary* | *Job Sharing or Shared Time* • Selection of Retrenchees | *The LIFO Principle* | *Other Acceptable Criteria* | *A Multifaceted Approach* | *Acceptability of Criteria* | *Final Selection* • Retrenchment Pay and the Retrenchment Package | *The Legal Requirements* | *Disputes about Retrenchment Pay* | *Disqualification for Retrenchment Pay* | *Employer Concerns* • Final Notification of Dismissal • Aftercare • The Undertaking to Re-employ • Organisations Employing more than 50 People | *The Legal Position* • Retrenchment of Employees who Refuse to Accept Organisational Restructuring | *Relevant Legislation* | *The New Dilemma*

MERGERS, TRANSFERS AND OUTSOURCING

The Legal Requirements • Clarification of Concepts | *Transfer of a Business as a Going Concern* • Contextual Framework | *Phase 1: Pre-integration Phase* | *Phase 2: Integration* | *Phase 3: Post-integration Phase* • The Role of the HR Manager/Labour Relations Specialist

CONCLUSION

SUGGESTED QUESTIONS/TASKS

SOURCES

## Overview

An employee can be dismissed for misconduct or breach of contract, but there are instances in which the employee's services may be terminated through no fault on their part or without them having committed misconduct. This happens in the case of incapacitation through illness or an accident, or when for some other reason the employee is unable to fulfil their duties. It may also happen where for operational reasons the employee's services are no longer required. In these instances, there are special procedures to be followed. These procedures take into consideration the fact that the employee is not to blame or not at fault and the effect that such termination will have on the employee personally, professionally and economically.

The termination of employee services through retrenchments or redundancies is of great concern to unions and employees, particularly in South Africa, where there is endemic unemployment and it is difficult for retrenchees to find new positions. Therefore, the labour legislation places special emphasis on the implementation of correct and considered retrenchment and redundancy procedures. The term 'retrenchment' is used where, due to operational requirements or economic factors, the company no longer needs a particular number of employees, while redundancy occurs when a job becomes obsolete or no longer required, leading to a reduction of employees in the organisation.

Furthermore, and in recent years, the number of business transfers and mergers has increased. This happens where, for instance, an organisation decides to sell a portion of or all its assets to new owners, which may then negatively affect the employment status of employees. Similar to the process of restructuring due to operational requirements, the company is required to implement measures to ensure the smooth integration of employees into the employ of new owners or to terminate the services of those affected according to the applicable provisions of the Labour Relations Act 66 of 1995. Therefore, the human resource (HR) department must fulfil a key role during the transition and integration process, through assisting with organisational re-structuring and promoting the desired culture of continued business effectiveness.

## The Concept of No-fault Terminations

The concept of no-fault termination refers to the reasons and the procedures which are accepted by the Labour Relations Act as sufficient to justify the termination of the employment contract, even though the employee has not committed any offence. Section 188 of the Act states that a dismissal will be unfair if the employer cannot prove:

- that the dismissal relates to the conduct or capacity of the employee or the operational requirements of the employer
- that a fair procedure has been followed.

Where the employee is guilty of repeated or serious misconduct, or where the employee, despite repeated efforts by the employer, continues to underperform, their subsequent dismissal can be attributed to the employee's own behaviour and would not be classified as a no-fault termination. On the other hand, where the employee is for some reason incapable of performing their duties or where the employer retrenches or declares the employee redundant, the employee themself has played no part in bringing about the termination. No-fault terminations also occur in the event of mergers and acquisitions, where the employer decides to sell a portion of or all its assets, with a concomitant impact on the talent profile of the organisation. Terminations in cases of incapacity, retrenchment or redundancy, and even transfer, are extremely contentious.

The Addendum to the Act contains the Codes of Good Practice that serve as guidelines to employers when dealing with terminations and retrenchments.

## Dismissal due to Ill Health or Injury

It sometimes happens that an employee becomes ill or sustains an injury, either while working or elsewhere. In most cases, the illness or injury is of short duration and is covered by the sick-leave provisions as contained in the Basic Conditions of Employment Act 75 of 1997. However, in some instances, the employee may be away from work for an unreasonably lengthy period or may not be able to return to work at all.

### Temporary Incapacity

The Code of Good Practice: Dismissals provides that in cases where the employee's illness or injury is of a temporary nature, the employer should consider alternatives, and should take into account:

- the nature of the employee's work
- the period of illness
- the seriousness of the injury or illness
- the possibility of employing a temporary replacement.

In these cases, the question of payment to the absent employee arises, since the 30- or 36-day period of paid sick leave in a three-year cycle is normally not sufficient, even if the employee still has the full sick-leave allowance to their credit. Whether the employer will pay the employee for the full period or most of their absence is a discretionary decision. Some employers will consider the employee's length of service and sick-leave record. Where an employee has frequently taken sick leave at regular intervals, for no really serious complaint, the employer may decide that further payment is not justified. On the other hand, if an employee has long service and has rarely or never taken sick leave, the employer may calculate the sick leave the employee could have taken during their service and pay them accordingly.

If the employee has contracted the illness or sustained the injury as a result of their work, payment may be claimed in terms of the Compensation for Occupational Injuries and Diseases Act 130 of 1993, as amended. Previously, the scope of the Act excluded domestic workers from accessing related social security benefits, but since 10 March 2021, and following the Constitutional Court judgment in *Mahlangu and Another v Minister of Labour and Others [2020] ZACC 24*, domestic workers are now covered for illness or injury contracted at work in terms of Section 80 of the Act.

## Permanent Incapacity

As South Africa has a high prevalence of HIV/AIDS, tuberculosis (TB) and lifestyle illnesses such as diabetes and heart conditions, most employers offer wellness programmes aimed at preserving the livelihoods of employees, and employers are required to adhere to the Code when managing permanent incapacity. Where the incapacity of the employee is more permanent, the Code of Good Practice states that the employer must consider one or more of the following:

- Providing the employee with another job which they may still be capable of performing
- Adapting the employee's duties
- Adapting their working conditions.

Where none of these possibilities exist, the employer may eventually decide that termination is unavoidable. Such termination must be undertaken with the utmost sensitivity. All possible assistance must be given to the employee – for example, to claim benefits from the Compensation Commissioner (if the illness or injury is work-related) or to obtain early retirement benefits (to be 'boarded').

Terminations for incapacity may be challenged as unfair dismissals. In such cases the following will be taken into account:

- Whether or not the employee is able to perform the job
- If not, the extent to which the employee is still capable of work
- The extent to which the employee can be accommodated by adapting their work conditions and/or duties
- The availability of suitable alternative employment.

It stands to reason that, throughout the process, the employee will be consulted and informed. The case review below shares some key insights and learnings for employers to consider when dealing with prolonged absence due to injury on duty.

## Case Review: The Need to Explore all Possibilities

*General Motors (Pty) Ltd and National Union of Metalworkers of South Africa obo Ruiters: (22 January 2015 LAC)*

### Background

Mr Ruiters had been employed as a team leader in the General Assembly and Manufacturing Department at General Motors. A problem arose when Ruiters injured his left hand. This meant that it was painful for him to perform the tasks required when standing in for an absent employee. On 20 April 2006, Ruiters visited Dr Struwig, the company doctor. On the latter's recommendation, he was moved to another part of the department where not so many stand-ins would be required, although the fact that he still had to perform those tasks at times was problematic. Sometime later, Struwig convened a meeting with a specialist and a Mr Heynsen, evidently the head of Ruiters' department. It was decided that HR should be requested to assist in finding alternative employment for Ruiters. During cross-examination, it was stated by the union's representative that a certain document was produced at Ruiters' incapacity inquiry stating that Ruiters could drive. Further, it was stated that one of the witnesses at the inquiry, Mr S Naidoo, the body shop manager, had said that if the issue of Ruiters' driving ability could be cleared with the appellant's doctor (presumably Dr Struwig) then Ruiters could be accommodated in the position of a driver. On 3 December 2007, following the incapacity enquiry, Ruiters was informed that he was being dismissed, since he could no longer perform his job.

### Argument and Pronouncements

#### At the CCMA

At the Commission for Conciliation, Mediation and Arbitration (CCMA) hearing, Dr Struwig's testimony related mainly to his appointments with Mr Ruiters and the recommendations made by him, while Ruiters repeated his claim that he had suggested that he could drive. After hearing the evidence, the commissioner declared the procedure to have been 'procedurally and substantively fair'.

#### At the Labour Court

The trade union appealed against the commissioner's finding and the Labour Court noted that the arbitrator had failed to evaluate the evidence and failed to 'give consideration to a material issue'. This had the effect of depriving the employee of a fair hearing. As a result, the Court overturned the arbitrator's decision and ordered that the matter be referred back to the CCMA for arbitration by a different arbitrator. Not satisfied with the outcome, the company lodged an appeal with the Labour Appeal Court.

### At the Labour Appeal Court

This Court commenced by stating that, in accordance with the criteria for fairness, the task at hand was to decide whether the ruling made by the Labour Court was one which a reasonable decision maker would have made in the same circumstances. The Court conceded that if it was impossible to accommodate an employee who cannot continue in their job, a dismissal would probably be fair, provided that a fair procedure had been followed. It was up to the employer to prove that the dismissal had been both procedurally and substantively fair.

The Court concluded by stating that, in ignoring the need to further investigate the possibility of placing Ruiters, the commissioner had acted unlawfully. His decision was 'not in the range of decisions that a reasonable decision maker would have made'. In light of the above, the Court declared that the appeal by the company had failed. The judge indicated that, instead of appealing the decision of the Labour Court, the company should have allowed the matter to be reheard by another commissioner, as ordered by that Court. The Labour Appeal Court also ruled that because it was the company which had chosen to appeal, it had to bear all the costs of the court action.

## Discussion

What this case shows is that having a procedure is of no use if it is not followed in practice, if managers are not trained in the process and if, in the case of incapacity, all avenues are not explored. There seemed to be some inkling among the managers that something should be done, but no one took responsibility and, as the Labour Appeal Court stated, the matter went back and forth for 12 months without any definitive action being taken. In the end, a great deal of time and money was wasted, and the arbitration had to start from scratch.

## Alcohol or Substance Abuse

Addiction to alcohol or other habit-forming substances results in incapacity and productivity problems related to absenteeism as well as low employee performance. To avoid such potential challenges, the employer must implement policies regulating such behaviours and procedures to facilitate the rehabilitation of the affected employees. The policy can incorporate the following key measures:

- The education of supervisors or managers on how to manage alcohol and substance abuse at the workplace
- Scientifically proven methods to treat alcohol or substance abuse

- A declaration regarding strict adherence to confidentiality
- The implementation of initiatives such as the employee assistance programme (EAP)
- The risk implications of safety, productivity, medical or personal problems
- The prevention of victimisation and harassment
- The provision of designated areas in the workplace for smokers, while at the same time regulating their smoking intervals
- The provision of possible consequences if the employee violates the policy or is not rehabilitated despite the attempts undertaken by the employer.

In terms of the procedure, the employer needs to ensure that proper processes are executed to manage alcohol or drug abuse among employees. Invariably, procedures aligned to policies should provide step-by-step guidelines dealing with:
- how pre-employment tests will be administered to identify potential alcohol or substance abuse
- periodic scheduled medical examinations in special dedicated facilities
- the identification of employees with alcohol or substance abuse problems and how to engage in the process of rehabilitation
- a monitoring and evaluation programme designed to support the rehabilitation of affected employees.

In such cases, consideration is first given to counselling and rehabilitation. Only if this fails can termination be considered.

## Abuse of Sick-leave Provisions

It is unfortunately true that many employees abuse the provision for paid sick leave as contained in the Basic Conditions of Employment Act 75 of 1997. This is particularly so because the Act allows employees to take two days' sick leave at a time without a medical certificate; furthermore, even when medical certificates are produced, these may be for relatively minor complaints. The employer may not question a medical certificate or request further details from the medical practitioner without the employee's permission. This leaves the employer seemingly powerless to act against what may be termed 'delinquent absentees'.

Employees should be made aware that if they use their sick leave indiscriminately, they may in the longer term be at a disadvantage. Should they contract a serious illness or injury, the employer might not readily pay them beyond the paid sick leave due to them. Yet, despite such admonitions, employees may continue to abuse sick leave provisions.

If an employee is habitually absent for a day or more at a time, the employer has the following options:

- If the employee is absent more than twice in an eight-week period without producing a medical certificate, the employer can demand that the employee produce a certificate for the third absence, whether for one day or longer.
- Where intermittent absence continues over a long period, the employer should first establish the nature of the employee's incapacity. The employer may then request that the employee disclose information about their illness or submit to a medical examination by an appointed practitioner. This will enable the employer to determine whether the illness as claimed by the employee is permanent or temporary.

This process would help the employer to decide the course of action to be followed. If the employee accedes and the illness is confirmed, the employer will apply the incapacity principles described above. If, however, the employee refuses or the illness is not confirmed, the employer may inform the employee that their repeated absence makes them unable to fulfil their contract and that, unless there is proof of incapacity, the employment may have to be terminated.

## Retrenchment and Redundancy

### Rationale

Previously, it was regarded as the right of management to reduce or enlarge the workforce as demanded by production and economic cycles and in terms of business rationale. However, with the growing emphasis on employee rights, and especially the right to job security, the position has changed. Employers can no longer claim that retrenchment or redundancy is entirely a managerial prerogative, nor can these be undertaken on an ad hoc basis without the involvement of the affected employees or their trade unions.

The necessity of retrenchments, particularly of those arising from a cyclical downturn, is questioned. Unionists claim that employers reduce employment levels as a first option in times of economic recession, without considering alternative measures. They argue that there is an obligation on the employer to keep employees in their jobs, since those employees contributed towards business growth. Furthermore, most trade unions argue against retrenchments, citing that poor employees suffer the aftermath of job loss, while business executives earn astronomical salary packages.

On the macro level, retrenchments are seen as a direct result of the inadequate workings of the capitalist system. As far as unions are concerned, the reasons employers give for retrenchment – such as falling demand, financial distress, the need for more effective utilisation of human capital, low investor confidence and so forth – are not acceptable. Nevertheless, if there is no alternative, union and worker representatives may have to accept retrenchments, but they will do so only if the retrenchments are undertaken in a fair and equitable manner.

In South Africa, especially since the Covid-19 pandemic started wreaking havoc in the economy in 2020, retrenchments have been escalating, leading to ever higher unemployment levels.

Additionally, and in recent years, the global technological advancements exacerbated by the Fourth Industrial Revolution (4IR) have affected traditional employment. This trend will escalate further, unless the state, employers and trade unions collectively devise measures to combat job losses. Quite clearly, retrenchments are not only a business issue but also a disturbing social phenomenon. These developments will require a new approach to employment and collaborative relations between organisations and the providers of labour.

## Retrenchment versus Redundancy

A distinction is made between retrenchment and redundancy. Retrenchment is attributed to cyclical downturns, market losses or other economic factors which oblige the employer to reduce their labour force. Redundancy, on the other hand, occurs when jobs are lost through restructuring or the introduction of technology. In the case of retrenchment, the jobs may be reinstated if economic circumstances improve, but where redundancy occurs, the loss of jobs is usually permanent. In the past unions have claimed that more responsibility should be placed on employers for redundancies than for retrenchments. However, they may have to change this stance in the light of future developments in the labour market.

## Recommendations by the ILO

Recommendation R119 by the International Labour Organization (ILO, 1963: Article 12), concerning termination of employment, provides for retrenchment procedures by stating, firstly: 'Positive steps should be taken by all parties concerned to avert or minimise as far as possible reductions of the workforce by the adoption of appropriate measures, without prejudice to the efficient operation of the undertaking, establishment or service.'

In Article 13(1) it is recommended that, when a reduction is contemplated, consultation with workers' representatives should take place 'as early as possible on all appropriate questions'. Matters suggested for consultation include:

- measures to avoid the reduction of the workforce
- restriction of overtime

- training and retraining
- transfer between departments
- spreading termination of employment over a certain period
- measures for minimising the effects of reduction on the workers concerned
- selection of workers to be affected.

On the question of selection of employees for retrenchment, Article 15(1) recommends that this should be done 'according to precise criteria which … should be established, wherever possible, in advance and which should give due weight both to the interests of the undertaking, establishment or service and to the interests of the workers'. According to Article 15(2), the criteria adopted may include:
- the need for the efficient operation of the undertaking
- the ability, experience, skill and occupational qualifications of individual workers
- employees' length of service
- employee age
- the family situation of employees.

Articles 16 and 17 recommend the following:
- Employees who have been retrenched should be given priority of re-engagement, depending on the available number of jobs.
- Such priority of re-engagement may be limited to a specific period of time (meaning that the offer will not be there indefinitely).
- The wages of employees who are re-engaged should not be adversely affected, with due regard to the differences between the previous and new occupations.
- National employment or other appropriate agencies should be fully utilised in attempts to place redundant workers in alternative employment.

### The Legal Requirements

Section 188 of the Labour Relations Act concedes that a dismissal arising from the employer's operational requirements is permitted as long as a fair procedure has been followed. This having been said, employers cannot claim a fair retrenchment process without following the requirements of the Act, as contained in sections 189 and 189A.

Retrenchment is a no-fault dismissal. Because of its human cost, the Act places particular obligations on an employer, most of which are meant to ensure that all possible alternatives to dismissal are explored and that the employees to be dismissed are treated fairly.

Section 189 states that when an employer contemplates dismissing one or more employees for reasons based on the employer's operational requirements, the employer must, inter alia:

- consult with either the trade unions involved, a workplace forum or the employees themselves, in that order
- issue a notice to employees or their representatives, setting out the relevant information
- allow the other party the right to make representations and respond to these
- select persons to be retrenched according to agreed criteria or, if no criteria have been agreed upon, criteria that are fair and objective.

(Section 189A contains special procedures for organisations employing more than 50 employees. This will be discussed later in this chapter.)

## Retrenchment Policy and Procedure

Because of the importance which the legislation places on retrenchments and redundancies, it is advisable for an undertaking to have a retrenchment policy. It is preferable to have a policy or procedure before the fact than to run around for solutions when the reality of retrenchment has to be faced. Companies that have agreements with unions will usually also have agreed retrenchment policies and procedures, but even those organisations which do not have a high-level union presence need to establish policies and procedures. Where workplace forums exist, retrenchments are subject to consultation with the forum.

## Notice of Intention to Retrench

Employers are obliged to inform the employees or their union as soon as the possibility of retrenchment arises. Section 189(3) of the Labour Relations Act obliges the employer to include the following information in the notification to employees:

- The reasons for the retrenchments
- The alternatives considered before reaching the decision to retrench
- The number of employees to be affected
- The proposed method for selection of retrenchees
- Proposed times and dates
- Proposed severance pay
- Assistance to employees
- The possibility of future re-employment
- The number of persons in employ
- The number of people retrenched in the previous 12 months.

## Consultation
### *The Requirement for Consultation*
Sections 189 and 189A place a high value on consultation. In fact, if the employer fails to consult with employees on retrenchment, it will be an unfair retrenchment and the employer will face an order for reinstatement or compensation. The purpose of consultation is to enable the parties, in the form of a joint problem-solving exercise, to strive for consensus, if that is possible.

In order for this to be effective, the consultation process must commence as soon as possible once a reduction of the workforce through retrenchments or redundancies is contemplated by the employer, so that possible alternative measures can be explored. The employer should, in all good faith, keep an open mind throughout and seriously consider alternative proposals.

### *Consultation when Establishing Policies and Procedures*
Consultation will be necessary at various stages of the retrenchment programme. Where plant-level representation exists, consultation (and probably also negotiation) will already occur when general policies and procedures for retrenchment are established. This type of consultation will probably culminate in a retrenchment agreement, which would facilitate consultation when the need for retrenchment or redundancy actually arises. Worker representatives would want to know under which circumstances the employer would regard retrenchment as necessary. They should agree on some mutually acceptable standards or methods by means of which such circumstances may be verified. Consideration will also be given to possible alternatives to retrenchments, but the most important issue during this phase would be the negotiation of mutually acceptable criteria for the selection of people to be retrenched, and agreement on the exact steps and procedures to be followed in the event of actual retrenchment.

### *Timing of Consultation*
Whether there is a prior retrenchment agreement or not, consultation will have to occur once retrenchment or cutbacks become imminent. This entails notification to the union or worker representatives that the employer may have to retrench or is actually planning retrenchment. Opinion differs as to the length of notice or the exact timing for this type of consultation. It will depend on the nature of the employer's business and the reason for the reduction – that is, whether the retrenchments are due to economic, organisational or technological changes. Unions maintain that the employer should notify and consult as soon as they become aware of the need to retrench. In the case of technological innovation, this may be a year or years in advance, and in other instances it may range from six months to two weeks.

## Parties to be Consulted

Section 189(1) of the Labour Relations Act provides that where an employer intends to retrench or make certain employees redundant, the employer has to consult with a party determined by a collective agreement or, where no agreement exists, with a workplace forum. The employer must also consult with any registered union whose members will be affected by the proposed retrenchments or, if no union or workplace forum exists, with the affected employees.

## Matters for Consultation

In terms of the Labour Relations Act, during consultation the parties must:

- reach consensus on measures to avoid dismissals
- consider minimising the number of dismissals
- debate the timing of dismissals
- consider measures to mitigate the adverse effects of the retrenchments
- agree on the criteria for the selection of people to be retrenched
- agree on the retrenchment package
- consider the possibility of re-employment when the business improves as well as the time frames and criteria for such re-employment
- grant the other party the opportunity to make proposals on any matter related to the proposed retrenchments
- consider and react to these proposals
- should the proposals be rejected, furnish reasons for not agreeing.

## Case Review: Reasons for Retrenchment and the Need to Consult

*SACCAWU, C Moeng and others v Woolworths (Pty) Ltd (Case no J3159/12 & JS1177/12: 9 June 2015)*

### Background

In 2012, Woolworths stopped employing full-time staff, as that arrangement proved 'too inflexible' for its business. Instead, all new employees were appointed as flexi-time workers. On 4 August of that year the company instituted what it called a 'voluntary phase', during which management consulted with the full-timers as individuals. On 23 August the South African Commercial Catering and Allied Workers' Union (SACCAWU), which represented about 15 per cent of Woolworths' employees, challenged what it termed the 'unilateral action' by management. Woolworths claimed that it had not been their intention to retrench during the voluntary phase and therefore consultation with the union had not been required. In the end, 413 of the 590 full-timers accepted one of the alternatives, while 177 rejected the proposals. The 'voluntary phase' ended on 4 September.

The second phase of the exercise was termed the Section 189 phase, meaning that the company would now comply with the procedures towards retrenchment as set out in that section of the Labour Relations Act. To this end, it sent notices to the remaining full-time employees, inviting them to consultations on this issue. Management also informed SACCAWU of its intentions. This phase ended on 3 November. On 4 November, all 92 employees were dismissed.

SACCAWU, acting on behalf of 44 of the dismissed employees, took the matter to the Labour Court, alleging that the dismissals had been unfair.

## Argument

The Court commenced by referring to Section 189A(19) of the Labour Relations Act and explained that it had to decide not only whether there was a fair reason, but also whether it was fair to the employees and whether there was a reasonable basis for the retrenchment. 'Fairness, not correctness' was the test to be applied. The Court further noted that, although it was stated in the proposed amendments that employees doing the same work should be treated equally, there was also a caveat in the clause allowing for different treatment if there is a 'justifiable reason'.

## Pronouncements

The Court noted that Woolworths had not explored the alternatives to dismissal. It was the opinion of the Court that the company had failed to engage in meaningful consultation from the start and had failed to consider alternatives. It had failed to prove that the dismissals were 'operationally justifiable'. The dismissals were, therefore, substantively unfair.

The Court then turned to the question of procedural fairness. In this respect the Court noted that when the union had questioned management's actions in the 'voluntary stage', management had not engaged with the union and had merely responded that it was not contemplating retrenchments. Woolworths should have foreseen this possibility much earlier and engaged with the union instead of conducting 'consultations' only with individuals. The very nature of the three options already offered at the initial stage showed that if the offer was not accepted, the alternative would be dismissal, indicating that at this stage there was already an intention to retrench workers who did not agree. The Court went on to note that in the second phase, Woolworths 'refused to budge' even when reasonable alternatives were suggested. Instead, it urged the union to convince its members that accepting the changes would be 'more beneficial than severance pay'. It was indicated that, before a scheduled meeting on 3 November, Woolworths had already decided to dismiss the employees who did not accept the offer. This was proved by the fact that Woolworths had already sent a termination letter to one employee (later claimed as a mistake) and had considered the date of termination to be 4 November.

On the basis of the above, the Court decided that Woolworths had failed to consult meaningfully and that its actions were also procedurally unfair. Woolworths was ordered to reinstate all the applicants as from the date of dismissal without loss of pay. The company was also ordered to pay all costs.

## Discussion

Instead of following the retrenchment process as set out in the Labour Relations Act, Woolworths decided to institute its own version of the process to be followed. When forced to follow the prescribed route, it merely went through the paces without any concession to the arguments of and for the other party. In fact, the company's actions from the beginning might be seen as unlawful and as an attempt to coerce employees into agreement. Those employees who initially accepted the offer may have been intimidated into doing so for fear of having no job at all. This, in the present South African context, is a frightening prospect.

The reasons which Woolworths added to that of operational requirements to justify its actions were not only 'mischievous', as alleged, but also unconvincing and constituted a strange approach to the concepts themselves. For example, the argument that equality is achieved by bringing all employees down to the same level is the very opposite of the usual understanding of equalisation, as confirmed by the relevant provisions in the Employment Equity Act 55 of 1998. Also, the then proposed amendments to the Labour Relations Act, as referred to by the company, were mainly intended to safeguard vulnerable employees against discriminatory practices and not to assist management in downgrading the existing benefits of other employees. Finally, to boast of a saving which, as the Court indicated, was achieved by persuading employees to forgo their rights has the appearance of insensitivity on the part of the managers concerned.

All in all, this case is a good lesson in how substantive and procedural fairness should be maintained in dismissals for operational requirements.

### Consideration of Alternatives

Before a final decision on retrenchment can be made, alternative measures must be considered and implemented. The first and most obvious of these is natural attrition.

### Natural Attrition

An organisation with a high labour turnover should, if it is considering retrenchment, first try to reduce staff by not replacing employees who leave and putting a moratorium on recruitment. The company can ban the employment of casual and contract labour.

### Transfers and Retraining

Once provision has been made for natural attrition and the organisation has stopped the recruitment of new employees and temporary labour, it should consider transferring and retraining some of the existing employees, particularly where a certain job has or may become redundant. Unions insist that this alternative be considered, not only within the company itself but also among other companies belonging to the same group. Employers are expected to do everything in their power to find other positions for employees whose positions will become redundant. The law does state that an employee who has unreasonably refused the offer of a transfer or another position will not be entitled to retrenchment pay.

### Cutting Back on Time Worked

Other alternatives to retrenchment will involve the employees themselves. These fall under the general heading of a cutback in time worked. They include a ban on overtime, short time, temporary lay-offs, cycled unpaid leave or shared time. These alternatives cannot be unilaterally instituted and need to be negotiated with employees or their representatives.

Short time, lay-offs and unpaid leave may precede, but not completely obviate, the need for final retrenchment. Also, a total ban on overtime, which appears to be an easy alternative, may sometimes not be feasible because of the nature of the company's operations. The operations of the undertaking should be carefully considered before agreeing to ban overtime completely.

### Voluntary Retrenchment/Retirement

The final alternative is to be found in voluntary retrenchment or early retirement of older employees. This can be offered only if the pension and retrenchment package is such that it makes it viable for the employee concerned. In South Africa, early retirement may be a viable option for higher-level employees and for employees of all types who are close to retirement age, but it is not a solution for many unskilled workers. Also, to be considered is the fact that, unless the pension fund is strong enough to bear additional payments, it will be up to management to make the retirement package more attractive, and this may prove quite costly. Voluntary retrenchment brings its own problems. If the package is attractive enough, the best employees may leave. Employers are advised to reserve the right to retain key employees.

### Temporary Reductions in Salary

Only through mutual consent or by means of a collective agreement may the employer consider reducing the salaries and related benefits of affected employees. This can be done for a duration agreed to between parties or indefinitely until the business of the employer improves. At that point the employer should reinstate the employees' previous conditions of service.

### Job Sharing or Shared Time

A less popular alternative is job sharing, where two people share the responsibilities of one full-time position, including the salary and benefits. This arrangement is beneficial in terms of preventing job loss, but will require proper redesign of the job to ensure collaboration between the employees in question for seamless execution.

## Selection of Retrenchees

### The LIFO Principle

The question as to the criteria to be adopted in selecting people to be retrenched is often one of the most contentious in the retrenchment argument. Unions favour the adoption of the last-in-first-out (LIFO) principle. They argue that it rewards length of service and that it is the most easily applicable and objective criterion, and that it prevents any type of favouritism or discrimination against union members. Yet it could be argued that the LIFO principle does not always favour unions, whose members are often among the younger employees. Employers, on the other hand, contend that there is no reason that they should not be allowed to retrench less competent employees, to which the union may respond that retrenchments should not be used for disciplinary purposes.

### Other Acceptable Criteria

Unions will agree that the employer may reserve the right to retain workers with shorter service than others but with special or critical skills necessary for the continued functioning of the organisation, provided that there is no employee with longer service who would be able to do that job or who could be trained for that purpose. Worker representatives may also insist that, besides the LIFO principle, employers should consider special circumstances, such as the fact that an employee is the sole breadwinner or has a disability which would make it difficult for them to find new employment.

*A Multifaceted Approach*

In the past, criteria for the selection of people to be retrenched were generally set by the union rather than negotiated with the employer. A one-factor approach, consisting of the primary adoption of the LIFO principle, with reference to special circumstances merely raised by the union, was generally demanded. Employers have gradually persuaded worker representatives that a multifaceted approach should be introduced, that the employer also wishes special circumstances to be considered and that an appropriate formula encompassing various criteria, perhaps with different weightings, should be worked out. In South Africa, the adoption of various criteria is supported by Labour Court judgments. These have not insisted on LIFO as the only criterion, but have advised that:

- criteria should be agreed upon
- criteria should be objective
- the selection should be done fairly in accordance with the agreed criteria.

*Acceptability of Criteria*

The Labour Relations Act does not stipulate the criteria to be applied. It merely provides for consultation on such criteria and for the implementation of agreed or fair criteria. This implies that where no agreement on the criteria can be achieved, the employer may (after reacting appropriately to the other party's proposals) implement their own criteria, provided that these are fair, provable and consistently applied.

Selection criteria that are generally accepted to be fair include length of service, skills and qualifications. Generally, the test for fair and objective criteria will be satisfied by the use of the LIFO principle. There may be instances where the LIFO principle or other criteria need to be adapted. The LIFO principle, for example, should not operate so as to undermine an agreed affirmative action programme. Although affirmative action will not automatically protect employees from retrenchment, it may be necessary to agree on specific criteria relating to under-represented or designated groups. At the same time, care should be exercised that criteria do not indirectly discriminate against certain individuals. Exceptions may also include the retention of employees who are fundamental to the successful operation of the business. These exceptions should, however, be treated with caution.

Employee representatives generally refuse to accept that a worker who has been transferred to another department will have their previous service disregarded and would be the first out if retrenchments occur in that department. A policy of this nature becomes even more difficult to justify if the work done in the new department requires little or no training. This leads naturally to the question as to whether, if one department becomes redundant, retrenchments should occur vertically in that department alone or horizontally across departments. It is accepted that, particularly where the LIFO principle is applied, the selection of people to be retrenched should be conducted throughout the company – or even within a group of companies – unless circumstances dictate otherwise.

*Final Selection*

After criteria have been agreed upon, it is management's job to draw up the list of affected roles, including the names of persons to be retrenched. It is good practice to present this to the union or workers' representatives for scrutiny and for representation as regards exceptional cases.

## Retrenchment Pay and the Retrenchment Package
*The Legal Requirements*

The Labour Relations Act provides that consultation on the amount of retrenchment pay must take place between the employer and the body representing employees. Section 196 of the Labour Relations Act provides that employees dismissed for reasons based on the employer's operational requirements are entitled to severance pay of at least one week's pay for each completed year of continuous service with the employer, unless the employer is exempted from the provisions of Section 196. This minimum requirement does not prevent unions from attempting to improve on retrenchment payments. The right of the trade union to seek an improvement on the statutory minimum severance pay, through collective bargaining, is not limited or reduced in any way.

An employer or group of employers may apply for exemption from this minimum payment by utilising the exemption procedure of the Basic Conditions of Employment Act. The minister may at any time – but subject to consultation with the National Economic Development and Labour Council (NEDLAC) and the Co-ordinating Bargaining Council for the Public Service – revise the minimum by publishing a new minimum rate in the *Government Gazette*.

*Disputes about Retrenchment Pay*

A dispute concerning the amount of retrenchment pay may be submitted first for conciliation by the CCMA or a bargaining council, and thereafter to arbitration. In dealing with a dispute about retrenchment pay, the Labour Court may investigate the circumstances and determine the amount of retrenchment pay for which the employer will be liable.

*Disqualification for Retrenchment Pay*

As indicated earlier, an employee who has unreasonably refused transfer or the offer of another job is not entitled to retrenchment pay. Reasonableness is determined by a consideration of the reasonableness of the offer of alternative employment and the reasonableness of the employee's refusal. In the first case, objective factors such as remuneration, status and job security are relevant. In the second case, the employee's personal circumstances, such as location and family responsibilities, play a greater role.

*Employer Concerns*

One concern of employers is that management may agree to substantial retrenchment packages only for the employee to be re-employed soon afterwards by the same or another employer. The first, namely re-employment at the same company, would speak of poor planning, since if it is envisaged that reduction will be of a temporary nature, provision should be made for temporary lay-offs with limited or no benefits but with the guarantee of re-employment by a specific date. Employees are given a choice between permanent retrenchment with the necessary severance pay and temporary lay-offs with a guarantee of re-employment.

## Final Notification of Dismissal

The period of notice to employees, once the retrenchments have been agreed upon and the people being retrenched selected, is often the most contested part of the process. Employers, to avoid a drop in morale and productivity, usually delay notification to the employees selected for retrenchment to the last moment. Their reasons for doing so may be sound, yet unions insist that sufficient notice of retrenchment be given to the employees concerned. One of the reasons for this is the very strong psychological effect that summary notice may have on employees. To be out of a job from one day to the next is a severe blow. In response, there is the counterargument that rapid severance of a relationship is preferable to a drawn-out or gradual parting. Other reasons for sufficient notice cited by employee representatives are the need to allow the retrenched employees an opportunity to find alternative employment and the time required to identify cases where particular hardship may result.

In South Africa the requirement is that 'reasonable notice' should be given. This allows for a great deal of discretion on the part of the decision maker. The courts have indicated that if, in their opinion, an employer has given insufficient notice, that employer will be ordered to pay compensation in lieu of notice.

A compromise could be found in allowing for an additional paid notice period, over and above the normal notice period. This means that the employee is told of their retrenchment shortly before they are due to leave but is paid as though they were employed until the end of the month, whereafter the notice period comes into effect. In granting the payment, a clear distinction should be made between 'pay in lieu of notice' and 'retrenchment pay'.

## Aftercare

Once retrenchments or redundancies have been effected, assistance should be given to employees in claiming from the Unemployment Insurance Fund (UIF) and other benefits. Even if the paperwork has been done before the actual retrenchments, there will invariably be queries and problems. Also, employers should fulfil their promise of assistance in the search for alternative employment. For these reasons it may be necessary, in the case of both partial retrenchments and a complete shutdown, and especially in the case of large-scale retrenchments, to set up a temporary aftercare centre, either as part of the HR department or – and perhaps preferably – completely separate from the employer's other operations. The centre should also deal with the effects of retrenchment on employees who have not been retrenched, such as:

- feelings of anxiety after fellow employees have departed
- fears regarding job insecurity
- turnover intentions indicating the probability of employees leaving their jobs
- lack of motivation and low morale
- planned and unplanned absenteeism.

Figure 12.1 illustrates the retrenchment process, from the point at which the employer becomes aware of the need for retrenchments, to providing aftercare for retrenched and non-retrenched employees.

## The Undertaking to Re-employ

Unions may demand that, for a specified period, retrenched employees be given priority should vacancies arise. The procedure requested is that unions concerned be advised of vacancies and that they be given sufficient opportunity to contact people who have been retrenched who could possibly fill such vacancies. The demand for an offer to re-employ is a reasonable one, but it should be carefully considered, and there should be strict compliance with the offer once it has been made.

The unfair labour practices provisions in the Labour Relations Act include as unfair the failure to re-employ where an agreement to this effect has been concluded. This means that an employer may be faced with an unfair labour practice allegation for employing completely new workers in preference to previously retrenched employees. This could happen if the employer did not

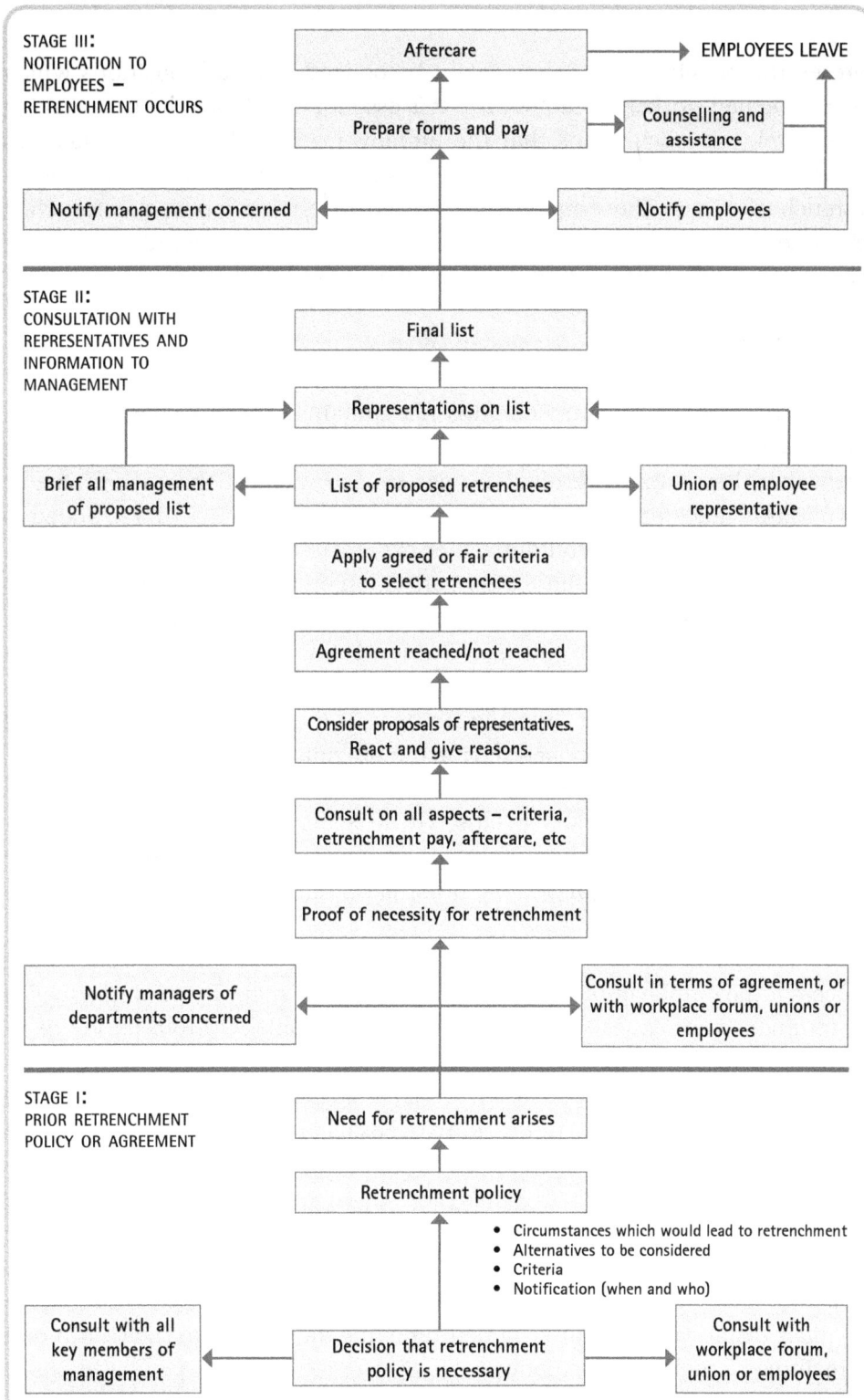

**STAGE III:**
NOTIFICATION TO
EMPLOYEES —
RETRENCHMENT OCCURS

Aftercare → EMPLOYEES LEAVE

Prepare forms and pay → Counselling and assistance

Notify management concerned ← → Notify employees

**STAGE II:**
CONSULTATION WITH
REPRESENTATIVES AND
INFORMATION TO
MANAGEMENT

Final list

Representations on list

Brief all management of proposed list ← List of proposed retrenchees → Union or employee representative

Apply agreed or fair criteria to select retrenchees

Agreement reached/not reached

Consider proposals of representatives. React and give reasons.

Consult on all aspects – criteria, retrenchment pay, aftercare, etc

Proof of necessity for retrenchment

Notify managers of departments concerned ← → Consult in terms of agreement, or with workplace forum, unions or employees

**STAGE I:**
PRIOR RETRENCHMENT
POLICY OR AGREEMENT

Need for retrenchment arises

Retrenchment policy

- Circumstances which would lead to retrenchment
- Alternatives to be considered
- Criteria
- Notification (when and who)

Consult with all key members of management ← Decision that retrenchment policy is necessary → Consult with workplace forum, union or employees

**Figure 12.1:** A retrenchment programme

foresee the possibility that they might be obliged to create positions which the retrenched workers could not fill. It is essential to phrase the undertaking to re-employ in such terms that the employer will still be able to take on completely new workers with special skills not held by the people who were retrenched. Where the employer is obliged to offer a job to a retrenched employee, a limit needs to be set on the time allowed for the union to fill the vacancy, as tracing retrenched employees may take too long.

## Organisations Employing more than 50 People
### The Legal Position

Section 189A of the Labour Relations Act contains special provisions which have to be adhered to by organisations employing more than 50 people in the event that they want to retrench 10 per cent or more of their workforce or have retrenched employees during the preceding 12 months which, added to the new retrenchments, would reach or exceed 10 per cent of the workforce. (There is one exception: where an organisation employs between 50 and 200 employees, this section of the Act also applies should they intend to retrench 10 or more employees.) In terms of Section 189A, the employer has to give written notice as provided for in Section 189(3). The employer must provide information regarding not only the number of employees to be retrenched but also the number retrenched during the previous 12 months.

The duty to consult remains. In fact, the Labour Relations Amendment Act 6 of 2014 added a new subclause (d) to Section 189A(2), stating that if one of the parties requests an extension of the 60-day period in the hope of reaching a workable agreement, the other party may not unreasonably refuse the request.

The CCMA must appoint a facilitator to assist with the retrenchment process if the employer or a union representing the majority of employees to be retrenched so requests. The request must be made within a period of 15 days following the notification of retrenchment. The purpose of facilitation is to help the parties reach consensus. If a facilitator has been appointed and 60 days have elapsed since the union/employees received notice of the proposed retrenchment, the employer may give notice that they intend to terminate the contracts of the affected employees. Upon receipt of such notice, the union may give notice of a strike action or refer the matter to the Labour Court on the basis that there is no fair reason for the dismissal. Because a facilitator has been appointed, the union is not obliged to follow normal strike or unfair dismissal procedures by first referring the dispute to the CCMA or a bargaining council for conciliation.

Where no facilitator has been requested, the parties can refer the dispute to the CCMA or bargaining council, provided that 30 days have elapsed since notice of retrenchment was given. After a further period of 30 days, as prescribed in Section 65, the employer may give notice of termination. On receipt of such notice, the union/employees may give notice of the intention to strike or to refer the matter to the Labour Court on the grounds that there is no fair reason for the dismissals.

The union/employees may immediately give notice of a strike if the employer gives notice of termination before the specified periods have elapsed. Where notice of a strike has been given, the employees may not refer the matter to the Labour Court. Equally, where the matter has been referred to the Labour Court, no strike action may be undertaken.

If the union/employee grievance differs from the reason for the strike, and is based on the fact that the employer did not follow a fair procedure, the union/employees may at any time request the Labour Court to issue an order compelling the employer to follow a fair procedure, interdicting or restraining the employer from dismissal before a fair procedure has been followed, or obliging the employer to reinstate a dismissed employee. Where none of these remedies are appropriate, the applicants may ask for compensation.

The detailed procedure related to retrenchments in this category reflects concern on the part of the state about the effect that large-scale retrenchments might have on the economy and also on the employees in a situation where unemployment levels are already high. Unfortunately, with increased mechanisation/digitalisation, the situation is not likely to improve. Employers will increasingly, and usually rightly so, argue that they have to employ the latest technology or outsource in order to remain competitive and cost-efficient. What is required is probably not more complex legal provisions, but for all parties to put their heads together to find new solutions to new problems.

## Case Review: Retrenchment – Employer Employing more than 50 Persons

*Leoni Wiring Systems (East London) (Pty) Ltd v National Union of Metalworkers of South Africa & Others (Labour Court: P413/2006)*

### Background

On 5 July 2006, Leoni Wiring, realising that it was not going to secure sufficient contracts for 2007 and that a shutdown was inevitable, issued a notice of intention to retrench in terms of Section 189A(2) of the Labour Relations Act. No application for a facilitator was made by any of the parties. At the first consultation meeting, which took place on 12 July, the employer explained that some employees would be retrenched at the end of September 2006 and the rest at the end of February 2007. The meeting ended with the understanding that the union would come back to management and provide feedback on the proposals made by management. When the union did not comply, management set up another consultative meeting, with a specific agenda point being feedback from the National Union of Metalworkers of South Africa (NUMSA) regarding alternatives to retrenchment. The union also demanded disclosure of the company's order book, its financial statements for the previous three years and other related financial information. On 15 August, the company responded by stating that the reason for the retrenchment did not lie with short-term financial problems (evidently more with long-term viability); however, if the union could show why the information being sought was relevant, the company might reconsider its stance.

On 27 September, NUMSA addressed a fax to the company in which the union alleged that the employees had been selected without discussions with the union and that the selection of permanent employees and the retention of contract employees was unfair. The next day, 28 September, the company received notification that the union intended calling its members out on strike in accordance with the provisions of Section 189A of the Labour Relations Act. The company immediately applied for an urgent interdict restraining the union from engaging in strike action. The employer applied for the interdict against the union to be granted as a matter of urgency. The Labour Court agreed.

## Pronouncements

In explaining its decision, the Labour Court declared itself satisfied that the employer had understandably been under the impression that no dispute existed and had therefore been justified in issuing the notice without referring the matter to conciliation. In the light of this, the proposed action by NUMSA was not lawful and stood to be interdicted.

## Discussion

Section 189A was inserted in terms of the Labour Relations Amendment Act 12 of 2002. As such, it was, at the time, a relatively new and untested piece of legislation. As the Labour Court indicated, no precedents could be found in South African law. What the case demonstrates is the complexity and, it might be said, the obtuseness of this section. Parties engaged in large-scale retrenchments should be warned to tread carefully and to check on every step taken. In fact, it might be advisable in all cases to request a facilitator, as the process appears to be simpler if one is appointed.

## Retrenchment of Employees who Refuse to Agree to Organisational Restructuring
*Relevant Legislation*

From the information provided in this chapter it is clear that the Labour Relations Act, and also the Basic Conditions of Employment Act, accepts the right of the employer to retrench employees who have become redundant and who, after a fair procedure and consideration of all alternatives, can no longer be accommodated in the organisation.

Until 2014, Section 189A(19) stated that if all the criteria listed in the relevant sections of the Act had been met, the Labour Court was obliged to rule that a dismissal for operational reasons had been fair if:

- it was based on a requirement related to the employer's economic, technological or structural needs or other similar needs
- it was operationally justifiable on rational grounds
- proper consideration had been given to possible alternatives
- the selection criteria were fair and objective.

Section 189A(19) has now been repealed, perhaps because the instruction to the Court might be too limiting, but the criteria still serve as sound guidelines and indicate that the law accepts the employer's right to dismiss for operational reasons.

However, in apparent direct contrast to the right of the employer to dismiss an employee who refuses to accept changed conditions of employment, Section 188(1)(c) of the Act declared that the dismissal of an employee in order to force them to accept a demand involving a matter of mutual interest would be an automatically unfair labour practice. This resulted in argument, especially by trade unions, that employers were prohibited from dismissing employees who refused to accept changed conditions of employment. The question which then arose was whether employers were obliged to retain these employees, even if there was a dire and well-proven need for implementing the suggested changes.

In 2002 the matter was seemingly clarified in the landmark judgment by Justice Zondo in *Fry's Metals* (see the case review that follows). Justice Zondo went to great lengths to demonstrate that the right of employers to retrench was reflected in numerous sections of the Labour Relations Act as well as in certain sections of the Employment Equity Act and the Basic Conditions of Employment Act. Most significantly, he clarified the intentions of a lockout as compared to those in an actual dismissal on operational grounds. Furthermore, he made a reasoned distinction between Section 188(1)(c) of the Labour Relations Act and the sections relating to retrenchment.

The result was that the dismissal of an employee who could no longer be accommodated was generally taken as justified, on condition that there was a clear reason for doing so, that a fair procedure had been followed and that there was no indication that the employer was trying to force the employee to accept. However, the matter did not end there, as is explored in the case review that follows.

## Case Review: The New Dilemma

*Fry's Metals (Pty) Ltd v National Union of Metalworkers of South Africa and Others (JA01) (2002) ZALAC25 (6 December 2002)*

### Background

In May 2000, Fry's Metals employed the services of a firm of consultants with a view to increasing productivity, as they regarded this as essential to the continued viability of the company. Following the advice of the consultants, the company, in June 2000, held meetings with the shop stewards to explain the situation that the company was in and the measures the company was proposing in order to 'ensure the continued viability of the organisation and continued employment'.

In essence, the proposed solution entailed a change to the conditions of employment for employees in certain departments by changing from a three-shift system of 8 hours per shift to a two-shift system of 12 hours per shift. The employees were given until 6 September to respond. At the meeting held on that date, they rejected some of the proposals and requested more time to decide on the others. On 3 October, a letter was sent to the union and the affected employees, giving notice of their retrenchment on 20 October.

The union immediately approached the Labour Court, requesting an urgent interdict ordering the company to refrain from dismissing the employees for 'failure to comply with a demand concerning a matter of mutual interest' and from introducing the new shift system. The Labour Court agreed with the union and interdicted the employer, who then appealed against the decision of the Labour Court.

### Argument and Findings

The Labour Appeal Court, under Justice Zondo, noted that the union had not based its case on a failure by the employer to adhere to the provisions of Section 188 of the Labour Relations Act, dealing with the retrenchment process, but instead had chosen to allege that the dismissals constituted a contravention in terms of Section 187(1)(c). The Court thus indicated that the matter had to be adjudicated with reference to this section.

The Court concluded that the pertinent question was whether the employer was dismissing the employees for operational reasons or to compel them to accept a demand. The Court maintained that the purpose of the dismissal was to make it possible to employ persons who would be willing to work the shifts; furthermore, that in the letter of 24 September the employer had specifically stated that the dismissals were for operational reasons and had even offered the employees concerned time off and assistance in finding new employment. All in all, this was not the language of someone who wants to force employees to comply.

The appeal by the employer was upheld by the Court.

The matter did not end there, as the union then requested leave to appeal against the decision of the Labour Appeal Court. In 2005 this application was finally denied.

## Discussion

It was conceded that not all dismissals/retrenchments for operational reasons would be judged in the same light. As an example, the Labour Appeal Court differentiated between the employer's actions in this case and that of an employer who waits until the matter is about to go to court before dismissing, evidently keeping the threat of dismissal only to persuade employees to accept changes. By contrast, the employer under discussion had, from the beginning, not varied the date of dismissal. Even when offering employees a chance to change their minds, management had indicated that this did not guarantee that they would be employed.

*The New Dilemma*

The relative certainty provided by the pronouncements in *Fry's Metals* was shattered when, in the Labour Relations Amendment Act 6 of 2014, the lawmakers saw fit to reword Section 188(1)(c) to read that a dismissal would be automatically unfair if it resulted from the refusal of an employee to accept a demand related to a matter of mutual interest.

The revised clause shifted the emphasis from the employer compelling to the employee refusing. It seems that this change, which is really an exercise in semantics, was aimed at nullifying Justice Zondo's assertion that an employer who finally retrenched an employee was, unlike one who locked out employees, not doing so to compel an employee to change their mind, but rather to make way for employing someone who would accept the new conditions.

With the shift to the employee refusing, it would seem that Judge Zondo's argument could no longer apply and that, if an employee refuses to accept a demand by the employer, including a demand that they agree to a change in working conditions, the employee cannot be dismissed. This is an untenable situation, as it literally ties the employer's hands. It ignores not only the nationally and internationally recognised right of the employer to reorganise and restructure, but also the necessity of doing so in existent and future economic conditions or due to organisational changes. Moreover, it ignores Justice Zondo's very clear distinction between Section 188, meant to deal with blatantly unfair dismissals, and Sections 189 and 189A, relating to retrenchments which, if conducted fairly, are sanctioned by the Act.

The only logical reason for the change in wording would be to cover grey areas where it might seem that the employer is acting fairly but their intention is to get the employee(s) to accept. However, this could still have been dealt with under the original wording, as was indicated by Justice Zondo when he explained that an employer who waits until the very last minute before dismissing might well have been trying to force the employees to change their minds by keeping the threat of dismissal hanging over their heads.

In essence, all the changed wording has done is to further confuse and complicate the issue, the likely result being another spate of cases until clarification is eventually achieved.

## Mergers, Transfers and Outsourcing

### The Legal Requirements
Section 197 of the Labour Relations Act deals with the issue of transfer. Where a business or part of a business is transferred as a going concern, the following precepts apply:
- The contracts of all employees are automatically transferred to the new employer.
- All the rights and obligations between the old employer and their employees are also transferred to the new employer.
- Any action or default committed by the old employer immediately before the transfer (eg unfair dismissals) is regarded as an action of the new employer.
- The service of all transferred employees is regarded as continuous – their length of service is calculated from the date they were first employed by the old employer.
- The conditions and benefits under the new employer do not have to be exactly the same, but must be equal to or similar in value and content.

Section 197A provides that in the case of insolvency, sequestration, schemes of arrangement or compromise, the contracts of employment are automatically transferred to the new employer. However, according to Section 189(1), an agreement concluded by both the old and new employers with a trade union, a workplace forum or the employees may provide for rights and obligations different from those under the old employer.

## Clarification of Concepts
### Transfer of a Business as a Going Concern
Section 197(1) of the Labour Relations Act states that 'business' includes the whole or part of any business, trade, undertaking or service, and the term 'transfer' refers to the transfer of a business as a going concern by one employer, to be known as 'the old employer', to another employer, 'the new employer'. It was obviously the intention that, besides mergers and takeovers, outsourcing, 'corporatisation' and privatisation could also be regarded as transfers of a going concern.

In the event of a transfer from one employer to another, the transferred entity must be the whole or part of a business (here, the test is whether there is an economic entity capable of being transferred) and the business must be transferred as a going concern (here, the test is whether the economic entity that is transferred retained its identity after the transfer). The phrase 'going concern' is not defined in the Act. What is transferred must be a business in operation 'so that the business remains the same but in different hands'. Whether that has occurred is a matter which must be determined objectively in light of the circumstances of each transaction.

In deciding whether a business has been transferred as a going concern, regard must be had to the substance and not the form of the transaction. A number of factors will be relevant to the question whether the transfer of a business as a going concern has taken place, namely:
- whether there was a transfer or otherwise of assets, both tangible and intangible
- whether customers were transferred
- whether the same business is being carried on by the new employer.

What must be stressed is that this list of factors is not exhaustive and that no individual factor is decisive. They must all be considered in the overall assessment, and therefore should not be considered in isolation. (see *NEHAWU v University of Cape Town & Others (2003) 24 ILJ 95 (CC)* and *Aviation Union of South Africa on behalf of Barnes & Others v South African Airways (Pty) Ltd & Others (2010 (4) SA604 (LAC))*.

Mergers, acquisitions and outsourcing involve a legalistic process, as described above, and there are fundamental contextual issues that need to be prioritised.

## Contextual Framework
Globalisation, and the need for ever-increasing efficiency, has forced organisations to revert to their core functions, to consolidate these functions and to cast off peripheral functions. The result has been a spate of mergers,

acquisitions and the outsourcing of certain functions. This may involve transfers and takeovers of entire non-core functions or business units of an organisation. It may also involve long-term contracts for the delivery of agreed services at agreed service levels for agreed remuneration, and may further involve the automatic transfer of a business/undertaking to the supplier.

In negotiating these 'deals', executives tend to concentrate on the financial, legal and operational requirements and pay little attention to the significant HR implications or to talent mobility, organisational structuring, culture alignment and system integration. Most disturbingly, HR leaders may not even be involved in the preliminary discussions that lead to the ultimate decision to engage in a merger or acquisition, but are often brought in only after the transactions have been finalised. This unfortunate state of affairs has much wider implications for benefits, policies, practices and organisational culture. Hence, the HR practitioner or labour relations specialist needs to be involved in the negotiations from the outset in order to provide input on organisational redesign. Figure 12.2 illustrates the three phases of the labour relations framework for mergers and acquisitions.

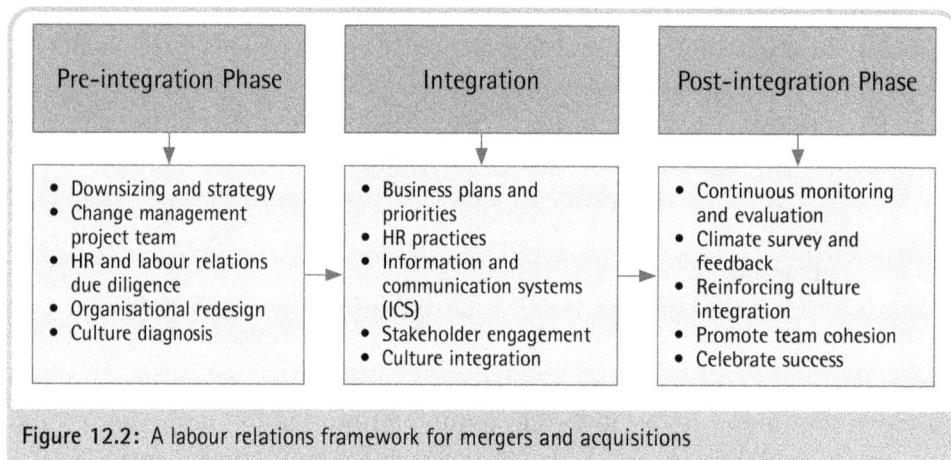

| Pre-integration Phase | Integration | Post-integration Phase |
|---|---|---|
| • Downsizing and strategy<br>• Change management project team<br>• HR and labour relations due diligence<br>• Organisational redesign<br>• Culture diagnosis | • Business plans and priorities<br>• HR practices<br>• Information and communication systems (ICS)<br>• Stakeholder engagement<br>• Culture integration | • Continuous monitoring and evaluation<br>• Climate survey and feedback<br>• Reinforcing culture integration<br>• Promote team cohesion<br>• Celebrate success |

**Figure 12.2:** A labour relations framework for mergers and acquisitions

*Phase 1: Pre-integration Phase*

Planned downsizing and the company's strategic intent to harmonise two or more companies into a single conglomerate should take into consideration the reasons for large-scale redundancies, the implications for talent mobility and employee resentment. It is therefore essential for HR professionals and/ or labour relations specialists to advise on key interventions to optimise employee performance and maintain order in the workplace.

A change management project team, including key business leaders, HR practitioners and labour relations specialists, must be formed to manage the entire business transformation process. In certain instances, and depending on whether the organisation is unionised, the members of the recognised trade union must also be involved as contemplated in the Labour Relations Act's provisions dealing with consultation in respect of mergers and acquisitions. The terms of reference, clearly stipulating roles and responsibilities, should also be spelt out to guide stakeholder engagement and the team towards realising a successful merger.

HR and labour relations due diligence, through determining the impact of the planned business transformation on employee engagement, is important. Moreover, the absence of HR practitioners or labour relations specialists in the early stages of this process could compromise plans to sustain the new business.

Organisational redesign, involving the rationalisation of multiple structures, functions, roles and responsibilities, should support a seamless business transformation. If formal governance processes are in place, the HR department will be able to encourage employee responsibility, empowerment, autonomy and the collaboration necessary to avoid silos and instead help employees to work towards the required synergies.

Culture diagnosis involves the formal examination of how the companies involved in the merger tend to do things. This aids in identifying inherent divergences and enables the formulation of plans to combine these habits, customs and routines to align with the new business.

### Phase 2: Integration

Business plans and priority synergies provide the context for HR alignment. Most importantly, labour relations specialists will be expected to facilitate employee engagement through communication, maintaining high standards of health and safety, improving trust-based relationships and managing dispute resolution.

HR practices related to labour relations, staffing and talent retention, training, remuneration and benefits, and continued employee performance improvement must be transformed to reflect the new business context.

Information and communication systems are at the heart of transitioning to the ideal business. Effective initiatives aimed at reducing uncertainty and promoting cohesion must be implemented through input from HR practitioners in collaboration with labour relations specialists.

Stakeholder engagement becomes more complex during this stage, as all parties from the various companies carry diverging expectations of the new merger. The realisation of commonality might well be unrealistic, especially if the labour relations specialists were not involved in the pre-integration phase.

Culture integration is a concerted effort that must be taken to restore calm, avoid confusion, manage uncertainties and improve trust by identifying and implementing common values that define the new way of doing things.

*Phase 3: Post-integration Phase*

Phases 1 and 2 demonstrate the extent to which companies invest in this business transformation process. Now, to realise the return on investment (ROI) of the merger and acquisition, efforts must be made to continuously monitor and evaluate key success factors (KSFs) and barriers. This is done through dedicated governance interventions such as audits and quality assurance.

Climate survey and feedback is often part of the monitoring and evaluation process. The purpose of this step is to assess the impact of the process on employee engagement and productivity and on sustainable growth.

Culture reinforcement is another investment undertaking that can be explored, through intrinsic and extrinsic motivators, depending on the level of integration and barriers impeding the new way of doing things. Hence, it is advisable for business leaders, including HR practitioners, to always act in exemplary ways and in accordance with the new value system. This will encourage employees to also align their behaviour, attitude and actions, and will possibly reduce the cost of extrinsic (tangible) rewards.

Managing teams from different organisations is a mammoth task which cannot be overlooked. Moreover, HR practitioners will be expected to implement initiatives to promote team homogeneity and cross-functional relationships. They will also need to support special-purpose teams through their capacity to diagnose business problems and present solutions for optimising business transformation.

Based on the complexity of the merger and acquisition process, a successful outcome should be celebrated by involving all stakeholders, particularly senior management and employee representatives of a recognised trade union, if the organisation is unionised.

It cannot be overemphasised that the involvement of the HR department – and trade union officials, where applicable – right from the pre-integration phase will help avoid any adverse post-acquisition consequences such as absenteeism, substandard employee performance, low productivity, uncertainty, low morale and even labour unrest.

## The Role of the HR Manager/Labour Relations Specialist

As indicated, the HR or labour relations practitioner needs to become involved from the outset in any plans regarding mergers, acquisitions, alliances and disposals that would culminate in the transfer of employees. HR or labour relations practitioners play a critical role in the pre-integration phase; in the integration of systems, processes and culture; and in the post-integration phase by assessing the successful transformation of a new entity.

Initial negotiations involving mostly senior management and small project teams should preferably also include HR practitioners, so that they can provide input on the following matters:

- Whether all contracts will be transferred, or whether there will have to be rationalisation and, if so, how this process will be undertaken
- If contracts are to be transferred, whether terms and conditions of service will be the same or similar (this will include the employer's contribution to pension and medical aid funds)
- Where two organisations are to merge, how different terms and conditions, as well as policies, can be brought together
- How a unified culture between two vastly different organisations will be achieved
- Whether salary bands and job evaluation systems can be integrated
- Whether there are existing arrangements and agreements with unions and how these will be transferred or amalgamated (the organisations may have different recognised unions)
- Promises made to, or obligations towards, existing employees, and how these are to be fulfilled or met by the new entity
- The possibility of varying job content and how this and other questions of promotion will be handled
- The cost of relocations, where these become necessary
- The provision of physical accommodation and facilities to transferred employees
- The continuation of affirmative action initiatives
- The possibility of outsourcing certain functions and the contractual implications, as dictated by Section 197 of the Labour Relations Act
- Where transfers are transnational, the differences between the labour legislation of the different countries involved and the effect of this on the objective of achieving unified terms and conditions of employment
- The possibility of transnational support among unions and union federations and the implications of this for the organisation
- The cost of possible redundancies, changes in conditions of service, changes in systems and monies to be paid to employees that need to be calculated before transactions are finalised.

Once the negotiations have been completed and the transfer becomes imminent, employees and their representatives need to be informed. A change of such dimensions causes a great deal of uncertainty and anxiety, with a concomitant effect on employee morale. Therefore, communication needs to be handled with great sensitivity. Employees need to be given detailed information, preferably in small groups where questions can be addressed and uncertainties dealt with. Where a recognised union exists, these employee representatives must be involved, particularly if redundancies are being considered. In terms of Section 197 of the Labour Relations Act, any change in terms and conditions of employment will have to be negotiated with a union and a collective agreement concluded. In this regard, employers are expected, in terms of the Act, to disclose the relevant information that will enable the union to participate meaningfully in the consultation process.

The need for communication is ongoing. Information cannot be supplied once off. Communication will have to continue, and feedback obtained, even after the transfer has been effected. The process is so complex that problems are bound to occur, and these have to be dealt with as they arise.

## Case Review: Transfer of Contract Following a Merger

### *Mwamweda v University of KwaZulu-Natal (CCMA: KNDB8712040, 18 March 2006)*

### Background

Mwamweda was appointed to the position of professor and Dean of Education at the University of Natal in January 2002. His appointment was for a fixed period of five years. Subsequent to his appointment, the University of Natal merged with the University of Durban-Westville to become the University of KwaZulu-Natal, the effective date being 1 January 2004. According to Mwamweda, he was first told that his contract would be transferred to the new institution and that there would be no change to his contract conditions. However, in November, a circular indicated that certain jobs, Mwamweda's included, were going to be advertised and that incumbents had to apply for positions. Mwamweda questioned the need to apply for his own position. When no information was forthcoming, he wrote a letter to the head of HR, a Ms Scheepers, enquiring what was happening to his contract, since his post was being advertised. Scheepers responded that nobody had a position at the new institution. Before this, Mwamweda had also spoken to Professor Mazibuko, at the time the Executive Dean of Humanities, who had informed him that his contract was with the University of Natal, and that he had no contract with the University of KwaZulu-Natal. Because of this uncertainty, Mwamweda decided to reapply for his position. Apparently, he and the Head of Education at the then University of Durban-Westville were the only applicants.

Mwamweda stated that he could not understand how the other candidate could have been appointed in his stead since, although she met the minimum requirements, she could not match him in experience. According to Mwamweda, he did not have a definite position after the merger, a situation he found devastating. To occupy himself, he had taken to teaching some classes.

## Argument

In bringing his case to the CCMA, Mwamweda alleged that he had been unfairly demoted. Although he was being paid the same salary as before, he had lost the status of dean. He had been appointed as a dean and not as a person receiving a certain salary package. The Senior Manager: Employee Relations, a Mr Finden, argued that although the contracts of all employees were transferred to the new institution, there was a difference between contracts and posts and that the latter were not transferred. With the merger, overlaps occurred, and it became necessary to deploy certain persons and advertise positions such as the deanships. According to Finden, after the merger and before the interview, Mwamweda did not occupy any post; in fact, nobody occupied a post, but employees had not been told this, as it might have caused consternation. After the merger had taken place, Mwamweda was 'merely performing the functions of a dean', but 'actually he was not a dean'.

Mazibuko indicated that she had discussed Mwamweda's position with him, an assertion denied by the latter. Her understanding of the situation was that he was an external candidate, as he had a fixed-term contract. Therefore, all deans had to apply for the eight positions, and those not successful would be redeployed. According to Mazibuko, Mwamweda was a dean until the new structure was put in place. When asked of which institution he was dean, she replied that he was 'dean full-stop'. She could not understand why Finden had said that the posts had fallen away.

## Pronouncements

In his analysis of argument, the commissioner pointed to the relevant provisions of Section 197 of the Labour Relations Act and Section 23 of the Higher Education Act 101 of 1997, as well as Mwamweda's contract of employment. Both Acts make provision for the automatic transfer of contracts and for the rights and obligations of the old employer to be transferred to the new employer. As the commissioner put it, the rights outlined in the Higher Education Act were placed there 'to assure all staff of employment in terms of their existing contracts. It informs them that their existing conditions of service, their benefits and salaries, will remain intact'.

It was noted that, while the university maintained that it had honoured Mwamweda's contract in every way and was paying him the same salary as before, the latter's case rested on the fact that he was no longer the Dean of Education. The commissioner went on to point out that the provisions of Section 197 of the Labour Relations Act are automatic unless otherwise agreed in a collective agreement. Therefore, the new institution was obliged to retain Mwamweda in the position of dean on terms no worse than those in his contract. The university was ordered to reinstate Mwamweda in the position of Dean of Education, with retrospective effect as from 8 December 2004, and to pay the applicant's costs.

## Discussion

This case illustrates the results of entering into a merger without following proper processes as regards the transfer of staff to the new institution. To justify their stance with regard to Mwamweda, the person responsible for employee relations engaged in a semantic exercise, asserting the difference between contracts and posts. As the commissioner rightly noted, this distinction is 'illusory rather than real'. In fact, it is absurd. An employee's contract is for a specific post. If the employee's contract is transferred, it is assumed that it will be for the same post. The fact that there may not be sufficient posts available in the new structure is a completely different matter.

Mergers do bring about problems of duplication, particularly in the higher echelons of institutions and organisations, where it is not easy to find similar positions for redundant persons. This is why it is necessary to be proactive and transparent, to discuss the problems which are foreseen with the incumbents and to consider alternatives, including the option of retrenchment, either before or after a merger. Keeping employees on a string, and then placing them where management sees fit, is not a recommended procedure.

# Conclusion

Dealing with no-fault terminations is the most difficult task of the HR practitioner. It is evident from the contents of this chapter that such terminations cannot be undertaken in haste. They require careful planning, consultation with all relevant parties, consideration of all possible problems and alternatives, and sensitivity to the fears and uncertainties of all employees as well as the hardships to be suffered by those who lose their jobs.

# Suggested Questions/Tasks

1. Draw up a detailed retrenchment policy and procedure for your organisation. Divide into three groups, namely management, the union and the Labour Court.
   a. Management and the union role-play their interactions and negotiations up to the point of dismissal of certain employees. They then produce a file containing all relevant correspondence as well as minutes of meetings.
   b. The matter is then taken to the Labour Court by the union. The union must set out grounds for the referral, while the company must respond in writing. Both parties then present their case and engage

in argument. The Court does the necessary questioning and finally produces a reasoned and substantiated verdict which is relayed verbally and in writing to the other parties.

2. You employ 250 persons. It is now May 2022. In September 2021, 20 employees were retrenched and the company now wants to make 10 more jobs redundant due to the introduction of new technology. What process would you follow and how could the union respond?

3. Indicate whether the following would qualify as 'the transfer of a business as a going concern'. Supply reasons for your answer and outline the process to be followed in each case:

   a. M and M is closing down its clothing factory. The factory has been bought by J and J, which intends to manufacture cardboard boxes.

   b. EXPO Consultants has decided to outsource its window-cleaning operation. The company to which the operation has been outsourced specialises in the cleaning of windows and already has a large full-time staff.

   c. The Getyou Bank has decided to acquire the Dontcare Insurance Company.

   d. Cantlast, a large funeral service, has declared itself insolvent. Nobody is interested in buying this business.

4. You are the HR manager in an organisation which is about to take over another business as a going concern. The directors are worried that they may not be able to employ the other party's employees.

   a. Could the directors possibly avoid taking over the employees? Explain. Also indicate what the other party would have to do as part of the transfer of a going concern.

   b. What advice would you give the directors in your organisation if avoidance proves impossible?

   c. What would have to be done if, six months down the line, your organisation wants to retrench some of the transferred employees?

   d. Explain the importance of involving HR practitioners, labour relations specialists and trade union officials in the merger and acquisition process.

## Sources

ILO (International Labour Organization). 1963. 'R119 – Termination of Employment Recommendation'. https://www.ilo.org/dyn/normlex/en/f?p = 1000:12100:1152855 8356405::NO::P12100_SHOW_TEXT:Y: (Accessed 28 September 2021).

# 13

# Collective Bargaining

## Chapter Outline

➤

THE RIGHT TO FREE COLLECTIVE BARGAINING

FREEDOM OF ASSOCIATION AND FREEDOM FROM VICTIMISATION

ORGANISATIONAL RIGHTS

Exercising Organisational Rights • Representative versus Majority Unions • Rights of Majority Trade Unions • Rights Granted to Representative Unions • New Rights for Non-majority Unions • Right to Establish Thresholds of Representativeness • The Right to Appoint Shop Stewards | *Election of Shop Stewards* | *Shop Steward Rights* • The Right to Disclosure of Information • The Right to Negotiate for Agency Shops and Closed Shops | *The Problem* | *Agency Shops* | *Closed Shops* | *Evaluation*

ENFORCEABILITY OF AGREEMENTS

CENTRALISED BARGAINING STRUCTURES

Legislation for Bargaining Councils • Establishing a Bargaining Council | *Voluntary Agreement by Parties* | *Constitution of a Bargaining Council* | *Registration of Bargaining Councils* • Functions of Bargaining Councils

BARGAINING COUNCIL AGREEMENTS

Contents of Agreements • Status of Bargaining Council Agreements • Extension of Agreements • Arguments for and against Extension • Exemptions from Agreements • Duration of an Agreement • Administration and Policing of Agreements

BARGAINING COUNCILS IN THE PUBLIC SERVICE

STATUTORY COUNCILS

WORKPLACE RIGHTS OF UNIONS PARTY TO BARGAINING COUNCILS

DECENTRALISED BARGAINING STRUCTURES

The Right to Recognition | *The Nature of Recognition* | *The Recognition Agreement* • Substantive Agreements at Plant Level • Other Procedural Agreements

THE ONGOING DEBATE ABOUT BARGAINING STRUCTURES

THE DUTY TO BARGAIN: LEGAL PRECEPTS

Voluntary Nature of Bargaining • Indirect Compulsion to Bargain • Good Faith Bargaining • Bargaining Levels and Bargaining Partners

WORKPLACE FORUMS

Definition of Workplace • Constitution of a Workplace Forum • Forum Meetings • Establishing a Workplace Forum | *Prerequisites* • Establishment and Functions • Definition of Employee • Matters for Consultation • Nature of Consultation • Matters Subject to Joint Decision Making • The Joint Decision-making Process • Applying for a Workplace Forum

ETHICS IN COLLECTIVE BARGAINING

CONCLUSION

SUGGESTED QUESTIONS/TASKS

SOURCES

# Overview

Collective bargaining is, in most labour relations systems, the central process in the conduct of the labour relationship. Once they have been unionised, employees will demand that the employer establish a bargaining relationship with them so that together they may attempt to resolve their conflicts and regulate their relationship. This relationship will be established because there is a common interest between the two parties. The purpose of the relationship is to prevent either party from using its coercive power to achieve its own ends. Nevertheless, the threat that a particular party may apply coercive power is always present in the bargaining relationship. It serves to pressure both sides into agreement.

The bargaining process will cover a wide range of items, some of them substantive and others procedural in nature. These may be dealt with by either distributive or integrative bargaining. Also, bargaining may be conducted in different types of bargaining units, and with employers at various levels. Bargaining units and bargaining levels determine bargaining structures, of which there are many forms.

The type of bargaining structure established in a particular labour relations system will define the relationships and interactions in that system. The structure is, in turn, dependent on a number of factors, most of them related to union or employer organisation and strategy. The state, too, may play an important role in determining bargaining structures and the bargaining relationship.

South African labour legislation has, since the advent of democracy, protected the right to free collective bargaining. This is supported by the rights to freedom of association and freedom from victimisation. The Labour Relations Act 66 of 1995 re-established these rights and granted unions a number of additional organisational rights, as well as the right to establish closed shops and agency shops. Closed shops can oblige employees who are not members of the union to join the majority union. In the case of an agency shop, employees who are not members of the union can be obliged to pay amounts equal to union dues into a union-administered fund. The argument can be made that the closed shop in particular contravenes the freedom-of-association provision.

The legislation does not enforce collective bargaining, but it does actively encourage it and it indirectly promotes the establishment of centralised bargaining bodies in the form of bargaining councils, whose agreements may be extended to non-parties. Some bargaining councils have become so big, so entrenched and so formalised that unions in these councils have lost touch with their grassroots membership. Therefore, it may become necessary to balance centralised negotiation with stronger representation at plant level, and even to establish more co-operative bodies in the form of, for example, workers' councils (but not those subject to the majority union as now provided for in the Labour Relations Act).

Finally, all parties need to continually bear in mind that we are on the brink of significant changes in the way business is done and therefore also in employment relations. Everyone involved should begin to gear their relationships towards these changes.

When looking at the theoretical principles of collective bargaining, it is important to consider:

- the important role played by collective bargaining in the labour relationship
- the use of power in the bargaining process
- distributive bargaining versus integrative bargaining
- centralised and decentralised bargaining units and bargaining levels.

## Collective Bargaining in the Labour Relationship

Convention No 154 of the International Labour Organization (ILO) defines collective bargaining as referring to (ILO, 1981: Article 2):

> *all negotiations which take place between an employer, a group of employers or one or more employers' organisations, on the one hand, and one or more workers' organisations, on the other, for –*
> *(a) determining working conditions and terms of employment; and/or*
> *(b) regulating relations between employers and workers; and/or*
> *(c) regulating relations between employers or their organisations and a workers' organisation or workers' organisations.*

The collective bargaining process, although it may be union-initiated, is a two-way process in which there is pressure and counterpressure from both sides. Just as the union might wish to gain concessions from management, so too might management wish to gain concessions from the union. To these ends, they bargain and eventually reach a compromise.

Furthermore, the collective bargaining process is, to some extent, a co-operative process. It might arise from a conflict of interests and goals, but it can take place only because there are common interests. Its purpose is to contain conflict and even to promote co-operation.

Collective bargaining has hitherto been the principal method by which employers and their employees as a collective have established and continued relationships which might otherwise prove difficult to maintain. Collective bargaining is a way for the two sides to get together, to talk about their problems, needs and goals, and to try to settle their differences.

Collective bargaining should not be an isolated process. Where there is an established relationship, it could be a continual process of give and take. How much a particular party gives will usually depend on the power of the other, but power is not static. The fulcrum of power continually shifts between the two parties. Also, collective bargaining is subject to external influences in the shape of economic and sociopolitical developments, technological innovation and demographic changes. These affect the power balance between the parties and lead to issues over which there might be disagreement.

Thus, the collective bargaining process may be more comprehensively described as a process which:

- is necessitated by a conflict of needs, interests, goals, values, perceptions or ideologies or any combination of these
- relies on a basic interdependency and commonality of interest
- involves the application of continual pressure and counterpressure by the employee collective and the employer collective
- is aimed at achieving some balance between the needs, goals and interests of management and those of employees – the extent to which either party achieves its objectives depending on:
  - the nature of the relationship
  - each party's source and use of power
  - the power balance between the parties
  - the organisational and strategic effectiveness of each party
  - the type of bargaining structure
  - the prevalent economic, sociopolitical and other conditions.

## Commonality as a Basis for Bargaining

Bargaining would not take place if there were no point of common interest between employer and employee. There would be no bargaining if it were not necessary for the parties to work together to produce goods or services and, in the long term, to ensure the future of the undertaking and the economy as a whole. Because both parties will benefit from the enterprise and because one needs the other to achieve their own goals, bargaining does take place. Thus, commonality of interest and interdependence form the basis of the bargaining relationship. Both parties have to acknowledge the existence of the relationship before bargaining can commence.

However, although common interests are at the basis of the labour relationship, the emphasis has usually been placed on conflict and the need to bargain about the parties' diverging interests.

## Force and Counterforce in the Bargaining Relationship

### Power as Regulator of the Bargaining Process

While commonality of interest may be the basis of the bargaining relationship and conflict the reason for bargaining, power could be described as the driving force. Despite their common interest and the need to control conflict, the parties would probably not agree to bargain if they did not believe that the other party held some form of power. Where one party holds all or most of the power, it will usually pursue its own interests to the detriment of the other party. Each party's pursuit of its own interests will be limited only by the power, or counterforce, which the other party can apply.

### Employer versus Employee Power

Power can take various forms, but the basis of the employer's power is the fact that they provide the employee with the opportunity to work and earn a living. The employee holds power because of their ability to withhold their work from the employer.

In the individual employer–employee relationship it is easier for the employer to withhold the opportunity to work from the employee than it is for the employee to withhold their labour from the employer. The employer may not be dependent on the work of one employee and probably could replace that employee with another worker or with machinery, whereas the employee depends on the employer for their livelihood and the ability to support their family. The employee will hold power only if they are irreplaceable or difficult to replace or if they can easily find another job.

In order to increase their power base, employees have to establish combinations, either informally or in the form of trade unions. A trade union, having behind it the power of the collective employee body and its collective threat of jointly withholding labour, can more easily counter the power of the employer. This places employees on a more equal footing with the employer. It is often only a display of joint employee/union power, sometimes in the form of threatened strike action, that obliges the employer to bargain with employees or their representatives.

### Coercive Power and the Bargaining Process

The purpose of establishing a bargaining relationship is to prevent the use of coercive power by either side. Yet the ability of each side to apply coercive power continues to influence the bargaining process. In establishing a bargaining relationship, the parties agree that they will attempt to settle their differences by negotiation, but that if negotiation does not succeed, each may use their coercive power against the other. Consequently, the freedom to engage in a strike or lockout is integral to the normal collective bargaining process.

### Other Sources of Power

Once they have established a bargaining relationship, the parties will bring whatever force they can to the relationship. Besides their basic coercive power, employers and trade unions will attempt to gain power from other sources. For example:

- An individual employer may combine with other employers. And, as a body, they may lobby the government to extend their power.
- The employer may use economic and other circumstances against the union.
- Unions may attempt to gain the sympathy of other employees or employers, other institutions or the community.
- Unions or employers may attempt to gain political influence or even political power.

### The Effect of Power on Bargaining Outcomes

At any stage during the bargaining process, the overall power of each party and its willingness to engage in a demonstration of coercive power will greatly influence the conduct and outcome of the negotiation. If, at a particular time, a union wields more overall power, and if it is willing to engage in strike action, it is more likely to gain concessions from the employer. Thus, traditional collective bargaining relies mainly on a continual power play between the parties. It is an ongoing, dynamic process in which even the rules of the game may change from time to time.

Figure 13.1 illustrates the interplay between commonality, conflict and power in the establishment of the bargaining relationship.

In certain circumstances, a party which actually has greater power may not engage in hard bargaining or try to impose its own conditions at any cost. This may happen when:

- socio-economic concerns militate against a forceful approach
- continued conflict threatens the relationship and may even completely destroy it
- the conflict will have wider implications
- legislation obliges interaction
- moral principles dictate the approach to the relationship.

If this happens, the relationship may become more co-operative than antagonistic, and bargaining is aimed at promoting the common good rather than settling opposing interests. Co-operation is, however, more likely where there is equal power and where employees have some share in the decision-making process.

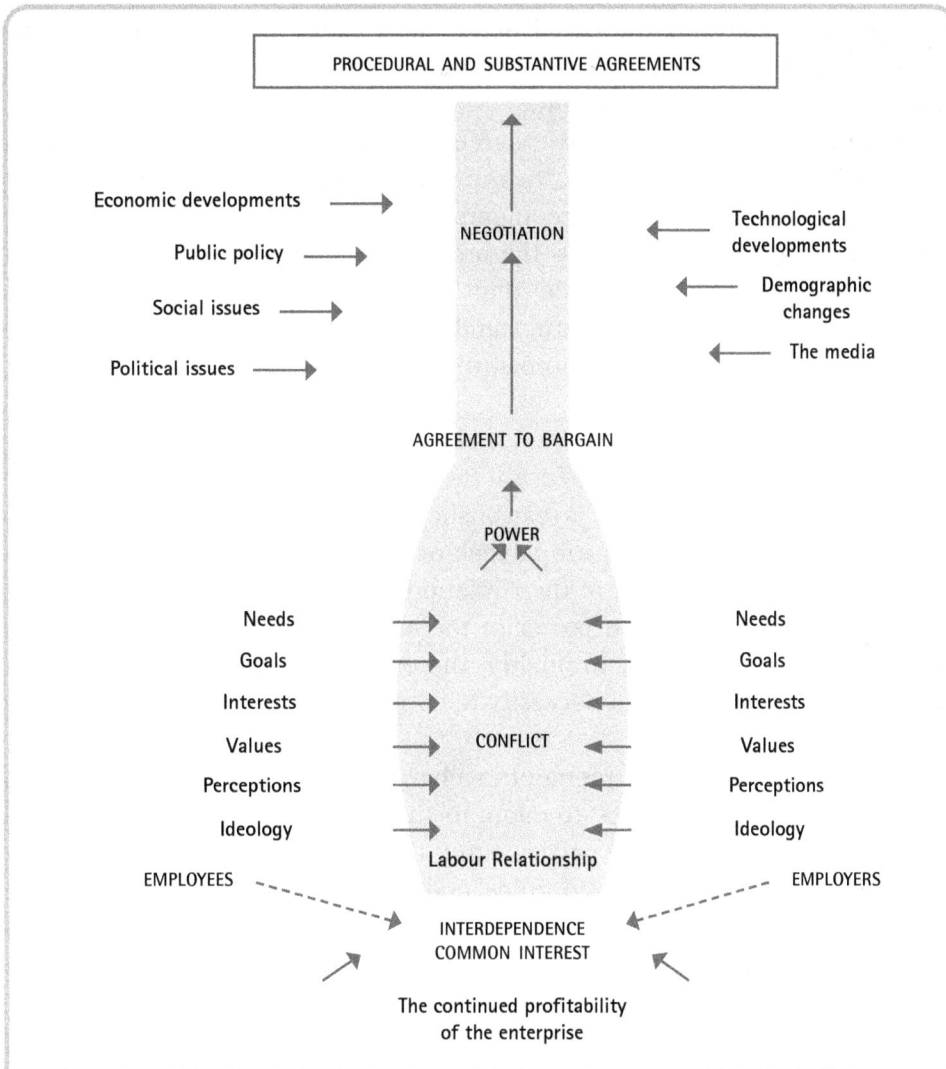

**Figure 13.1:** Establishing the collective bargaining relationship

## Characteristics of a Bargaining Relationship

### The Purpose and Role of Collective Bargaining Agreements

The purpose of concluding a collective agreement is mainly to have legal certainty on aspects regulating the relationship between bargaining partners in the workplace. Collective bargaining is a formal and predictable group process, aimed at ensuring a continuous relationship between parties at the workplace. Collective bargaining as a decision-making process is flexible, and should ideally work towards good faith, trust and the integrity of the bargaining partners. The process itself is very dynamic and based on the principle of social and industrial democracy. Ideally, a mature collective relationship is complementary rather than competitive, and one in which growth and agreements can result.

In South Africa, a collective agreement binds all parties, including the members of a trade union, to the agreement for the entire period of the agreement. Collective agreements take precedence over individual employment agreements, unless the terms and conditions of the individual agreement are more favourable than those contained in the collective agreement or any other minimum standards statute, or unless the collective agreement is contrary to the Constitution of the Republic of South Africa, 1996.

### The Bargaining Relationship as a Formal Relationship

The bargaining relationship is established when the employer agrees to enter into negotiations with employees or their representative union with a view to mutual regulation of their relationship. In agreeing to bargain, the employer acknowledges the power of the employees and their standing as equal negotiating partners. Implicitly, the employer accepts that there is a conflict of interests, and the necessity of containing this conflict through the bargaining process.

In a voluntary system, agreement to a bargaining relationship also implies acceptance of the employees' freedom to strike and the employer's freedom to lock out employees. The parties agree that they will interact within the framework of mutually agreed rules and procedures. As Harrison (2004: 189) has stated: 'The rules embodied in collective bargaining procedures represent a voluntary undertaking by employers and trade unions alike to act in accordance with accepted norms of behaviour.'

A number of trends in the changing nature of the collective bargaining landscape has been noted over the last decade. These include deregulation, flexicurity and an enhanced interest in the productivity debate. Structural changes in the economy have resulted in shifts within industries, resulting in changes in the number and types of employees retained. The international view on the changing nature of collective bargaining suggests that where increases in competitiveness in a country result in a general emphasis on deregulation and decentralisation of employment relations, there is a link to greater economic competitiveness. Berton et al (2019) confirm that one such an advantage is that company-level collective agreements affect workplace training, a key ingredient in competitiveness.

### The Bargaining Relationship as an Employer–Union Relationship

The bargaining relationship differs from the normal employer–employee relationship in that an outside party, in the form of the union, usually represents the interests of employees. Equally, an employer may be represented by an employers' organisation. Thus, the bargaining relationship is often described as an employer–union relationship or a relationship between an employers' organisation and a union. The entry of a third party greatly formalises the relationship. Such formalisation is necessary, but it may, at times, adversely affect the relationship.

## Establishment of the Relationship

Where a union has managed to enrol a large number of employees at a particular enterprise, it will demand recognition of the union as representative of employees in the organisation and as an equal bargaining partner. If the employer agrees to enter into the relationship, the next step will be for the parties to draw up a recognition agreement.

At this stage, the parties have merely formalised the relationship and have not yet begun to negotiate on the real issues, but they will already have engaged in collective bargaining. The recognition agreement establishes the parameters for further negotiation. It sets the stage for consultation, negotiation and even co-operation in respect of those matters which are of mutual interest to the parties concerned. Furthermore, where a union or a number of unions acting jointly have managed to recruit a substantial number of employees in a particular industry or sector, they will demand that the employers concerned recognise these unions for collective bargaining at a more centralised level, in what may be known as a bargaining council.

## The Scope and Content of Collective Bargaining

The scope of collective bargaining varies from one bargaining relationship to another and from system to system. Bargaining initially hinges on procedural issues and any bargaining arrangement will, at the least, cover procedures for meetings, arrangements for negotiations and procedures for the settlement of disputes between the parties. Provision will also be made for the winding up of the relationship, should either party so desire. The issues mentioned will be contained in the bargaining council's constitution or in the recognition agreement.

Next, the main focus is usually on remuneration and the work situation. The parties agree that they will, at regular intervals or when circumstances require, bargain on substantive issues such as wages and conditions of service. In some cases, the bargaining scope extends only to this point. Employers may not want to negotiate on the procedures used in the undertaking. Unions, on the other hand, may demand a say in grievance, disciplinary and retrenchment procedures and in the procedures adopted to safeguard the health and safety of employees. They may, furthermore, demand to be consulted before new technology is introduced and to have some say in decisions which will directly or indirectly affect employees.

Management, for its part, will raise issues of its own. These may include matters such as productivity, training, salary and wage structures, worker commitment and even a possible decrease in wages in times of financial difficulty.

The scope of collective bargaining can, in effect, be extended to include all areas of conflict or mutual concern in the relationship. Hence, the scope of collective bargaining includes the prevention of disputes, or at least the peaceful resolution of disputes, to regulate the terms and conditions of matters of mutual interest in labour relations. Thus, there is a direct link between the sources of conflict and the issues raised in the bargaining arena. Table 13.1 serves to illustrate this point.

## General Requirements for an Effective Collective Bargaining Process

The South African Board for People Practices (SABPP, 2021) has proposed the following requirements for a good collective bargaining process:

- In the interest of establishing good faith, there should be an acceptance of management and trade unions and of the legitimate position of each.
- Parties should have a sound knowledge of labour relations legislation and the sociopolitical and economic environment.
- All participants in collective bargaining should be well trained.
- Collective bargaining processes require clear frameworks and rules. Therefore, the recognition and procedural agreement is a critical first step in the relationship between the employer and trade union(s).
- Collective bargaining should function on the basis of accurate and complete information shared by both parties.
- Preparation for bargaining should include an analysis of issues to be bargained so that the bargaining parties can identify and agree on which issues are suitable for bargaining.

**Table 13.1:** Collective bargaining issues and problems

| Source of conflict | | Issues | Type of issue |
|---|---|---|---|
| Employer Orientation | Employee Orientation | | |
| Higher profits | Higher income | Wages | Substantive |
| Development of business | | Hours of work | Substantive |
| | | Holidays | Substantive |
| | | Sick leave | Substantive |
| | | Benefits | Substantive |
| | | Allowances | Substantive |
| | | Bonuses | Substantive |
| | | Productivity | Substantive |
| Flexibility | Security | Dismissals | Procedural and substantive |
| | | Discipline | Procedural |
| | | Short time | Procedural and substantive |
| | | Retrenchment | Procedural and substantive |
| | | Technology | Procedural |
| | | Pensions | Substantive |
| | | Seniority rights | Procedural and substantive |
| Control | Shared decision making | Grievance handling | Procedural |
| | | Discipline | Procedural |
| | | Consultation | Procedural |
| | | Worker participation | Procedural |
| | | Rights of shop stewards | Procedural |
| | | Union rights | Procedural |
| | | Committees | Procedural |

| Source of conflict | | Issues | Type of issue |
|---|---|---|---|
| **Employer Orientation** | **Employee Orientation** | | |
| Worker commitment Productivity | Leisure | Premiums | Substantive |
| | | Working hours | Substantive |
| | | Leave | Substantive |
| | | Absenteeism | Procedural and substantive |
| | | Productivity | Procedural and substantive |
| Profitability | Ensured health and safety | Health and safety procedures | Procedural |
| | | Health and safety committees | Procedural |
| Competitive salaries | Development Job satisfaction Social needs Status | Training | Procedural |
| | | Productivity bonuses | Procedural and substantive |
| | | Organisation of work | Procedural |
| | | Wage structure | Procedural and substantive |
| | | Organisational structure | Procedural |
| | | Job descriptions | Procedural |
| Concentration on business matters | Concentration on social problems | Housing | Substantive |
| | | Education | Procedural and substantive |
| | | Rehabilitation of employees with alcohol or substance abuse problems | Procedural |
| | | Bursaries | Substantive |
| | | Social responsibility | Procedural and substantive |
| | | Equal opportunities | Procedural |
| | | The environment | Procedural and substantive |

# Bargaining Styles

### Distributive Bargaining

This is the most common type of bargaining that usually occurs in the labour relations situation. Distributive bargaining takes place when management and the union are in opposing positions and when a gain for one party represents a loss for the other.

Distributive bargaining items are described as issues. The most prevalent issues between management and the union are usually economic.

Distributive bargaining involves the use of power tactics and every other possible strategy by both sides. Each party strives towards an outcome favourable for itself, and will carefully assess the position, strengths and weaknesses of its own side and of the other party. Each party wants to gauge just how far it can press its own demands without the other side using coercive power in the form of a strike or a lockout or other action. In the extreme, each will consider the possibility of allowing the other to apply coercive power and will assess its own ability to withstand it.

### Integrative Bargaining

Integrative bargaining occurs when both parties have the same preference for a successful outcome or are equally concerned to solve a problem. In distributive bargaining there is a clear distinction between losses and gains, resulting in a win-lose situation. Integrative bargaining strives for a win-win solution. In practice, it may happen that either party loses a little, but neither suffers a total loss. Overall, both parties gain. It is a case of granting concessions and gaining concessions, so that both parties move from the status quo to a better position.

Items subjected to integrative bargaining are described as problems. These include job security, procedures, promotion, benefits and institutional security. Retrenchment and promotion could be regarded as problems rather than issues.

Important objectives can be achieved by integrative bargaining. Supplementing distributive with integrative bargaining may contribute to a better overall bargaining climate. Instead of the parties being in continual opposition, there should be times when they work together and engage in what is essentially integrative problem solving.

# Bargaining Structure

## Bargaining Units and Bargaining Levels

The term 'bargaining structure' encompasses 'bargaining units' and 'bargaining levels'. A bargaining unit is composed of the employees who will be covered by an agreement. Expressed simply, the composition of a bargaining unit will determine on behalf of whom, and with whom, bargaining will take place. It also determines whether bargaining will be conducted with one union only or with a number of unions and with one employer or a number of employers. Thus, an agreement can apply to:

- a single group of employees at one plant
- all employees or most of the employees at a plant
- a certain type of employee working at various plants but for the same company
- all or most of the employees of a company
- certain types of workers in an industry or area
- all or most of the employees in an industry or sector
- artisans or other specialists across industries.

The bargaining unit will determine whether negotiations will be conducted with:

- plant-level management
- the head office of a company
- a number of employers in an industry, sector or area
- employers from different industries.

This leads to the establishment of bargaining levels – that is, whether bargaining will take place at a decentralised level or at a more centralised level.

## Importance of the Bargaining Structure

There are many types of bargaining structures. The kind of structure established will vary from company to company, from industry to industry and from one labour relations system to another.

The type of bargaining structure and the bargaining level established will determine:

- which employees will be covered by an agreement
- who will receive protection from an agreement (especially if it is enforceable by law)
- how much influence the union will have in a company or industry

- how much power a union and employers can exercise during negotiations (sometimes a union is able to wield more influence if it bargains at plant level, and at other times it is more powerful if it engages in collective bargaining at company or industry level)
- at what level union members will be able to participate in decision making (the more centralised bargaining becomes, the less unions will be able to receive direct input from their membership).

## Types of Bargaining Structure

Kochan (1980) identified four types of bargaining units or bargaining levels: narrow decentralised units, broad decentralised units, narrow centralised units and broad centralised units. These are discussed below.

### Narrow Decentralised Units

This type of bargaining unit is established when a union represents the interests of one group of workers at a particular plant or where various unions, each constituting a different bargaining unit, represent the interests of different groups of workers at that plant.

As far as the union is concerned, a narrow decentralised unit will:
- minimise conflict between union members
- maximise commonality of interest
- increase worker participation at plant level
- carry the risk of:
  - strengthening management power
  - encouraging union rivalry
  - allowing the employer to apply the 'divide and rule' principle
  - minimising the effect of strike action, as production may be able continue without the members of one of the unions
  - not reaching the real locus of power, as top management may be at a centralised level.

For the employer, a narrow decentralised unit has the following implications:
- The danger of multiple strikes increases.
- Negotiations become time-consuming if the employer has to deal separately with more than one union at the plant.
- The danger of whipsawing (with the aim of securing the greatest possible number of concessions) exists (Greer & Hauptmeier, 2016).
- The highest negotiated wage may have to be paid to all employees.

## Broad Decentralised Units

In this instance, all or a number of unions at a particular plant combine to form one bargaining unit. They may bargain as a team or engage in coalition bargaining, whereby each union will retain its independence and may negotiate special conditions for its members or withdraw from an agreement, if it so wishes. Broad decentralised units could:

- advance the special interests of workers at that plant
- allow for maximum employee participation
- deprive management of the power it would wield against a single union representing a particular group
- lead to a total loss of production, as strike action is likely to be instituted by all or most of the employees at that plant
- if there is inter-union rivalry, allow management to apply the 'divide and rule' principle
- involve prolonged intra-organisational bargaining so as to accommodate different interests
- still not allow unions to reach the real locus of power in the organisation.

## Narrow Centralised Units

This type of structure is established when one union or a number of unions representing a particular type or level of employee at a company, in an industry or in different industries bargain centrally with the company head office, with a number of employers from the same industry, or with employers from different industries.

With narrow centralised units, unions might:

- retain uniformity of interests, but not to the same extent as with narrow decentralised units
- have less employee participation at plant level or member participation in actual negotiations
- run the risk of agreements reached at centralised level being undermined by management at particular plants
- be able to negotiate with the real decision makers in management
- not wield so much power with strike action
- achieve increased prominence in the organisation(s) concerned.

Employers, on the other hand, may be faced with:

- the risk of different unions whipsawing from agreement to agreement
- the problem of having to deal with a number of unions in different bargaining units
- union rivalry, which may complicate bargaining or lead to multiple strikes.

In general, bargaining in these units may have the effect that:

- there is less direct conflict between individual management and employees
- the impact of strike action is minimised (unless the strikers occupy strategic positions)
- strikes are more widespread, but less frequent
- the bargaining process is depersonalised
- where all employers in an industry are involved, the wages of that group of workers are taken out of competition.

### Broad Centralised Units

A broad centralised unit is established when one union or a number of unions representing diverse interests bargain with a number of employers at industry or sectoral level. This is a very complex structure, but it holds a number of advantages for both employers and unions:

- Wage levels and benefits apply to all employers and employees.
- Employers need not be concerned that wage increases granted will increase their costs and prices in relation to their competitors.
- Unions are not faced with an employer who, because of this concern, attempts to keep wages at the lowest possible level.
- The centralised body can establish benefit structures and training programmes which individual employers would not have been able to provide.
- Negotiations are conducted on a more depersonalised basis, and on a more professional level.
- The danger of spontaneous strike action decreases, although strike action, when it does occur, is on a much larger scale.

### Evaluation of Bargaining Structures

Whether employer or union power increases or decreases with greater centralisation depends greatly on the circumstances. A strong union may actually lose strategic power by engaging in centralised negotiations, but it may do so for the sake of other advantages such as wider influence and control in an industry. Likewise, it may be more advantageous for a strong employer to bargain individually with a union. Weaker or smaller employers and unions may benefit from the support of others, but they may equally find that wages and conditions negotiated are not favourable to their particular circumstances or, in the case of unions, do not meet the demands of their members.

Broad centralised agreements are usually concluded at the cost of worker participation in decision making at plant level and membership participation in the bargaining process, unless separate provisions are made for plant-level participation and the union or employers' association adopts alternative strategies to allow for maximum member participation in negotiations. Also, there is the increased possibility of inter-union and inter-employer conflict and a greater need for intra-organisational bargaining. As a result, negotiations may be lengthy and cumbersome. This might eventually negate the cost reduction achieved by joint negotiation. (See 'Arguments for and against Extension' later in this chapter.)

### Towards Greater Flexibility

The question as to whether centralised bargaining is preferable to decentralised bargaining has been widely debated. Both have advantages and disadvantages, as explored in Table 13.2. Furthermore, an advantage for one party may prove a disadvantage to the other. Employers and unions may opt for a two-tier system, where, for example, minimum conditions and benefits are negotiated at central level and more particular or improved conditions and procedures are established by plant-level negotiations. Alternatively, strong centralised arrangements may be balanced by allowing for employee participation in decision making at plant or organisational level.

### Variables Determining Bargaining Structures

The type of bargaining structure established will depend, interactively, on:
- union organisation policy and strategy
- employer organisation and strategy
- the type of bargaining issue
- government policy and legislation
- economic factors.

Both parties will want to bargain at the level where they can wield the most power. Where unions and employers are organised at a highly centralised level, they will opt for centralised units. Union strategy in particular will be influenced by the extent of the union's organisation. If this is local, they would prefer to bargain at decentralised level, but will continually strive for wider influence. However, if there is strong inter-union competition, some unions may not want to co-operate in centralised units. Equally, smaller employers may not want to be part of highly centralised bodies where larger employers predominate.

Certain issues, such as organisational procedures, may be better dealt with at a decentralised level, while government policy and legislation may enforce or encourage the use of particular bargaining units.

Finally, the state of the economy might oblige individual employers to move away from centralised units, but unions might prefer to remain at this level in order to take wages out of competition.

**Table 13.2:** Advantages and disadvantages of centralised and decentralised bargaining

| CENTRALISED BARGAINING | | DECENTRALISED BARGAINING | |
|---|---|---|---|
| Advantages | Disadvantages | Advantages | Disadvantages |
| Wages out of competition (pro for unions and employers) | | Wages differentiated according to particular organisation | Danger of whipsawing (con for employers)<br><br>Employers afraid to become uncompetitive (con for unions) |
| Better benefits at less cost | | Benefits tailormade for individual needs | Fewer benefits provided |
| Larger-scale training programmes | | Programmes tailormade for specific needs | Less likelihood of large-scale training programmes |
| Fewer strike actions | Labour action on a wider scale | | Likelihood of spontaneous strikes increases |
| | Does not diffuse workplace tensions | Diffuses workplace tensions | |
| Limits power of workplace organisation (management and employees) | | Increases power of workplace organisation | Workplace representatives may become too independent of union |
| | Possibility of democratic decision making in unions and employers' organisations decreases | Greater opportunity for democratic decision making | |
| | Diverse interests represented | Caters for specific needs | |
| | Greater intra-organisational conflict | Intra-organisational conflict minimised | |

| CENTRALISED BARGAINING | | DECENTRALISED BARGAINING | |
| --- | --- | --- | --- |
| Advantages | Disadvantages | Advantages | Disadvantages |
| | More inflexible | More flexible | |
| Bargainers are usually more professional | | | Bargainers may not be sufficiently experienced |
| Long-term objectives | | | Objectives may be short term |
| Provides overall, uniform standards and minimum safeguards | | | May lead to employer playoffs and wage inflation |

## Pluralism and Collective Bargaining

The emphasis on collective bargaining relies on the pluralist approach to the labour relationship. This approach rests on the presumption that:

- with different groups representing competing interests, power will be widely and fairly distributed
- employees, by joining unions, will equal the power of management
- the free exercise of power by one group will be constrained by the countervailing power of the other
- the state will act as neutral watchdog
- the parties will engage in mutually beneficial collective bargaining
- both parties will moderate their demands for the sake of the common good
- conflict will be contained at manageable levels.

Unfortunately, such ideal interactions are difficult to achieve. In the first place, the employer holds the initial power and the union has to continually challenge this power.

The effects of collective agreements on wage increases and job satisfaction differ because the preferences and bargaining power of the parties differ in different settings (Kauhanen, Maczulskij & Riukula, 2020).

Addison (2020) found the following:

- Trade unions, under certain bargaining structures, can achieve favourable macro consequences by being less aggressive in their wage bargaining.

- Trade unions can achieve favourable micro outcomes by stimulating workers' voice.
- Where there are benefits to a long-term relationship between the employer and the worker, trade unions can facilitate contracting.

The tendency towards increased competition should be balanced by the recognition of interdependence and a focus on common goals. However, the parties often do not recognise or admit that they are dependent on each other, nor do employees see employer goals as being in alignment with their own goals and interests.

In these circumstances, the importance of collective bargaining may be questioned. Collective bargaining could then be replaced by a search for more co-operative or less confrontational processes.

## Part Two: Collective Bargaining in South Africa

In looking at collective bargaining in South Africa, it is necessary to pay particular attention to:
- the need for freedom of association and freedom from victimisation to be guaranteed in a free collective bargaining system
- various organisational rights granted to unions in terms of South African legislation
- the controversial issue of closed shops and agency shops
- bargaining councils which have hitherto been central institutions in the South African system
- the advantages and disadvantages of centralised bargaining
- the concept of good faith.

## The Right to Free Collective Bargaining

South Africa, in its official labour relations policy, supports the principles of:
- voluntarism
- free collective bargaining
- freedom of association.

Collective bargaining is, in principal, voluntary. However, the Labour Relations Act 66 of 1995 confers rights at the workplace on unions which have majority representation, and even those who have 'sufficient' representation (see 'Representative versus Majority Unions'). By doing so it facilitates and, it could be said, even enforces a bargaining relationship with employers. The

Act also promotes (but does not enforce) centralised bargaining in national, regional or sectoral bargaining councils.

## Freedom of Association and Freedom from Victimisation

In order to engage in effective collective bargaining, employees in particular, but also employers in some instances, will join collective organisations.

If power is to be balanced and free collective bargaining is to take place, it is essential that:

- individuals should have the freedom to join the organisations of their choice
- no manipulation of membership should occur
- the collective organisations themselves should have free choice and be free from influence
- members of such organisations or their office bearers should not fear victimisation.

For these reasons, any free collective bargaining system is based on the joint principles of freedom of association and freedom from victimisation.

The Labour Relations Act stresses the importance of these precepts by providing for protection of these rights in sections 1 to 10. (The contents of these sections are discussed in detail in Chapter 3.)

## Organisational Rights

Meaningful collective bargaining in the workplace cannot be conducted without the guarantee of freedom of association. The realisation of the fundamental principle of freedom of association is set out in the Freedom of Association and Protection of the Right to Organise Convention (ILO, 1948), as an essential precondition for the effective realisation of the right to collective bargaining. The foundation is further strengthened by the Constitution of South Africa, which states that everyone is equal before the law (Section 9(1)), has freedom of association (Section 18) and has specific rights within the employment relations context (Section 23(2) and Chapter 3 of the Labour Relations Act).

### Exercising Organisational Rights

The Labour Relations Act also sets out the procedure to be followed if a union wishes to exercise organisational rights. According to Section 21 of the Act, a registered union wishing to exercise any of the rights provided for in the Act should inform the employer in writing of its intention to do so. Such notice should:

- be accompanied by a certified copy of the union's registration certificate
- specify the workplace where the union wants to exercise these rights
- provide proof of the union's representativeness
- list the rights which the union wishes to exercise.

The employer is obliged to meet with the union within 30 days of receiving such notice, whereafter the parties should attempt to reach agreement on the manner in which these rights will be exercised. If no agreement can be reached, either party may refer the dispute to the Commission for Conciliation, Mediation and Arbitration (CCMA), which will attempt conciliation. If conciliation fails, either party may request that the matter be taken to arbitration.

### Representative versus Majority Unions

The Act distinguishes between rights granted to 'representative' unions and those accorded to 'majority' unions. Section 14 of the Act describes a majority trade union as one which (either singly or acting jointly with another union) has as members the majority of persons employed in a workplace. The term 'representative union' refers to a union (or two or more unions acting jointly) which has 'sufficient' representation of employees employed in a workplace.

The lack of clarity in the definition of the meaning of 'sufficient' has resulted in a number of disputes. This is further complicated by the unclear definition of a workplace in the Act. A workplace is defined as 'the place or places where the employees of an employer work'. The Act goes on to state that workplaces under the same employer will be regarded as separate only if they are 'independent by virtue of their "size, organisation or function"'. It is the interpretation of the latter phrase that raises problems. In practice, unions may be regarded as representative if they represent 30 per cent or more of employees in the bargaining unit.

### Rights of Majority Trade Unions

Majority unions are entitled to:

- enter the employer's premises
- hold meetings on the employer's premises outside working hours
- conduct ballots
- request stop-order facilities
- request time off for office bearers
- elect shop stewards/union representatives
- demand disclosure of relevant information

- establish, with the employer, thresholds of representativeness (see 'The Right to Establish Thresholds of Representativeness')
- negotiate an agency-shop or a closed-shop agreement.

## Rights Granted to Representative Unions

In terms of sections 12, 13 and 15 of the Labour Relations Act, representative unions are entitled to:

- gain access to the employer's premises for the purpose of recruiting members
- communicate with members or otherwise serve their interests
- hold meetings with employees on the premises of the employer outside working hours
- conduct ballots among employees
- arrange for stop-order facilities (for the payment of union dues)
- get time off for union office bearers to perform their functions.

The rights granted to unions are not absolute. They are subject to reasonable arrangements with the employer regarding time and place, insofar as this is necessary for security purposes, and to avoid disruption.

Once the right to stop orders has been granted, employees must apply in writing for union dues to be deducted from their wages. The employer must pay over these amounts to the representative union by the 15th day of the following month. An employee may withdraw permission for the deductions by giving the employer one month's written notice (three months in the case of a public service employee). With each month's payment, the employer must furnish the union with copies of any notices of withdrawal, a statement containing the names of every employee from whose wages deductions have been made, and the necessary details about the amounts deducted.

## New Rights for Non-majority Unions

Recognising that trade union representativity develops or varies over time, Section 21 of the Labour Relations Act was amended (by Act 6 of 2014) by the insertion of subclauses 8A and 8B in Section 21 relating to a situation where a non-majority union (or two or more unions acting jointly) has requested the CCMA to adjudicate on a matter related to organisational rights. In terms of the amendments, a commissioner may grant the union(s) the right to appoint shop stewards and to disclosure of information, on condition that:

- the union already qualifies for the rights of a representative union
- no other union has been accorded those rights.

Where organisational rights have been granted to a union representing employees of a temporary employment service, the rights granted will also apply to the client or clients of the temporary employment service.

It is obvious from these amendments and those discussed in the next section that the government intends to provide increasing protection to employees not represented by a big union and to those not in a traditional employment relationship. The amendment erodes, to some extent, the distinction between majority and representative unions. It also indicates that the legislators are increasingly adapting legislation to the changing nature of work.

### The Right to Establish Thresholds of Representativeness

A majority union or unions at a workplace or in a bargaining council may conclude an agreement with the employer(s) in which thresholds of representativeness are specified. This means that these parties can decide that a union which does not meet the threshold will not be regarded as a sufficiently representative union at the workplace and will therefore not be given the rights in terms of the Act.

An agreement which sets high thresholds could ensure the presence of one or two unions, and make it impossible for any other union, even if it has sufficient representation, to operate at that workplace or in a bargaining council. This type of arrangement could be both advantageous and disadvantageous to the employer. On the one hand, it discourages multi-unionism, but on the other it may prevent effective representation of all employee interests. (See the discussion in Chapter 2 of events in the mining industry, where certain mining companies and the National Union of Mineworkers [NUM] established thresholds which effectively prevented the Association of Mining and Construction Workers Union [AMCU] from gaining recognition.)

Probably because of the use of thresholds to exclude other unions, the Labour Relations Amendment Act 6 of 2014 brought in a new Section 21(8C). This section refers to a union (or two or more unions acting jointly) which does not meet a threshold of representation established by the other parties. The amendment allows a commissioner, in arbitrating a dispute about organisational rights, to grant the union(s) the rights of a representative union, on condition that they represent a 'significant interest' and that the parties who set the threshold (namely the employer and the majority union) have had the opportunity to participate in the arbitration proceedings.

As in all other disputes about organisational rights, the commissioner, when making a decision, must take into account:
- the nature of the workplace
- the nature of the sector in which it operates

- the organisational history of the workplace or any other workplace of the employer.

The commissioner should also try to minimise:
- the proliferation of trade unions at the workplace
- the additional financial and administrative burden placed on the employer.

These restrictions indicate that the unions concerned might not easily be granted the rights in question, but it does give a union which may represent neglected or other interests, a foot in the door. The term 'significant' has not been defined. It will be up to the commissioner to make a decision according to the particular circumstances.

### The Right to Appoint Shop Stewards
*Election of Shop Stewards*
In terms of Section 14 of the Labour Relations Act, a majority union, or two or more unions which together represent the majority of employees at a workplace (and now also a union which has been granted Section 14 rights by a Commissioner), have the right to elect shop stewards (union representatives). The number of shop stewards allowed is as follows:
- In any workplace where 10 union members are employed: one shop steward
- In a workplace with 10 to 50 union members: two shop stewards
- In a workplace with 51 to 300 union members: one additional shop steward for every 50 members, up to a maximum of seven
- In a workplace with 301 to 600 union members: seven shop stewards for the first 300 members and one for every additional 100 members, up to a maximum of 10
- In a workplace with 601 to 1 000 union members: one shop steward for every 200 members in excess of 600, up to a maximum of 12
- In a workplace with more than 1 000 union members: one shop steward for every 500 additional members, up to a maximum of 20.

The nomination, election, terms of office and removal of a shop steward are determined by the union's constitution.

*Shop Steward Rights*
Sections 14(4) and (5) and Section 15 of the Labour Relations Act spell out the rights of shop stewards and union office bearers at the workplace. These include the right to:
- represent co-employees
- monitor the employer's implementation of the Act

- report any transgression of the Act
- take reasonable paid time off during working hours to perform the duties of a shop steward or to receive training.

## The Right to Disclosure of Information

Section 16 of the Act provides that a majority union and the shop stewards of that union are entitled to demand all relevant information, including copies of documents, which they require to carry out their functions at the workplace.

If an employer is engaged in negotiation with the union concerned, the employer is obliged to furnish the union with all relevant information required by the union for effective representation, consultation, co-decision-making or collective bargaining. Where the information requested is confidential, the employer must inform the union in writing to this effect. A union cannot demand information which:

- is legally privileged
- cannot be furnished without disobeying a court order
- could cause the employer substantial damage if it becomes public
- is private to a person (unless such person grants permission).

Disputes regarding disclosure may be referred to the CCMA, which will attempt to mediate and, failing an agreement, resort to arbitration.

The commissioner hearing the dispute must first decide whether the information requested is relevant or not. If the commissioner finds it to be relevant, they need to consider the disadvantage which either side may suffer if the information is disclosed (or not disclosed). If the commissioner decides that the information ought to be disclosed, they may set conditions aimed at limiting the damage. The commissioner is also charged with considering whether breach of confidentiality has previously occurred in the relationship. Where previous breaches have occurred, the commissioner may withdraw the right to information at that workplace for a specified period.

## Case Review: Demand for Disclosure

### SA Commercial Catering & Allied Workers Union & Koppel Bacher & Co (Pty) Ltd t/a GS Vickers & Co (CCMA: KNDB 5989-07)

### Background

The union in question, which was at the time engaged in wage negotiations with the company, had demanded disclosure of the organisation's financial statements for the years 2005 and 2006, as well as the management accounts for 2007. It had based its demand on Section 16 of the Labour Relations Act, maintaining that it needed the information to engage in meaningful negotiation. The employer maintained that the information sought was not relevant and consequently refused to disclose it, whereupon the union requested that the CCMA make a ruling on the issue.

### Argument

At the CCMA, the union explained that the information sought was not unique, was not confidential and would not be disclosed by the union to the company's competitors. It needed the information to back up its wage claims and to challenge management on increases granted to those who were not members of the union, including directors. The union argued further that their members had to be able to compare the performance of the company with their wage demands.

The company argued that the information was not relevant, because the organisation had not based its offer on affordability but on inflation and market-related increases. The information was confidential, and a breach of confidentiality could cause considerable harm.

### Pronouncements

The commissioner noted that the onus was on the union to prove, on the balance of probabilities, that the information sought was relevant. This would, to a large extent, depend on the purpose for which it was required. If the information was required for collective bargaining purposes, only information which would allow the union to engage in effective consultation and bargaining needed to be disclosed.

Referring to the judgment in *SACCAWU v Pep Stores 1998 19 ILJ 939 (CCMA) 946G*, the commissioner set out the purpose of disclosure as being to:

- facilitate the consultative process
- enable the union to engage in meaningful attempts to reach consensus
- provide an understanding of the problem
- enable the union to contribute to a solution

- bring knowledge and reason to a situation
- introduce rationality into the participative process.

According to the commissioner, the employer is not obliged to respond to a 'generalised' demand for information. On the other hand, it was not up to the employer to decide whether information was relevant or not. The decision should be based on the purpose of disclosure and on whether the information would add to the union's ability to engage in meaningful consultation and negotiation – in other words, whether it would be 'effective'.

The commissioner concluded that the information sought by the union was not relevant. The ambit in which the union was bargaining was fairly narrow, while the information it sought was quite wide and encompassed the entire business of the employer. The commissioner advised the union to establish a link between the information and the purpose for which it was required. The commissioner suggested that, in the existing context, a demand for specific information on unit labour costs, gross sales figures and net income before tax would have been more appropriate.

## Discussion

As noted during this hearing, there is a shortage of case law on the disclosure of information in the collective bargaining context. Most of the cases on disclosure have related to information demanded during a retrenchment exercise, which involves consultation and problem solving, and not collective bargaining. Those cases, too, have pointed to fitness for purpose and the context in which disclosure is demanded. If, for example, the employer in the case above had argued that it could not afford increases, more comprehensive disclosure of its financial situation may have been justified.

There are commentators who argue that as much information as possible should be disclosed, but others, such as the commissioner in this case, argue that this would result in unions going on a 'shopping expedition'. What is obvious is that there are no clear guidelines as to the type and extent of information to be disclosed, and that each case will be judged in terms of its particular circumstances.

### The Right to Negotiate for Agency Shops or Closed Shops
*The Problem*

Unions generally have a problem with so-called 'free riders'. These are employees who do not belong to the union and do not pay union dues, but who fall within the bargaining unit. This means that when improved wages and conditions of service are negotiated, they too are beneficiaries. Trade union members argue that these employees are benefiting unfairly from the sacrifices of those who pay the dues. The solution, as found in many labour relations systems, is the establishment of agency shops or closed shops.

## Agency Shops

Section 25 of the Labour Relations Act provides for the establishment of agency shops, subject to agreement between an employer and a majority union. An agency-shop agreement does not oblige employees to become union members, but it may oblige non-members who are eligible for union membership to pay a subscription. The amount of the subscription should not exceed the amount payable in dues by union members. These subscriptions are paid into a separate fund, administered by the majority union. The fund should be used to advance the socio-economic welfare of all employees. Thus, the union could apply the funds to support its bargaining initiatives, but also for more general purposes, such as the establishment of a crèche or recreation facilities at the workplace.

## Closed Shops

Section 26 of the Act contains provision for closed-shop agreements between a majority union or unions and an employer or an employers' association in a bargaining council. A closed-shop agreement obliges all eligible employees to become members of the majority union. However, the legislation does provide that persons already in employ at the time that the agreement is concluded, or persons who are conscientious objectors, cannot be obliged to join the union. The conditions of an agency shop may then be applied to them.

A closed-shop agreement may be concluded only if two-thirds of the employees to be covered have voted in favour of such agreement. The agreement must stipulate that no portion of the subscriptions should be used to pay for affiliation to a political party or as a contribution to a political party or candidate; nor may the funds be applied for any other purpose than the promotion and protection of the socio-economic welfare of the employees.

Closed-shop agreements have to be subjected to a vote every three years, or when one-third of the employees covered by the agreement so request. Also, a union which is not party to such agreement, but which has a significant interest in or representation among the employees concerned, can apply to be admitted to the agreement. If its application is refused, the dispute may be referred to the CCMA.

## Evaluation

A union party to a closed-shop agreement may, in terms of its constitution, withhold membership from an employee or may terminate an employee's membership for 'fair' reasons, including (but not limited to) behaviour which hampers 'the collective exercise of trade union rights', according to Section 26(6) of the Labour Relations Act. The same section also states that it is not unfair for an employer to dismiss an employee who refuses to join a closed-shop union, who has been refused membership of a trade union which is party to a closed shop, or whose membership has been terminated by the union. This could mean that an employee or group of employees who refuse to take part in a strike could have their membership terminated. The employer would then be placed in a position where they have to dismiss such employee(s).

The situation is even more serious where a closed shop has been negotiated at centralised level and then applied to an entire sector or industry. Non-party employees who refuse to take part in a national strike may have to be dismissed. The Labour Court may find such dismissal to be unfair, but only if the reasons for withholding or terminating membership are found to be unfair.

While the concept of an agency shop may still be defensible, the closed shop has long been the subject of great controversy. The main criticism is that it negates the individual's right to freedom of association, guaranteed in terms of both labour legislation and the Constitution.

Although rights are never absolute, the rights entrenched in the Constitution may, according to Section 36(1) of the Constitution, be limited 'only if the limitation is reasonable and justifiable in an open and democratic society based on human dignity, equality and freedom, taking into account all relevant factors'. These factors include:

- the nature of the right
- the importance and purpose of the limitation
- the nature and extent of the limitation
- the relation between the limitation and its purpose
- the existence of less restrictive means of achieving this purpose.

It could be argued that, if the above criteria are applied, the infringement of a right as perpetrated by the closed shop should not be allowed. The right in question, namely freedom of association, is one of the cornerstones of a democratic system. Consequently, any effort to limit it must be for very sound and important reasons. The only reasons for allowing a closed shop are either to further the interests of the majority union or to facilitate collective bargaining. These are hardly important enough to justify limiting a right and there is thus very little relation between the limitation and its purpose. Also, the provision for agency shops already addresses the main problem of free riders. It does so by less restrictive means, and without infringing on freedom of association.

In addition to the above, the clause relating to closed shops directly conflicts with the Act in which it appears. The Labour Relations Act entrenches not only the right to freedom of association, but also the right of employees not to be unfairly dismissed. An unfair dismissal is one for which there is no fair reason. A fair reason would be one related to the employee's work, performance or behaviour in the relationship with the employer. The closed-shop legislation allows for a dismissal unrelated to the actual employment relationship and to the employee's action in that relationship.

There is, moreover, a strong tendency among closed-shop unions to become entrenched in often cosy relationships and to neglect servicing their members. It is interesting to note that closed shops were a feature of the pre-1979 labour dispensation, when the system was not open to all race groups and when the then dominant Trade Union Council of South Africa (TUCSA) unions were entrenched in bargaining councils and closed-shop arrangements.

## Case Review: Agency Shop

### National Manufactured Fibre Employers' Association & Another v Bikwani & Others (Labour Court: C639/98)

### Background

The applicants in this case were the relevant employers' association, SANS Fibre (Pty) Ltd, and the Southern African Clothing and Textile Workers' Union (SACTWU).

SANS had recognised SACTWU as the majority union in the organisation. At the time the issue arose, the company already had a long-standing relationship with this union, which was also represented on the bargaining council. Another union, the South African Chemical Workers' Union (SACWU), had for some time sought to make inroads at SANS, but although it did have members in the organisation, these were not sufficient to entitle it to organisational rights.

In 1998, SANS and SACTWU concluded an agreement, one clause of which was headed 'Agency Shop'. The agreement, which was in accordance with the bargaining council agreement, provided that employees who were not union members pay an agency-shop fee to SACTWU. Following the agreement, SANS commenced deducting the fee from those eligible employees who did not belong to any union at all, as well as from the SACWU members.

SACWU, whose members now had to pay double dues, declared a dispute and the matter was arbitrated by the CCMA. The commissioner interpreted the phrase pertaining to 'non-union members' to relate only to those eligible employees who were not members of any union at all. He explained that the word 'union' had not been written with a capital letter in the relevant sentence and consequently did not, in his opinion, refer to all persons who were not members of the majority union, irrespective of whether they were members of another union. The finding was that SANS had erred by deducting the agency-shop fee from SACWU members and the company was ordered to repay all monies so deducted.

The company and SACTWU subsequently submitted the matter for review by the

Labour Court on the grounds that the award was not justifiable in terms of the reasons given, nor was it rationally justifiable. SACWU, on the other hand, contended that it was logical that an agency-shop agreement should apply only to those eligible employees who were not members of any union.

## Pronouncements

The Labour Court rejected SACWU's contention, arguing that it would not be logical for the majority union to enter into an agreement excluding employees who belonged to another union. Non-union employees would then merely join the other union in order to avoid paying the agency-shop fee. They would continue to 'free-ride' at the expense of the majority while enjoying benefits, such as representation, from the other union.

Before considering the case in detail, the Court first pronounced that employees, irrespective of their membership of the other union, remained free riders as 'they make no contribution towards the collective bargaining costs of the representative union and yet they receive the benefits of that union's efforts in the same way as that union's members who foot the bill thereof'. In order to establish whether the commissioner had exceeded his powers, the Court turned to sections 25(1) and (2) of the Labour Relations Act. Referring to the phrase 'who are not members of the trade union', it concluded that because the only union mentioned previously in the paragraph was the 'representative trade union' and because the definite article ('the') had been used in the phrase mentioned, it was clear that the legislature intended the agency shop to apply to all persons who were not members of the representative (majority) union. The Court concluded that the commissioner's interpretation was 'at complete variance with the very essence of the agency-shop agreement as contemplated by S25'. The opinion expressed by the Court was that

> an agency-shop agreement as contemplated by S25 is not concerned with whether an employee is or is not a member of a minority union but is concerned with whether or not the employee does or does not contribute to the collective bargaining costs of the representative union the fruit of whose sweats he enjoys.

## Discussion

Agency-shop agreements are bound to cause dissatisfaction among those employees who already belong to another union, as well as those employees who do not belong to any union at all.

While the 'free rider' problem of the majority union is understood, it could be argued that these persons gain from collective bargaining by the majority union only because it suits both management and that union to include them in the bargaining unit. Uniformity works in favour of the majority union, and it could be regarded as unreasonable for it still to extract a fee from non-members. The situation becomes even more complicated when, as in the case above, certain employees pay dues to two unions while receiving only half a service from each: bargaining benefits from the majority union and representation from the union of their choice. A further problem arises when more than one union is party to the agency shop. Non-unionised employees may be obliged to pay a fee equal to that of the union charging the highest subscription. Thus, non-unionised employees pay a higher amount than those belonging to the other union, which levies a lower subscription fee.

Whatever the objections to agency-shop agreements, provision is made for them in the Act and unions will continue to demand that employers enter into such agreements. Furthermore, as has been indicated, the courts tended to interpret disputes arising from these agreements solely in terms of the provisions of the Act, which gives majority unions the right to bargain for closed shops and agency shops.

## Case Review: Closed Shop

### South African Transport and Allied Workers Union and Northwest Star (2008) 29 ILJ 224 (BCA)

### Background

The South African Transport and Allied Workers Union (SATAWU), which had originally been the dominant union at Northwest Star, had, in terms of a previous recognition agreement, had a closed shop in the organisation. The original recognition agreement expired in 2000 and the new recognition agreement stated only that the parties 'may' conclude an agreement allowing for a closed shop. However, when SATAWU in 2005 requested the establishment of a closed shop, the company refused. When no agreement could be reached, the union declared a dispute, claiming that the employer was obliged by Section 26(1) of the Labour Relations Act to enter into negotiations towards a closed shop.

During the proceedings it emerged that union representation at the organisation had changed significantly since another union, the Transport and Allied Workers Union (TAWU), had come on the scene in 2000. The latter union now enjoyed 40 per cent representativeness, as against SATAWU's 60 per cent. Management argued that it would be unfair to TAWU, with which it also had a recognition agreement, and with which it had a good relationship, to force its members to join SATAWU. (In its original submission, the employer party also argued that it would be unconstitutional, but the arbitrator did not deal with this aspect, as it was beyond his powers.)

The arbitrator noted that SATAWU already had an agency-shop agreement which would allow for dues to be paid to it by all employees in the bargaining unit.

At the time of the hearing, Northwest Star was under judicial management and looking to sell off part of its operations. Management argued that granting SATAWU a closed shop could lead to labour unrest, which would deter would-be buyers.

## Pronouncements

The arbitrator noted that before 1995 the Labour Relations Act had contained a duty to bargain, but that the Act of 1995 contained no such compulsion. Instead, it provided for organisational rights to facilitate the bargaining process.

On the matter of the closed shop, the arbitrator expressed the opinion that closed shops were viable when the union in question was the only union in the organisation or where any other union that existed did not have significant representation. He did pose the rhetorical question as to why, if the company could grant the union an agency shop, it could not also grant it a closed shop. The arbitrator then answered his own question, explaining that an agency shop merely obliged the payment of union dues, while a closed shop forced employees to join a union not of their choice. Indirectly it was also suggested that in this context the only reason for wanting a closed shop in addition to an agency shop was to force the other union out of the organisation.

In reaching his decision that SATAWU's application should fail, the arbitrator cited the purpose of the Labour Relations Act, which is to achieve economic development, social justice, labour peace and democratisation of the workplace. Granting a closed shop in the organisation's present circumstances would affect its economic prospects, lead to labour unrest and retard democratisation in the workplace.

## Commentary

SATAWU's reasons for wanting a closed shop while it already had an agency shop were indeed questionable. It is encouraging that other factors were seen as weightier than the letter of the law. While the agency shop may still be acceptable, the closed shop does negate freedom of association. At the time of these hearings the Labour Courts were hesitant to entertain arguments relating to the constitutionality of the agency shop, but the Constitutional Court itself has since declared that any arrangement which negates freedom of choice and freedom of association principles, should be judged as unlawful (see *Police and Prisons Civil Rights Union v South African Correctional Services Workers' Union and Others (CCT152/17) [2018] ZACC 24; [2018] 11 BLLR 1035 (CC); 2018 (11) BCLR 1411 (CC); (2018) 39 ILJ 2646 (CC); 2019 (1) SA 73 (CC) (23 August 2018)).* The time has perhaps come for a review of the relevant provisions.

# Enforceability of Agreements

Centralised bargaining council agreements have always been enforceable in terms of the Labour Relations Act. However, recognition and other plant-level agreements were regarded merely as contracts at common law and were, therefore, enforceable only by the lengthy processes of the civil courts. Section 23 of the Labour Relations Act made all collective agreements binding on the parties to the agreement, as well as on employees who are not members of a party union, if such employees are identified or bound in the agreement and if the union is a majority union. Agreements remain binding for their duration even on a member of a union or employers' association who withdraws or becomes a member during the currency of such agreement. Collective agreements automatically change individual contracts of employment.

Where a dispute arises concerning the interpretation or implementation of a collective agreement, and if there is no existent or operative dispute-settling agreement between the parties, or if one party has obstructed settlement, the dispute may be submitted to the CCMA for conciliation and, failing settlement, for arbitration.

# Centralised Bargaining Structures
## Legislation for Bargaining Councils
The Labour Relations Act promotes the use of centralised bargaining structures. In essence, it retains the previous industrial councils, now renamed bargaining councils, and extends these also to the public service. Some aspects of councils have been modified, and provision has been made for statutory councils in areas where unions may not be sufficiently representative.

## Establishing a Bargaining Council
### Voluntary Agreement by Parties
A bargaining council may be established by one (or more) employer party and one (or more) employee party. The employee party must be a registered trade union (or unions), while the employer party can be a registered employers' association (or associations). The state may also be regarded as the employer party in a sector or area in which it acts as the employer.

Bargaining councils are established when these parties voluntarily come together and agree to bargain with each other, but the council will come into existence in the official sense only after it has been registered by the Labour Relations Registrar.

## Constitution of a Bargaining Council

In order to register, a council needs to have a constitution. Section 30 of the Labour Relations Act provides that a bargaining council constitution must:

- state how representatives on the council and their alternatives are to be appointed (half the representatives have to be appointed by the employer party and half by the employee party)
- provide for representation by small and medium enterprises
- provide rules for the appointment, removal, duties and powers of office bearers and officials
- state how representatives will vacate their seats
- state how decisions are to be made
- provide procedures for the calling and conduct of meetings, including requirements for a quorum and the keeping of minutes
- provide for the establishment and functioning of committees
- establish procedures for dealing, by way of arbitration, with disputes regarding the interpretation and implementation of the council's constitution
- establish procedures for dealing with disputes between the parties to the council
- set out procedures for dealing with disputes between employers and employees (unions) covered by the council
- state under which circumstances additional members will be allowed to join the council
- state for which purposes funds will be applied
- state how funds will be deposited and excess funds invested
- provide for alteration of the constitution and the winding up or liquidation of the council
- establish a procedure for granting exemptions from collective agreements (by a party independent of the council).

## Registration of Bargaining Councils

Once a constitution has been approved by all parties, it is submitted to the registrar, together with the prescribed application and any other information which might be of use to the registrar. The registrar publishes in the *Government Gazette* a notice of the application received, and allows time for objections to be lodged. The registrar will satisfy themselves that:

- the council has complied with all prescribed procedures
- the constitution contains all the prescribed provisions
- no other council is registered for the same scope
- the parties are sufficiently representative.

Once the registrar is satisfied, they must register the council.

## Functions of Bargaining Councils

In terms of Section 27 of the Labour Relations Act, bargaining councils may:

- conclude and enforce collective agreements
- prevent and settle disputes
- conduct conciliation and arbitration in terms of the Act, or provide for such conciliation and arbitration
- establish a fund for the settlement of disputes
- establish and promote education and training schemes
- establish and administer pension, provident, medical aid, sick, holiday and unemployment funds
- make representations to the National Economic Development and Labour Council (NEDLAC) (or an appropriate body) regarding policy or law affecting their industries
- determine, by collective agreement, issues which for the purposes of a strike or lockout will be regarded as 'issues in dispute'
- delegate additional matters for consultation to workplace forums
- provide industrial support services in their sector
- extend their functions and services to home workers and the informal sector.

A bargaining council thus has two basic functions: a collective bargaining function and a dispute settlement function. The council is obliged by law to attempt settlement of all disputes in the industry or sector irrespective of whether the parties to the dispute are members of the council or not. However, the main purpose in establishing a bargaining council is to create a forum for collective bargaining. Through negotiations on the bargaining council, the parties regulate the relationship between them and reach agreement on substantive issues such as wages and working conditions.

The Labour Relations Act, by specifically granting bargaining councils powers to establish funds and have an input into policy and law, envisaged also a broader level of operation for these councils in the industries or sectors in which they operate, even to the point of determining matters for consultation with workplace forums in their industries and providing support services to all persons employed in their sector.

# Bargaining Council Agreements

## Contents of Agreements

Bargaining council agreements are largely substantive agreements dealing with wages and conditions of service, but they may also contain procedural items such as job evaluation and grading systems, retrenchment procedures and even grievance and disciplinary procedures. Usually the substantive items in the agreements, and particularly wage rates, are renegotiated from year to year or, where the agreement so determines, every two or three years.

Matters dealt with in council agreements include:

- minimum rates, average minimum rates and method of calculation
- wage and salary scales
- grading systems
- piecework rates
- payment of council levies
- pension, insurance and sick fund contributions
- limitations or prohibitions on overtime
- payment of money in lieu of notice
- prohibitions on deducting from the employee's wages monies other than those specified in the agreement
- prohibitions on set-off debts
- regulations regarding time and manner of payment to employees
- regulations regarding the maximum number of employees in each section, or regarding proportionate distribution of employees
- prohibitions on piecework
- prohibitions on the employment of persons under a specified age
- prohibitions on 'payments in kind'
- prohibitions on contract work
- provision for a closed shop
- regulations regarding hours of work, maximum working hours per week, payment for overtime and for work on Sundays and public holidays
- notice periods for different categories of employees
- regulations pertaining to paid public holidays, annual leave, sick leave, lay-offs, short time and desertion.

## Status of Bargaining Council Agreements

It becomes obvious from the above that these agreements deal in detail with the regulation of substantive conditions of employment – so much so that they resemble the Basic Conditions of Employment Act 75 of 1997. They are, in fact, basic-condition regulations for particular industries or sectors. Once gazetted, the agreement becomes subsidiary legislation and supersedes similar provisions in the Basic Conditions of Employment Act (with the exception of the core conditions in that Act).

## Extension of Agreements

The parties to a bargaining council do not necessarily include all employers and employees in that industry sector or area. Since one of the main purposes of a centralised bargaining forum is to establish uniformity, the parties will want all employers and employees to be covered by their agreement. This they may do by requesting the Minister of Labour to extend their agreement to non-parties who fall within the registered scope of the council. To do so they need to prove to the minister that one or more unions whose members constitute a majority among the unions party to the council, and one or more employers' associations whose members supply employment to the majority of persons employed by party employers, have voted in favour of such extension. The minister in turn must satisfy themself that:

- the unions on the council are representative of the majority of employees within the registered scope of the council
- the employer parties employ the majority of employees in the council's registered scope
- the non-parties mentioned in the request fall within the registered scope
- the agreement makes provision for an independent body to hear appeals regarding exemptions from the agreement
- the agreement contains criteria to be applied by this body in hearing the appeals
- the agreement does not discriminate against non-parties.

Despite the requirement that parties should have majority representation, Section 32(4) of the Labour Relations Act allows the minister to extend an agreement by parties which do not have majority representation if the minister is satisfied that the council is sufficiently representative and that failure to extend the agreement will be detrimental to collective bargaining at sectoral level. Since the term 'sufficiently representative' is not defined, this leaves the minister with a great deal of discretion to promote centralised bargaining arrangements.

## Arguments for and against Extension

The extension of centralised agreements to non-parties is a contentious issue. Smaller organisations argue that this gives councils unwarranted powers of control and does not allow for freedom of association. They argue that smaller enterprises struggle and even go under because they have to comply with the conditions, including wage levels, set out in the agreement, and also pay levies to the council.

The original purpose of extending agreements was to prevent the exploitation of non-unionised employees. This presupposed that councils would set only minimum-level wages and conditions of service. The Basic Conditions of Employment Act now establishes relatively satisfactory employment conditions, and it is to be doubted that wage levels set by councils (particularly those dominated by large employers) are minimum-level wages. It could be argued that parties to councils, and the government, may have lost sight of the actual purpose of these councils, and may be using the system merely to extend the control and influence of the council, rather than to protect employees and promote the industry.

A case in point can be found in developments some years ago in one of the oldest and largest councils in the country, namely the Metal Industry Bargaining Council. It has long been alleged that, although several employers' organisations and various unions are party to the council, it is dominated by the Steel and Engineering Industries Federation of South Africa (SEIFSA) and the National Union of Metal Workers of South Africa (NUMSA). The perception of some employers in the industry is that the purpose of extending the agreement to all parties in the industry is to keep wages out of competition. The smaller employers in the industry have repeatedly claimed that the wages established by the council are slowly putting them out of business, although SEIFSA insists that the majority of its members are small employers. The 2017 wage negotiations in this industry did not go smoothly, with NUMSA at one stage threatening a strike and claims that some of the employers' associations would not support the proposed settlement. A settlement agreement was eventually reached in August 2017, but questions as to the council's representativeness remain, as well as concerns about the financial status of the council, which some parties claim is almost bankrupt.

## Exemptions from Agreements

An employer covered by the extension of a bargaining council agreement may apply to the council for exemption from a part or the whole of the agreement. In the past, councils did not easily grant exemptions. For this reason, the Labour Relations Act makes provision for an independent body to hear appeals in cases where a council refuses to grant an exemption or withdraws an exemption.

In an effort to fine-tune and speed up the appeals process, the Labour Relations Amendment Act 6 of 2014 amended Section 32 (dealing with extension of agreements). The amendments include the following:

- The minister, before agreeing to extend an agreement, should satisfy themself that the bargaining council concerned has an effective procedure in place to deal with applications for exemptions.
- The independent body established to deal with exemptions must do so within a period of 30 days from the date on which the appeal was lodged.
- The council must ensure that the independent body adheres to the time frames.
- No official, office bearer or representative of the union(s) or the employers' association party to the council should be allowed to sit on the appeals body or participate in its proceedings.
- Upon receiving a request for extension, the minister must put the application out for public comment within a time frame of 21 days.
- When determining the representativeness of parties to the council, the minister now has to also take into account non-standard employees, such as those provided by temporary employment services, persons on fixed-term contracts and part-time employees, as this might very well affect representation ratios.

These amendments arise from concerns about labour market rigidity and should be viewed in the context of the National Development Plan (NDP).

## Duration of an Agreement

The1 parties themselves decide on the period for which the agreement will be binding. Usually, an agreement is effective for between one and three years, and a new agreement is negotiated before the previous agreement expires.

## Administration and Policing of Agreements

Most bargaining councils will appoint administrative assistants, the number of assistants depending on the size of the council. The actual policing of agreements is left to agents or inspectors, who are appointed in terms of the Labour Relations Act and who have wide-ranging powers. These agents visit organisations which are subject to the jurisdiction of the council. They ensure that such organisations are registered and that there is compliance with the terms of the bargaining council agreement. Any transgression (particularly the underpayment of wages) is reported to the council. The council will first try to persuade the employer to rectify the situation; if this fails, the council will institute proceedings.

## Bargaining Councils in the Public Service

Sections 35 to 38 of the Labour Relations Act make provision for specific regulations regarding bargaining councils in this sector and for a compulsory co-ordinating bargaining council for the public sector. This body concerns itself with norms and standards which are applicable throughout the public service, or with matters applicable to two or more sectors. The co-ordinating bargaining council designates an area of the public service as a sector for which a bargaining council should be established.

A bargaining council established for a particular public service sector will have sole jurisdiction in that sector as regards matters which are to be subject to negotiations with the state as employer.

## Statutory Councils

The Labour Relations Act makes provision for a trade union/unions or an employers' organisation/organisations representing 30 per cent of employees or employers in a sector, industry or area to apply for the registration of a statutory council.

The registrar will apply more or less the same procedure as with the application for registration of the bargaining council, except that representativeness is measured in terms of the stated percentage. If the registrar is satisfied that all the requirements have been met, they will publish a notice in the *Government Gazette* establishing the statutory council and inviting all registered unions and employers' associations (or any other interested parties) in the sector or area to a meeting, to be presided over by the CCMA. The purpose of the meeting is to reach an agreement on representation in the statutory council. If no agreement is reached, another attempt at a meeting will be made. Following this, the statutory council will be established with the applicant union or employers' association and other parties which may be allowed as representatives. Where there is no union or employers' association, the minister will appoint representatives of employees or employers in that industry or area as parties to the statutory council.

A statutory council may perform the same dispute settlement functions as a bargaining council. In addition, it may establish and promote education and training schemes, establish various funds and perform any of the functions of a bargaining council.

A statutory council which is sufficiently representative may apply to the minister to have its agreements on education, training and funds gazetted as determinations. In making such determinations, the minister may impose a levy on all employers and employees in the registered scope of the statutory council.

The provision for statutory councils opens up the possibility for hitherto unregulated sectors, such as agriculture, to be subjected to centralised agreements or determinations, but these determinations are, as discussed above, limited in scope.

## Workplace Rights of Unions Party to Bargaining Councils

In terms of Section 19 of the Labour Relations Act, a union that is party to a bargaining council has the right of access to any workplace within the registered scope of the bargaining council. It will further be entitled to hold meetings and to request stop-order facilities at that workplace. This applies even if the business in question is not party to the bargaining council.

## Decentralised Bargaining Structures

### The Right to Recognition

Where a union cannot or does not wish to operate at a centralised level, it will approach individual employers for recognition at a particular plant or undertaking, and then bargain on behalf of employees at that plant or undertaking or in a specific bargaining unit.

Previously, union efforts at plant-level recognition were often hampered by the employer's refusal to grant the union access (or permission to hold meetings). In terms of the organisational rights accorded to unions by the Labour Relations Act, a union has merely to prove sufficient or majority representation in order to exercise these and other rights in a particular undertaking.

### The Nature of Recognition

Although unions have prescribed organisational rights, there is no compulsion on the employer to bargain with a particular union. The union still has to approach the employer to demand that it be recognised as the representative of and bargaining agent for a particular group of employees. Theoretically, the employer could refuse to enter into a bargaining relationship, but this would be difficult if the union already has a presence at the workplace, and particularly where a majority union has requested the appointment of shop stewards. Thus, the logical step is to enter into a formal or informal agreement with the union.

*The Recognition Agreement*

Where the arrangement is formal, the parties enter into a recognition agreement. The recognition agreement (also known as a relationship agreement) confirms that the employer accepts the union as a bargaining agent for all or a defined group of employees, known as the bargaining unit. It will also stipulate the rules and procedures for the further conduct of the relationship and the issues and procedures which will be subject to bargaining or joint decision making.

The recognition agreement resembles the constitution of a bargaining council. However, the recognition agreement, because it entails closer involvement of the union with the organisation, may encompass not only collective bargaining but also a certain measure of joint decision making.

A recognition agreement is, in essence, a collective contract between an employer and the union representing employees. Parties are free to structure the agreement as they choose, but most will at least contain the following clauses:

- **Preamble:** This spells out the principles and objectives of the relationship.
- **Definitions:** This section explains certain terms in the agreement.
- **Recognition:** This clause defines the employees on behalf of whom the union will bargain. This can be done by inserting a definition of 'eligible employees' or by stating that the union may bargain for all employee classes where it is sufficiently representative.
- **Access:** This clause states when and under which conditions the union will be allowed on the premises and the procedures to be followed in requesting access.
- **Check-off facilities:** This provides for union dues to be deducted from the wages of union members, subject to written consent from these employees.
- **Shop stewards:** This contains an agreement on the number of shop stewards and their constituencies, the procedures for elections, the powers of and rules for shop stewards when performing their duties, and time off for training or union affairs.
- **Victimisation:** This constitutes an undertaking that shop stewards will not be victimised for performing their duties.
- **Negotiations:** The procedures to be followed in initiating and conducting negotiations are spelt out.
- **Disputes procedure:** This details in-house and external procedures to be followed in the event that a dispute arises during negotiations.
- **Peace obligation:** This is a declaration of good faith and an undertaking not to engage in action against the other party without following agreed processes.

- **Duration and termination of the agreement:** This sets out the period for which the agreement will be in force (usually indefinite) and the conditions under which it may be terminated.
- **Amendments:** This details the procedures to be followed if the agreement is amended, suspended or cancelled.

### Substantive Agreements at Plant Level

Once a recognition agreement has been concluded, the parties will from time to time engage in negotiations on substantive issues. The procedures and the nature of the issues will depend on the terms agreed upon in the recognition document. Such substantive agreements will be similar in form to bargaining council agreements, but may not be quite as detailed, as they do not cater for a whole industry.

### Other Procedural Agreements

Numerous other matters may be subject to negotiation between the union and management. These would include training, discipline, grievances, retrenchment, job grading and so forth. Each of these would require a special procedural agreement setting out the steps to be taken.

## The Ongoing Debate about Bargaining Structures

Employers have not, as a body, shown a preference for a particular bargaining level. However, it may be assumed that the larger organisations are quite comfortable with centralised bargaining – and especially with the fact that it takes wages out of competition, thus preventing smaller employers from paying lower wages and undercutting prices.

On the other hand, there are employers who have displayed increasing unwillingness to bargain in bargaining councils, arguing that there is a greater tendency towards decentralisation in organisations.

Being at the centre of bargaining arrangements throughout the country gives a union a great deal of power, and this is the main reason why COSATU supports the concept of bargaining councils. Also, it facilitates the union function of obtaining agreements, since unions do not have to approach individual employers. This being said, the federation itself admits that this could pose a threat to the democratic principles on which unions are built. As mentioned previously, union representatives on bargaining councils can become ensconced in their positions and fail to service their membership. Although unions may claim that they consult and obtain mandates from members, it is not easy to do so continually and on a national or sectoral basis.

The result may be that office bearers and negotiators make the decisions, which are then relayed to the membership. This may also include the decision to engage in strike action. The very fact that non-strikers are intimidated, and that violence often erupts, points to the possibility that decisions may not be as democratic as claimed.

It could be argued that unions are adequately represented by shop stewards at plant and organisational level. Shop stewards are important in this context, but unless they are adequately trained, they will revert to the union for important decisions, and the union's take on matters might not suit the employees or the employer at that organisation. The powers of shop stewards are limited, and they would not be allowed to negotiate with management on substantive issues such as, for example, productivity bonuses, although this might have the support of all parties in the organisation.

The reasoning behind the legislation relating to workplace forums was sound. In numerous systems, strong centralised collective bargaining is balanced by legally enforced participation at the workplace. However, the problem with the South African legislation is that, in its quest to appease competing interests, it gives with the one hand and takes with the other. Employees themselves and the employer are unable to establish statutory forums, and union supremacy remains.

## The Duty to Bargain: Legal Precepts

In South Africa, there is *no* duty to bargain nor to recognise a trade union. Disputes concerning matters such as wages, terms and conditions of employment and trade union recognition are resolved by a 'power play'. Established agreements could be challenged via arbitration or adjudication.

### Voluntary Nature of Bargaining
As stated earlier, the institution of collective bargaining in South Africa has, since its inception, been based on the principle of voluntarism. If this is accepted, then no duty to bargain can by law be imposed on the employer or employee party. In these circumstances the issues surrounding the bargaining relationship would be resolved by a 'power play' between the parties concerned. Where the union holds more power, it would be able to oblige the employer to recognise it and to bargain at a particular level, but where the union is weak, the preference of the employer would dominate. In the extreme, the employer could refuse to bargain with a union which does not hold sufficient power.

## Indirect Compulsion to Bargain

However, a system of complete voluntarism does not exist. The state, in its efforts to maintain labour peace, will usually establish parameters for the relationship. It will attempt to create a power balance between the parties and will protect both against exploitation and unfair labour practices. It is within these constraints that the freedom to bargain, or not, will have to be judged.

Although the Labour Relations Act contains no explicit duty to bargain, the legislation does provide that where a dispute centres on the refusal to bargain, such dispute must be subjected to advisory arbitration. Section 64(2) of the Act describes the refusal to bargain as:

- the refusal to recognise a union as collective bargaining agent
- the refusal to agree to the establishment of a bargaining council
- the withdrawal of recognition as a bargaining agent
- resignation from a bargaining council
- a dispute about appropriate bargaining units, bargaining levels or bargaining subjects.

In advisory arbitration, the parties do not have to accept the decision of the arbitrator. If a settlement is not reached, either party may follow the procedures for a legal strike or lockout.

## Good Faith Bargaining

The agreement to bargain implies a duty to bargain in good faith. This means that the party concerned should:

- display a sincere intention to achieve a settlement
- make proposals and concessions indicative of good faith
- not unilaterally institute changes
- not use delaying tactics
- not set unreasonable preconditions for bargaining
- not bypass acknowledged bargaining partners
- supply sound arguments for adopting a particular position
- not suddenly change bargaining conditions
- not unnecessarily withhold information
- never engage in insulting behaviour
- disclose any information which is needed for collective bargaining purposes (employers are compelled to do so in terms of the Labour Relations Act).

## Bargaining Levels and Bargaining Partners

There has been some controversy about the issue of bargaining levels and the choice of bargaining partners. A number of cases have hinged around union demands that employers party to bargaining councils should bargain also at plant level. The courts have been hesitant to set any definitive guidelines, but the general stance has been that bargaining at industry level does not preclude plant-level bargaining, and vice versa. Where the bargaining level was at issue, consideration would be given to the practical implications and to the circumstances and practices of each party. The Labour Court has stated that the choice of bargaining levels is a strategic question with which the law should not readily interfere (see *National Union of Food Beverage Wine Spirits & Allied Workers v Universal Product Network (Pty) Ltd (2016) 37 ILJ 476 (LC) [2017] PER 81*).

The subject of bargaining partners – and therefore bargaining units – has been equally controversial. The freedom of association principle does dictate that no employee should be denied representation by the body of their choice, yet practicalities prevent the employer from dealing on a permanent basis with each and everybody which claims to represent a particular group of employees. On the other hand, the majoritarian principle is not always democratic, particularly where various interest groups exist and where the majority gained is negligible. In light of this, the tendency in the past was to promote negotiations with unions with a stable and substantial presence, or those representing special workplace interests. The Labour Relations Act substantiates this line of thinking by granting organisational rights, as the precursors of bargaining, to unions which are sufficiently representative.

On the other hand, the Act also allows a majority union and an employer or a bargaining council to conclude an agreement establishing levels of representativeness. Effectively, the majority union could then achieve sole bargaining rights.

As noted in a previous section, the Labour Relations Amendment Act 6 of 2014 sought to rectify some of the problems identified by proposing that a commissioner may grant a sufficiently representative union the rights of a majority union. The commissioner would also be allowed to ignore the threshold set by the majority union and the employer and grant representation to a union which has a significant presence in an organisation.

All in all, the issue of bargaining levels and bargaining partners remains relatively fluid.

## Workplace Forums

According to Section 79 of the Labour Relations Act, workplace forums may be established in workplaces where there are more than 100 workers, to promote the workers' interests and to make joint decisions. The majority trade union (or the trade unions that together represent the majority of workers) may apply at the CCMA to form a workplace forum. The roles of a workplace forum are to:

- promote the interests of all workers
- enhance workplace efficiency
- consult with the employer
- participate in decision making.

Workplace forums are constituted by representatives from all occupational levels in the organisation. However, a statutory workplace forum can be established only at the request of the majority union in the organisation.

Majority unions already have significant rights at the workplace and would probably be consulted on – or be bargaining with management regarding – most of the matters dealt with by workplace forums. Majority unions may therefore see little need for also establishing forums, particularly forums which include employees who are not union members, where their power base would be diluted. Consequently, relatively few workplace forums have been established since the legislation was passed.

### Definition of Workplace

The term 'workplace' is defined in the Labour Relations Act as

> *the place or places where the employees of an employer work. If an employer carries on or conducts two or more operations that are independent of one another by reason of their size, function or organisation, the place or places where employees work in connection with each independent operation, constitutes the workplace for that operation.*

This wide and rather ambiguous definition may cause confusion, but the word 'independent' should be regarded as crucial.

### Constitution of a Workplace Forum

Section 82 of the Labour Relations Act specifies the various matters to be covered by the constitution of a workplace forum, including the manner in which representatives are to be elected. An employee may be nominated to the workplace forum by any registered trade union with members at the workplace or by means of a petition signed by 100 employees or 20 per cent of the workforce, whichever is the lesser.

(Schedule 2 as appended to the Act provides further information and advice on the constitution of the workplace forum.)

Forum Meetings

The legislation explicitly provides that the workplace forum must:

- meet regularly as a forum
- hold regular meetings with the employer/employer representatives, at which the employer must report to the forum about:
  - the financial and employment situation
  - the performance of the organisation since the last report
  - expected short- and long-term performance
  - any matter arising which may affect employees at the workplace
- at regular intervals hold meetings with employees at the workplace, during which the forum should report on:
  - the forum's activities in general
  - the matters regarding which it has engaged in consultation and co-decision-making with management.

The employer must also call an annual meeting with employees, at which the employer must present a report on:

- the financial and employment situation
- the overall performance of the organisation
- plans and prospects.

Meetings with employees must take place during working hours, without loss of pay by employees, at a time and place agreed upon between the forum and the employer.

Establishing a Workplace Forum

*Prerequisites*

The expressed purpose of workplace forums is to promote co-operation and greater efficiency and productivity in the organisation. Whether they achieve this purpose will depend to a large extent on:

- the manner in which they are established
- the manner in which they function
- the attitudes of unions, non-unionised employees and management towards the forum
- whether unions can separate their bargaining function from their co-operative function.

Establishment and Functions

Chapter 5 of the Labour Relations Act provides that a statutory workplace forum may, at the request of a majority union or unions, be established in any workplace which employs 100 or more persons. The purpose of the forum is to promote a co-operative relationship between employees and management through consultation and co-decision-making on specific issues. It is hoped that this will promote a more peaceful labour relationship, co- responsibility and, consequently, improved productivity and efficiency.

Although a forum can be initiated only by a representative union, the eventual distribution of seats on the forum must reflect the composition of the workforce. In terms of the Act, a workplace forum should strive to promote the interests of all employees at the workplace, whether they are union members or not, and to improve efficiency/productivity at the workplace.

## Definition of Employee

The term 'employee' is specifically defined in the relevant section of the Labour Relations Act. It includes all persons employed at the workplace, with one exception. Senior management staff are not included if their service contracts or status allow them to:

- represent the employer in interactions with the workplace forum
- determine policy
- take decisions which may lead to conflict with employee representatives at the workplace.

## Matters for Consultation

Except where a collective agreement (in the public service, this refers only to a bargaining council agreement) determines otherwise, a workplace forum is entitled to be consulted on proposals relating to any of the following matters:

- The restructuring of the workplace
- The introduction of new technology and work processes
- Changes in the organisation of work
- Partial or complete plant closure
- Mergers and transfers of property rights, insofar as these affect employees
- The dismissal of employees based on organisational requirements (retrenchments and redundancies)
- Exemptions from agreements or from any legal provision
- Job grading
- Criteria for the granting of merit increases or discretionary bonuses
- Education and training
- Export promotion.

A bargaining council having jurisdiction may grant workplace forums the right to consultation on additional matters. Furthermore, the employer and the majority union(s) may conclude an agreement on additional matters for consultation, or another law may determine that additional matters be subject to consultation.

## Nature of Consultation

The purpose of consultation is to reach agreement/consensus. According to Section 85 of the Labour Relations Act, the employer must:

- consult with the forum on any matter required by law
- allow forum members to make representations and suggest alternatives
- seriously consider all suggestions
- if the employer does not agree with the forum, furnish reasons for such disagreement
- if no agreement can be reached, follow an agreed procedure aimed at reconciling differences before implementing plans.

It is evident that the Act intends consultation to be taken seriously but that, once procedures have been exhausted, the employer may make the final decision.

## Matters Subject to Joint Decision Making

The Act obliges the employer to engage in joint decision making with workplace forums on any proposal relating to the issues listed below (unless they have already been dealt with in a collective agreement):

- Disciplinary codes and procedures
- Rules relating to the regulation of conduct (in terms of the disciplinary code but not work performance)
- Measures aimed at protecting and developing employees previously disadvantaged by unfair discrimination
- Changes to rules regulating social benefits which are controlled by the employer.

A newly constituted workplace forum may request an employer to produce for review the existent criteria for merit increases and discretionary bonuses, disciplinary procedures and the rules for regulating conduct.

Where the employer and majority union(s) agree, additional matters may be subjected to joint decision making, or certain matters may be removed from the list. Any other law can grant workplace forums the right to co-decision-making on matters other than those listed above.

## The Joint Decision-making Process

The aim of the joint decision-making process is to achieve consensus. This means that all parties should be persuaded that the solution offered is the best possible one. Consensus differs from agreement in that agreement entails compromise and is sometimes reached by majority decision, whereas consensus implies unanimity.

A joint problem-solving approach should be adopted and the parties should search for viable alternatives which are acceptable to everyone. Consensus is not easily achieved. For this reason, the legislation determines that where consensus is not possible, the employer may submit the matter to arbitration in terms of an agreed procedure or, if there is no procedure, to the CCMA. The CCMA will attempt to conciliate, and if this is unsuccessful, the employer may request the CCAM to engage in arbitration.

The Labour Relations Act is mute on the steps to be followed should the employer decide not to submit the dispute to arbitration. However, since the employer may not implement proposals or procedures until consensus is achieved, it is doubtful that an employer will choose this alternative. It would appear preferable for both parties to reach agreement on consensus-achieving mechanisms, such as fact-finding or task groups, and to build these into their own procedures.

### Applying for a Workplace Forum

A majority union or two or more unions acting together and forming a majority at a particular workplace can apply to the CCMA for the establishment of a workplace forum. The application must be accompanied by proof that a copy has been served on the employer concerned.

Once the CCMA receives the application, it has to make sure that:

- there are more than 100 employees at the workplace
- the applicant union(s) represents the majority of employees at the workplace
- another functioning forum, operating in terms of the Act, has not yet been established.

Thereafter, the CCMA will appoint a commissioner, whose role will be to assist the parties in reaching a collective agreement relating to the establishment of a workplace forum. The commissioner has to call a meeting between the employer and all registered unions in the workplace or, at the very least, between the employer and the applicant union. Once an agreement is reached, the role of the commissioner is complete. If no agreement is reached, the commissioner will once again attempt to bring about agreement. Failing this, the commissioner will establish a forum, appoint an electoral officer and set a date for the election of the first forum members.

In the case of the public sector, the CCMA does not need to be involved, as the relevant minister has the right, after consultation with the co-ordinating public service bargaining council, to publish a notice in the *Government Gazette*. A schedule regulating the establishment of workplace forums in the public service is appended to the Labour Relations Act.

Where a union is recognised by way of a collective agreement as representative of all employees at the workplace, it may apply for the establishment of a union-based forum, and may then select representatives to the forum solely from its own ranks. The nomination, election and removal from office of representatives would then be regulated by the constitution of the applicant union. A union-based forum will be dissolved if the agreement ends or the union concerned no longer has majority representation.

This provision would, in practice, mean that shop stewards could have two representational bodies: the shop stewards' committee and the workplace forum.

## Ethics in Collective Bargaining

Labour negotiators negotiate regarding the livelihoods of other people. Arriving at the best possible agreement between employer(s) and employees requires skill, knowledge, leadership and a fine sense of judgement. Contrary to when people negotiate to buy car or a house for the best possible deal, labour negotiators' deal-making abilities, bluffing techniques, comments and behaviour at the table, in caucuses and outside the negotiation chambers are constantly being monitored and evaluated by a variety of stakeholders. Ethics in collective bargaining seems to be a subject field on its own. Or is it?

When a labour negotiator's ethical judgements are challenged, will they be able to defend them? An ethical belief system is inherently prejudicial. It is influenced by the opinions and experiences of many generations, and by the people, institutions and the media in a person's life. A person's behaviour reflects their belief system. When it comes to ethics in labour negotiations, the negotiator has to know who they are (have self-awareness), be able to analyse who the other party is, and understand the issues on the table. All these aspects will influence how the negotiator deals with dilemmas in the negotiation process. Essentially, every ethical dilemma in the workplace has economic consequences.

The father of ethics, Aristotle (a Greek philosopher born in 384 BCE), once said: 'It is the mark of an educated mind to be able to entertain a thought without accepting it' (Gilbert, 2021). In labour negotiations, the Aristotelian principle implies the art of being able to agree or disagree on an issue, and to have a robust discussion around the issue. Disagreeing, or seeing a situation from a different angle, does not mean that the parties around the negotiation table hate each other. Rather, it implies an acceptance of the fact that people are different and have different belief systems, life experiences, levels of education, religions and value systems, and that those differences influence their behaviours and decisions. Those differences influence the ethical orientation of a person – what is known as their ethical framework – and may or may not change over time. Ideally, a person's personal, business, family and professional ethics should be aligned.

A variety of ethical frameworks exist, for example African, Western and Asian ethical frameworks. These focus on how ethical decisions are made by a collective culture of people. There are also ethical frameworks based on occupation, such as research, medical, accounting or business ethics. Historically, the ethical framework for labour relations has been influenced by social perspectives such as unitarism, pluralism and radicalism as it concerns economic, organisational, leadership and collective behaviour. Based on these perspectives, we can suggest a foundational ethical or normative choice for labour negotiation management, namely the choice between consequential versus non-consequential ethics.

Demosthenes (a Greek statesman born in 384 BCE) suggested a consequential framework of ethics, where the rightness of action will be judged by the outcome (Osama & Siddiqui, 2020). This framework flows from a unitarian social perspective. It embraces the orientation that the end or solution to a problem justifies the means – or how the solution is achieved – because the action (means) was for the greater good (solution). The problem on the negotiation table needs to be resolved and the behaviour required to change it is therefore justified. A consequential ethical orientation calls for the assessment of the negotiation dilemma and supports the idea that the outcome must be for the greater good – resulting in greater happiness, which is the best or the most preferred outcome for the followers of this orientation. The solution must bring the maximum benefit for most people, with rules of conduct which will work the best for all. This framework supports order and structure. Predetermined general rules must be followed.

Non-consequential ethics (Singer, 1972) flows from the individual's moral compass, with the focus being on the principles of how a solution can be achieved. The means by which the parties achieve the solution (professional behaviour) is more important that the solution. This framework accepts that people do not all have the same value systems, and that in rules of conduct there are many shades of right and wrong. In labour negotiations, the principles these negotiators are committed to are established in a code of conduct, with the negotiators who are following a non-consequential ethical compass being committed to specific norms. In labour negotiations these norms (such as trust, integrity, respect, recognition, legality, good faith and fairness) are agreed upon through a collective agreement. The way in which a problem is resolved is guided by shared values instead of a set of rules. These negotiators have a sense of duty and are held accountable through reporting systems. They have a holistic view of their reactions to problems and an understanding that their action or non-action impacts on others. One blind spot of this framework is the concept of reversibility: While the golden rule for this framework suggests that one must do unto others as you would like to be done to you, negotiators should be aware that others might not necessarily appreciate their efforts to do unto them what the negotiators think is good for themselves.

Considering that organisations have to rapidly adapt to a very uncertain future with regard to issues such as pandemics, global warming and industrialisation, it is becoming less likely that an ideal solution in labour negotiations can be predicted at the commencement of negotiations. Participation in the creation of a shared future for a workplace is likely to produce more benefits for parties around the labour negotiation table.

## Conclusion

The Covid-19 pandemic has resulted in an economic and humanitarian crisis far greater than the international recession of 2008–2009. To recover from this pandemic, the world requires unusual, creative recovery plans towards the transformation of workplace systems, policies and relationships. Stakeholders at collective bargaining tables would need to reconsider existing collective bargaining arrangements, the anticipated future bargaining relationship as well as their far greater obligations towards the community, environmental practices and the way in which people collaborate and work.

While labour legislation in South Africa will not disappear, there is likely to be a significant shift regarding how and with which bargaining partners change in the workplace will happen.

## Suggested Questions/Tasks

1. What are the main roles of collective bargaining in South Africa? Substantiate your answer.
2. A number of international and African organisations are influencing the issues placed on collective bargaining tables for the next decade. These include the ILO, with its decent job goals; the United Nations (UN), with its Sustainable Development Goals (SDGs); and the African Union (AU), with its transformational goals. For each organisation, select three goals that will have a direct influence on the current labour relations landscape and explain what is expected from these goals.

3. Discuss the primary objectives of collective bargaining in South Africa.

4. Evaluate the requirements for a good collective bargaining process as suggested by the SABPP (see https://www.sabpp.co.za/).

5. Differentiate between recognition/procedural agreements, substantive agreements and transformational agreements, and present an example of each.

6. Does an employer in South Africa have a duty to bargain? Substantiate your argument.

7. Before 1 January 2015, only majority and sufficiently representative trade unions were recognised by the Labour Relations Act. However, with the amendments to the Act, three more levels of organisational rights to parties can be recognised. Explain these levels.

8. Critically evaluate the forces that influence the conclusion of specific collective agreements.

9. Differentiate between a bargaining unit and a bargaining level and give an example of each.

10. Specify whether workplace forums and recognition agreements are structures of collective bargaining. Substantiate your argument.

11. Discuss the issues in respect of which the employer(s) need to consult with a workplace forum.

12. Employment relationships at all levels of an organisation require high levels of trust, which is strongly related to high levels of compliance, fairness and good faith. It is therefore important that employees know what each of the aforementioned requirements entails. Explain the nature of good faith and the basic requirements for good faith in relationship behaviour.

13. Discuss the influence of the minimum wage on collective bargaining and sectoral determinations.

14. Explain how lawful the extension of collective agreements is. In your argument, also include the constitutionality of these extensions.

15. Imagine a scenario where the employer has recognised your union as a majority trade union but refuses to share confidential information on management training. Utilising the relevant sections in the Labour Relations Act, explain your recourse and arguments.

16. Debate the following statement: 'The government should/should not take complete control of the labour relations system.'

17. Your union has decided that it wishes to establish a statutory workplace forum at Strong Leather, which has branches all over the country. The largest branch sources and processes leather for the other branches. Another branch manufactures saddles for horses. Others are footwear manufacturers, while yet others make children's toys from leather scraps.

a. Under what conditions would the union be allowed to request that a forum be established?
b. What advantages would the union see in the establishment of a forum?
c. Could a forum be established to cover all Strong Leather's operations? Explain.
d. What would the parties have to consider before drawing up their constitution?
e. Draw up a constitution for the proposed forum.
f. What would be the next step? Provide details.
g. Who could be represented on the forum if your union is the majority union?
h. What would your union have to prove if it wanted to appoint only its own shop stewards as employee members?
i. What would be the first matters to be addressed by the forum?
j. How would you go about training forum members to engage in joint problem solving or more co-operative processes?
k. Provide your own assessment as to the future success of the forum.

## Sources

Addison, JT. 2020. 'The consequences of trade union power erosion'. Institute of Labour Economics. https://wol.iza.org/articles/consequences-of-trade-union-power-erosion/long (Accessed 29 October 2021).

Berton, F, Carreri, A, Devicienti, F & Ricci, A. 2019. 'Workplace unionism, collective bargaining and skill formation: New results from mixed methods'. Institute of Labour Economics (IZA) Discussion Papers No 12712. http://hdl.handle.net/10419/207536 (Accessed 29 October 2021).

Gilbert, PR. 2021. 'Virtue and authenticity: Heidegger's interpretation of Aristotle's ethical concepts'. In *Phenomenological Interpretations of Ancient Philosophy*, edited by K. Larsen and PR Gilbert. Leiden: Brill: 92–131.

Greer, I & Hauptmeier, M. 2016. 'Management whipsawing: The staging of labor competition under globalization'. *ILR Review* 69(1): 29–52.

Harrison, DS. 2004. Collective bargaining within the labour relationship, in a South African context. PhD dissertation, North-West University.

ILO (International Labour Organization). 1948. 'C087 – Freedom of Association and Protection of the Right to Organise Convention, 1948'. https://www.ilo.org/dyn/normlex/en/f?p=NORMLEXPUB:12100:0::NO::P12100_INSTRUMENT_ID:312232 (Accessed 30 September 2021).

ILO. 1981. 'C154 – Collective Bargaining Convention, 1981'. http://www.ilo.org/dyn/normlex/en/f?p = NORMLEXPUB:12100:0::NO::P12100_ILO_CODE:C154 (Accessed 30 September 2021).

Kauhanen, A, Maczulskij, T & Riukula, K. 2020. 'Heterogeneous impacts of the decentralization of collective bargaining'. IZA Discussion Paper No 13867. https://ssrn.com/abstract = 3730465 (Accessed 29 October 2021).

Kochan, TA. 1980. *Collective Bargaining and Industrial Relations*. Homewood: Richard D. Irwin.

Labour Relations Act (66 of 1995). *Government Gazette* vol 366 no 16861. Pretoria: Government Printer.

Osama, M & Siddiqui, DA. 2020. 'Right is what that benefits all, or that which is morally correct: An enquiry on how ethical predispositions (consequentialism vs formalism) influence the effect of role models on ethical leader'. December 29, 2020. https://ssrn.com/abstract = 3756685 (Accessed 29 October 2021).

SABPP (South African Board of People Practices). 2021. 'SABPP Labour Market Scenarios 2030: People and work – How will the South African labour market change over the next 14 years?'. https://cdn.ymaws.com/www.sabpp.co.za/resource/resmgr/website_files_1/publications/labour_market_scenario/labour-market-2030-scenarios.pdf (Accessed 29 October 2021).

Singer, P. 1972. 'Famine, affluence, and morality'. *Philosophy and Public Affairs* 1(3): 229–243.

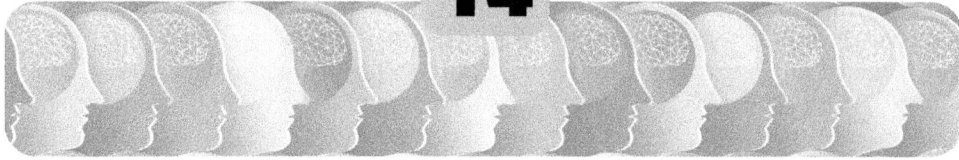

**14**

# Industrial Action

## Chapter Outline

# Overview

In the approach to labour relations from a pluralistic perspective, employers have the right to manage – this is termed the managerial prerogative. The process of collective bargaining and joint decision making is aimed at acknowledging mutual interdependency and achieving a balance of power in the relationship by means of supporting freedom of association. Strike action is seen as a means of levelling the playing field between employers and employees in the workplace through the collective bargaining framework. Strike action is regarded as part of the collective bargaining process; without the threat of strike action, collective bargaining would be pointless.

The Labour Relations Act 66 of 1995 attempts to redress inequality and injustices within the labour relations system. The Act endorses and regulates strike action, and aims to promote orderly collective bargaining in the management of the workplace relationship. If parties engage in conflict management and negotiations through collective bargaining, then disputes should be resolved speedily and amicably without the need for the role players to resort to strikes and lockouts. Avoiding disrupted production in the workplace and workdays lost would result in an increase in productivity as well as a potential improvement of the labour relationship.

In recent years, strike action in South Africa has been a growing concern. In some cases it is due to employees demanding unrealistic salary increases rather than approaching the negotiating table with an attitude of co-operation and collaboration. Unfortunately, civil unrest, violence, intimidation, harassment and the destruction of property have all been linked to strike action at some point. It is disturbing that members of society and the country have at times been negatively affected by strikes, to such an extent that the actions of disorderly strikers have had negative consequences for the economy. Violent industrial action jeopardises the aims of the labour legislation, which are to promote economic growth, social justice, labour peace, workplace democracy, worker participation and joint decision making.

Conflict can lead to disputes in the workplace. Disputes in the workplace tend to centre around interests and not rights. Therefore, in industrial action, coercive action is taken by either the employer or the employee to show their power in the labour relationship. Ongoing antagonistic relationships in the South African labour market have resulted in many challenges that have impacted negatively on the economy as a whole. The antagonism that continues to characterise employment relationships in the South African workplace has impacted equally negatively on employment relations satisfaction and the fulfilment of the psychological contract (Ntimba, Lessing & Swarts, 2020).

Sometimes, disputes may occur before procedures have been utilised, and at other times after the procedures have been exhausted. A free labour relations system will not provide for compulsory arbitration of all disputes and will entrench the right to coercive action, and particularly to a strike or a lockout.

Coercive action is the ultimate manifestation of conflict in the workplace, and is used in situations where employees feel that no other means will result in their opinions being heard. Strikes and lockouts constitute the most visible expression of the conflict that exists between employers and employees. They are the direct result of the power struggle between employers and employees. Coercive action, of which strikes are but one manifestation, can emerge in different forms. These can range from organised strikes to overtime bans, go-slows, work-to-rule, and so forth.

➤

Strikes occur more often than lockouts, and most lockouts instituted by employers are in response to actions or demands by employees; these types of lockouts are known as defensive lockouts. The employer may also lock out employees in order to compel them to agree to a demand.

Section 23(2)(c) of the Constitution of the Republic of South Africa, 1996, provides that every worker has the right to strike, but, like any other constitutional right, the right to strike is not absolute. The Labour Relations Act, while it grants employees the right to strike, also grants employers the right to a lockout, but only in particular circumstances and only if they follow the prescribed procedures. The strike or lockout will only be legal if the party concerned adheres to the prescriptions. Moreover, in the case of a strike, the legality of the action protects the employees from dismissal. Hence, legal strikes are also known as protected strikes. In the case of a lockout, the employer is protected from being sued for breach of contract. The Act also allows for sympathy strikes by employees in other organisations and for strikes in protest at socio-economic conditions.

In certain circumstances, industrial action is prohibited, for example where legislation or an agreement provides for arbitration of a dispute. For example, the Act prohibits strike action in essential services or in designated maintenance services. The Labour Relations Amendment Act 8 of 2018 also provides for an advisory arbitration panel to arbitrate a dispute which may lead to or has led to a strike. The purpose is to reach an agreed solution and thereby to avoid an action which might adversely affect individuals or society at large.

Persons who engage in a strike or a lockout without following due process are not protected by the Act, and the aggrieved party may apply to the Labour Court to interdict the offender. Employees who engage in an illegal strike may be dismissed by the employer, but only after the employer has followed a fair procedure, which includes the issuing of an ultimatum to return to work or face the consequences.

Strikes and lockouts have the potential to be traumatic events and both parties should be adequately prepared for their occurrence. Protest action in South Africa must be seen and understood in the context of the country: it is regarded as the essence of democracy given the country's history and it manifests in the form of protests and social mobilisation. In the South African context it must be mentioned that protest action or strike action has been sometimes violent in nature; this constitutes a contradiction in terms of the true nature and the intention of democracy.

# Strike Action

## Definition

A strike may be broadly defined as a temporary, collective withholding of labour, its objective being to stop or impede the continuation of business and thereby to oblige the employer to take notice of employee demands.

The fact that a strike is of a temporary nature is important. Employees engaged in strike action do not intend to permanently withhold their labour from the employer, but merely to oblige the employer to enter into negotiations or, where negotiations are already under way or deadlocked, to persuade the employer to change their position regarding the demands of the employees.

Section 213 of the Labour Relations Act defines a strike as:

> *the partial or complete concerted refusal to work, or the retardation or obstruction of work, by persons who are or have been employed by the same employer or by different employers, for the purpose of remedying a grievance or solving a dispute in respect of any matter of mutual interest between employer and employee, and every reference to work in this definition includes overtime work, whether it is voluntary or compulsory ...*

This definition has the following main elements:

- **Refusal to work:** The refusal to work can be partial or complete and can also include retardation or obstruction of work. A strike does not need to amount to a complete withdrawal of labour. A partial refusal means that employees perform some of their tasks but not others. The retardation of work is manifested in the so-called go-slow, where employees continue to work but do so at a slower rate. Obstruction of work refers to instances where employees in one way or another hamper production or the work process. The refusal to work overtime is also viewed as a strike. (This refers only to contractual overtime – where the employee has contracted to work overtime or where they have usually worked overtime and therefore contractually accepted it. Employees who do not normally work overtime would not be striking if they refuse to do so.)
- **Collective action:** One employee cannot strike. Strike action is by its very nature a collective action and by implication it will always involve two or more employees. Employees can organise themselves to embark on industrial action. The collective action can also be initiated under the guidance of the trade union representing the employees in the organisation.
- **Following from a grievance or dispute:** Strike action usually emanates from failed negotiations, demands by employees or protests at management actions or decisions. If employees refuse to work but they do not have any demand or are not seeking to remedy a grievance or resolve a dispute, there is no strike in terms of the statutory definition. Furthermore, a union may not strike in support of a demand that is unlawful. Once an employer has agreed to the demands of employees there is no longer any valid purpose for the strike.

In order for any form of labour action to constitute a strike in terms of the Labour Relations Act, it must comply with all three of the above elements. It should also be noted that the definition refers to persons who are in the employ of the same 'or different' employers. This not only caters for strikes by employees in the same industry, but also allows for sympathy strikes (discussed later in this chapter).

## Reasons for Strike Action

The most common reasons for strike action include general dissatisfaction among employees, an adversarial employment relationship, economic concerns, dissatisfaction with conditions of service, personal problems, solidarity with other employees, lack of consultation, socio-economic issues, the need to demonstrate strength, and trade union rivalry. All these are discussed below.

### General Dissatisfaction among Employees

This normally starts with unhappiness or dissatisfaction with current circumstances in the workplace, whether it is related to the employment relationship itself, the physical work environment/workplace situation, or labour market problems in society. As the unhappiness becomes more serious, tempers flare and workers become involved in heated group discussions, which can then lead to demands being made and protest action and, eventually, to a strike.

The problems often lie in unrealistic expectations of role players in the labour market and the socio-economic problems found in our highly unequal and divided society. These have a negative effect on the trust relationship in the workplace. Added to this is a lack of co-operation in labour–employer relations, a very rigid labour relations system, and the difficulties involved in employing and dismissing workers as a result of stringent labour legislation.

It is no surprise that the primary labour relationships occur within relationships between an employee and their immediate supervisor. The primary labour relationship is the one relationship where the lack of trust results in low levels of compliance, fairness and good faith in the relationship. Supervisors and shop stewards work closely together in the workplace and levels of distrust can also result in damage to the trust relationship. A lack of trust will become evident when employers or employees fail to maintain levels of compliance, fairness or good faith in primary labour relationships. The failure to maintain a trust relationship can also be perceived by employees as a breach of the employment contract or the policies, procedures and workplace regulations (Ehlers, 2020).

### An Adversarial Employment Relationship

The escalation in conflict and destructive nature of protest and strike action not only harms the economy of the organisation and country, but also has a highly negative impact on the trust relationship between employer and employees, which results in an employment relationship that is adversarial in nature.

## Economic Concerns

These concerns include wages and the increasing cost of electricity, transport, food, health services, clothing, rent and so forth – in short, an increase in the general cost of living. Concerns of this nature lead to demands for higher wages and improvement of terms and conditions of employment and benefits. Any attempts by employers to reduce wages may have a negative effect and will be met with resistance and protest action by employees and their trade unions, which can escalate to strike action.

## Dissatisfaction with Conditions of Service

The unhappiness and frustration of some workers with the conditions of service agreed upon in their contracts of employment can lead to strike action over time if these conditions are not revised and adapted according to the prevailing situation. Some examples of issues which can breed dissatisfaction are working hours, flexibility of working conditions, health care support, ineffective training and a lack of benefits such as medical aid and pension provision.

## Personal Problems

Personal issues may have an impact on the workplace and it can be difficult for employees to separate their personal lives from their work lives. It is not uncommon for people to bring their personal problems to work, which has an effect on the workplace environment as well as the relationship between employee and employer. The complexity of the personal problems found in society and at home can spill over into the workplace and lead to a shift in focus of the workforce. Personal and social issues such as poor housing, inadequate transport infrastructure and access to health care facilities are only some of the most prominent issues that employees deal with on a daily basis. Others include family issues, financial issues, substance addiction, disability or health-related complications. These problems affect the focus of the employees and could lead to financial losses for the organisation. It can even result in accidents at the workplace and it leads to poor performance and lower productivity. Ultimately, this situation can also affect the wellbeing of other people in the organisation.

## Solidarity with Other Employees

Solidarity between people is one of the main elements of social order and social conflict. It can manifest in political coalitions and social routines and is present in the workplace and the society that we live in. Workers are very aware of the value of their labour and the impact that withholding labour can have on organisations. Unions also promote solidarity among all employees and very often call on other unions to support the causes of their members by also engaging in strike action.

### Lack of Consultation

Unions and employees want to be consulted on issues that might affect them and very often claim that employers fail to consult with them, which leads to dissatisfaction and, sometimes, strikes. Consultation is defined in the workplace context as a process by which one party informs another party about an issue and their viewpoints thereon. The issue is systematically considered before a final decision regarding the issue is made. There is no obligation or understanding in the consultation process that the decision-making party will or must incorporate the viewpoint of the consulting partner in the decision.

Section 189(1) of the Labour Relations Act provides that, before dismissal based on operational requirements (retrenchment) is contemplated, employers must consult with the individual employee and with the employee's representative and/or trade union in terms of any collective agreement. In the absence of a collective agreement, meetings should be held with all employees that could be affected by the retrenchment. In Section 189(2) of the Labour Relations Act provision is made that the consulting parties must attempt to reach consensus on matters such as avoiding dismissals, suitable measures to minimise dismissals, changes in the timing of the dismissals, applicable measures to mitigate the effects of retrenchment, methods of selecting the employees to be dismissed, and severance pay.

### Socio-economic Issues

Workers may not be satisfied with the socio-economic status quo and, through their unions, may engage in collective action to raise awareness of their concerns. In South Africa, the focus has been on improving the lives of citizens by targeting inequality, unemployment and poverty. Currently, a critical aspect is access to health care. The majority of the South African population depend on the public health care system and expect the system to take care of their needs. Furthermore, ongoing initiatives and efforts by government to address gender inequality in South Africa have not had the desired effect, and gender equality remains a big stumbling block for socio-economic development.

## The Need to Demonstrate Strength

Where the employer is not taking a union seriously, a strike may be called, seemingly for a work-related reason, but with the real purpose of showing the employer that the employees and their union can wield power if the employer does not co-operate. During strikes in South Africa, people are often seen toyi-toying at these mass gatherings and marches. Unrealistic demands and power play are part of the process and the unions sometimes show their strength through violence, intimidation and damage to property during protest action.

## Trade Union Rivalry

Individual unions and trade union federations want to be viewed by their members and supporters in terms of what services and benefits they can provide and of the role they play during collective bargaining and negotiations. This has unfortunately led to some trade unions becoming militant and demanding economically unfeasible salaries and benefits. If the employer does not give in to their demands, they declare a dispute or revert to industrial action that is characterised by violence and destruction. Some trade unions become radicalised and revert to politics and militancy instead of focusing on their primary mandate of improving employee terms and conditions of employment and negotiating salary increases within an economically viable and sustainable business environment.

Some people claim that the South African labour framework is undemocratic and results in union rivalry, but we need to remember that the Labour Relations Act supports freedom of association and that fair labour practices are entrenched in the Constitution. Rival trade unions sometimes use strike action as a tool to increase trade union membership and to mobilise employees in order to give a particular union a political edge over its rivals. Some noteworthy occurrences are mentioned by Murwirapachena and Sibanda (2014), such as where competitiveness between unions weakened effective negotiations in the mining industry. In the past, there have been instances where negotiations were conducted in a manner described as 'bad faith negotiations', as the demands were unrealistic and not achievable. For example, in July 2013 gold producers, represented by the Chamber of Mines of South Africa (CMSA), proposed a wage increase of five per cent. The Association of Mineworkers and Construction Union (AMCU) negotiated for unprecedented increases as high as 150 per cent, and the National Union of Mineworkers (NUM) asked for a 60 per cent increase on the minimum entry-level salary for gold miners.

## Classification

The classification of strikes is related to the reasons for particular strikes. Because the reasons are wide-ranging, numerous types may be identified. These include the following:

- **General strikes:** Strike action that is general in nature involves a diverse group of employees. In the current South African context, the demands in general strikes seem to be geared towards addressing inequality. Attempts by workers to intensify the impact of their strikes by using various tactics which have a negative impact on the lives and property of other people have been observed. This includes damage to property during strike action, such as trashing city infrastructure; vandalising property; forming picket lines at organisations, municipality buildings and government departments; and even preventing shoppers from doing business with their chosen businesses.
- **Economic strikes:** Strikes of this nature are the most common form of strike action. They relate to management's refusal or failure to satisfy the demands of employees regarding wages and other economic issues such as service benefits and working conditions.
- **Grievance strikes:** These normally occur when employees do not agree with the way in which management deals with normal day-to-day problems. These issues can include the introduction of new technology, downsizing, restructuring or any other work-related problems.
- **Demonstration strikes:** This refers to actions intended primarily to display dissatisfaction, as a preliminary to negotiation or a precursor to further negotiation.
- **Recognition strikes:** These are actions in which it is intended, by a show of strength, to make management recognise the employees' right to representation or to closer consideration of their demands.
- **Procedural strikes:** This type of strike occurs after procedures or negotiations have been exhausted, or are thought to have been exhausted, where no agreement has been reached and a deadlock situation has arisen. In these circumstances, strike action may be seen as a last-resort attempt to break the deadlock and to continue with negotiations under different conditions.
- **Strategic strikes:** These strikes are instituted to consolidate the union's position at a particular plant or in a particular industry or area. They are, in part, a show of strength and are often not caused by immediate grievances or demands.
- **Go-slows:** The go-slow is a method of withholding labour and affecting production without actually bringing operations to a standstill. For employees, it holds the advantage that they do not lose their wages as easily and that it is more difficult for management to take action against

them. Also, since employees are still manning their positions, they cannot be replaced by temporary labour. A go-slow amounts to a partial withdrawal of labour and managements may treat a go-slow in the same manner as a strike.

- **Overtime bans:** Where overtime is regulated by contract or agreement, a ban on overtime constitutes strike action and would be subject to the same regulations as a strike. Bans on overtime may be directly linked to employee perceptions that wages are being kept deliberately low and that overtime is used as a means of enticing employees to supplement their incomes.
- **Sympathy or solidarity strikes:** Employees at plants belonging to the same company, in other organisations in the same industry/sector, or belonging to the same union or federation may institute strike action to display solidarity with striking employees. These sympathy strikers have no issue with their own employer, but their purpose is to pressurise the employer against whom the original action was launched. By engaging in sympathy action, strikers may persuade their own employer to place pressure for settlement on the 'offending' employer. Sympathy actions could extend nationally and internationally, particularly where multinational employers are involved.
- **Sociopolitical protest actions (also known as general strikes):** These are union-initiated actions aimed at sociopolitical grievances and are usually regionally or nationally based.
- **Wildcat strikes:** These strikes occur without any prior warning. The element of surprise is used to bring certain issues to management's attention. These strikes are mostly unprotected strikes.
- **Grasshopper strikes (also known as rotating strikes):** This type of strike action is used by employees to impede operations. It is normally very well planned and co-ordinated. Employees start their strike action in a specific section of the organisation. As soon as the 'problems' in that section have been sorted out, strike action commences in another section. This process continues until some solution to employee grievances is found.
- **Sit-down strikes:** During this type of strike action the employees refuse to leave the work area; in that way they prevent the employer from making use of replacement labour. Normal production is disrupted, as workers are occupying working areas.

Strikes may also be classified in terms of their location. Thus, a certain action may be described as a plant-level strike, an industry strike, a company-wide strike or a general strike.

## Factors Contributing to Strike Action

Although every strike is, in essence, a unique occurrence, certain general problems can be discerned by studying strike actions in different countries over a number of years. Factors usually regarded as contributing to strike-proneness, or as influencing the occurrence of strike action, are discussed below:

- **Shifts in the business cycle:** Unions will more readily engage in strike action during a period of economic growth than during a recession. In times of economic prosperity there is a higher demand for labour and employers cannot afford to lose production owing to a strike. During a recession, when jobs are in high demand and the employer may have produced more than they can sell, the position could be reversed. The employer would be more willing or ready to sustain strike action and may even welcome the temporary closure of the plant or part of the plant. This is the theoretical situation. In practice, employees might suffer during a recession and might continue making demands while employers try not to concede. This might lead to drawn-out actions.
- **Homogeneous work groups:** Kerr and Siegel (1954) found that strikes are more likely to occur where employees come from the same community, and particularly if such communities are themselves homogeneous and isolated from others. Thus, miners who work together and live in the same community, separated from other communities, may more readily engage in strike action than manufacturing workers who are drawn from different, geographically spread-out communities.
- **Community support:** Closely related to the previous factor is the influence of community support. Such support sustains strikers in their action and increases the pressure on employers for the settlement of disputes.
- **Location:** Organisations situated close to other concerns, particularly those of the same kind, are more susceptible to labour action than would otherwise be the case. News travels rapidly along the employee grapevine, and it is easier for unions to organise employees who are in the same geographical area.
- **The work process:** Unpleasant, monotonous work lends itself more easily to strike action than work of a lighter or more interesting nature. Hard work may draw more militant workers. Also, where work is dirty or hard or has become so mechanised that it is boring, employees may engage in strike action merely to gain temporary relief.
- **The labour relationship:** Where employers are reluctant to recognise unions or to concede to any union demands, and where relationships remain fragile, strike action is more likely to occur. Furthermore, there tends to be a greater incidence of strike action if bargaining takes place on

a decentralised level, although centralised actions, when they do occur, are on a larger scale.

- **The strength of the union movement:** A strong union which is organised effectively and is assured of the support of its members will more easily engage in strike action than a weaker counterpart. On the other hand, unions in the process of growth may, despite relatively weak positions, stage strategic strike actions to create awareness of their existence; however, these strikes are usually short-lived.
- **Inter-union rivalry:** Multi-unionism, and the subsequent heightened inter-union rivalry, is likely to lead to an escalation in strike activity as unions try to outdo one another.
- **Legislation:** Where a government has imposed severe limitations on strike action, or has provided effective dispute settlement machinery, the incidence of strikes may decrease. The converse is also true.
- **Size of the organisation:** Studies have proven that larger organisations tend to be more strike-prone than their smaller counterparts. This is attributed mainly to the fact that large undertakings have cumbersome organisational structures, leading to insufficient communication and to depersonalisation of the employee, encouraging individuals to act as one of a collective. Also, a union wishing to demonstrate its power to the public will target the larger organisations.
- **Profitability and costs:** Companies which are highly profitable may suffer from more labour action. Employees may feel that they are receiving too small a share of the wealth generated.
- **Worker-related factors:** In general, employees who are materially deprived and have little to lose, or who see themselves as completely disadvantaged in society, will more readily engage in strike action than their more privileged counterparts.
- **Public opinion and the press:** Where the press and the public support actions undertaken by unions, the propensity for strikes increases.
- **High-profile employers:** Employers who have a prominent public image may be more frequently subjected to labour unrest. Actions against these employers are highly publicised and add to the union's standing.

### The Freedom to Strike

The question as to whether employees should be entitled to undertake strike action at all times is a controversial one. Some theorists say that strike action should be completely outlawed, as it is a disruption of normal employment relations. This faction argues that conflict should be contained within the other labour relations processes, and that strike action is an indication of a breakdown in these procedures. By contrast, there are those who argue that strike action is an integral part of the labour relations process and a legitimate means of expressing conflict or of exerting pressure. In the pluralist approach it is accepted that the freedom to strike, as a last resort and as a final display of power, cannot be denied to employees. Otherwise, they would be in an unequal power relationship with the employer. Therefore, the freedom to strike, within certain parameters, is legitimised in most Western systems.

The parameters mentioned may include the imposition of cooling-off periods or conciliation processes before strike action can occur, or there may be regulations regarding, for example, the holding of ballots or liability for damages caused. Where the state has imposed certain limitations on strike action, there is differentiation between legal and illegal strikes. Legal strikes are those which are instituted within the parameters of government legislation, whereas employees engaged in illegal strike action do not follow the legislated procedures.

### The Question of Dismissal: The Right to Strike

Another subject for debate is whether employers should be entitled to dismiss striking employees. The arbitrary dismissal of strikers effectively ends the negotiation process. If it is accepted that strike action is part of the negotiation process and a legitimate means of exerting pressure, then the dismissal of strikers defeats the purpose. This argument is supported by the fact that strike action is defined as a temporary, and not a permanent, withholding of labour.

A further argument is that the ability of employers to dismiss striking workers may result in a permanently unequal power balance in the relationship. Therefore, the equivalent for employers of the right to strike is the right to a lockout and not the right to dismiss strikers. Where a government has provided for legal strikes, it may also provide that employees engaged in a legal strike may not be dismissed by an employer, or at least not until prescribed procedures have been followed.

## Other Employee Actions

### Withdrawal of Co-operation

Employees may withdraw their support of co-operative actions. This can include the refusal to participate in profit-sharing schemes and quality circles. They may also raise grievances and refuse to co-operate when the employer tries to solve work-related problems.

### Work-to-Rule

This is a very difficult form of collective action to manage, as employees do not transgress any rules; instead, they insist on a very rigid interpretation of the duties specified in their contracts of employment or in the collective agreement. Employees ask for very minute and detailed instructions on how to complete work. This has the effect of slowing down work. It is not the same as a go-slow, in that employees are merely doing what they are supposed to do, but it also impacts on production.

### Product and Service Boycotts

A boycott is an attempt to stop consumers from buying a product marketed by a particular undertaking or from using a service provided by the employer. It is a means of exerting pressure on an employer and affecting the profitability of the undertaking without direct action being taken by employees. A boycott requires extensive publicity, organisation and persuasion of the consumers in the marketplace. It is best implemented where workers – or other members of the public who would be sympathetic to the cause – constitute a significant proportion of such consumers. Also, boycotts are more successful where a company markets one or two well-known products rather than a diversity of lesser-known goods.

### External Pressures

Employees who are at issue with their employers may attempt to extend their influence by gaining the sympathy of other employees and employers, suppliers, consumers, the public at large, community leaders and national or international organisations. These persons or organisations are persuaded to interfere in the negotiations or to exert whatever pressure they can bring to bear on the employer concerned. Where the external pressures are numerous and varied, or where the person or organisation exerting the pressure is of importance to the employer, this form of action may prove quite effective.

## Labour Market Trends and Labour Unrest in the Covid-19 Era

The lockdown measures instituted during the Covid-19 pandemic, together with load shedding, have weakened the South African economy. (The Covid-19 vaccination programme, run by the government, is an initiative to curb the devastating effects of the pandemic.) In response, companies introduced various cost-saving measures, including retrenchments and restructuring. At the time of writing, the unemployment rate had worsened, notwithstanding the reopening of various sectors of the economy. All these aspects bring the potential for workplace conflict, and if this is not managed properly it can lead to labour unrest and to industrial action.

Trade unions need to take note of the following aspects:

- **Collective bargaining for trade unions:** South Africa's economy was fragile even before the Covid-19 pandemic, and at the time of writing, the situation had worsened. The reintroduction of lockdown measures in 2021, sporadic load shedding and the slow roll-out of Covid-19 vaccinations are some of the issues that could affect the economic recovery going forward. This, in turn, could have an effect on the ability to bargain collectively during wage negotiations. Unresolved negotiations and the failure to reach agreements can lead to parties declaring disputes and reverting to protest action.

- **Retrenchments impacting on trade union representativeness:** Unions will need to challenge the fact that executives continue to receive high bonuses while workers are retrenched in times of hardship. Unions need to engage in consultation and see to it that retrenchments are the last resort. Collective bargaining and negotiations must be supported with evidence of a proper analysis of the available financial information of a company when demands are made. A bigger focus must be placed on efforts to find alternative means to avoid retrenchment, and the viability of reskilling and transferring people to different business units needs to be investigated.

- **The shift to remote working:** Remote working has brought about new collective bargaining issues, such as time management and communication costs. In some instances benefits achieved through union bargaining, such as transport and food allowances, have been eroded with the implementation of remote working.

- **The effects of Covid-19 on women:** The pandemic has put inequality firmly in the spotlight and has highlighted the most vulnerable workers. Women who earn less that the minimum wage, who are self-employed and who are temporary workers have been hit the hardest by the pandemic. A review of organisational, government and trade union policies regarding women's economic empowerment is important.

- **The value of work:** The need for employers and trade unions to re-evaluate the value of work, which has in the past been diminished by worker exploitation, has been brought to the fore by the pandemic. Essential workers have been redefined to include health practitioners such as medical practitioners, nurses and caretakers of the fragile and elderly. Essential services include workers performing services such as medical health, laboratory and medical services; fire prevention and fire fighting; services related to grocery stores; fuel production, supply and maintenance; funeral services; newspaper, broadcasting and telecommunication services; waste and refuse removal services. Note that this list is not exhaustive.

- **Precarious employment as an alternative form of employment:** A dramatic change in the manner in which work has traditionally been executed has come about as a result of the uncertainty caused by the pandemic. Business managers have had to look for innovative ways to reduce costs in a challenging economic climate. Employers have been forced to appoint previously permanent contract workers in flexible, non-permanent part-time positions, with the possibility of being laid off until the economy recovers.
- **The establishment of new employment relationships:** Unions have had to face the informalisation of employment relationships and the disintegration of their bargaining units. Trade unions need to adapt to work with the informal sector, as informal economic activities are vital to the livelihoods of many in South Africa. This may signal the beginnings of a new understanding of how work is organised and what it means for the employment relationship.
- **Reduced compliance with labour standards:** Non-compliance with labour laws and the difficulties of enforcing sectoral determinations and the national minimum wage in South Africa are challenges. Trade unions play an important role in the enforcement of labour standards by exposing non-compliance where they experience it. Health and safety standards in the workplace are non-negotiable and the pandemic proved that unions cannot rely on all employers to implement the required labour standards. The introduction of new shared social values or norms in communities and organisations will need to be entrenched in such a way that societies adhere to and comply with labour standards as set out by government.

Statistics released by the Commission for Conciliation, Mediation and Arbitration (CCMA) have shown that, out of 71 099 workers who were at risk to be retrenched by the end of December 2020, only 30 199 (42 per cent) workers' jobs were saved. During that period, 39 566 workers were retrenched (DEL, 2021: 11). This is relatively significant in the context of the triple challenges of high unemployment, inequality and poverty in the country.

## Lockouts by the Employer

Just as employees may decide to engage in strike action if their demands are not met by an employer, so the employer may temporarily withhold employment from employees if they do not agree to the employer's demands or to a settlement proposed by the employer.

The Labour Relations Act defines a lockout as:

> *the exclusion by the employer of employees from the employer's workplace for the purpose of compelling the employees to accept a demand in respect of any matter of mutual interest between employer and employee, whether or not the employer breaches those employees' contracts of employment in the course or for the purpose of the exclusion.*

During a lockout, the employer prevents employees from working and therefore earning their wages. As in the case of a strike, there must be a demand made and it must relate to a matter of mutual interest. The employer is also safeguarded from claims of breach of contract if they legally lock out employees.

In practice, lockouts occur far less frequently than strikes, first because, in this context, employers are more reactive than proactive, and secondly because an employer has far more to lose, in total, by closing down operations than an individual employee loses by engaging in strike action.

## Strikes and Lockouts in South Africa

The South African labour market is known for the intense and violent nature of protest action during strikes, which are to a great extent characterised by the destruction of property. In South Africa, strike and lockout actions, with the exception of those in essential and maintenance services, are not forbidden, but they are regulated by means of the distinction between protected and unprotected strikes according to the Labour Relations Act. Nonetheless, a strike or lockout will be legal only if the prescribed dispute settlement machinery has been used. This does not mean that so-called spontaneous strikes do not occur, but these have no legal status.

### Protected versus Unprotected Actions

Prior to the Labour Relations Act of 1995, the terms 'legal strike' or 'illegal strike' were used. Currently, the terms 'protected' and 'unprotected' are more commonly applied to strikes.

A protected strike is one where employees cannot legally be dismissed if they have followed the rules and continue to do so. Nevertheless, where a strike continues and has an increasingly adverse effect on the organisation, the employer may have a case for dismissing employees on the grounds of operational requirements. Also, the Labour Relations Amendment Act 8 of 2018 proposes that if a continuing strike has an adverse effect on society and the economy, a special advisory arbitration panel may be set up for the purpose of facilitating settlement.

The term 'unprotected strike' refers to strikes where the necessary statutory requirements have not been met and where employees participating in such strike action can be dismissed, since they are in breach of contract.

An employer who locks out employees after following the prescribed procedures is also protected in the sense that the employer may not be sued for breach of contract or accused of an unfair labour practice. The employer is also not obliged to pay employees during a lockout.

## Protected Strikes and Legal Lockouts
### Procedures towards a Protected Strike/Lockout
The formal process towards strike action normally begins after options for negotiation in the workplace have been exhausted and if the parties were not able to reach an agreement among themselves. To engage in a legal strike or lockout, the party concerned must:
- refer the issue in dispute for conciliation to the CCMA or to a bargaining council having jurisdiction
- produce a certificate issued by the CCMA or the bargaining council indicating that conciliation has failed, or produce proof that 30 days have elapsed from the date of the initial referral
- give the other party 48 hours' written notice of the planned action (this notice must indicate on which day and at what time a strike will commence)
- if the employer party is the public service (a state department), give seven days written notice of a proposed strike or lockout
- where the dispute involves an agreement concluded in a bargaining council, or involves an employers' organisation, give the necessary notice to these parties
- where the dispute involves the refusal to bargain, first go to advisory arbitration before embarking on any action.

### Waiver of Procedures
The procedures outlined above need not be followed where:
- a strike is in response to an illegal lockout by the employer
- a lockout follows an illegal strike by employees
- a collective agreement sets out the procedure to be followed
- a bargaining council has handled the strike in terms of its procedures.

Moreover, where the dispute concerns a unilateral change in conditions of employment, the union may demand that the employer restores the conditions or does not implement changes while due process is being followed. The employer will have 48 hours to comply. If the employer fails to do so, the employees may immediately engage in legal strike action without following the prescribed procedures.

### Dismissals

As stated previously, participation in a protected strike does not constitute breach of contract and the employees cannot be dismissed. Nevertheless, striking employees may be dismissed should they make themselves guilty of offences (such as intimidation, assault, damage to property, etc) that justify dismissal in terms of the employer's disciplinary code. In these cases, normal disciplinary procedures should be followed by the employer.

If employees participate in strike action where the statutory procedures have not been followed, they are not protected against dismissal, but the employer will still have to follow fair procedures, including an ultimatum to employees to return to work (see the case review later in this chapter). The employer may also approach the Labour Court for an interdict against illegal strikers.

### Replacement Labour and Payment of Strikers

There is no prohibition on the use of replacement ('scab') labour during a strike, except where a workplace has been designated as a maintenance service. Nevertheless, striking employees will try to discourage 'scabs' by organising pickets at the entrance to the premises.

The employer does not need to remunerate any employees participating in a strike, irrespective of whether the strike was protected or unprotected. The principle of 'no work, no pay' applies. However, during any strike action an employer must, if so requested by an employee, continue any payment in kind such as accommodation, or other basic amenities. Once the strike is over, arrangements may be made for the employer to recover the value of payment in kind.

## Unprotected Strike and Lockout Actions

### General Prohibitions

Strikes and lockouts are prohibited where:

- the parties are bound by a collective agreement prohibiting strike or lockout action in certain kinds of dispute
- an agreement obliges the parties to take the issue to arbitration
- the issue in dispute must, in terms of the Labour Relations Act, be taken to arbitration or to the Labour Court
- the parties are engaged in an essential or maintenance service
- the parties are bound by an arbitration award, a determination by a statutory council or a determination in terms of the Basic Conditions of

Employment Act 75 of 1997 (unless a period of 12 months has expired since the determination came into effect).

The ban on strikes where a matter is subject to arbitration means that in most disputes of right, the parties may not legally engage in labour action. The exceptions to this are disputes centring on the granting of organisational rights and those related to retrenchments in organisations employing more than 50 people. (The regulations regarding the latter situation have been discussed in Chapter 13.) Unions are entitled to strike or to go to arbitration over organisational rights. Section 65(2)(b) of the Labour Relations Act provides that if a union gives notice of a strike over organisational rights, it may not, for a period of 12 months, take the dispute to arbitration.

### Essential Services

An essential service is defined in Section 213 of the Labour Relations Act as 'any service the interruption of which may endanger the lives, personal health or safety of the entire population or a part of the population'.

It is obvious that any medical or emergency service, such as firefighting, would be classified as an essential service. Persons involved with the supply of water to the general public may be regarded as involved in an essential service, while the interruption of rubbish collection over a long period may eventually render this, too, an essential service. Parliamentary services and the South African Police Service (SAPS) are also classified as essential services.

Disputes in these sectors, regardless of whether they constitute disputes of right or of interest, cannot be settled by the use of economic power. The only alternative, therefore, is to use mediation and arbitration or legal adjudication. (See Chapter VII of the Act.)

Section 70A(1) of the Act provides that the minister, after consultation with the National Economic Development and Labour Council (NEDLAC), must establish an Essential Services Committee under the auspices of the CCMA. According to Section 70B(1)(d) of the Act, the function of this Essential Services Committee is to hear representations from concerned parties, and to decide which services should be designated 'essential services'.

### Minimum Services

Sometimes it is not necessary for the entire organisation to be classified as an essential service, but there may be special parts of its operations which need to continue functioning. The Essential Services Committee may endorse any collective agreement providing for the maintenance of minimum services, which are then classified as essential services as regards that employer and their employees.

*Maintenance Services*

Section 75 of the Labour Relations Act also makes provision for the designation of certain services as maintenance services. These are services which cannot be interrupted, since this would result in 'material physical destruction to a working area, plant or machinery'. Like minimum services, these are also classified as essential services.

The continued incidence of illegal strike action by persons employed in essential services has proven problematic. For this reason, the Labour Relations Amendment Act 6 of 2014 contained detailed proposals aimed at further empowering the Essential Services Committee and encouraging the use of alternative dispute settlement procedures.

## Recourse against Illegal Actions
*Urgent Interdicts*

The Labour Relations Act grants the Labour Court sole jurisdiction as regards illegal strikes and lockouts, and enables it to grant urgent interdicts prohibiting such actions.

Where a party engages or intends to engage in a strike or lockout which is illegal in terms of the Act, the other party may apply to the Labour Court for an urgent interdict. The applicant must give the respondent 48 hours' notice of their intention to apply for such interdict, but the Court may condone shorter notice if:

- the applicant has informed the other party in writing of their intention to lodge an application
- the respondent has had a reasonable opportunity to be heard
- there are sound reasons for allowing a shorter notice period.

(Notice periods are not applicable in the case of an essential or maintenance service.)

In granting the interdict, the Labour Court may make an order prohibiting participation in, or the promotion of, an illegal strike or lockout. It may order compensation for any losses suffered, but only after it has considered:

- efforts made to conform to the provisions of the Act and the extent of such efforts
- whether the strike or lockout was pre-planned
- whether it was a reaction to an unfair practice by the other party
- the duration of the action
- the financial position of each party
- the promotion of orderly collective bargaining.

## Dismissal of Unprotected (Illegal) Strikers

As mentioned above, employees engaged in a protected strike may not be dismissed merely for participating in such a strike, whereas employees embarking on an unprotected strike can be dismissed. The Labour Relations Act states that participation in an unprotected strike is viewed as misconduct. Although this type of behaviour cannot always be equated with other instances of misconduct, a fair procedure must be followed before the employee involved can be dismissed.

If the employer is of the opinion that the employees' actions justify dismissal, the employer should issue an ultimatum in clear and unambiguous terms. This ultimatum should:

- inform the employees that they are participating in an unprotected strike
- state very clearly what the employees are required to do, namely to return to work within a reasonable time
- provide the employees with a 'cooling off' period where they can calmly consider their actions and possible consequences
- state what sanction will be imposed if the employees fail to comply with the ultimatum
- give employees sufficient time to respond to the ultimatum.

There is no general agreement among judges and experts about the procedure to be followed if the employees do not return to work. Some maintain that the ultimatum is sufficient warning and the employer can then proceed with the dismissal, while others would have the employer engaging in further consultation, if not with employees then at least with the union, and even hearing representations by employees. (See the case review later in this chapter.)

Disputes about dismissal related to strike action are conciliated by the CCMA. Should conciliation fail to settle the disputes, they will be adjudicated by the Labour Court.

## Advisory Arbitration

The Labour Relations Act has provided mainly for conciliation as a method of possibly resolving disputes of interest. Should conciliation fail, the parties are then free to resort to a legal strike or lockout once they have followed the procedure outlined above. Section 150A makes provision for a deadlock-breaking mechanism for a protracted and violent strike, in the form of compulsory arbitration undertaken by a statutory advisory arbitration panel. Sections 150A, B, C and D in the Labour Relations Amendment Act 8 of

2018 allows the director of the CCMA to appoint a panel to engage in advisory arbitration of a dispute if:

- the minister orders the director to do so
- one of the parties has requested that a panel be appointed
- the Labour Court has issued an order to that effect
- the parties have agreed to resort to advisory arbitration.

The decision to order a panel can only be made when the Labour Court declares a dispute to be unresolved or with the commencement of a strike, whichever occurs first.

Section 150A(3) of the Act determines that the director may order a panel to be appointed only if the director has reasonable grounds to believe that:

- the strike or lockout is no longer functional to the collective bargaining process
- there is an imminent danger of constitutional rights being violated
- there is a threat of violence or damage to property
- the strike causes or can cause 'an acute national or local crisis which affects the normal functioning of a community or society'.

The Labour Court will order that a panel be appointed if it believes that there are reasonable grounds for doing so and that a national crisis may arise, or that constitutional rights may be violated.

The panel must consist of a senior commissioner as chairperson and four assessors, two of whom should be nominated by the employer party and two by the employee party. If the parties fail to do so, they will be a presented by NEDLAC with a list of assessors, from which each party can choose two persons. Should either or both of the parties fail to participate, the director must appoint assessors on their behalf.

The chairperson, together with the assessors, will conduct the arbitration. In doing so, the chairperson will have the same powers as a commissioner in terms of the Act and may request disclosure of all the necessary information. The panel has seven days to complete its task, but may request an extension from the director. Following this, the panel makes an award, setting out its findings and recommendations, which are then served on the parties. Thereafter the employer and employee parties have seven days to indicate their agreement or otherwise, but they may request an extension or that they reconvene. If a party does not respond, it will be assumed that they agree.

The minister must publish the findings of the panel, whether the parties have agreed or not. Where there is agreement, the aspects agreed upon may be extended to non-parties within their jurisdiction (for example, where the parties represent a bargaining council).

The original provision for advisory arbitration is contained in Section 150 of the Act (Labour Relations Amendment Bill, 2012). In terms of that section, parties who do not accept the arbitration are still free to engage in a strike or a lockout. According to the Explanatory Memorandum, this would also apply where an advisory panel has been appointed (Memorandum of Objects, 2012).

A party bound by the award and/or its members, as well as any other person to whom the award has been made, may not strike or effect a lockout concerning the subject matter of the award. This is in line with and encourages parties to comply with the provisions of the Labour Relations Act relating to the limitation of the right to strike. Section 65(3) states that no person may take part in a strike or a lockout, or in any conduct in contemplation or furtherance of a strike or lockout, if that person is bound by an arbitration award or a collective agreement that regulates the issue in dispute.

The amendments have been widely criticised as interfering in the hitherto accepted process. However, there is no indication that there will be unnecessary interference and this kind of intervention should occur only when the circumstances as outlined call for a possible alternative solution.

## Sympathy Strikes

The Labour Relations Act grants employees the right to engage in sympathy strikes.

### Definition

A sympathy strike may be defined as an action initiated by employees of one employer (secondary employer) in support of striking employees at another employer (primary employer) (Section 66(1) of the Labour Relations Act).

A sympathy strike is also known as a solidarity strike or secondary strike, as defined in the Act, Section 66(1). The issue in dispute at the workplace of the primary employer may have little or nothing to do with the secondary employer.

### Legal Requirements

In terms of the Act, a secondary strike will be protected if:

- the strike that is being supported, namely the primary strike, is a protected strike and all procedural requirements have been followed
- the secondary strikers have given their employer, or a representative employers' organisation, at least seven days' notice before going on strike
- the nature and extent of the secondary strike is reasonable in relation to the possible direct or indirect effect it might have on the business of the primary employer

- there is some kind of correlation between the businesses of the primary and the secondary employers (for example, Spar employees going on strike in support of employees striking at Checkers).

The law therefore accepts that a secondary action, in order to be legitimate, must be instituted for the purpose of exerting pressure on the first employer to change their position and that it should not be undertaken merely to express solidarity with other strikers.

### Recourse by the Secondary Employer

An employer faced with a secondary strike that, in their opinion, does not comply sufficiently with the above requirements may lodge an application in the Labour Court to prohibit the strike action by means of a court interdict. The Court or any party to the action may then request the CCMA to investigate the extent to which the sympathy action will have any effect on the first employer.

## Picketing

Picketing normally goes hand in hand with a strike. It can be viewed as action undertaken by employees or their supporters to publicise the existence of a labour dispute by patrolling or standing outside or near to the location where the dispute has arisen. More often than not it is marked by the waving of placards indicating the nature of the dispute.

Picketing is allowed in terms of Section 17 of the Constitution, which gives all citizens the right to – peacefully and unarmed – demonstrate, picket and present petitions.

### Purpose

Picketing is undertaken in order to:

- persuade employees who are not participating in the strike to stop production and to join or support the strike
- deter customers from entering the employer's premises
- hamper the delivery of supplies necessary for production
- prevent, disrupt or limit the delivery of goods to customers
- communicate grievances to the wider public.

*The Legal Position*

The Labour Relations Act accepts that picketing is a legitimate action in support of a strike. In terms of Section 69(1) of the Act, a picket will be protected if:

- the picket has been authorised by a registered trade union
- the picketers engage in a peaceful demonstration
- it is held in support of a protected strike or in opposition to a lockout.

Picket lines may be formed in any public place outside the premises of the employer or, with the permission of the employer, on the actual premises. Permission for picketing on the premises may not be unreasonably withheld.

*Picketing Agreements/Rules*

It is advisable for employers and worker representatives to establish rules regarding picketing. In the event of a strike or a contemplated strike, either party may request the CCMA to facilitate an agreement setting out the rules applicable to picketing in that undertaking. If the parties cannot agree, the CCMA will itself establish picketing rules for the organisation. Concerns about continuing violence on picket lines have led the lawmakers to insert a new clause into Section 69 of the Labour Relations Amendment Act of 2018. This would oblige a commissioner conciliating a dispute of interest to make sure that there are picketing rules in place. Where there are no rules and it is evident that a strike will occur, the commissioner will be obliged to establish the rules.

The Code of Good Practice: Collective Bargaining, Industrial Action and Picketing has been issued by the Department of Labour (DoL, 2018). For an example of a collective agreement on picketing rules, see the Annexures online (Western Cape Government, 2019). Where an agreement regarding picketing has been concluded and such agreement is broken, or where the union is unable to exercise its right to picket, the dispute may be referred to the CCMA for conciliation and, if no agreement is achieved, to the Labour Court. Where the dispute involves the rights afforded to the parties by the Act, it may be referred directly to the Labour Court.

## Sociopolitical Protest Actions

Much argument has revolved around the question as to whether a protest action – and, therefore, the absence from work of employees engaged in such action – should constitute employment-related action. The Labour Relations Act does provide for legal (and therefore protected) protests or stayaways, the purpose of which is to promote the socio-economic interests of workers in general. No definition of 'socio-economic interests' is provided, but the term can be taken to include such matters as the imposition of certain taxes, cuts in government spending or employment creation, the provision of housing, and privatisation.

Employees engaged in protest actions will be accorded the same protection as legal strikers, provided that:

- the action has been instituted by a registered trade union or federation
- the union or federation has sent a notice by registered mail to NEDLAC, stating the reason for and nature of the proposed action
- the union or federation has, at least 14 days before the commencement of such action, given notice to NEDLAC of its intention to continue with the action.

Where the procedures outlined have not been followed, the Labour Court will have sole jurisdiction to grant an order prohibiting a person or persons from taking part in such protest or from taking any action in furtherance of the protest.

The Court may also issue a declaratory order taking into account:

- the nature and duration of the protest
- the steps taken by the union or federation to minimise the unfavourable effects of such action
- the behaviour of those participating in the protest action.

Any employee who acts in contempt of an order of the Labour Court in respect of a protest action loses the protection granted by the law.

## Case Review: Dismissal of Strikers Bound by Bargaining Council Constitution

### SA Clothing and Textile Workers Union & Others v Yarntex (Pty) Ltd t/a Bertrand Group (2013) 34 ILJ 2199 (LAC)

#### Background

The organisation concerned, Bertrand, falls under a subsector of the Textile Bargaining Council. This council provided, in its constitution, that conditions of employment, including wage rates, could be negotiated only at subsector or section level (and therefore not at individual companies). At the beginning of 2008, the South African Clothing and Textile Workers' Union (SACTWU) negotiated new wage rates for the subsector under which Bertrand was classified.

The dispute in question arose over the fact that the Bertrand Group, because it operated in a disadvantaged area, had previously been granted a concession to pay

80 per cent of negotiated rates. The exemption was due to end in 2009. The union and Bertrand employees were not satisfied with the fact that Bertrand would still be paying less than the negotiated rates.

In July 2008, workers engaged in a wildcat strike. After receiving a final written warning, they returned to work, but in the same month the union declared a dispute with the company, demanding that they pay the full negotiated rate. However, in August it withdrew the dispute and instead declared a dispute in the bargaining council. When this initiative failed, the union gave notice to commence a strike on 17 September. Later, while in consultation with the company's lawyers, the union agreed to continue negotiations, but on the 17th the workers went out on strike.

The company warned both the union and the employees that the strike was unprotected and issued an ultimatum to return to work. In the meantime, strikers had stormed the premises and threatened violence against non-strikers. The company posted notices around the premises warning that disciplinary action would be taken. A notice to this effect was also sent to the union.

On 18 September, the union met with management representatives and agreed that the action would be suspended, and negotiations would continue. However, when, on 22 September, a union official met with the workers, they refused to return to work. At this stage SACTWU withdrew from the situation. The company issued a final ultimatum to employees and at the same time invited them to elect representatives who could make submissions on their behalf. No representations were made and all the strikers were dismissed, whereupon they declared an unfair dismissal dispute.

In court, the union representative argued that the bargaining council constitution did not expressly forbid strike action.

## Pronouncements

The Labour Court pointed out that the bargaining council's constitution was an all-embracing document intended to regulate collective bargaining and labour action in the industry and that it was itself a product of bargaining. The starting point was the promotion of organised centralised bargaining intended to avoid coercive action and, as this was the intent, the constitution did not have to state specifically that strikes could not occur at other levels. The Labour Appeal Court therefore upheld the earlier decision of the Labour Court that the dismissals had been fair under the circumstances.

## Comments

The finding that the dismissals were fair indicates that the Labour Appeal Court agreed with the employer that the strikes were illegal, as they contravened a provision implicit in the council's constitution forbidding labour action at that level. The employer did not react to the threats but followed the necessary procedures. The strikers were given ample opportunity to rectify the situation, which they refused to do.

*Modise & Others v Steve's Spar Blackheath 2001 (2) SA 406
(LAC)*

## Background

This case was brought by four employees of Steve's Spar who, with others, had been dismissed for engaging in an illegal or unprotected strike. The four claimed that they were not members of the union and that they had been unwilling participants in the strike; instead, they had not reported for work for fear of reprisals. They further claimed that they had been in contact with the employer to inform him that they were willing but scared to work. This the employer denied.

The Labour Court did not accept their explanation and their claim was denied. The employees subsequently appealed against this judgment on the grounds that they had been dismissed without being given the opportunity to plead their case.

## Pronouncements

Dissenting judgments were given by Justice Zondo and Justice Conradie, respectively. Justice Mogoeng concurred with Justice Zondo, whose award thus stood.

### *Zondo AJP*

Justice Zondo commenced by noting that the *audi alteram partem* rule was 'part of the rules of natural justice which are deeply entrenched in our law'. This was particularly so in labour law, under which the employer became 'obliged to hear the employee's side before he could dismiss him'. According to Justice Zondo this applies to all dismissals, whatever the reason for such action. The only possible exceptions could arise from 'crisis zone situations', waivers or possible waivers (when the employees denied themselves the right to a hearing). In *A Guide to SA Labour Law*, Rycroft and Jordaan (1992) approve of this opinion and, referring specifically to strike dismissals, state that, although an illegal strike was sufficient reason for dismissal, the employer had to provide an opportunity for the employees to address the problem either through the union or through an elected committee. This would give them the chance to debate whether they wanted to go on strike. Rycroft and Jordaan (1992) also note that an ultimatum must be issued so that employees are given enough time to return to work.

Justice Zondo also referred to Article 7 of the International Labour Organization's Convention on Termination of Employment (ILO, 1982), which, in his opinion, made it clear that a hearing was imperative in all cases of misconduct. Illegal strikes were not exempted from this rule.

Justice Zondo concluded that

> it can be said with a sufficient degree of certainty that, in the context of dismissal, an employer is obliged to observe the audi rule where the decision may adversely affect the employee's rights. Were these rights not to be given to strikers, they would be receiving different treatment to an employee who, for example, stole from the employer.

It was conceded that there were a large number of cases in which the courts had not found the dismissal of strikers to be unfair, despite the fact that no hearing had been held. However, in these cases, the courts had 'acknowledged the general rule' that a hearing should take place, but had found justification for the failure to hold a hearing. In some of the cases cited it had been found that 'the strikers had waived or abandoned their right to a hearing or that a hearing would have been pointless or would have served no purpose or that in the particular circumstances the employer could not reasonably have been expected to give the strikers a hearing'.

It was Justice Zondo's considered opinion that the failure to hold a hearing should only be condoned under very exceptional conditions. In this regard he referred to Hoexter JA in *Zenzile & Others v Administrator of the Transvaal & Others (1989) 10 ILJ 34 (W) at 38I–41A*, where it was pronounced that 'even if the offence cannot be disputed, there is always something which can be said about sentence and if there is something that can be said about it, there is something that should be heard'.

Another argument raised was that an ultimatum replaced the necessity for a hearing. To this Justice Zondo replied that a hearing and an ultimatum are 'two different things' which serve different purposes. The one could not be substituted for the other. It would, according to Justice Zondo, probably be preferable to allow a hearing before an ultimatum was issued. This could, for example, be done by sending a letter to the union inviting them to make representations as to why employees should not be dismissed. Justice Zondo clarified that the employer could deal with the strikers as a group by 'calling for collective representations [as to] why the strikers should not be dismissed'.

## Conradie JA

Justice Conradie commenced by noting that the fact that a strike was illegal did not necessarily mean that the strikers should be dismissed. The decision as to dismissal depended on whether the strike was 'functional to collective bargaining' or not. In this case the strike was 'totally dysfunctional'. In fact, the employees and their union had been interdicted from continuing with the strike but had continued regardless and had made no effort to discuss the matter with the employer. He therefore could 'see no reason why the appellants should not be penalised for their non-compliance'.

Justice Conradie accepted the employer's version that an ultimatum had been issued to the assembled strikers together with the court order, that the ultimatum had been extended to the following morning and that they had been dismissed only when they did not comply with the extended ultimatum.

Turning to the question as to whether the strikers should have been afforded a hearing, Justice Conradie had the following to say:

> The only general principle that I can discern in both administrative and labour law is that a hearing should be afforded if it is in the circumstances fair to give one. Usually the circumstances are such that it is fair to give a hearing. It is only in this sense that there may be said to be an obligation on an employer: if he encounters circumstances where it is fair to do so, he must give a hearing.

In support of the contention that a hearing was not necessary, Justice Conradie referred, among others, to *National Union of Mineworkers of SA v Haggie Rand Ltd (1991) 12 ILJ 1022 (LAC)*, where the presiding judge had expressed the opinion that there was no merit in the argument for a pre-dismissal hearing in the event of an illegal strike. The judge also said the following:

> If one postulates a hearing in the present circumstances one necessarily emasculates the ultimatum, for it would have to read that workers are to return to work or be dismissed but subject to a disciplinary hearing ... There is also something quite artificial and unacceptable in requiring an employer who is directly affected by the flagrant, unmistakable behaviour of an employee to conduct an enquiry himself into such misbehaviour after such employer has himself deemed it necessary to issue a dismissal ultimatum as a result thereof.

This opinion was supported in other cases cited by Justice Conradie. The judge then went on to explore the purpose of the ultimatum. An illegal strike was, he stated, misconduct of a special kind which could be 'purged' by compliance with an ultimatum. Once the employee returned to work, they were no longer guilty of misconduct relating to participation in the strike. Unlike a disciplinary enquiry, an ultimatum was 'not directed at establishing the existence of an offence and then imposing a sanction', but rather 'a device for getting strikers back to work'. This presupposed the unlawfulness of the workers' action. It was both a means of avoiding a dismissal and a prerequisite for effecting one. Thus 'the question of dismissing a striker can only logically arise after non-compliance with an ultimatum'.

At this point, Justice Conradie noted that the Code of Good Practice did, in any event, provide for a pre-ultimatum discussion in that it required the employer to contact the union, at the earliest possible opportunity, to discuss the intended ultimatum. In Justice Conradie's opinion, the employer's obligation went no further. He could not see why this discussion should be 'supplemented by another and discreet hearing of some kind and another'. Justice Zondo's suggestion of a pre-ultimatum hearing, which could be individual, seemed to him to be useless. Would the employees then attempt to convince the employer that they should not be dismissed, yet proceed to ignore the ultimatum and continue with the strike? Equally, a post-ultimatum hearing would be futile:

*They would be able to urge the employer either to withdraw the ultimatum on account of the strike being lawful, if that was their intention, or, it is said, to urge that they should, by virtue of their excellent employment records or family commitments or advanced age or their ignorance of the lawfulness of the strike, or their unwillingness to participate in it, be permitted to continue striking unlawfully.*

Justice Conradie conceded that in normal cases of misconduct, there was usually no excuse for not holding individual disciplinary enquiries. However, in a collective action such as a strike, the employee or the union was not entitled to present individual motivations. If this were to be allowed, the employer could selectively dismiss. It would also undermine union solidarity and be unfair to the union. Even the argument that certain strikers were unwilling participants did, in Justice Conradie's opinion, not hold:

*There would, in every strike, legal or illegal, almost certainly be reluctant participants, for example, those who voted against the strike but participate because they bow to the will of the majority. It would in my judgment be grossly unfair to require an employer to hold an enquiry into each striker's enthusiasm for the cause before being able to issue an ultimatum against those, and only those, found to be in favour of the strike ... The absurd result of this would be that the 'willing' strikers would be dismissed, but that those who make allegations of intimidation which the employer is unable to disprove, may remain on strike unhindered.*

In conclusion, it was noted that the union was involved from the beginning, that an application had been brought to interdict the strike and that this was an open invitation to the union to defend its position, which it did not do. It was also noted: 'In a strike situation, discussion (or attempted discussion) with a union acquits an employer of his duty to listen to the other side.'

## Reply of Zondo AJP

Justice Zondo replied to the argument regarding fairness that 'the audi approach' introduced certainty into labour law and that the 'no audi approach' would perpetuate uncertainty. With the 'audi approach' every employer would know in advance what they should do even though this rule was not absolute, and the existence of exceptions was acknowledged. It provided for a principled approach as opposed to deciding each case on its own.

Justice Zondo consequently concluded as follows:

*In the light of the above, I have no hesitation in concluding that in our law an employer is obliged to observe the audi rule when he contemplates dismissing strikers. As is the case with all general rules, there are exceptions to this general rule ... The form which the observance of the audi rule must take will depend on the circumstances of each case including whether there are contractual or statutory provisions which apply in a particular case. In some cases, a formal hearing may be called for. In others an informal hearing will do. In some cases, it will suffice for the employer to send a letter or memorandum to the strikers or their union or their representatives inviting them to make representations by a given time why they should not be dismissed for participating in an illegal strike ... In some cases, a collective hearing may be called for whereas in others ... probably a few ... individual hearings may be needed for certain individuals.*

The employer was ordered to reinstate the four employees with retrospective effect.

## Discussion

Certain issues arise from these judgments, the first being whether participation in an illegal strike can be equated with other forms of serious misconduct or whether, as Justice Conradie stated, it is misconduct of a special kind. The facts would seem to favour the latter interpretation, as the Labour Relations Act specifically declares participation in a strike without following due process or without an enforceable demand as unlawful. This it does not do in other cases of misconduct. Furthermore, the Act makes special provisions for strike dismissals, different from those related to other forms of misconduct.

If it is accepted that strike dismissals are different from other dismissals, then the question arises as to how they differ. The primary difference is that guilt exists from the outset and does not have to be proved. The employees have not tendered their services. This renders them in breach of contract. The only possible excuses would be a belief that the strike is legal or that they were intimidated into participation. The illegality of the strike therefore has to be conveyed to the strikers from the outset. Secondly, employees need to know that if they are being intimidated, they can, before or at the beginning of the strike, bring this to the employer's attention, not when the possibility of dismissal is imminent. In this case, there were employees who did just that and who kept in constant contact with the employer. They were not dismissed. Allowing employees to bring representations regarding intimidation when they are threatened with dismissal is to invite everyone to use that excuse. A further difference was pointed out by Justice Conradie when he noted that in strike dismissals the misconduct can be rectified. All the employees have to do is to return to work. Other misconducts cannot be rectified in this manner.

The second issue arises from the fact that these dismissals are different. If they are, does it then signify a different procedure? The Act has already answered this question, but, as evidenced by this case, the general principle of the hearing remains. The Act does state that a discussion should be held with the union. Both judgments accepted that this would be sufficient to satisfy the 'audi' rule, but differed as to the content of the discussion. Moreover, Justice Zondo intimated that there might be cases for individual hearings. In these circumstances it may be advisable to address both the union and employees beforehand and to indicate that representations citing exceptional circumstances can be made, but that these exceptional circumstances would not include normal arguments in mitigation.

Finally, there is the matter of reality. A strike situation is a crisis situation. Not all employees may agree with the strike. Some might go along with it for the sake of solidarity while others are intimidated into joining. Employers need to deal with this reality and cannot in these circumstances be judged by absolutes. All that could be expected of them is to do the best they can and to be as fair as possible. They cannot be expected to consider all possibilities and all possible exceptions. As far as they are concerned, their employees as a collective are out on strike, and they deal, through the union, with this collective. Where they sense that the union is not acting in good faith, they should address the employees themselves, but they cannot, when it comes to the ultimatum, which is the final step in the conflict, be expected to engage in a lengthy process of consultation and the hearing of representations. This would lead to a litany of mostly fabricated excuses and would, as has been correctly stated, emasculate the entire process.

## Addressing Protracted, Violent Strikes

A strike that takes an unreasonably long period to be resolved can have devastating effects on the economy. It also increases levels of unemployment, thereby perpetuating poverty, with serious effects on the lives of people. The question that arises is how to put a stop to a lengthy strike and protect the economy from shrinking, with negative effects on existing jobs.

Strikes should only be allowed to continue if they are lawful. The definition of 'strike' lends itself to any obstruction of work that is lawful. So, if workers refuse to undertake 'work' that is illegal and unlawful, this will not constitute a strike. Where employees refuse to work in support of an unlawful demand (for example the removal of a supervisor without following due process), this will also not constitute a strike. Therefore, where the action involved does not constitute a strike, participants do not enjoy the protection offered by Section 67(1) of the Labour Relations Act.

If the means used by strikers to obstruct work constitute unlawful conduct such as violence, then the conduct will not qualify as a strike, and will thus not be protected. If a strike becomes violent and no longer pursues legitimate or lawful demands, the Labour Court should intervene, as violent and unruly conduct is the antithesis of the aim of a strike, which is to persuade the employer through peaceful withholding of work to agree to the union's demands. For a court to intervene, Rycroft and Jordaan (1992) argue that one must ask whether the misconduct has resulted in the strike no longer being functional to collective bargaining, in which case it would no longer deserve protected status.

The Labour Court, in *National Union of Food Beverage Wine Spirits & Allied Workers v Universal Product Network (Pty) Ltd 2016 37 ILJ 476 (LC)*, adopted Rycroft's functionality test, which entails that the Court could assume the power to alter the protected status of a strike to unprotected action on the basis of violence. This entails the weighing up of the level of violence against the efforts of the trade union to curb it in order for a court to determine whether a strike's protected status is still functional to collective bargaining.

Rycroft and Jordaan (1992) further argue that there is an inseparable link between strikes and functional collective bargaining. He justifies this on three grounds. First, the Interim Constitution of South Africa 200 of 1993 provided that 'workers have the right to strike for the purposes of collective bargaining'. Secondly, strikes must be orderly. And, lastly, the strike must not involve misconduct. This he infers from the fact that employees engaged in misconduct can be dismissed irrespective of whether the strike is protected or not.

Informed by the decision of *Afrox Ltd v SACWU 2*, Rycroft and Jordaan (1992) argue that a strike can lose its protection if it is no longer functional to collective bargaining. So if a strike is no longer functional to collective bargaining, it is bound to lose protection, and those who participate in such activities will face dismissal or an action for damages can be instituted against those responsible.

## Handling Strike Action

Both employers and unions need to plan for and handle strike action as effectively as possible.

### The Union
The primary tasks of the union are to:
- maintain the morale of the workforce
- ensure that strikers are effectively looked after so that material considerations do not oblige a return to work
- undertake talks towards the settlement of a strike or towards the recommencement of negotiations with management.

The union will attempt to elicit as much sympathy action as possible and to exert pressure through other agencies. Publicity is important. This it will gain through pamphlets and the press and also by picketing, where this action is legally permissible. The union will also attempt, as far as is legally possible, to prevent the replacement of striking workers with 'scab' labour, but it will have to be careful, as attempts to prevent 'scabbing' may develop into actual intimidation.

## Management: The Need for a Contingency Plan

Management will attempt to minimise the effects of a strike and bring about a return to work by negotiation with representatives of the striking workers. Any management team, irrespective of its relationship with its employees or representative unions, should be prepared for the event that employees, or a group of employees, stage a work stoppage or strike, particularly where such actions are spontaneous or illegal. They prepare for this by drawing up a contingency plan.

### Purpose of the Contingency Plan

The purpose of a contingency plan is to:

- avoid impulsive reaction on the part of management and panic among managers or among those employees who are not on strike
- establish a uniform policy and plan of action
- formulate guidelines for the handling of striking employees
- ensure the necessary protection of persons and property
- arrange for the continuation of production, or for shutdown or partial shutdown
- ensure that a negotiation forum is established
- make the necessary practical or administrative arrangements for the return (or non-return) of striking employees.

### Ensuring Preparedness

Certain concrete steps can be taken to ensure that all key managerial personnel have the information they will need immediately once a strike or work stoppage occurs, and that co-ordinated action will be initiated. One person, in the form of the general manager or another senior manager, should be responsible for co-ordinating all actions. Everyone else will report to that person, who will act as spokesperson for management. This person will also be charged with the task of dealing with the press. Management should deal honestly with the press, since sensationalism and unguarded statements may lead to an escalation in tension. All other persons should be prohibited from making any public statements.

The manager in charge should be assisted by a negotiating committee, appointed beforehand, which will be charged with the function of planning strategy and negotiating with employee representatives. The method of selection of employee representatives should be decided on during the preparatory stage. Management may decide that it will negotiate with shop stewards, union officials, workers' committee members or a number of persons elected by the striking employees. To attempt negotiation with an entire contingent of strikers is usually not feasible. For this reason management should also decide whether or not it will allow strikers to remain on the property and, if so, where they will be allowed to gather and how representatives will be elected.

Practical contingencies need to be foreseen. A list of persons or institutions such as suppliers, customers and subsidiary agencies who will need to be contacted, and the telephone numbers of each, should be drawn up.

Arrangements need to be made for the protection of other employees, for example by moving them away from premises close to the strikers. The necessary security has to be arranged and provision will have to be made for the protection of buildings and property, as well as for the shutting off of machinery. In each instance, persons to be held responsible must be appointed.

If preparation is made for production or delivery to continue, a list of available manpower should be drawn up. The list will describe the skills of each person in the organisation, including managerial- and supervisory-level staff, so that planning and training for redeployment can occur before the event. The manager who will co-ordinate redeployment should be specified. The possibility of obtaining additional manpower may also be considered, although this may incense the strikers. Furthermore, the operation of each section needs to be studied with the purpose of providing for different or extended shifts or cycles in the event of any irregularity.

Finally, there are administrative details which require attention. These include the issue of notices and ultimatums to striking employees, as well as provision for the rapid paying out of wages and for new employment or re-employment, should the strike be illegal and dismissals eventually prove unavoidable. The manager responsible must already have devised a plan or made the necessary arrangements.

*The Action Plan*

The action plan should be drafted beforehand and will include provisions for:

- the immediate reporting of a work stoppage or strike action
- an assessment of the extent of the action and the possible cause
- the handling of striking employees
- the evacuation of strikers, or their movement to a particular venue
- the shutdown of machinery and equipment and the institution of security measures
- the movement or evacuation of non-striking employees
- the manning of key positions
- the provision of information to outside agencies

- the convening of the negotiating committee
- communication among managers and between management and non-striking employees
- the keeping of a strike diary
- communication with the strikers and the appointment of representatives
- the establishment of a negotiation forum
- notice to striking employees that they will not be paid for the time that they do not work
- attempts to persuade employees to return to work while negotiations continue
- the prevention of violence and intimidation
- the monitoring of picketing
- redeployment, continued production and delivery
- dealing with the media
- issuing statements to striking employees
- a notification of settlement
- the return to work of employees
- in the case of an illegal strike, an ultimatum and notification of dismissals and procedures for payment, employment or re-employment.

(A detailed strike contingency plan is included in the Annexures available online.)

### Aftercare

The conflict which gave rise to a strike is not necessarily settled when employees return to work. Also, the prior existence of conflict, even where resolution is achieved, leads to a heightened conflict potential. Consequently, the necessary aftercare (which does not mean management should pander to employees) should be instituted. Aftercare should include the following:

- All agreements and promises made must be acted upon as soon as possible.
- No further recriminations should be made.
- Measures to improve communication channels and procedures should be put in place.
- The necessary precautions to prevent a recurrence should be taken.
- After a cooling-down period, a follow-up, in the form of a meeting with employee representatives, should be arranged.

### Ensuring Effectiveness

Unfortunately, the effectiveness of a contingency plan can be assessed only once an action has occurred. It is never possible to foresee all contingencies, and some ad hoc action may become necessary. Nevertheless, managerial representatives should be trained in the execution of the plan, possibly by the use of simulation exercises. The plan does ensure that:

- there is a degree of preparedness
- there is certainty as to the action which should be taken
- cohesion is maintained among members of management.

Unions might, equally, draw up their own strike action or lockout contingency plan, which will deal with matters such as meetings, strategies, pickets and the dissemination of information to strikers.

### The Role of the South African Police Service

The police are not responsible for enforcing the provisions of the Labour Relations Act, but the police have the duty to serve and protect the citizens of the country, to act as protectors of the public interest and to enforce criminal law. The police have no role to play in the management of strikes. They are not tasked to act on behalf of management and to disperse strikers or force employees to return to work. The police cannot get involved or express themselves on the merits of any dispute that led to a strike or a lockout.

Police officers have a general duty to uphold the law and may take action to ensure peaceful gatherings, whether on the picket line or elsewhere. If a picket is not peaceful and is likely to lead to violence, the police may take steps to protect property and human lives. The police force may intervene if there is public disturbance by striking workers or if they pose a physical threat to people, but the police's duty towards employers and striking employees is the same as towards the general public, and they should not favour any of the parties.

## Conclusion

To the public at large and to some students of the subject, strike and lock-out actions constitute the most important and most sensational aspect of labour relations. While these actions are important, they need to be handled with care. They are only one part of a web of interrelated processes and should preferably constitute the last resort following a period of protracted negotiation. The South African industrial relations landscape is unfortunately often characterised by violence and labour action of long duration. There are limited mechanisms in place to deal with violent strikes, even though the effects have been seen all over the country. Violent and prolonged strike action has devastating effects on the economy, and often results in injuries to members of the community and non-striking workers.

## Suggested Questions/Tasks

1. Discuss how you would advise employers to put a stop to violent and lengthy strike action and protect the economy from shrinking.

2. Describe briefly what Rycroft's functionality test is as described in *National Union of Food Beverage Wine Spirits & Allied Workers v Universal Product Network (Pty) Ltd 2016 37 ILJ 476 (LC)*.

3. Gather information on the protracted strike of 2014 in the platinum industry, and then answer the following questions:
   a. Was this a protected strike? Support your opinion and explain the procedure.
   b. What was the reason for the strike? Could there have been more than one reason? Explain.
   c. Which of the factors contributing to strike action were present in this case?

4. What would a union have to do if it wanted to demonstrate outside the employer's premises, and what would be the purpose of such demonstrations?

5. Do you think a strike that lasts for six months will ultimately benefit the workers?

6. Some observers believe that the legislation is insufficient in that it does not cater for strikes which have become 'dysfunctional'. Under which conditions could a strike be described as dysfunctional and what could the legislators do about this?

7. Access the Code of Good Practice on Picketing. Divide into two groups, one representing management and lecturers and the other the students. The two parties are now in dispute, and the students have given notice of their intention to engage in strike action. Come together and negotiate a picketing agreement.

8. Do your own research and discuss the most prominent reasons for recent industrial action in the labour market.

9. Explain the current labour market problems in the South African context that can lead to labour unrest and industrial action.

10. Debate the role of the SAPS in strike action and the resolution of disputes between employer and employees/trade unions.

11. Do you believe that picketing can take place in South Africa without employees and trade unions reverting to destructive and violent behaviour? Motivate your answer in detail.

# Sources

DEL (Department of Employment and Labour). 2021. 'Annual Performance Plan 2021/22'. Pretoria: Government Printer. http://www.labour.gov.za/DocumentCenter/Reports/Annual%20Reports/Annual%20Perfomance%20Plan/2021%20-2022/APP%20202021%20updated%20.pdf (Accessed 29 October 2021).

DoL (Department of Labour). 2018, 'Code of Good Practice: Collective Bargaining, Industrial Action and Picketing' issued by the Department of Labour, *Government Gazette* vol 642, no 42121. Pretoria: Government Printer. https://www.gov.za/sites/default/files/gcis_document/201812/42121rg10899gon1396s.pdf (Accessed 29 October 2021).

Ehlers, LI. 2020. 'Trust and perceptions of compliance, fairness and good faith in primary labour relationships'. *South African Journal of Economic and Management Sciences* 23(1): 1–9.

ILO (International Labour Organization). 1982. 'C158 – Termination of Employment Convention, 1982'. https://www.ilo.org/dyn/normlex/en/f?p=NORMLEXPUB:12100:0::NO::P12100_ILO_CODE:C158 (Accessed 1 October 2021).

Kerr, C & Siegel, A (eds). 1954. 'The inner industry propensity to strike', in *Industrial Conflict*, edited by A Kornhauser, R Dubin, AM Ross, Society for the Psychological Study of Social Issues. McGraw-Hill: New Yori McGraw-Hill.

Labour Relations Act (66 of 1995). *Government Gazette* vol 366 no 16861. Pretoria: Government Printer.

Memorandum of Objects. 2012. 'Labour Relations Amendment Bill, 2012'. http://www.labour.gov.za/DocumentCenter/Bills/Proposed%20Amendment%20Bills/memoofobjectslra.pdf (Accessed 29 October 2021).

Murwirapachena, G & Sibanda, K. 2014. 'Exploring the incidents of strikes in post-apartheid South Africa'. *International Business and Economics Research Journal* 13(3): 553–560.

Ntimba, DI, Lessing, KF & Swarts, I. 2020. 'The relationship between employment relationship, employment relations satisfaction and psychological contracts in the South African public sector workplace'. *African Journal of Employee Relations* 44: Art. 8129.

Rycroft, AJ & Jordaan, B. 1992. *A Guide to South African Labour Law*, 2nd edition. Cape Town: Juta.

Western Cape Government. 2019. 'Circular 0013-2019'. https://wcedonline.westerncape.gov.za/circulars/circulars19/Circular0013-2019.pdf (Accessed 29 October 2021).

**15**

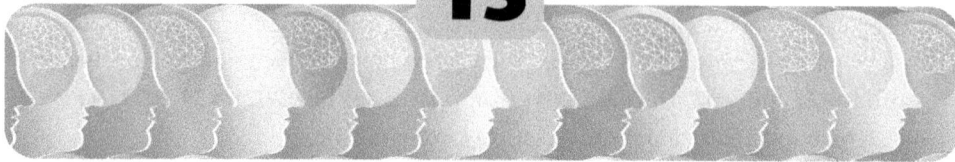

# Organisational Development in the New Millennium

## Chapter Outline

## Overview

Chapter 14 emphasised the need for democratic and forward-looking practices at the workplace. These involve change. In order to keep in step with a rapidly changing world, organisations (and especially South African organisations) have to continually reassess their position.

Throughout the twentieth century, technology – and, with it, workplace practices – developed at an ever-increasing rate. To manage this change, the scientific field of organisation development (OD) emerged.

OD is a range of intentional, systematic and planned interventions aimed at creating alignment between an organisation's goals and activities in order to ensure a particular result which will increase the performance of the organisation in terms of health and effectiveness (CIPD, 2020). In recent years, the focus of OD has moved towards sustainability (Lozano and Garcia, 2020). These interventions include the implementation of a range of carefully developed systems, practices and techniques to steer the organisation towards a goal. The process is initiated by the stakeholders in the organisation. The agendas of international organisations such as the International Labour Organization (ILO), the African Union (AU), and the European Union (EU) play a significant role in OD, as these organisations hold member states responsible for achieving the elements on their agendas. In turn, states need to implement guidelines and reporting systems in organisations to track progress on these elements, which implies creating awareness and implementing changes in organisations to comply with the guidelines.

While the purpose of this chapter is not to present an academic overview of OD, it is important for human resource (HR) and particularly employment relations practitioners to realise that the modern workplace is a site of constant change and transformation and that this must be managed to develop the organisation to be optimally effective, given the internal and external challenges and opportunities it faces. Whereas previously the job content of these practitioners had a narrower focus, the rapid rate and extent of changes in recent times mean that employment relations practitioners must remain vigilant of the changing environment and constantly upskill themselves.

## Managing Internal and External Forces

There are a number of internal and external forces to which employment relations practitioners must pay attention if they are to address them.

### Internal Forces of Change in Organisations

The following are important forces within the organisation that HR and employment relations practitioners must take into account:

- **Linking HR management to organisational strategy:** This includes the organisation's orientation towards various aspects of its vision and mission, such as its orientation towards collective bargaining and employee involvement in the organisational strategy.

- **Level of digitalisation and the use of data analytics:** Digitalisation increases the use of data analytics in the management of the performance of the organisation (Betti, Sarens & Poncin, 2021: 872). Data analytics has become central to the operation of most businesses, making it a necessary skill for every manager and for all functions across an organisation (Kaufmann & Tan, 2021). In turn, digitalisation has an impact on traditional jobs and work security arrangements and causes a variety of changes to processes and procedures, which may be upsetting to most employees. While there is a duty on employers to reasonably consider alternatives, such as training, to assist employees to adapt to the new expectations and job content, there is a growing responsibility on employees to take ownership of their own development. Digitalisation ultimately results in changes to the structure and nature of the workforce.
- **Corporate culture:** Hirsch (2021) notes that currently, many organisations the world over are experiencing a shortage of talent, and the way in which they handle corporate culture will be increasingly important. Corporate leaders have diverged significantly in their attitudes to the potentially permanent increase in remote working brought about by the Covid-19 pandemic. There is a notable shift in what companies can do to create appealing workplace environments for a new generation of workers emerging from the special circumstances created by the global pandemic, especially around issues of gender, parental roles, empathy, demography, virtual communication and human interaction.
- **Quality of teamwork in a learning organisation:** Teamwork, supported by social potential, contributes towards shaping the level of collaborative working in a learning organisation (Jasińska, 2020).
- **Leadership:** Dumas and Beinecke (2018: 867) state that change champions need to encourage their organisations to learn, innovate, experiment and question. They must prepare their organisations for change by constantly seeking new perspectives, and encourage participation throughout the organisation.
- **Organisational processes driving change:** Cimini et al (2021) note that lean organisational structures with new job profiles and higher levels of technology adoption have become a feature of workplaces in the past decade.

## External Drivers of Change

Dmitrijeva et al (2020: 1077) suggest a number of change factors influencing the transformation and development of organisations:

- **Economic drivers:** As the movement from an industrial economy towards a knowledge-based economy grows, new ways of thinking about how we manage change and innovation processes have to be found (Lewis et al, 2020: 1).
- **Political drivers:** Government policies on welfare and public service influence transitional change within organisations (Dahlstedt &Vesterberg, 2021: 16).
- **Social drivers:** Management, organisational and contextual factors are social drivers of change in an organisation. The management factors include the characteristics of the entrepreneur/innovator and the managerial practices engaged in, with those practices that facilitate teamwork and the participation of all involved being best suited. In terms of contextual factors, the need for support from policy makers; community participation; and the demand for innovations that consider local context are recognised as OD drivers. Organisational factors include the type of business model, partnerships, culture and intrapreneurship, and continuous learning (João-Roland & Granados, 2020: 775).
- **Competitive factors:** Intangible assets such as reputation and legitimacy are recognised as key factors for gaining a sustained competitive advantage (Miotto, Del-Castillo-Feito & Blanco-González, 2020).
- **Organisational justice to achieve corporate social responsibility (CSR):** The definitions of business ethics, organisational justice and CSR are still under development. However, there is a pressing international drive to ensure that businesses and the people in businesses behave professionally and morally in their conduct towards each other, stakeholders and the environment while improving their business, their community and society at large (Chen and Khuangga, 2021: 389).
- **Financial infrastructure:** From the beginning of the Covid-19 pandemic it became clear that instability and uncertainty in the environmental, economic and social dimensions will remain in the medium and long term. In the wake of the pandemic, HR management and investments in upgrading information technology has become crucial pillars to ensure the reliability and sustainability of organisations (Marques, Serrasqueiro & Nogueira, 2021).
- **Corporate environmental management:** Hamdoun (2020) suggests that organisations will need to foster the implementation of environmental management plans and practices regarding their benefits, resources and capabilities, institutional and stakeholder pressures and organisational

size. They will also need to determine the role of managers in their environmental programmes to achieve a competitive advantage and increase organisational performance – particularly financial performance, economic performance and environmental performance. For labour relations practitioners, environmental management could result in greater communication opportunities with employees and trade unions on particular practices and procedures.

## Implementing a Change Process

### The Role of the Employment Relations Specialist

Employee relations has a mediating role to play, in the form of the employee relations climate, in the relationship between strategic HR management and organisational performance in organisations (Ali, Lei & Wei, 2018).

More progressive organisational styles centre on the continual development of both the work situation and the relations between those involved. It is envisaged that this will become the main task of the HR/industrial relations specialist, and that this practitioner will be closely involved with – and, in fact, mostly responsible for – OD. In fact, some more progressive organisations have already realised that employment relations specialists should be the drivers of new organisational processes and initiatives.

Employment relations specialists would be wise to upskill themselves by obtaining a good foundation in a variety of change methodologies. Some suggestions of change methods to explore are the ADKAR model, Lewin's model of change, theory E and theory O of organisational change and Kotter's model (Bekmukhambetova, 2021: 99). It would also be beneficial for employment relations specialists to have an awareness of the aspects of change discussed in the following subsections.

### Complexity of the Process

Awareness of the need for change and acceptance of the prerequisites for change form the foundation of a change initiative, but the change process itself is the most complex. The process of evolutionary change does not rest on a single initiative or set of initiatives, but on continuous, dynamic interaction which will take years to climax. The process is often discouraging, because it may seem that nothing is happening. Furthermore, it is not a smooth process. All aspects of the process are interrelated, and the exact format will differ from one institution to another and from one year to the next.

## Gaining Commitment

As a first step in the change process, the main players have to be made aware of the need for change. They must themselves believe in and be totally committed to the change process. If they merely pay lip service to the principle, other stakeholders will either relapse into apathy or eventually engage in revolt. Transformation workshops, encompassing interaction and sensitivity training, are required at this stage, as the greatest resistance is bound to come from those in positions of power.

## Initiating Change
### Spreading the Message

In the second stage, the initiative goes public. This commences with a sincere expression of intent by management, followed by an indaba of internal stakeholder representatives, supported by similar indabas at all other levels. The purpose is to build support, commitment and trust, but this cannot be done before the organisation and all participants have taken a clear and honest look at themselves and admitted to past mistakes.

The initial stages would entail employees and management engaging in an open exchange and clearly identifying areas of dissatisfaction with the organisation, each other, other stakeholders or the work process. The facilitator will assist in depersonalising issues and translating them into problems. All stakeholders should be given the opportunity to say what they expect from the process.

This type of interchange requires that positions of equality be established, that previous power holders relinquish assumptions of power and control, and that an atmosphere is created in which all views are accepted and valued. All parties should display a willingness to move on from existent paradigms and attitudes, to enter into new relationship patterns and to accept responsibility for the change process. Certain problems may be minimised or eliminated merely by speaking about them and exchanging opinions.

Major problems will have to be addressed, but, when doing so, parties should stay with that which is real and possible (reality testing). Representative committees need to be appointed to deal with particular problems. Their main task will be to remove existing obstacles, such as unnecessary regulations and bureaucratic controls, in order to facilitate future change processes.

During this phase the principles of democracy, transparency and accountability should be clearly established as a basis for any future interactions. These are fundamentals in the light of which all future actions will be judged, and without which trust, the remaining fundamental, cannot be engendered, thus dooming all future initiatives to 'half-life' or to absolute failure.

Admittedly, the process as described above is not without its obstacles. The employer/management may doggedly cling to power and resort to using existing systems of control and regulations as a camouflage. Employees may not initially be capable of handling their new roles and may at first pursue only their own objectives. They may have been dulled into apathy or scepticism by previous practices or unsuccessful attempts at change in the past. These obstacles should be openly addressed and unpacked, and strategies for overcoming them must be put in place.

This discussion clearly illustrates the complexity of every stage of the change process and the need for continued communication and workshopping. The situation should be reassessed on an ongoing basis. Further initiatives towards transformation can be undertaken only after a basic cultural shift has occurred.

## The Environmental Scan

This phase entails a thorough scanning of the environment and of the organisation's position in that environment. Questions to be asked include the following:

- Is emphasis being placed on the most relevant areas?
- In which areas of business and industry will new needs arise?
- What changes have occurred in the general population?
- What is the educational, social and experiential profile of this population?
- What external policy frameworks are being developed or are likely to be developed?
- Are existing systems and structures suited to the new demands?
- Which technologies are available to facilitate the task?
- What is being done in South Africa and elsewhere in the world?
- On which financial resources could the organisation draw?
- What changes are likely to occur?
- How can the organisation best position itself in the existing and future environment?

## The Internal Audit

While the environmental scan will provide the organisation with a broad framework for establishing its mission and objectives, specific objectives are only established once the second part of the exercise – the audit of existing and potential internal resources – is undertaken. This entails a thorough assessment of the financial, material and human resources of the organisation, and is the 'reality check' which will prevent the parties from setting unrealistic objectives. It may equally create awareness of untapped resources. At the very least, it will lead to the formulation of short-term strategies aimed at expanding or improving the resources – for example, retraining or development of HR potential or renewed attempts to access financial resources.

### Formulating a Vision, Mission and Objectives

It is accepted that, in line with the new culture, the above steps will have been undertaken in collaboration with representatives of all stakeholders. The next stage would commence with the joint establishment of a vision and mission for the organisation and the setting of realistic yet ambitious objectives. A thorough environmental scan and a meaningful vision and mission will lead to the setting of objectives aimed at both effectiveness and efficiency. Once these broad organisational objectives (sometimes supplemented by more specific objectives) have been established, short- and long-term strategies to achieve the objectives are put in place.

### Obtaining 'Buy-in'

Once a new mission and vision have been established and the necessary objectives and strategies have been framed, these must be taken to the coalface. The employer/management should contract with employees for concrete change and display a willingness to embrace new paradigms and experiment with new structures and procedures. Functional units or teams need to be created, responsibilities reassessed and reassigned, and new leadership styles implemented. Functionality and expertise, and not status or administrative ability, must become the dominant criteria.

### 'Panel-beating' the Organisational Structure

The change process will probably involve decentralisation and delegation of power, decision making and responsibility. This may entail that each section or department becomes an independent profit centre, that administrative functions are decentralised as far as possible and that the overall structure of the organisation becomes flatter than before. Each centre should be allowed maximum flexibility and autonomy within the framework of the overall objectives.

### Continuing Development and Training

In all areas, participants should be encouraged to share responsibility and decision making and to engage in self-direction, self-motivation and self-control. These persons have to be equipped and supported to play their new roles. It may also be necessary to establish support systems which encourage employees to take responsibility for their own development and which promote a general culture of continuous development.

Close liaison with customers is another imperative, as is the assessment of both individual and group performance in terms of jointly established competencies and criteria. The role of the leader becomes that of facilitator, co-ordinator and supporter – the creator of opportunities for people and the organisation.

### Continuous Reassessment

The change process is dynamic and indefinite and frequent reassessment is essential. Participants need to workshop frequently, to assess where they are and where they are going, and to identify dysfunctional aspects. If necessary, they may have to backtrack and go in a different direction. This is all part of the process. Even once all the phases have been implemented, new horizons and challenges will already have emerged. This will necessitate a move forward by repeating the process – hopefully, now at a more advanced level.

## Conclusion

At the start of the second decade of the new millennium, the Covid-19 pandemic emerged and created havoc in terms of the traditional knowledge of how to deal with change. According to Mendy (2020), new research directions have emerged, such as:

- how to better manage change within and beyond a crisis situation
- the extent of crisis management and the repercussions for staff members' overall learning and resilience-building capacity
- emerging recovery mechanisms that could address the survivability of small and medium enterprises
- resilience building
- dealing with financial and non-financial challenges in the context of a change environment.

In this rapidly changing world, organisations (and especially South African organisations) have to continually reassess their position and adapt to the changing environment.

## Sources

Ali, M, Lei, S & Wei, XY. 2018. 'The mediating role of the employee relations climate in the relationship between strategic HRM and organizational performance in Chinese banks'. *Journal of Innovation and Knowledge* 3(3): 115–122.

Bekmukhambetova, A. 2021. 'Comparative analysis of change management models based on an exploratory literature review', in *New Horizons in Business and Management Studies*. Conference Proceedings. Corvinus University of Budapest: 98–110.

Betti, N, Sarens, G & Poncin, I. 2021. 'Effects of digitalisation of organisations on internal audit activities and practices'. *Managerial Auditing Journal* 36(6): 872–888.

Chen, LF & Khuangga, DL. 2021. 'Configurational paths of employee reactions to corporate social responsibility: An organizational justice perspective'. *Corporate Social Responsibility and Environmental Management* 28(1): 389–403.

Cimini, C, Boffelli, A, Lagorio, A, Kalchschmidt, M & Pinto, R. 2021. 'How do industry 4.0 technologies influence organisational change? An empirical analysis of Italian SMEs'. *Journal of Manufacturing Technology Management* 32(3): 695–721.

CIPD (Chartered Institute of Personnel and Development). 2020. 'Organisational development'. 25 November 2020. https://www.cipd.co.uk/knowledge/strategy/organisational-development/factsheet#gref (Accessed 14 October 2021).

Dahlstedt, M & Vesterberg, V. 2021. 'Politics of makeover: initiating organisational change and positioning the unemployed in a Swedish reality TV series'. *International Journal of Politics, Culture, and Society* 1–19.

Dmitrijeva, J, Schroeder, A, Ziaee Bigdeli, A & Baines, T. 2020. 'Context matters: How internal and external factors impact servitization'. *Production Planning and Control* 31(13): 1077–1097.

Dumas, C & Beinecke, RH. 2018. 'Change leadership in the 21st century'. *Journal of Organizational Change Management* 31(4): 867–876.

Hamdoun, M. 2020. 'The antecedents and outcomes of environmental management based on the resource-based view: A systematic literature review'. *Management of Environmental Quality: An International Journal* 31(2): 451–469.

Hirsch, PB. 2021. 'Sustaining corporate culture in a world of hybrid work'. *Journal of Business Strategy* 42(5): 358–361.

Jasińska, M. 2020. 'Synergy: An enhancement of learning organisations undergoing a change'. *Entrepreneurship and Sustainability Issues* 7(3): 1902.

João-Roland, IDS & Granados, ML. 2020. 'Social innovation drivers in social enterprises: systematic review'. *Journal of Small Business and Enterprise Development* 27(5): 775–795.

Kaufmann, UH & Tan, AB. 2021. *Data analytics for organisational development: Unleashing the potential of your data.* Chichester: John Wiley & Sons.

Lewis, MA, Schweitzer, J, Cunningham, R & Jacobs, B. 2020. 'Navigating complex organisational change: Putting sustainable transitions theory to practice', in *ISPIM Conference Proceedings.* The International Society for Professional Innovation Management (ISPIM), virtual, 6–8 December 2020. LUT Scientific and Expertise Publications.

Lozano, R & Garcia, I. 2020. 'Scrutinizing sustainability change and its institutionalization in organizations'. *Frontiers in Sustainability* 1: 1.

Marques, ICP, Serrasqueiro, Z & Nogueira, F. 2021. 'Covid-19 and organisational development: Important signs of a new pillar for sustainability'. *Social Responsibility Journal* 11 October 2021. https://doi.org/10.1108/SRJ-10-2020-0415.

Mendy, JA. 2020. 'Review of SMEs' COVID-19 theorised challenges: New directions for managing recovery-oriented organisational change'. https://www.researchgate.net/profile/John-Mendy/publication/352479419_A_Review_of_SMEs'_COVID-19_Theorised_Challenges_New_Directions_for_Managing_Recovery-Oriented_Organisational_Change/links/60cb203392851ca3aca7ea4f/A-Review-of-SMEs-COVID-19-Theorised-Challenges-New-Directions-for-Managing-Recovery-Oriented-Organisational-Change.pdf (Accessed 19 October 2021).

Miotto, G, Del-Castillo-Feito, C & Blanco-González, A. 2020. 'Reputation and legitimacy: Key factors for higher education institutions' sustained competitive advantage'. *Journal of Business Research* 112: 342–353.

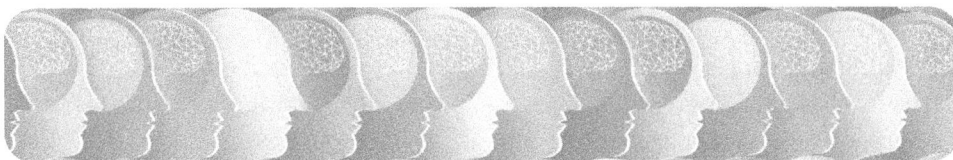

# Index

Note: Page numbers in *italics* refer to tables and figures

effects on women  587

and Fifth Industrial Revolution (5IR)  58

labour market trends  586–588

labour unrest  586–588

law of demand and supply and  246–247, *247*

remote working  12, 258

social distancing  12

and value of work  587

craft trade unions  316

crime and employment levels  295

CUSA *see* Council of Unions of South Africa (CUSA)

custom and tradition in employment relationship  26–27

cyclical unemployment  278–279


**D**

deadlocks during negotiations  404

decentralised bargaining  527–528, 530, *531–532*, 556–558

defects and irregularities, addressed by Labour Relations Act 66 of 1995  148

demand *see* law of demand and supply

demand-deficient unemployment  278–279

democracy in workplaces *see* workers' participation

demographics
 affirmative action  196–197
 influence on negotiations  374

demonstration strikes  581

Department of Employment and Labour  313

Department of Labour  105–106

designated groups, definition  154, 190

developments post 1990  80–87

Dialectical Materialism  45

digitalisation
 effect on labour markets  255
 internal force of change in organisations  616

disabled persons *see* people with disabilities

disciplinary procedures, flowing from collective bargaining and workers' participation  42

disclosure of information *see also* protected disclosures
 to forum members  470
 mergers, transfers and outsourcing  507–508
 referral of disputes to CCMA  539
 right to  539

discrimination
 applicants for position  152
 burden of proof  153, 166, 167
 contraventions of Employment Equity Act  152–153
 different conditions of service for same work  166, 185–186
 dismissals automatically unfair  167
 disputes arising from  153
 elimination of  108–109
 fair vs unfair  151–152, 173
 HIV testing  168
 inherent requirements of job  172
 justified differentiation  185–186
 medical and psychological testing of employees  152, 166
 protection of job-seekers  166
 recruitment and selection  189–190
 reverse  195

disguised employment/ unemployment  124, 274

dismissals *see also* retrenchments and redundancies

general trade unions  318
Gini coefficient  88, 255, 297
good faith bargaining  373, 519, 560
go-slows  581–582
government *see also* State
  as employer  286
  labour market initiatives 1994–
    2008  287–293
  and labour markets  285–293
  programmes to combat youth
    unemployment  291–292
grasshopper strikes  582
grievance procedures  42
  employment equity plans  206
grievance strikes  581
groups
  formation  419–420
  heterogeneous  420–421
  intergroup relationships  420
  storming  420
  virtual  421
Growth Employment and
  Redistribution Strategy (GEAR)
    81–82, 86, 290–291, 342

**H**
harassment
  definition  169
  employer liability  170
  form of discrimination  166
  policy and procedure  170
  sexual  91, 153, 167, 169–170, 171–
    172, 458
health and safety *see* occupational
  health and safety
HIV testing  168
HRDS *see* Human Resource
  Development Strategy for South
  Africa (HRDS)
human capital labour market theory
  251

Human Resource Development
  Strategy for South Africa (HRDS)
    296

**I**
ICWU *see* Industrial & Commercial
  Workers' Union of South Africa
    (ICWU)
ideologies in labour relations system
  Classical Liberalism  44
  definition of ideology  42
  Free Market  44–45
  Individualism vs
    Communitarianism  43
  libertarianism  48
  Socialism  45–47
  in South Africa  58–59
illegal strike disputes  469
immigration, and employment levels
  294–295
incapacity
  dispute settlement  461, 469–470
  permanent or temporary  476–477
incompetence, dispute settlement
  461, 469–470
indefinite contracts  127–128
independent contractors
  vs employees  116–118, 119, 124
  tests for  117–118
individualism
  vs communitarianism  43
  economic  45
induction programmes  211
Industrial & Commercial Workers'
  Union of South Africa (ICWU)
    61–62
industrial councils  62
industrial relations
  institutionalisation of conflict  6
  origins  6

economic and social realities in new millennium 87–94
industrialisation in South Africa (1880–1924) 59–63
industrial revolutions 56–58
manufacturing and service industries (1925–1948) 63–66
Nationalist government (1948–1970) 66–71
pluralist mode 93
labour relations systems
components 41
effect on society 56
ideological basis 42–48
legal framework 42
parties to relationship 41
processes and procedures 41–42
role of State 48–56
labour standards, reduced compliance in Covid-19 era 588
labour unrest *see also* strikes
and collective bargaining 93
in Covid-19 era 586–588
and employment levels 295
post 1990 83
labour/work relations *see* employment relationship
last-in-first-out (LIFO) principle 214–215, 490, 491–492
law of demand and supply
Covid-19 pandemic and 246–247, *247*
demand schedule 233–234, *234*
elasticity of demand 241–242, *242*, 253–254, 372
elasticity of supply 242–244, *243*, *244*
market equilibrium 234–239, *235*
same principles as price theory 233
law of diminishing returns 244

legal practitioner, definition 149
legislation
purpose 99
rationale of framework 99–100
regulating employment relationship 27
legitimate power 24, 377
libertarianism 48
LIFO *see* last-in-first-out (LIFO) principle
lockouts 588–589
definition 149, 589
regulation 142–143

**M**

maintenance services, prohibition of strike action by employees 143, 593
majority trade unions
vs representative trade unions 535–536
rights 535–536
thresholds of representativeness 537–538
management
handling of strike action 608–611
role in employment relationship 17–18
mandatorism
pro-capital 52
pro-labour 52, 86
and voluntarism 49
marginal utility of labour 245–246, *245*, *246*
market equilibrium 234, *235*
elasticity 241–244, 253
factors causing shifts in demand curve 239
factors causing shifts in supply curve 240

New Partnership for Africa's Development (NEPAD) 313
no-fault termination of employment
  concept of no-fault 475–476
  dismissal due to ill health or injury 476–481
  mergers, transfers and outsourcing 502–508
  retrenchment and redundancy 481–502
non-majority trade unions, rights 536–537
'no work, no pay' principle 591
NUM *see* National Union of Mineworkers (NUM)
NUMSA *see* National Union of Metalworkers of South Africa (NUMSA)

## O
occupational detriment *see* protected disclosures
occupational health and safety 134
occupational injuries and diseases 134
occupational trade unions 315–317
operational requirements, definition 149
organisational development in new millennium
  external drivers of change 617–618
  implementation of change process 618–622
  internal forces of change in organisations 615–616
organisational rights of unions
  agency shops 541–542, 544–546
  appointment of shop stewards 538–539

closed shops 541, 542–544, 546–547
disclosure of information 539, 540–541
dispute settlement 468
exercise of 332–333, 534–535
majority trade unions 535–536
non-majority trade unions 536–537
notice of strike action 592
recognition agreements 557
refusal to grant 467
representation thresholds 537–538
representative rights 536
representative trade unions 535, 536
outsourcing, changes in roles in employment relationship 18
overtime bans 582

## P
participation schemes 360
people with disabilities
  affirmative action 215
  definition 154
performance appraisals, affirmative action 211
permanent contracts 127–128
picketing 142–143
  agreements/rules 598
  legitimate action in support of strikes 598
  purpose 597
  right to picket 597
plant-level
  committees 358
  dispute settlement processes 472
pluralism 33–34, 80, 86, 93, 532–533
police role in labour relations system 55

**T**